Pro Entity Framework Core 2 for ASP.NET Core MVC

Adam Freeman

Apress®

Pro Entity Framework Core 2 for ASP.NET Core MVC

Adam Freeman
London, UK

ISBN-13 (pbk): 978-1-4842-3434-1
https://doi.org/10.1007/978-1-4842-3435-8

ISBN-13 (electronic): 978-1-4842-3435-8

Library of Congress Control Number: 2018939926

Managing Director, Apress Media LLC: Welmoed Spahr
Acquisitions Editor: Gwenan Spearing
Development Editor: Laura Berendson
Coordinating Editor: Mark Powers

Cover designed by eStudioCalamar

Cover image designed by Freepik (www.freepik.com)

Distributed to the book trade worldwide by Springer Science+Business Media New York, 233 Spring Street, 6th Floor, New York, NY 10013. Phone 1-800-SPRINGER, fax (201) 348-4505, e-mail orders-ny@springer-sbm.com, or visit www.springeronline.com. Apress Media, LLC is a California LLC and the sole member (owner) is Springer Science + Business Media Finance Inc (SSBM Finance Inc). SSBM Finance Inc is a **Delaware** corporation.

For information on translations, please e-mail editorial@apress.com; for reprint, paperback, or audio rights, please email bookpermissions@springernature.com.

Apress titles may be purchased in bulk for academic, corporate, or promotional use. eBook versions and licenses are also available for most titles. For more information, reference our Print and eBook Bulk Sales web page at www.apress.com/bulk-sales.

Any source code or other supplementary material referenced by the author in this book is available to readers on GitHub via the book's product page, located at www.apress.com/9781484234341. For more detailed information, please visit www.apress.com/source-code.

Printed on acid-free paper

Dedicated to my lovely wife, Jacqui Griffyth.
(And also to Peanut.)

Contents

About the Author

Adam Freeman is an experienced IT professional who has held senior positions in a range of companies, most recently serving as chief technology officer and chief operating officer of a global bank. Now retired, he spends his time writing and long-distance running.

About the Technical Reviewer

Fabio Claudio Ferracchiati is a senior consultant and a senior analyst/developer using Microsoft technologies. He works for BluArancio (`www.bluarancio.com`). He is a Microsoft Certified Solution Developer for .NET, a Microsoft Certified Application Developer for .NET, a Microsoft Certified Professional, and a prolific author and technical reviewer. Over the past ten years, he's written articles for Italian and international magazines and coauthored more than ten books on a variety of computer topics.

PART I

Introducing Entity Framework Core 2

The first part of this book is designed to help you understand broadly the foundational ideas of Entity Framework Core 2 development and to experience in practice what the framework is like to use in an ASP.NET Core MVC project.

CHAPTER 1

Entity Framework Core in Context

Entity Framework Core—also known as EF Core—is an object-relational mapping (ORM) package produced by Microsoft that allows .NET Core applications to store data in relational databases.

Understanding Entity Framework Core

Entity Framework Core has one key task: storing.NET objects in a database and retrieving them again later. Put another way, Entity Framework Core acts as the bridge between an ASP.NET Core MVC application and a database, as shown in Figure 1-1.

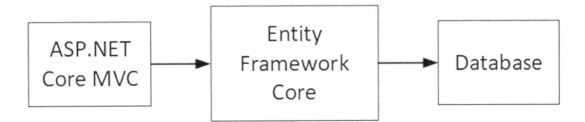

Figure 1-1. Entity Framework Core in context

Storing .NET objects in a database can be a surprisingly complex process. Databases don't exist in isolation. They are created and managed by *database servers*, which are specialized applications focused solely on the storage and management of data. Database servers provide the persistent storage for most applications, and the most popular database servers have been under development for decades, resulting in high-performance and robust software that is packed with features. Database servers support a core set of common features, but they differentiate themselves with custom additions, and getting the best results from a database server means taking advantage of them.

There are different types of database server available; the kind that Entity Framework Core works with is called a *relational database server*, also known as a *relational database management system* (RDBMS). A relational database server manages *relational databases*, where data is stored as rows in tables, not unlike a spreadsheet. Relational database servers typically accept commands expressed in the *Structured Query Language* (SQL), which allows data operations—such as storing or deleting data—to be expressed. There is a SQL standard, but database servers use slightly different dialects, especially when it comes to accessing the nonstandard features.

© Adam Freeman 2018
A. Freeman, *Pro Entity Framework Core 2 for ASP.NET Core MVC*,
https://doi.org/10.1007/978-1-4842-3435-8_1

Note I am simplifying here for the sake of brevity. The world of databases is filled with distinctions between different types of data and different types of databases and database servers, none of which has much bearing on using ASP.NET Core MVC or Entity Framework Core.

To store .NET objects in a database, Entity Framework Core has to be able to translate objects into a form that can be stored in a database table and formulate a SQL command that the database server can process. To deal with the differences between database servers, Entity Framework Core relies on a *database provider*, which is responsible for communicating with the database and formulating the SQL commands.

To retrieve .NET objects from the database, Entity Framework Core has to be able to reverse the process. It has to be able to create a SQL query that will ask the database server for the data values that represent the object and use them to populate the properties of a .NET object. To make this process as natural as possible, Entity Framework Core supports LINQ for querying the database, which makes working with collections of objects stored in a database similar to working with collections of objects in memory.

About This Book

In this book, I explain how to use Entity Framework Core in ASP.NET Core MVC applications. I show you the different ways that Entity Framework Core can be added to a project and the pitfalls that await the unwary. Entity Framework Core is a powerful, tool but it is important to pay attention to the details; otherwise, you will end up with an application that doesn't perform well or doesn't behave as expected.

What Do You Need to Know?

To get the most from this book, you should already be familiar with ASP.NET Core MVC development. You will struggle if you don't already know how controllers and actions work and how Razor views behave. If you are not familiar with ASP.NET Core MVC, then consult `https://docs.microsoft.com/en-us/aspnet/core` or my book *Pro ASP.NET Core MVC 2*, published by Apress.

What Software Do You Need?

To follow the examples in this book, you will need a PC running Windows, the .NET Core SDK, and the latest version of Visual Studio. With the exception of Windows, all the tools that I use in this book are available without charge, and I explain how to set up your development environment in Chapter 2.

What If You Don't Want to Use Windows?

I have relied on Windows and Visual Studio throughout this book because that is what most readers use, and being able to use LocalDB—the Windows-only developer version of SQL Server—makes the examples more predictable and reliable. With a little effort, you can run all of the examples in this book on any platform that .NET Core supports, although you will need to install the full SQL Server product (or use Docker containers). Contact me at `adam@adam-freeman.com` if you want to use Linux or macOS, and I will try to help you get started.

What Is the Structure of This Book?

This book is split into three parts, each of which covers a set of related topics.

Part 1: Introducing Entity Framework Core 2

The best way to learn is by doing, and in this part of the book, you get a high-level view of how Entity Framework Core works and how it integrates with ASP.NET Core MVC. In Chapter 2, you create your first ASP.NET Core MVC application that uses Entity Framework Core to store data. In Chapter 3, I provide a primer for working with databases and using SQL so that you can understand how Entity Framework Core works and follow the examples throughout this book. Chapters 4–10 are given over to the development of a project called SportsStore, through which I show you a realistic development process, touching on the most important Entity Framework Core features and explaining where in the book each of them is described in detail.

Part 2: Entity Framework Core 2 in Detail

In Part 2, I describe the core features of Entity Framework Core that you will use on a day-to-day basis in your ASP.NET Core MVC projects. I show you how each feature works, explain the role it plays, and describe alternative techniques when they are available.

Part 3: Advanced Entity Framework Core 2

In Part 3, I describe the advanced features that Entity Framework Core provides. These are the features that you are unlikely to need often but that are invaluable when the default Entity Framework Core behavior doesn't solve your problem.

Where Can You Get the Example Code?

You can download the example projects for all the chapters in this book from `https://github.com/apress/pro-ef-core-2-for-asp.net-core-mvc`. The download is available without charge and contains all of the classes, views, and other assets required to follow the examples without having to type in all of the code.

Where Can You Get Corrections for This Book?

You can find errata for this book at `https://github.com/apress/pro-ef-core-2-for-asp.net-core-mvc`.

How Can You Contact Me?

If you have problems making the examples in this chapter work or if you find a problem in the book, then you can e-mail me at `adam@adam-freeman.com`, and I will try my best to help. Please check the errata for this book to see whether it contains a solution to your problem before contacting me.

Summary

In this chapter, I introduced Entity Framework Core and explained the role it plays and described the structure and contents of this book. In the next chapter, you will see ASP.NET Core MVC and Entity Framework Core in action in a simple demonstration of how these two powerful tools can work together.

CHAPTER 2

Your First Entity Framework Core Application

The best way to get started with Entity Framework Core is to jump right in and use it. In this chapter, I create a simple application using Entity Framework Core and ASP.NET Core MVC so you can see how everything fits together. To keep the example simple, I skip over some of the details that are described in later chapters.

Getting Ready

To prepare for the example in this chapter—and the ones in the chapters that follow—you will need to install some development tools. There are zero-cost versions of all of the tools required for ASP.NET Core MVC and Entity Framework Core development, and it is these versions that I use throughout this book.

UPDATES TO THIS BOOK

Microsoft has an active development schedule for .NET Core, ASP.NET Core MVC, and Entity Framework Core, which means that there may be new releases available by the time you read this book. It doesn't seem fair to expect you to buy a new book every few months, especially since most changes are relatively minor.

Instead, I will post free updates to the GitHub repository for this book (`https://github.com/apress/pro-ef-core-2-for-asp.net-core-mvc`) for breaking changes caused by minor releases.

This kind of update is an experiment for me (and for Apress), and I don't yet know what form those updates may take—not least because I don't know what the future major releases of ASP.NET Core MVC or Entity Framework Core will contain—but the goal is to extend the life of this book by supplementing the examples it contains.

I am not making any promises about what the updates will be like, what form they will take, or how long I will produce them before folding them into a new edition of this book. Please keep an open mind and check the repository for this book when new ASP.NET Core MVC versions are released. If you have ideas about how the updates could be improved, then e-mail me at `adam@adam-freeman.com` and let me know.

A. Freeman, *Pro Entity Framework Core 2 for ASP.NET Core MVC*,
https://doi.org/10.1007/978-1-4842-3435-8_2

Installing .NET Core

The .NET Core Software Development Kit (SDK) includes the runtime and development tools needed to build and run .NET projects. To install the .NET Core SDK on Windows, download the installer from `https://www.microsoft.com/net/download/thank-you/dotnet-sdk-2.1.4-windows-x64-installer`. This URL is for the 64-bit .NET Core SDK version 2.1.4, which is the version that I use throughout this book and which you should install to ensure that you get the expected results from the examples. (Microsoft also publishes a runtime-only installer, but this does not contain the tools that are required for this book.)

Run the installer and, once the install process is complete, open a new PowerShell window or command prompt and run the command shown in Listing 2-1 to check that .NET Core is working.

Listing 2-1. Testing .NET Core

```
dotnet --version
```

The output from this command will display the version of the latest version of the .NET Core runtime that is installed. If you have installed only the version specified earlier, this will be 2.1.4.

Installing Visual Studio 2017

Visual Studio is the traditional development environment for ASP.NET Core and Entity Framework Core projects. Download the installer from `https://www.visualstudio.com/vs`. There are different editions of Visual Studio 2017 available, but the free Community edition is sufficient for the examples in this book. Run the installer and ensure that the .NET Core Cross-Platform Development workload is selected, as shown in Figure 2-1.

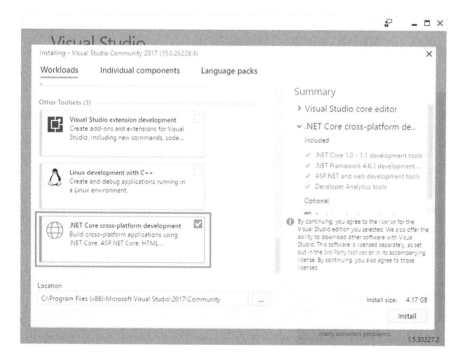

Figure 2-1. *Selecting the Visual Studio packages*

This workload includes the LocalDB version of SQL Server that I use throughout this book, along with the Visual Studio features required for ASP.NET Core MVC and Entity Framework Core development. Click the Install button to begin the process of downloading and installing the Visual Studio features.

Adding the Visual Studio Extensions

Two Visual Studio extensions are essential for working on ASP.NET Core MVC projects. The first is called Razor Language Service, and it provides IntelliSense support for tag helpers when editing Razor views. The second is called Project File Tools, and it provides automatic completion for editing .csproj files, which simplifies the process of adding NuGet packages to projects. (You may find that these extensions are already installed since Microsoft changes the ones that are added by default from time to time.)

Select Extensions and Updates from the Visual Studio Tools menu, select the Online section, and use the search box to locate the extensions. Click the Download button, as shown in Figure 2-2, to download the extension files.

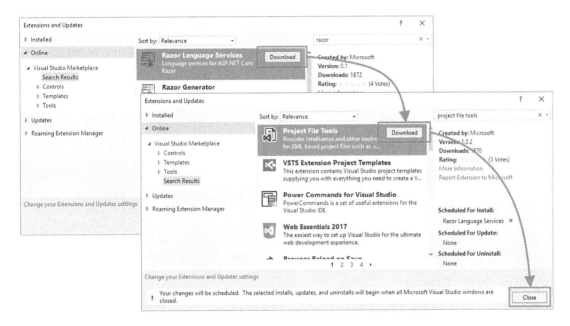

Figure 2-2. *Downloading Visual Studio extensions*

Click the Close button to dismiss the list of extensions and then close Visual Studio, which will trigger the installation process for the extensions you downloaded. You will be prompted to accept the changes that will be made and the license terms, as shown in Figure 2-3. Click the Modify button to install the extensions. Once the process has completed, you can start Visual Studio and begin development.

Figure 2-3. *Installing Visual Studio extensions*

Creating the Project

To get started with Entity Framework Core, I will show how to create a simple data-entry application that stores its data in a database. I am going to go through the process quickly, without going into too much detail, just to give you a sense of how ASP.NET Core MVC and Entity Framework Core can work together. But don't worry: everything that I do in this chapter is explained in depth in later chapters.

Setting the Scene

Imagine that a friend has decided to host a New Year's Eve party and that she has asked me to create a web app that allows her invitees to electronically RSVP. She has asked for these four key features:

- A home page that shows information about the party

- A form that can be used to RSVP

- Validation for the RSVP form, which will display a thank-you page

- A summary page that shows who is coming to the party

This is the same data-entry app that I created in my *Pro ASP.NET MVC Core 2* book, and the difference for this book is that I am going to store the responses in a database using Entity Framework Core.

Creating the Project

To create the project, start Visual Studio and select New ➤ Project from the File menu. Select the ASP.NET Core Web Application project template, set the Name field to PartyInvites, and click the Browse button to select a convenient location to store the project, as shown in Figure 2-4.

■ **Tip** You can download this project from the GitHub repository for this book, `https://github.com/apress/pro-ef-core-2-for-asp.net-core-mvc`.

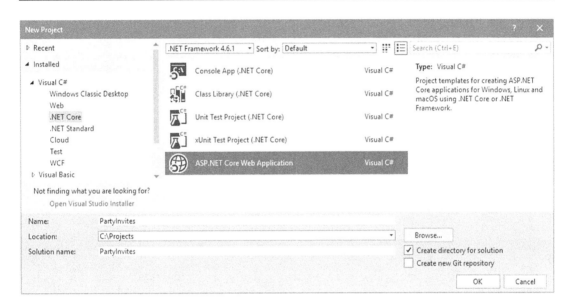

Figure 2-4. *Creating the example project*

Click the OK button to continue the project setup. Ensure that .NET Core and ASP.NET Core 2.0 are selected at the top of the window and click the Empty template, as shown in Figure 2-5. Visual Studio includes templates that set up ASP.NET Core MVC and Entity Framework Core in a project, but the result hides some useful details.

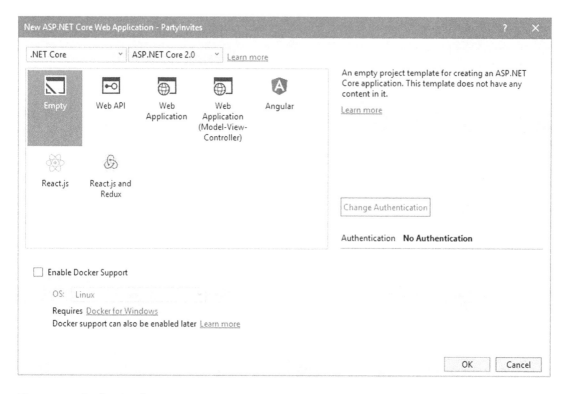

Figure 2-5. *Configuring the ASP.NET Core project*

Click the OK button and Visual Studio will create the PartyInvites project with a basic configuration that sets up ASP.NET Core but doesn't configure the MVC framework or Entity Framework Core.

Adding the Bootstrap CSS Framework

I use the Bootstrap CSS framework throughout this book to style the HTML elements. To add Bootstrap to the project, right-click the PartyInvites item in the Solution Explorer, select Add ➤ New Item from the pop-up menu, and use the JSON File template (found in the ASP.NET Core ➤ Web ➤ General category) to create a file called .bowerrc with the content shown in Listing 2-2. (It is important to pay attention to this file name: it starts with a period, contains the letter r twice and has no file extension).

Listing 2-2. The Contents of the .bowerrc File in the PartyInvites Folder

```
{
  "directory": "wwwroot/lib"
}
```

Use the JSON File template again to create a file called bower.json and add the content shown in Listing 2-3.

Listing 2-3. The Contents of the bower.json File in the PartyInvites Folder

```json
{
  "name": "asp.net",
  "private": true,
  "dependencies": {
    "bootstrap": "4.0.0"
  }
}
```

When you save the changes to the file, Visual Studio will download the new version of the Bootstrap package and install it in the wwwroot/lib folder.

Configuring the HTTP Port

Changing the port that will be used by ASP.NET Core to receive requests will make the examples easier to follow. Edit the launchSettings.json file in the Properties folder and change the URLs as shown in Listing 2-4.

Listing 2-4. Changing the HTTP Ports in the launchSettings.json File in the Properties Folder

```json
{
  "iisSettings": {
    "windowsAuthentication": false,
    "anonymousAuthentication": true,
    "iisExpress": {
      "applicationUrl": "http://localhost:5000/",
      "sslPort": 0
    }
  },
  "profiles": {
    "IIS Express": {
      "commandName": "IISExpress",
      "launchBrowser": true,
      "environmentVariables": {
        "ASPNETCORE_ENVIRONMENT": "Development"
      }
    },
    "PartyInvites": {
      "commandName": "Project",
      "launchBrowser": true,
      "environmentVariables": {
        "ASPNETCORE_ENVIRONMENT": "Development"
      },
      "applicationUrl": "http://localhost:5000/"
    }
  }
}
```

The URLs in this file are used to configure the application when it is started using IIS Express and when it is run from the command line. All of the examples in this book are run from the command line so that logging messages can easily be seen.

Creating the Data Model and Context Classes

When you are creating an application that uses both ASP.NET Core MVC and Entity Framework Core, the data model becomes especially important. To create the data model class for the example application, I added a Models folder to the project, created within it a file called GuestResponse.cs, and added the code shown in Listing 2-5.

Listing 2-5. The Contents of the GuestResponse.cs File in the Models Folder

```
namespace PartyInvites.Models {

    public class GuestResponse {

        public long Id { get; set; }

        public string Name { get; set; }
        public string Email { get; set; }
        public string Phone { get; set; }
        public bool? WillAttend { get; set; }
    }
}
```

Entity Framework Core is able to store instances of regular C# classes, just as long as they have a property whose value uniquely identifies each object, known as the *primary key property*. In the case of the GuestResponse class, the Id property is the primary key property.

Entity Framework Core features are provided by a database context class, which identifies the data model classes to Entity Framework Core and is used to access the data in the database. To create the context class, I added a file called DataContext.cs to the Models folder and added the code shown in Listing 2-6.

Listing 2-6. The Contents of the DataContext.cs File in the Models Folder

```
using Microsoft.EntityFrameworkCore;

namespace PartyInvites.Models {

    public class DataContext : DbContext {

        public DataContext(DbContextOptions<DataContext> options)
            : base(options) { }

        public DbSet<GuestResponse> Responses { get; set; }
    }
}
```

When you create a database context class, it is important that you include a constructor that receives a configuration object and passes it to the constructor of the base class. For each data model class that you want to access, the context class defines a property that returns a DbSet<T> object, and it is through this object that data is stored and retrieved. I defined a property that returns a DbSet<GuestResponse> object so I can store and retrieve GuestResponse objects.

Creating the Controller and Views

To provide the application with a controller, I created the Controllers folder and added to it a file called HomeController.cs with the code shown in Listing 2-7.

Listing 2-7. The Contents of the HomeController.cs File in the Controllers Folder

```
using Microsoft.AspNetCore.Mvc;
using PartyInvites.Models;
using System.Linq;

namespace PartyInvites.Controllers {

    public class HomeController : Controller {
        private DataContext context;

        public HomeController(DataContext ctx) => context = ctx;

        public IActionResult Index() => View();

        public IActionResult Respond() => View();

        [HttpPost]
        public IActionResult Respond(GuestResponse response) {
            context.Responses.Add(response);
            context.SaveChanges();
            return RedirectToAction(nameof(Thanks),
                new { Name = response.Name, WillAttend = response.WillAttend });
        }

        public IActionResult Thanks(GuestResponse response) => View(response);

        public IActionResult ListResponses() =>
            View(context.Responses.OrderByDescending(r => r.WillAttend));
    }
}
```

The controller receives a DataContext object as a constructor parameter and uses it to access the data managed by Entity Framework Core. The DbSet<GuestResponse> object returned by the database context class's Responses property implements the IEnumerable<GuestResponse> interface and will automatically query the database for the stored GuestResponse objects when it is enumerated.

The DbSet<GuestResponse> object is also used to store objects. The Add method is used to give Entity Framework Core an object that you want to store, and the SaveChanges method performs the update.

 Tip   In more complex projects, I recommend using the repository pattern to access the Entity Framework Core features, as explained in Chapter 10. For the simple project in this chapter, the controller is working directly with the database context class.

I created the Views/Home folder and added to it a file called _Layout.cshtml with the content shown in Listing 2-8. This layout will provide the common layout for all of the other views in this chapter and includes a link element that includes the Bootstrap CSS file.

Listing 2-8. The Contents of the _Layout.cshtml File in the Views/Home Folder

```
<!DOCTYPE html>

<html>
<head>
    <meta name="viewport" content="width=device-width" />
    <title>Party Invites</title>
    <link rel="stylesheet" href="/lib/bootstrap/dist/css/bootstrap.css" />
</head>
<body>
    @RenderBody()
</body>
</html>
```

To use the layout by default in the application's view, I added a file called _ViewStart.cshtml in the Views folder with the content shown in Listing 2-9.

Listing 2-9. The Contents of the _ViewStart.cshtml File in the Views Folder

```
@{
    Layout = "_Layout";
}
```

To create the view that will provide a landing page, I added a file called Index.cshtml in the Views/Home folder with the content shown in Listing 2-10.

Listing 2-10. The Contents of the Index.cshtml File in the Views/Home Folder

```
<div class="text-center m-4">
    <h3>We're going to have an exciting party!</h3>
    <h4>And you are invited</h4>
    <a class="btn btn-primary" asp-action="Respond">RSVP Now</a>
</div>
```

To receive details of a response from a user, I added a file called Respond.cshtml to the Views/Home folder with the contents shown in Listing 2-11.

Listing 2-11. The Contents of the Respond.cshtml File in the Views/Home Folder

```
@model GuestResponse

<div class="bg-primary p-2 text-white text-center">
    <h2>RSVP</h2>
</div>

<form asp-action="Respond" method="post" class="m-4">
    <div class="form-group">
        <label>Your Name</label>
        <input asp-for="Name" class="form-control" />
    </div>
    <div class="form-group">
        <label>Your Email</label>
        <input asp-for="Email" class="form-control" />
    </div>
    <div class="form-group">
        <label>Your Phone Number</label>
        <input asp-for="Phone" class="form-control" />
    </div>
    <div class="form-group">
        <label>Will You Attend?</label>
        <select asp-for="WillAttend" class="form-control">
            <option value="">Choose an option</option>
            <option value="true">Yes, I'll be there</option>
            <option value="false">No, I can't come</option>
        </select>
    </div>

    <div class="text-center">
        <button type="submit" class="btn btn-primary">Submit RSVP</button>
    </div>
</form>
```

To confirm the responses provided by users, I added a file called Thanks.cshtml to the Views/Home folder with the content shown in Listing 2-12.

Listing 2-12. The Contents of the Thanks.cshtml File in the Views/Home Folder

```
@model GuestResponse

<div class="text-center mt-3">
    <h1>Thank you, @Model.Name!</h1>
    @if (Model.WillAttend == true) {
        <div>
            It's great that you're coming. The drinks are already in the fridge!
        </div>
    } else {
        <div>
            Sorry to hear that you can't make it, but thanks for letting us know.
        </div>
    }
    Click <a asp-action="ListResponses">here</a> to see who is coming.
</div>
```

To create the final view, I added a file called ListResponses.cshtml to the Views/Home folder with the content shown in Listing 2-13, which lists all of the responses that the application has received.

Listing 2-13. The Contents of the ListResponses.cshtml File in the Views/Home Folder

```
@model IEnumerable<GuestResponse>

<h3 class="bg-primary p-2 text-white text-center">Here is the list of people who have
responded</h3>

<div class="container-fluid">
    <div class="row p-1">
        <div class="col font-weight-bold">Name</div>
        <div class="col font-weight-bold">Email</div>
        <div class="col font-weight-bold">Phone</div>
        <div class="col font-weight-bold">Attending</div>
    </div>
    @foreach (GuestResponse r in Model) {
        <div class="row p-1">
            <div class="col">@r.Name</div>
            <div class="col">@r.Email</div>
            <div class="col">@r.Phone</div>
            <div class="col">@(r.WillAttend == true ? "Yes" : "No")</div>
        </div>
    }
</div>
```

To complete the configuration for the application's views, I added a file called _ViewImports.cshtml in the Views folder, with the content shown in Listing 2-14.

Listing 2-14. The Contents of the _ViewImports.cshtml File in the Views Folder

```
@using PartyInvites.Models
@addTagHelper *, Microsoft.AspNetCore.Mvc.TagHelpers
```

These statements allow the classes in the Models namespace to be used without qualification in views and activate the tag helpers feature, which I have relied on in the views to configure some of the HTML elements.

Configuring Entity Framework Core

When Visual Studio creates a new ASP.NET Core project, it adds almost all of the NuGet packages required for ASP.NET Core MVC and Entity Framework Core development. One further addition is required to add support for the command-line tools that Entity Framework Core uses to prepare databases to store data. Right-click the PartyInvites item in the Solution Explorer, select Edit PartyInvites.csproj from the pop-up menu, and add the element shown in Listing 2-15.

Listing 2-15. Adding a Package in the PartyInvites.csproj File in the PartyInvites Folder

```
<Project Sdk="Microsoft.NET.Sdk.Web">

  <PropertyGroup>
    <TargetFramework>netcoreapp2.0</TargetFramework>
  </PropertyGroup>

  <ItemGroup>
    <Folder Include="wwwroot\" />
  </ItemGroup>

  <ItemGroup>
    <PackageReference Include="Microsoft.AspNetCore.All" Version="2.0.5" />
    <DotNetCliToolReference Include="Microsoft.EntityFrameworkCore.Tools.DotNet"
                            Version="2.0.1" />
  </ItemGroup>

</Project>
```

Packages that provide command-line tools must be added using a DotNetCliToolReference element. Visual Studio provides tools for managing NuGet packages but isn't able to add this kind of package. When you save the file, Visual Studio will download the package and add to the project.

Configuring the Connection String

When you use a database, you must provide a connection string, which tells Entity Framework Core how to connect to the database and often includes additional information such as authentication credentials. Right-click the PartyInvites item in the Solution Explorer, select Add ➤ New Item from the pop-up menu, and select the ASP.NET Configuration File item template; make sure that the Name field is set to appsettings.json, as shown in Figure 2-6.

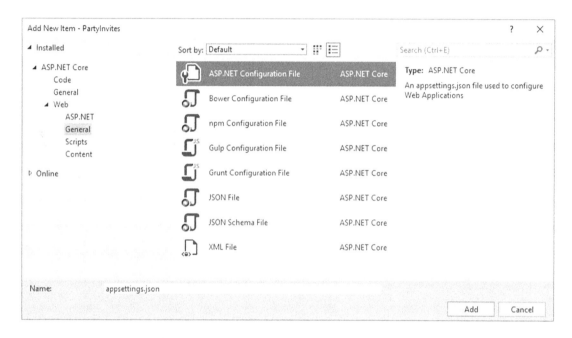

Figure 2-6. *Creating an application configuration file*

Click the Add button to create the file and change the connection string as shown in Listing 2-16.

Listing 2-16. Defining the Connection String in the appsettings.json File in the PartyInvites Folder

```
{
  "ConnectionStrings": {
    "DefaultConnection": "Server=(localdb)\\MSSQLLocalDB;Database=PartyInvites"
  }
}
```

This connection string tells Entity Framework Core to use a database called PartyInvites using LocalDB, which was installed along with Visual Studio.

Configuring the Startup Class

The next step is to configure the application to set up ASP.NET Core MVC and Entity Framework Core by adding the statements shown in Listing 2-17 to the Startup class.

Listing 2-17. Configuring the Application in the Startup.cs File in the PartyInvites Folder

```
using System;
using System.Collections.Generic;
using System.Linq;
using System.Threading.Tasks;
using Microsoft.AspNetCore.Builder;
using Microsoft.AspNetCore.Hosting;
using Microsoft.AspNetCore.Http;
using Microsoft.Extensions.DependencyInjection;
using Microsoft.EntityFrameworkCore;
using Microsoft.Extensions.Configuration;
using PartyInvites.Models;

namespace PartyInvites {

    public class Startup {

        public Startup(IConfiguration config) => Configuration = config;

        public IConfiguration Configuration { get; }

        public void ConfigureServices(IServiceCollection services) {
            services.AddMvc();
            string conString = Configuration["ConnectionStrings:DefaultConnection"];
            services.AddDbContext<DataContext>(options =>
                options.UseSqlServer(conString));
        }

        public void Configure(IApplicationBuilder app, IHostingEnvironment env) {
            app.UseDeveloperExceptionPage();
            app.UseStatusCodePages();
            app.UseStaticFiles();
            app.UseMvcWithDefaultRoute();
        }
    }
}
```

The changes load the settings in the appsettings.json file and use them to configure the database context class so that it will be used by Entity Framework Core and available as a service through the dependency injection feature, which allows other parts of the application to easily obtain a context object and access the Entity Framework Core features.

Preparing the Database

Entity Framework Core has to create and configure a database so that it can be used to store GuestResponse objects. This is done by creating a *migration*. Entity Framework Core inspects the application's data model and figures out how it can be stored in a relational database. The result—the migration—contains a set of instructions that the database provider class translates into SQL commands that tell the database server to create the database that Entity Framework Core needs. I explain how migrations work in detail in Chapter 12.

Migrations are created and applied using command-line tools. Open a new PowerShell window or command prompt, navigate to the PartyInvites project folder (the folder that contains the bower.json and Startup.cs files), and run the command shown in Listing 2-18.

Listing 2-18. Creating a New Migration

```
dotnet ef migrations add Initial
```

To apply the migration and create the database, run the command shown in Listing 2-19 in the PartyInvites folder.

Listing 2-19. Applying a Migration

```
dotnet ef database update
```

Testing the Application

To start the application, run the command shown in Listing 2-20 in the PartyInvites project folder. Although you can start applications using Visual Studio, many of the examples in this book depend on logging messages generated by the application, and these are more easily seen when the application is started from the command line; this is the approach that I take in all of the chapters that follow.

Listing 2-20. Starting the Application

```
dotnet run
```

Once the application has started, open a new browser window and navigate to `http://localhost:5000` to see the content shown in Figure 2-7.

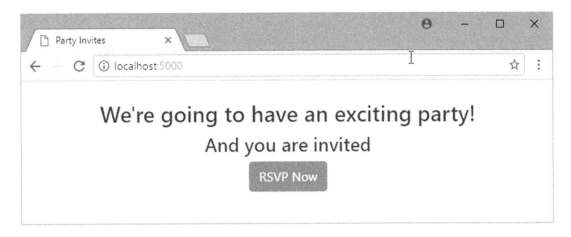

Figure 2-7. *Running the example application*

Click the RSVP Now button, fill out the form, and click the Submit RSVP button. You will see the response shown in Figure 2-8.

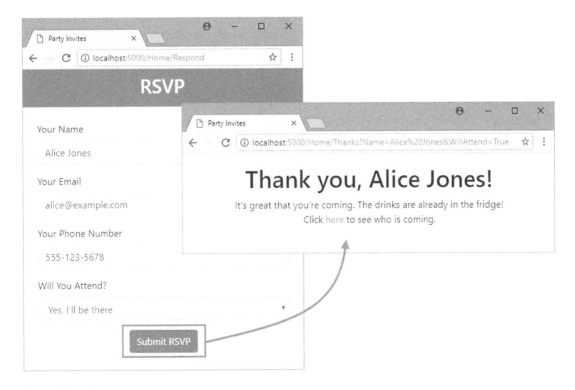

Figure 2-8. *Creating a response*

23

Click the link to see the list of responses. You will see content similar to that shown in Figure 2-9, which shows additional responses I created.

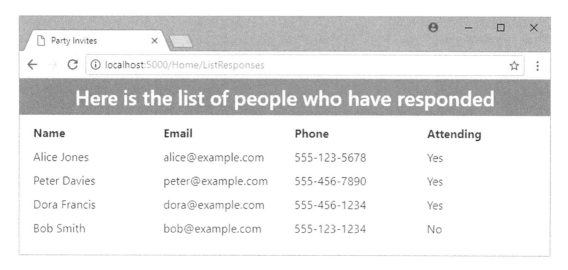

Figure 2-9. *Displaying a list of responses*

The GuestResponse objects that are created by the MVC model binder from the values in the HTTP POST requests are stored in the database. When you request the list of responses, the database is queried for the data, and Entity Framework Core uses the results to create a sequence of GuestResponse objects that are used to generate the list.

Summary

In this chapter, I created a new ASP.NET Core project and used it to create a simple data entry application that stores its data in a LocalDB database using Entity Framework Core. You saw how easy it is to add Entity Framework Core to an MVC application and how few changes are required to store data persistently, at least for a simple application. In the next chapter, I provide an overview of the tools that Visual Studio provides for working with databases and use them to explain the most important SQL commands that Entity Framework Core relies on.

CHAPTER 3

Working with Databases

Using Entity Framework Core makes using databases easier, but it doesn't free the developer from understanding how they work and how actions performed by the application are translated into SQL commands, especially when unexpected results occur. In this chapter, I show you the tools that Visual Studio provides for examining databases and show you how to execute different kinds of SQL commands. You don't need to be an expert in SQL to use Entity Framework Core, but having an understanding of the basics can be helpful when you don't get the outcome you intended.

CHOOSING A DATABASE SERVER AND PROVIDER PACKAGE

It is hard to go wrong when choosing a database server because all of the available options are good products. It doesn't matter whether you prefer commercial products or want open source or whether you want to run your own servers or use the cloud.

If you already have a database server, perhaps because of a corporate purchasing standard or site-licensing deal, then that's the one to use. Entity Framework Core smooths out the differences between database servers, and it doesn't really matter which one you use. It certainly isn't worth fighting against your company's technology standards unless you have very specific requirements.

If you don't already have a database server, then there are plenty of good options available. Microsoft SQL Server is the database server that I use most often because it has a wide range of pricing schemes, including zero-cost options for developers and small projects and hosted versions available on Azure. I use the zero-configuration developer version of SQL Server—known as LocalDB—for the examples in this book.

(I receive no reward of any kind for recommending SQL Server or any of the products I use or mention in books. It is important to use the software I specify to follow the examples, but that doesn't restrict your choices in any way for real projects.)

If you prefer open source, then MySQL is an excellent choice, albeit one that is managed by Oracle, which has a mixed open source track record. MariaDB is a fork of the MySQL project that doesn't involve Oracle but that aims to maintain compatibility. There are many providers that offer MySQL or its derivatives as hosted/cloud services, including Amazon Web Services and Microsoft Azure.

Once you have chosen your database server, you can then select the database provider for use with Entity Framework Core. Microsoft maintains a list of providers for the most popular databases at `https://docs.microsoft.com/en-us/ef/core/providers`. Most provider packages are free to use, but there are some commercial products available, too. If you want to use the Oracle database server (the commercial product, not MySQL), then you will need to license a third-party provider since Oracle has yet to produce its own package.

© Adam Freeman 2018

A. Freeman, *Pro Entity Framework Core 2 for ASP.NET Core MVC*,

https://doi.org/10.1007/978-1-4842-3435-8_3

Preparing for This Chapter

In this chapter, I continue using the PartyInvites project created in Chapter 2. To prepare for this chapter, open a new PowerShell window or command prompt, navigate to the `PartyInvites` project folder (the one that contains the `bower.json` file) and run the commands shown in Listing 3-1. These commands delete and re-create the database used by the application, which will help ensure that you get the expected results for the examples in this chapter.

Listing 3-1. Resetting the Example Application Database

```
dotnet ef database drop --force
dotnet ef database update
```

Add the configuration statements shown in Listing 3-2 to the `appsettings.json` file. These statements disable logging messages for all .NET packages except Entity Framework Core, which will make it easier to follow the examples.

Listing 3-2. Configuring Logging Messages in the appsettings.json File in the PartyInvites Folder

```
{
  "ConnectionStrings": {
    "DefaultConnection": "Server=(localdb)\\MSSQLLocalDB;Database=PartyInvites"
  },
  "Logging": {
    "LogLevel": {
      "Default": "None",
      "Microsoft.EntityFrameworkCore": "Information"
    }
  }
}
```

This logging configuration will let you see the messages produced by Entity Framework Core that reveal the SQL commands that are sent to the database and prevent them from being lost in a stream of other messages.

Start the application by executing the `dotnet run` command in the project folder and use a browser window to navigate to `http://localhost:5000`. Click the RSVP Now button and create four RSVP responses using the values shown in Table 3-1.

Table 3-1. The Data Values Required for the Example Application

Name	Email	Phone	WillAttend
Alice Jones	alice@example.com	555-123-5678	Yes
Peter Davies	peter@example.com	555-456-7890	Yes
Dora Francis	dora@example.com	555-456-1234	Yes
Bob Smith	bob@example.com	555-123-1234	No

When you have added the responses, navigate to `http://localhost:5000/home/listresponses` and you will see the list shown in Figure 3-1.

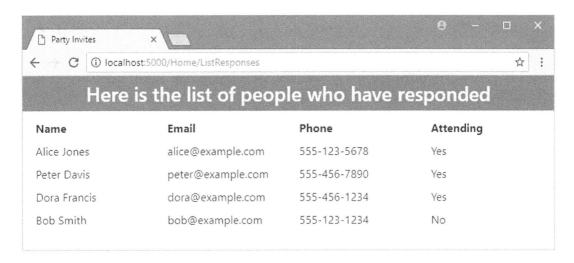

***Figure 3-1.** Adding data to the example application*

Exploring the Database

Visual Studio includes a set of tools that allow you to explore the databases you work with. Select Connect to Database from the Visual Studio Tools menu, and you will be presented with the dialog box shown in Figure 3-2, which lets you select the type of database server you want to connect to.

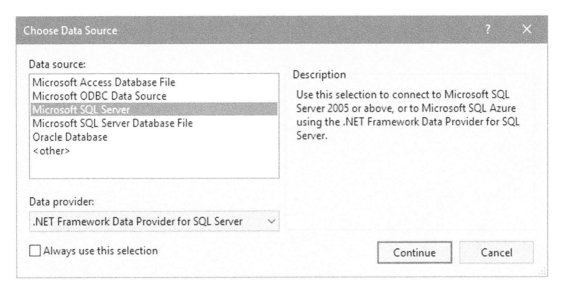

***Figure 3-2.** Selecting the database server type*

In this book, I use LocalDB for all the examples. LocalDB is a version of Microsoft SQL Server that was installed as part of the Visual Studio workload in Chapter 2 and is designed to be used by developers. It implements all the key SQL Server features, but it requires no configuration and isn't licensed for production systems. Select Microsoft SQL Server from the list of options presented by Visual Studio and click the Continue button.

The next dialog box lets you specify the details of the database server and database you want to work with, as shown in Figure 3-3. Enter **(localdb)\MSSQLLocalDB** into the Server Name field and select PartyInvites for the "Select or Enter a Database Name" field, as shown in Figure 3-3.

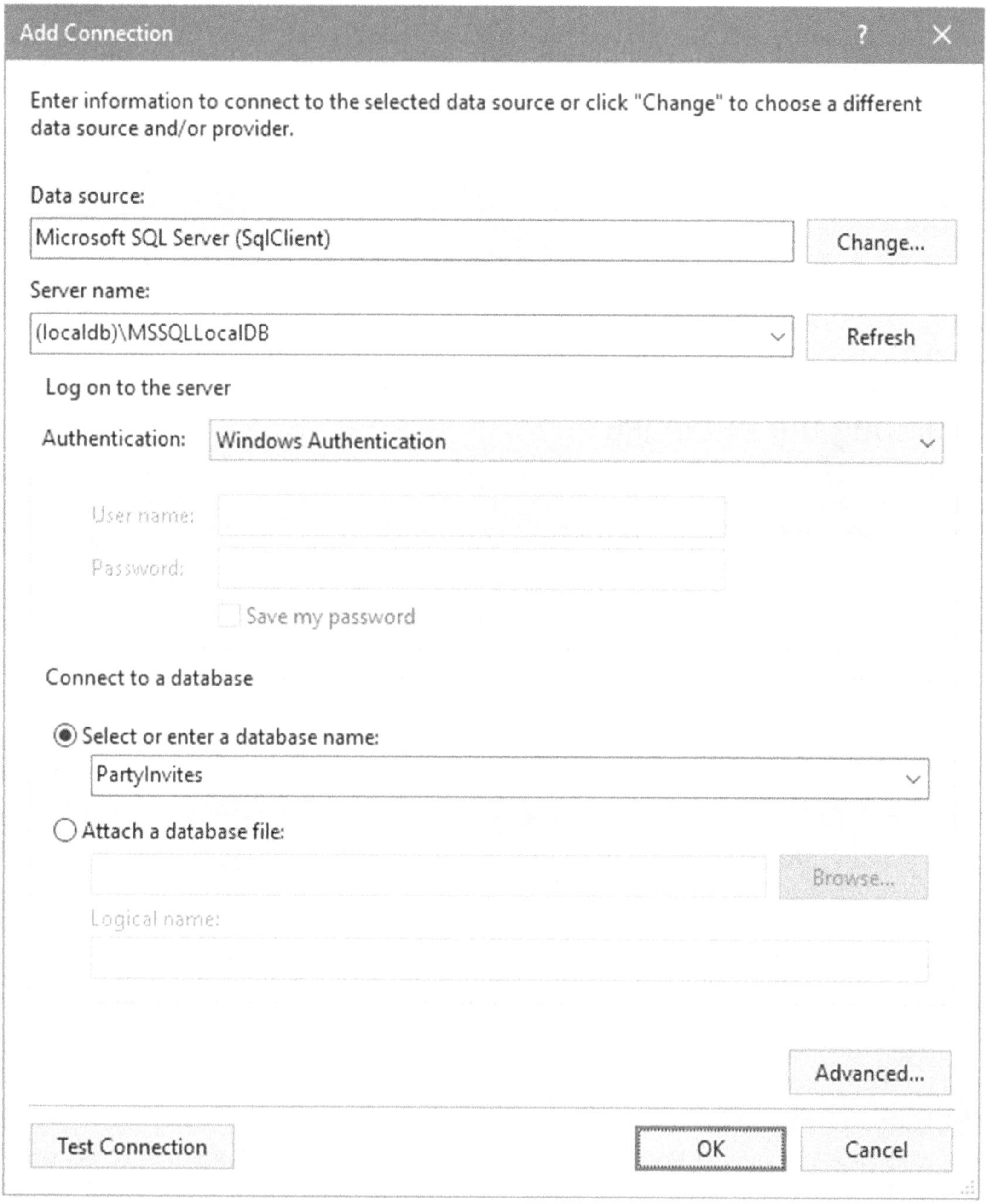

Figure 3-3. Selecting the database server and database

> ■ **Tip** The string required to connect to LocalDB can cause confusion. The first part is localdb surrounded by parentheses. Then there is a single \ character, followed by MS_SQL_LocalDB but without the underscores: (localdb)\MSSQLLocalDB. An additional \ character is required when you specify connection strings in the appsetting.json file because the backward slash has special meaning and must be escaped: (localdb)\\ MSSQLLocalDB.

Click the OK button and Visual Studio will connect to the database server and display the details in the Server Explorer window (select View ➤ Server Explorer if the window doesn't open). In the Data Connections section of the display, you will see an entry for the PartyInvites, which you can expand to see details of the database, as shown in Figure 3-4.

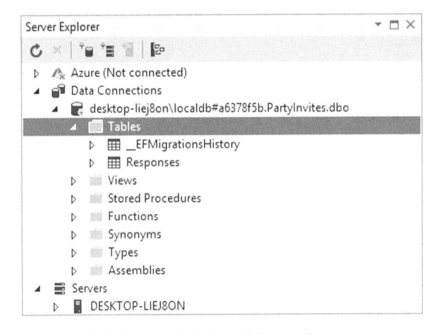

Figure 3-4. *The database entry in the Server Explorer window*

Examining the Database Tables

If you expand the Tables item, you will see two entries. The __EFMigrationsHistory table is used to keep track of the migrations that have been applied to the database to keep it synchronized with the application's data model. I explain how migrations work in detail in Chapter 13, and this table isn't of interest for this chapter. The Responses table is used to store the application's GuestResponse objects. Expand this table in the Server Explorer and you can see the table columns, as shown in Figure 3-5.

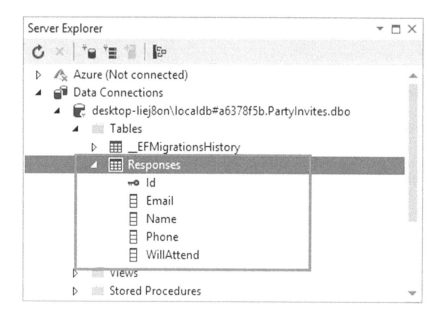

Figure 3-5. *The structure of the Responses table in the database*

You can see how Entity Framework Core has used details from the application to create the table that will store GuestResponse objects. The name of the table is taken from the property in the database context class, and the names of the columns correspond to the properties defined by the GuestResponse class. These decisions are conventions that Entity Framework Core follows by default, and I explain how to override them in Part 2.

The data types used by .NET have to be translated into data types that are supported by the database server. Entity Framework Core works out what database types should be used when it creates the database, and you can examine its decisions by right-clicking the Responses item in the Server Explorer window and selecting Open Table Definition from the pop-up menu. Visual Studio will open a new editor pane that contains details of the table structure, as shown in Figure 3-6.

Figure 3-6. *Exploring structure of a database table*

You can see the SQL data type that has been selected to represent the value of each GuestResponse property. Entity Framework Core relies on the database provider to select the best SQL data types, and there can be differences in the types selected for different database servers. For SQL Server, you can see that the Id property will be stored as a SQL bigint, corresponding to a .NET long; the WillAttend property will be stored as a bit, corresponding for a .NET nullable bool; and the other properties will be stored as nvarchar(MAX), which corresponds to the .NET string.

■ **Tip**   For most projects, the data types that Entity Framework Core selects will be perfectly acceptable, but you can use the features described in Chapter 21 to specify different types.

Examining the Database Content

Right-click the table in the Server Explorer window and select Show Table Data from the pop-up menu to see the data in the table. Visual Studio will query the database and display the results, as shown in Figure 3-7.

Figure 3-7. *Displaying the data in a database table*

The grid that Visual Studio uses to display the data is editable, which means you can update the existing data values and add new rows to the table without needing to use SQL directly.

Add a new response by using the values shown in Table 3-2 to fill out the fields in the bottom row of the grid and then press the Tab key. You won't be able to enter a value for the Id column, but the database server will assign a value for you when the data is added to the database.

Table 3-2. *The Data Values for Adding a Row to the Database Table*

Email	Name	Phone	WillAttend
jane@example.com	Jane Marshall	555-123-1212	True

When you press the Tab button, Visual Studio will add the new data to the database. You can see the new data in the application by navigating to http://localhost:5000/home/listresponses, as shown in Figure 3-8.

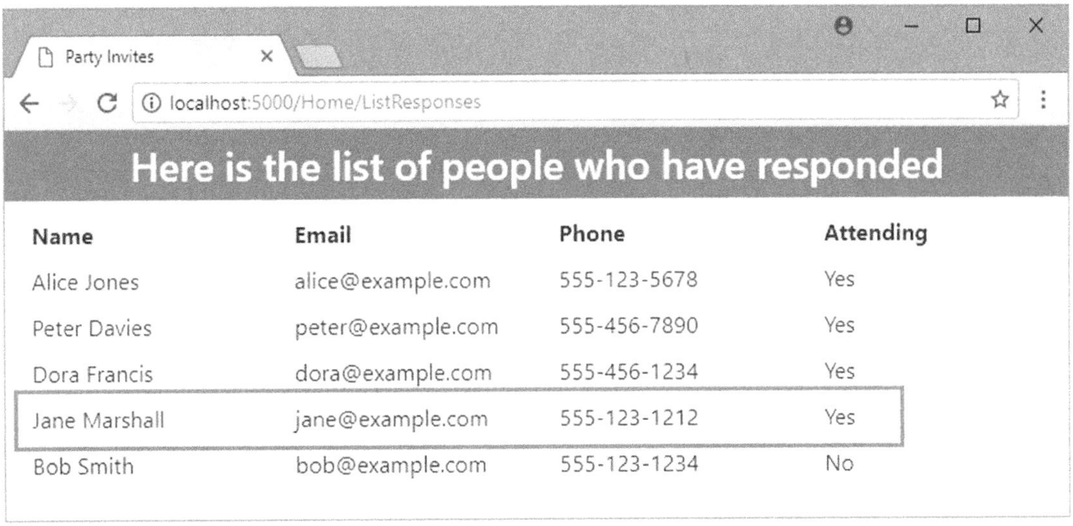

Figure 3-8. New data displayed by the application

Understanding SQL

It can often be useful to understand how Entity Framework Core translates your application's actions into commands for the database server. You don't have to be an expert in SQL to use Entity Framework Core, but it helps to know the basics so you can tell when you are not getting the results you expect. In the sections that follow, I describe the basic SQL commands and explain how they are used by Entity Framework Core.

Querying Data

The fundamental SQL feature is the query, which retrieves data from the database. If you navigate to http://localhost:5000/home/listresponses and examine the logging messages generated by the application, you will be able to see the SQL command that Entity Framework Core used to get the data from the database, shown here:

```
...
SELECT [r].[Id], [r].[Email], [r].[Name], [r].[Phone], [r].[WillAttend]
FROM [Responses] AS [r]
ORDER BY [r].[WillAttend] DESC
...
```

If you are familiar with LINQ, you will have a sense of what this SQL command does just by reading it, but it is worth exploring a little further to understand what Entity Framework Core is doing.

Manually Querying the Database

You can query the database directly using the Visual Studio Server Explorer window by right-clicking the table and selecting New Query from the pop-up menu. When working with SQL Server, I prefer to use a different Visual Studio feature by selecting New Query from the Tools ➤ SQL Server menu. When you see the Connect dialog window shown in Figure 3-9, enter **(localdb)\MSSQLLocalDB** in the Server Name field, leave the Database Name field as <default>, and click the Connect button.

33

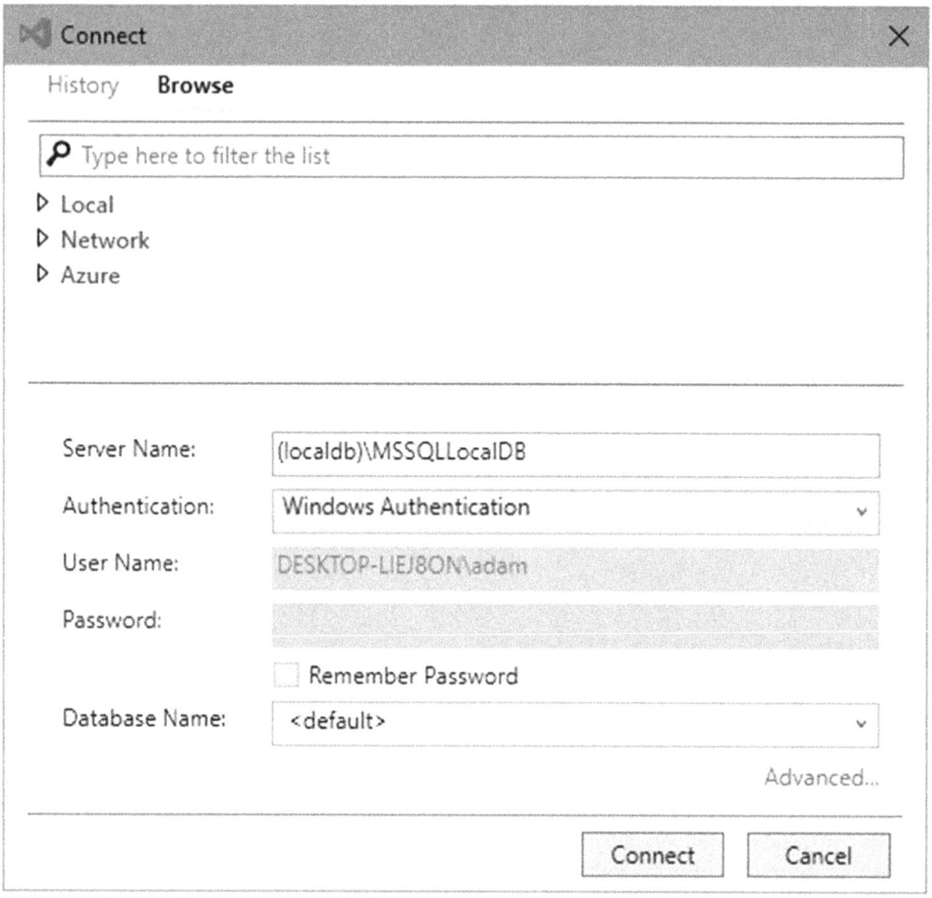

Figure 3-9. *Connecting to the database*

■ **Tip**   Once you have connected to a database, the connection settings are saved in the `History` table of the Connect dialog window and can be used to connect in the future without having to reenter the details.

Click the Connect button, and Visual Studio will connect to the database server and open a new editor pane, into which you can enter SQL commands. Enter the commands shown in Listing 3-3 into the new editor.

Listing 3-3. A Basic SQL Query

```
USE PartyInvites

SELECT * FROM Responses
```

Click the green arrow in the top-left corner of the editor pane or right-click the window and select Execute from the pop-up menu to execute the commands. Visual Studio will send the SQL to the database server and display the results, as shown in Figure 3-10.

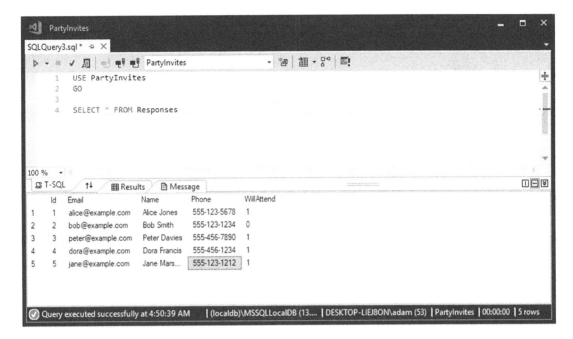

Figure 3-10. *Querying the database*

Since this is the first SQL command you have executed directly, I will break down each part of it and explain what it means. Here is the first part:

```
...
USE PartyInvites
...
```

This command selects the PartyInvites database. A database server can manage many databases, and it is important to select the database that you want to work with. (You can select the database when you create the connection or use the drop-down list at the top of the query window, but I prefer to make the selection explicitly.)

The second part of the SQL from Listing 3-3 is the actual query, shown here:

```
...
SELECT * FROM Responses
...
```

The SELECT keyword denotes a SQL query. The FROM keyword specifies the database table whose data is required. The asterisk specifies that the query should return values for all the columns in the table. Put together, this query tells the database server "give me all of the columns from the Responses table." This query produces the results shown in Table 3-3.

Table 3-3. *The Results from the Basic Query*

Id	Email	Name	Phone	WillAttend
1	alice@example.com	Alice Jones	555-123-5678	1
2	bob@example.com	Bob Smith	555-123-1234	0
3	peter@example.com	Peter Davies	555-456-7890	1
4	dora@example.com	Dora Francis	555-456-1234	1
5	jane@example.com	Jane Marshall	555-123-1212	1

Filtering Data

A query will return all the rows in a table by default. That is perfectly reasonable for applications that store small amounts of data, such as the example project, but in most real projects you will want to query for a subset of the data. The WHERE keyword is used to select specific rows from a database table. Enter the SQL shown in Listing 3-4 into the Visual Studio query window to see how this works.

STRUCTURED QUERY LANGUAGE CONVENTIONS

You will notice that I use uppercase characters for the SQL keywords in this chapter. This is not required, but it is common practice to do so, and it can help make complex SQL easier to read. The world of SQL is as full of conventions and preferences—just like C# development—and you will inevitably encounter database administrators and developers who insist on a certain style. Database servers are adept at parsing SQL, and my advice is to adopt a style that you and your team find easy to read, even if that means writing commands that tends toward the C# coding conventions rather than those associated with SQL.

Listing 3-4. Querying for Selected Rows

```
USE PartyInvites

SELECT * FROM Responses
WHERE WillAttend = 1
```

The WHERE keyword is followed by an expression that will match the rows that should be included in the results. In this case, I have specified that rows that have a WillAttend value of 1 should be included in the results and other rows should be excluded. Execute this command, and you will see just the matching responses, as shown in Table 3-4.

Table 3-4. *Results from Using the WHERE Keyword*

Id	Email	Name	Phone	WillAttend
1	alice@example.com	Alice Jones	555-123-5678	1
3	peter@example.com	Peter Davies	555-456-7890	1
4	dora@example.com	Dora Francis	555-456-1234	1
5	jane@example.com	Jane Marshall	555-123-1212	1

Selecting and Ordering Columns

The asterisk (the * character) in the query asks for all the columns for the rows that are included in the results. You won't always need all of the columns, and you may want to specify the order in which the columns are presented in the results. A SQL query can be selective about the columns that are included in the results, as shown in Listing 3-5.

Listing 3-5. Selecting and Ordering Columns

```
USE PartyInvites
SELECT Id, Name, Email FROM Responses
WHERE WillAttend = 'true'
```

In this query, I have specified that I only want values for the Id, Name, and Email columns. When you execute the query, you will see the results shown in Table 3-5, and values from the other columns are excluded. Notice that the results are presented in the order in which I specified the columns.

Table 3-5. *Results Selecting Columns*

Id	Name	Email
1	Alice Jones	alice@example.com
3	Peter Davies	peter@example.com
4	Dora Francis	dora@example.com
5	Jane Marshall	jane@example.com

Ordering Rows

The order in which the matching rows are returned in the results can be specified using the ORDER BY keywords. In Listing 3-6, I have used ORDER BY to tell the database server that I want the results ordered by the value of the Email column.

Listing 3-6. Ordering Results

```
USE PartyInvites

SELECT Id, Name, Email FROM Responses
WHERE WillAttend = 'true'
ORDER BY Email
```

When you execute the query, the results will be ordered by the value of the Email column, as shown in Table 3-6.

Table 3-6. *Results Ordering Rows*

Id	Name	Email
1	Alice Jones	alice@example.com
4	Dora Francis	dora@example.com
5	Jane Marshall	jane@example.com
3	Peter Davies	peter@example.com

Examining the Entity Framework Core Query

There are lots of SQL query features, but the ones shown in the previous sections are enough to get a sense of the data that is being requested from the database. There are some slight differences in the queries that Entity Framework Core produces that are worth explaining. In Listing 3-7, I have changed the LINQ query used in the ListResponses action method of the Home controller to be more selective about the data it requests.

Listing 3-7. Changing the LINQ Query in the HomeController.cs File in the Controllers Folder

```
using Microsoft.AspNetCore.Mvc;
using PartyInvites.Models;
using System.Linq;

namespace PartyInvites.Controllers {

    public class HomeController : Controller {
        private DataContext context;

        public HomeController(DataContext ctx) => context = ctx;

        public IActionResult Index() => View();

        public IActionResult Respond() => View();

        [HttpPost]
        public IActionResult Respond(GuestResponse response) {
            context.Responses.Add(response);
            context.SaveChanges();
            return RedirectToAction(nameof(Thanks),
                new { Name = response.Name, WillAttend = response.WillAttend });
        }

        public IActionResult Thanks(GuestResponse response) => View(response);
```

```
public IActionResult ListResponses() =>
    View(context.Responses
        .Where(r => r.WillAttend == true)
        .OrderBy(r => r.Email));
    }
}
```

Start the application using `dotnet run` in the project folder and navigate to `http://localhost:5000/home/listresponses`. The HTML displayed to the user will contain only responses from those attending the party, ordered by their e-mail addresses, as shown in Figure 3-11.

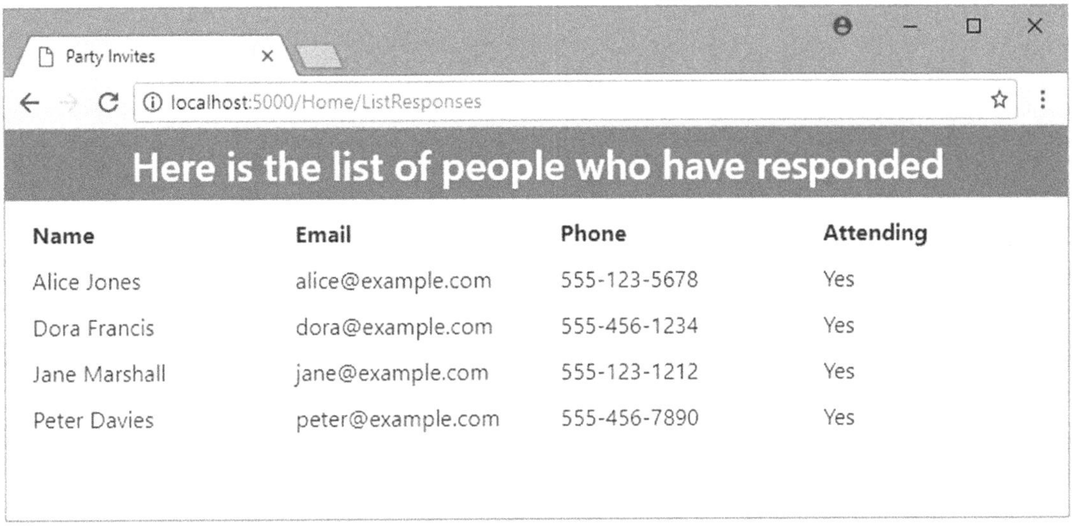

Figure 3-11. *Using a more selective query in the example application*

If you examine the logging messages generated by the application, you will see the SQL that Entity Framework Core produced from the LINQ query.

```
...
SELECT [r].[Id], [r].[Email], [r].[Name], [r].[Phone], [r].[WillAttend]
FROM [Responses] AS [r]
WHERE [r].[WillAttend] = 1
ORDER BY [r].[Email]
...
```

You can see that the structure of the query follows the same pattern as the one that I built in the previous sections. The use of square brackets (the [and] characters) allows column names to contain special characters, such as spaces. This isn't required for the data model in the example application, but Entity Framework Core does it anyway.

The AS keyword is used to create a temporary alias. Entity Framework Core uses the AS keyword to refer to the Responses table using r. This is something that doesn't have benefit in a simple query but that can be helpful in more complex queries that combine data from multiple tables.

Understanding Query Parameters

There is one further difference that you might see when examining the queries that are created by Entity Framework Core. To demonstrate, I have changed the query used by the ListResponses action method, as shown in Listing 3-8.

Listing 3-8. Changing the LINQ Query in the HomeController.cs File in the Controllers Folder

```
using Microsoft.AspNetCore.Mvc;
using PartyInvites.Models;
using System.Linq;

namespace PartyInvites.Controllers {

    public class HomeController : Controller {
        private DataContext context;

        public HomeController(DataContext ctx) => context = ctx;

        public IActionResult Index() => View();

        public IActionResult Respond() => View();

        [HttpPost]
        public IActionResult Respond(GuestResponse response) {
            context.Responses.Add(response);
            context.SaveChanges();
            return RedirectToAction(nameof(Thanks),
                new { Name = response.Name, WillAttend = response.WillAttend });
        }

        public IActionResult Thanks(GuestResponse response) => View(response);

        public IActionResult ListResponses(string searchTerm = "555-123-5678") =>
            View(context.Responses
                .Where(r => r.Phone == searchTerm)
                .OrderBy(r => r.Email));
    }
}
```

The LINQ query uses the Where method to select GuestResponse objects whose Phone value matches a search parameter. If you start the application, navigate to http://localhost:5000/home/listresponses, and examine the logging messages generated by the application, you will see how this has been translated into SQL.

```
...
SELECT [r].[Id], [r].[Email], [r].[Name], [r].[Phone], [r].[WillAttend]
FROM [Responses] AS [r]
WHERE [r].[Phone] = @__searchTerm_0
ORDER BY [r].[Email]
...
```

The @ character is used to denote a parameter in a SQL query. Parameters are used when Entity Framework Core is dealing with variables, and they allow the database server to recognize similar queries and improve performance by processing them the same way. Parameters also provide protection against SQL injection attacks, where a user enters a data value that can be interpreted as part of the SQL command.

Using parameters is a good idea—especially since Entity Framework Core doesn't know whether the source of the data value can be trusted—but it does make it more difficult to understand what SQL is being sent to the database because the parameter value isn't displayed in the logging messages by default. This isn't a problem most of the time because it is the structure of the query that is of interest, but in Listing 3-9, I have changed the configuration of the example application so that Entity Framework Core will include parameter values in the logging messages it generates.

Caution   Don't leave this option enabled in production because sensitive data will end up in the application's log files.

Listing 3-9. Enabling Parameter Value Logging in the Startup.cs File in the PartyInvites Folder

```
using System;
using System.Collections.Generic;
using System.Linq;
using System.Threading.Tasks;
using Microsoft.AspNetCore.Builder;
using Microsoft.AspNetCore.Hosting;
using Microsoft.AspNetCore.Http;
using Microsoft.Extensions.DependencyInjection;
using Microsoft.EntityFrameworkCore;
using Microsoft.Extensions.Configuration;
using PartyInvites.Models;

namespace PartyInvites {

    public class Startup {

        public Startup(IConfiguration config) => Configuration = config;

        public IConfiguration Configuration { get; }

        public void ConfigureServices(IServiceCollection services) {
            services.AddMvc();
            string conString = Configuration["ConnectionStrings:DefaultConnection"];
            services.AddDbContext<DataContext>(options => {
                options.EnableSensitiveDataLogging(true);
                options.UseSqlServer(conString);
            });
        }
```

```
        public void Configure(IApplicationBuilder app, IHostingEnvironment env) {
            app.UseDeveloperExceptionPage();
            app.UseStatusCodePages();
            app.UseStaticFiles();
            app.UseMvcWithDefaultRoute();
        }
    }
}
```

Using the EnableSensitiveDataLogging method tells Entity Framework Core to include the parameter values in its logging messages. Restart the application using dotnet and navigate to http://localhost:5000/home/listresponses. In the logging messages generated by the application, Entity Framework Core will include parameter values in the message displayed immediately before the query.

```
...
Executed DbCommand (58ms) [Parameters=[@__searchTerm_0='555-123-5678' (Size = 4000)],
    CommandType='Text', CommandTimeout='30']
SELECT [r].[Id], [r].[Email], [r].[Name], [r].[Phone], [r].[WillAttend]
FROM [Responses] AS [r]
WHERE [r].[Phone] = @__searchTerm_0
ORDER BY [r].[Email]
...
```

Storing and Updating Data

In most applications, queries are the most common type of command, but storing new data and updating existing data are important, too. The INSERT command is used to insert a new row of data into a table, and the SQL command shown in Listing 3-10 adds a new row to the Responses table.

Listing 3-10. Inserting Data into a Table

```
USE PartyInvites

INSERT INTO Responses(Name, Email, Phone, WillAttend)
VALUES ('Joe Dobbs', 'joe@example.com', '555-888-1234', 1)
```

The INSERT INTO keywords are followed by a list of the columns for which you want to provide values. Then the VALUES keyword is used, followed by the values that are to be stored in the database, expressed in the same order as the list of columns. The command in the listing adds a new row with values for the Name, Email, Phone, and WillAttend columns. No value is required for the Id column, which Entity Framework Core configures so that the database server will generate a value when the rest of the columns are stored.

Tip   Notice that strings are demarked with single quotes (the ' character) in SQL, rather than the double quotes (the " character) used by C#.

When you execute the command in Listing 3-10, you will see the following message:

```
...
(1 row(s) affected)
...
```

The database server responds to commands that modify the database by indicating how many rows were changed. To see the INSERT command used by Entity Framework Core, navigate to http://localhost:5000, click the RSVP Now button, and create a response using the values in Table 3-7.

Table 3-7. *The Values for Creating a Response*

Name	Email	Phone	WillAttend
Anna Roth	anna@example.com	555-204-7692	False

If you examine the logging messages generated by the application when it stores the new data in the database, you will see that the same basic style of INSERT command has been used but with a few differences.

```
...
Executed DbCommand (3ms) [Parameters=[@p0='anna@example.com' (Size = 4000),
    @p1='Anna Roth' (Size = 4000), @p2='555-204-7692' (Size = 4000),
    @p3=False' (Nullable = true)], CommandType='Text', CommandTimeout='30']

SET NOCOUNT ON;

INSERT INTO [Responses] ([Email], [Name], [Phone], [WillAttend])
VALUES (@p0, @p1, @p2, @p3);
...
```

The SET NOCOUNT ON command disables reporting on the number of rows that are affected by a command. It has little effect on simple commands like the one in this chapter, but it can improve performance for more complex operations. You can see that the INSERT command used by Entity Framework Core is similar to the one from Listing 3-10 but with parameterized values.

Immediately after the INSERT, Entity Framework Core sends another command to the database server.

```
...
SELECT [Id]
FROM [Responses]
WHERE @@ROWCOUNT = 1 AND [Id] = scope_identity();
...
```

Entity Framework Core uses this command to check the number of rows that have been affected by the INSERT command and to determine the value unique value that the database server has assigned to the Id column. Knowing the Id value is important for subsequent operations performed on the new stored data, and Entity Framework Core performs this query even though there are no such operations in the example application.

Updating Existing Data

The UPDATE command is used to modify data that has been previously stored in the database and can be used to select modify multiple rows in a single operation. The command shown in Listing 3-11 modifies the rows in the Responses table whose WillAttend value is 1 and changes their phone number. (This isn't an especially useful change in its own right, but it does demonstrate the basic structure of an UPDATE.)

Listing 3-11. Updating Existing Data

```
USE PartyInvites

UPDATE Responses
SET Phone='404-204-1234'
WHERE WillAttend = 1
```

The UPDATE keyword is followed by the name of the table, and the SET keyword is used to specify the columns and values to be changed. The WHERE keyword is followed by an expression that selects the rows to be modified. When you execute this command, the database server will respond with the number of rows that have been affected.

```
...
(5 row(s) affected)
...
```

Execute the command shown in Listing 3-12 to query for all the rows in the Responses table.

Listing 3-12. Querying for All Rows

```
USE PartyInvites

SELECT * FROM Responses
```

Table 3-8 shows the results of this query and highlights the effect of the update performed in Listing 3-11.

Table 3-8. *The Effect of Updating Existing Data*

Id	Email	Name	Phone	WillAttend
1	alice@example.com	Alice Jones	**404-204-1234**	1
2	bob@example.com	Bob Smith	555-123-1234	0
3	peter@example.com	Peter Davies	**404-204-1234**	1
4	dora@example.com	Dora Francis	**404-204-1234**	1
5	jane@example.com	Jane Marshall	**404-204-1234**	1
6	joe@example.com	Joe Dobbs	**404-204-1234**	1
7	anna@example.com	Anna Roth	555-204-7692	0

Deleting Data

The last command is the one that removes data from the database: the DELETE command. This command must be used carefully because it has a WHERE clause that allows a single command to select many rows for deletion, and it is easy to accidentally remove more data from the database than intended. The command shown in Listing 3-13 removes all of the rows from the Responses table that have a WillAttend value of zero.

Listing 3-13. Deleting Data

```
USE PartyInvites

DELETE FROM Responses
WHERE WillAttend = 0
```

Execute this command and then repeat the query from Listing 3-12 to confirm that the declined invitations have been removed from the database. There is no support in the example application for deleting data, but you will see this type of command used in later chapters, including as part of the SportsStore application that I start building in the next chapter.

Joining Data

Databases can contain relationships between tables, which Entity Framework Core uses to keep track of relationships between objects. This feature is built on the INSERT and UPDATE commands described earlier in this chapter but depends on a more complex type of query, known as a *join*, which incorporates data from multiple tables. Joins can be confusing; you don't need to understand them to work with Entity Framework Core, but having a basic knowledge can be useful.

▪ **Note** Don't worry if you don't follow this section immediately. It will make more sense once you have read Chapter 14, which includes the Entity Framework Core feature that uses joins and which is described in depth in Chapters 15 and 16.

Preparing the Database

To demonstrate how a join works, I need to add another table to the database. Execute the command shown in Listing 3-14, which will create a table called Preferences.

Listing 3-14. Creating a New Table in the Database

```
USE PartyInvites

DROP TABLE IF EXISTS Preferences

CREATE TABLE Preferences (
    Id bigint IDENTITY,
    Email nvarchar(max),
    NutAllergy bit,
    Teetotal bit,
    ResponseId bigint,

)
```

The DROP TABLE command tells the database server to delete the Preferences table if it already exists, which means that you can execute the commands shown in Listing 3-14 repeatedly without causing an error.

The CREATE TABLE command is used to create a new table. The name of the table is specified, along with a list of the columns that the table will contain and the type of each column. The table created by the command in Listing 3-14 has Id, Email, NutAllergy, and Teetotal columns. The Id column has been configured with the IDENTITY keyword, which makes the database server responsible for creating unique values and which Entity Framework Core applies by default to primary key columns. The command shown in Listing 3-15 inserts new rows into the Responses and Preferences tables.

Listing 3-15. Storing Related Data

```
USE PartyInvites

INSERT INTO Responses(Name, Email, Phone, WillAttend)
VALUES ('Dave Habbs', 'dave@example.com', '555-777-1234', 1)

INSERT INTO Preferences (Email, NutAllergy, Teetotal)
VALUES ('dave@example.com', 0, 1)
```

The first INSERT command adds a row to the Responses table. The second INSERT command adds a row to the Preferences table. Execute the commands shown in Listing 3-16 to query these tables and see the new data.

Listing 3-16. Querying for the New Data

```
USE PartyInvites

SELECT * FROM Responses
SELECT * FROM Preferences
```

The first SELECT command queries the database for all the Response rows and includes the row shown in Table 3-9, which was created by the first INSERT command in Listing 3-15.

Table 3-9. *The New Responses Row*

Id	Email	Name	Phone	WillAttend
8	dave@example.com	Dave Habbs	555-777-1234	1

The second SELECT command queries the database for all the Preferences rows and produces the result shown in Table 3-10. Notice that the ResponseId property of the row in the Preferences table matches the Id value for the row shown in Table 3-9.

Table 3-10. *The New Preferences Row*

Id	Email	NutAllergy	Teetotal
1	dave@example.com	0	1

Performing a Join

There are different types of joins, but the kind that is used by Entity Framework Core is known as an *inner join*, which selects rows from tables that share a common value. Listing 3-17 contains a query that performs an inner join on the Responses and Preferences tables.

Listing 3-17. Performing an Inner Join

```
USE PartyInvites

SELECT Responses.Email, Responses.Name, Preferences.NutAllergy, Preferences.Teetotal
FROM Responses
INNER JOIN Preferences ON Responses.Email = Preferences.Email
```

The SELECT command asks the database server for columns from both tables and the INNER JOIN keywords are used to specify that rows from the Responses table should be joined with rows from the Preferences table where both have the same Email value. The result is that data values from both rows created in Listing 3-16 are combined into a single result, as shown in Table 3-11.

Table 3-11. *The JOIN Results*

Email	Name	NutAllergy	Teetotal
dave@example.com	Dave Habbs	0	1

This is a simple join, but it shows the basic mechanism and will help you make sense of the queries that Entity Framework Core uses to get data from databases used to store complex data models.

Summary

In this chapter, I showed you how to use Visual Studio to inspect the database that is used to store an application's data. I also showed you how to execute basic SQL commands so that you have a sense of how Entity Framework Core is using the database and you can check you are getting the results that you expect. In the next chapter, I start the process of creating a more complex and realistic application: SportsStore.

CHAPTER 4

SportsStore: A Real (Data) Application

In this chapter, I start the process of building a more realistic project that demonstrates how ASP.NET Core MVC and Entity Framework Core are used together. The project will be simple but realistic and focus on the most commonly used Entity Framework Core features. The application will be a variation on the SportsStore application that I use in many of my books, with an increased focus on data and data storage.

In this chapter, I build a simple self-contained ASP.NET Core MVC application. In the next chapter, I add Entity Framework Core and store the application data in a database. In the chapters that follow, I add more data operations, expand the data model, add support for customer features, and show you how to scale up the application. Throughout the SportsStore chapters, I point you at the chapters that describe key features in isolation and in more detail. Starting in Chapter 5, when I add Entity Framework Core to the project, I also describe the most common problems that you are likely to encounter and explain how to resolve them.

Note My focus in this book is on Entity Framework Core and how it can be used in an MVC application. I have omitted some SportsStore features, such as authentication for administration features, and expanded on others, such as the data model.

Creating the Project

To create the SportsStore project, start Visual Studio and select New ➤ Project from the File menu. Select the ASP.NET Core Web Application project template, set the Name field to SportsStore, and click the Browse button to select a convenient location to store the project, as shown in Figure 4-1.

Tip You can download this project from the GitHub repository for this book, `https://github.com/apress/pro-ef-core-2-for-asp.net-core-mvc`.

© Adam Freeman 2018
A. Freeman, *Pro Entity Framework Core 2 for ASP.NET Core MVC*,
https://doi.org/10.1007/978-1-4842-3435-8_4

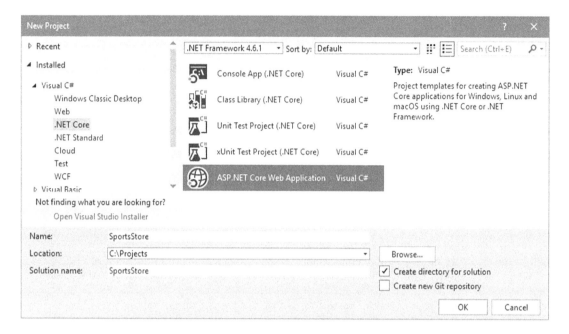

Figure 4-1. *Creating the example project*

Click the OK button to continue the project setup. Ensure that .NET Core and ASP.NET Core 2.0 are selected at the top of the window and click the Empty template, as shown in Figure 4-2. Visual Studio includes templates that set up ASP.NET Core MVC and Entity Framework Core in a project, but the result hides some useful details. I start with a basic ASP.NET Core project and build it up step-by-step in the chapters that follow so you can see how the different components work together.

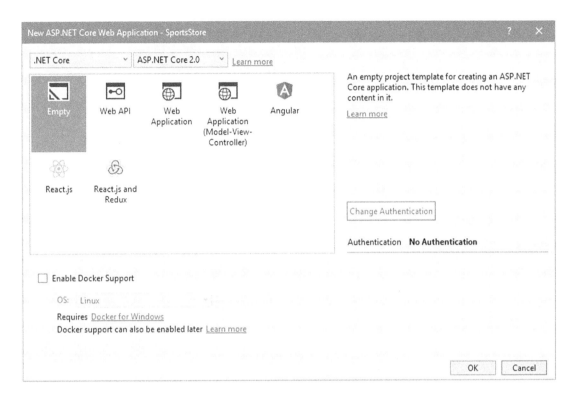

Figure 4-2. *Configuring the ASP.NET Core project*

Click the OK button and Visual Studio will create the SportsStore project with a basic configuration that sets up ASP.NET Core but doesn't configure the MVC framework or Entity Framework Core.

Configuring the MVC Framework

The next step is to add the basic configuration for the MVC framework so that I can add controllers and views to handle HTTP requests. I added the MVC middleware to the ASP.NET Core request pipeline, as shown in Listing 4-1.

Listing 4-1. Configuring MVC in the Startup.cs File in the SportsStore Folder

```
using System;
using System.Collections.Generic;
using System.Linq;
using System.Threading.Tasks;
using Microsoft.AspNetCore.Builder;
using Microsoft.AspNetCore.Hosting;
using Microsoft.AspNetCore.Http;
using Microsoft.Extensions.DependencyInjection;
```

```
namespace SportsStore {
    public class Startup {

        public void ConfigureServices(IServiceCollection services) {
            services.AddMvc();
        }

        public void Configure(IApplicationBuilder app, IHostingEnvironment env) {
            app.UseDeveloperExceptionPage();
            app.UseStatusCodePages();
            app.UseStaticFiles();
            app.UseMvcWithDefaultRoute();
        }
    }
}
```

These changes configure the MVC framework using the default routing schema, add support for static files, and configure the error pages so they provide details useful for developers.

Adding the Model

The model for this application will be based around a list of products. I created the Models folder and added to it a class file called Product.cs with the code shown in Listing 4-2.

Listing 4-2. The Contents of the Product.cs File in the Models Folder

```
namespace SportsStore.Models {

    public class Product {
        public string Name { get; set; }
        public string Category { get; set; }
        public decimal PurchasePrice { get; set; }
        public decimal RetailPrice { get; set; }
    }
}
```

This is a variation on the Product class that I usually use in my books so that I can better demonstrate useful Entity Framework Core features.

Adding a Repository

To provide consistent access to the data in an application, I like to use the repository pattern, where an interface defines the properties and methods used to access the data and an implementation class is used to work with the data storage mechanism. The advantages of using the repository pattern are that unit testing the MVC part of an application is easier and details of how the data is stored are hidden from the rest of the application.

■ **Tip** Using a repository is a good idea for most projects, but it is not a requirement for working with Entity Framework Core. In Part 3, for example, most of examples don't have a repository because there are a lot of complex code changes and I didn't want to have to repeatedly work changes through multiple classes and interfaces. Don't worry if you are unconvinced about the benefits of the repository pattern because you can always add one later, albeit with some refactoring.

To create the repository interface, I added a file called IRepository.cs to the Models folder and added the code shown in Listing 4-3.

Listing 4-3. The Contents of the IRepository.cs File in the Models Folder

```
using System.Collections.Generic;

namespace SportsStore.Models {

    public interface IRepository {

        IEnumerable<Product> Products { get; }

        void AddProduct(Product product);
    }
}
```

The Products property will provide read-only access to all the products that the application knows about. The AddProduct method will be used to add new products.

For this chapter, I am going to store the model objects in memory, which I then replace with Entity Framework Core in Chapter 4. I added a class called DataRepository.cs to the Models folder and added the code shown in Listing 4-4.

Listing 4-4. The Contents of the DataRepository.cs File in the Models Folder

```
using System.Collections.Generic;

namespace SportsStore.Models {

    public class DataRepository : IRepository {
        private List<Product> data = new List<Product>();

        public IEnumerable<Product> Products => data;

        public void AddProduct(Product product) {
            this.data.Add(product);
        }
    }
}
```

The DataRepository class implements the IRepository interface and uses a List to keep track of Product objects, which means that the data will be lost as soon as the application is stopped or restarted. I introduce a persistent repository in Chapter 4, but this is enough to get the ASP.NET Core MVC part of the project working before I introduce Entity Framework Core.

I added the statement shown in Listing 4-5 to the Startup class to register the DataRepository class as the implementation to use for dependencies on the IRepository interface.

Listing 4-5. Configuring Dependency Injection in the Startup.cs File in the SportsStore Folder

```
using System;
using System.Collections.Generic;
using System.Linq;
using System.Threading.Tasks;
using Microsoft.AspNetCore.Builder;
using Microsoft.AspNetCore.Hosting;
using Microsoft.AspNetCore.Http;
using Microsoft.Extensions.DependencyInjection;
using SportsStore.Models;

namespace SportsStore {
    public class Startup {

        public void ConfigureServices(IServiceCollection services) {
            services.AddMvc();
            services.AddSingleton<IRepository, DataRepository>();
        }

        public void Configure(IApplicationBuilder app, IHostingEnvironment env) {
            app.UseDeveloperExceptionPage();
            app.UseStatusCodePages();
            app.UseStaticFiles();
            app.UseMvcWithDefaultRoute();
        }
    }
}
```

The statement in Listing 4-5 registers the DataRepository class using the AddSingleton method, which means that a single object will be created the first time that a dependency on the IRepository interface is resolved and then used for all subsequent dependencies.

Adding a Controller and View

The emphasis for the example application is going to be the administration of product objects because that provides the greatest scope for demonstrating different data features. I need a controller that will receive HTTP requests and translate them into operations on Product objects, so I created the Controllers folder, added to it a code file called HomeController.cs, and used it to define the controller shown in Listing 4-6.

Listing 4-6. The Contents of the HomeController.cs File in the Controllers Folder

```
using Microsoft.AspNetCore.Mvc;
using SportsStore.Models;

namespace SportsStore.Controllers {

    public class HomeController : Controller {
        private IRepository repository;

        public HomeController(IRepository repo) => repository = repo;

        public IActionResult Index() => View(repository.Products);

        [HttpPost]
        public IActionResult AddProduct(Product product) {
            repository.AddProduct(product);
            return RedirectToAction(nameof(Index));
        }
    }
}
```

The Index action passes the collection of Product objects from the repository to its view, which will display a table of data to the user. The AddProduct method stores new Product objects based on the data received in an HTTP POST request.

Next, I created the Views/Home folder and added to it a file called Index.cshtml, with the content shown in Listing 4-7. This is the view that will display the application's Product data and allow the user to create new objects.

Listing 4-7. The Contents of the Index.cshtml File in the Views/Home Folder

```
@model IEnumerable<Product>

<h3 class="p-2 bg-primary text-white text-center">Products</h3>

<div class="container-fluid mt-3">
    <div class="row">
        <div class="col font-weight-bold">Name</div>
        <div class="col font-weight-bold">Category</div>
        <div class="col font-weight-bold text-right">Purchase Price</div>
        <div class="col font-weight-bold text-right">Retail Price</div>
        <div class="col"></div>
    </div>
    <form asp-action="AddProduct" method="post">
        <div class="row">
            <div class="col"><input name="Name" class="form-control" /></div>
            <div class="col"><input name="Category" class="form-control" /></div>
            <div class="col">
                <input name="PurchasePrice" class="form-control" />
            </div>
            <div class="col">
```

```
                    <input name="RetailPrice"  class="form-control" />
                </div>
                <div class="col">
                    <button type="submit" class="btn btn-primary">Add</button>
                </div>
            </div>
        </form>
        @if (Model.Count() == 0) {
            <div class="row">
                <div class="col text-center p-2">No Data</div>
            </div>
        } else {
            @foreach (Product p in Model) {
                <div class="row p-2">
                    <div class="col">@p.Name</div>
                    <div class="col">@p.Category</div>
                    <div class="col text-right">@p.PurchasePrice</div>
                    <div class="col text-right">@p.RetailPrice</div>
                    <div class="col"></div>
                </div>
            }
        }
    }
</div>
```

A grid layout is used to display an inline form for creating new objects, along with details of all the existing Product objects known to the application or a placeholder if there are no objects.

Adding the Finishing Touches

I right-clicked the SportsStore project item in the Solution Explorer, selected Add ➤ New Item, and select the JSON File template (found in the ASP.NET Core ➤ Web ➤ General category) to create a file called .bowerrc with the content shown in Listing 4-8. (It is important to pay attention to this file name: it starts with a period, contains the letter r twice and has no file extension).

Listing 4-8. The Contents of the .bowerrc File in the SportsStore Folder

```
{
  "directory": "wwwroot/lib"
}
```

I used the JSON File template again to create a file called bower.json, with the content shown in Listing 4-9.

Listing 4-9. The Contents of the bower.json File in the SportsStore Folder

```
{
  "name": "asp.net",
  "private": true,
  "dependencies": {
    "bootstrap": "4.0.0"
  }
}
```

When you save the changes to the file, Visual Studio will download the new version of the Bootstrap package and install it in the `wwwroot/lib` folder.

■ **Note** Bower, the client-side package management tool that I use to install Bootstrap in this chapter, has been deprecated and will eventually be replaced. Bower remains under active support, and there is integrated support for using it in Visual Studio, which is why I have used it in this book.

Next, I created the `Views/Shared` folder and added a file to it called `_Layout.cshtml` that I used to define the shared layout shown in Listing 4-10.

Listing 4-10. The Contents of the _Layout.cshtml File in the Views/Shared Folder

```
<!DOCTYPE html>
<html>
<head>
    <meta name="viewport" content="width=device-width" />
    <title>SportsStore</title>
    <link rel="stylesheet" href="~/lib/bootstrap/dist/css/bootstrap.min.css" />
</head>
<body>
    <div class="p-2">
        @RenderBody()
    </div>
</body>
</html>
```

This simple layout provides the structure of the HTML document required by browsers so that I don't have to include it in every view. It also includes a `link` element that tells browsers to request the CSS file containing the Bootstrap styles, which I use to style content throughout this book.

To use the layout in Listing 4-10 by default, I added a file called `_ViewStart.cshtml` in the Views folder with the content shown in Listing 4-11. (If you use the MVC View Start Page item template to create this file, then Visual Studio will add the content shown in the listing automatically.)

Listing 4-11. The Contents of the _ViewStart.cshtml File in the Views Folder

```
@{
    Layout = "_Layout";
}
```

To enable the ASP.NET Core MVC tag helpers and make the model class easier to reference, I added a file called `_ViewImports.cshtml` to the Views folder and added the content shown in Listing 4-12.

Listing 4-12. The Contents of the _ViewImports.cshtml File in the Views Folder

```
@using SportsStore.Models
@addTagHelper *, Microsoft.AspNetCore.Mvc.TagHelpers
```

The final step is to configure the application so that it will listen for HTTP requests on port 5000. I edited the launchSettings.json file in the Properties folder to replace the randomly assigned ports, as shown in Listing 4-13. There is no special significance of port 5000, other than I use it throughout the examples in this book.

Listing 4-13. Changing the Service Ports in the launchSettings.json File in the Properties Folder

```
{
  "iisSettings": {
    "windowsAuthentication": false,
    "anonymousAuthentication": true,
    "iisExpress": {
      "applicationUrl": "http://localhost:5000/",
      "sslPort": 0
    }
  },
  "profiles": {
    "IIS Express": {
      "commandName": "IISExpress",
      "launchBrowser": true,
      "environmentVariables": {
        "ASPNETCORE_ENVIRONMENT": "Development"
      }
    },
    "SportsStore": {
      "commandName": "Project",
      "launchBrowser": true,
      "environmentVariables": {
        "ASPNETCORE_ENVIRONMENT": "Development"
      },
      "applicationUrl": "http://localhost:5000/"
    }
  }
}
```

Running the Example Application

To build and start the example application, open a new command prompt or PowerShell window, navigate to the SportsStore project folder (the one that contains the bower.json file), and run the command shown in Listing 4-14.

Listing 4-14. Starting the Example Application

```
dotnet run
```

The application will begin listening for HTTP requests on port 5000. Open a browser window and navigate to http://localhost:5000. You will see the initial placeholder, which will be replaced once you fill out the form fields and click the Add button, as illustrated in Figure 4-3.

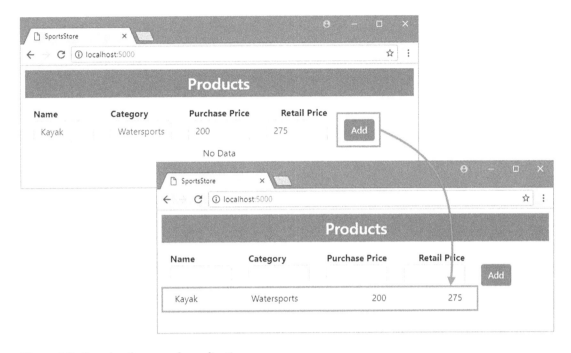

Figure 4-3. *Running the example application*

Summary

In this chapter, I created a simple ASP.NET Core MVC application that I will use in the following chapters. At the moment, the application's data is stored in memory, which means that all products are lost when the application is stopped or restarted. In the next chapter, I add Entity Framework Core to the project and store data persistently in a database.

■ ■ ■

CHAPTER 5

SportsStore: Storing Data

In this chapter, I demonstrate how to store the data in the SportsStore application in a database. I show you how to add Entity Framework Core to the project, how to prepare the data model, how to create and use a database, and how to adapt the application so that it makes efficient SQL queries. I also describe the problems that you are most likely to encounter when adding Entity Framework Core to a project and explain how to solve them.

Preparing for this Chapter

I continue to use the SportsStore project I created in Chapter 4. No changes are required for this chapter. Open a command prompt or PowerShell window, navigate to the SportsStore project folder (the one that contains the bower.json file), and use dotnet run to start the application. Use a browser to navigate to http://localhost:5000 and you will see the content shown in Figure 5-1. You can use the HTML form to store Product objects, but they will be lost when the application is stopped or restarted because the data is stored only in memory.

Tip You can download the SportsStore project—and the projects for all the other chapters in this book—from https://github.com/apress/pro-ef-core-2-for-asp.net-core-mvc.

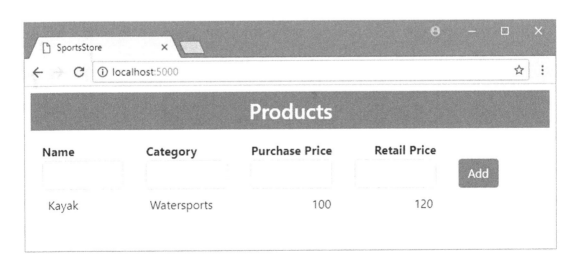

Figure 5-1. *Running the example application*

© Adam Freeman 2018
A. Freeman, *Pro Entity Framework Core 2 for ASP.NET Core MVC*,
https://doi.org/10.1007/978-1-4842-3435-8_5

Configuring Entity Framework Core

The default configuration that Visual Studio creates for ASP.NET Core projects includes the NuGet packages required to run Entity Framework Core applications. A separate package is required to add the command-line tools that manage databases, and it must be installed manually.

Right-click the SportsStore project item in the Solution Explorer window, select Edit SportsStore.csproj from the pop-up menu, and add the configuration element shown in Listing 5-1.

Listing 5-1. Adding a Package in the SportsStore.csproj File in the SportsStore Folder

```
<Project Sdk="Microsoft.NET.Sdk.Web">

  <PropertyGroup>
    <TargetFramework>netcoreapp2.0</TargetFramework>
  </PropertyGroup>

  <ItemGroup>
    <Folder Include="wwwroot\" />
  </ItemGroup>

  <ItemGroup>
    <PackageReference Include="Microsoft.AspNetCore.All" Version="2.0.3" />
    <DotNetCliToolReference Include="Microsoft.EntityFrameworkCore.Tools.DotNet"
        Version="2.0.0" />
  </ItemGroup>

</Project>
```

Packages that include command-line tools must be added manually using the `DotNetCliToolReference` element. The package shown in the listing includes the `dotnet ef` commands that are used to manage databases in projects that use Entity Framework Core.

Configuring Entity Framework Core Logging Messages

It is important to understand the SQL queries and commands that Entity Framework Core sends to the database server, even in a project that stores only a small amount of data. To configure Entity Framework Core to generate logging messages that will display the SQL queries it uses, I added a file called `appsettings.json` to the SportsStore folder using the ASP.NET Configuration File item template and added the configuration statements shown in Listing 5-2.

Listing 5-2. The Contents of the appsettings.json File in the SportsStore Folder

```
{
  "ConnectionStrings": {
    "DefaultConnection": "Server=(localdb)\\MSSQLLocalDB;Database=_CHANGE_ME;
    Trusted_Connection=True;MultipleActiveResultSets=true"
  },
  "Logging": {
    "LogLevel": {
```

```
    "Default": "None",
    "Microsoft.EntityFrameworkCore": "Information"
   }
  }
 }
}
```

The default content that Visual Studio uses for this type of file includes a connection string for a database, which I'll change shortly. The highlighted additions in Listing 5-2 set the default logging level to None, which disables all logging messages. This is then overridden for the `Microsoft.EntityFrameworkCore` package using the `Information` setting, which will provide details of the SQL that Entity Framework Core uses. You don't have to disable all other logging messages in real projects, but this combination will make it easier to follow the examples.

Preparing the Data Model

In the following sections, I prepare the data model that already exists in the SportsStore project for use with Entity Framework Core.

Defining a Primary Key Property

To store data in a database, Entity Framework Core needs to be able to uniquely identify each object, which requires selecting a property that will be used as the primary key. For most projects, the simplest way to define a primary key is to add a `long` property called `Id` to the data model class, as shown in Listing 5-3.

Listing 5-3. Adding a Primary Key Property in the Product.cs File in the Models Folder

```
namespace SportsStore.Models {

    public class Product {

        public long Id { get; set; }

        public string Name { get; set; }
        public string Category { get; set; }
        public decimal PurchasePrice { get; set; }
        public decimal RetailPrice { get; set; }
    }
}
```

This approach means that Entity Framework Core will configure the database so that the database server will generate primary key values so you don't have to worry about avoiding duplicates. Using a `long` value ensures that there is a large range of primary key values available and means that most projects will be able to store data indefinitely without worrying about running out of keys.

Creating the Database Context Class

Entity Framework Core relies on a database context class to provide an application with access to the data in a database. To provide the example application with a context, I added a class called `DataContext.cs` to the `Models` folder with the code shown in Listing 5-4.

Listing 5-4. The Contents of the DataContext.cs File in the Models Folder

```
using Microsoft.EntityFrameworkCore;

namespace SportsStore.Models {

    public class DataContext : DbContext {

        public DataContext(DbContextOptions<DataContext> opts) : base(opts) {}

        public DbSet<Product> Products { get; set; }
    }
}
```

When you use Entity Framework Core to store a simple data model like the one in the SportsStore application, the database context class is correspondingly simple—although this will change as the data model becomes more complex in later chapters. For the moment, there are three important characteristics of the database context class.

The first characteristic is that the base class is DbContext, which is defined in the Microsoft. EntityFrameworkCore namespace. Using DbContext as the base class is what makes a database context and provides access to Entity Framework Core functionality.

The second characteristic is that the constructor receives a DbContextOptions<T> object (where T is the context class), which must be passed to the constructor of the base class using the base keyword, like this:

```
...
public DataContext(DbContextOptions<DataContext> opts) : base(opts) { }
...
```

The constructor parameter will provide Entity Framework Core with the configuration information it needs to connect to the database server. You will receive an error if you don't define the constructor parameter or don't pass on the object.

The third characteristic is a property whose type is DbSet<T>, where T is the class that is going to be stored in the database.

```
...
public DbSet<Product> Products { get; set; }
...
```

The data model class is Product, so the property in Listing 5-4 returns a DbSet<Product> object. The property must be defined with get and set clauses. The set clause allows Entity Framework Core to assign an object that provides convenient access to the data. The get clause provides access to that data to the rest of the application.

Updating the Repository Implementation

The next step is to update the repository implementation class so that data is accessed through the context class defined in the previous section, as shown in Listing 5-5.

Listing 5-5. Using the Context Class in the DataRepository.cs File in the Models Folder

```
using System.Collections.Generic;

namespace SportsStore.Models {

    public class DataRepository : IRepository {
        //private List<Product> data = new List<Product>();
        private DataContext context;

        public DataRepository(DataContext ctx) => context = ctx;

        public IEnumerable<Product> Products => context.Products;

        public void AddProduct(Product product) {
            this.context.Products.Add(product);
            this.context.SaveChanges();
        }
    }
}
```

In an ASP.NET Core MVC application, access to data context objects is managed using dependency injection, and I added a constructor to the DataRepository class that receives a DataContext object, which will be provided by dependency injection at runtime.

The Products property defined by the repository interface can be implemented by returning the DbSet<Product> property defined by the context class. Similarly, the AddProduct method can be easily implemented because the DbSet<Product> object defines an Add method that accepts Product objects and stores them persistently.

The most significant change is the call to the SaveChanges method, which tells Entity Framework Core to send any pending operations—such as requests to the Add method to store data—to the database.

Preparing the Database

In the sections that follow, I go through the process of configuring the SportsStore application to describe the database that I want to use and then asking Entity Framework Core to create it. This is known as a *code-first* project, where you start with one or more C# classes and use them to create and configure the database. The alternative is known as a *database-first* project, where you create a data model from an existing database—a process that I describe in Chapters 17 and 18.

Configuring the Connection String

Entity Framework Core relies on connection strings to provide details of how to contact the database server used by the context class. The format of connection strings differs based on the database server you are using but generally includes the server name and network port of the database server, the name of the database, and authentication credentials. Connection strings are defined in the appsettings.json file, and in Listing 5-6, I have defined the connection string for the SportsStore database. In this book, I am using the LocalDB version of SQL Server, which is designed specifically for developers and doesn't require any configuration or credentials.

> **Tip**   You must ensure that the connection string is on a single unbroken line. The fixed width of a book page makes it hard to show the connection string, but you will get an error if you split the connection string into multiple lines to make it easier to read.

The format of connection strings is specific to each database server. For the connection string in Listing 5-6, there are four configuration properties, as described in Table 5-1.

Listing 5-6. Adding a Connection String in the appsettings.json File in the SportsStore Folder

```
{
  "ConnectionStrings": {
    "DefaultConnection": "Server=(localdb)\\MSSQLLocalDB;Database=SportsStore;Trusted_
    Connection=True;MultipleActiveResultSets=true"
  },
  "Logging": {
    "LogLevel": {
      "Default": "None",
      "Microsoft.EntityFrameworkCore": "Information"
    }
  }
}
```

Table 5-1. *The Four Configuration Properties of the LocalDB Connection String*

Name	Description
Server	This property specifies the name of the database server that Entity Framework Core will connect to. For LocalDB, this value is (localdb)\\ MSSQLLocalDB, which allows a connection to the database server without requiring any further configuration.
Database	This property specifies the name of the database that Entity Framework Core will use. In Listing 5-6, I removed the placeholder that Visual Studio added to the file and specified SportsStore as the name.
Trusted_Connection	When set to true, Entity Framework Core will authenticate with the database server using Windows account credentials. This property isn't required for LocalDB even though Visual Studio adds it by default when it creates the appsettings.json file.
MultipleActiveResultSets	This property configures the connection to the database server so that the results from multiple queries can be read at the same time.

Configuring the Database Provider and Context Class

I added the configuration statements shown in Listing 5-7 to the Startup class to tell Entity Framework Core how to use the connection string, which database provider should be used, and how to manage the context class.

Listing 5-7. Configuring Entity Framework Core in the Startup.cs File in the SportsStore Folder

```
using System;
using System.Collections.Generic;
using System.Linq;
using System.Threading.Tasks;
using Microsoft.AspNetCore.Builder;
using Microsoft.AspNetCore.Hosting;
using Microsoft.AspNetCore.Http;
using Microsoft.Extensions.DependencyInjection;
using SportsStore.Models;
using Microsoft.EntityFrameworkCore;
using Microsoft.Extensions.Configuration;

namespace SportsStore {
    public class Startup {

        public Startup(IConfiguration config) => Configuration = config;

        public IConfiguration Configuration { get; }

        public void ConfigureServices(IServiceCollection services) {
            services.AddMvc();
            services.AddTransient<IRepository, DataRepository>();
            string conString = Configuration["ConnectionStrings:DefaultConnection"];
            services.AddDbContext<DataContext>(options =>
                options.UseSqlServer(conString));
        }

        public void Configure(IApplicationBuilder app, IHostingEnvironment env) {
            app.UseDeveloperExceptionPage();
            app.UseStatusCodePages();
            app.UseStaticFiles();
            app.UseMvcWithDefaultRoute();
        }
    }
}
```

The constructor and the Configuration property are used to access the configuration data in the appsettings.json file, which allows me to read the connection string. The AddDbContext<T> extension method is used to set up the context class and tells Entity Framework Core which database provider to use (through the UseSqlServer method, in this case, but a different method is used for each database provider) and provides the connection string.

Notice that I also changed the method that configures dependency injection for the IRepository interface, like this:

```
...
services.AddTransient<IRepository, DataRepository>();
...
```

In Chapter 4, I used the AddSingleton method to ensure that a single DataRepository object was used to resolve all dependencies on the IRepository interface, which was important because the application data was stored in a List and I wanted the same objects to always be used. Now that I am using Entity Framework Core, I have switched to the AddTransient method, which ensures that a new DataRepository object is created each time a dependency on the IRepository is resolved. This is important because Entity Framework Core expects to create a new context object for each HTTP request in an ASP.NET Core MVC application.

Creating the Database

The steps in the previous section told Entity Framework Core what type of data I want to store and how to connect to the database server. The next step is to create the database.

Entity Framework Core manages databases through a feature called *migrations*, which are sets of changes that create or modify a database to synchronize it with the data model (and which I describe in detail in Chapter 13). To create a migration that will set up the database, open a new command prompt or PowerShell window, navigate to the SportsStore project folder (the one that contains the bower.json file), and run the command shown in Listing 5-8.

Listing 5-8. Creating a Migration

```
dotnet ef migrations add Initial
```

The dotnet ef commands access the features in the package added in Listing 5-1. The migrations add arguments tell Entity Framework Core to create a new migration, and the final argument specifies the name for the migration, Initial, which is the conventional name to use for the migrations that first prepares a database.

When you run the command in Listing 5-8, Entity Framework Core will inspect the project, find the context class, and use it to create a migration. The result will be a Migrations folder visible in the Solution Explorer that contains class files whose statements will prepare the database.

It isn't enough to just create the migration, which is just a set of instructions. These instructions must be executed to create the database so that it can store the application data. To execute the instructions in the Initial migration, run the command shown in Listing 5-9 in the SportsStore project folder.

Tip If you have already followed the examples in this chapter and see an error telling you that there is already an object named Products, then run dotnet ef database drop --force in the project folder to remove the database before running the command in Listing 5-9.

Listing 5-9. Applying a Migration

```
dotnet ef database update
```

Entity Framework Core will connect to the database server specified in the connection string and execute the statements in the migration. The result will be a database that can be used to store Product objects.

Running the Application

The basic support for storing Product objects persistently is in place, and the application is ready to be tested, even though there is still some work to be done. Start the application using dotnet run in the SportsStore project folder, navigate to http://localhost:5000, and use the HTML form to create Product objects using the values shown in Table 5-2.

Table 5-2. *The Values for Creating Test Product Objects*

Name	Category	Purchase Price	Retail Price
Kayak	Watersports	200	275
Lifejacket	Watersports	30	48.95
Soccer Ball	Soccer	17	19.50

Click the Add button for each set of data values, and Entity Framework Core will store the object in the database, producing the result shown in Figure 5-2.

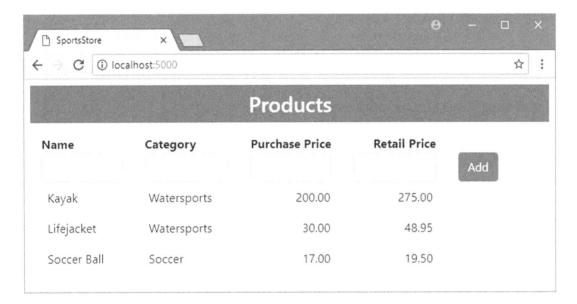

Figure 5-2. *Testing data storage*

The user experience has remained the same, but, behind the scenes, the data is being stored by Entity Framework Core in the database. Stop and restart the application using dotnet run, and the data you entered will still be available.

Avoiding the Query Pitfalls

The application is working, and data is being stored in the database, but there is still work to be done to get the best from Entity Framework Core. In particular, there are two common pitfalls to be avoided. These are problems that can be recognized by examining the SQL queries that Entity Framework Core sends to the database, and in Listing 5-10, I have added a statement to the Index action of the Home controller that will help make the queries triggered by an HTTP request easier to see.

Listing 5-10. Adding a Console Statement in the HomeController.cs File in the Controllers Folder

```
using Microsoft.AspNetCore.Mvc;
using SportsStore.Models;

namespace SportsStore.Controllers {

    public class HomeController : Controller {
        private IRepository repository;

        public HomeController(IRepository repo) => repository = repo;

        public IActionResult Index() {
            System.Console.Clear();
            return View(repository.Products);
        }

        [HttpPost]
        public IActionResult AddProduct(Product product) {
            repository.AddProduct(product);
            return RedirectToAction(nameof(Index));
        }
    }
}
```

The System.Console.Clear method will clear the console when the Index action is invoked so that queries from previous requests won't be visible. Start the application, navigate to http://localhost:5000, and examine the logging messages that are displayed.

■ **Note** The System.Console.Clear method will work only when you use dotnet run to start the application from PowerShell or the command prompt. It will cause an exception if you try to start the application using the Visual Studio debugger.

You will see that there are two logging messages that show two queries sent to the database, like this:

```
...
SELECT [p].[Id], [p].[Category], [p].[Name], [p].[PurchasePrice], [p].[RetailPrice]
FROM [Products] AS [p]
...
SELECT [p].[Id], [p].[Category], [p].[Name], [p].[PurchasePrice], [p].[RetailPrice]
FROM [Products] AS [p]
...
```

In the following sections, I explain why there are two requests and why one of them doesn't take full advantage of the capabilities of the database server.

Understanding the IEnumerable<T> Pitfall

Entity Framework Core makes it easy to query a database using LINQ, although it doesn't always work the way you might expect. In the Index view used by the Home controller, I use the LINQ Count method to determine how many Product objects have been stored in the database, like this:

```
...
@if (Model.Count() == 0) {
    <div class="row">
        <div class="col text-center p-2">No Data</div>
    </div>
} else {
    @foreach (Product p in Model) {
        <div class="row p-2">
            <div class="col">@p.Name</div>
            <div class="col">@p.Category</div>
            <div class="col text-right">@p.PurchasePrice</div>
            <div class="col text-right">@p.RetailPrice</div>
            <div class="col"></div>
        </div>
    }
}
...
```

To determine how many Product objects have been stored in the database, Entity Framework Core uses a SQL SELECT statement to get all of the Product data that is available, uses that data to create a series of Product objects, and then counts them. As soon as the counting is complete, the Product objects are discarded.

This isn't a problem when there are only three objects in the database, but the amount of work required to count objects this way becomes an issue as the amount of data increases. A more effective approach is to ask the database server to do the counting, which will spare Entity Framework Core the need to transfer all of the data and create the objects. This can be done with a simple change to the view model type, as shown in Listing 5-11.

Listing 5-11. Changing the View Model in the Index.cshtml File in the Views/Home Folder

```
@model IQueryable<Product>

<h3 class="p-2 bg-primary text-white text-center">Products</h3>

<div class="container-fluid mt-3">
    <!-- ...other elements omitted for brevity... -->
</div>
```

If you reload the browser window, you will see that the first of the two queries that Entity Framework Core sends to the database server has changed.

```
...
SELECT COUNT(*)
FROM [Products] AS [p]
...
SELECT [p].[Id], [p].[Category], [p].[Name], [p].[PurchasePrice], [p].[RetailPrice]
FROM [Products] AS [p]
...
```

The SELECT COUNT query asks the database server to count the Product objects and doesn't retrieve data or create any objects in the application.

Getting different queries for different view model types may seem like counterintuitive behavior, and understanding why it happens is essential to ensuring that Entity Framework Core can query databases efficiently.

LINQ is implemented as a set of extension methods that operate on objects that implement the IEnumerable<T> interface. This interface represents a sequence of objects, and it is implemented by the generic collection classes and arrays.

Entity Framework Core includes a duplicate set of LINQ extension methods that operate on objects that implement the IQueryable<T> interface. This interface represents a database query, and these duplicate methods means that operations such as Count can be performed as easily on data stored in the database as on in-memory objects.

The DbSet<T> class used in the database context class created in Listing 5-4 implements both of these interfaces so that the Products property, for example, implements both the IEnumerable<Product> and IQueryable<T> interfaces. When the view model in the Index view was set to IEnumerable<Product>, the standard version of the Count method was used. The standard Count implementation has no understanding of Entity Framework Core and just counts up the objects in the sequence. This triggers the SELECT query and produces the inefficient behavior where all of the data is read and used to create objects that are counted and discarded.

When I changed the view model to IQueryable<Product>, the Entity Framework Core version of the Count method was used. This version of the method allows Entity Framework Core to translate the complete query into SQL and produces the more efficient version that uses SELECT COUNT to get the number of stored objects without needing to retrieve any data.

UNDERSTANDING THE RAZOR VIEW MODEL CAST

You might be surprised that I can treat the view model object as an IQueryable<Product> object, even though the result of the repository class's Products property is IEnumerable<T>. When views are compiled, the C# class that Razor produces includes an explicit conversion to the type specified by the view model, similar to including this statement in the action method:

```
...
public IActionResult Index() {
    System.Console.Clear();
    return View(repository.Products as IQueryable<Product>);
}
...
```

In the case of this example, this feature means I can switch between working with the IQueryable<T> and IEnumerable<T> interfaces just by changing the @model expression. The type conversion is done at runtime, which is why any mismatches between the object provided by the controller and the object expected by the view won't become apparent until the application is running.

Understanding the Duplicate Query Pitfall

Making one of the queries more efficient doesn't explain why there are two queries in the first place. As I explained in the previous section, the DbSet<T> class implements the IQueryable<T> interface, which represents a database query and which allows LINQ to be used even on data in the database.

By default, Entity Framework Core doesn't execute the query until the IQueryable<T> object is enumerated. This allows queries to be composed gradually and for new queries to be created by calling a LINQ method on an existing query, rather than on the data it returns. But this behavior also means a fresh SQL query is sent to the database each time an IQueryable<T> is enumerated. This can be helpful for some applications because it means you can use the same object to get the latest data from the database, but in an ASP.NET Core MVC application, this usually ends up producing multiple queries for the same data just a few milliseconds apart.

In the example application, the IQueryable<T> view model object is enumerated twice in the Index view, like this:

```
...
@if (Model.Count() == 0) {
    <div class="row">
        <div class="col text-center p-2">No Data</div>
    </div>
} else {
    @foreach (Product p in Model) {
        <div class="row p-2">
            <div class="col">@p.Name</div>
            <div class="col">@p.Category</div>
            <div class="col text-right">@p.PurchasePrice</div>
            <div class="col text-right">@p.RetailPrice</div>
            <div class="col"></div>
        </div>
    }
}
...
```

It isn't just foreach loops that enumerate sequences of objects; LINQ methods that produce a single result, such as the Count method, will also trigger a query. The IQueryable<T> behavior and its use in the Index view combine to produce two queries.

The situation may seem improved now that the two queries are no longer identical, but further improvements are possible, as I describe in the following sections.

AVOIDING UNINTENDED QUERIES

There is nothing wrong with triggering multiple queries from a single IQueryable<T> object, just as long as that is what you intend to do. The problem is when you forget how IQueryable<T> objects behave, treat them like IEnumerable<T> objects, and accidentally make queries without noticing. In a busy application, the resources wasted by accidental queries can be significant and will drive up the capacity costs for a project.

Avoiding a Query Using CSS

The Index view shows one of the most common causes for duplicate requests in an ASP.NET Core MVC application, where the Count method is used to see whether there is any data so that placeholder content can be shown to the user. An alternative way of providing a "no data" placeholder is to make it the responsibility of the browser by relying on CSS. In Listing 5-12, I have added a style element to the layout used by the views in the example application and used it to define two custom styles.

Listing 5-12. Defining Styles in the _Layout.cshtml File in the Views/Shared Folder

```
<!DOCTYPE html>
<html>
<head>
    <meta name="viewport" content="width=device-width" />
    <title>SportsStore</title>
    <link rel="stylesheet" href="~/lib/bootstrap/dist/css/bootstrap.min.css" />
    <style>
        .placeholder { visibility: collapse; display: none }
        .placeholder:only-child { visibility: visible; display: flex }
    </style>
</head>
<body>
    <div class="p-2">
        @RenderBody()
    </div>
</body>
</html>
```

An HTML element assigned to the placeholder class will have its visibility property set to collapse and its display property set to none by default, which will prevent it from being seen by the user. But when the HTML element is the only child of its containing element, the property values will be changed, which is achieved by using the only-child pseudoclass. In Listing 5-13, I have revised the Index view used by the Home controller to remove the call to the LINQ Count method and rely on the CSS classes instead.

Listing 5-13. Relying on CSS Classes in the Index.cshtml File in the Views/Home Folder

```
@model IQueryable<Product>

<h3 class="p-2 bg-primary text-white text-center">Products</h3>
```

```
<div class="container-fluid mt-3">
    <div class="row">
        <div class="col font-weight-bold">Name</div>
        <div class="col font-weight-bold">Category</div>
        <div class="col font-weight-bold text-right">Purchase Price</div>
        <div class="col font-weight-bold text-right">Retail Price</div>
        <div class="col"></div>
    </div>
    <form asp-action="AddProduct" method="post">
        <div class="row">
            <div class="col"><input name="Name" class="form-control" /></div>
            <div class="col"><input name="Category" class="form-control" /></div>
            <div class="col">
                <input name="PurchasePrice" class="form-control" />
            </div>
            <div class="col">
                <input name="RetailPrice" class="form-control" />
            </div>
            <div class="col">
                <button type="submit" class="btn btn-primary">Add</button>
            </div>
        </div>
    </form>
    <div>
        <div class="row placeholder">
            <div class="col text-center p-2">No Data</div>
        </div>
        @foreach (Product p in Model) {
            <div class="row p-2">
                <div class="col">@p.Name</div>
                <div class="col">@p.Category</div>
                <div class="col text-right">@p.PurchasePrice</div>
                <div class="col text-right">@p.RetailPrice</div>
                <div class="col"></div>
            </div>
        }
    </div>
</div>
```

I have added a div element so that the only-child pseudoclass will work and removed the if clause with its call to the Count method. The result is the element assigned to the placeholder class will always be included in the HTML sent to the browser but will be visible only if the foreach loop doesn't generate any elements, which will happen when no Product objects have been stored in the database. If you reload the browser window, you will see that there is now only one query sent to the database.

```
...
SELECT [p].[Id], [p].[Category], [p].[Name], [p].[PurchasePrice], [p].[RetailPrice]
FROM [Products] AS [p]
...
```

Forcing Query Execution in the Repository

The problem with working directly with IQueryable<T> objects is that details of how data storage has been implemented have leaked into other parts of the application, which undermines the sense of functional separation that the MVC pattern follows.

TAKING A BALANCED APPROACH TO PATTERNS

Patterns are useful templates for building projects that are easy to understand and easy to test, but a balanced approach is required when it comes to implementing them. It doesn't matter which parts of a pattern you adopt and which parts you ignore—just as long as you make those decisions consciously.

In the example application, for example, there is a tension between the repository pattern, which aims to hide details of how data is stored, and the reality of working with Entity Framework Core.

By containing the IQueryable<T> object to the repository implementation class, I am limiting the proportion of the application that has to know about Entity Framework Core queries. But it doesn't do this completely because the rest of the application still has to know about the primary key property that I defined in Listing 5-13 and that I will use to identify objects in later chapters.

For me, this is a reasonable balance between practicality (objects have to be uniquely identified) and principle (containing data storage details to the repository). You may prefer to avoid using a repository entirely or choose to adhere more rigidly to the repository pattern (by using a different key strategy, for example, as described in Chapter 19).

An alternative approach is to have the repository implementation class take responsibility for dealing with the quirks of IQueryable<T> objects and presenting the rest of the application with regular collections of in-memory objects that implement the IEnumerable<T> interface and can be enumerated without worrying about unexpected effects. In Listing 5-14, I have changed the repository class so that it no longer passes on the DbSet<T> objects returned by the context class Products property.

Listing 5-14. Forcing Query Evaluation in the DataRepository.cs File in the Models Folder

```
using System.Collections.Generic;
using System.Linq;

namespace SportsStore.Models {

    public class DataRepository : IRepository {
        private DataContext context;

        public DataRepository(DataContext ctx) => context = ctx;

        public IEnumerable<Product> Products => context.Products.ToArray();

        public void AddProduct(Product product) {
            this.context.Products.Add(product);
            this.context.SaveChanges();
        }
    }
}
```

The LINQ ToArray and ToList methods trigger the execution of the query and produce an array or a list that contains the results. These are regular in-memory collections of objects that implement only the IEnumerable<T> interface, which means that I have to change the view model in the Index view used by the Home controller again, as shown in Listing 5-15. It also means that I can safely return to performing multiple LINQ operations in the view, without having to give thought to how the data has been obtained.

■ **Note** One consequence of this approach is that the repository must be able to provide the rest of the application with the data it requires, which leads to complex queries being consolidated in the repository class. I tend to prefer this approach because it makes it easier to see and manage all of the queries that Entity Framework Core will have to deal with. But that's just my personal preference, and you should choose the approach that suits you best.

Listing 5-15. Changing the View Model in the Index.cshtml File in the Views/Home Folder

```
@model IEnumerable<Product>

<h3 class="p-2 bg-primary text-white text-center">Products</h3>

<div class="container-fluid mt-3">
    <div class="row">
        <div class="col font-weight-bold">Name</div>
        <div class="col font-weight-bold">Category</div>
        <div class="col font-weight-bold text-right">Purchase Price</div>
        <div class="col font-weight-bold text-right">Retail Price</div>
        <div class="col"></div>
    </div>
    <form asp-action="AddProduct" method="post">
        <div class="row">
            <div class="col"><input name="Name" class="form-control" /></div>
            <div class="col"><input name="Category" class="form-control" /></div>
            <div class="col">
                <input name="PurchasePrice" class="form-control" />
            </div>
            <div class="col">
                <input name="RetailPrice" class="form-control" />
            </div>
            <div class="col">
                <button type="submit" class="btn btn-primary">Add</button>
            </div>
        </div>
    </form>
    <div>
        @if (Model.Count() == 0) {
        <div class="row">
            <div class="col text-center p-2">No Data</div>
        </div>
```

```
    } else {
        @foreach (Product p in Model) {
            <div class="row p-2">
                <div class="col">@p.Name</div>
                <div class="col">@p.Category</div>
                <div class="col text-right">@p.PurchasePrice</div>
                <div class="col text-right">@p.RetailPrice</div>
                <div class="col"></div>
            </div>
        }
    }
    </div>
</div>
```

Restart the application using `dotnet run` and navigate to `http://localhost:5000`; you will see the familiar output shown in earlier figures. The user experience hasn't changed throughout this section, but if you examine the logging messages generated by the application, you will see that there is only one query to the database, even though the view model object is enumerated twice.

```
...
SELECT [p].[Id], [p].[Category], [p].[Name], [p].[PurchasePrice], [p].[RetailPrice]
FROM [Products] AS [p]
...
```

Common Problems and Solutions

Using Entity Framework Core to store and retrieve data is straightforward once you get the basic feature in place, but there are pitfalls to avoid. In the sections that follow, I describe the problems you are most likely to encounter and explain how to resolve them.

Problems Creating or Accessing the Database

The most fundamental problems arise when trying to create the database or access it from the application. For the most part, these are problems caused by misconfiguration, as I explain in the following sections.

The "No executable found matching command dotnet-ef" Error

The `dotnet ef` commands are used to create and manage migrations, but they are not enabled by default and rely on a package being added to the application. If you receive a "no executable found" error when you try to run any of the `dotnet ef` commands, then open the `.csproj` file and make sure that there is a `DotNetCliToolReference` reference for the `Microsoft.EntityFrameworkCore.Tools.DotNet` package, as shown in Listing 5-1.

If you have added the package, then make sure you are running the commands in the project folder, which is the one that contains the `.csproj` file and the `Startup.cs` file. If you try to use `dotnet ef` in any other folder, then the .NET Core runtime won't be able to find the commands you are using.

The "Build Failed" Error

The project is automatically compiled when you run a `dotnet ef` command, and the "build failed" error is reported if there are any problems in the code, although no details about the cause of the problem are provided.

If you want to see what is preventing the compiler from building the project, then run `dotnet build` in the project folder. You can then resolve the problem and run the `dotnet ef` command again.

■ **Note** This error can also be caused by trying to run one of the `dotnet ef` commands after you have started the application using `dotnet run` in another command prompt or PowerShell window. The build process tries to override files that are held open by the running application, which causes a failure. Stop the application and your `dotnet ef` command should succeed.

The "The entity type requires a primary key to be defined" Error

If you see this error when trying to create a migration, then the most likely cause is that you have not selected a primary key. For simple applications, the best approach is the one shown in Listing 5-3. For complex applications, the advanced features for working with keys are described in Chapter 19.

The "There is already an object named <Name> in the database" Exception

This exception occurs when you try to apply a migration that tries to create a database table that already exists. This usually happens when you remove a migration from a project, re-create it, and then try to apply it to the database again. The database already contains the tables created by the migration, which prevents it from succeeding.

This problem is most likely to arise during development, and the easiest solution is to delete and re-create the database by running the commands in Listing 5-16 in the project folder. These commands will remove the database and the data it contains, which means that it should not be used on production systems.

Listing 5-16. Resetting a Database

```
dotnet ef database drop --force
dotnet ef database update
```

The "A Network-Related or Instance-Specific Error Occurred" Exception

This exception tells you that Entity Framework Core has been unable to contact the database server. The most common cause of this exception is a mistake in the connection string in the `appsettings.json` file. If you are using LocalDB for development, then make sure that you have set the `Server` configuration property to `(localdb)//MSSQLLocalDb`, where there are two / characters and the second part of the name is `MS_SQL_Local_Db` (but without the underscore characters). If you are using the full SQL Server product—or another database server entirely—then make sure that you have used the correct hostname and TCP port, ensure that the hostname resolves to the correct IP address, and test your network to make sure that you can reach the server.

The "Cannot Open Database Requested By The Login" Exception

If you receive this exception, then Entity Framework Core is able to communicate with the database server but has asked to access a database that does not exist. The first thing to check is that you have specified the correct database name in the connection string in the appsettings.json file. For LocalDB (and the full SQL Server products), this means correctly setting the Database property, as shown in Listing 5-6. If you are using a different database server, then check the documentation to see how the database name should be specified.

■ **Tip** It can be hard to figure out what connection strings should contain, especially when you switch database server or provider package. The website https://www.connectionstrings.com provides a useful reference for a wide range of database servers and connection options.

If you have entered the correct database name, then it is possible that you have created a migration but not applied it, which means that the database server has never been asked to create the database that Entity Framework Core is asking to access. Run dotnet ef database update in the project folder to apply the migration.

Problems Querying Data

The biggest problem when querying data is duplicate requests to the database server, as described in the "Avoiding the Query Pitfalls" section. But that's not the only problem that can arise, as I explain in the following sections.

The "Property Could Not Be Mapped" Exception

This exception occurs when you add a property to the data model class but don't create and apply a migration to update the database. See Chapter 13 for details of how to use migrations to keep the data model and the database synchronized.

The "Invalid Object Name" Exception

This exception usually means that Entity Framework Core has tried to query data from a table that does not exist in the database. This is a variation of the problem described in the previous section and usually means that the database has not been updated to reflect a change in the application's data model. See Chapter 13 for details of how migrations work and how to manage them.

The "There is Already an Open DataReader" Exception

This exception occurs when you are trying to start a query before reading all of the results from the previous one. If you are using SQL Server, you can enable the multiple active result set (MARS) feature in the connection string, as shown in Listing 5-6. For other databases, you can use the ToArray or ToList method to force one query to be fully read before starting the next query.

The "Cannot Consume Scoped Service from Singleton" Exception

The AddDbContext method in the Startup class uses the AddedScoped method to set up the dependency injection for the context class. This means you must use the AddTransient or AddScoped method, as shown in Listing 5-7, to configure any service that depends on the context class, such as repository implementation classes. If you use the AddSingleton method to register your services, you will receive an exception when ASP.NET Core tries to resolve dependencies.

The Stale Context Data Problem

In an ASP.NET Core MVC application, Entity Framework Core expects a new context object to be created for each HTTP request. A common problem, however, is to keep hold of context objects and try to use them for subsequent requests.

The problem this presents is that each Entity Framework Core context object keeps track of the objects it has created to use a cache and to detect changes. Keeping context objects and reusing them can produce unexpected results because the data is out of date or incomplete. Even though you may have an aversion to creating objects for a single request, it is already the pattern used by the rest of the application—the MVC framework creates new controller and view objects for each HTTP request—and it is how Entity Framework Core expects its context objects to be used.

Problems Storing Data

For the most part, few changes are required to allow Entity Framework Core to store instances of classes in an MVC data model. There are some common problems, however, which I describe in the sections that follow.

Objects Are Not Stored

If the application seems to be working but objects are not stored in the database, then the first thing to check is that you remembered to call the SaveChanges method in your repository implementation class. Entity Framework Core will only update the database after the SaveChanges method is called and will silently discard changes if you forget.

Only Some Property Values Are Not Stored

If only some of the data values associated with an object are being stored in the database, then make sure that you only use properties and that all of them have set and get clauses. Entity Framework Core will only store the value of properties and will ignore any methods or fields by default. If the constraints of your application prevent you from using only properties in your data model classes, then see Chapter 20 for the advanced Entity Framework Core features for changing the way that data model classes are used.

The "Cannot Insert Explicit Value for Identity Column" Exception

If you have selected a primary key as shown in Listing 5-3, then Entity Framework Core will configure the database so that the database server is responsible for generating the values that will allow objects to be uniquely identified.

This means that multiple applications—or instances of the same application—can share the same database without coordination to avoid duplicate values. It also means that an exception will be thrown if you try to store a new object with a key value that is not the default for the key type. For the Product class, the primary key type is long, so new objects can be stored only when the Id value is zero, which is the default long value. The most common cause of this exception is including an input element in the view that is used to create new objects and allowing the user to provide a value, which is then used by the MVC model binder and passed on to the database via Entity Framework Core.

■ **Tip**   See Chapter 19 for the advanced primary key options if you don't want the database server to generate values for you.

Summary

In this chapter, I added support for storing data in a database and querying it. I explained the process of moving to a persistent data store and demonstrated how the queries that an application makes must be adapted to work efficiently with Entity Framework Core. I also described the most common problems that you are likely to encounter when you introduce Entity Framework Core to an existing application and told you how to resolve each of them. In the next chapter, I add features to the SportsStore application to modify and delete the data in the database.

CHAPTER 6

SportsStore: Modifying and Deleting Data

At the moment, the SportsStore application can store Product objects in the database and perform queries to read them back again. Most applications also require the ability to make changes to the data after it has been stored, including removing objects entirely. In this chapter, I add support for updating and deleting Product objects. I also describe the problems that you are likely to encounter adding these features in your own projects and explain how to resolve them.

Preparing for This Chapter

In this chapter I continue using the SportsStore project created in Chapter 4 and to which I added Entity Framework Core in Chapter 5. Run the commands shown in Listing 6-1 in the SportsStore project folder to delete and re-create the database, which will help ensure that you get the expected results from the examples.

Tip You can download the SportsStore project for this chapter—and the projects for every other chapter—from the GitHub repository for this book: https://github.com/apress/pro-ef-core-2-for-asp.net-core-mvc.

Listing 6-1. Deleting and Re-creating the Database

```
dotnet ef database drop --force
dotnet ef database update
```

Start the application using dotnet run and navigate to http://localhost:5000; you will see the content shown in Figure 6-1.

© Adam Freeman 2018
A. Freeman, *Pro Entity Framework Core 2 for ASP.NET Core MVC*,
https://doi.org/10.1007/978-1-4842-3435-8_6

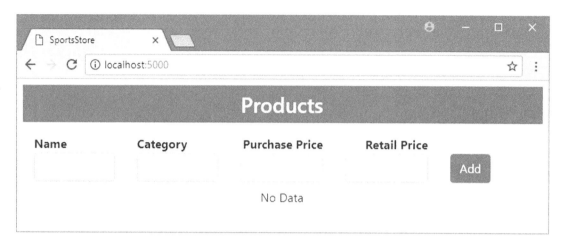

Figure 6-1. *Running the example application*

Fill out the HTML form using the data values in Table 6-1, which will provide data for the examples in this chapter.

Table 6-1. *The Values for Creating Test Product Objects*

Name	Category	Purchase Price	Retail Price
Kayak	Watersports	200	275
Lifejacket	Watersports	30	48.95
Soccer Ball	Soccer	17	19.50

When you have added details of all three products, you should see the results shown in Figure 6-2.

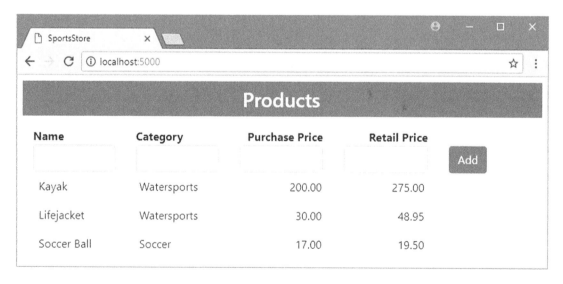

Figure 6-2. *Adding the test data*

Modifying Objects

Entity Framework Core supports a number of different ways of updating objects, which I describe in Chapters 12 and 21. In this chapter, I start with the simplest technique, in which an object created by the MVC model binder is used to completely replace the object stored in the database.

Updating the Repository

To get started, I have changed the IRepository interface to add methods that the rest of the application can use to retrieve and update an existing object, as shown in Listing 6-2.

Listing 6-2. Adding Methods in the IRepository.cs File in the Models Folder

```
using System.Collections.Generic;

namespace SportsStore.Models {

    public interface IRepository {

        IEnumerable<Product> Products { get; }

        Product GetProduct(long key);

        void AddProduct(Product product);

        void UpdateProduct(Product product);
    }
}
```

The GetProduct method will provide a single Product object using its primary key value. The UpdateProduct method receives a Product object and does not return a result. In Listing 6-3, I have added the new method to the repository implementation class.

Listing 6-3. Adding a Method in the DataRepository.cs File in the Models Folder

```
using System.Collections.Generic;
using System.Linq;

namespace SportsStore.Models {

    public class DataRepository : IRepository {
        private DataContext context;

        public DataRepository(DataContext ctx) => context = ctx;

        public IEnumerable<Product> Products => context.Products.ToArray();

        public Product GetProduct(long key) => context.Products.Find(key);

        public void AddProduct(Product product) {
            context.Products.Add(product);
```

```
            context.SaveChanges();
        }

        public void UpdateProduct(Product product) {
            context.Products.Update(product);
            context.SaveChanges();
        }
    }
}
```

The DbSet<Product> returned by the database context's Products property provides the feature that I need to implement the new methods. The Find method accepts a primary key value and queries the database for the object it corresponds to. The Update method accepts a Product object and uses it to update the database, replacing the object in the database that has the same primary key. As with all operations that change the database, I have to call the SaveChanges method after the Update method.

Tip   It can be awkward to have to remember to call the SaveChanges method, but it soon becomes second nature, and this approach means you can set up multiple changes by calling the context object's methods and then send them all to the database at the same time with a single SaveChanges call. I explain how this works in detail in Chapter 24.

Updating the Controller and Creating a View

The next step is to update the Home controller so there are action methods that will allow the user to select a Product object for editing and send changes to the application, as shown in Listing 6-4. I have also commented out the line that clears the console so that the SQL queries that Entity Framework Core performs for the new methods will be easier to see.

Listing 6-4. Adding Actions in the HomeController.cs File in the Controllers Folder

```
using Microsoft.AspNetCore.Mvc;
using SportsStore.Models;

namespace SportsStore.Controllers {

    public class HomeController : Controller {
        private IRepository repository;

        public HomeController(IRepository repo) => repository = repo;

        public IActionResult Index() {
            //System.Console.Clear();
            return View(repository.Products);
        }

        [HttpPost]
        public IActionResult AddProduct(Product product) {
            repository.AddProduct(product);
```

```
            return RedirectToAction(nameof(Index));
        }

        public IActionResult UpdateProduct(long key) {
            return View(repository.GetProduct(key));
        }

        [HttpPost]
        public IActionResult UpdateProduct(Product product) {
            repository.UpdateProduct(product);
            return RedirectToAction(nameof(Index));
        }
    }
}
```

You can see how the action methods are mapped onto the features provided by the repository and through to the database context class. To provide the controller with a view for the new actions, I added a file called UpdateProduct.cshtml to the Views/Home folder with the content shown in Listing 6-5.

Listing 6-5. The Contents of the UpdateProduct.cshtml in the Views/Home Folder

```
@model Product

<h3 class="p-2 bg-primary text-white text-center">Update Product</h3>

<form asp-action="UpdateProduct" method="post">
    <div class="form-group">
        <label asp-for="Id"></label>
        <input asp-for="Id" class="form-control" readonly />
    </div>
    <div class="form-group">
        <label asp-for="Name"></label>
        <input asp-for="Name" class="form-control" />
    </div>
    <div class="form-group">
        <label asp-for="Category"></label>
        <input asp-for="Category" class="form-control" />
    </div>
    <div class="form-group">
        <label asp-for="PurchasePrice"></label>
        <input asp-for="PurchasePrice" class="form-control" />
    </div>
    <div class="form-group">
        <label asp-for="RetailPrice"></label>
        <input asp-for="RetailPrice" class="form-control" />
    </div>
    <div class="text-center">
        <button class="btn btn-primary" type="submit">Save</button>
        <a asp-action="Index" class="btn btn-secondary">Cancel</a>
    </div>
</form>
```

The view presents the user with an HTML form that can be used to change the properties of a Product object, with the exception of the Id property, which is used as the primary key. Primary keys cannot be easily changed once they have been assigned, and it is simpler to delete an object and create a new one if a different key value is required. For this reason, I have added the readonly attribute to the input element that shows the value of the Id property but doesn't allow it to be changed.

To integrate the update feature into the rest of the application, I added a button element for each of the Product objects displayed by the Index view, as shown in Listing 6-6. I also added a column to the grid that displays the Id property.

Listing 6-6. Integrating Updates in the Index.cshtml File in the Views/Home Folder

```
@model IEnumerable<Product>

<h3 class="p-2 bg-primary text-white text-center">Products</h3>

<div class="container-fluid mt-3">
    <div class="row">
        <div class="col-1 font-weight-bold">Id</div>
        <div class="col font-weight-bold">Name</div>
        <div class="col font-weight-bold">Category</div>
        <div class="col font-weight-bold text-right">Purchase Price</div>
        <div class="col font-weight-bold text-right">Retail Price</div>
        <div class="col"></div>
    </div>
    <form asp-action="AddProduct" method="post">
        <div class="row p-2">
            <div class="col-1"></div>
            <div class="col"><input name="Name" class="form-control" /></div>
            <div class="col"><input name="Category" class="form-control" /></div>
            <div class="col">
                <input name="PurchasePrice" class="form-control" />
            </div>
            <div class="col">
                <input name="RetailPrice" class="form-control" />
            </div>
            <div class="col">
                <button type="submit" class="btn btn-primary">Add</button>
            </div>
        </div>
    </form>
    <div>
        @if (Model.Count() == 0) {
            <div class="row">
                <div class="col text-center p-2">No Data</div>
            </div>
        } else {
            @foreach (Product p in Model) {
                <div class="row p-2">
                    <div class="col-1">@p.Id</div>
                    <div class="col">@p.Name</div>
                    <div class="col">@p.Category</div>
                    <div class="col text-right">@p.PurchasePrice</div>
```

```
            <div class="col text-right">@p.RetailPrice</div>
            <div class="col">
                <a asp-action="UpdateProduct" asp-route-key="@p.Id"
                        class="btn btn-outline-primary">
                    Edit
                </a>
            </div>
        </div>
    }
}
    </div>
</div>
```

Start the application using `dotnet run` and navigate to `http://localhost:5000`; you will see the new elements, which show the primary key and provide an Edit button for each product, as shown in Figure 6-3.

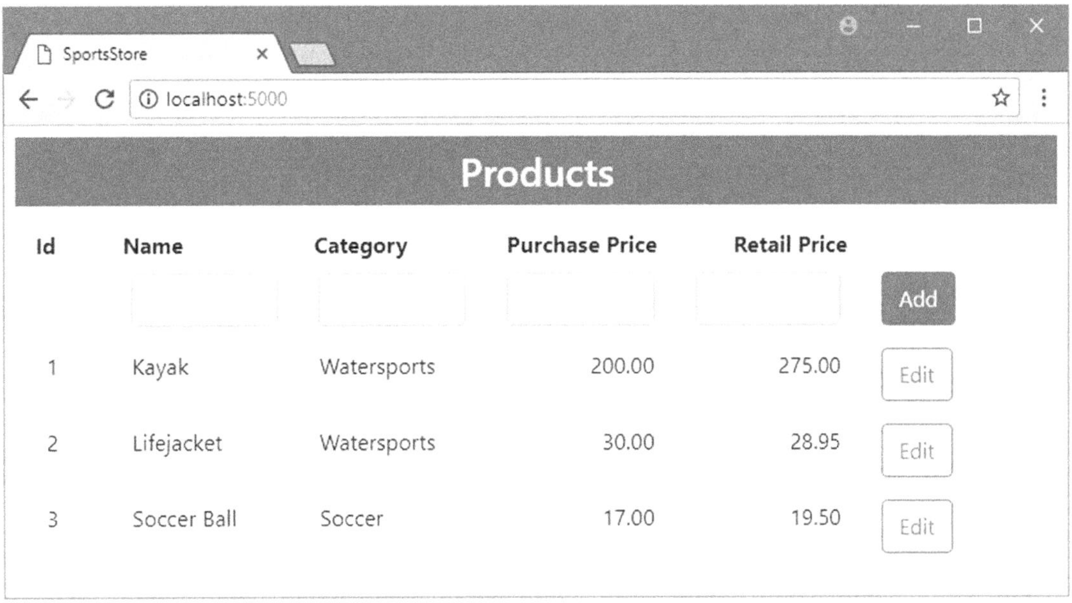

Figure 6-3. *Adding elements to the Index view*

Click the Edit button for the Soccer Ball product, change the value of the Purchase Price field to 16.50, and click the Save button. The browser will send the form data to the `UpdateProduct` action method on the `Home` controller, which will receive a `Product` object that has been created by the MVC model binder. The `Product` object will be passed on to the `Update` method of the database context class, and when the `SaveChanges` method is called, the form data values will be stored in the database, as shown in Figure 6-4.

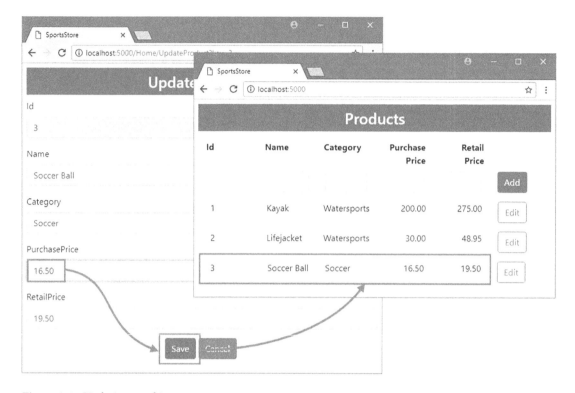

Figure 6-4. *Updating an object*

If you examine the logging messages generated by the application, you can see how the actions you performed result in SQL commands being sent to the database server. When you clicked the Edit button, Entity Framework Core queried the database for the details of the Soccer Ball object with this command:

```
...
SELECT TOP(1) [e].[Id], [e].[Category], [e].[Name], [e].[PurchasePrice],
    [e].[RetailPrice]
FROM [Products] AS [e]
WHERE [e].[Id] = @__get_Item_0
...
```

The Find method that I used in Listing 6-6 is translated into a SELECT command for a single object, which is specified using the TOP keyword. When you clicked the Save button, Entity Framework Core updated the database using this command:

```
...
UPDATE [Products] SET [Category] = @p0, [Name] = @p1, [PurchasePrice] = @p2,
    [RetailPrice] = @p3
WHERE [Id] = @p4;
...
```

The Update method is translated into a SQL UPDATE command that stores the form values that have been received from the HTTP request.

Updating Only Changed Properties

The basic building blocks for performing updates are in place, but the result is inefficient because Entity Framework Core has no baseline against which to figure out what has changed and so has no choice but to store all of the properties. To see the problem, click the Edit button for one of the products and then click Save without making any changes. Even though there are no new data values, the logging messages generated by the application show that the UPDATE command produced by Entity Framework Core sends the values for all of the properties defined by the Product class.

```
...
UPDATE [Products] SET [Category] = @p0, [Name] = @p1, [PurchasePrice] = @p2,
    [RetailPrice] = @p3
WHERE [Id] = @p4;
...
```

Entity Framework Core includes a change-detection feature that can work out which properties have changed. For a data model class as simple as Product, this is unlikely to be an issue, but for more complex data models, detecting changes can be important.

The change detection feature requires a baseline against which the data received from the user can be compared. There are different ways of providing the baseline, which I describe in Chapter 12, but I use the easiest approach in this chapter, which is to query the database for the existing data. In Listing 6-7, I have updated the repository implementation class so that it queries the database for the stored Product object and uses it to avoid updating properties that have not changed.

Tip   The cost of the query must be balanced against the benefit of avoiding unnecessary updates, but this approach is simple and reliable and works well with the features that Entity Framework Core provides to stop two users trying to update the same data, as described in Chapter 20.

Listing 6-7. Avoiding Unnecessary Updates in the DataRepository.cs File in the Models Folder

```
using System.Collections.Generic;
using System.Linq;

namespace SportsStore.Models {

    public class DataRepository : IRepository {
        private DataContext context;

        public DataRepository(DataContext ctx) => context = ctx;

        public IEnumerable<Product> Products => context.Products.ToArray();

        public Product GetProduct(long key) => context.Products.Find(key);

        public void AddProduct(Product product) {
            context.Products.Add(product);
            context.SaveChanges();
        }
```

```
    public void UpdateProduct(Product product) {
        Product p = GetProduct(product.Id);
        p.Name = product.Name;
        p.Category = product.Category;
        p.PurchasePrice = product.PurchasePrice;
        p.RetailPrice = product.RetailPrice;
        // context.Products.Update(product);
        context.SaveChanges();
    }
  }
}
```

This code bridges two different features in the application. Entity Framework Core performs change tracking on objects that it creates from query data, while the MVC model binder creates objects from HTTP data. These two sources of objects are not integrated, and problems occur if care is not taken to keep them separate. The safest way of taking advantage of change tracking is to query the database and then copy the values from the HTTP data, as I have done in the listing. When the SaveChanges method is called, Entity Framework Core will work out which values are changed and update only those properties in the database.

Tip   Notice that I have commented out the call to the Update method, which is not required when a query provides baseline data.

To see how this works, start the application using dotnet run, navigate to http://localhost:5000, and click the Edit button for the Kayak product. Change the Retail Price value to 300 and click the Save button. Examine the logging messages generated by the application, and you will see that the UPDATE command that Entity Framework Core has sent to the database only modifies the property that was changed.

```
...
UPDATE [Products] SET [RetailPrice] = @p0
WHERE [Id] = @p1;
...
```

Performing Bulk Updates

Bulk updates are often required in applications where there are dedicated administration roles that need to make changes to multiple objects in a single operation. The exact nature of the updates will differ, but common reasons for bulk updates include correcting data entry mistakes or reassigning objects to new categories, both of which can be time-consuming to perform on individual objects. Bulk updates are easy to perform using Entity Framework Core, but they require a little effort to get them working smoothly with the ASP.NET Core MVC part of the application.

Updating the Views and Controller

To add support for performing bulk updates, I updated the Index view to contain an Edit All button that targets the UpdateAll action. I also added a ViewBag property called UpdateAll, which will lead to the display of a partial view called InlineEditor.cshtml when true, as shown in Listing 6-8.

Listing 6-8. Supporting Bulk Updates in the Index.cshtml File in the Views/Home Folder

```
@model IEnumerable<Product>

<h3 class="p-2 bg-primary text-white text-center">Products</h3>

<div class="container-fluid mt-3">
@if (ViewBag.UpdateAll != true) {
    <div class="row">
        <div class="col-1 font-weight-bold">Id</div>
        <div class="col font-weight-bold">Name</div>
        <div class="col font-weight-bold">Category</div>
        <div class="col font-weight-bold text-right">Purchase Price</div>
        <div class="col font-weight-bold text-right">Retail Price</div>
        <div class="col"></div>
    </div>
    <form asp-action="AddProduct" method="post">
        <div class="row p-2">
            <div class="col-1"></div>
            <div class="col"><input name="Name" class="form-control" /></div>
            <div class="col"><input name="Category" class="form-control" /></div>
            <div class="col">
                <input name="PurchasePrice" class="form-control" />
            </div>
            <div class="col">
                <input name="RetailPrice" class="form-control" />
            </div>
            <div class="col">
                <button type="submit" class="btn btn-primary">Add</button>
            </div>
        </div>
    </form>
    <div>
        @if (Model.Count() == 0) {
            <div class="row">
                <div class="col text-center p-2">No Data</div>
            </div>
        } else {
            @foreach (Product p in Model) {
                <div class="row p-2">
                    <div class="col-1">@p.Id</div>
                    <div class="col">@p.Name</div>
                    <div class="col">@p.Category</div>
                    <div class="col text-right">@p.PurchasePrice</div>
                    <div class="col text-right">@p.RetailPrice</div>
                    <div class="col">
                        <a asp-action="UpdateProduct" asp-route-key="@p.Id"
                                class="btn btn-outline-primary">
                            Edit
                        </a>
                    </div>
```

```
                    </div>
                }
            }
        </div>
        <div class="text-center">
            <a asp-action="UpdateAll" class="btn btn-primary">Edit All</a>
        </div>
} else {
    @Html.Partial("InlineEditor", Model)
}
</div>
```

I created the partial view by adding a file called InlineEditor.cshtml to the Views/Home folder with the content shown in Listing 6-9.

Listing 6-9. The Contents of the InlineEditor.cshtml File in the Views/Home Folder

```
@model IEnumerable<Product>

<div class="row">
    <div class="col-1 font-weight-bold">Id</div>
    <div class="col font-weight-bold">Name</div>
    <div class="col font-weight-bold">Category</div>
    <div class="col font-weight-bold">Purchase Price</div>
    <div class="col font-weight-bold">Retail Price</div>
</div>
@{ int i = 0; }
<form asp-action="UpdateAll" method="post">
    @foreach (Product p in Model) {
        <div class="row p-2">
            <div class="col-1">
                @p.Id
                <input type="hidden" name="Products[@i].Id" value="@p.Id" />
            </div>
            <div class="col">
                <input class="form-control" name="Products[@i].Name"
                    value="@p.Name" />
            </div>
            <div class="col">
                <input class="form-control" name="Products[@i].Category"
                    value="@p.Category" />
            </div>
            <div class="col text-right">
                <input class="form-control" name="Products[@i].PurchasePrice"
                    value="@p.PurchasePrice" />
            </div>
            <div class="col text-right">
                <input class="form-control" name="Products[@i].RetailPrice"
                    value="@p.RetailPrice" />
            </div>
```

```
        </div>
        i++;
    }
    <div class="text-center m-2">
        <button type="submit" class="btn btn-primary">Save All</button>
        <a asp-action="Index" class="btn btn-outline-primary">Cancel</a>
    </div>
</form>
```

The partial view creates a set of form elements whose name follows the MVC convention for a collection of objects so that the Id property is given the names Products[0].Id, Products[1].Id, and so on. Setting up the names for the input elements requires a counter, which produces the awkward mix of Razor and C# expressions.

In Listing 6-10, I have added action methods to the Home controller, which will allow the user to start the bulk edit process and submit the data.

Listing 6-10. Adding Action Methods in the HomeController.cs File in the Controllers Folder

```
using Microsoft.AspNetCore.Mvc;
using SportsStore.Models;

namespace SportsStore.Controllers {

    public class HomeController : Controller {
        private IRepository repository;

        public HomeController(IRepository repo) => repository = repo;

        public IActionResult Index() {
            //System.Console.Clear();
            return View(repository.Products);
        }

        [HttpPost]
        public IActionResult AddProduct(Product product) {
            repository.AddProduct(product);
            return RedirectToAction(nameof(Index));
        }

        public IActionResult UpdateProduct(long key) {
            return View(repository.GetProduct(key));
        }

        [HttpPost]
        public IActionResult UpdateProduct(Product product) {
            repository.UpdateProduct(product);
            return RedirectToAction(nameof(Index));
        }

        public IActionResult UpdateAll() {
            ViewBag.UpdateAll = true;
            return View(nameof(Index), repository.Products);
        }
```

```
[HttpPost]
public IActionResult UpdateAll(Product[] products) {
    repository.UpdateAll(products);
    return RedirectToAction(nameof(Index));
}
    }
}
```

The POST version of the UpdateAll method accepts an array of Product objects, which the MVC model binder will create from the form data and pass on to the repository method of the same name.

Updating the Repository

In Listing 6-11, I have added a new method to the repository interface that will perform a bulk update.

Listing 6-11. Adding a Method in the IRepository.cs File in the Models Folder

```
using System.Collections.Generic;

namespace SportsStore.Models {

    public interface IRepository {

        IEnumerable<Product> Products { get; }

        Product GetProduct(long key);

        void AddProduct(Product product);

        void UpdateProduct(Product product);

        void UpdateAll(Product[] products);
    }
}
```

To complete the feature, I added an UpdateAll method to the repository implementation that updates the database using the data received from the HTTP request, as shown in Listing 6-12.

Listing 6-12. Performing a Bulk Edit in the DataRepository.cs File in the Models Folder

```
using System.Collections.Generic;
using System.Linq;

namespace SportsStore.Models {

    public class DataRepository : IRepository {
        private DataContext context;

        public DataRepository(DataContext ctx) => context = ctx;

        public IEnumerable<Product> Products => context.Products.ToArray();

        public Product GetProduct(long key) => context.Products.Find(key);
```

96

```
public void AddProduct(Product product) {
    context.Products.Add(product);
    context.SaveChanges();
}

public void UpdateProduct(Product product) {
    Product p = GetProduct(product.Id);
    p.Name = product.Name;
    p.Category = product.Category;
    p.PurchasePrice = product.PurchasePrice;
    p.RetailPrice = product.RetailPrice;
    //context.Products.Update(product);
    context.SaveChanges();
}

public void UpdateAll(Product[] products) {
    context.Products.UpdateRange(products);
    context.SaveChanges();
}
    }
}
```

The DbSet<T> class provides methods for working on both individual objects and collections of objects. In this example, I have used the UpdateRange method, which is the collection counterpart to the Update method. When the SaveChanges method is called, Entity Framework Core will send a series of SQL UPDATE commands to update the server. Start the application using dotnet run, navigate to http://localhost:5000, and click the Edit All button to display the bulk editing feature, as shown in Figure 6-5.

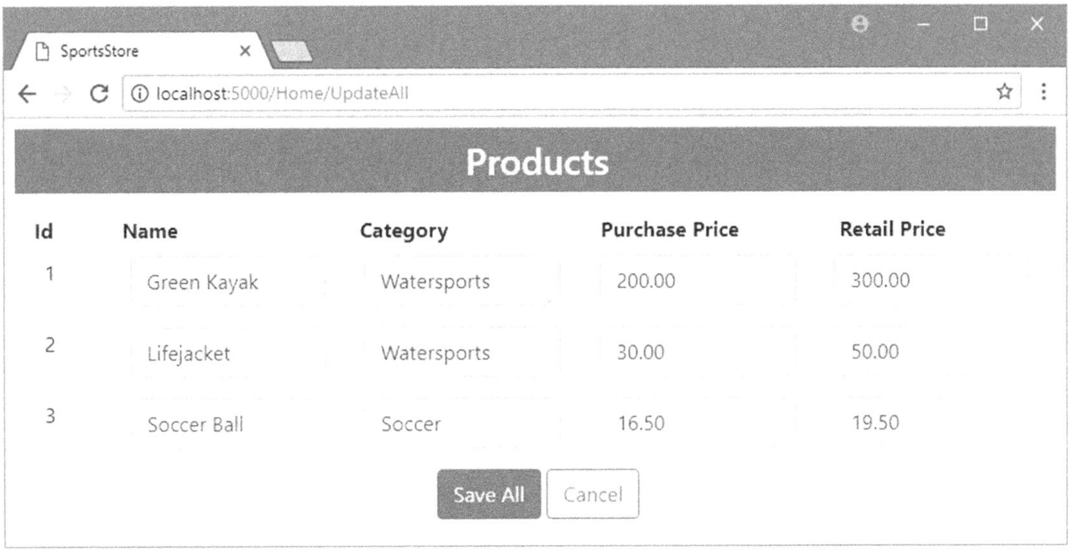

Figure 6-5. *Editing multiple objects*

Using Change Detection for Bulk Updates

The code in Listing 6-12 doesn't use the Entity Framework Core change-detection feature, which means that all of the properties for all of the Product objects will be updated. To update only changed values, I modified the UpdateAll method in the repository class, as shown in Listing 6-13.

Listing 6-13. Using Change Detection in the DataRepository.cs File in the Models Folder

```
...
public void UpdateAll(Product[] products) {
    //context.Products.UpdateRange(products);

    Dictionary<long, Product> data = products.ToDictionary(p => p.Id);
    IEnumerable<Product> baseline =
        context.Products.Where(p => data.Keys.Contains(p.Id));

    foreach(Product databaseProduct in baseline) {
        Product requestProduct = data[databaseProduct.Id];
        databaseProduct.Name = requestProduct.Name;
        databaseProduct.Category = requestProduct.Category;
        databaseProduct.PurchasePrice = requestProduct.PurchasePrice;
        databaseProduct.RetailPrice = requestProduct.RetailPrice;
    }
    context.SaveChanges();
}
...
```

The process for performing the update can be convoluted. I start by creating a dictionary of the Product objects received from the MVC model binder, using the Id property for keys. I use the collection of keys to query for the corresponding objects in the database, like this:

```
...
IEnumerable<Product> baseline =
        context.Products.Where(p => data.Keys.Contains(p.Id));
...
```

I enumerate the query objects and copy the property values from the request objects. When the SaveChanges method is called, Entity Framework Core performs change-detection and updates only those values that have changed. Start the application using dotnet run, navigate to http://localhost:5000, and click the Edit All button. Change the Name field of the first product to Green Kayak and the Retail Price field of the Lifejacket to 50. Click the Save All button and examine the logging messages generated by the application. To get the baseline data for change-detection, Entity Framework Core sends this query to the database:

```
...
SELECT [p].[Id], [p].[Category], [p].[Name], [p].[PurchasePrice], [p].[RetailPrice]
FROM [Products] AS [p]
WHERE [p].[Id] IN (1, 2, 3)
...
```

The objects that are created from this data are used for change detection. Entity Framework Core works out which properties have new values and sends two UPDATE commands to the database.

```
...
UPDATE [Products] SET [Name] = @p0
WHERE [Id] = @p1;
...
UPDATE [Products] SET [RetailPrice] = @p2
WHERE [Id] = @p3;
...
```

You can see that the Name value is changed by the first command and the RetailPrice value is changed by the second command, corresponding to the changes made using the MVC part of the application.

Deleting Data

Deleting objects from the database is a simple process, although it can become more involved as the data model grows, as I explain in Chapter 7. In Listing 6-14, I have added Delete method to the repository interface.

Listing 6-14. Adding a Method in the IRepository.cs File in the Models Folder

```
using System.Collections.Generic;

namespace SportsStore.Models {

    public interface IRepository {

        IEnumerable<Product> Products { get; }

        Product GetProduct(long key);

        void AddProduct(Product product);

        void UpdateProduct(Product product);

        void UpdateAll(Product[] products);

        void Delete(Product product);
    }
}
```

In Listing 6-15, I have updated the repository implementation class to add support for the Delete method.

Listing 6-15. Deleting Objects in the DataRepository.cs File in the Models Folder

```
using System.Collections.Generic;
using System.Linq;

namespace SportsStore.Models {

    public class DataRepository : IRepository {
        private DataContext context;
```

```
        public DataRepository(DataContext ctx) => context = ctx;

        public IEnumerable<Product> Products => context.Products.ToArray();

        public Product GetProduct(long key) => context.Products.Find(key);

        // ...other methods omitted for brevity...

        public void Delete(Product product) {
            context.Products.Remove(product);
            context.SaveChanges();
        }
    }
}
```

The DbSet<T> class has Remove and RemoveRange methods for deleting one or several objects from the database. As with other operations that modify the database, no data will be deleted until the SaveChanges method is called.

Working through the application, I added an action method to the Home controller that receives details of the Product object to delete from the HTTP request and passes them on to the repository, as shown in Listing 6-16.

Listing 6-16. Adding an Action Method in the HomeController.cs File in the Controllers Folder

```
using Microsoft.AspNetCore.Mvc;
using SportsStore.Models;

namespace SportsStore.Controllers {

    public class HomeController : Controller {
        private IRepository repository;

        public HomeController(IRepository repo) => repository = repo;

        // ...other action methods omitted for brevity...

        [HttpPost]
        public IActionResult Delete(Product product) {
            repository.Delete(product);
            return RedirectToAction(nameof(Index));
        }
    }
}
```

To complete the feature, I added a form element for each Product objects displayed by the Index view used by the Home controller so that the user can trigger a delete, as shown in Listing 6-17.

■ **Tip**   The form contains the existing Edit button element just so that the two buttons will be displayed side by side by the browser.

Listing 6-17. Adding a Form in the Index.cshtml File in the Views/Home Folder

```
@model IEnumerable<Product>

<h3 class="p-2 bg-primary text-white text-center">Products</h3>

<div class="container-fluid mt-3">
    @if (ViewBag.UpdateAll != true) {
        <div class="row">
            <div class="col-1 font-weight-bold">Id</div>
            <div class="col font-weight-bold">Name</div>
            <div class="col font-weight-bold">Category</div>
            <div class="col font-weight-bold text-right">Purchase Price</div>
            <div class="col font-weight-bold text-right">Retail Price</div>
            <div class="col"></div>
        </div>
        <form asp-action="AddProduct" method="post">
            <div class="row p-2">
                <div class="col-1"></div>
                <div class="col"><input name="Name" class="form-control" /></div>
                <div class="col"><input name="Category" class="form-control" /></div>
                <div class="col">
                    <input name="PurchasePrice" class="form-control" />
                </div>
                <div class="col">
                    <input name="RetailPrice" class="form-control" />
                </div>
                <div class="col">
                    <button type="submit" class="btn btn-primary">Add</button>
                </div>
            </div>
        </form>
        <div>
            @if (Model.Count() == 0) {
                <div class="row">
                    <div class="col text-center p-2">No Data</div>
                </div>
            } else {
                @foreach (Product p in Model) {
                    <div class="row p-2">
                        <div class="col-1">@p.Id</div>
                        <div class="col">@p.Name</div>
                        <div class="col">@p.Category</div>
                        <div class="col text-right">@p.PurchasePrice</div>
                        <div class="col text-right">@p.RetailPrice</div>
                        <div class="col">
                            <form asp-action="Delete" method="post">
                                <a asp-action="UpdateProduct" asp-route-key="@p.Id"
                                   class="btn btn-outline-primary">
                                    Edit
                                </a>
```

```
                              <input type="hidden" name="Id" value="@p.Id" />
                              <button type="submit" class="btn btn-outline-danger">
                                  Delete
                              </button>
                          </form>
                      </div>
                  </div>
              }
          }
      </div>
      <div class="text-center">
          <a asp-action="UpdateAll" class="btn btn-primary">Edit All</a>
      </div>
  } else {
      @Html.Partial("InlineEditor", Model)
  }
</div>
```

Notice that the form contains only an input element for the Id property. That's all that Entity Framework Core uses to delete an object from the database, even though the operation is performed on a complete Product object. Rather than send additional data that isn't going to be used, I have sent just the primary key value, which the MVC model binder will use to create a Product object, leaving all the other properties null or the default value for the type.

Note   This is another example of how much implementation detail is allowed to leak into the rest of the application. Sending just an Id value for a delete operation is efficient and simple, but it does rely on knowledge of how Entity Framework Core works, and that creates a dependency on how the data is being stored. The alternative is not to rely on the behavior of Entity Framework Core, but that means sending values for properties that are going to be ignored and that will increase the amount of bandwidth required by the application. Some design decisions are clear-cut, but others require difficult choices between suboptimal alternatives.

To test the delete feature, start the application using dotnet run, navigate to http://localhost:5000, and click the Delete button for the Soccer Ball item. The Product object will be removed from the database, as shown in Figure 6-6.

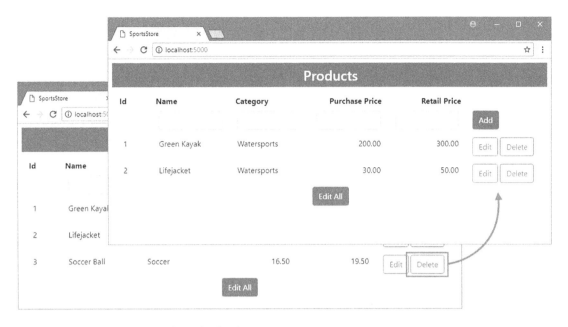

Figure 6-6. *Deleting an object from the database*

Common Problems and Solutions

The Entity Framework Core features for updating and deleting data are reasonably straightforward although there can be difficulties when using these features with objects that have been created by the MVC model binder from HTTP requests. In the sections that follow, I describe the problems you are most likely to encounter and explain how to resolve them.

Objects Are Not Updated or Deleted

If the application seems to be working but objects are not being modified, then the first thing to check is that you remembered to call the SaveChanges method in your repository implementation class. Entity Framework Core will only update the database after the SaveChanges method is called and will quietly discard changes if you forget.

The "Reference Not Set to an Instance of an Object" Exception

This exception is caused by trying to update an object whose primary property is set to null or zero. The most common reason for this problem is forgetting to include a value for the primary key property in the HTML form that is used to update an object. Although you cannot change the primary key value, you must ensure that a value is provided as part of the HTML form. Use a hidden input element if you don't want the user to see the primary key value.

The "Instance of Entity Type Cannot be Tracked" Exception

This exception is caused when you call the Entity Framework Core Update method using an object created by the MVC model binder after you have queried the database for the same object using Entity Framework Core. The database context class keeps track of the objects it creates to make change-detection work, and Entity Framework Core can't cope when you try to introduce a conflicting object that has been created by the MVC framework.

You can only use the Update method if you have not queried for baseline data. To avoid this problem, copy the properties from the object created by the MVC model binder to the object created by Entity Framework Core, as shown in Listing 6-7.

The "Property Has a Temporary Value" Exception

This exception occurs when you try to send an HTTP request to the application to delete an object but forget to include a value for the primary key property. The MVC model binder will create an object whose primary key value is the default for the property type, which is used to indicate a temporary value when waiting for the database server to allocate a value when storing a new object. To prevent this exception, ensure you include an input element that provides the primary key value in the HTML form. The type of the input element can be set to hidden to prevent the user from changing the value.

Updates Result in Zero Values

If numeric properties are set to zero by an update, the likely cause is either that the HTML form doesn't include a value for this property or the value entered by the user cannot be parsed into the property data type by the MVC model binder. To fix the first problem, ensure that there are values for all the properties defined by the data model class. To fix the second problem, use the MVC validation features to make partial updates when data values cannot be processed.

Summary

In this chapter, I added support for updating and deleting objects in the SportsStore application. I showed you how to modify individual objects and perform bulk updates and how to provide Entity Framework Core with baseline data for its change-detection feature. I also showed you how to delete data, which is simple to do with a one-class data model but becomes more complex as the data model grows. In the next chapter, I expand the data model for the SportsStore application.

CHAPTER 7

SportsStore: Expanding the Model

In this chapter, I expand the data model for the SportsStore application beyond the single Product class. I show you how to normalize data by replacing a string property with a separate class and explain how to access the data once you have created it. I also add support for representing customer orders, which is an essential part of any online store.

Preparing for This Chapter

In this chapter, I continue using the SportsStore project created in Chapter 4 and modified in the chapters since. To prepare for this chapter, I am going to consolidate the process for creating and editing Product objects into a single view. In Listing 7-1, I combined the action methods that add or update Product objects in the Home controller and removed the actions for performing bulk updates.

Tip　You can download the SportsStore project for this chapter—and the projects for every other chapter—from the GitHub repository for this book: https://github.com/apress/pro-ef-core-2-for-asp.net-core-mvc.

Listing 7-1.　Consolidating Actions in the HomeController.cs File in the Controllers Folder

```
using Microsoft.AspNetCore.Mvc;
using SportsStore.Models;

namespace SportsStore.Controllers {

    public class HomeController : Controller {
        private IRepository repository;

        public HomeController(IRepository repo) => repository = repo;

        public IActionResult Index() {
            return View(repository.Products);
        }

        public IActionResult UpdateProduct(long key) {
            return View(key == 0 ? new Product() : repository.GetProduct(key));
        }
```

```
    [HttpPost]
    public IActionResult UpdateProduct(Product product) {
        if (product.Id == 0) {
            repository.AddProduct(product);
        } else {
            repository.UpdateProduct(product);
        }
        return RedirectToAction(nameof(Index));
    }

    [HttpPost]
    public IActionResult Delete(Product product) {
        repository.Delete(product);
        return RedirectToAction(nameof(Index));
    }
}
}
```

The consolidated actions rely on the default value for long properties to determine whether the user wants to modify an existing object or create a new one. In Listing 7-2, I have updated the Index view to reflect the changes in the controller.

Listing 7-2. Reflecting Controller Changes in the Index.cshtml File in the Views/Home Folder

```
@model IEnumerable<Product>

<h3 class="p-2 bg-primary text-white text-center">Products</h3>

<div class="container-fluid mt-3">
    <div class="row">
        <div class="col-1 font-weight-bold">Id</div>
        <div class="col font-weight-bold">Name</div>
        <div class="col font-weight-bold">Category</div>
        <div class="col font-weight-bold text-right">Purchase Price</div>
        <div class="col font-weight-bold text-right">Retail Price</div>
        <div class="col"></div>
    </div>
    @foreach (Product p in Model) {
        <div class="row p-2">
            <div class="col-1">@p.Id</div>
            <div class="col">@p.Name</div>
            <div class="col">@p.Category</div>
            <div class="col text-right">@p.PurchasePrice</div>
            <div class="col text-right">@p.RetailPrice</div>
            <div class="col">
                <form asp-action="Delete" method="post">
                    <a asp-action="UpdateProduct" asp-route-key="@p.Id"
                        class="btn btn-outline-primary">
                        Edit
                    </a>
                    <input type="hidden" name="Id" value="@p.Id" />
                    <button type="submit" class="btn btn-outline-danger">
```

```
                    Delete
                </button>
            </form>
        </div>
    </div>
    }
    <div class="text-center p-2">
        <a asp-action="UpdateProduct" asp-route-key="0"
            class="btn btn-primary">Add</a>
    </div>
</div>
```

Run the commands shown in Listing 7-3 in the SportsStore project folder to delete and re-create the database, which will help ensure that you get the expected results from the examples.

Listing 7-3. Deleting and Re-creating the Database

```
dotnet ef database drop --force
dotnet ef database update
```

Start the application using dotnet run and navigate to http://localhost:5000; you will see the content shown in Figure 7-1. Don't add any data to the database because it will be updated with a new migration in the next section and data added now will produce an exception.

Figure 7-1. *Running the example application*

Creating a Data Model Relationship

At the moment, each Product object is created with a Category value that is expressed as a string value. In a real project, it would only be a matter of time before a typo puts a product into an unintended category. To avoid this kind of problem, relationships can be used to normalize the application's data, which has the effect of reducing duplication and ensuring consistency, as I demonstrate in the sections that follow.

Adding a Data Model Class

The starting point is to create a new data model class. I added a file called `Category.cs` to the `Models` folder and used it to define the class shown in Listing 7-4.

Listing 7-4. The Contents of the Category.cs File in the Models Folder

```
namespace SportsStore.Models {

    public class Category {
        public long Id { get; set; }
        public string Name { get; set; }
        public string Description { get; set; }
    }
}
```

The `Category` class will represent a category of products. The `Id` property is the primary key property, and the `Name` and `Description` properties will be provided by the user when a new category is created and stored in the database.

Creating the Relationship

The next step is to create a relationship between the two data model classes, which is done by adding properties to one of those classes. In any data relationship, one of the classes is known as the dependent entity, and it is this class to which the properties are added. To work out which class is the dependent entity, ask yourself which type of object cannot exist without the other. In the case of the SportsStore application, a category will be able to exist without containing any products, but I want every product to belong to a category—and that means the `Product` class is the dependent entity in this situation. In Listing 7-5 I have added two properties to the `Product` class that create the relationship with the `Category` class.

■ **Tip**   Don't worry if selecting the dependent entity doesn't make sense at the moment. I return to this topic in more detail in Chapter 14, and you will become more comfortable with the concept as you gain experience with Entity Framework Core.

Listing 7-5. Adding Relationship Properties in the Product.cs File in the Models Folder

```
namespace SportsStore.Models {

    public class Product {

        public long Id { get; set; }

        public string Name { get; set; }
        //public string Category { get; set; }
        public decimal PurchasePrice { get; set; }
        public decimal RetailPrice { get; set; }
```

```
    public long CategoryId { get; set; }
    public Category Category { get; set; }
    }
}
```

The first property I added is called `CategoryId` and is an example of a foreign key property, which Entity Framework Core will use to track the relationship by assigning a primary key value that identifies a `Category` object. The name of a foreign key property is composed of the class name plus the primary key property name, which is how I arrived at `CategoryId`.

The second property replaces the existing `Category` property and is an example of a navigation property. Entity Framework Core will populate this property with the `Category` object that is identified by the foreign key property, which makes it more natural to work with the data in the database.

Updating the Context and Creating the Repository

To access the `Category` objects, I added a `DbSet<T>` property to the database context class, as shown in Listing 7-6.

Listing 7-6. Adding a Property in the DataContext.cs File in the Models Folder

```
using Microsoft.EntityFrameworkCore;

namespace SportsStore.Models {

    public class DataContext : DbContext {

        public DataContext(DbContextOptions<DataContext> opts) : base(opts) {}

        public DbSet<Product> Products { get; set; }

        public DbSet<Category> Categories { get; set; }
    }
}
```

The new property follows the same pattern as the existing one: it is a `public` property with `get` and `set` clauses, and it returns `DbSet<T>`, where `T` is the class I want to store in the database.

When you expand the data model, you can provide the rest of the application with access to the new data types by adding members to the existing repository or by creating a new one. For the SportsStore application, I am going to create a separate repository just to demonstrate how it is done. I added a class file called `CategoryRepository.cs` to the `Models` folder and used it to define the interface and implementation class shown in Listing 7-7.

Listing 7-7. The Contents of the CategoryRepository.cs File in the Models Folder

```
using System.Collections.Generic;

namespace SportsStore.Models {

    public interface ICategoryRepository {

        IEnumerable<Category> Categories { get; }
```

```
        void AddCategory(Category category);
        void UpdateCategory(Category category);
        void DeleteCategory(Category category);
    }

    public class CategoryRepository : ICategoryRepository {
        private DataContext context;

        public CategoryRepository(DataContext ctx) => context = ctx;

        public IEnumerable<Category> Categories => context.Categories;

        public void AddCategory(Category category) {
            context.Categories.Add(category);
            context.SaveChanges();
        }

        public void UpdateCategory(Category category) {
            context.Categories.Update(category);
            context.SaveChanges();
        }

        public void DeleteCategory(Category category) {
            context.Categories.Remove(category);
            context.SaveChanges();
        }
    }
}
```

I have defined the repository interface and implementation class in a single file and used the simplest approach to performing updates, without relying on the change-detection features. In Listing 7-8, I registered the repository and its implementation in the Startup class for use with the dependency injection feature.

Listing 7-8. Registering a Repository in the Startup.cs File in the SportsStore Folder

```
using System;
using System.Collections.Generic;
using System.Linq;
using System.Threading.Tasks;
using Microsoft.AspNetCore.Builder;
using Microsoft.AspNetCore.Hosting;
using Microsoft.AspNetCore.Http;
using Microsoft.Extensions.DependencyInjection;
using SportsStore.Models;
using Microsoft.EntityFrameworkCore;
using Microsoft.Extensions.Configuration;

namespace SportsStore {
    public class Startup {
```

```
    public Startup(IConfiguration config) => Configuration = config;

    public IConfiguration Configuration { get; }

    public void ConfigureServices(IServiceCollection services) {
        services.AddMvc();
        services.AddTransient<IRepository, DataRepository>();
        services.AddTransient<ICategoryRepository, CategoryRepository>();
        string conString = Configuration["ConnectionStrings:DefaultConnection"];
        services.AddDbContext<DataContext>(options =>
            options.UseSqlServer(conString));
    }

    public void Configure(IApplicationBuilder app, IHostingEnvironment env) {
        app.UseDeveloperExceptionPage();
        app.UseStatusCodePages();
        app.UseStaticFiles();
        app.UseMvcWithDefaultRoute();
    }
  }
}
```

Creating and Applying a Migration

Entity Framework Core can't store Category objects until the database has been updated to match the changes in the data model. To update the database, a new migration must be created and applied to the database, which is done by running the commands shown in Listing 7-9 in the SportsStore project folder.

■ **Tip**   If you get an exception when you run the dotnet ef database update command, then the likely reason is you added Product data to the database after running the commands in Listing 7-3. Run the commands in Listing 7-3 again, and the database will be reset and updated to the migration created in Listing 7-9.

Listing 7-9. Creating and Applying a Database Migration

```
dotnet ef migrations add Categories
dotnet ef database update
```

The first command creates a new migration called Categories, which will contain the commands required to prepare the database to store new objects. The second command executes those commands to update the database.

Creating a Controller and View

I have created a *required* relationship between the Product and Category classes, which means that every Product must be associated with a Category object. With this kind of relationship, it is helpful to provide the user with the means to manage the Category objects in the database. I added a class file called CategoriesController.cs to the Controllers folder and used it to create the controller shown in Listing 7-10.

Tip The alternative to a required relationship is an optional one, where a Product object can be associated with a Category but doesn't have to be. I explain how to create both kinds of relationship in detail in Part 2.

Listing 7-10. The Contents of the CategoriesController.cs File in the Controllers Folder

```
using Microsoft.AspNetCore.Mvc;
using SportsStore.Models;

namespace SportsStore.Controllers {

    public class CategoriesController : Controller {
        private ICategoryRepository repository;

        public CategoriesController(ICategoryRepository repo) => repository = repo;

        public IActionResult Index() => View(repository.Categories);

        [HttpPost]
        public IActionResult AddCategory(Category category) {
            repository.AddCategory(category);
            return RedirectToAction(nameof(Index));
        }

        public IActionResult EditCategory(long id) {
            ViewBag.EditId = id;
            return View("Index", repository.Categories);
        }

        [HttpPost]
        public IActionResult UpdateCategory(Category category) {
            repository.UpdateCategory(category);
            return RedirectToAction(nameof(Index));
        }

        [HttpPost]
        public IActionResult DeleteCategory(Category category) {
            repository.DeleteCategory(category);
            return RedirectToAction(nameof(Index));
        }
    }
}
```

The Categories controller receives a repository to access category data through its constructor and defines actions that support querying the database and creating, updating, and deleting Category objects. To provide the controller with a view, I created the Views/Categories folder and added to it a file called Index.cshtml with the content shown in Listing 7-11.

Listing 7-11. The Contents of the Index.cshtml File in the Views/Categories Folder

```
@model IEnumerable<Category>

<h3 class="p-2 bg-primary text-white text-center">Categories</h3>

<div class="container-fluid mt-3">
    <div class="row">
        <div class="col-1 font-weight-bold">Id</div>
        <div class="col font-weight-bold">Name</div>
        <div class="col font-weight-bold">Description</div>
        <div class="col-3"></div>
    </div>
    @if (ViewBag.EditId == null) {
        <form asp-action="AddCategory" method="post">
            @Html.Partial("CategoryEditor", new Category())
        </form>
    }
    @foreach (Category c in Model) {
        @if (c.Id == ViewBag.EditId) {
            <form asp-action="UpdateCategory" method="post">
                <input type="hidden" name="Id" value="@c.Id" />
                @Html.Partial("CategoryEditor", c)
            </form>
        } else {
            <div class="row p-2">
                <div class="col-1">@c.Id</div>
                <div class="col">@c.Name</div>
                <div class="col">@c.Description</div>
                <div class="col-3">
                    <form asp-action="DeleteCategory" method="post">
                        <input type="hidden" name="Id" value="@c.Id" />
                        <a asp-action="EditCategory" asp-route-id="@c.Id"
                            class="btn btn-outline-primary">Edit</a>
                        <button type="submit" class="btn btn-outline-danger">
                            Delete
                        </button>
                    </form>
                </div>
            </div>
        }
    }
</div>
```

This view provides an all-in-one interface for managing categories and delegates creating, and editing objects to a partial view. To create the partial view, I added a file called CategoryEditor.cshtml to the Views/Categories folder and added the content shown in Listing 7-12.

Listing 7-12. The Contents of the CategoryEditor.cshtml File in the Views/Categories Folder

```
@model Category

<div class="row p-2">
    <div class="col-1"></div>
    <div class="col">
        <input asp-for="Name" class="form-control" />
    </div>
    <div class="col">
        <input asp-for="Description" class="form-control" />
    </div>
    <div class="col-3">
        @if (Model.Id == 0) {
            <button type="submit" class="btn btn-primary">Add</button>
        } else {
            <button type="submit" class="btn btn-outline-primary">Save</button>
            <a asp-action="Index" class="btn btn-outline-secondary">Cancel</a>
        }
    </div>
</div>
```

To make it easier to move around the application, I added the elements shown in Listing 7-13 to the shared layout.

Listing 7-13. Adding Elements in the _Layout.cshtml File in the Views/Shared Folder

```
<!DOCTYPE html>
<html>
<head>
    <meta name="viewport" content="width=device-width" />
    <title>SportsStore</title>
    <link rel="stylesheet" href="~/lib/bootstrap/dist/css/bootstrap.min.css" />
    <style>
        .placeholder { visibility: collapse; display: none }
        .placeholder:only-child { visibility: visible; display: flex }
    </style>
</head>
<body>
    <div class="container-fluid">
        <div class="row p-2">
            <div class="col-2">
                <a asp-controller="Home" asp-action="Index"
                        class="@GetClassForButton("Home")">
                    Products
                </a>
                <a asp-controller="Categories" asp-action="Index"
                        class="@GetClassForButton("Categories")">
                    Categories
                </a>
            </div>
```

```
        <div class="col">
            @RenderBody()
        </div>
    </div>
</div>
</body>
</html>

@functions {
    string GetClassForButton(string controller) {
        return "btn btn-block " + (ViewContext.RouteData.Values["controller"]
            as string == controller ? "btn-primary" : "btn-outline-primary");
    }
}
```

I have added buttons that select the Product and Categories controllers with a simple inline function that uses Bootstrap CSS styles to highlight the button for the currently displayed controller.

■ **Note** I don't often use inline Razor functions because I prefer to keep all of the C# code in class files. But in this case, the function has the benefit of keeping the example concise, and it is related only to the content in the view and is easier than creating a view component.

Populating the Database with Categories

It will be helpful to have some data to work with while completing the data relationship. Start the application using dotnet run, click the Categories button, and use the HTML form to create categories using the values in Table 7-1.

Table 7-1. *The Data Values for Creating Categories*

Name	Description
Watersports	Make a splash
Soccer	The world's favorite game
Running	Run like the wind

When you have added all three categories, you should see the content illustrated in Figure 7-2.

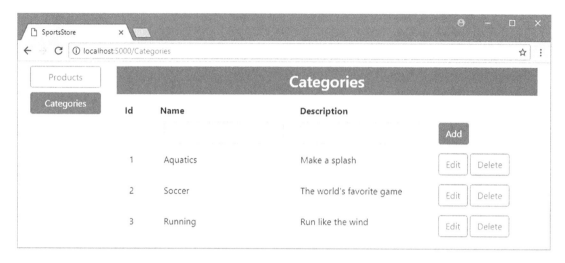

Figure 7-2. *Adding category data to the application*

Using a Data Relationship

The part of the application that deals with `Product` objects must be updated to reflect the new relationship in the database. There are two parts to this process: including the category data when querying the database and allowing the user to select a category when creating or editing a product.

Working with Related Data

Entity Framework Core ignores relationships unless you explicitly include them in queries. This means that navigation properties such as the `Category` defined by the `Product` class will be left `null` by default. The `Include` extension method is used to tell Entity Framework Core to populate a navigation property with related data and is called on the `IQueryable<T>` object that represents a query. In Listing 7-14, I have used the `Include` method to include the related `Category` objects in the queries made by the product repository.

Listing 7-14. Including Related Data in the DataRepository.cs File in the Models Folder

```
using System.Collections.Generic;
using System.Linq;
using Microsoft.EntityFrameworkCore;

namespace SportsStore.Models {

    public class DataRepository : IRepository {
        private DataContext context;

        public DataRepository(DataContext ctx) => context = ctx;

        public IEnumerable<Product> Products => context.Products
            .Include(p => p.Category).ToArray();

        public Product GetProduct(long key) => context.Products
            .Include(p => p.Category).First(p => p.Id == key);
```

```
    public void AddProduct(Product product) {
        context.Products.Add(product);
        context.SaveChanges();
    }

    public void UpdateProduct(Product product) {
        Product p = context.Products.Find(product.Id);
        p.Name = product.Name;
        //p.Category = product.Category;
        p.PurchasePrice = product.PurchasePrice;
        p.RetailPrice = product.RetailPrice;
        p.CategoryId = product.CategoryId;
        context.SaveChanges();
    }

    public void UpdateAll(Product[] products) {
        Dictionary<long, Product> data = products.ToDictionary(p => p.Id);
        IEnumerable<Product> baseline =
            context.Products.Where(p => data.Keys.Contains(p.Id));

        foreach(Product databaseProduct in baseline) {
            Product requestProduct = data[databaseProduct.Id];
            databaseProduct.Name = requestProduct.Name;
            databaseProduct.Category = requestProduct.Category;
            databaseProduct.PurchasePrice = requestProduct.PurchasePrice;
            databaseProduct.RetailPrice = requestProduct.RetailPrice;
        }
        context.SaveChanges();
    }

    public void Delete(Product product) {
        context.Products.Remove(product);
        context.SaveChanges();
    }
  }
}
```

The Include method is defined in the Microsoft.EntityFrameworkCore namespace, and it accepts a lambda expression that selects the navigation property you want Entity Framework Core to include in the query. The Find method that I used for the GetProduct method cannot be used with the Include method, so I have replaced it with the First method, which achieves the same effect. The result of these changes is that Entity Framework Core will populate the Product.Category navigation property for the Product objects created by the Products property and the GetProduct method.

Notice the changes that I made to the UpdateProduct method. First, I query for the baseline data directly, rather than through the GetProduct method because I don't want to load related data when performing an update. Second, I commented out the statement that sets the Category property and added a statement that sets the CategoryId property instead. Setting the foreign key property is all that Entity Framework Core needs to update the relationship between two objects in the database.

Selecting a Category for a Product

In Listing 7-15, I have updated the Home controller so that it has access to the Category data through the repository and passes on the data to its view. This will allow the view to select from the complete set of categories when editing or creating a Product object.

Listing 7-15. Using Category Data in the HomeController.cs File in the Controllers Folder

```
using Microsoft.AspNetCore.Mvc;
using SportsStore.Models;

namespace SportsStore.Controllers {

    public class HomeController : Controller {
        private IRepository repository;
        private ICategoryRepository catRepository;

        public HomeController(IRepository repo, ICategoryRepository catRepo) {
            repository = repo;
            catRepository = catRepo;
        }

        public IActionResult Index() {
            return View(repository.Products);
        }

        public IActionResult UpdateProduct(long key) {
            ViewBag.Categories = catRepository.Categories;
            return View(key == 0 ? new Product() : repository.GetProduct(key));
        }

        [HttpPost]
        public IActionResult UpdateProduct(Product product) {
            if (product.Id == 0) {
                repository.AddProduct(product);
            } else {
                repository.UpdateProduct(product);
            }
            return RedirectToAction(nameof(Index));
        }

        [HttpPost]
        public IActionResult Delete(Product product) {
            repository.Delete(product);
            return RedirectToAction(nameof(Index));
        }
    }
}
```

To allow the user to choose one of the categories when creating or editing a Product, I added a select element to the UpdateProduct view, as shown in Listing 7-16.

Listing 7-16. Displaying Categories in the UpdateProduct.html File in the Views/Home Folder

```
@model Product

<h3 class="p-2 bg-primary text-white text-center">Update Product</h3>

<form asp-action="UpdateProduct" method="post">
    <div class="form-group">
        <label asp-for="Id"></label>
        <input asp-for="Id" class="form-control" readonly />
    </div>
    <div class="form-group">
        <label asp-for="Name"></label>
        <input asp-for="Name" class="form-control" />
    </div>
    <div class="form-group">
        <label asp-for="Category"></label>
        <select class="form-control" asp-for="CategoryId">
            @if (Model.Id == 0) {
                <option disabled selected>Choose Category</option>
            }
            @foreach (Category c in ViewBag.Categories) {
                <option selected=@(Model.Category?.Id == c.Id)
                    value="@c.Id">@c.Name</option>
            }
        </select>
    </div>
    <div class="form-group">
        <label asp-for="PurchasePrice"></label>
        <input asp-for="PurchasePrice" class="form-control" />
    </div>
    <div class="form-group">
        <label asp-for="RetailPrice"></label>
        <input asp-for="RetailPrice" class="form-control" />
    </div>
    <div class="text-center">
        <button class="btn btn-primary" type="submit">Save</button>
        <a asp-action="Index" class="btn btn-secondary">Cancel</a>
    </div>
</form>
```

I include a placeholder option element if the view is being used to create a new Product object and use a Razor expression to apply the selected attribute if an existing object is being edited.

All that remains is to update the Index view to follow the navigation property and display the name of the selected category for each Product object, as shown in Listing 7-17.

Listing 7-17. Following a Navigation Property in the Index.cshtml File in the Views/Home Folder

```
@model IEnumerable<Product>

<h3 class="p-2 bg-primary text-white text-center">Products</h3>

<div class="container-fluid mt-3">
    <div class="row">
        <div class="col-1 font-weight-bold">Id</div>
        <div class="col font-weight-bold">Name</div>
        <div class="col font-weight-bold">Category</div>
        <div class="col font-weight-bold text-right">Purchase Price</div>
        <div class="col font-weight-bold text-right">Retail Price</div>
        <div class="col"></div>
    </div>
    @foreach (Product p in Model) {
        <div class="row p-2">
            <div class="col-1">@p.Id</div>
            <div class="col">@p.Name</div>
            <div class="col">@p.Category.Name</div>
            <div class="col text-right">@p.PurchasePrice</div>
            <div class="col text-right">@p.RetailPrice</div>
            <div class="col">
                <form asp-action="Delete" method="post">
                    <a asp-action="UpdateProduct" asp-route-key="@p.Id"
                        class="btn btn-outline-primary">
                        Edit
                    </a>
                    <input type="hidden" name="Id" value="@p.Id" />
                    <button type="submit" class="btn btn-outline-danger">
                        Delete
                    </button>
                </form>
            </div>
        </div>
    }
    <div class="text-center p-2">
        <a asp-action="UpdateProduct" asp-route-key="0"
            class="btn btn-primary">Add</a>
    </div>
</div>
```

Creating and Editing Products with Categories

Start the application using `dotnet run`, navigate to `http://localhost:5000`, click the Add button, and use the form to create `Product` objects using the data shown in Table 7-2. As you create each object, use the `select` element to pick the category from the list.

Table 7-2. *The Values for Creating Test Product Objects*

Name	Category	Purchase Price	Retail Price
Kayak	Watersports	200	275
Lifejacket	Watersports	30	48.95
Soccer Ball	Soccer	17	19.50

As you create each object, the Index action will be executed to display the results, which will cause Entity Framework Core to query the database for the Product data and its related Category objects. You can see how this is translated into a SQL query by examining the logging messages generated by the application, like this:

```
...
SELECT [p].[Id], [p].[CategoryId], [p].[Name], [p].[PurchasePrice],
    [p].[RetailPrice], [p.Category].[Id], [p.Category].[Description],
    [p.Category].[Name]
FROM [Products] AS [p]
INNER JOIN [Categories] AS [p.Category] ON [p].[CategoryId] = [p.Category].[Id]
...
```

Entity Framework Core uses the foreign key to query for the data it needs to create the Category objects related to each Product and uses an inner join to combine data from the Products and Categories tables.

Once you have created all three Product objects, click Categories, click the Edit button for the Watersports category, and change the value of the Name field to Aquatics. Click the Save button and click Products, and you will see that both the Product objects in the edited category are shown with the new name, as illustrated in Figure 7-3.

Caution If you delete a Category object, then the Product objects that are related to it will also be deleted, which is the default configuration for required relationships. I explain how this works and the alternative configuration options in Chapter 22.

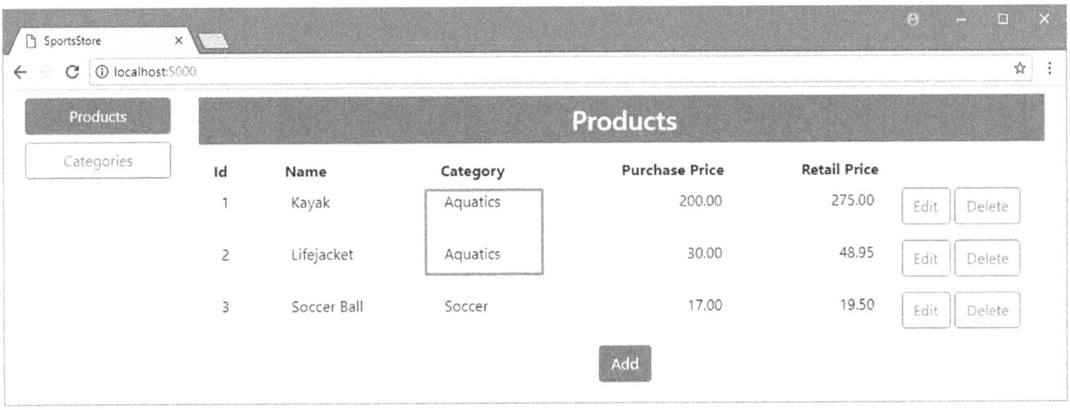

Figure 7-3. *The effect of changing a category name*

Adding Support for Orders

To demonstrate a more complex relationship, I am going to add support for creating and storing orders and use them to represent product selections made by customers. In the sections that follow, I expand the data model with additional classes, update the database, and add a controller to manage the new data.

Creating the Data Model Classes

I started by adding a file called Order.cs to the Models folder and using it to define the class shown in Listing 7-18.

Listing 7-18. The Contents of the Order.cs File in the Models Folder

```
using System.Collections.Generic;

namespace SportsStore.Models {

    public class Order {
        public long Id { get; set; }
        public string CustomerName { get; set; }
        public string Address { get; set; }
        public string State { get; set; }
        public string ZipCode { get; set; }
        public bool Shipped { get; set; }

        public IEnumerable<OrderLine> Lines { get; set; }
    }
}
```

The Order class has properties that store the customer's name and address and whether the products have been shipped. There is also a navigation property that provides access to the related OrderLine objects, which will represent an individual product selection. To create this class, I added a file called OrderLine.cs to the Models folder with the code shown in Listing 7-19.

Listing 7-19. The Contents of the OrderLine.cs File in the Models Folder

```
namespace SportsStore.Models {

    public class OrderLine {
        public long Id { get; set; }

        public long ProductId { get; set; }
        public Product Product { get; set; }

        public int Quantity { get; set; }

        public long OrderId { get; set; }
        public Order Order { get; set; }
    }
}
```

Each OrderLine object is related to an Order and a Product and has a property that indicates how many of that product the customer requires. To make it convenient to access the Order data, I added the properties shown in Listing 7-20 to the context class.

Listing 7-20. Adding Properties in the DataContext.cs File in the Models Folder

```
using Microsoft.EntityFrameworkCore;

namespace SportsStore.Models {

    public class DataContext : DbContext {

        public DataContext(DbContextOptions<DataContext> opts) : base(opts) {}

        public DbSet<Product> Products { get; set; }

        public DbSet<Category> Categories { get; set; }

        public DbSet<Order> Orders { get; set; }
        public DbSet<OrderLine> OrderLines { get; set; }
    }
}
```

Creating the Repository and Preparing the Database

To provide consistent access to the new data to the rest of the application, I added a file called IOrdersRepository.cs to the Models folder and used it to define the interface shown in Listing 7-21.

Listing 7-21. The Contents of the IOrdersRepository.cs File in the Models Folder

```
using System.Collections.Generic;

namespace SportsStore.Models {

    public interface IOrdersRepository {

        IEnumerable<Order> Orders { get; }
        Order GetOrder(long key);
        void AddOrder(Order order);
        void UpdateOrder(Order order);
        void DeleteOrder(Order order);
    }
}
```

Next, I added a file called OrdersRepository.cs to the Models folder and used it to create the implementation class shown in Listing 7-22.

Listing 7-22. The Contents of the OrdersRepository.cs File in the Models Folder

```
using Microsoft.EntityFrameworkCore;
using System.Collections.Generic;
using System.Linq;

namespace SportsStore.Models {

    public class OrdersRepository : IOrdersRepository {
        private DataContext context;

        public OrdersRepository(DataContext ctx) => context = ctx;

        public IEnumerable<Order> Orders => context.Orders
            .Include(o => o.Lines).ThenInclude(l => l.Product);

        public Order GetOrder(long key) => context.Orders
            .Include(o => o.Lines).First(o => o.Id == key);

        public void AddOrder(Order order) {
            context.Orders.Add(order);
            context.SaveChanges();
        }

        public void UpdateOrder(Order order) {
            context.Orders.Update(order);
            context.SaveChanges();
        }

        public void DeleteOrder(Order order) {
            context.Orders.Remove(order);
            context.SaveChanges();
        }
    }
}
```

The repository implementation follows the pattern established for the other repositories and forgoes change detection in favor of simplicity. Note the use of the `Include` and `ThenInclude` methods to navigate around the data model and add related data to queries—a process I describe in detail in Chapters 14–16.

In Listing 7-23, I added a statement to the `Startup` class so that dependencies on the `IOrderRepository` interface will be resolved using transient `OrderRepository` objects by the dependency injection system.

Listing 7-23. Configuring Dependency Injection in the Startup.cs File in the SportsStore Folder

```
using System;
using System.Collections.Generic;
using System.Linq;
using System.Threading.Tasks;
using Microsoft.AspNetCore.Builder;
using Microsoft.AspNetCore.Hosting;
using Microsoft.AspNetCore.Http;
using Microsoft.Extensions.DependencyInjection;
```

```
using SportsStore.Models;
using Microsoft.EntityFrameworkCore;
using Microsoft.Extensions.Configuration;

namespace SportsStore {
    public class Startup {

        public Startup(IConfiguration config) => Configuration = config;

        public IConfiguration Configuration { get; }

        public void ConfigureServices(IServiceCollection services) {
            services.AddMvc();
            services.AddTransient<IRepository, DataRepository>();
            services.AddTransient<ICategoryRepository, CategoryRepository>();
            services.AddTransient<IOrdersRepository, OrdersRepository>();
            string conString = Configuration["ConnectionStrings:DefaultConnection"];
            services.AddDbContext<DataContext>(options =>
                options.UseSqlServer(conString));
        }

        public void Configure(IApplicationBuilder app, IHostingEnvironment env) {
            app.UseDeveloperExceptionPage();
            app.UseStatusCodePages();
            app.UseStaticFiles();
            app.UseMvcWithDefaultRoute();
        }
    }
}
```

Run the commands shown in Listing 7-24 in the SportsStore project folder to prepare the database to store the new data model classes by creating and applying an Entity Framework Core migration.

Listing 7-24. Creating and Applying a New Database Migration

```
dotnet ef migrations add Orders
dotnet ef database update
```

Creating Controllers and Views

All of the Entity Framework Core plumbing is in place to work with Order objects, and the next step is to add the MVC features that will allow instances to be created and managed. I added a class file called OrdersController.cs to the Controllers folder and used it to define the controller shown in Listing 7-25. I have left out the code for the AddOrUpdateOrder method, which I'll complete when the rest of the features are in place.

Listing 7-25. The Contents of the OrdersController.cs File in the Controllers Folder

```csharp
using Microsoft.AspNetCore.Mvc;
using SportsStore.Models;
using System.Collections.Generic;
using System.Linq;

namespace SportsStore.Controllers {

    public class OrdersController : Controller {
        private IRepository productRepository;
        private IOrdersRepository ordersRepository;

        public OrdersController(IRepository productRepo,
                IOrdersRepository orderRepo) {
            productRepository = productRepo;
            ordersRepository = orderRepo;
        }

        public IActionResult Index() => View(ordersRepository.Orders);

        public IActionResult EditOrder(long id) {
            var products = productRepository.Products;
            Order order = id == 0 ? new Order() : ordersRepository.GetOrder(id);
            IDictionary<long, OrderLine> linesMap
                = order.Lines?.ToDictionary(l => l.ProductId)
                ?? new Dictionary<long, OrderLine>();
            ViewBag.Lines = products.Select(p => linesMap.ContainsKey(p.Id)
                ? linesMap[p.Id]
                : new OrderLine { Product = p, ProductId = p.Id, Quantity = 0 });
            return View(order);
        }

        [HttpPost]
        public IActionResult AddOrUpdateOrder(Order order) {

            // ...action method to be completed...

            return RedirectToAction(nameof(Index));
        }

        [HttpPost]
        public IActionResult DeleteOrder(Order order) {
            ordersRepository.DeleteOrder(order);
            return RedirectToAction(nameof(Index));
        }
    }
}
```

The LINQ statements in the EditOrder action method may look convoluted, but they prepare the OrderLine data so that there is one object for every Product, even if there has been no previous selection for that product.

For a new order, this means that the ViewBag.Lines property will be populated with a sequence of OrderLine objects, corresponding to each Product in the database, with Id and Quantity properties set to zero. When the object is stored in the database, the zero Id value will indicate this is a new object, and the database server will assign a new unique primary key.

For existing orders, the ViewBag.Lines property will be populated with the OrderLine objects read from the database, filled out with extra objects with zero Id properties for the remaining products.

This structure takes advantage of the way that ASP.NET Core MVC and Entity Framework Core fit together and simplifies the process of updating the database, as you will see when you work through the rest of the example.

The next step is to create a view that will list all of the objects in the database. I created the Views/Orders folder and added to it a file named Index.cshtml with the content shown in Listing 7-26.

Listing 7-26. The Contents of the Index.cshtml File in the Views/Orders Folder

```
@model  IEnumerable<Order>

<h3 class="p-2 bg-primary text-white text-center">Orders</h3>

<div class="container-fluid mt-3">
    <div class="row">
        <div class="col-1 font-weight-bold">Id</div>
        <div class="col font-weight-bold">Name</div>
        <div class="col font-weight-bold">Zip</div>
        <div class="col font-weight-bold">Total</div>
        <div class="col font-weight-bold">Profit</div>
        <div class="col-1 font-weight-bold">Status</div>
        <div class="col-3"></div>
    </div>
    <div>
        <div class="row placeholder p-2"><div class="col-12 text-center">
            <h5>No Orders</h5>
        </div></div>
        @foreach (Order o in Model) {

            <div class="row p-2">
                <div class="col-1">@o.Id</div>
                <div class="col">@o.CustomerName</div>
                <div class="col">@o.ZipCode</div>
                <div class="col">@o.Lines.Sum(l => l.Quantity
                    * l.Product.RetailPrice)</div>
                <div class="col">@o.Lines.Sum(l => l.Quantity
                    * (l.Product.RetailPrice - l.Product.PurchasePrice))</div>
                <div class="col-1">@(o.Shipped ? "Shipped" : "Pending")</div>
                <div class="col-3 text-right">
                    <form asp-action="DeleteOrder" method="post">
                        <input type="hidden" name="Id" value="@o.Id" />
                        <a asp-action="EditOrder" asp-route-id="@o.Id"
                            class="btn btn-outline-primary">Edit</a>
                        <button type="submit" class="btn btn-outline-danger">
                            Delete
                        </button>
                    </form>
```

```
                    </div>
                </div>
            }
        </div>
    </div>
</div>
<div class="text-center">
    <a asp-action="EditOrder" class="btn btn-primary">Create</a>
</div>
```

This view presents a summary of the Order objects in the database and displays both the total price of the products ordered and the amount of profit that will be made. There are buttons to create a new order and to edit and delete an existing one.

To provide the view for creating or editing an order, I added a file called EditOrder.cshtml to the Views/Orders folder and added the content shown in Listing 7-27.

Listing 7-27. The Contents of the EditOrder.cshtml File in the Views/Orders Folder

```
@model Order

<h3 class="p-2 bg-primary text-white text-center">Create/Update Order</h3>

<form asp-action="AddOrUpdateOrder" method="post">
    <div class="form-group">
        <label asp-for="Id"></label>
        <input asp-for="Id" class="form-control" readonly />
    </div>
    <div class="form-group">
        <label asp-for="CustomerName"></label>
        <input asp-for="CustomerName" class="form-control" />
    </div>
    <div class="form-group">
        <label asp-for="Address"></label>
        <input asp-for="Address" class="form-control" />
    </div>
    <div class="form-group">
        <label asp-for="State"></label>
        <input asp-for="State" class="form-control" />
    </div>
    <div class="form-group">
        <label asp-for="ZipCode"></label>
        <input asp-for="ZipCode" class="form-control" />
    </div>
    <div class="form-check">
        <label class="form-check-label">
            <input type="checkbox" asp-for="Shipped" class="form-check-input" />
            Shipped
        </label>
    </div>
```

```html
<h6 class="mt-1 p-2 bg-primary text-white text-center">Products Ordered</h6>
<div class="container-fluid">
    <div class="row">
        <div class="col font-weight-bold">Product</div>
        <div class="col font-weight-bold">Category</div>
        <div class="col font-weight-bold">Quantity</div>
    </div>
    @{ int counter = 0; }
    @foreach (OrderLine line in ViewBag.Lines) {
        <input type="hidden" name="lines[@counter].Id" value="@line.Id" />
        <input type="hidden" name="lines[@counter].ProductId"
            value="@line.ProductId" />
        <input type="hidden" name="lines[@counter].OrderId" value="@Model.Id" />
        <div class="row mt-1">
            <div class="col">@line.Product.Name</div>
            <div class="col">@line.Product.Category.Name</div>
            <div class="col">
                <input type="number" name="lines[@counter].Quantity"
                    value="@line.Quantity" />
            </div>
        </div>
        counter++;
    }
</div>
<div class="text-center m-2">
    <button type="submit" class="btn btn-primary">Save</button>
    <a asp-action="Index" class="btn btn-secondary">Cancel</a>
</div>
</form>
```

This view provides the user with a form containing input elements for the properties defined by the Order class, as well as elements for each of the Product objects in the database, which will be populated with selected quantities when editing existing objects.

To make the new features easier to access, I added the element shown in Listing 7-28 to the layout shared by all the views.

Listing 7-28. Adding an Element in the _Layout.cshtml File in the Views/Shared Folder

```html
<!DOCTYPE html>
<html>
<head>
    <meta name="viewport" content="width=device-width" />
    <title>SportsStore</title>
    <link rel="stylesheet" href="~/lib/bootstrap/dist/css/bootstrap.min.css" />
    <style>
        .placeholder { visibility: collapse; display: none }
        .placeholder:only-child { visibility: visible; display: flex }
    </style>
</head>
```

```html
<body>
    <div class="container-fluid">
        <div class="row p-2">
            <div class="col-2">
                <a asp-controller="Home" asp-action="Index"
                        class="@GetClassForButton("Home")">
                    Products
                </a>
                <a asp-controller="Categories" asp-action="Index"
                        class="@GetClassForButton("Categories")">
                    Categories
                </a>
                <a asp-controller="Orders" asp-action="Index"
                        class="@GetClassForButton("Orders")">
                    Orders
                </a>
            </div>
            <div class="col">
                @RenderBody()
            </div>
        </div>
    </div>
</body>
</html>

@functions {
    string GetClassForButton(string controller) {
        return "btn btn-block " + (ViewContext.RouteData.Values["controller"]
            as string == controller ? "btn-primary" : "btn-outline-primary");
    }
}
```

Start the application using dotnet run, navigate to http://localhost:5000, click the Orders button, and click Create. You will see an empty form that contains elements for all the products in the database. Since this is a new order, all the Quantity fields are zero, as shown in Figure 7-4.

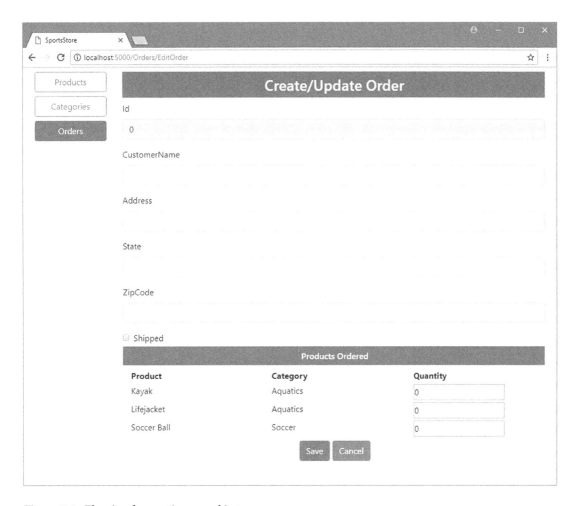

Figure 7-4. *The view for creating new objects*

Storing Order Data

No data is stored when you click the Save button because I left the AddOrUpdateOrder method incomplete in Listing 7-25. To complete the controller, I added the code shown in Listing 7-29 to the action method.

Listing 7-29. Storing Data in the OrdersController.cs File in the Controllers Folder

```
...
[HttpPost]
public IActionResult AddOrUpdateOrder(Order order) {
    order.Lines = order.Lines
        .Where(l => l.Id > 0 || (l.Id == 0 && l.Quantity > 0)).ToArray();
    if (order.Id == 0) {
        ordersRepository.AddOrder(order);
    } else {
```

```
        ordersRepository.UpdateOrder(order);
    }
    return RedirectToAction(nameof(Index));
}
...
```

The code statements I used in the action method rely on a useful Entity Framework Core feature: when I pass an Order object to the AddOrder or UpdateOrder repository method, the Entity Framework Core will store not only the Order object but also its related OrderLine objects. This may not seem important, but it simplifies a process that would otherwise require a series of carefully coordinated updates.

To see the SQL commands that are produced, start the application using dotnet run, navigate to http://localhost:5000/orders, click the Create button, and fill out the form. It doesn't matter what details you use for the customer, but make sure you enter the quantities for the products shown in Table 7-3.

Table 7-3. *The Quantities Values Required to Create an Order*

Product	Quantity
Kayak	1
Lifejacket	2
Soccer Ball	0

When you click the Save button, you will see several SQL commands in the logging messages generated by the application. The first stores the Order object, and the second gets the value assigned for the primary key.

```
...
INSERT INTO [Orders] ([Address], [CustomerName], [Shipped], [State], [ZipCode])
VALUES (@p0, @p1, @p2, @p3, @p4);

SELECT [Id]
FROM [Orders]
WHERE @@ROWCOUNT = 1 AND [Id] = scope_identity();
...
```

Entity Framework Core then uses the primary key of the Order object to store the OrderLine objects, like this:

```
...
DECLARE @inserted0 TABLE ([Id] bigint, [_Position] [int]);
MERGE [OrderLines] USING (
VALUES (@p5, @p6, @p7, 0),
 (@p8, @p9, @p10, 1)) AS i ([OrderId], [ProductId], [Quantity], _Position) ON 1=0
WHEN NOT MATCHED THEN
    INSERT ([OrderId], [ProductId], [Quantity])
    VALUES (i.[OrderId], i.[ProductId], i.[Quantity])
    OUTPUT INSERTED.[Id], i._Position
INTO @inserted0;
...
```

Finally, Entity Framework Core queries the database to get the primary keys assigned to the `OrderLine` objects, like this:

```
...
SELECT [t].[Id] FROM [OrderLines] t
INNER JOIN @inserted0 i ON ([t].[Id] = [i].[Id])
ORDER BY [i].[_Position];
...
```

Don't worry if you can't make complete sense of the SQL commands. The point to note is that Entity Framework Core takes care of storing the related data and generates the SQL commands automatically. The final point to note about the code in Listing 7-29 relates to this statement:

```
...
order.Lines = order.Lines
        .Where(l => l.Id > 0 || (l.Id == 0 && l.Quantity > 0)).ToArray();
...
```

This statement excludes any `OrderLine` object for which no quantity has been selected, except for objects that have already been stored in the database. This ensures that the database isn't full of `OrderLine` objects that are not part of an order but does allow updates to be made to previously stored data.

When you save the data, a summary of the order will be displayed, as illustrated in Figure 7-5.

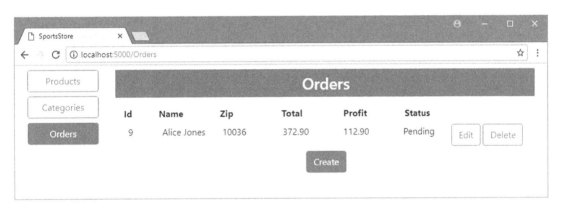

Figure 7-5. *A summary of order data*

Common Problems and Solutions

The features for creating and working with related data can be awkward, and in the following sections, I describe common problems and explain how to resolve them.

The "ALTER TABLE conflicted with the FOREIGN KEY" Exception

This exception usually occurs when you apply a migration to a database that contains constraints that the existing data in the database doesn't conform to. For the SportsStore application, for example, you would have seen this exception if you had created `Product` objects in the database before applying the migration that added support for separate `Category` objects. The existing data in the database would not have conformed to the requirement to have a foreign key relationship with a category and so the database update would have failed.

The simplest way to solve this problem is to drop and re-create the database, which will remove any data it contains. This isn't a suitable approach in a production system, however, where the data will have to be carefully modified before the migration can be applied.

The "UPDATE Conflicted with the FOREIGN KEY" Exception

This exception occurs when you try to store a new object or update an existing one using data that doesn't match the constraints applied to the database to support related data. The most likely cause is omitting a key value for the related data. In the context of the SportsStore application, for example, this exception will occur if you try to store or update a Product object without including a value for the CategoryId property. If you receive this exception, make sure that your HTML form contains input elements for all of the foreign key properties defined by your data model classes.

The "The Property Expression 'x => x.<name>' is Not Valid" Exception

This exception occurs when you forget to add get and set clauses to a navigation property and then select it using the Include method. Omitting the clauses creates a field rather than a property and the Include method cannot follow it in a query. To solve the problem, add get and set clauses to create a property. You may also have to re-create and reapply the migration that defines the relationship.

The "Type of Navigation Property <name> Does Not Implement ICollection<OrderLine>" Exception

Entity Framework Core is sensitive to the data types assigned to its navigation properties, and this exception can result when you perform a LINQ query on a navigation property collection before storing data, as I did in Listing 7-29 for the SportsStore application. To fix the problem, call the ToArray method on the result of your LINQ query, which will produce a result that implements the interface that Entity Framework Core expects.

The "The Property <name> is Not a Navigation Property of Entity Type <name>" Exception

This exception occurs when you use the Include method to select a property that Entity Framework Core cannot follow for related data. The most common cause of this problem is selecting the foreign key property rather than the navigation property it is paired with. In the case of the SportsStore application, you would see this error if you use the Include method to select the ProductId property from an OrderLine object, rather than the Product property.

The "Invalid Object Name <name>" Exception

This exception usually occurs when you create a migration that expands the data model with a relationship but have forgotten to apply it to the database. Use the dotnet ef database update command to apply the migrations in your project, and see Chapter 13, where I explain how migrations work in detail.

Objects Are Deleted Instead of Being Updated

If you find that trying to update an object actually results in it being deleted, then the likely cause is that you are loading related data and then setting the navigation property to null when getting the baseline data for change detection. In the case of the SportsStore application, for example, you can see this behavior by querying for a baseline Product object, using the Include method to load the related Category object, and then setting the Category property to null before calling the SaveChanges method. This combination of actions leads Entity Framework Core to quietly delete the object you had intended to update. To fix this problem, don't load the related data and don't set the navigation property to null.

The Class Name for Related Data Is Displayed in a View

This problem is caused by using a Razor expression that selects the value of the navigation property, which returns the related object. Razor then calls the ToString method, which returns the class name. To include a data value from related data in a view, select one of the related object's properties so that you use @Category.Name and not just @Category, for example.

Summary

In this chapter, I expanded the SportsStore data model by adding new classes and creating relationships between them. I explained how to query for related data, how to perform updates, and how to resolve the most common problems these features are likely to cause. In the next chapter, I show you how to adapt the MVC and Entity Framework Core parts of the application to deal with large amounts of data.

CHAPTER 8

SportsStore: Scaling Up

When you create an application, the focus is usually on getting the right foundation, and that's the approach I have taken with the SportsStore project. As the application progresses, it can be useful to increase the amount of data you are working with so that you can see the impact it has on the operations that the user has to perform and the amount of time they take. In this chapter, I add test data to the database to show the flaws in the way that SportsStore presents data to the user and address these by adding support for paginating, ordering, and searching data. I also show you how to improve the performance of these operations by using the Entity Framework Core that supports advanced data model configuration options, known as the Fluent API.

Preparing for This Chapter

I continue to use the SportsStore project that was created in Chapter 4 and updated in the chapters since. Run the commands shown in Listing 8-1 in the SportsStore project folder to delete and re-create the database.

Tip You can download the SportsStore project for this chapter—and the projects for every other chapter—from the GitHub repository for this book: `https://github.com/apress/pro-ef-core-2-for-asp.net-core-mvc`.

Listing 8-1. Deleting and Re-creating the Database

```
dotnet ef database drop --force
dotnet ef database update
```

Creating a Seed Data Controller and View

For this chapter, I need a controller that can populate the database with test data. I added a file called `SeedController.cs` to the `Controllers` folder and used it to define the controller shown in Listing 8-2.

Listing 8-2. The Contents of the SeedController.cs File in the Controllers Folder

```
using Microsoft.AspNetCore.Mvc;
using Microsoft.EntityFrameworkCore;
using SportsStore.Models;
using System.Linq;
```

```
namespace SportsStore.Controllers {

    public class SeedController : Controller {
        private DataContext context;

        public SeedController(DataContext ctx) => context = ctx;

        public IActionResult Index() {
            ViewBag.Count = context.Products.Count();
            return View(context.Products
                .Include(p => p.Category).OrderBy(p => p.Id).Take(20));
        }

        [HttpPost]
        public IActionResult CreateSeedData(int count) {
            ClearData();
            if (count > 0) {
                context.Database.SetCommandTimeout(System.TimeSpan.FromMinutes(10));
                context.Database
                    .ExecuteSqlCommand("DROP PROCEDURE IF EXISTS CreateSeedData");
                context.Database.ExecuteSqlCommand($@"
                    CREATE PROCEDURE CreateSeedData
                            @RowCount decimal
                    AS
                        BEGIN
                        SET NOCOUNT ON
                      DECLARE @i INT = 1;
                        DECLARE @catId BIGINT;
                        DECLARE @CatCount INT = @RowCount / 10;
                        DECLARE @pprice DECIMAL(5,2);
                        DECLARE @rprice DECIMAL(5,2);
                        BEGIN TRANSACTION
                            WHILE @i <= @CatCount
                                BEGIN
                                    INSERT INTO Categories (Name, Description)
                                    VALUES (CONCAT('Category-', @i),
                                     'Test Data Category');
                                    SET @catId = SCOPE_IDENTITY();
                                    DECLARE @j INT = 1;
                                    WHILE @j <= 10
                                        BEGIN
                                            SET @pprice = RAND()*(500-5+1);
                                            SET @rprice = (RAND() * @pprice)
                                            + @pprice;
                                            INSERT INTO Products (Name, CategoryId,
                                             PurchasePrice, RetailPrice)
                                            VALUES (CONCAT('Product', @i, '-', @j),
                                           @catId, @pprice, @rprice)
                                            SET @j = @j + 1
                                        END
                            SET @i = @i + 1
                            END
```

```
                        COMMIT
                    END");
                context.Database.BeginTransaction();
                context.Database
                    .ExecuteSqlCommand($"EXEC CreateSeedData @RowCount = {count}");
                context.Database.CommitTransaction();
            }
            return RedirectToAction(nameof(Index));
        }

        [HttpPost]
        public IActionResult ClearData() {
            context.Database.SetCommandTimeout(System.TimeSpan.FromMinutes(10));
            context.Database.BeginTransaction();
            context.Database.ExecuteSqlCommand("DELETE FROM Orders");
            context.Database.ExecuteSqlCommand("DELETE FROM Categories");
            context.Database.CommitTransaction();
            return RedirectToAction(nameof(Index));
        }
    }
}
```

When it comes to generating large quantities of test data, creating .NET objects and storing them in the database is inefficient. The Seed controller uses the Entity Framework Core features for working directly with SQL to create and execute a stored procedure that produces test data much more quickly. (I describe these features in detail in Chapter 23.)

DON'T DO THIS IN REAL PROJECTS

The approach I have taken in Listing 8-2 should be used only for generating test data and not for any other part of an application.

For this chapter, I needed a mechanism so you can reliably generate large amounts of test data without requiring complex database tasks or using third-party tools. (There are some excellent commercial tools available for generating SQL data, but they generally require a license for anything more than a few hundred rows.)

Working directly with SQL should be done with caution because it bypasses a lot of the useful protections that Entity Framework Core provides, is difficult to test and maintain, and often ends up working on a single database server. You should also avoid creating stored procedures in C# code, which I have done in Listing 8-2 for simplicity.

In short, don't use any aspect of this technique in the production parts of your applications.

To provide the controller with a view, I created the Views/Seed folder and added to it a file called Index.cshtml with the content shown in Listing 8-3.

Listing 8-3. The Contents of the Index.cshtml File in the Views/Seed Folder

```
@model IEnumerable<Product>

<h3 class="p-2 bg-primary text-white text-center">Seed Data</h3>

<form method="post">
    <div class="form-group">
        <label>Number of Objects to Create</label>
        <input class="form-control" name="count" value="50" />
    </div>

    <div class="text-center">
        <button type="submit" asp-action="CreateSeedData" class="btn btn-primary">
            Seed Database
        </button>
        <button asp-action="ClearData" class="btn btn-danger">
            Clear Database
        </button>
    </div>
</form>

<h5 class="text-center m-2">
    There are @ViewBag.Count products in the database
</h5>

<div class="container-fluid">
    <div class="row">
        <div class="col-1 font-weight-bold">Id</div>
        <div class="col font-weight-bold">Name</div>
        <div class="col font-weight-bold">Category</div>
        <div class="col font-weight-bold text-right">Purchase</div>
        <div class="col font-weight-bold text-right">Retail</div>
    </div>
    @foreach (Product p in Model) {
        <div class="row">
            <div class="col-1">@p.Id</div>
            <div class="col">@p.Name</div>
            <div class="col">@p.Category.Name</div>
            <div class="col text-right">@p.PurchasePrice</div>
            <div class="col text-right">@p.RetailPrice</div>
        </div>
    }
</div>
```

The view lets you specify how much test data should be generated and displays the first 20 Product objects, which are provided by the query in the Index action of the Seed controller. To make the Seed controller easier to use, I added the element shown in Listing 8-4 to the shared layout.

Listing 8-4. Adding an Element in the _Layout.cshtml File in the Views/Shared Folder

```html
<!DOCTYPE html>
<html>
<head>
    <meta name="viewport" content="width=device-width" />
    <title>SportsStore</title>
    <link rel="stylesheet" href="~/lib/bootstrap/dist/css/bootstrap.min.css" />
    <style>
        .placeholder { visibility: collapse; display: none }
        .placeholder:only-child { visibility: visible; display: flex }
    </style>
</head>
<body>
    <div class="container-fluid">
        <div class="row p-2">
            <div class="col-2">
                <a asp-controller="Home" asp-action="Index"
                        class="@GetClassForButton("Home")">
                    Products
                </a>
                <a asp-controller="Categories" asp-action="Index"
                    class="@GetClassForButton("Categories")">
                    Categories
                </a>
                <a asp-controller="Orders" asp-action="Index"
                        class="@GetClassForButton("Orders")">
                    Orders
                </a>
                <a asp-controller="Seed" asp-action="Index"
                        class="@GetClassForButton("Seed")">
                    Seed Data
                </a>
            </div>
            <div class="col">
                @RenderBody()
            </div>
        </div>
    </div>
</body>
</html>

@functions {
    string GetClassForButton(string controller) {
        return "btn btn-block " + (ViewContext.RouteData.Values["controller"]
            as string == controller ? "btn-primary" : "btn-outline-primary");
    }
}
```

Start the application using dotnet run, navigate to http://localhost:5000, and click the Seed Data button. Set the value in the input element to 1000 and click the Seed Database button. It will take a moment to generate the data, after which you will see the result shown in Figure 8-1.

Tip   The values for the prices for the test data are generated randomly, which means you may receive slightly different results for some of the examples.

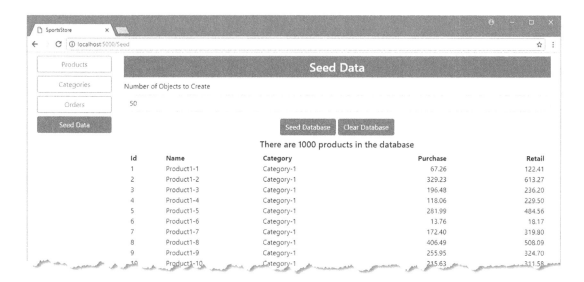

Figure 8-1. Running the example application

Scaling Up Data Presentation

It doesn't take a great deal of data to show flaws in the way that the SportsStore application presents its data. With a thousand objects, the way that the data is presented to the user becomes unusable, and that is still a relatively small amount of data for an application to deal with. In the sections that follow, I change the way that the SportsStore application presents its data to help the user perform basic operations and locate the objects they require.

Adding Support for Pagination

The first problem I am going to tackle is breaking up the data presented to the user so that it isn't just one long list. Using simple tables that include all of the objects is a useful approach when laying out the foundations of an application, but tables containing thousands of rows are unusable in most applications. To address this, I am going to add support for querying for smaller amounts of data from the database and allow the user to navigate by paging through these smaller amounts.

When dealing with large amounts of data, it is important to ensure that access to that data is managed consistently so that there is no way for one part of the application to accidentally query for millions of objects. The approach I am going to take is to create a collection class that incorporates pagination.

Creating the Paginated Collection Class

To define the collection that provides access to paginated data, I created the Models/Pages folder, added to it a class called PagedList.cs, and used it to define the class shown in Listing 8-5.

Listing 8-5. The Contents of the PagedList.cs File in the Models/Pages Folder

```
using System.Collections.Generic;
using System.Linq;

namespace SportsStore.Models.Pages {

    public class PagedList<T> : List<T> {

        public PagedList(IQueryable<T> query, QueryOptions options = null) {
            CurrentPage = options.CurrentPage;
            PageSize = options.PageSize;

            TotalPages = query.Count() / PageSize;
            AddRange(query.Skip((CurrentPage - 1) * PageSize).Take(PageSize));
        }

        public int CurrentPage { get; set; }
        public int PageSize { get; set; }
        public int TotalPages { get; set; }

        public bool HasPreviousPage => CurrentPage > 1;
        public bool HasNextPage => CurrentPage < TotalPages;

    }
}
```

I have used a strongly typed `List` as the base class, which will let me build on the base collection behavior easily. The constructor accepts an `IQueryable<T>`, which represents the query that will provide the data to display to the user. This query will be executed twice—once to get the total number of objects that the query could return and once to get just the objects that will be displayed on the current page. This is the trade-off inherent in pagination, where an additional `COUNT` query is balanced against queries for smaller numbers of objects overall. The other constructor arguments specify the page required for the query and the number of objects to be displayed per page.

To represent the options required for the query, I added a class file called `QueryOptions.cs` to the Models/Pages folder, with the code in Listing 8-6.

Listing 8-6. The Contents of the QueryOptions.cs File in the Models/Pages Folder

```
namespace SportsStore.Models.Pages {

    public class QueryOptions {
        public int CurrentPage { get; set; } = 1;
        public int PageSize { get; set; } = 10;
    }
}
```

Updating the Repository

To ensure that pagination is used consistently, I am going to return a `PagedList` object as the result of queries performed through the repository. In Listing 8-7, I added a method called `GetProduct` method, which returns the data for a single page.

Listing 8-7. Returning Pages of Data in the IRepository.cs File in the Models Folder

```
using System.Collections.Generic;
using SportsStore.Models.Pages;

namespace SportsStore.Models {

    public interface IRepository {

        IEnumerable<Product> Products { get; }

        PagedList<Product> GetProducts(QueryOptions options);

        Product GetProduct(long key);

        void AddProduct(Product product);

        void UpdateProduct(Product product);

        void UpdateAll(Product[] products);

        void Delete(Product product);
    }
}
```

In Listing 8-8, I have made the corresponding change to the implementation class for the repository.

Listing 8-8. Returning Pages of Data in the DataRepository.cs File in the Models Folder

```
using System.Collections.Generic;
using System.Linq;
using Microsoft.EntityFrameworkCore;
using SportsStore.Models.Pages;

namespace SportsStore.Models {

    public class DataRepository : IRepository {
        private DataContext context;

        public DataRepository(DataContext ctx) => context = ctx;

        public IEnumerable<Product> Products => context.Products
            .Include(p => p.Category).ToArray();

        public PagedList<Product> GetProducts(QueryOptions options) {
            return new PagedList<Product>(context.Products
                .Include(p => p.Category), options);
        }

        // ..other methods omitted for brevity...
    }
}
```

The new method returns a `PagedList` collection of `Product` objects for the page specified by the arguments.

Updating the Controller and View

To add support for pagination to the `Home` controller, I updated the `Index` action so that it accepts the arguments required to select a page and so it uses the new repository method, as shown in Listing 8-9.

Listing 8-9. Using Paged Data in the HomeController.cs File in the Controllers Folder

```
using Microsoft.AspNetCore.Mvc;
using SportsStore.Models;
using SportsStore.Models.Pages;

namespace SportsStore.Controllers {

    public class HomeController : Controller {
        private IRepository repository;
        private ICategoryRepository catRepository;

        public HomeController(IRepository repo, ICategoryRepository catRepo) {
            repository = repo;
            catRepository = catRepo;
        }

        public IActionResult Index(QueryOptions options) {
            return View(repository.GetProducts(options));
        }

        public IActionResult UpdateProduct(long key) {
            ViewBag.Categories = catRepository.Categories;
            return View(key == 0 ? new Product() : repository.GetProduct(key));
        }

        [HttpPost]
        public IActionResult UpdateProduct(Product product) {
            if (product.Id == 0) {
                repository.AddProduct(product);
            } else {
                repository.UpdateProduct(product);
            }
            return RedirectToAction(nameof(Index));
        }

        [HttpPost]
        public IActionResult Delete(Product product) {
            repository.Delete(product);
            return RedirectToAction(nameof(Index));
        }
    }
}
```

The base class of the paged data collection implements the IEnumerable<T> interface, which minimizes the extent of the changes required to support paged data. The only change required to the view for the Index action of the Home controller is to display a partial view that will provide details of the pagination, as shown in Listing 8-10. The rest of the view doesn't need to change since it will enumerate data in the same way regardless of whether the sequence it operates on contains all of the available data or just a page of it.

Listing 8-10. Using a Partial View in the Index.cshtml File in the Views/Home Folder

```
@model IEnumerable<Product>

<h3 class="p-2 bg-primary text-white text-center">Products</h3>

<div class="text-center">
    @Html.Partial("Pages", Model)
</div>

<div class="container-fluid mt-3">
    <div class="row">
        <div class="col-1 font-weight-bold">Id</div>
        <div class="col font-weight-bold">Name</div>
        <div class="col font-weight-bold">Category</div>
        <div class="col font-weight-bold text-right">Purchase Price</div>
        <div class="col font-weight-bold text-right">Retail Price</div>
        <div class="col"></div>
    </div>
    @foreach (Product p in Model) {
        <div class="row p-2">
            <div class="col-1">@p.Id</div>
            <div class="col">@p.Name</div>
            <div class="col">@p.Category.Name</div>
            <div class="col text-right">@p.PurchasePrice</div>
            <div class="col text-right">@p.RetailPrice</div>
            <div class="col">
                <form asp-action="Delete" method="post">
                    <a asp-action="UpdateProduct" asp-route-key="@p.Id"
                       class="btn btn-outline-primary">
                        Edit
                    </a>
                    <input type="hidden" name="Id" value="@p.Id" />
                    <button type="submit" class="btn btn-outline-danger">
                        Delete
                    </button>
                </form>
            </div>
        </div>
    }
    <div class="text-center p-2">
        <a asp-action="UpdateProduct" asp-route-key="0"
           class="btn btn-primary">Add</a>
    </div>
</div>
```

To complete the pagination support for Product objects, I defined the partial view by adding a file called Pages.cshtml to the Views/Shared folder and adding the elements shown in Listing 8-11.

Listing 8-11. The Contents of the Pages.cshtml File in the Views/Shared Folder

```
<form id="pageform" method="get" class="form-inline d-inline-block">

    <button name="options.currentPage" value="@(Model.CurrentPage -1)"
        class="btn btn-outline-primary @(!Model.HasPreviousPage ? "disabled" : "")"
            type="submit">
        Previous
    </button>

    @for (int i = 1; i <= 3 && i <= Model.TotalPages; i++) {
        <button name="options.currentPage" value="@i" type="submit"
            class="btn btn-outline-primary @(Model.CurrentPage == i ? "active" : "")">
            @i
        </button>
    }
    @if (Model.CurrentPage > 3 && Model.TotalPages - Model.CurrentPage >= 3) {
        @:...
        <button class="btn btn-outline-primary active">@Model.CurrentPage</button>
    }
    @if (Model.TotalPages > 3) {
        @:...
        @for (int i = Math.Max(4, Model.TotalPages - 2);
                    i <= Model.TotalPages; i++) {
            <button name="options.currentPage" value="@i" type="submit"
                    class="btn btn-outline-primary
                    @(Model.CurrentPage == i ? "active" : "")">
                @i
            </button>
        }
    }
    <button name="options.currentPage" value="@(Model.CurrentPage +1)" type="submit"
            class="btn btn-outline-primary @(!Model.HasNextPage? "disabled" : "")">
        Next
    </button>

    <select name="options.pageSize" class="form-control ml-1 mr-1">
        @foreach (int val in new int[] { 10, 25, 50, 100 }) {
            <option value="@val" selected="@(Model.PageSize == val)">@val</option>
        }
    </select>
    <input type="hidden" name="options.currentPage" value="1" />
    <button type="submit" class="btn btn-secondary">Change Page Size</button>
</form>
```

The view contains an HTML form that is used to send GET requests back to the action method for pages of data and to change the page size. The Razor expressions look messy, but they adapt the pagination buttons displayed to the user to the number of pages available. To see the effect, start the application using

147

dotnet run and navigate to http://localhost:5000. The list of products will be broken into pages of ten items, which can be paged through using a series of buttons, as shown in Figure 8-2.

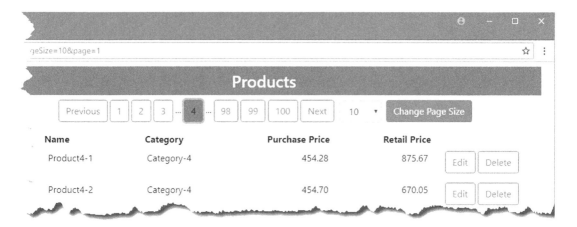

Figure 8-2. *Paging data*

Adding Search and Ordering Support

Displaying pages is a good start, but it is still difficult to focus on a specific set of objects. To give the user the tools they need to locate data, I am going to build on the pagination feature to add support for changing the display order and for performing searches. The starting point is to expand the PagedList class so that it can perform searches and order the results of queries using property names, rather than lambda expressions that select properties, as shown in Listing 8-12. This requires some convoluted code to perform the operations, but the result can be applied to any data model class and integrates more easily with the ASP.NET Core MVC parts of the application.

Listing 8-12. Adding Features in the PagedList.cs File in the Models Pages Folder

```
using System.Collections.Generic;
using System.Linq;
using System;
using System.Linq.Expressions;

namespace SportsStore.Models.Pages {

    public class PagedList<T> : List<T> {

        public PagedList(IQueryable<T> query, QueryOptions options = null) {
            CurrentPage = options.CurrentPage;
            PageSize = options.PageSize;
            Options = options;

            if (options != null) {
                if (!string.IsNullOrEmpty(options.OrderPropertyName)) {
                    query = Order(query, options.OrderPropertyName,
                        options.DescendingOrder);
                }
```

```
            if (!string.IsNullOrEmpty(options.SearchPropertyName)
                    && !string.IsNullOrEmpty(options.SearchTerm)) {
                query = Search(query, options.SearchPropertyName,
                    options.SearchTerm);
            }
        }

        TotalPages = query.Count() / PageSize;
        AddRange(query.Skip((CurrentPage - 1) * PageSize).Take(PageSize));
    }

    public int CurrentPage { get; set; }
    public int PageSize { get; set; }
    public int TotalPages { get; set; }
    public QueryOptions Options { get; set; }

    public bool HasPreviousPage => CurrentPage > 1;
    public bool HasNextPage => CurrentPage < TotalPages;

    private static IQueryable<T> Search(IQueryable<T> query, string propertyName,
            string searchTerm) {
        var parameter = Expression.Parameter(typeof(T), "x");
        var source = propertyName.Split('.').Aggregate((Expression) parameter,
            Expression.Property);
        var body = Expression.Call(source, "Contains", Type.EmptyTypes,
            Expression.Constant(searchTerm, typeof(string)));
        var lambda = Expression.Lambda<Func<T, bool>>(body, parameter);
        return query.Where(lambda);
    }

    private static IQueryable<T> Order(IQueryable<T> query, string propertyName,
            bool desc) {
        var parameter = Expression.Parameter(typeof(T), "x");
        var source = propertyName.Split('.').Aggregate((Expression) parameter,
            Expression.Property);
        var lambda = Expression.Lambda(typeof(Func<,>).MakeGenericType(typeof(T),
            source.Type), source, parameter);
        return typeof(Queryable).GetMethods().Single(
                method => method.Name == (desc ? "OrderByDescending"
                            : "OrderBy")
                && method.IsGenericMethodDefinition
                && method.GetGenericArguments().Length == 2
                && method.GetParameters().Length == 2)
            .MakeGenericMethod(typeof(T), source.Type)
            .Invoke(null, new object[] { query, lambda }) as IQueryable<T>;
    }
}
}
```

Listing 8-13 shows the corresponding changes to the QueryOptions class.

Listing 8-13. Adding Properties in the QueryOptions.cs File in the Models/Pages Folder

```
namespace SportsStore.Models.Pages {

    public class QueryOptions {

        public int CurrentPage { get; set; } = 1;
        public int PageSize { get; set; } = 10;

        public string OrderPropertyName { get; set; }
        public bool DescendingOrder { get; set; }

        public string SearchPropertyName { get; set; }
        public string SearchTerm { get; set; }
    }
}
```

To create a generalized view that will present the search and ordering options to the user, I added a file called PageOptions.cshtml in the Views/Shared folder and added the content shown in Listing 8-14.

Listing 8-14. The Contents of the PageOptions.cshtml File in the Views/Shared Folder

```
<div class="container-fluid mt-2">
    <div class="row m-1">
        <div class="col"></div>
        <div class="col-1">
            <label class="col-form-label">Search</label>
        </div>
        <div class="col-3">
            <select form="pageform" name="options.searchpropertyname"
                    class="form-control">
                @foreach (string s in ViewBag.searches as string[]) {
                    <option value="@s"
                            selected="@(Model.Options.SearchPropertyName == s)">
                        @(s.IndexOf('.') == -1 ? s : s.Substring(0, s.IndexOf('.')))
                    </option>

                }
            </select>
        </div>
        <div class="col">
            <input form="pageform" class="form-control" name="options.searchterm"
                value="@Model.Options.SearchTerm" />
        </div>

        <div class="col-1 text-right">
            <button form="pageform" class="btn btn-secondary" type="submit">
                Search
            </button>
        </div>
        <div class="col"></div>
    </div>
```

```
    <div class="row m-1">
        <div class="col"></div>
        <div class="col-1">
            <label class="col-form-label">Sort</label>
        </div>
        <div class="col-3">
            <select form="pageform" name="options.OrderPropertyName"
                    class="form-control">
                @foreach (string s in ViewBag.sorts as string[]) {
                    <option value="@s"
                            selected="@(Model.Options.OrderPropertyName == s)">
                        @(s.IndexOf('.') == -1 ? s : s.Substring(0, s.IndexOf('.')))
                    </option>
                }
            </select>
        </div>
        <div class="col form-check form-check-inline">
                <input form="pageform" type="checkbox" name="Options.DescendingOrder"
                       id="Options.DescendingOrder"
                       class="form-check-input" value="true"
                        checked ="@Model.Options.DescendingOrder" />
                <label class="form-check-label">Descending Order</label>
        </div>
        <div class="col-1 text-right">
            <button form="pageform" class="btn btn-secondary" type="submit">
                Sort
            </button>
        </div>
        <div class="col"></div>
    </div>
</div>
```

This view relies on the HTML 5 feature of associating elements with forms outside of the form element, which means that I can extend the form defined in the Pages view with elements that are specific to searching and ordering.

I don't want to hard-code the list of properties that the user can use to search or order data into the view, so, for simplicity, I get these values from the ViewBag. This is not an ideal solution, but it does provide a lot of flexibility, and it allows me to easily adapt the same content to different views and different data. To display the search and ordering elements to the user alongside the Product list, I added the content shown in Listing 8-15 to the Index view used by the Home controller.

Listing 8-15. Displaying the Product Features in the Index.cshtml File in the Views/Home Folder

```
@model IEnumerable<Product>

<h3 class="p-2 bg-primary text-white text-center">Products</h3>

<div class="text-center">
    @Html.Partial("Pages", Model)
    @{
        ViewBag.searches = new string[] { "Name", "Category.Name" };
        ViewBag.sorts = new string[] { "Name", "Category.Name",
```

151

```
              "PurchasePrice", "RetailPrice"};
    }
    @Html.Partial("PageOptions", Model)
</div>
<div class="container-fluid mt-3">
    <!-- ...other elements omitted for brevity... -->
</div>
```

The code block specifies the Product properties by which the user will be able to search and order Product objects, while the @Html.Partial expression renders the elements for these features.

To see the results, start the application using dotnet run and navigate to http://localhost:5000. You will see a new series of elements that make navigating the data easier, as shown in Figure 8-3.

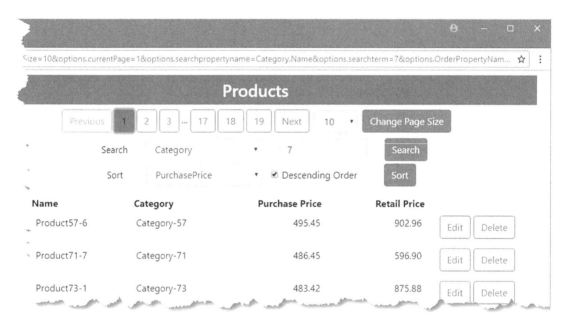

Figure 8-3. *Searching and ordering Product objects*

Applying the Data Presentation Features to Categories

The process for putting the pagination, search, and sorting features in place has been awkward, but now that the foundation is in place, I can apply them to other data types in the application, such as the management of Category objects. To begin, I updated the repository interface and implementation classes to add a method that accepts a QueryOptions object and returns a PagedList result, as shown in Listing 8-16.

Listing 8-16. Adding Page Support in the CategoryRepository.cs File in the Models Folder

```
using System.Collections.Generic;
using SportsStore.Models.Pages;

namespace SportsStore.Models {
```

```
    public interface ICategoryRepository {

        IEnumerable<Category> Categories { get; }

        PagedList<Category> GetCategories(QueryOptions options);

        void AddCategory(Category category);
        void UpdateCategory(Category category);
        void DeleteCategory(Category category);
    }

    public class CategoryRepository : ICategoryRepository {
        private DataContext context;

        public CategoryRepository(DataContext ctx) => context = ctx;

        public IEnumerable<Category> Categories => context.Categories;

        public PagedList<Category> GetCategories(QueryOptions options) {
            return new PagedList<Category>(context.Categories, options);
        }

        public void AddCategory(Category category) {
            context.Categories.Add(category);
            context.SaveChanges();
        }

        public void UpdateCategory(Category category) {
            context.Categories.Update(category);
            context.SaveChanges();
        }

        public void DeleteCategory(Category category) {
            context.Categories.Remove(category);
            context.SaveChanges();
        }
    }
}
```

In Listing 8-17, I have added a QueryOptions parameter to the Index action of the controller that manages Category objects and used it to query the repository.

Listing 8-17. Adding Page Support in the CategoriesController.cs File in the Controllers Folder

```
using Microsoft.AspNetCore.Mvc;
using SportsStore.Models;
using SportsStore.Models.Pages;

namespace SportsStore.Controllers {

    public class CategoriesController : Controller {
        private ICategoryRepository repository;
```

```
    public CategoriesController(ICategoryRepository repo) => repository = repo;

    public IActionResult Index(QueryOptions options)
        => View(repository.GetCategories(options));

    [HttpPost]
    public IActionResult AddCategory(Category category) {
        repository.AddCategory(category);
        return RedirectToAction(nameof(Index));
    }

    public IActionResult EditCategory(long id) {
        ViewBag.EditId = id;
        return View("Index", repository.Categories);
    }

    [HttpPost]
    public IActionResult UpdateCategory(Category category) {
        repository.UpdateCategory(category);
        return RedirectToAction(nameof(Index));
    }

    [HttpPost]
    public IActionResult DeleteCategory(Category category) {
        repository.DeleteCategory(category);
        return RedirectToAction(nameof(Index));
    }
    }
}
```

Finally, I can present the features to the user by adding the elements shown in Listing 8-18 to the Index view used by the Categories controller.

Listing 8-18. Adding Features in the Index.cshtml File in the Views/Categories Folder

```
@model IEnumerable<Category>

<h3 class="p-2 bg-primary text-white text-center">Categories</h3>

<div class="text-center">
    @Html.Partial("Pages", Model)
    @{
        ViewBag.searches = new string[] { "Name", "Description" };
        ViewBag.sorts = new string[] { "Name", "Description" };
    }
    @Html.Partial("PageOptions", Model)
</div>

<div class="container-fluid mt-3">
    <!-- ...other elements omitted for brevity... -->
</div>
```

To see the new features, start the application, navigate to `http://localhost:5000`, and click the Categories button. The list of categories is presented in pages, and the user can search and order them as required, as shown in Figure 8-4.

Figure 8-4. *Paging, sorting and searching categories*

Indexing the Database

Adding a thousand test objects to the database is enough to show the scaling limitations of the way that data was presented to the user, but it isn't enough data to reveal the limitations of the database. To see the effect of working with larger amounts of data, I have added statements to the PagedList constructor that measure how long it takes to perform a query and write the elapsed time to the console, as shown in Listing 8-19.

■ **Tip** There are many ways to measure performance, and most database servers provide tools that will help you understand how long queries take to execute. In the case of SQL Server, the SQL Server Profiler and the SQL Server Management Studio tools provide endless amounts of detail. These tools can be useful, but I generally rely on the approach that I take in Listing 8-19 because it is simple and accurate enough to understand the magnitude of any performance problems.

Listing 8-19. Timing the Query in the PagedList.cs File in the Models/Pages Folder

```
using System.Collections.Generic;
using System.Linq;
using System;
using System.Linq.Expressions;
using System.Diagnostics;
```

```
namespace SportsStore.Models.Pages {

    public class PagedList<T> : List<T> {

        public PagedList(IQueryable<T> query, QueryOptions options = null) {
            CurrentPage = options.CurrentPage;
            PageSize = options.PageSize;
            Options = options;

            if (options != null) {
                if (!string.IsNullOrEmpty(options.OrderPropertyName)) {
                    query = Order(query, options.OrderPropertyName,
                        options.DescendingOrder);
                }
                if (!string.IsNullOrEmpty(options.SearchPropertyName)
                        && !string.IsNullOrEmpty(options.SearchTerm)) {
                    query = Search(query, options.SearchPropertyName,
                        options.SearchTerm);
                }
            }

            Stopwatch sw = Stopwatch.StartNew();
            Console.Clear();

            TotalPages = query.Count() / PageSize;
            AddRange(query.Skip((CurrentPage - 1) * PageSize).Take(PageSize));

            Console.WriteLine($"Query Time: {sw.ElapsedMilliseconds} ms");
        }

        // ...other members omitted for brevity...
    }
}
```

Start the application using dotnet run, navigate to http://localhost:5000, click the Seed Data button, and populate the database with the number of objects you want to test. When the database has been seeded, click the Products button, select the Purchase Price property for the Sort select element, select the Descending Order option, and click the Sort button.

If you examine the logging messages generated by the application, you will see the queries that have been used to get the data and the amount of time they took.

```
...
SELECT COUNT(*)
FROM [Products] AS [p]
...
SELECT [p].[Id], [p].[CategoryId], [p].[Name], [p].[PurchasePrice],
    [p].[RetailPrice], [p.Category].[Id], [p.Category].[Description],
    [p.Category].[Name
FROM [Products] AS [p]
INNER JOIN [Categories] AS [p.Category] ON [p].[CategoryId] = [p.Category].[Id]
ORDER BY [p].[PurchasePrice] DESC
```

```
OFFSET @__p_0 ROWS FETCH NEXT @__p_1 ROWS ONLY
...
Query Time: 14 ms
...
```

Table 8-1 shows the amount of time it takes to perform these queries on my development machine for different amounts of seed data. You may see different times when you perform the tests, but what's important is the way that the amount of time taken to perform the queries increases along with the amount of data.

Table 8-1. *The Time Taken to Perform Queries*

Objects	Time
1,000	14ms
10,000	17ms
100,000	185ms
1,000,000	2453ms
2,000,000	5713ms

Creating and Applying Indexes

Part of the performance problem is that the database server has to examine a lot of data rows to find the data that the application requires. An effective way to reduce the amount of work that the database server has to perform is to create indexes, which speed up queries but do so after taking some initial time to prepare and a little additional work after every update. For the SportsStore application, I am going to add indexes for the properties of the Product and Category classes that the user can use to search for or order data. Indexes are created in the database context class, as shown in Listing 8-20.

Listing 8-20. Creating Indexes in the DataContext.cs File in the Models Folder

```csharp
using Microsoft.EntityFrameworkCore;

namespace SportsStore.Models {

    public class DataContext : DbContext {

        public DataContext(DbContextOptions<DataContext> opts) : base(opts) {}

        public DbSet<Product> Products { get; set; }

        public DbSet<Category> Categories { get; set; }

        public DbSet<Order> Orders { get; set; }
        public DbSet<OrderLine> OrderLines { get; set; }
```

```
protected override void OnModelCreating(ModelBuilder modelBuilder) {

    modelBuilder.Entity<Product>().HasIndex(p => p.Name);
    modelBuilder.Entity<Product>().HasIndex(p => p.PurchasePrice);
    modelBuilder.Entity<Product>().HasIndex(p => p.RetailPrice);

    modelBuilder.Entity<Category>().HasIndex(p => p.Name);
    modelBuilder.Entity<Category>().HasIndex(p => p.Description);
    }
  }
}
```

The OnModelCreating method is overridden to customize the data model using the Entity Framework Core Fluent API feature, which I describe in detail in Parts 2 and 3 of this book. The Fluent API allows you override the default Entity Framework Core behaviors and to access advanced features, such as creating indexes. In the listing, I have created indexes for the Name, PurchasePrice, and RetailPrice properties of the Product class and for the Name and Description properties of the Category class. I don't need to create indexes for the primary or foreign key properties because Entity Framework Core does that for me by default.

Creating indexes requires a new migration to be created and applied to the database. Run the commands shown in Listing 8-21 in the SportsStore project folder to create a migration called Indexes and apply it to the database.

■ **Tip**   It can take a while to apply a migration that creates indexes when there is a lot of data in the database because all of the existing data has to be added to the index. You may want to use the Seed controller to reduce the amount of test data before executing the migration commands.

Listing 8-21. Creating and Applying a Database Migration

```
dotnet ef migrations add Indexes
dotnet ef database update
```

Once the migration has been applied, restart the application and repeat the query tests to see the impact on performance. Table 8-2 shows the query times before and after the indexes were added for my PC.

Table 8-2. The Time Taken to Perform Queries

Objects	Time	Indexed Time
1,000	14ms	9ms
10,000	17ms	10ms
100,000	185ms	23ms
1,000,000	2453ms	143ms
2,000,000	5713ms	158ms

UNDERSTANDING THE COUNT QUERY PERFORMANCE

There is still a small increase in the amount of time taken as the amount of data increases. The query that I make to get the number of objects that have been stored in the database is translated into a SQL `SELECT COUNT` command, the performance of which drops for a large number of objects. Database servers generally offer alternative methods of counting data, and in the case of SQL Server, you can query the metadata that the database server maintains about the database, like this:

```
...
select sum (spart.rows)
from sys.partitions spart
where spart.object_id = object_id('Products') and spart.index_id < 2
...
```

This type of query cannot be performed using LINQ. Instead, see Chapter 23 for details of using the Entity Framework Core features that support executing SQL commands directly.

Common Problems and Solutions

Scaling up the amount of data that the application supports requires a careful balance of adapting the ASP.NET Core MVC part of the application to ask Entity Framework Core for smaller amounts of data and providing tools for ordering and searching data. In the sections that follow, I describe the problems that you are most likely to encounter and explain how to resolve them.

Queries for Pages Are Too Slow

The most likely reason for slow queries is that the application is retrieving all of the objects from the database and then sorting or searching them in memory before taking just those objects required for a single page. Each time the user switches to a new page, this process is repeated, creating large amounts of work to retrieve and process objects that are then discarded.

This problem is usually caused by LINQ methods being called on the IEnumerable<T> interface, rather than the IQueryable<T> interface, as described in Chapter 5. The quickest way to diagnose this problem is to look application's logging messages to see the SQL queries that Entity Framework Core produces. Although the details will vary, using the IQueryable<T> interface with the OrderBy and Skip LINQ methods will produce queries with ORDER BY and OFFSET clauses.

If you are using the IQueryable<T> interface, then you should check for duplicate queries, as described in Chapter 5. It is easy to forget that enumerating the sequence of objects will trigger a query, especially when working out how many page buttons are required, for example.

Applying the Index Migration Times Out

When you apply a migration to the database that adds indexes, the database server has to populate the index using the data that has already been stored. This can be a lengthy process for large databases, and the dotnet ef command can time out before the process is complete, which will cause the migration to fail and prevent the indexes from being created. To solve this problem in development, drop and re-create the database so that the indexes are applied when there is no data. For production systems, back up the database, remove the data, and then apply the migrations. Once the indexes have been created, you can populate the database again using small blocks of data so that each update only requires a small amount of work.

Creating an Index Does Not Improve Performance

If you find that an index does not improve your query times, then the first thing to check is that the migration that creates the indexes has been applied to the database. The next most likely problem is that indexes have not been created for all of the properties that the application uses for queries. If your application uses combinations of properties for searches, you may need to create additional indexes, as described in Part 3.

Summary

In this chapter, I showed adapted the SportsStore application to deal with larger amounts of data. I added support for paging, sorting, and searching the data, which allow the user to work with manageable numbers of objects at a time. I also used the Fluent API to customize the data model and add indexes to improve query performance. In the next chapter, I add the customer-facing features to the SportsStore application.

CHAPTER 9

SportsStore: Customer Features

In this chapter, I am going to build the customer-facing parts of the SportsStore application, which will allow a user to select products, see their shopping cart, and check out to create an order. The features that I add in this chapter are largely related to the ASP.NET Core MVC framework and build on the Entity Framework Core foundation created in previous chapters.

I pick up the pace in this chapter because most of the work is building features using ASP.NET Core MVC on top of the foundation created with Entity Framework Core in previous chapters.

Preparing for This Chapter

I continue to use the SportsStore project that was created in Chapter 4 and updated in the chapters since.

Tip You can download the SportsStore project for this chapter—and the projects for every other chapter—from the GitHub repository for this book: https://github.com/apress/pro-ef-core-2-for-asp.net-core-mvc.

Removing the Timing Statements

In Chapter 8, I measured the time taken to perform queries. The statements that timed the query are no longer required, and I have commented them out in Listing 9-1.

Listing 9-1. Commenting Out Statements in the PagedList.cs File in the Models/Pages Folder

```
using System.Collections.Generic;
using System.Linq;
using System;
using System.Linq.Expressions;
using System.Diagnostics;

namespace SportsStore.Models.Pages {

    public class PagedList<T> : List<T> {

        public PagedList(IQueryable<T> query, QueryOptions options = null) {
            CurrentPage = options.CurrentPage;
            PageSize = options.PageSize;
            Options = options;
```

© Adam Freeman 2018
A. Freeman, *Pro Entity Framework Core 2 for ASP.NET Core MVC*,
https://doi.org/10.1007/978-1-4842-3435-8_9

```
        if (options != null) {
            if (!string.IsNullOrEmpty(options.OrderPropertyName)) {
                query = Order(query, options.OrderPropertyName,
                    options.DescendingOrder);
            }
            if (!string.IsNullOrEmpty(options.SearchPropertyName)
                    && !string.IsNullOrEmpty(options.SearchTerm)) {
                query = Search(query, options.SearchPropertyName,
                    options.SearchTerm);
            }
        }

        //Stopwatch sw = Stopwatch.StartNew();
        //Console.Clear();
        TotalPages = query.Count() / PageSize;
        AddRange(query.Skip((CurrentPage - 1) * PageSize).Take(PageSize));
        //Console.WriteLine($"Query Time: {sw.ElapsedMilliseconds} ms");
    }

    // ...other members omitted for brevity...
    }
}
```

Adding a View Import

In Chapter 8, I used the PagedList class in views without changing the view model, just to demonstrate that I could add scale up features to an application with the minimum of changes. In this chapter, I am going to use the PagedList class directly in views, so I added the containing namespace to the view imports file, as shown in Listing 9-2.

Listing 9-2. Adding a Namespace in the _ViewImports.cshtml File in the Views Folder

```
@using SportsStore.Models
@using SportsStore.Models.Pages
@addTagHelper *, Microsoft.AspNetCore.Mvc.TagHelpers
```

Modifying the Data Model

To prepare the data model for the customer-facing features, I added a Description property to the Product class so that customers can learn a little about the products they see, as shown in Listing 9-3.

Listing 9-3. Adding a Property in the Products.cs File in the Models Folder

```
namespace SportsStore.Models {

    public class Product {

        public long Id { get; set; }

        public string Name { get; set; }
        public string Description { get; set; }
```

```
        public decimal PurchasePrice { get; set; }
        public decimal RetailPrice { get; set; }

        public long CategoryId { get; set; }
        public Category Category { get; set; }
    }
}
```

To make it easier to query and store data by category, I added a navigation property to the `Category` class that Entity Framework Core will be able to populate with the related `Product` objects, as shown in Listing 9-4.

Listing 9-4. Adding a Navigation Property in the Category.cs File in the Models Folder

```
using System.Collections.Generic;

namespace SportsStore.Models {

    public class Category {
        public long Id { get; set; }
        public string Name { get; set; }
        public string Description { get; set; }

        public IEnumerable<Product> Products { get; set; }
    }
}
```

Adding Product Seed Data

I want to be able to switch between large amounts of test data and small amounts of more realistic data. To that end, I added the code shown in Listing 9-5 to the Seed controller to add the standard SportsStore categories and products.

Listing 9-5. Adding Production Seed Data in the SeedController.cs File in the Controllers Folder

```
using Microsoft.AspNetCore.Mvc;
using Microsoft.EntityFrameworkCore;
using SportsStore.Models;
using System.Linq;

namespace SportsStore.Controllers {

    public class SeedController : Controller {
        private DataContext context;

        public SeedController(DataContext ctx) => context = ctx;

        public IActionResult Index() {
            ViewBag.Count = context.Products.Count();
            return View(context.Products
                .Include(p => p.Category).OrderBy(p => p.Id).Take(20));
        }
```

```
// ...other actions omitted for brevity...

[HttpPost]
public IActionResult CreateProductionData() {
    ClearData();

    context.Categories.AddRange(new Category[] {
        new Category {
            Name = "Watersports",
            Description = "Make a splash",
            Products = new Product[] {
                new Product {
                    Name = "Kayak", Description = "A boat for one person",
                    PurchasePrice = 200, RetailPrice = 275
                },
                new Product {
                    Name = "Lifejacket",
                    Description = "Protective and fashionable",
                    PurchasePrice = 40, RetailPrice = 48.95m
                },
            }
        },
        new Category {
            Name = "Soccer",
            Description = "The World's Favorite Game",
            Products = new Product[] {
                new Product {
                    Name = "Soccer Ball",
                    Description = "FIFA-approved size and weight",
                    PurchasePrice = 18, RetailPrice = 19.50m
                },
                new Product {
                    Name = "Corner Flags", Description
                        = "Give your playing field a professional touch",
                    PurchasePrice = 32.50m, RetailPrice = 34.95m
                },
                new Product {
                    Name = "Stadium",
                    Description = "Flat-packed 35,000-seat stadium",
                    PurchasePrice = 75000,   RetailPrice = 79500
                }
            }
        },
        new Category {
            Name = "Chess",
            Description = "The Thinky Game",
            Products = new Product[] {
                new Product {
                    Name = "Thinking Cap",
                    Description = "Improve brain efficiency by 75%",
                    PurchasePrice = 10, RetailPrice = 16
                },
```

```
                    new Product {
                        Name = "Unsteady Chair", Description
                            = "Secretly give your opponent a disadvantage",
                        PurchasePrice = 28, RetailPrice = 29.95m
                    },
                    new Product {
                        Name = "Human Chess Board",
                        Description = "A fun game for the family",
                        PurchasePrice = 68.50m, RetailPrice = 75
                    },
                    new Product {
                        Name = "Bling-Bling King",
                        Description = "Gold-plated, diamond-studded King",
                        PurchasePrice = 800, RetailPrice = 1200
                    }
                }
            }
        });
        context.SaveChanges();
        return RedirectToAction(nameof(Index));
    }
  }
}
```

The new action method creates a series of Category objects and sets the Products navigation property to a collection of Product objects. All of the objects are passed to the AddRange method and are stored in the database by the SaveChanges method. To target the new action method, I added the elements shown in Listing 9-6 to the Index view used by the Seed controller.

Listing 9-6. Adding an Element in the Index.cshtml File in the Views/Seed Folder

```
@model IEnumerable<Product>

<h3 class="p-2 bg-primary text-white text-center">Seed Data</h3>

<form method="post">
    <div class="form-group">
        <label>Number of Objects to Create</label>
        <input class="form-control" name="count" value="50" />
    </div>

    <div class="text-center">
        <button type="submit" asp-action="CreateProductionData"
                class="btn btn-outline-primary">
            Production Seed
        </button>
        <button type="submit" asp-action="CreateSeedData" class="btn btn-primary">
            Seed Database
        </button>
```

```
        <button asp-action="ClearData" class="btn btn-danger">
            Clear Database
        </button>
    </div>
</form>

<h5 class="text-center m-2">
    There are @ViewBag.Count products in the database
</h5>

<div class="container-fluid">
    <div class="row">
        <div class="col-1 font-weight-bold">Id</div>
        <div class="col font-weight-bold">Name</div>
        <div class="col font-weight-bold">Category</div>
        <div class="col font-weight-bold text-right">Purchase</div>
        <div class="col font-weight-bold text-right">Retail</div>
    </div>
    @foreach (Product p in Model) {
        <div class="row">
            <div class="col-1">@p.Id</div>
            <div class="col">@p.Name</div>
            <div class="col">@p.Category.Name</div>
            <div class="col text-right">@p.PurchasePrice</div>
            <div class="col text-right">@p.RetailPrice</div>
        </div>
    }
</div>
```

The button element sends an HTTP POST request, which will have the effect of clearing the database and seeding it with the standard SportsStore products and categories.

Preparing the Database

To prepare the database for this chapter, run the commands shown in Listing 9-7 in the SportsStore project folder. These commands add a new migration that reflects the change to the data model and then delete and re-create the database.

Listing 9-7. Preparing the Database

```
dotnet ef migrations add Customer
dotnet ef database drop --force
dotnet ef database update
```

Start the application using dotnet run, navigate to http://localhost:5000, click the Seed Data button, and then click the Production Seed button. Products and categories will be added to the database and displayed, as shown in Figure 9-1.

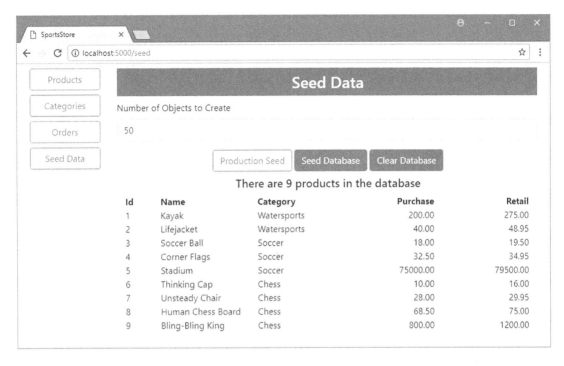

Figure 9-1. *Running the example application*

Displaying Products to the Customer

In the sections that follow, I add the support required to display a list of products to the user, allowing them to filter by category and paginate through the products available to purchase. To do this, I will build on the features I added in previous chapters.

Preparing the Data Model

To start the customer-facing part of the application, I added the ability to query Product objects by their category, starting with the repository interface, as shown in Listing 9-8.

Listing 9-8. Querying by Category in the IRepository.cs File in the Models Folder

```
using System.Collections.Generic;
using SportsStore.Models.Pages;

namespace SportsStore.Models {

    public interface IRepository {

        IEnumerable<Product> Products { get; }

        PagedList<Product> GetProducts(QueryOptions options, long category = 0);

        Product GetProduct(long key);
```

```
        void AddProduct(Product product);

        void UpdateProduct(Product product);

        void UpdateAll(Product[] products);

        void Delete(Product product);
    }
}
```

In Listing 9-9, I made the corresponding change in the implementation class, using the LINQ Where method to query based on the foreign key property that associates a Product with its related Category.

Listing 9-9. Querying by Category in the DataRepository.cs File in the Models Folder

```
using System.Collections.Generic;
using System.Linq;
using Microsoft.EntityFrameworkCore;
using SportsStore.Models.Pages;

namespace SportsStore.Models {

    public class DataRepository : IRepository {
        private DataContext context;

        public DataRepository(DataContext ctx) => context = ctx;

        public IEnumerable<Product> Products => context.Products
            .Include(p => p.Category).ToArray();

        public PagedList<Product> GetProducts(QueryOptions options,
                long category = 0) {
            IQueryable<Product> query = context.Products.Include(p => p.Category);
            if (category !=- 0) {
                query = query.Where(p => p.CategoryId == category);
            }
            return new PagedList<Product>(query, options);
        }

        // ...other methods omitted for brevity...
    }
}
```

The IQueryable<T> interface allows me to compose the query based on the method parameters, creating an object that will query the database only when it is enumerated. This is the advantage of working with IQueryable<T> objects, although the drawback is the ease with which duplicate queries can be accidentally triggered.

Creating the Store Controller, Views, and Layout

To provide the controller that will present the data to the customer, I added a file called StoreController.cs to the Controllers folder and added the code shown in Listing 9-10.

Listing 9-10. The Contents of the StoreController.cs File in the Controllers Folder

```
using Microsoft.AspNetCore.Mvc;
using SportsStore.Models;
using SportsStore.Models.Pages;

namespace SportsStore.Controllers {

    public class StoreController : Controller {
        private IRepository productRepository;
        private ICategoryRepository categoryRepository;

        public StoreController(IRepository prepo, ICategoryRepository catRepo) {
            productRepository = prepo;
            categoryRepository = catRepo;
        }

        public IActionResult Index([FromQuery(Name = "options")]
                QueryOptions productOptions,
                QueryOptions catOptions,
                long category) {
            ViewBag.Categories = categoryRepository.GetCategories(catOptions);
            ViewBag.SelectedCategory = category;
            return View(productRepository.GetProducts(productOptions, category));
        }

    }
}
```

I use two QueryOptions objects to manage the display of Product and Category data. These are used to obtain a PagedList<Product> object, which is passed to the view as its model, and a PagedList<Category> object, which is added to the ViewBag.

To provide a layout for the customer-facing features, I created the Views/Store folder and added to it a file called _Layout.cshtml with the content shown in Listing 9-11.

Listing 9-11. The Contents of the _Layout.cshtml File in the Views/Store Folder

```
<!DOCTYPE html>

<html>
<head>
    <meta name="viewport" content="width=device-width" />
    <link rel="stylesheet" href="~/lib/bootstrap/dist/css/bootstrap.min.css" />
    <title>SportsStore</title>
</head>
<body>
    <div class="container-fluid">
```

```
            <div class="row bg-dark p-4 text-white">
                <div class="col-auto"><h4>SPORTS STORE</h4></div>
                <div class="col"></div>
                <div class="col-auto text-right">
                    (Cart Goes Here)
                </div>
            </div>
        </div>
        @RenderBody()
</body>
</html>
```

This layout presents the standard SportsStore header I use in most of my books, with a placeholder for the summary of the customer's shopping cart, which I'll add to the application later. To display the list of products, I added a file called Index.cshtml to the Views/Store folder with the content shown in Listing 9-12.

Listing 9-12. The Contents of the Index.cshtml File in the Views/Store Folder

```
@model PagedList<Product>

<div class="container-fluid">
    <div class="row no-gutters">
        <div class="col-auto">
            @Html.Partial("Categories", ViewBag.Categories as PagedList<Category>)
        </div>
        <div class="col">
            <div class="container-fluid">
                <div class="row pt-4 pb-1">
                    <div class="col text-center">
                        @Html.Partial("Pages", Model)
                    </div>
                </div>
                <div class="row pt-1 pb-1">
                    <div class="col"></div>
                    <div class="col-6 text-center form-group">
                        <input form="pageform" type="hidden"
                                name="options.searchpropertyname" value="Name" />
                        <input form="pageform" name="options.searchterm"
                                placeholder="Seach..." class="form-control" />
                    </div>
                    <div class="col">
                        <button form="pageform" class="btn btn-secondary"
                                type="submit">Search</button>
                    </div>
                    <div class="col"></div>
                </div>
                @foreach (Product p in Model) {
                    <div class="row">
                        <div class="col">
                            <div class="card m-1 p-1 bg-light">
                                <div class="bg-faded p-1">
                                    <h4>
```

```
                    @p.Name
                    <span class="badge badge-pill badge-primary"
                            style="float:right">
                        <small>$@p.RetailPrice</small>
                    </span>
                </h4>
            </div>
            <form id="@p.Id" asp-action="AddToCart"
                asp-controller="Cart" method="post">
                <input type="hidden" name="Id" value="@p.Id" />
                <input type="hidden" name="Name"
                    value="@p.Name" />
                <input type="hidden" name="RetailPrice"
                    value="@p.RetailPrice" />
                <input type="hidden" name="returnUrl" value=
                "@ViewContext.HttpContext.Request.PathAndQuery()"
                />
                <span class="card-text p-1">
                    @(p.Description
                        ?? "(No Description Available)")
                    <button type="submit"
                        class="btn btn-success btn-sm pull-right"
                            style="float:right">
                        Add To Cart
                    </button>
                </span>
            </form>
        </div>
    </div>
</div>
    }
</div>
        </div>
    </div>
</div>
```

This view brings together a number of features to display products, including pagination and search support. To display the list of categories to the user, I added a file called Categories.cshtml to the Views/Store folder with the content shown in Listing 9-13.

Listing 9-13. The Contents of the Categories.cshtml File in the Views/Store Folder

```
@model PagedList<Category>

<div class="container-fluid mt-4">

    <div class="row no-gutters">
        <div class="col mt-1">
            <button form="pageform" name="category" value="0" type="submit"
                class="btn btn-block @(ViewBag.SelectedCategory == 0
                    ? "btn-primary" : "btn-outline-primary")">
                All
```

```
                </button>
            </div>
        </div>

        <div class="row no-gutters mt-4"></div>

        <div class="row no-gutters">
            <div class="col mt-1">
                <button form="pageform"
                        name="catoptions.currentPage" value="@(Model.CurrentPage -1)"
                        class="btn btn-block btn-outline-secondary
                            @(!Model.HasPreviousPage ? "disabled" : "")"
                        type="submit">
                    Previous
                </button>
            </div>
        </div>

        @foreach (Category c in Model) {
            <div class="row no-gutters">
                <div class="col mt-1">
                    <button form="pageform" name="category" value="@c.Id"
                        type="submit"
                        class="btn btn-block @(ViewBag.SelectedCategory == c.Id
                            ? "btn-primary" : "btn-outline-primary")">
                        @c.Name
                        </button>
                    </div>
                </div>
        }

        <div class="row no-gutters">
            <div class="col mt-1">
                <button form="pageform"
                        name="catoptions.currentPage" value="@(Model.CurrentPage +1)"
                        class="btn btn-block btn-outline-secondary
                            @(!Model.HasNextPage? "disabled" : "")"
                        type="submit">
                    Next
                </button>
            </div>
        </div>
    </div>
</div>
```

This view lists the categories that are available and provides Previous and Next buttons to page through the list. The button elements that select categories use the HTML form called pagesform to target the controller with the chosen category's primary key value.

Creating the Return URL

I need to know which URL to navigate back to after the user has selected a product, and to make the process easier, I created the Infrastructure folder and added to it a class file called UrlExtensions.cs, with the code shown in Listing 9-14.

Listing 9-14. The Contents of the UrlExtensions.cs File in the Infrastructure Folder

```
using Microsoft.AspNetCore.Http;

namespace SportsStore.Infrastructure {

    public static class UrlExtensions {

        public static string PathAndQuery(this HttpRequest request) =>
            request.QueryString.HasValue
                ? $"{request.Path}{request.QueryString}"
                : request.Path.ToString();
    }
}
```

This class defines the PathAndQuery extension method that I used in a form element in Listing 9-13. To enable the use of the extension method in the view, I added the statement shown in Listing 9-15 to the view imports file.

Listing 9-15. Adding a Namespace in the _ViewImports.cshtml File in the Views Folder

```
@using SportsStore.Models
@using SportsStore.Models.Pages
@using SportsStore.Infrastructure
@addTagHelper *, Microsoft.AspNetCore.Mvc.TagHelpers
```

Testing the Store Display

To see the effect of the changes, start the application using dotnet run and navigate to http://localhost:5000/store. You will see the list of products, which can be filtered by category, as shown in Figure 9-2.

⬛ **Tip** You can see how the display deals with larger amounts of data by navigating to http://localhost:5000/seed and generating test data.

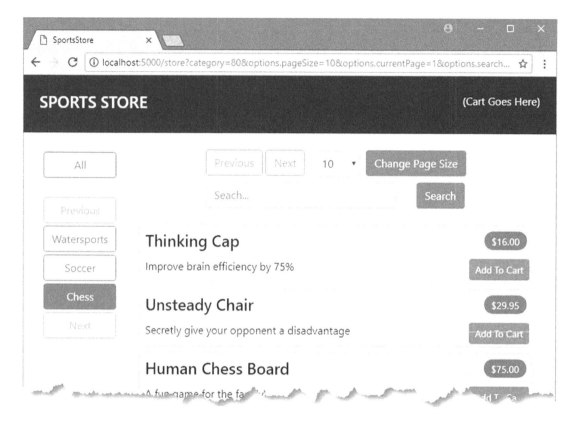

Figure 9-2. *Displaying products*

Adding the Shopping Cart

The next step is to add support for selecting products and storing them in a cart, which can then be used to complete an order. In the sections that follow, I configure the application to store session data and use this as a temporary store for product selections.

Enabling Persistent Session Data

Some of the features needed to complete the SportsStore application need to store data across HTTP requests, which I will do using the ASP.NET Core session data feature configured to store its data using Entity Framework Core. To add the package required to configure the session database, I right-clicked the SportsStore project item in the Solution Explorer, selected Edit SportsStore.csproj from the pop-up menu, and made the changes shown in Listing 9-16.

Listing 9-16. Adding Packages in the SportsStore.csproj File in the SportsStore Folder

```
<Project Sdk="Microsoft.NET.Sdk.Web">

  <PropertyGroup>
    <TargetFramework>netcoreapp2.0</TargetFramework>
  </PropertyGroup>
```

```
<ItemGroup>
  <Folder Include="wwwroot\" />
</ItemGroup>

<ItemGroup>
  <PackageReference Include="Microsoft.AspNetCore.All" Version="2.0.3" />
  <DotNetCliToolReference Include="Microsoft.EntityFrameworkCore.Tools.DotNet"
      Version="2.0.0" />
  <DotNetCliToolReference Include="Microsoft.Extensions.Caching.SqlConfig.Tools"
      Version="2.0.0" />
</ItemGroup>

</Project>
```

Save the change and Visual Studio will download and install the new package. Open a new command prompt and run the command shown in Listing 9-17 in the SportsStore project folder to create the session database.

■ **Caution**   You might be tempted to create your own session data feature, but don't underestimate the amount of work that is required, especially to ensure that expired sessions are periodically purged from the database. My advice is to use your time and skills to create features for your application and not to reinvent something that Microsoft has already provided.

Listing 9-17.   Creating the Session Database

```
dotnet sql-cache create "Server=(localdb)\MSSQLLocalDB;Database=SportsStore" "dbo"
"SessionData"
```

The dotnet sql-cache create command prepares the session database but is awkward to work with because it doesn't read its configuration from the appsettings.json file, meaning that the arguments must be carefully typed. The first argument is the connection string for the database, the second argument is the schema name (which is dbo by default), and the final argument is the name of the table that will be added to the database and for which I have specified SessionData.

Configuring Sessions in the Application

To enable sessions in the database, I added the statements shown in Listing 9-18 to the Startup class.

Listing 9-18.   Enabling Sessions in the Startup.cs File in the SportsStore Folder

```
using System;
using System.Collections.Generic;
using System.Linq;
using System.Threading.Tasks;
using Microsoft.AspNetCore.Builder;
using Microsoft.AspNetCore.Hosting;
using Microsoft.AspNetCore.Http;
using Microsoft.Extensions.DependencyInjection;
using SportsStore.Models;
```

```
using Microsoft.EntityFrameworkCore;
using Microsoft.Extensions.Configuration;

namespace SportsStore {
    public class Startup {

        public Startup(IConfiguration config) => Configuration = config;

        public IConfiguration Configuration { get; }

        public void ConfigureServices(IServiceCollection services) {
            services.AddMvc();
            services.AddTransient<IRepository, DataRepository>();
            services.AddTransient<ICategoryRepository, CategoryRepository>();
            services.AddTransient<IOrdersRepository, OrdersRepository>();
            string conString = Configuration["ConnectionStrings:DefaultConnection"];
            services.AddDbContext<DataContext>(options =>
                options.UseSqlServer(conString));

            services.AddDistributedSqlServerCache(options => {
                options.ConnectionString = conString;
                options.SchemaName = "dbo";
                options.TableName = "SessionData";
            });
            services.AddSession(options => {
                options.Cookie.Name = "SportsStore.Session";
                options.IdleTimeout = System.TimeSpan.FromHours(48);
                options.Cookie.HttpOnly = false;
            });
        }

        public void Configure(IApplicationBuilder app, IHostingEnvironment env) {
            app.UseDeveloperExceptionPage();
            app.UseStatusCodePages();
            app.UseStaticFiles();
            app.UseSession();
            app.UseMvcWithDefaultRoute();
        }
    }
}
```

The session feature will only store string values. To make this feature easier to use, I added a file called SessionExtensions.cs to the Infrastructure folder and added the code shown in Listing 9-19.

Listing 9-19. The Contents of the SessionExtensions.cs File in the Infrastructure Folder

```
using Microsoft.AspNetCore.Http;
using Newtonsoft.Json;

namespace SportsStore.Infrastructure {

    public static class SessionExtensions {
```

```
    public static void SetJson(this ISession session, string key, object value) {
        session.SetString(key, JsonConvert.SerializeObject(value));
    }

    public static T GetJson<T>(this ISession session, string key) {
        var sessionData = session.GetString(key);
        return sessionData == null
            ? default(T) : JsonConvert.DeserializeObject<T>(sessionData);
    }
  }
}
```

This class defines extensions methods that serialize objects to the JSON format and restore them again, allowing me to easily store simple objects as session data.

Creating the Cart Model Class

To represent the customer's product selections, I added a file called Cart.cs to the Models folder and used it to define the class shown in Listing 9-20.

Listing 9-20. The Contents of the Cart.cs File in the Models Folder

```
using System.Collections.Generic;
using System.Linq;

namespace SportsStore.Models {

    public class Cart {
        private List<OrderLine> selections = new List<OrderLine>();

        public Cart AddItem(Product p, int quantity) {
            OrderLine line = selections
                .Where(l => l.ProductId == p.Id).FirstOrDefault();
            if (line != null) {
                line.Quantity += quantity;
            } else {
                selections.Add(new OrderLine {
                    ProductId = p.Id,
                    Product = p,
                    Quantity = quantity
                });
            }
            return this;
        }

        public Cart RemoveItem(long productId) {
            selections.RemoveAll(l => l.ProductId == productId);
            return this;
        }
```

```
        public void Clear() => selections.Clear();

        public IEnumerable<OrderLine> Selections { get => selections; }
    }
}
```

The Cart class manages a collection of OrderLine objects, which represent individual product selections and which can be easily stored in the database when an order is created.

Creating the Controller and Views

To provide the logic that will support working with Cart objects, I added a file called CartController.cs to the Controllers folder with the code shown in Listing 9-21.

Listing 9-21. The Contents of the CartController.cs File in the Controllers Folder

```
using Microsoft.AspNetCore.Mvc;
using SportsStore.Models;
using SportsStore.Infrastructure;
using Microsoft.AspNetCore.Mvc.ViewComponents;
using Microsoft.AspNetCore.Mvc.ViewFeatures;
using Microsoft.AspNetCore.Http;
using System.Linq;

namespace SportsStore.Controllers {

    [ViewComponent(Name = "Cart")]
    public class CartController : Controller {
        private IRepository productRepository;
        private IOrdersRepository ordersRepository;

        public CartController(IRepository prepo, IOrdersRepository orepo) {
            productRepository = prepo;
            ordersRepository = orepo;
        }

        public IActionResult Index(string returnUrl) {
            ViewBag.returnUrl = returnUrl;
            return View(GetCart());
        }

        [HttpPost]
        public IActionResult AddToCart(Product product, string returnUrl) {
            SaveCart(GetCart().AddItem(product, 1));
            return RedirectToAction(nameof(Index), new { returnUrl });
        }

        [HttpPost]
        public IActionResult RemoveFromCart(long productId, string returnUrl) {
            SaveCart(GetCart().RemoveItem(productId));
            return RedirectToAction(nameof(Index), new { returnUrl });
        }
```

```
    public IActionResult CreateOrder() {
        return View();
    }

    [HttpPost]
    public IActionResult CreateOrder(Order order) {
        order.Lines = GetCart().Selections.Select(s => new OrderLine {
            ProductId = s.ProductId,
            Quantity = s.Quantity
        }).ToArray();
        ordersRepository.AddOrder(order);
        SaveCart(new Cart());
        return RedirectToAction(nameof(Completed));
    }

    public IActionResult Completed() => View();

    private Cart GetCart() =>
        HttpContext.Session.GetJson<Cart>("Cart") ?? new Cart();

    private void SaveCart(Cart cart) =>
        HttpContext.Session.SetJson("Cart", cart);

    public IViewComponentResult Invoke(ISession session) {
        return new ViewViewComponentResult() {
            ViewData = new ViewDataDictionary<Cart>(ViewData,
                session.GetJson<Cart>("Cart"))
        };
    }
  }
}
```

The controller defines actions that add and remove items from the cart, display the contents of the cart, and allow the customer to create an order. Some of these methods accept a `returnUrl` parameter that allows the user to return to the product list without losing the query string parameters that configure the pagination and category filtering options. This class is also a view component, which I will use to display a summary of the cart in the customer-facing layout.

Creating the Views

To provide the new controller with a view for managing the cart, I created the Views/Cart folder and added to it a file called `Index.cshtml` with the contents shown in Listing 9-22.

Listing 9-22. The Contents of the Index.cshtml File in the Views/Cart Folder

```
@model Cart
@{
    Layout = "~/Views/Store/_Layout.cshtml";
}

<h2 class="m-3">Your Cart</h2>
```

```
<div class="container-fluid">
    <div class="row">
        <div class="col font-weight-bold">Quantity</div>
        <div class="col font-weight-bold">Product</div>
        <div class="col font-weight-bold text-right">Price</div>
        <div class="col font-weight-bold text-right">Subtotal</div>
        <div class="col"></div>
    </div>
    @if (Model.Selections.Count() == 0) {
        <div class="row mt-2"><div class="col-12"><h4>Cart is Empty</h4></div></div>
    } else {
        @foreach (OrderLine line in Model.Selections) {
            <div class="row mt-1">
                <div class="col">@line.Quantity</div>
                <div class="col">@line.Product.Name</div>
                <div class="col text-right">
                    $@line.Product.RetailPrice.ToString("f2")
                </div>
                <div class="col text-right">
                    $@((line.Product.RetailPrice
                        * line.Quantity).ToString("f2"))
                </div>
                <div class="col">
                    <form asp-action="RemoveFromCart">
                        <button type="submit" name="productId"
                            value="@line.ProductId"
                            class="btn btn-sm btn-outline-danger">Remove</button>
                    </form>
                </div>
            </div>
        }
    }
    <div class="row mt-2">
        <div class="col"></div>
        <div class="col"></div>
        <div class="col text-right font-weight-bold">Total:</div>
        <div class="col text-right font-weight-bold">
            $@(Model.Selections.Sum(l => l.Product.RetailPrice
                * l.Quantity).ToString("f2"))
        </div>
        <div class="col"></div>
    </div>
</div>
<div class="text-center m-2">
    @if (ViewBag.returnUrl != null) {
        <a href="@ViewBag.returnUrl" class="btn btn-outline-primary">
            Continue Shopping
        </a>
    }
```

```
    <a asp-action="CreateOrder" class="btn btn-primary">
        Place Order
    </a>
</div>
```

The view displays a summary of the customer's selection and provides buttons that return to the product list or continue to create an order. To gather the information required to create an order, I added a file called CreateOrder.cshtml to the Views/Cart folder with the content shown in Listing 9-23.

Listing 9-23. The Contents of the CreateOrder.cshtml File in the Views/Cart Folder

```
@model Order
@{
    Layout = "~/Views/Store/_Layout.cshtml";
}

<h2 class="m-3">Your Details</h2>

<form asp-action="CreateOrder" method="post" class="m-4">
    <div class="form-group">
        <label>Your Name:</label>
        <input asp-for="CustomerName" class="form-control" />
    </div>
    <div class="form-group">
        <label> Your Address</label>
        <input asp-for="Address" class="form-control" />
    </div>
    <div class="form-group">
        <label>Your State:</label>
        <input asp-for="State" class="form-control" />
    </div>
    <div class="form-group">
        <label>Your Zip Code:</label>
        <input asp-for="ZipCode" class="form-control" />
    </div>
    <div class="text-center m-2">
        <button type="submit" class="btn btn-primary">Place Order</button>
        <a asp-action="Index" class="btn btn-secondary">Cancel</a>
    </div>
</form>
```

To display a message to the user once an order has been created, I added a file called Completed.cshtml to the Views/Cart folder with the content shown in Listing 9-24.

Listing 9-24. The Contents of the Completed.cshtml File in the Views/Cart Folder

```
@{
    Layout = "~/Views/Store/_Layout.cshtml";
}
<div class="text-center m-4">
    <h2>Thanks!</h2>
    <p>Thanks for placing your order.</p>
    <p>We'll ship your goods as soon as possible.</p>
```

```
    <a asp-action="Index" asp-controller="Store"
            class="btn btn-primary">
        OK
    </a>
</div>
```

To create the view for the cart summary widget, I created the Views/Shared/Components/Cart folder and added to it a file called Cart.cshtml, with the content shown in Listing 9-25.

Listing 9-25. The Contents of the Default.cshtml File in the Views/Shared/Components/Cart Folder

```
@model Cart

@if (Model?.Selections?.Count() > 0) {
    <div>@Model.Selections.Count() items,
        $@(Model.Selections.Sum(l => l.Quantity
            * l.Product.RetailPrice).ToString("f2"))
    </div>
    if (ViewContext.RouteData.Values["controller"] as string != "Cart") {
        <a asp-action="Index" asp-controller="Cart"
                class="btn btn-sm btn-light">
            Checkout
        </a>
    }
}
```

This view displays the number of items in the cart and their total cost. There is also a button that will navigate to the Cart controller if that is not the controller that has rendered the view. To display the cart widget, I used the Component.InvokeAsync method to add the view component to the layout used for the store features, as shown in Listing 9-26.

Listing 9-26. Adding an Element in the _Layout.cshtml File in the Views/Store Folder

```
<!DOCTYPE html>

<html>
<head>
    <meta name="viewport" content="width=device-width" />
    <link rel="stylesheet" href="~/lib/bootstrap/dist/css/bootstrap.min.css" />
    <title>SportsStore</title>
</head>
<body>
    <div class="container-fluid">
        <div class="row bg-dark p-4 text-white">
            <div class="col-auto"><h4>SPORTS STORE</h4></div>
            <div class="col"></div>
            <div class="col-auto text-right">
                @await Component.InvokeAsync("Cart", Context.Session)
            </div>
        </div>
    </div>
```

```
    @RenderBody()
</body>
</html>
```

Testing the Ordering Process

To test the ordering process, start the application using `dotnet run` and navigate to `http://localhost:5000/store`. Click the Add to Cart button for one or more products and then click the Place Order button. Enter the customer details and click the Place Order button; you will see the completion messages. Figure 9-3 shows the sequence.

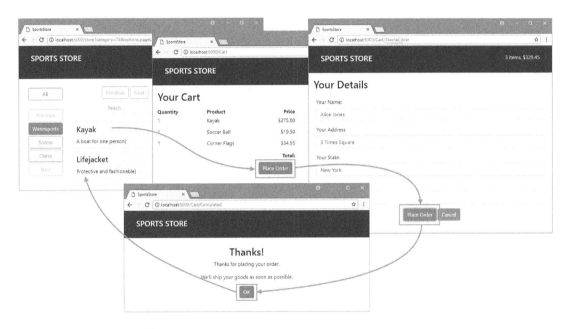

Figure 9-3. Placing an order

Common Problems and Solutions

This chapter has largely been about building application features using MVC, and there have been few additions that are likely to cause problems with Entity Framework Core.

Clicking a Page Button Manages the Wrong Data Type

If you click the button to change the page of `Categories`, for example, but find that the `Product` page changes, then the likely cause is that the HTML forms in your views are updating the wrong `PageOptions` object. Pay close attention to the names of the parameters in your action methods and make sure that you use these names as prefixes in the `name` attributes of your HTML elements. If in doubt, use the browser's F12 developer tools to see what form values are being sent to the application.

Clicking a Page Button Has No Effect

The most common cause of buttons that have no effect is omitting the form attribute, which is used to associate an HTML element with a form. This is a feature of HTML 5 but often causes confusion because developers are not used to extending a form beyond its form element.

The "Cannot Insert Explicit Value for Identity Column" Exception

This is an exception that I described previously, but it is worth noting again because it occurs often. In the context of this chapter, the likely cause is to have queried the database for objects and then stored them as session data, just as I did with the Product objects associated with an OrderLine. The objects that you queried for already have primary keys, and the exception is thrown because Entity Framework Core attempts to add them to the database as new objects.

When you subsequently get the object from session data and store it in the database, you must ensure that you remove references to the related data for which you queried previously. For the OrderLine objects that I stored in the Cart as session data and then stored in the database with an Order, I used the following code to remove the references to Product objects and produce a clean set of OrderLine objects:

```
...
order.Lines = GetCart().Selections.Select(s => new OrderLine {
    ProductId = s.ProductId, Quantity = s.Quantity
}).ToArray();
...
```

Session Objects Are Null

If you see errors indicating that the objects you expect to access via session data are null, then you may have forgotten to create the session database, using the command shown in Listing 9-17.

Session Objects Are Lost or Inconsistently Available

This is most likely caused by configuring the session feature to store its data in memory rather than in a database. An in-memory session store can be quicker, but the data is lost when the application is restarted, which is especially problematic if you using application containers, such as Docker containers, and are adapting to demand by starting and stopping containers.

Similarly, using an in-memory session store can lead to inconsistent session data when there are multiple instances of the MVC application running and you have not configured the network to ensure that HTTP requests from the same client are always handled by the same MVC instance. If you encounter either of these problems, then consider storing session data in a database as demonstrated in this chapter.

Summary

In this chapter, I completed the SportsStore application by adding the customer-facing features. I created a product list that the user can page through, search, or filter by category. Product selections are added to a cart, which can then be used to create an order, which is stored in the database. Most of the features that I added in this chapter used the MVC framework to build on the Entity Framework Core foundation created in earlier chapters, and this is a pattern than you will see in your own project—a lot of initial data model configuration and code and then a series of user-facing features that fall into place quickly. In the chapter, I complete the SportsStore project by creating a RESTful API.

CHAPTER 10

▓ ▓ ▓

SportsStore: Creating a RESTful Web Service

Web services are useful for providing data to client-side applications that are written with frameworks such as Angular or React. These applications are typically run in browsers and don't require the HTML content that the rest of the SportsStore provides. Instead, these applications interact with the ASP.NET Core MVC application using HTTP requests and receive data formatting using the JavaScript Object Notation (JSON) standard.

In this chapter, I am going to complete the SportsStore application by adding a RESTful web service that can provide web clients with access to the application's data. ASP.NET Core MVC has excellent support for creating RESTful web services, but care has to be taken to get the right results when using Entity Framework Core.

There are no hard-and-fast rules for how web services should work, but the most common approach is to adopt the Representational State Transfer (REST) pattern. There is no authoritative specification for REST, and there is no consensus about what constitutes a RESTful web service, but there are some common themes that are widely used for web services.

The core premise of REST—and the only aspect for which there is broad agreement—is that a web service defines an API through a combination of the URLs and HTTP methods such as GET and POST. The HTTP method specifies the type of operation, while the URL specifies the data object or objects that the operation applies to.

Preparing for This Chapter

For this chapter, I continue using the SportsStore project that was created in Chapter 4 and that I have been building up in in the chapters since. Run the commands shown in Listing 10-1 in the SportsStore project folder to reset the database.

Listing 10-1. Resetting the Example Application Database

```
dotnet ef database drop --force
dotnet ef database update
```

Start the application using dotnet run, navigate to http://localhost:5000, click the Seed Data button, and then click Production Seed. The database will be seeded with a small number of products, as shown in Figure 10-1.

© Adam Freeman 2018
A. Freeman, *Pro Entity Framework Core 2 for ASP.NET Core MVC*,
https://doi.org/10.1007/978-1-4842-3435-8_10

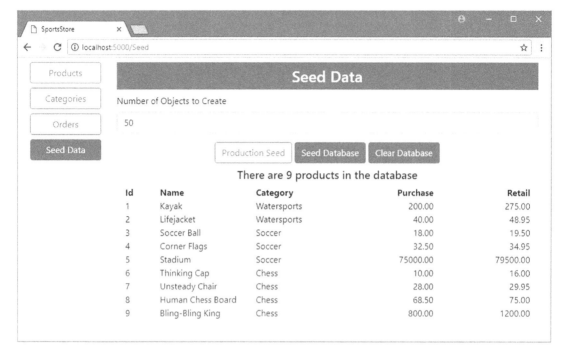

Figure 10-1. *Running the example application*

Tip You can download the SportsStore project for this chapter—and the projects for every other chapter—from the GitHub repository for this book: `https://github.com/apress/pro-ef-core-2-for-asp.net-core-mvc`.

Creating a Web Service

In the sections that follow, I build a simple web service that provides access to the Product data stored by the SportsStore application.

Creating the Repository

When adding a web service to an application, it is a good idea to create a separate repository because the queries that client-side applications perform can be different from those of a regular ASP.NET Core MVC application. For the SportsStore web service, I added a file called IWebServiceRepository.cs to the Models folder and used it to define the interface shown in Listing 10-2.

Listing 10-2. The Contents of the IWebServiceRepository.cs File in the Models Folder

```
namespace SportsStore.Models {

    public interface IWebServiceRepository {

        object GetProduct(long id);

    }
}
```

I am starting with just a GetProduct method, which will accept a primary key value and return the corresponding Product object from the database. The GetProduct method returns an object result, rather than a Product, so that I can demonstrate how to present Entity Framework Core data from a web service.

For the repository implementation class, I added a file called WebServiceRepository.cs to the Models folder and used it to define the class shown in Listing 10-3.

Listing 10-3. The Contents of the WebServiceRepository.cs File in the Models Folder

```
using System.Linq;

namespace SportsStore.Models {

    public class WebServiceRepository : IWebServiceRepository {
        private DataContext context;

        public WebServiceRepository(DataContext ctx) => context = ctx;

        public object GetProduct(long id) {
            return context.Products.FirstOrDefault(p => p.Id == id);
        }
    }
}
```

The class implements the GetProduct method by using the LINQ FirstOrDefault method to locate the object stored in the database that has the specified Id value. When creating a web service, it is important that you deal with requests for nonexistent data, which is why I have used the FirstOrDefault method.

To register the repository and its implementation class, I added the statements shown in Listing 10-4 to the Startup class.

Listing 10-4. Configuring the Repository in the Startup.cs File in the SportsStore Folder

```
using System;
using System.Collections.Generic;
using System.Linq;
using System.Threading.Tasks;
using Microsoft.AspNetCore.Builder;
using Microsoft.AspNetCore.Hosting;
using Microsoft.AspNetCore.Http;
using Microsoft.Extensions.DependencyInjection;
using SportsStore.Models;
using Microsoft.EntityFrameworkCore;
using Microsoft.Extensions.Configuration;
```

```
namespace SportsStore {
    public class Startup {

        public Startup(IConfiguration config) => Configuration = config;

        public IConfiguration Configuration { get; }

        public void ConfigureServices(IServiceCollection services) {
            services.AddMvc();
            services.AddTransient<IRepository, DataRepository>();
            services.AddTransient<ICategoryRepository, CategoryRepository>();
            services.AddTransient<IOrdersRepository, OrdersRepository>();
            services.AddTransient<IWebServiceRepository, WebServiceRepository>();
            string conString = Configuration["ConnectionStrings:DefaultConnection"];
            services.AddDbContext<DataContext>(options =>
                options.UseSqlServer(conString));

            services.AddDistributedSqlServerCache(options => {
                options.ConnectionString = conString;
                options.SchemaName = "dbo";
                options.TableName = "SessionData";
            });
            services.AddSession(options => {
                options.Cookie.Name = "SportsStore.Session";
                options.IdleTimeout = System.TimeSpan.FromHours(48);
                options.Cookie.HttpOnly = false;
            });
        }

        public void Configure(IApplicationBuilder app, IHostingEnvironment env) {
            app.UseDeveloperExceptionPage();
            app.UseStatusCodePages();
            app.UseStaticFiles();
            app.UseSession();
            app.UseMvcWithDefaultRoute();
        }
    }
}
```

Creating the API Controller

ASP.NET Core MVC makes it easy to add web services to an application using standard controller features.
I added a class called ProductValuesController.cs to the Controllers folder and add the code shown in
Listing 10-5.

Listing 10-5. The Contents of the ProductValuesController.cs File in the Controllers Folder

```
using Microsoft.AspNetCore.Mvc;
using SportsStore.Models;

namespace SportsStore.Controllers {

    [Route("api/products")]
    public class ProductValuesController : Controller {
        private IWebServiceRepository repository;

        public ProductValuesController(IWebServiceRepository repo)
            => repository = repo;

        [HttpGet("{id}")]
        public object GetProduct(long id) {
            return repository.GetProduct(id) ?? NotFound();
        }
    }
}
```

The name of this new controller class is ProductValuesController, which follows the convention of including the word Values in the name to indicate that the controller will return data to its clients rather than HTML. Another convention for web service controllers is to create a separate part of the routing schema dedicated to handling requests for data. The most common way to do this is to create URLs for web services that start with /api, followed by the plural form of the name of the data type that the web service handles. For a web service handling Product objects, this means that HTTP requests should be sent to the /api/products URL, which I have configured using the Route attribute, like this:

```
...
[Route("api/products")]
...
```

The only action currently defined by the controller is the GetProduct method, which returns a single Product object based on its primary key, which is the value assigned to its Id property. The action method is decorated with the HttpGet method, which will allow ASP.NET Core MVC to use this action to handle HTTP GET requests.

```
...
[HttpGet("{id}")]
public Product GetProduct(long id) {
...
```

The attribute's argument extends the URL schema defined by the Route attribute so that the GetProduct method can be reached by a URL in the form /api/products/{id}. Action methods for web services return .NET objects, which are automatically serialized and sent to the client.

To prevent the web service serializing a null response when a nonexistent object is requested, the action method uses the null-coalescing operator to call the NotFound method, like this:

```
...
return repository.GetProduct(id) ?? NotFound();
...
```

This will return a 404 - Not Found status code, which signals to the client that the request could not be satisfied.

Testing the Web Service

To test the new web service, start the application using dotnet run. Open a new PowerShell window and execute the command shown in Listing 10-6 to send an HTTP get request to the API controller.

Note I use the PowerShell Invoke-RestMethod command throughout this chapter to simulate requests from a client-side application.

Listing 10-6. Testing the Web Service

```
Invoke-RestMethod http://localhost:5000/api/products/1 -Method GET | ConvertTo-Json
```

The HTTP request is dispatched to the GetProduct method on the ProductValues controller, which uses the Find method to retrieve a Product object from the database. The Product object is serialized into the JSON format and returned to the browser, which will display the data it receives.

```
{
 "id":1,
 "name":"Kayak",
 "description":"A boat for one person",
 "purchasePrice":200.00,
 "retailPrice":275.00,
 "categoryId":1,
 "category":null
}
```

Notice that the category navigation property is set to null because I didn't ask Entity Framework Core to load the related data for the Product object.

Projecting a Result to Exclude Null Navigation Properties

Sending a client application data that contains null properties can lead to confusion because it may not be obvious whether there is no related data or there is related data but it just hasn't been included in the response. You know enough about the data model to realize that the categoryId value indicates that there is related data, but expecting a client application to make that distinction is problematic, especially if it is being developed by a different team of programmers. If you don't want to include related data properties, you can avoid confusion by using LINQ to project a result that excludes the foreign key and navigation properties from the result, as shown in Listing 10-7.

Listing 10-7. Excluding Properties in the WebServiceRepository.cs File in the Models Folder

```
using System.Linq;

namespace SportsStore.Models {

    public class WebServiceRepository : IWebServiceRepository {
        private DataContext context;

        public WebServiceRepository(DataContext ctx) => context = ctx;

        public object GetProduct(long id) {
            return context.Products
                .Select(p => new { Id = p.Id, Name = p.Name,
                    Description = p.Description, PurchasePrice = p.PurchasePrice,
                    RetailPrice = p.RetailPrice})
                .FirstOrDefault(p => p.Id == id);
        }
    }
}
```

I use the LINQ Select method to pick the properties that I want included in the result and use the FirstOrDefault method to select the object with the specified primary key value. Restart the application using dotnet run and use a separate PowerShell window to execute the command shown in Listing 10-8.

Listing 10-8. Requesting a Product Object

```
Invoke-RestMethod http://localhost:5000/api/products/1 -Method GET | ConvertTo-Json
```

The result from this request is the following JSON data, which excludes the related data properties:

```
{
 "id":1,
 "name":"Kayak",
 "description":"A boat for one person",
 "purchasePrice":200.00,
 "retailPrice":275.00
}
```

If you examine the logging messages generated by the application, you will see that Entity Framework Core has requested only the specified properties from the database.

```
...
SELECT TOP(1) [p].[Id], [p].[Name], [p].[Description], [p].[PurchasePrice],
    [p].[RetailPrice]
FROM [Products] AS [p]
WHERE [p].[Id] = @__id_0
...
```

Including Related Data in a Web Service Response

Care is required if you want to include related data in a web service response. To demonstrate the problem, I have changed the query used by the repository so that it uses the Include method to select the Category object with which the Product object is associated, as shown in Listing 10-9.

Listing 10-9. Including Related Data in the WebServiceRepository.cs File in the Models Folder

```
using System.Linq;
using Microsoft.EntityFrameworkCore;

namespace SportsStore.Models {

    public class WebServiceRepository : IWebServiceRepository {
        private DataContext context;

        public WebServiceRepository(DataContext ctx) => context = ctx;

        public object GetProduct(long id) {
            return context.Products.Include(p => p.Category)
                .FirstOrDefault(p => p.Id == id);
        }
    }
}
```

To see the problem that this code hides, start the application using dotnet run and use a separate PowerShell window to execute the command shown in Listing 10-10.

Listing 10-10. Requesting Related Data

```
Invoke-RestMethod http://localhost:5000/api/products/1 -Method GET | ConvertTo-Json
```

Instead of JSON data, you will see the following error message:

```
Invoke-RestMethod : Unable to read data from the transport connection: The connection was closed.
```

ASP.NET Core MVC uses a package called Json.NET to deal with serialization, and a configuration change is required to reveal the cause of the error, as shown in Listing 10-11.

Listing 10-11. Changing the Serializer Configuration in the Startup.cs File in the SportsStore Folder

```
using System;
using System.Collections.Generic;
using System.Linq;
using System.Threading.Tasks;
using Microsoft.AspNetCore.Builder;
using Microsoft.AspNetCore.Hosting;
using Microsoft.AspNetCore.Http;
using Microsoft.Extensions.DependencyInjection;
using SportsStore.Models;
using Microsoft.EntityFrameworkCore;
using Microsoft.Extensions.Configuration;
using Newtonsoft.Json;
```

```
namespace SportsStore {
    public class Startup {

        public Startup(IConfiguration config) => Configuration = config;

        public IConfiguration Configuration { get; }

        public void ConfigureServices(IServiceCollection services) {
            services.AddMvc().AddJsonOptions(opts =>
                opts.SerializerSettings.ReferenceLoopHandling
                    = ReferenceLoopHandling.Serialize);
            services.AddTransient<IRepository, DataRepository>();
            services.AddTransient<ICategoryRepository, CategoryRepository>();
            services.AddTransient<IOrdersRepository, OrdersRepository>();
            services.AddTransient<IWebServiceRepository, WebServiceRepository>();
            string conString = Configuration["ConnectionStrings:DefaultConnection"];
            services.AddDbContext<DataContext>(options =>
                options.UseSqlServer(conString));

            services.AddDistributedSqlServerCache(options => {
                options.ConnectionString = conString;
                options.SchemaName = "dbo";
                options.TableName = "SessionData";
            });
            services.AddSession(options => {
                options.Cookie.Name = "SportsStore.Session";
                options.IdleTimeout = System.TimeSpan.FromHours(48);
                options.Cookie.HttpOnly = false;
            });
        }

        public void Configure(IApplicationBuilder app, IHostingEnvironment env) {
            app.UseDeveloperExceptionPage();
            app.UseStatusCodePages();
            app.UseStaticFiles();
            app.UseSession();
            app.UseMvcWithDefaultRoute();
        }
    }
}
```

Restart the application using dotnet run. Rather than use PowerShell, open a new browser window and request the http://localhost:5000/api/products/1 URL. When the browser requests the data, you will see that the application reports the following error and exits:

```
...
Process is terminating due to StackOverflowException
...
```

The content displayed by the browser reveals what has happened. Even though the URL you requested targeted a single Product object and its related Category, a lot of data was sent by the application before it crashed.

```
...
{"id":1,"name":"Kayak","description":"A boat for one person",
    "purchasePrice":200.00,"retailPrice":275.00,"categoryId":1,
    "category": {"id":1,"name":"Watersports",
        "description":"Make a splash",
        "products":[{"id":1,"name":"Kayak",
            "description":"A boat for one person",
            "purchasePrice":200.00,"retailPrice":275.00,
            "categoryId":1,
            "category":{"id":1,"name":"Watersports",
                "description":"Make a splash",
                "products":[{"id":1,"name":"Kayak","description":"A boat for one
...
```

There is an endless loop where the Category navigation property of the Product object points to its related Category object, whose Products navigation property includes the Product object and so on. This is caused by an Entity Framework Core feature called *fixing up*, in which objects that have been received from the database are used as the values for navigation properties. I describe the fixing up process in detail in Chapter 14 and explain when it can be useful, but for RESTful web services, this feature causes problems because the JSON serializer just keeps following the navigation properties until the application encounters a stack overflow. The configuration change in Listing 10-11 tells the JSON serializer to keep following references even when it has already serialized an object. The default behavior is to throw an exception when a loop is detected, which is what caused the error in Listing 10-10.

Avoiding Circular References in Related Data

There is no way to disable the fixing up feature, so the best solution for avoiding endless loops of related data is to set the navigation property to null before it reaches the JSON serializer to create a dynamic type so that there are no null values included in the result, which is the approach that I have taken in Listing 10-12.

Listing 10-12. Avoiding an Endless Loop in the WebServiceRepository.cs File in the Models Folder

```
using System.Linq;
using Microsoft.EntityFrameworkCore;

namespace SportsStore.Models {

    public class WebServiceRepository : IWebServiceRepository {
        private DataContext context;

        public WebServiceRepository(DataContext ctx) => context = ctx;

        public object GetProduct(long id) {
            return context.Products.Include(p => p.Category)
                .Select(p => new {
                    Id = p.Id, Name = p.Name, PurchasePrice = p.PurchasePrice,
                    Description = p.Description, RetailPrice = p.RetailPrice,
                    CategoryId = p.CategoryId,
                    Category = new {
                        Id = p.Category.Id,
                        Name = p.Category.Name,
                        Description = p.Category.Description
```

```
            }
        })
        .FirstOrDefault(p => p.Id == id);
    }
}
}
```

Start the application using `dotnet run` and use a separate PowerShell window to execute the command shown in Listing 10-13.

Listing 10-13. Requesting Related Data

```
Invoke-RestMethod http://localhost:5000/api/products/1 -Method GET | ConvertTo-Json
```

The command produces the following JSON result, which includes all of the related data but doesn't contain a circular reference:

```
...
{
    "id":  1,
    "name":  "Kayak",
    "purchasePrice":  200.00,
    "description":  "A boat for one person",
    "retailPrice":  275.00,
    "categoryId":  1,
    "category":
    {
      "id":  1,
      "name":  "Watersports",
      "description":  "Make a splash"
    }
}
...
```

Querying for Multiple Objects

When handling queries for multiple objects, it is important to restrict the amount of data you send to the client application. If you simply return all of the objects in the database, then you will drive up the cost of running your application and may even overwhelm the client application. In Listing 10-14, I have added a method to the web service repository interface that allows a client to specify a start index for the results and the number of objects they require.

Listing 10-14. Adding a Method in the IWebServiceRepository.cs File in the Models Folder

```
namespace SportsStore.Models {

    public interface IWebServiceRepository {

        object GetProduct(long id);

        object GetProducts(int skip, int take);
    }
}
```

195

In Listing 10-15, I have added the method in the implementation class and used the technique from the previous section to avoid circular references with the related data.

Listing 10-15. Adding a Method in the WebServiceRepository.cs File in the Models Folder

```
using System.Linq;
using Microsoft.EntityFrameworkCore;

namespace SportsStore.Models {

    public class WebServiceRepository : IWebServiceRepository {
        private DataContext context;

        public WebServiceRepository(DataContext ctx) => context = ctx;

        public object GetProduct(long id) {
            return context.Products.Include(p => p.Category)
                .Select(p => new {
                    Id = p.Id, Name = p.Name, PurchasePrice = p.PurchasePrice,
                    Description = p.Description, RetailPrice = p.RetailPrice,
                    CategoryId = p.CategoryId,
                    Category = new {
                        Id = p.Category.Id,
                        Name = p.Category.Name,
                        Description = p.Category.Description
                    }
                })
                .FirstOrDefault(p => p.Id == id);
        }

        public object GetProducts(int skip, int take) {
            return context.Products.Include(p => p.Category)
                .OrderBy(p => p.Id)
                .Skip(skip)
                .Take(take)
                .Select(p => new {
                    Id = p.Id, Name = p.Name, PurchasePrice = p.PurchasePrice,
                    Description = p.Description, RetailPrice = p.RetailPrice,
                    CategoryId = p.CategoryId,
                    Category = new {
                        Id = p.Category.Id,
                        Name = p.Category.Name,
                        Description = p.Category.Description
                    }
                });
        }
    }
}
```

In Listing 10-16, I have added an action to the web service controller that allows clients to request multiple objects.

Listing 10-16. Adding an Action in the ProductValuesController.cs File in the Controllers Folder

```
using Microsoft.AspNetCore.Mvc;
using SportsStore.Models;

namespace SportsStore.Controllers {

    [Route("api/products")]
    public class ProductValuesController : Controller {
        private IWebServiceRepository repository;

        public ProductValuesController(IWebServiceRepository repo)
            => repository = repo;

        [HttpGet("{id}")]
        public object GetProduct(long id) {
            return repository.GetProduct(id) ?? NotFound();
        }

        [HttpGet]
        public object Products(int skip, int take) {
            return repository.GetProducts(skip, take);
        }
    }
}
```

To test the new action method, start the application using dotnet run and use a separate PowerShell window to execute the command shown in Listing 10-17.

Listing 10-17. Querying for Multiple Objects

```
Invoke-RestMethod http://localhost:5000/api/products?skip=2"&"take=2 -Method GET | ConvertTo-Json
```

The HTTP requests asks the web service to skip the first two objects and then return the next two, which produces the following results:

```
...
{
  "value": [
    {
      "id": 3,
      "name": "Soccer Ball",
      "purchasePrice": 18.00,
      "description": "FIFA-approved size and weight",
      "retailPrice": 19.50,
      "categoryId": 2,
      "category": {
        "id": 2,
        "name": "Soccer",
        "description": "The World\u0027s Favorite Game"
      }
    },
    {
```

```
    "id":  4,
    "name":  "Corner Flags",
    "purchasePrice":  32.50,
    "description":  "Give your playing field a professional touch",
    "retailPrice":  34.95,
    "categoryId":  2,
    "category":  {
      "id":  2,
      "name":  "Soccer",
      "description":  "The World\u0027s Favorite Game"
    }
  }],
  "Count":  2
}
...
```

Completing the Web Service

The complexity in a web service that uses Entity Framework Core data is in the serialization of responses, as described in the previous section. The other standard data operations follow the same pattern as shown in earlier chapters. In Listing 10-18, I have added methods to the repository to allow objects to be stored, updated, and deleted.

Listing 10-18. Adding Methods in the IWebServiceRepository.cs File in the Models Folder

```
namespace SportsStore.Models {

    public interface IWebServiceRepository {

        object GetProduct(long id);

        object GetProducts(int skip, int take);

        long StoreProduct(Product product);

        void UpdateProduct(Product product);

        void DeleteProduct(long id);
    }
}
```

In Listing 10-19, I have added the new methods to the repository implementation class.

Listing 10-19. Adding Methods in the WebServiceRepository.cs File in the Models Folder

```
using System.Linq;
using Microsoft.EntityFrameworkCore;

namespace SportsStore.Models {

    public class WebServiceRepository : IWebServiceRepository {
        private DataContext context;
```

```
    public WebServiceRepository(DataContext ctx) => context = ctx;

    public object GetProduct(long id) {
        return context.Products.Include(p => p.Category)
            .Select(p => new {
                Id = p.Id, Name = p.Name, PurchasePrice = p.PurchasePrice,
                Description = p.Description, RetailPrice = p.RetailPrice,
                CategoryId = p.CategoryId,
                Category = new {
                    Id = p.Category.Id,
                    Name = p.Category.Name,
                    Description = p.Category.Description
                }
            })
            .FirstOrDefault(p => p.Id == id);
    }

    public object GetProducts(int skip, int take) {
        return context.Products.Include(p => p.Category)
            .OrderBy(p => p.Id)
            .Skip(skip)
            .Take(take)
            .Select(p => new {
                Id = p.Id, Name = p.Name, PurchasePrice = p.PurchasePrice,
                Description = p.Description, RetailPrice = p.RetailPrice,
                CategoryId = p.CategoryId,
                Category = new {
                    Id = p.Category.Id,
                    Name = p.Category.Name,
                    Description = p.Category.Description
                }
            });
    }

    public long StoreProduct(Product product) {
        context.Products.Add(product);
        context.SaveChanges();
        return product.Id;
    }

    public void UpdateProduct(Product product) {
        context.Products.Update(product);
        context.SaveChanges();
    }

    public void DeleteProduct(long id) {
        context.Products.Remove(new Product { Id = id });
        context.SaveChanges();
    }
}
}
```

Notice that the StoreProduct methods return the primary key value assigned to the Product object by the database server. Client-side applications often keep their own data model, and it is important to ensure they have the information they require to perform subsequent operations without needing to perform additional queries.

Updating the Controller

In Listing 10-20, I have updated the web service controller to add actions that correspond to the new repository methods.

Listing 10-20. Adding Actions in the ProductValuesController.cs File in the Controllers Folder

```
using Microsoft.AspNetCore.Mvc;
using SportsStore.Models;

namespace SportsStore.Controllers {

    [Route("api/products")]
    public class ProductValuesController : Controller {
        private IWebServiceRepository repository;

        public ProductValuesController(IWebServiceRepository repo)
            => repository = repo;

        [HttpGet("{id}")]
        public object GetProduct(long id) {
            return repository.GetProduct(id) ?? NotFound();
        }

        [HttpGet]
        public object Products(int skip, int take) {
            return repository.GetProducts(skip, take);
        }

        [HttpPost]
        public long StoreProduct([FromBody] Product product) {
            return repository.StoreProduct(product);
        }

        [HttpPut]
        public void UpdateProduct([FromBody] Product product) {
            repository.UpdateProduct(product);
        }

        [HttpDelete("{id}")]
        public void DeleteProduct(long id) {
            repository.DeleteProduct(id);
        }
    }
}
```

To test storing a new object, start the application using `dotnet run` and use a separate PowerShell window to execute the command shown in Listing 10-21.

Listing 10-21. Storing New Data

```
Invoke-RestMethod http://localhost:5000/api/products -Method POST -Body (@{Name="Scuba
Mask"; Description="Spy on the Fish"; PurchasePrice=21; RetailPrice=40;CategoryId=1} |
ConvertTo-Json) -ContentType "application/json"
```

This command is awkward to type in, but it sends an HTTP POST request to the server with values for all of the properties that are needed to store a `Product` object in the database. Once the command has completed, use a browser window to navigate to `http://localhost:5000` and you will see the new object, as shown in Figure 10-2.

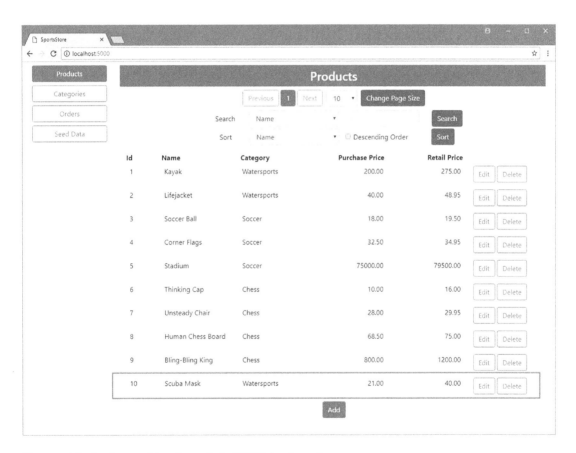

Figure 10-2. *Storing an object through the RESTful web service*

To test the update feature, use a PowerShell window to run the command shown in Listing 10-22, which modifies the Kayak product.

Listing 10-22. Modifying Data

```
Invoke-RestMethod http://localhost:5000/api/products -Method PUT -Body (@{Id=1;Name="Green
Kayak"; Description="A Tiny Boat"; PurchasePrice=200; RetailPrice=300;CategoryId=1} |
ConvertTo-Json) -ContentType "application/json"
```

Reload the browser window, and you will see that the RetailPrice value for the Kayak product has been changed to 300, and its name is now Green Kayak.

To test the ability to delete data, use a PowerShell window to run the command shown in Listing 10-23.

Listing 10-23. Deleting an Object

```
Invoke-RestMethod http://localhost:5000/api/products/1 -Method DELETE
```

Common Problems and Solutions

Most problems with web services are related to the serialization issues I described earlier in the chapter. There are some less common issues, however, and I describe them in the sections that follow.

Null Property Values When Storing or Updating Objects

If the object created by the MVC model binder has null or zero values for some of its properties, then the most likely cause is that you omitted the FromBody attribute from the action method parameter. Only the URL is used for values by default, and you must explicitly select the source of data when you want the MVC framework to use other parts of the request.

Slow Web Service Requests

The most common cause of slow requests is enumerating an IQueryable<T> object and accidentally triggering a query. This is easily done if you are processing data prior to JSON serialization, and it is important to remember that an IQueryable<T> object will query the database wherever it is enumerated and not just in Razor views.

The "Cannot Insert Explicit Value for Identity Column" Exception

If you receive this exception when writing a web service, then the most likely cause is that the client has included a primary key value in an object that is to be stored in the database. If you are writing the client application, then you can ensure the HTTP request doesn't include a value. If your web service is being used by a third-party application, then you can explicitly zero the primary key property in your action method before asking Entity Framework Core to store the data.

Summary

In this chapter, I completed the SportsStore application by adding a simple RESTful web service that can be used to provide client-side applications with data. I showed you the common problems that working with related data can cause and showed you how to avoid them by creating dynamic types. In the next part of the book, I start to describe the Entity Framework Core features in more depth.

PART II

Entity Framework Core 2 in Detail

In Part 2 of this book, I dig into the details. I start with an exploration of the basic data operations that Entity Framework Core supports and explain how databases are managed and how relationships between objects are handled. I also demonstrate the different ways that Entity Framework Core can be used with existing databases.

CHAPTER 11

Working with Entity Framework Core

In this chapter, I explain how Entity Framework Core is applied to an ASP.NET Core MVC project, starting with the addition of NuGet packages and working through the creation of a basic data model, a database schema, and the infrastructure to use it. The project created in this chapter sets the foundation for those that follow, which add Entity Framework Core features. Table 11-1 summarizes the chapter.

Table 11-1. *Chapter Summary*

Problem	Solution	Listing
Enable the EF Core command-line tools	Add an entry to the `.csproj` file using a `DotNetCliToolReference` element	10
Provide an application with access to EF Core features	Create a database context class	11
Prepare a data model class for database storage	Ensure that all of the properties have get and set clauses and add a primary key property	12
Provide EF Core with details of the database it should use	Define a connection string	14
Prepare a database for use with EF Core	Create and apply a database migration	17
Ensure that queries are processed by the database	Use the `IQueryable<T>` interface	24–26
Avoid duplicate queries	Force queries to be executed before enumerating the results	27, 28

© Adam Freeman 2018
A. Freeman, *Pro Entity Framework Core 2 for ASP.NET Core MVC*,
https://doi.org/10.1007/978-1-4842-3435-8_11

Creating the ASP.NET Core MVC Project

For this chapter, I am going to create a project with just the minimum content required by ASP.NET Core. I will then add the packages, classes, and configuration components to create an MVC application that uses Entity Framework Core.

To create the project, select New ➤ Project from the Visual Studio File menu and use the ASP.NET Core Web Application template to create a new project called DataApp, as shown in Figure 11-1.

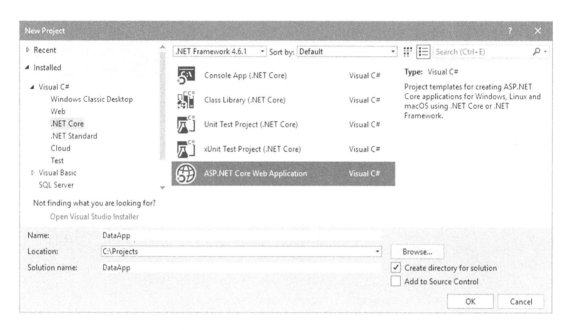

Figure 11-1. *Creating a new application*

Click the OK button to move to the next dialog window. Ensure that ASP.NET Core 2.0 is selected from the list and click the Empty template, as shown in Figure 11-2. Click OK to close the dialog window and create the project.

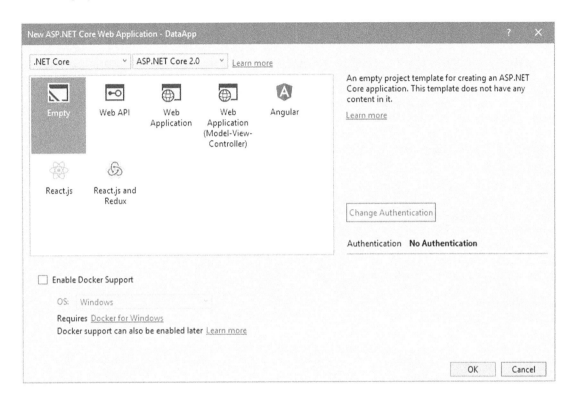

Figure 11-2. *Configuring the project*

Creating the Data Model Class

The data model in an MVC application is defined using regular C# classes, conventionally defined in a folder called Models. Entity Framework Core doesn't have any special requirements for the location of the data model classes and will happily work with the MVC convention.

To add a data model class to the example project, create the Models folder and add to it a C# file called Product.cs with the code shown in Listing 11-1.

Listing 11-1. The Contents of the Product.cs File in the Models Folder

```
namespace DataApp.Models {

    public class Product {

        public string Name { get; set; }
        public string Category { get; set; }
        public decimal Price { get; set; }
    }
}
```

Data model classes tend to be simple collections of properties, which makes them easy to work with and ensures they can be represented in formats such as JSON, which is often used by HTTP web services, as demonstrated in Chapter 10. The Product class in Listing 11-1 defines Name, Category, and Price properties and is a simplification of the data model from the SportsStore example in Part 1. I'll add more complexity to the data model in later chapters, but this is enough to get started.

Configuring Services and Middleware

The Empty template creates a basic ASP.NET Core project that requires additional configuration to enable the MVC framework. Add the statements shown in Listing 11-2 to the Startup class to enable the MVC framework and middleware components that are useful for development.

Listing 11-2. Enabling Services and Middleware in the Startup.cs File in the DataApp Folder

```
using System;
using System.Collections.Generic;
using System.Linq;
using System.Threading.Tasks;
using Microsoft.AspNetCore.Builder;
using Microsoft.AspNetCore.Hosting;
using Microsoft.AspNetCore.Http;
using Microsoft.Extensions.DependencyInjection;

namespace DataApp {
    public class Startup {

        public void ConfigureServices(IServiceCollection services) {
            services.AddMvc();
        }

        public void Configure(IApplicationBuilder app, IHostingEnvironment env) {
            app.UseDeveloperExceptionPage();
            app.UseStatusCodePages();
            app.UseStaticFiles();
            app.UseMvcWithDefaultRoute();
        }
    }
}
```

These changes enable developer-friendly error messages, add support for static content (such as HTML and CSS files), and set up the MVC framework with the default routing configuration.

Adding a Controller and View

Now that the MVC framework has been enabled, I can create a controller and a view to handle HTTP requests. Create a Controllers folder and add to it a C# class file called HomeController.cs with the code shown in Listing 11-3.

Listing 11-3. The Content of the HomeController.cs File in the Controllers Folder

```
using Microsoft.AspNetCore.Mvc;
using DataApp.Models;

namespace DataApp.Controllers {
    public class HomeController : Controller {

        public IActionResult Index() {
            return View(new Product[] {
                new Product { Name = "P1", Category = "Cat1", Price = 10 },
                new Product { Name = "P2", Category = "Cat2", Price = 20 },
                new Product { Name = "P3", Category = "Cat3", Price = 30 },
            });
        }
    }
}
```

There is one action method in this controller, named Index, and it creates a collection of placeholder Product objects that is passed as the view model objects to the default view. These static objects will be replaced later in the chapter when the database and Entity Framework Core are up and running.

To provide a consistent layout for the application, create a folder called Views/Shared and add a Razor layout page called _Layout.cshtml with the content shown in Listing 11-4.

Listing 11-4. The Content of the _Layout.cshtml File in the Views/Shared Folder

```
<!DOCTYPE html>
<html>
<head>
    <meta name="viewport" content="width=device-width" />
    <title>@ViewData["Title"]</title>
    <link rel="stylesheet" href="~/lib/bootstrap/dist/css/bootstrap.min.css" />
</head>
<body>
    <div class="p-2">
        <h4 class="bg-primary text-center p-2 text-white">@ViewData["Title"]</h4>
        @RenderBody()
    </div>
</body>
</html>
```

To create the view for the `Index` action method on the `Home` controller, create the `Views/Home` folder and add to it a Razor view called `Index.cshtml` with the content shown in Listing 11-5.

Listing 11-5. The Contents of the Index.cshtml File in the Views/Home Folder

```
@model IEnumerable<Product>
@{
    ViewData["Title"] = "Products";
    Layout = "_Layout";
}

<table class="table table-sm table-striped">
    <thead>
        <tr><th>Name</th><th>Category</th><th>Price</th></tr>
    </thead>
    <tbody>
        @foreach (var p in Model) {
            <tr>
                <td>@p.Name</td>
                <td>@p.Category</td>
                <td>$@p.Price.ToString("F2")</td>
            </tr>
        }
    </tbody>
</table>
```

The view uses the collection of `Product` objects it receives from the controller as its view model to generate rows in an HTML table, displaying the value of the Name, `Category`, and `Price` properties.

To enable tag helpers, I created a view imports page called `_ViewImports.cshtml` in the `Views` folder and added the statements shown in Listing 11-6.

Listing 11-6. The Contents of the _ViewImports.cshtml File in the Views Folder

```
@using DataApp.Models
@addTagHelper *, Microsoft.AspNetCore.Mvc.TagHelpers
```

Adding the Bootstrap CSS Framework

The layout file you created in Listing 11-4 includes a `link` element for the CSS stylesheet from the Bootstrap framework, which I use to style the HTML content throughout this book. To add Bootstrap to the project, right-click the DataApp item in the Solution Explorer, select Add ➤ New Item from the pop-up menu, and use the the JSON File template (found in the ASP.NET Core ➤ Web ➤ General category) to create a file called `.bowerrc` with the content shown in Listing 11-7. (It is important to pay attention to this file name: it starts with a period, contains the letter r twice and has no file extension).

Listing 11-7. The Contents of the .bowerrc File in the DataApp Folder

```
{
  "directory": "wwwroot/lib"
}
```

Use the JSON File template once again to create a file called `bower.json`, with the content shown in Listing 11-8.

Listing 11-8. The Contents of the bower.json File in the DataApp Folder

```
{
  "name": "asp.net",
  "private": true,
  "dependencies": {
    "bootstrap": "4.0.0"
  }
}
```

When you save the changes to the file, Visual Studio will download the new version of the Bootstrap package and install it in the `wwwroot/lib` folder.

Configuring the HTTP Port

Changing the port that will be used by ASP.NET Core to receive requests will make the examples easier to follow. Edit the `launchSettings.json` file in the `Properties` folder and change the URLs as shown in Listing 11-9.

Listing 11-9. Changing the HTTP Ports in the launchSettings.json File in the Properties Folder

```
{
  "iisSettings": {
    "windowsAuthentication": false,
    "anonymousAuthentication": true,
    "iisExpress": {
      "applicationUrl": "http://localhost:5000/",
      "sslPort": 0
    }
  },
  "profiles": {
    "IIS Express": {
      "commandName": "IISExpress",
      "launchBrowser": true,
      "environmentVariables": {
        "ASPNETCORE_ENVIRONMENT": "Development"
      }
    },
    "DataApp": {
      "commandName": "Project",
      "launchBrowser": true,
      "environmentVariables": {
        "ASPNETCORE_ENVIRONMENT": "Development"
      },
      "applicationUrl": "http://localhost:5000/"
    }
  }
}
```

The URLs in this file are used to configure the application when it is started using IIS Express and when it is run from the command line. The examples in this book are run from the command line so that logging messages can easily be seen.

Running the Example Application

Working with Entity Framework Core requires a lot more command line work than you may be used to, which means that starting the application from the command line can often be the most natural way to work, especially since it provides easy access to useful logging messages. Open a command prompt or PowerShell window, navigate to the DataApp project folder (the one that contains the Startup.cs class file), and run the command shown in Listing 11-10.

Listing 11-10. Testing the Example Application

```
dotnet run
```

Open a new browser window and navigate to http://localhost:5000 and you will see the response shown in Figure 11-3. Once you have confirmed that the application is running correctly, use Control+C to stop it.

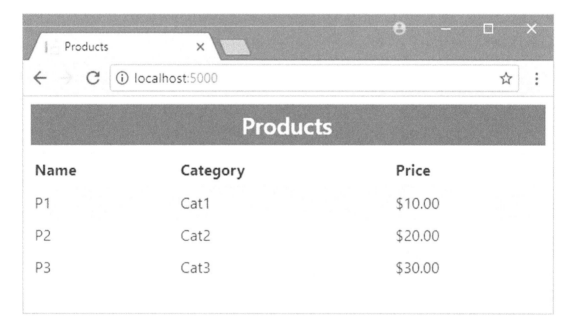

Figure 11-3. *Testing the example application*

Adding and Configuring Entity Framework Core

Now that there is a basic ASP.NET Core MVC application to work with, it is time to configure Entity Framework Core so that it is able to store and retrieve data on behalf of the MVC application.

Adding the NuGet Package

The project created by Visual Studio is configured to use the ASP.NET Core meta-package, which was introduced with ASP.NET Core 2. A single NuGet package provides access to all of the individual packages required to start development on a project, including ASP.NET Core, the MVC framework, and Entity Framework Core, which is in contrast to earlier releases that required a long list of NuGet packages to be manually added before development could begin.

As useful as the meta-package can be, one addition is still required for projects that use Entity Framework Core. Many important Entity Framework Core operations are performed using command-line tools, and the NuGet package that provides the command-line features is not part of the meta-package and must be installed manually.

Listing 11-11 shows the addition of the tools package to the DataApp.csproj file, which you can access by right-clicking the DataApp project item in the Solution Explorer and selecting Edit DataApp.csproj from the pop-up menu.

Listing 11-11. Adding the Tools Package in the DataApp.csproj File in the DataApp Folder

```
<Project Sdk="Microsoft.NET.Sdk.Web">

  <PropertyGroup>
    <TargetFramework>netcoreapp2.0</TargetFramework>
  </PropertyGroup>

  <ItemGroup>
    <Folder Include="wwwroot\" />
  </ItemGroup>

  <ItemGroup>
    <PackageReference Include="Microsoft.AspNetCore.All" Version="2.0.5" />
    <DotNetCliToolReference Include="Microsoft.EntityFrameworkCore.Tools.DotNet"
        Version="2.0.0" />
  </ItemGroup>

</Project>
```

This package is added using a DotNetCliToolReference element rather than the PackageReference used for regular packages. The DotNetCliToolReference element is used to add command-line tool packages to a project and isn't supported by the regular NuGet tools and is the reason that the file must be added manually. When you save the change to the csproj file, Visual Studio will download the package and add it to the project.

Creating the Database Context Class

A database context class provides Entity Framework Core with details of the data model classes whose instances will be stored in the database. The context class is one of the most important components for working with Entity Framework Core. To create the context class, add a class file called EFDatabaseContext.cs in the DataApp/Models folder with the code shown in Listing 11-12.

Listing 11-12. The Contents of the EFDatabaseContext.cs File in the Models Folder

```
using Microsoft.EntityFrameworkCore;
using Microsoft.EntityFrameworkCore.Design;
using Microsoft.Extensions.DependencyInjection;

namespace DataApp.Models {
    public class EFDatabaseContext : DbContext {

        public EFDatabaseContext(DbContextOptions<EFDatabaseContext> opts)
            : base(opts) { }

        public DbSet<Product> Products { get; set; }
    }
}
```

The constructor for the EFDatabaseContext class accepts a DbContextOptions object, which is used to configure Entity Framework Core. For ASP.NET Core MVC applications, this configuration is performed in the Startup class, as demonstrated later in this chapter, and so the constructor simply passes on the options object to the base class.

░ **Tip**   The context class must define a constructor, even though it does not contain any code statements. You will receive an error if you create a context class without the constructor.

Database context classes tell Entity Framework Core which data model classes are to be stored in the database by defining properties that return DbSet<T>, where the type parameter, T, specifies the data model class.

Preparing the Entity Class

Entity Framework Core needs to be able to uniquely identify Product objects so that they can be stored in the database and assigned a primary key. By default, Entity Framework Core looks for a property called Id or <Type>Id to use as the key, which means that for the Product class, the key property can be called Id or ProductId. To prepare the Product class for storage by Entity Framework Core, edit the Product class to add the property shown in Listing 11-13.

Listing 11-13. Adding a Key Property in the Product.cs File in the Models Folder

```
namespace DataApp.Models {

    public class Product {

        public long Id { get; set; }

        public string Name { get; set; }
        public string Category { get; set; }
        public decimal Price { get; set; }
    }
}
```

The type of the key property affects how it is handled by Entity Framework Core. For numeric types, such as int and long, the schema will be configured so that the database is responsible for generating the unique key value. This is useful for ASP.NET Core MVC applications where there can be multiple instances of the application sharing the same database and coordinating unique values can be complex. For other types, such as string, the property will still be used as a key, but the application is responsible for generating the values. I describe the advanced options for working with keys in Chapter 19.

Updating the Controller

To replace the static data with objects obtained using Entity Framework Core, open the HomeController.cs file and make the changes shown in Listing 11-14.

Listing 11-14. Using Real Data in the HomeController.cs File in the Controllers Folder

```
using Microsoft.AspNetCore.Mvc;
using DataApp.Models;

namespace DataApp.Controllers {
    public class HomeController : Controller {
        private EFDatabaseContext context;

        public HomeController(EFDatabaseContext ctx) {
            context = ctx;
        }

        public IActionResult Index() {
            return View(context.Products);
        }
    }
}
```

The controller's constructor will receive a context object, which will be provided by the ASP.NET Core dependency injection feature, providing the link between the MVC and Entity Framework Core parts of the application.

The job of the Index action method is to provide its view with a collection of Product objects to display. This collection is now obtained by reading the database context's Products property, which returns a DbSet<Product> object. The DbSet<Product> class implements the IEnumerable<Product> interface, which means that the Index.cshtml view can enumerate the sequence of Product objects without any changes. (However, as I explain in the "Avoiding the IEnumerable vs. IQueryable Pitfall" section, care must be taken with when using this interface.)

Configuring the Database Provider

Entity Framework Core isn't tied to any specific database server. Instead, all of the functionality that is required for a specific database server, such as MySQL or Microsoft SQL Server, is contained in a package called the *database provider*. This means that Entity Framework Core can be used with any database for which a provider is available. There are typically two steps required to configure the database provider: setting up the *connection string* so that the database provider knows how to communicate with the database server and configuring the application so that Entity Framework Core knows which database provider should be used for the context class and

A connection string gives a database provider the information it needs to connect to a specific database server. Each provider uses a different format of connection string, but they usually include the hostname and port required for the network connection, the user credentials required for authentication, and the name of the database that the application wants to use. Most projects use different instances of the database server so that the actions performed by developers are kept separate from real customer data, and this means that different connection strings will be required at different times. Configuration settings that change often are defined in the appsettings.json file so that they can be altered without needing to recompile the project, and this file is the usual home of connection strings in applications that use Entity Framework Core.

Defining the Connection String

Right-click the DataApp project item in the Solution Explorer, select Add ➤ New Item, and use the ASP.NET Configuration File item template to create a file called appsettings.json with the content shown in Listing 11-15.

■ **Caution** The connection string must be entered as a single unbroken line. The connection string is too long to show on a single line on the printed page, which is the cause of the awkward formatting in Listing 11-15. If in doubt, take a look at the appsettings.json file for this chapter on the GitHub repository for this book (https://github.com/apress/pro-ef-core-2-for-asp.net-core-mvc).

Listing 11-15. The Contents of the appsettings.json File in the DataApp Folder

```
{
  "ConnectionStrings": {
    "DefaultConnection": "Server=(localdb)\\MSSQLLocalDB;Database=DataAppDb;MultipleActive
    ResultSets=true"
  }
}
```

The connection string contains the details that will be used to connect to SQL Server. Each part of this connection string is described in Table 11-2.

■ **Note**   This connection string is simpler than most because it uses the configuration-free LocalDB feature, which is installed with Visual Studio. Connection strings for deployment database servers will be more complex and will usually include details of the hostname and TCP port for the network connection, along with credentials for authentication.

Table 11-2.   *The Elements of the Database Connection String*

Name	Description
Server	This setting specifies the hostname for the server. For the example, this is (localdb)\\MSSQLLocalDB because the database is accessed via the SQL Server LocalDB feature. For other types of database, the connection string will usually include the hostname and TCP port that should be used to connect to the database server.
Database	This setting specifies the name of the database. For the example, this is DataAppDb.
MultipleActiveResultSets	This setting determines whether a client can execute multiple active SQL statements on a single connection. For MVC applications, this is usually set to true because it avoids common exceptions when enumerating collections of data objects in Razor views.

Configuring the Application

You must configure the application so that Entity Framework Core knows which database provider you need and which connection string it should use to access the database. This is done in the Startup class, as shown in Listing 11-16.

Listing 11-16.   Configuring the Database Provider in the Startup.cs File in the DataApp Folder

```
using System;
using System.Collections.Generic;
using System.Linq;
using System.Threading.Tasks;
using Microsoft.AspNetCore.Builder;
using Microsoft.AspNetCore.Hosting;
using Microsoft.AspNetCore.Http;
using Microsoft.Extensions.DependencyInjection;
using DataApp.Models;
using Microsoft.EntityFrameworkCore;
using Microsoft.Extensions.Configuration;
```

```
namespace DataApp {
    public class Startup {

        public Startup(IConfiguration config) => Configuration = config;

        public IConfiguration Configuration { get; }

        public void ConfigureServices(IServiceCollection services) {
            services.AddMvc();
            string conString = Configuration["ConnectionStrings:DefaultConnection"];
            services.AddDbContext<EFDatabaseContext>(options =>
                options.UseSqlServer(conString));
        }

        public void Configure(IApplicationBuilder app, IHostingEnvironment env) {
            app.UseDeveloperExceptionPage();
            app.UseStatusCodePages();
            app.UseStaticFiles();
            app.UseMvcWithDefaultRoute();
        }
    }
}
```

ASP.NET Core automatically loads the contents of the appsettings.json file when the application starts and makes the configuration settings it contains, including connection strings, available through the IConfiguaton interface. In Listing 11-16 the constructor receives the IConfiguraton object and assigns it to a property called Configuration, which is then used in the ConfigureServices method to configure Entity Framework Core.

The configuration of Entity Framework Core is done in the ConfigureServices method, starting with getting the connection string from the configuration data. I have used the most direct approach to get the connection string, which is to use an array-style indexer to specify the name of the configuration property in a single string. The sections of the string represent the structure in the appsettings.json file so that ConnectionStrings:DefaultConnection corresponds to the DefaultConnection property in the ConnectionStrings section of the appsettings.json file, like this:

```
...
string conString = Configuration["ConnectionStrings:DefaultConnection"];
...
```

Once I have the connection string, I configure the database provider and associate it with the database context class using the AddDbContext extension method. The type parameter for the AddDbContext method specifies the context class, and the method receives a DbContextOptionsBuilder object that is used to select and configure the database provider, like this:

```
...
services.AddDbContext<EFDatabaseContext>(options => options.UseSqlServer(conString));
...
```

This statement identifies the EFDatabaseContext class for Entity Framework Core. The UseSqlServer method selects the database provider for SQL Server and tells it to connect to the database using the connection string read from the appsettings.json file.

Configuring Entity Framework Core Logging

Many of the examples in this book rely on understanding how C# statements in the application are translated into SQL queries that are sent to the database. To configure the ASP.NET Core logging system so that it will display useful messages from Entity Framework Core, make the additions to the `appsettings.json` file shown in Listing 11-17.

Listing 11-17. Enabling EF Core Logging in the appsettings.json File in the DataApp Folder

```
{
  "ConnectionStrings": {
    "DefaultConnection": "Server=(localdb)\\MSSQLLocalDB;Database=DataAppDb;MultipleActiveR
esultSets=true"
  },
  "Logging": {
    "LogLevel": {
      "Default": "None",
      "Microsoft.EntityFrameworkCore": "Information"
    }
  }
}
```

The logging system is configured as part of the ASP.NET Core initialization process performed by the Program class. The logging system reads the `Logging:LogLevel` configuration data and uses it to select the log messages that will be displayed. The logging configuration in Listing 11-17 selects `Information`-level messages from the `Microsoft.EntityFrameworkCore` namespace, which will include details of the SQL queries sent from the application to the database server. Logging messages from other namespaces are disabled.

Generating and Applying the Migration

Entity Framework Core uses migrations to create or modify the database so that it can be used to store the application's data. Use a command prompt or PowerShell window to run the commands shown in Listing 11-18 in the DataApp folder. The first command creates a new migration that contains the commands that will create the schema. The second command applies the migration to the database.

■ **Tip**   If you receive a "build failed" message when you run the commands in Listing 11-18, the likely cause is that the application is still running. Stop the application, wait a moment, and then run the commands to create and apply the migration again.

Listing 11-18. Creating and Applying the Database Migration

```
dotnet ef migrations add Initial
dotnet ef database update
```

I explain how migrations work in detail in Chapter 13, but the combined effect of these commands is to create the DataAppDb database, with a table called Products that has Id, Name, Category, and Price columns that correspond to the properties defined by the Product entity class.

The logging configuration created in Listing 11-17 ensures that you will see the SQL commands that are sent to the database by the dotnet ef database update command as it applies the migration. The most important part shows you how the migration has created a new table Products, like this:

```
...
CREATE TABLE [Products] (
    [Id] bigint NOT NULL IDENTITY,
    [Category] nvarchar(max) NULL,
    [Name] nvarchar(max) NULL,
    [Price] decimal(18, 2) NOT NULL,
    CONSTRAINT [PK_Products] PRIMARY KEY ([Id])
);
...
```

You can see that the SQL CREATE TABLE command creates columns in the Products table that correspond to the properties defined by the Product model class. This is how Entity Framework Core stores application data: .NET objects are stored as rows in a table with the value of each property being stored in its own column. Entity Framework Core does a lot more, of course, but as long as you keep the object-to-table-row mapping in mind, everything else will be a little easier to understand.

The migration also created a table called __EFMigrationsHistory that Entity Framework Core uses to keep track of which migrations have been applied, but it is the Products table that is important for the example application because it will be used to store Product objects.

Populating the Database

To populate the database with some initial data, select Tools ➤ SQL Server ➤ New Query and enter **(localdb)\MSSQLLocalDB** in the Server Name field. (Note that there is one \ character in this string, rather than the two that are required to define the connection string in the appsettings.json file.)

Ensure that Windows Authentication is selected for the Authentication field and click the Database Name menu to select DataAppDb from the drop-down list, which will display a complete list of the databases that have been created using LocalDB. Click Connect and enter the contents of Listing 11-19 into the editor.

Listing 11-19. Seeding the Database

```
USE DataAppDb

INSERT INTO Products (Name, Category, Price) VALUES
    ( 'Kayak', 'Watersports', 275),
    ( 'Lifejacket', 'Watersports', 48.95),
    ( 'Soccer Ball', 'Soccer', 19.50),
    ( 'Corner Flags', 'Soccer', 34.95),
    ( 'Stadium', 'Soccer', 79500),
    ( 'Thinking Cap', 'Chess', 16),
    ( 'Unsteady Chair', 'Chess', 29.95),
    ( 'Human Chess Board', 'Chess', 75),
    ( 'Bling-Bling King', 'Chess', 1200)

SELECT Id, Name, Category, Price from Products
```

The statements in this file add rows to the Products table in the DataAppDb database, providing values for the Name, Category, and Price columns. There are no values for the Id columns because they will be generated by the database to ensure that they are unique.

Select Execute from the Visual Studio SQL menu. Visual Studio will send the SQL statements to SQL Server, where they will be executed and produce the output shown in Table 11-3.

Table 11-3. *The Seed Data*

Id	Name	Category	Price
1	Kayak	Watersports	275.00
2	Lifejacket	Watersports	48.95
3	Soccer Ball	Soccer	19.50
4	Corner Flags	Soccer	34.95
5	Stadium	Soccer	79500.00
6	Thinking Cap	Chess	16.00
7	Unsteady Chair	Chess	29.95
8	Human Chess Board	Chess	75.00
9	Bling-Bling King	Chess	1200.00

Starting the Example Application

All of the pieces are in place, and it is time to start the application. Using a command prompt or PowerShell window to navigate to the DataApp project folder and run the command shown in Listing 11-20.

Listing 11-20. Running the Example Application

```
dotnet run
```

The application will be compiled and started, and the integrated ASP.NET Core web server will start listening for requests on HTTP port 5000.

Open a new browser window, request http://localhost:5000, and you will see that Entity Framework Core has provided the application with the data shown in Figure 11-4. Once you have confirmed that the application is operating correctly, press Control+C at the command prompt to exit.

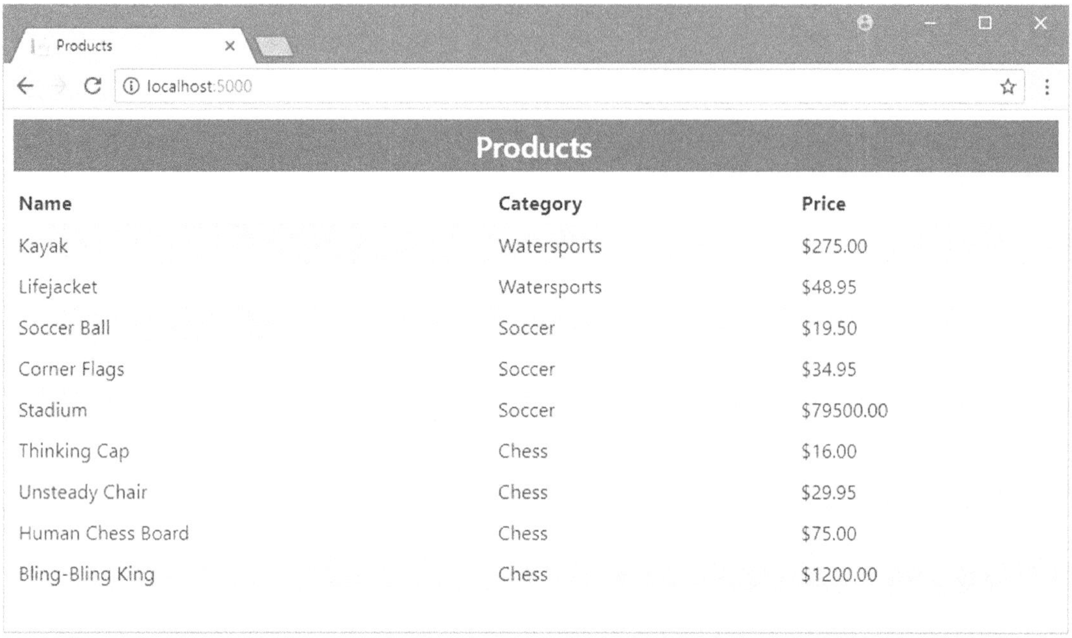

Figure 11-4. *Using Entity Framework Core in the example application*

UNDERSTANDING HOW THE APPLICATION WORKS

Before moving on, it is worth spending a moment to understand how the application has received the data displayed in Figure 11-4.

When the ASP.NET Core runtime received the HTTP request from the browser on port 5000, it dispatched it to the MVC framework, which used its routing system to select the Index action on the Home controller to generate a response.

The Index action read the Products property of the EFDatabaseContext object that the controller received through its constructor and received a sequence of Product objects. This sequence was passed as the view model to Views/Home/Index.cshtml view, which enumerated the objects it contained to generate rows in an HTML table.

When the sequence of Product objects was enumerated, Entity Framework Core read the contents of the Products table from the DataAppDb database, managed by SQL Server through its LocalDB feature. The name of the database and details of how to connect to the database server were contained in the connection string, defined in the appsettings.json file, and read in the Startup class.

```
...
"DefaultConnection":  "Server=(localdb)\\MSSQLLocalDB;Database=DataAppDb;
    MultipleActiveResultSets=true"
...
```

The name of the table that contains the data was taken from the name given to the DbSet<T> property defined by the EFDatabaseContext context class.

```
...
public DbSet<Product> Products { get; set; }
...
```

Entity Framework Core used this name in the migration that was used to generate the schema for the database. The data rows that were read from the table contained values from the Id, Name, Category, and Price columns, and these were used to create the Product objects that were processed by the Index.cshtml view.

The elegance of this approach is how little each part of the application needs to know about the rest of the project to do its job. The Index.cshtml view, for example, didn't need to be changed to work with the data from the database; it was written to process an IEnumerable<Product> before Entity Framework Core was added to the project, and that's what it still uses. Entity Framework Core takes care of translating the rows in the database into Product objects and makes the process of working with data largely seamless. Some changes were required for the controller, but, as you will see in the next section, this can be minimized by implementing the repository pattern.

If you find yourself confused by how some features work in later chapters, then remind yourself of this example and how the sequence of classes, configuration settings, and database features combined to provide the MVC part of the application with data. It will help remind you that Entity Framework Core isn't magic, even if it can sometimes feel like it. As you progress through the chapters that follow, you will see how each feature is implemented, and you will see that everything builds on a foundation revealed by this example.

Implementing the Repository Pattern

The Home controller in the example application works directly with an EFDatabaseContext object to access the data in the database. This is a perfectly functional approach, but it can be improved upon by implementing the repository pattern.

A *repository* consists of an interface that defines the data operations that can be performed in an application and an implementation class that does the actual work. The MVC parts of the application only use the interface, while, behind the scenes, the implementation class performs the data operations using the database context.

Using a repository makes it easier to isolate MVC components and consolidates the code that deals with Entity Framework Core, which makes it easier to unit test the different parts of the application and to switch to a different database (or even replace Entity Framework Core entirely and use a different data access layer). Without a repository, the code that deals with data tends to spread throughout the project, leading to code duplication and making effective unit testing difficult.

Defining the Repository Interface and Implementation Class

The starting point for a repository is to define an interface that allows data to be read through Entity Framework Core. Create a class file called IDataRepository.cs in the Models folder and add the code shown in Listing 11-21.

■ **Caution**　Don't implement the repository pattern in a real project until you have read the "Avoiding the IEnumerable vs. IQueryable Pitfall" section. The code shown in Listing 11-21 and Listing 11-22 contains a trap for the unwary.

Listing 11-21. The Contents of the IDataRepository.cs File in the Models Folder

```
using System.Collections.Generic;

namespace DataApp.Models {
    public interface IDataRepository {

        IEnumerable<Product> Products { get; }
    }
}
```

The repository interface will become more complex as features are added in later sections, but for the moment it defines only a single property called Products, which will return a sequence of Product objects. Create an implementation of the repository interface by adding a class file called EFDataRepository.cs to the Models folder with the code shown in Listing 11-22.

Listing 11-22. The Contents of the EFDataRepository.cs File in the Models Folder

```
using System.Collections.Generic;

namespace DataApp.Models {

    public class EFDataRepository : IDataRepository {
        private EFDatabaseContext context;

        public EFDataRepository(EFDatabaseContext ctx) {
            context = ctx;
        }

        public IEnumerable<Product> Products => context.Products;
    }
}
```

The implementation class receives an EFDatabaseContext object through its constructor, which it uses to implement the Products property required by the IRepository interface. This may not seem like a big step forward, but it means that the Home controller can be updated to depend on the repository interface without needing any knowledge of the context class, as shown in Listing 11-23.

Listing 11-23. Using the Repository in the HomeController.cs File in the Controllers Folder

```
using Microsoft.AspNetCore.Mvc;
using DataApp.Models;

namespace DataApp.Controllers {
    public class HomeController : Controller {
        private IDataRepository repository;

        public HomeController(IDataRepository repo) {
            repository = repo;
        }

        public IActionResult Index() {
            return View(repository.Products);
        }
    }
}
```

The Index action method works in the same way as it did before the repository was introduced but obtains its collection of Product objects via the repository interface. This makes it easy to create mock implementation classes for unit testing or to create different implementations that work with different data layers.

Configure the dependency injection feature to use the EFDataRepository class as the implementation of the IRepository interface by making the change to the Startup class shown in Listing 11-24.

Listing 11-24. Configuring Dependency Injection in the Startup.cs File in the DataApp Folder

```
using System;
using System.Collections.Generic;
using System.Linq;
using System.Threading.Tasks;
using Microsoft.AspNetCore.Builder;
using Microsoft.AspNetCore.Hosting;
using Microsoft.AspNetCore.Http;
using Microsoft.Extensions.DependencyInjection;
using DataApp.Models;
using Microsoft.EntityFrameworkCore;
using Microsoft.Extensions.Configuration;

namespace DataApp {
    public class Startup {

        public Startup(IConfiguration config) => Configuration = config;

        public IConfiguration Configuration { get; }

        public void ConfigureServices(IServiceCollection services) {
            services.AddMvc();
            string conString = Configuration["ConnectionStrings:DefaultConnection"];
            services.AddDbContext<EFDatabaseContext>(options =>
                options.UseSqlServer(conString));
            services.AddTransient<IDataRepository, EFDataRepository>();
        }
```

```
        public void Configure(IApplicationBuilder app, IHostingEnvironment env) {
            app.UseDeveloperExceptionPage();
            app.UseStatusCodePages();
            app.UseStaticFiles();
            app.UseMvcWithDefaultRoute();
        }
    }
}
```

Run the application again using the `dotnet run` command, and you will see the same data. The difference is that the data is obtained through the repository interface, which has broken the tight coupling between the MVC and EF Core parts of the application.

Avoiding the IEnumerable vs IQueryable Pitfall

There is a trap for the unwary in the way that I implemented the repository interface in the previous section. A change to the application is required to reveal the problem, as shown in Listing 11-25, which updates the `Index` action method on the `Home` controller so that it uses LINQ to filter the objects that are passed to the view.

Listing 11-25. Filtering Objects in the HomeController.cs File in the Controllers Folder

```
using Microsoft.AspNetCore.Mvc;
using DataApp.Models;
using System.Linq;

namespace DataApp.Controllers {
    public class HomeController : Controller {
        private IDataRepository repository;

        public HomeController(IDataRepository repo) {
            repository = repo;
        }

        public IActionResult Index() {
            return View(repository.Products.Where(p => p.Price > 25));
        }
    }
}
```

The LINQ query selects only those Product objects whose Price property has a value of greater than 25. Start the application using the dotnet run command in the DataApp folder, and use a web browser to request http://localhost:5000. You will see that only those Product objects whose Price property is greater than 25 are displayed, as shown in Figure 11-5.

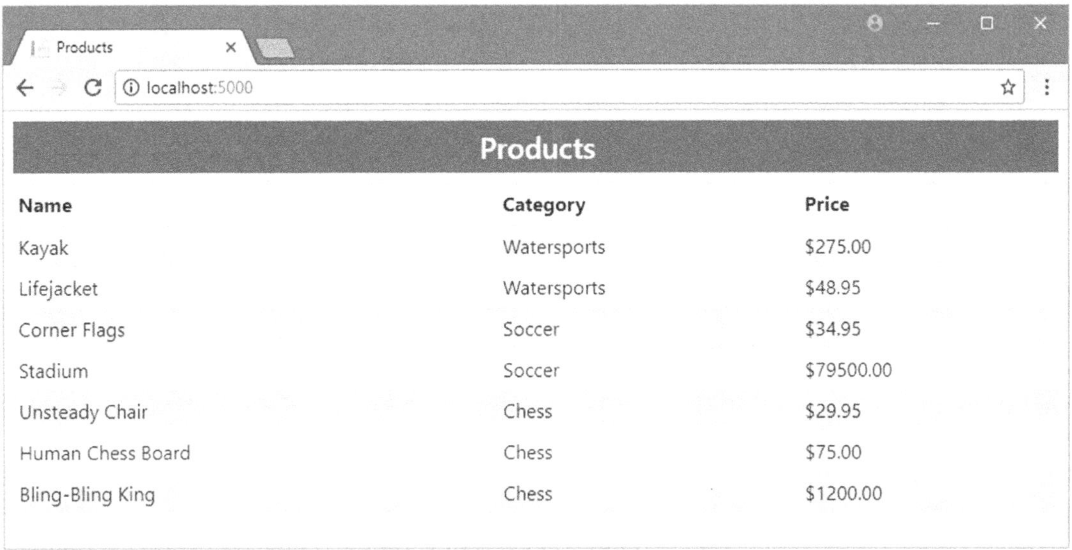

Figure 11-5. *Filtering data*

If you examine the logging messages written to the command prompt, you can see the SQL query that Entity Framework Core uses to get the data from the database.

```
...
SELECT [p].[Id], [p].[Category], [p].[Name], [p].[Price]
FROM [Products] AS [p]
...
```

Even though only some of the rows in the Products table are required, the query used by Entity Framework Core doesn't perform any filtering and asks the database for all the Product data. This is a quirk in the way that LINQ evaluates its queries, which means that all of the Product objects stored in the database are retrieved into the application, only after which is the filtering specified by the Where method applied.

For the example application, this means that all of the data is read from the Products table in the database and used to create Product objects, which are then inspected by the LINQ Where method and discarded if their Price value is too low.

This isn't a problem for applications that have small amounts of data. There are nine Product objects stored in the database in the example application. All nine will be read by the SQL query and then used to create Product objects, but only seven of them will be selected by the Where method. For such a small amount of data, the fact that two extra objects are retrieved by Entity Framework Core and then discarded by the MVC controller isn't worth worrying about. But the situation is different for applications that have substantial amounts of data, where retrieving a large number of table rows, using them to create objects, and then discarding them is a wasteful and expensive operation.

To fix the problem, changes are required to the repository interface and its implementation class. Listing 11-26 shows the change to the interface.

Listing 11-26. Fixing the Data Retrieval Issue in the IDataRepository.cs File in the Models Folder

```
using System.Collections.Generic;
using System.Linq;

namespace DataApp.Models {
    public interface IDataRepository {

        IQueryable<Product> Products { get; }
    }
}
```

The IQueryable interface is derived from IEnumerable but represents a query that should be processed by the database. Listing 11-27 makes the corresponding change to the implementation class so that it reflects the new return type for the Products property.

Listing 11-27. Fixing the Data Retrieval Issue in the EFDataRepository.cs File in the Models Folder

```
using System.Collections.Generic;
using System.Linq;

namespace DataApp.Models {

    public class EFDataRepository : IDataRepository {
        private EFDatabaseContext context;

        public EFDataRepository(EFDatabaseContext ctx) {
            context = ctx;
        }

        public IQueryable<Product> Products => context.Products;
    }
}
```

Restart the application with the dotnet run command and use the browser to request http://localhost:5000. In the messages written to the command prompt, you will see that a different query has been sent to SQL Server.

```
...
SELECT [p].[Id], [p].[Category], [p].[Name], [p].[Price]
FROM [Products] AS [p]
WHERE [p].[Price] > 25.0
...
```

The use of the IQueryable interface changes the way that the LINQ query is evaluated and ensures that the filtering is performed by the database server rather than by the MVC application. Only the data in the database that meets the filter criteria is retrieved, and no objects are created only to be immediately discarded.

Understanding and Avoiding the Additional Query Problem

The drawback of using the IQueryable<T> interface is that it is easy to accidentally generate more database queries than you intended. To demonstrate the problem, I have modified the action method in the Home controller so that it performs multiple operations on the data it receives from Entity Framework Core, as shown in Listing 11-28.

Listing 11-28. Multiple Data Operations in the HomeController.cs File in the Controllers Folder

```
using Microsoft.AspNetCore.Mvc;
using DataApp.Models;
using System.Linq;

namespace DataApp.Controllers {
    public class HomeController : Controller {
        private IDataRepository repository;

        public HomeController(IDataRepository repo) {
            repository = repo;
        }

        public IActionResult Index() {
            var products = repository.Products.Where(p => p.Price > 25);
            ViewBag.ProductCount = products.Count();
            return View(products);
        }
    }
}
```

The new statement in the Index method calls the Count method on the collection of objects that are obtained from the repository. This seems innocuous enough, but if you start the application using dotnet run and request http://localhost:5000, the logging messages will reveal that two queries were sent to the database. The first query asks the database server to count the number of products that match the filter, like this:

```
...
SELECT COUNT(*)
FROM [Products] AS [p]
WHERE [p].[Price] > 25.0
...
```

The second query actually retrieves the data objects.

```
...
SELECT [p].[Id], [p].[Category], [p].[Name], [p].[Price]
FROM [Products] AS [p]
WHERE [p].[Price] > 25.0
...
```

The IQueryable<T> interface triggers a new query every time that it is evaluated, which means that one query is sent when the Count method is called, and the second query occurs when the Razor view enumerates the Product objects to populate the HTML table sent to the browser. The queries appear in a different order from the code statements because the Razor view isn't rendered until after action method has completed.

The underlying problem is that Entity Framework Core doesn't have enough insight into the LINQ queries to realize that both data operations could be handled using a single database query. In this situation, you can avoid the additional queries by converting the IQueryable<T> object into a regular IEnumerable<T> using the ToArray or ToList methods, as shown in Listing 11-29.

Listing 11-29. Avoiding Additional Queries in the HomeController.cs File in the Controllers Folder

```
using Microsoft.AspNetCore.Mvc;
using DataApp.Models;
using System.Linq;

namespace DataApp.Controllers {
    public class HomeController : Controller {
        private IDataRepository repository;

        public HomeController(IDataRepository repo) {
            repository = repo;
        }

        public IActionResult Index() {
            var products = repository.Products.Where(p => p.Price > 25).ToArray();
            ViewBag.ProductCount = products.Count();
            return View(products);
        }
    }
}
```

The ToArray method forces evaluation of the query and produces a collection of objects that can be processed further without triggering additional queries, which means that the Count method operates on the data that has already been retrieved from the database, rather than triggering a new query.

■ **Note**   The examples in this section may give you the impression that you face the constant risk of either querying for more data or sending more queries than you need. The key is to examine the logging messages from the application to make sure you are getting the behavior you required, and this will become second nature once you get used to working with Entity Framework Core.

Hiding the Data Operations

A knock-on problem with using the IQueryable<T> interface is that it exposes details of how the data is managed to the rest of the application. This means that every time a new action method is written, for example, you must pay attention to whether the IQueryable<T> interface is being used and make sure you are requesting only the data you require using only the essential number of queries.

An alternative better approach is to hide away the detail of how the data is acquired in the repository so that the data can be used without having to worry about how it has been obtained. For the example application, this means moving the code that selects data from the controller into the repository. In Listing 11-30, I have replaced the Products property defined by the repository interface with a method that performs the query that was being done by the controller. This allows the repository to return an IEnumerable<Product> object that doesn't leak implementation details but that also doesn't retrieve and then discard data or trigger unexpected queries.

■ **Tip** You don't have to hide the data operations in your application. If you do, you are less likely to produce unexpected queries or request too much data, but the result can be less flexible and does have the effect of shifting complexity into the repository. I tend to mix and match approaches in my own projects (and the examples in this book), and I keep a careful eye on the logging messages produced by the application to ensure that I understand the way that the code in the MVC part of the application is being translated into SQL queries.

Listing 11-30. Defining Query Methods in the IDataRepository.cs File in the Models Folder

```
using System.Collections.Generic;
using System.Linq;

namespace DataApp.Models {
    public interface IDataRepository {

        IEnumerable<Product> GetProductsByPrice(decimal minPrice);
    }
}
```

The Products property has been replaced with a GetProductsByPrice method. The MVC part of the application will use this method rather than make its own queries directly using LINQ. Listing 11-31 shows the changes required to the repository implementation class.

Listing 11-31. Defining Query Methods in the EFDataRepository.cs File in the Models Folder

```
using System.Collections.Generic;
using System.Linq;

namespace DataApp.Models {

    public class EFDataRepository : IDataRepository {
        private EFDatabaseContext context;

        public EFDataRepository(EFDatabaseContext ctx) {
            context = ctx;
        }

        public IEnumerable<Product> GetProductsByPrice(decimal minPrice) {
            return context.Products.Where(p => p.Price >= minPrice).ToArray();
        }
    }
}
```

The context class's DbSet<Product> property implements the IQueryable<Product> interface. This means that I could simply have returned the result from the LINQ query without any kind of casting or conversion, but I have used the ToArray method to ensure that the onward use of the data won't trigger any additional queries.

Listing 11-32 updates the Index action method of the Home controller so that it uses the GetProductsByPrice method, leaving the repository to deal with filtering the data.

Listing 11-32. Using a Data Query Method in the HomeController.cs File in the Controllers Folder

```
using Microsoft.AspNetCore.Mvc;
using DataApp.Models;
using System.Linq;

namespace DataApp.Controllers {
    public class HomeController : Controller {
        private IDataRepository repository;

        public HomeController(IDataRepository repo) {
            repository = repo;
        }

        public IActionResult Index() {
            var products = repository.GetProductsByPrice(25);
            ViewBag.ProductCount = products.Count();
            return View(products);
        }
    }
}
```

The action method is able to get the filtered data it requires without worrying about how it is obtained and can perform additional operations on that data—such as using the LINQ Count method—without needing to consider if doing so will have an undesirable side effect.

Test the changes by starting the application with dotnet run and using a browser to navigate to http://localhost:5000. There is no change in the objects displayed in the browser, but the repository no longer exposes any implementation details, which improves the separation between the Entity Framework Core and MVC framework parts of the application and makes working with the application's data a less fraught process, albeit a less flexible one because the controller can receive only a specific subset of the data from the database.

Completing the Example MVC Application

To finish this chapter, I am going to complete the MVC part of the application by adding action methods and views for the most common operations that an application requires, along with methods in the repository to support them, completing the MVC part of the application. The implementation of the operations using Entity Framework Core is the subject the next chapter, so the repository class will just write out a message to the command prompt for now.

Completing the Repository

There are five core data operations that are required by most MVC applications: retrieving a single item, retrieving all items, creating a new item, updating an existing item, and deleting an item. Once you have these five operations set up and working, everything else will fall into place. Edit the repository interface to add the methods shown in Listing 11-33.

Listing 11-33. Adding Methods in the IDataRepository.cs File in the Models Folder

```
using System.Collections.Generic;
using System.Linq;

namespace DataApp.Models {
    public interface IDataRepository {

        Product GetProduct(long id);

        IEnumerable<Product> GetAllProducts();

        void CreateProduct(Product newProduct);

        void UpdateProduct(Product changedProduct);

        void DeleteProduct(long id);
    }
}
```

The GetProduct and DeleteProduct methods define parameters that accept a primary key value for a stored object, corresponding to the Id property. The CreateProduct and UpdateProduct accept Product objects, and the GetAllProducts has no parameters.

Edit the EFDataRepository class and add the methods shown in Listing 11-34 as placeholders for functionality that will be added in later chapters. The exception is the GetAllProducts method, which simply returns the value of the context object's Product property to provide access to all of the Product objects in the database.

Listing 11-34. Adding Methods in the EFDataRepository.cs File in the Models Folder

```
using System;
using System.Collections.Generic;
using System.Linq;
using Newtonsoft.Json;

namespace DataApp.Models {

    public class EFDataRepository : IDataRepository {
        private EFDatabaseContext context;

        public EFDataRepository(EFDatabaseContext ctx) {
            context = ctx;
        }
```

```
        public Product GetProduct(long id) {
            Console.WriteLine("GetProduct: " + id);
            return new Product();
        }

        public IEnumerable<Product> GetAllProducts() {
            Console.WriteLine("GetAllProducts");
            return context.Products;
        }

        public void CreateProduct(Product newProduct) {
            Console.WriteLine("CreateProduct: "
                + JsonConvert.SerializeObject(newProduct));
        }

        public void UpdateProduct(Product changedProduct) {
            Console.WriteLine("UpdateProduct : "
                + JsonConvert.SerializeObject(changedProduct));
        }

        public void DeleteProduct(long id) {
            Console.WriteLine("DeleteProduct: " + id);
        }
    }
}
```

The Newtonsoft.Json package is one that ASP.NET Core MVC relies on and that is installed as a dependency of the MVC packages. In this listing, it is used to serialize the objects received by the CreateProduct and UpdateProduct methods so they can be written to the console and easily examined.

Adding the Action Methods

To add the actions that will use the new data operations, edit the Home controller to add the methods shown in Listing 11-35. These methods use the ASP.NET Core MVC conventions and features for handling requests, including POST-only methods and model binding.

Listing 11-35. Adding Action Methods in the HomeController.cs File in the Controllers Folder

```
using Microsoft.AspNetCore.Mvc;
using DataApp.Models;
using System.Linq;

namespace DataApp.Controllers {
    public class HomeController : Controller {
        private IDataRepository repository;

        public HomeController(IDataRepository repo) {
            repository = repo;
        }
```

```
    public IActionResult Index() {
        return View(repository.GetAllProducts());
    }

    public IActionResult Create() {
        ViewBag.CreateMode = true;
        return View("Editor", new Product());
    }

    [HttpPost]
    public IActionResult Create(Product product) {
        repository.CreateProduct(product);
        return RedirectToAction(nameof(Index));
    }

    public IActionResult Edit(long id) {
        ViewBag.CreateMode = false;
        return View("Editor", repository.GetProduct(id));
    }

    [HttpPost]
    public IActionResult Edit(Product product) {
        repository.UpdateProduct(product);
        return RedirectToAction(nameof(Index));
    }

    [HttpPost]
    public IActionResult Delete(long id) {
        repository.DeleteProduct(id);
        return RedirectToAction(nameof(Index));
    }
  }
}
```

Updating and Adding Views

To complete the MVC side of the application, add a new Razor view called Editor.cshtml to the Views/
Shared folder and add the markup shown in Listing 11-36. This view will be used when the user wants to edit
or create an item and relies on the view bag property set by the Create and Edit methods in Listing 11-35 to
change its appearance and the action to which the HTML form is submitted.

Listing 11-36. The Contents of the Editor.cshtml File in the Views/Shared Folder

```
@model DataApp.Models.Product
@{
    ViewData["Title"] = ViewBag.CreateMode ? "Create" : "Edit";
    Layout = "_Layout";
}
```

```
<form asp-action="@(ViewBag.CreateMode ? "Create" : "Edit")" method="post">
    <div class="form-group">
        <label asp-for="Name"></label>
        <input asp-for="Name" class="form-control" />
    </div>
    <div class="form-group">
        <label asp-for="Category"></label>
        <input asp-for="Category" class="form-control" />
    </div>
    <div class="form-group">
        <label asp-for="Price"></label>
        <input asp-for="Price" class="form-control" />
    </div>
    <div class="text-center">
        <button class="btn btn-primary" type="submit">Save</button>
        <a asp-action="Index" class="btn btn-secondary">Cancel</a>
    </div>
</form>
```

Finally, edit the Index view to add buttons that will delete items and start the create and editing processes, as shown in Listing 11-37.

Listing 11-37. Adding Buttons to the Index.cshtml File in the Views/Home Folder

```
@model IEnumerable<DataApp.Models.Product>
@{
    ViewData["Title"] = "Products";
    Layout = "_Layout";
}

<table class="table table-sm table-striped">
    <thead>
        <tr><th>ID</th><th>Name</th><th>Category</th><th>Price</th></tr>
    </thead>
    <tbody>
        @foreach (var p in Model) {
            <tr>
                <td>@p.Id</td>
                <td>@p.Name</td>
                <td>@p.Category</td>
                <td>$@p.Price.ToString("F2")</td>
                <td>
                    <form asp-action="Delete" method="post">
                        <a asp-action="Edit"
                            class="btn btn-sm btn-warning" asp-route-id="@p.Id">
                            Edit
                        </a>
                        <input type="hidden" name="id" value="@p.Id" />
                        <button type="submit" class="btn btn-danger btn-sm">
                            Delete
                        </button>
                    </form>
```

```
            </td>
        </tr>
    }
    </tbody>
</table>
<a asp-action="Create" class="btn btn-primary">Create New Product</a>
```

Start the application using `dotnet run` and navigate to `http://localhost:5000` to see the result, shown in Figure 11-6. The MVC part of the application is complete, and the repository pattern has been implemented, which provides the foundation for adding features in the next chapter.

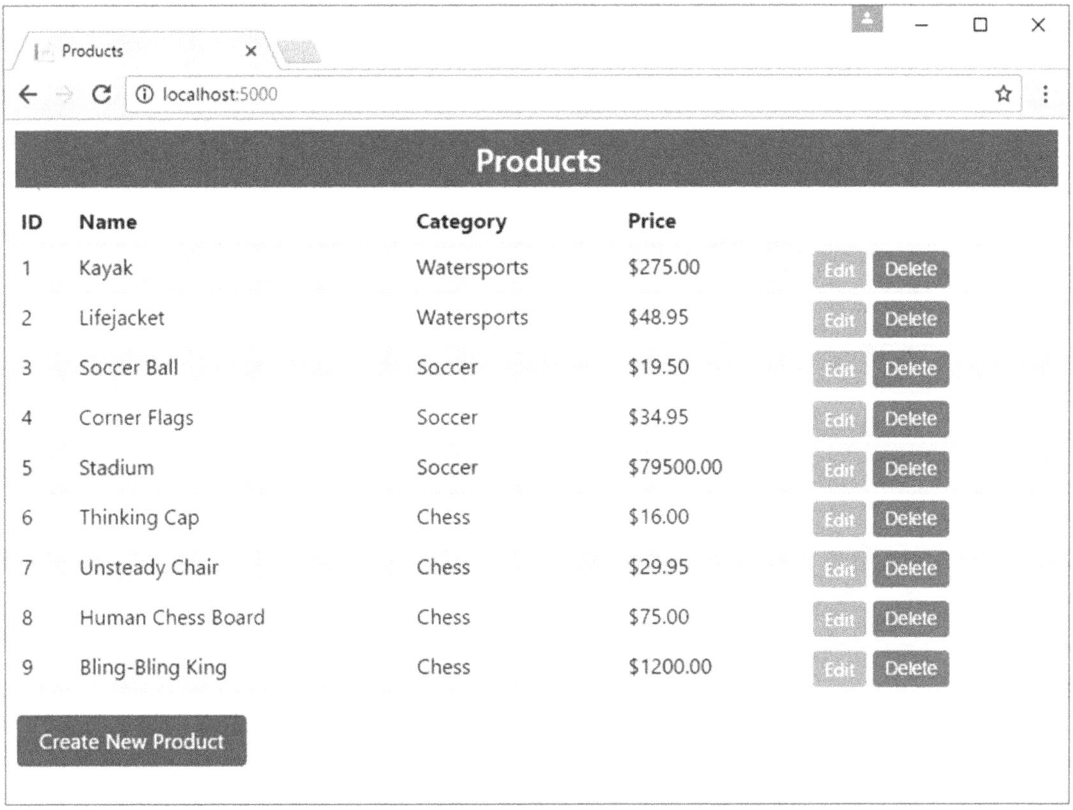

Figure 11-6. *Completing the MVC part of the application*

Summary

In this chapter, I demonstrated how to add Entity Framework Core to an ASP.NET Core MVC application and showed you the different ways that the repository pattern can be applied. I will enhance the example project in the chapters that follow, starting with the next chapter, in which I introduce the basic data operations that Entity Framework Core supports.

CHAPTER 12

Performing Data Operations

The data model in the example application is too simple to be representative of real projects, but it does allow me to easily explain how the four core data operations (creating, reading, updating, and deleting data) can be performed using Entity Framework Core. I show you how to create more complex data models in later chapters, but, as you will see in this chapter, even a simple model can reveal much about how Entity Framework Core works. Table 12-1 puts basic data operations in context.

Table 12-1. *Putting Basic Data Operations in Context*

Question	Answer
What are they?	The basic data operations allow you to read, store, update, and delete data from a database.
Why are they useful?	These operations are the basic building blocks of working with Entity Framework Core.
How are they used?	The database context class defines a property that provides methods for storing, updating, and deleting data and on which LINQ queries can be performed to read data from the database.
Are there any pitfalls or limitations?	These operations can be inefficient and require the database server to perform more work unless steps are taken to use features such as change detection.
Are there any alternatives?	If you are using Entity Framework Core, then these features are the foundation for working with data.

© Adam Freeman 2018
A. Freeman, *Pro Entity Framework Core 2 for ASP.NET Core MVC*,
https://doi.org/10.1007/978-1-4842-3435-8_12

Table 12-2 summarizes the chapter.

Table 12-2. *Chapter Summary*

Problem	Solution	Listing
Get a single object from the database	Use the `Find` method defined by the `DbSet<T>` object returned the context class	5
Get all of the objects of a given type from the database	Enumerate the `DbSet<T>` object returned by the context class property	6
Get a subset of objects	Use LINQ to express the constraints that select the objects you require	7–10
Add an object to the database	Pass the object to the `DbSet<T>.Add` method and call `SaveChanges`	11–12
Update an object in the database	Pass the object to the `DbSet<T>.Update` method and call `SaveChanges`	13
Use change detection to minimize updates	Query the database to get the baseline object, change its property values, and call `SaveChanges`	14–15
Use change detection without querying for baseline data	Include the original state of the object in the HTTP request and use it to provide the baseline	16–19
Remove an object from the database	Pass the object to the `DbSet<T>.Remove` method and call `SaveChanges`	21

Preparing for This Chapter

This chapter uses the DataApp project created in Chapter 11. To prepare for this chapter, open a command prompt or PowerShell window in the DataApp project folder and run the command shown in Listing 12-1.

■ **Tip** If you don't want to follow the process of building the example project, you can download all of the required files from this book's source code repository, `https://github.com/apress/pro-ef-core-2-for-asp.net-core-mvc`.

Listing 12-1. Resetting the Database

```
dotnet ef database drop --force
```

This command removes the database, which will help ensure that you get the expected results from the examples in this chapter. Run the command shown in Listing 12-2 in the DataApp project folder to re-create the database.

Listing 12-2. Preparing the Database

```
dotnet ef database update
```

To seed the database with data, select Tools ➤ SQL Server ➤ New Query and enter **(localdb)\MSSQLLocalDB** in the Server Name field. Ensure that Windows Authentication is selected for the Authentication field and click the Database Name menu to select DataAppDb from the drop-down list, which will display a complete list of the databases that have been created using LocalDB. Click Connect to open a connection to the database.

■ **Tip** The History tab keeps track of the databases you have connected to using Visual Studio and allows you to reconnect to databases without needing to enter the connection details again.

Enter the SQL shown in Listing 12-3 into the editor. Select Execute from the Visual Studio SQL menu. Visual Studio will ask the database server to execute the SQL, which will ensure that there is data for the example application to work with.

Listing 12-3. Seeding the Database

```
USE DataAppDb

INSERT INTO Products (Name, Category, Price)
VALUES
    ('Kayak', 'Watersports', 275),
    ('Lifejacket', 'Watersports', 48.95),
    ('Soccer Ball', 'Soccer', 19.50),
    ('Corner Flags', 'Soccer', 34.95),
    ('Stadium', 'Soccer', 79500),
    ('Thinking Cap', 'Chess', 16),
    ('Unsteady Chair', 'Chess', 29.95),
    ('Human Chess Board', 'Chess', 75),
    ('Bling-Bling King', 'Chess', 1200)
```

When you execute the SQL, you will see the following result, which indicates that nine rows of data were added to the database:

```
(9 row(s) affected)
```

Starting the Example Application

Start the application by running the command shown in Listing 12-4 in the DataApp folder.

Listing 12-4. Starting the Example Application

```
dotnet run
```

Open a browser window and request `http://localhost:5000`. The ASP.NET Core MVC application will use Entity Framework Core to retrieve data from the database and generate the response shown in Figure 12-1.

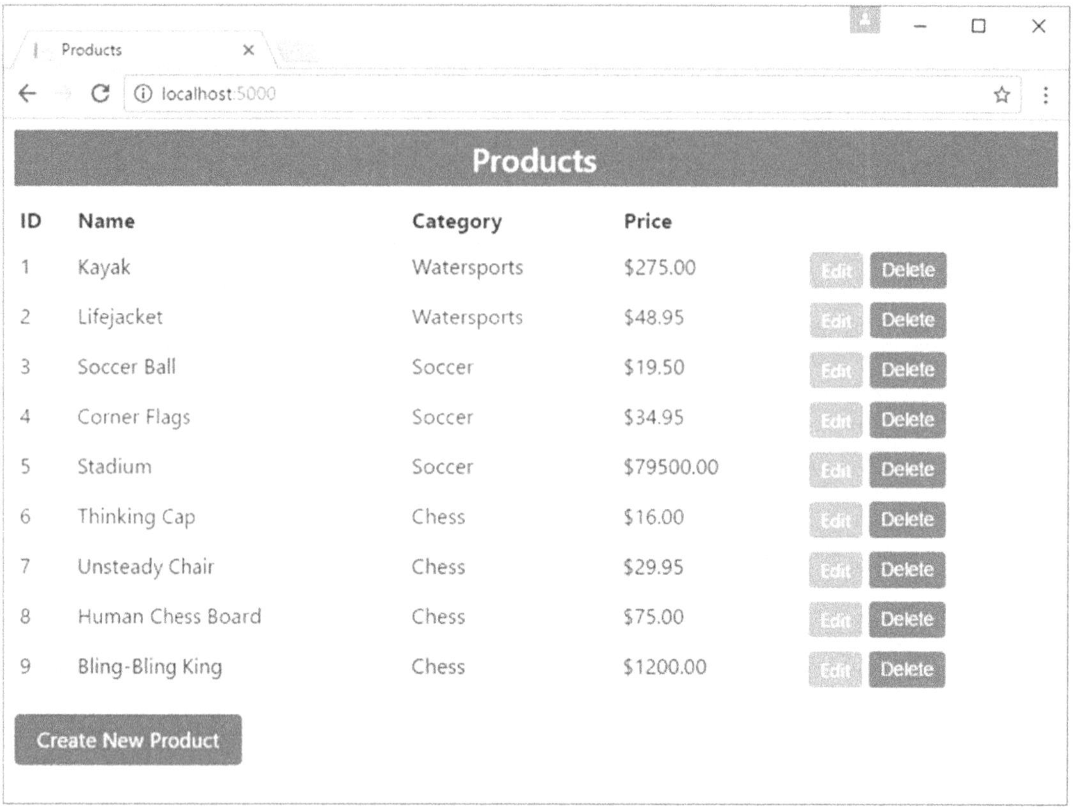

Figure 12-1. *Running the example application*

Reading Data

To understand how Entity Framework Core works, the best place to start is by querying the database and retrieving the data it contains. In the sections that follow, I explain how to query for a single entity object, all objects, and just some objects.

Reading an Object by Key

The key to the data operations used in this chapter is the DbSet<T> class, which is used as the result for the properties defined by the database context class. Here is the definition of the Products property from the EFDatabaseContext class, defined in Chapter 11:

```
...
public DbSet<Product> Products { get; set; }
...
```

Properties like this have two roles. The first role is to tell Entity Framework Core that the Product class is an *entity class*, meaning that Product objects will be stored in the database. This is important information when Entity Framework Core creates a migration because it influences the tables and rows that must be created to store the data in the database.

The second role is to provide a property that allows operations to be performed on the database, meaning that Product objects can be created, read, updated, and deleted using Entity Framework Core. The DbSet<T> class implements interfaces and defines methods that make these operations possible. The first, and most basic, of these methods is called Find, and it is described in Table 12-3 for quick reference.

Table 12-3. *The DbSet<T> Method for Querying by Key*

Name	Description
Find(key)	This method reads the row in the table that has the specified key and returns an object that represents it. If there is no row with that key, null is returned. If the table requires multiple keys, as described in Chapter 19, they can be specified as multiple parameters: Find(key1, key2, key3).

The Find method is useful when you have a key and want the object that is associated with it. In terms of the example application, that means you have the value assigned to the Id property of a Product object that has been stored in the database and you want to retrieve the complete Product object.

This is the purpose of the GetProduct method in the repository, which means that the Find method can be used to implement this method, as shown in Listing 12-5.

Listing 12-5. Querying by Key in the EFDataRepository.cs File in the Models Folder

```
using System;
using System.Collections.Generic;
using System.Linq;
using Newtonsoft.Json;

namespace DataApp.Models {

    public class EFDataRepository : IDataRepository {
        private EFDatabaseContext context;

        public EFDataRepository(EFDatabaseContext ctx) {
            context = ctx;
        }

        public Product GetProduct(long id) {
            return context.Products.Find(id);
        }

        public IEnumerable<Product> GetAllProducts() {
            Console.WriteLine("GetAllProducts");
            return context.Products;
        }
```

```
    public void CreateProduct(Product newProduct) {
        Console.WriteLine("CreateProduct: "
            + JsonConvert.SerializeObject(newProduct));
    }

    public void UpdateProduct(Product changedProduct) {
        Console.WriteLine("UpdateProduct : "
            + JsonConvert.SerializeObject(changedProduct));
    }

    public void DeleteProduct(long id) {
        Console.WriteLine("DeleteProduct: " + id);
    }
  }
}
```

The GetProduct method is used to provide the current property values for a Product object when the user starts the editing process in the MVC part of the application. Start the application using dotnet run, use a browser to navigate to http://localhost:5000, and click one of the Edit buttons. The form that is shown will be populated with data obtained from the Product object created by the Find method, as shown in Figure 12-2.

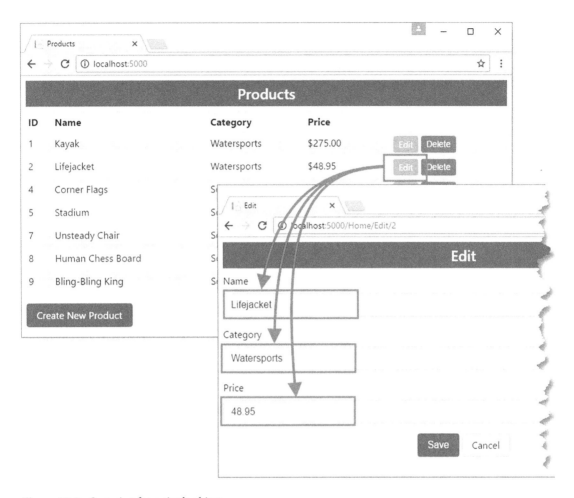

Figure 12-2. *Querying for a single object*

If you examine the logging output from the application on the command prompt, you will see the SQL query sent to the database.

```
...
SELECT TOP(1) [e].[Id], [e].[Category], [e].[Name], [e].[Price]
FROM [Products] AS [e]
WHERE [e].[Id] = @__get_Item_0
...
```

The query retrieves values for each of the properties defined by the Product class for the first row in the table that has the specified value for the Id column. These values are used by the Find method to create the Product object that it returns. This object is then passed to the MVC part of the application so that it can be displayed to the user.

Querying All Objects

To retrieve all the data objects stored in the database, you can read the value of the context class's Products property, which returns a DbSet<Product> object. The DbSet<T> class implements the IQueryable<T> and IEnumerable<T> interfaces, which means you can enumerate the sequence of Product objects read from the database using a foreach loop.

The repository class already includes support for reading all of the data objects, through the GetAllProducts method that I defined in Chapter 11, as follows:

```
...
public IEnumerable<Product> GetAllProducts() {
    return context.Products;
}
...
```

Entity Framework Core doesn't read the data from the database until you enumerate the DbSet<T> property, which can be a source of confusion. To demonstrate how Entity Framework Core defers reading the data, update the Index action on the Home controller, as shown in Listing 12-6.

Listing 12-6. Querying All Objects in the HomeController.cs File in the Controllers Folder

```
using Microsoft.AspNetCore.Mvc;
using DataApp.Models;
using System.Linq;

namespace DataApp.Controllers {
    public class HomeController : Controller {
        private IDataRepository repository;

        public HomeController(IDataRepository repo) {
            repository = repo;
        }

        public IActionResult Index() {
            var products = repository.GetAllProducts();
            System.Console.WriteLine("Property value has been read");
            return View(products);
        }

        public IActionResult Create() {
            ViewBag.CreateMode = true;
            return View("Editor", new Product());
        }

        // ...other actions omitted for brevity...
    }
}
```

The System.Console.WriteLine statement in Listing 12-6 writes out a message when the Products property has been read and before the value is passed to the View method.

Restart the application using `dotnet run` and request `http://localhost:5000`. Examine the logging output from the application, and you will see that the statement from Listing 12-6 appears before the SQL query is sent to the database, as follows:

```
...
Property value has been read
...
info: Microsoft.EntityFrameworkCore.Database.Sql[1]
      Executed DbCommand (6ms) [Parameters=[], CommandType='Text',
         CommandTimeout='30']
      SELECT [p].[Id], [p].[Category], [p].[Name], [p].[Price]
      FROM [Products] AS [p]
...
```

The data is retrieved from the database only when an operation is performed on the sequence, such as enumeration with a `foreach` loop or when using LINQ to convert the sequence to an array or a list (using the `ToArray` or `ToList` methods).

Querying for Specific Objects

The `DbSet<T>` properties defined by context objects also allow more complex queries to be created using the LINQ to Entities feature. The `DbSet<T>` class implements the `IQueryable<T>` interface, which, as explained in Chapter 11, is used to create queries that select objects from the database. This allows the use of LINQ to query and process data but with the benefit that the query is executed by the database server so that only the matching data objects are read from the database.

When using a `DBSet<T>` property, the query isn't sent to the database until the sequence of objects is enumerated. This means queries can be built up by chaining together multiple LINQ methods across multiple code statements, which fits nicely into the model of working with MVC applications.

As a demonstration, edit the `Index.cshtml` view to add an HTML form that will allow the user to filter the list of products that is displayed in the table, as shown in Listing 12-7.

Listing 12-7. Adding Filtering in the Index.cshtml File in the Views/Home Folder

```
@model IEnumerable<DataApp.Models.Product>
@{
    ViewData["Title"] = "Products";
    Layout = "_Layout";
}

<div class="m-1 p-2">
    <form asp-action="Index" method="get" class="form-inline">
        <label class="m-1">Category:</label>
        <select name="category" class="form-control">
            <option value="">All</option>
            <option selected="@(ViewBag.category == "Watersports")">
                Watersports
            </option>
            <option selected="@(ViewBag.category == "Soccer")">Soccer</option>
            <option selected="@(ViewBag.category == "Chess")">Chess</option>
        </select>
```

```html
        <label class="m-1">Min Price:</label>
        <input class="form-control" name="price" value="@ViewBag.price" />
        <button class="btn btn-primary m-1">Filter</button>
    </form>
</div>
<table class="table table-sm table-striped">
    <thead>
        <tr><th>ID</th><th>Name</th><th>Category</th><th>Price</th></tr>
    </thead>
    <tbody>
        @foreach (var p in Model) {
            <tr>
                <td>@p.Id</td>
                <td>@p.Name</td>
                <td>@p.Category</td>
                <td>$@p.Price.ToString("F2")</td>
                <td>
                    <form asp-action="Delete" method="post">
                        <a asp-action="Edit" class="btn btn-sm btn-warning"
                           asp-route-id="@p.Id">
                            Edit
                        </a>
                        <input type="hidden" name="id" value="@p.Id" />
                        <button type="submit" class="btn btn-danger btn-sm">
                            Delete
                        </button>
                    </form>
                </td>
            </tr>
        }
    </tbody>
</table>
<a asp-action="Create" class="btn btn-primary">Create New Product</a>
```

The new elements present the user with a select element to pick a category and with an input element to specify a minimum price. The values of these elements will be included in the GET request sent to the application when the Filter button is clicked.

To receive the filter criteria in the application, edit the Index action on the Home controller as shown in Listing 12-8.

Listing 12-8. Receiving Filter Criteria in the HomeController.cs File in the Controllers Folder

```csharp
using Microsoft.AspNetCore.Mvc;
using DataApp.Models;
using System.Linq;

namespace DataApp.Controllers {
    public class HomeController : Controller {
        private IDataRepository repository;

        public HomeController(IDataRepository repo) {
            repository = repo;
        }
```

```
public IActionResult Index(string category = null, decimal? price = null) {
    var products = repository.GetFilteredProducts(category, price);
    ViewBag.category = category;
    ViewBag.price = price;
    return View(products);
}

public IActionResult Create() {
    ViewBag.CreateMode = true;
    return View("Editor", new Product());
}

// ...other actions omitted for brevity...
    }
}
```

The Index action method defines two optional parameters that are passed to a repository method called GetFilteredProducts. To create the GetFilteredProducts method used by the Index action, extend the repository interface as shown in Listing 12-9.

■ **Tip** I used a nullable decimal value for the price parameter in Listing 12-8 to differentiate between the user entering nothing (in which case the parameter will be null) and the user entering zero (in which case the parameter will be 0). Using a regular decimal parameter would result in a zero value for both situations.

Listing 12-9. Adding a Method in the IDataRepository.cs File in the Models Folder

```
using System.Collections.Generic;
using System.Linq;

namespace DataApp.Models {
    public interface IDataRepository {

        Product GetProduct(long id);

        IEnumerable<Product> GetAllProducts();

        IEnumerable<Product> GetFilteredProducts(string category = null,
            decimal? price = null);

        void CreateProduct(Product newProduct);

        void UpdateProduct(Product changedProduct);

        void DeleteProduct(long id);
    }
}
```

The final step is to implement the method to build up the LINQ query based on the values that the user has provided. Edit the repository class to implement the GetFilteredProducts method, as shown in Listing 12-10.

Listing 12-10. Building a Query in the EFDataRepository.cs File in the Models Folder

```
using System;
using System.Collections.Generic;
using System.Linq;
using Newtonsoft.Json;

namespace DataApp.Models {

    public class EFDataRepository : IDataRepository {
        private EFDatabaseContext context;

        public EFDataRepository(EFDatabaseContext ctx) {
            context = ctx;
        }

        public Product GetProduct(long id) {
            return context.Products.Find(id);
        }

        public IEnumerable<Product> GetAllProducts() {
            Console.WriteLine("GetAllProducts");
            return context.Products;
        }

        public IEnumerable<Product> GetFilteredProducts(string category = null,
                decimal? price = null) {

            IQueryable<Product> data = context.Products;
            if (category != null) {
                data = data.Where(p => p.Category == category);
            }
            if (price != null) {
                data = data.Where(p => p.Price >= price);
            }
            return data;
        }

        // ...other methods omitted for brevity...
    }
}
```

The implementation of this method starts by reading the value of the context's Product property and assigning it to an IQueryable<Product> variable. As explained in Chapter 11, using the IQueryable<Product> interface ensures that the data filtering is done in the database, rather than loading all of the objects and then filtering them.

The query is built up based on whether values have been received for the `category` and `price` parameters. If there are parameter values, then the value of the `IQuerable<Product>` variable is updated using the LINQ `Where` method. The database isn't queried until the `IQueryable<T>` object is enumerated in the view, which is how the LINQ methods can be used to selectively compose the query across several lines of code.

To see the effect of the changes, restart the application, request `http://localhost:5000`, and use the form fields shown in Figure 12-3 to filter the data displayed by the application.

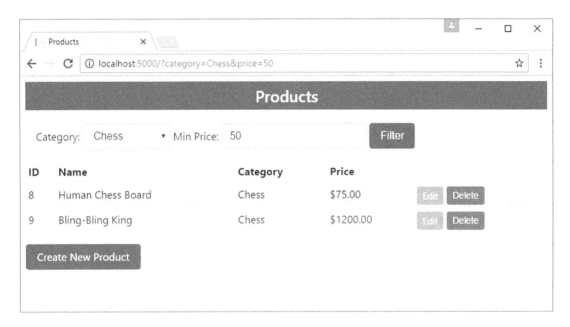

Figure 12-3. *Filtering data in the example application*

There are four possible types of query that can be produced.

- Querying all objects, when both parameters are null

- Querying for objects in a specific category and no minimum price

- Querying for objects with a minimum price in all categories

- Querying for objects in a specific category and with a minimum price

You can see each of the queries that will be sent to the database server by selecting category values and entering numbers into the price field. For example, this is the query that will be sent if you select a category but do not enter a minimum price:

```
...
SELECT [p].[Id], [p].[Category], [p].[Name], [p].[Price]
FROM [Products] AS [p]
WHERE [p].[Category] = @__category_0
...
```

This is the query that is used when both a category and a minimum price have been selected:

```
...
SELECT [p].[Id], [p].[Category], [p].[Name], [p].[Price]
FROM [Products] AS [p]
WHERE ([p].[Category] = @__category_0) AND ([p].[Price] >= @__price_1)
...
```

The key point is that the selection of the data is performed by the query that is sent to the database, ensuring that only matching data is returned to the application.

Storing New Data

The next step is to add the ability to store new objects in the database. Edit the repository class to implement the CreateProduct method as shown in Listing 12-11.

Listing 12-11. Storing Data in the EFDataRepository.cs File in the Models Folder

```
...
public void CreateProduct(Product newProduct) {
    newProduct.Id = 0;
    context.Products.Add(newProduct);
    context.SaveChanges();
}
...
```

There are two sources of Product objects in the example application: the MVC model binding process and the database context object. The model binding process creates Product objects when it receives an HTTP POST request, and the context object creates Product objects when it reads data from the database.

Entity Framework Core is responsible for the Product objects that are created by the database context object but has no visibility of the ones created by the MVC model binder. The Add method, which is called on the context's DbSet<T> property, makes Entity Framework Core aware of a Product object that has been created elsewhere in the application so that it can be written to the database.

Tip The DbSet<T> property also defines an AddRange method that can be used to store multiple objects in a single method call, as demonstrated in Chapter 13.

The SaveChanges method saves outstanding changes made to the Product objects that are being managed by Entity Framework Core to the database. This includes any Product objects that have been passed to the Add method. The effect of the code in Listing 12-11 is to make Entity Framework Core aware of a Product object and store it in the database.

To see the effect, restart the application using dotnet run, use a browser to navigate to http://localhost:5000, and click the Create button. Fill out the form fields and click the Save button.

When the Create action method on the Home controller is invoked to handle the HTTP POST request, it receives a Product object created by the model binder as its parameter. The action method calls the CreateProduct method on the repository, which makes Entity Framework Core aware of the Product object with the Add method and uses the SaveChanges method to store it in the database. The new data will be displayed in the table of products, as shown in Figure 12-4.

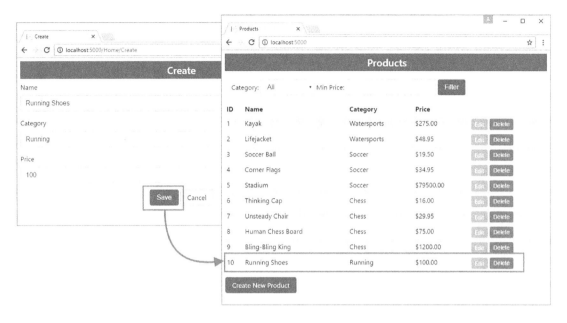

Figure 12-4. *Storing new data*

Understanding Key Assignment

Notice that the CreateProduct method explicitly sets the value of the Id property of the Product object to zero:

```
...
newProduct.Id = 0;
...
```

The primary key values for new objects are allocated by the database server when new rows in the table are created, and an exception will be thrown if the value for the Id property isn't zero. In Listing 12-11, I explicitly set the Id property to zero to ensure that the value received from the HTTP request isn't used.

■ **Note** I could have configured the MVC model binder to ignore values for the Id property in the HTTP request, but this presumes that the model binder is the only source of Product objects passed to the CreateProduct method. I like to make sure that the Entity Framework Core part of the application is robust in its own right, which is why I explicitly set the property to zero in Listing 12-11.

When Entity Framework Core stores a new object, it immediately performs a SQL query to discover the value that the database server has assigned to the Id column of the new table row. You can see this in the SQL statements that are logged to the command prompt when a new product is created, like this:

```
...
INSERT INTO [Products] ([Category], [Name], [Price])
VALUES (@p0, @p1, @p2);
```

```
SELECT [Id]
FROM [Products]
WHERE @@ROWCOUNT = 1 AND [Id] = scope_identity();
...
```

The INSERT statement tells the database server to create a new row in the Products table and provides values for the Category, Name, and Price columns. The SELECT statement queries the value for the Id column that has been used to create the new row. The value that is returned is used to update the Product object, ensuring that the object is consistent with its representation in the database.

You can see how this works by reading the value of the Id property after the SaveChanges method, as shown in Listing 12-12.

Listing 12-12. Determining the Key Value in the EFDataRepository.cs File in the Models Folder

```
...
public void CreateProduct(Product newProduct) {
    newProduct.Id = 0;
    context.Products.Add(newProduct);
    context.SaveChanges();
    Console.WriteLine($"New Key: {newProduct.Id}");
}
...
```

Restart the application using dotnet run and repeat the process of creating a new data item. Examine the output from the application, and you will see that there is a message that shows the key value assigned to the new Product, like this:

```
New Key: 11
```

The key value is also displayed in the table of products displayed by the browser.

Updating Data

The process for modifying existing data is similar to storing new data but requires a little work to get it working efficiently. There are three different ways to approach updates, which are described in the sections that follow.

Updating a Complete Object

The simplest approach to performing an update is to put the Product object created by the MVC model binding process under the management of Entity Framework Core, similar to the process for storing new data. To add support for updating data in this way, edit the UpdateProduct method in the EFDataRepository class, as shown in Listing 12-13.

Listing 12-13. Updating Data in the EFDataRepository.cs File in the Models Folder

```
...
public void UpdateProduct(Product changedProduct) {
    context.Products.Update(changedProduct);
    context.SaveChanges();
}
...
```

The DbSet<T>.Update method is used to let Entity Framework Core know a Product object that has been modified, and the context's SaveChanges method writes the object to the database.

■ **Tip** The DbSet<T> property also defines an UpdateRange method that can be used to update multiple objects in a single method call, as demonstrated in Chapter 15.

To see the effect, restart the application using the dotnet run command, click the Edit button for the Stadium product, and change the value of the Name field to Stadium (Large). Click the Save button; the database will be updated, and the change will then be reflected in the list of products when the browser is redirected to the Index action, as shown in Figure 12-5.

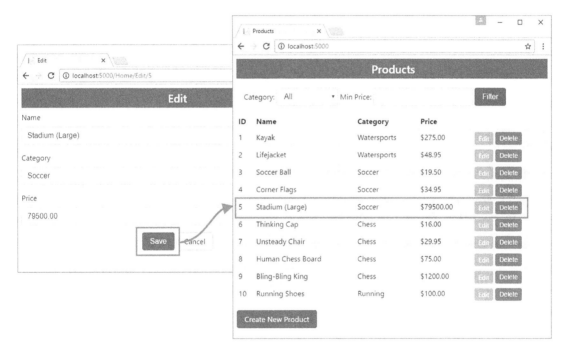

Figure 12-5. *Updating an object*

The advantage of this approach is simplicity: only two lines of code are required to handle updates. The disadvantage is that Entity Framework Core knows that the Product object has changed but doesn't have enough information to determine that only one property has changed. This means the values for all the Product object's properties have to be stored in the database, where you can see all three properties are updated.

```
...
UPDATE [Products] SET [Category] = @p0, [Name] = @p1, [Price] = @p2
WHERE [Id] = @p3;
...
```

Only one property has changed, but all three properties are updated in the database. For simple objects, writing unchanged properties isn't a significant issue. For real projects with complex data models, this approach can be inefficient.

⬛ **Tip** If you examine the console output from the application, you will see that the UPDATE statement is the middle of three that are sent to the database server. First is SET NOCOUNT ON, which disables the feature that reports on how many rows are affected by a query to improve performance. Next, the UPDATE statement updates the modified row or rows in the table. The third statement is SELECT @@ROWCOUNT, which reports on how many rows have been affected by the UPDATE. Entity Framework Core always checks that the expected number of rows has been changed.

Querying the Existing Data Before Updating

Entity Framework Core has the ability to work out exactly which properties in an object have been modified, which can be used to avoid writing unchanged data to the database. To understand how Entity Framework Core handles change detection, modify the UpdateProduct method in the repository as shown in Listing 12-14.

Listing 12-14. Using Change Detection in the EFDataRepository.cs File in the Models Folder

```
...
public void UpdateProduct(Product changedProduct) {
    Product originalProduct = context.Products.Find(changedProduct.Id);
    originalProduct.Name = changedProduct.Name;
    originalProduct.Category = changedProduct.Category;
    originalProduct.Price = changedProduct.Price;
    context.SaveChanges();
}
...
```

There are two Product objects in this example. The changedProduct object is received as the action method parameter and has been created by the MVC model binder using the HTTP POST request data. The originalProduct object is created by Entity Framework Core as the result of the Find method and represents the data that is currently in the database.

Entity Framework Core keeps track of the objects it creates using data from the database and works out when the value of properties has changed. To take advantage of this feature, I assign the values of the properties of the changedProduct object to the originalProduct object and then call the SaveChanges method. Entity Framework Core will inspect the property values of the originalProduct object to see whether they have changed since the object was created and will update only the ones that are different.

Restart the application, click the Edit button for the Stadium product again, and change the Name field from Stadium (Large) to Stadium (Small). When you click the Save button, the logging messages will show a SQL statement that only updates the property that has changed, like this:

```
...
UPDATE [Products] SET [Name] = @p0
WHERE [Id] = @p1;
...
```

The change detection process has identified that the Name property has changed, and the statement sent to the database server performs an update on just that property.

Understanding Change Detection

The base class for database contexts, DbContext, defines an Entry method that returns an EntityEntry object. This object is used by Entity Framework Core to detect changes in the objects that it creates. Table 12-4 describes the most useful EntityEntry properties.

Table 12-4. *Useful EntityEntry Properties*

Name	Description
State	This property returns a value from the EntityState enum to indicate the state of the object. The values are Added, Deleted, Detached, Modified, and Unchanged.
OriginalValues	This property returns a collection of the original property values, indexed by property name.
CurrentValues	This property returns a collection of the current property values, indexed by property name.

These properties can be used to inspect the status of entity objects, which can reveal how the change tracking process works. Listing 12-15 changes the repository's UpdateProduct method to write out change tracking information, using the EntityEntry object.

Listing 12-15. Inspecting Tracking Details in the EFDataRepository.cs File in the Models Folder

```
using System;
using System.Collections.Generic;
using System.Linq;
using Newtonsoft.Json;
using Microsoft.EntityFrameworkCore.ChangeTracking;

namespace DataApp.Models {

    public class EFDataRepository : IDataRepository {
        private EFDatabaseContext context;

        public EFDataRepository(EFDatabaseContext ctx) {
            context = ctx;
        }

        // ...methods omitted for brevity...

        public void UpdateProduct(Product changedProduct) {
            Product originalProduct = context.Products.Find(changedProduct.Id);
            originalProduct.Name = changedProduct.Name;
            originalProduct.Category = changedProduct.Category;
            originalProduct.Price = changedProduct.Price;
```

```
        EntityEntry entry = context.Entry(originalProduct);
        Console.WriteLine($"Entity State: {entry.State}");
        foreach (string p_name in new string[]
                { "Name", "Category", "Price" }) {
            Console.WriteLine($"{p_name} - Old: " +
                $"{entry.OriginalValues[p_name]}, " +
                $"New: {entry.CurrentValues[p_name]}");
        }
        context.SaveChanges();
    }

    public void DeleteProduct(long id) {
        Console.WriteLine("DeleteProduct: " + id);
    }
  }
}
```

The changes to the UpdateProduct method get the EntityEntry for the Product object created by the Find method and write out the value of the State properties and the current and original values for the Name, Category, and Price properties.

To see the tracking information, start the application using dotnet run and edit one of the products shown in the table. When the Save button is clicked, the data that the browser sends to the application will be applied to the entity object, and the tracking data will be written out to the command prompt.

```
...
Entity State: Modified
Name - Old: Kayak, New: Green Kayak
Category - Old: Watersports, New: Watersports
Price - Old: 275.00, New: 275.00
...
```

This tracking data shows that I edited the Name property of the Kayak product, changing it to Green Kayak. The State property returns the Modified value, and Entity Framework Core will only write properties whose values have changed to the database, avoiding updating values that have not changed.

Updating in a Single Database Operation

The previous example avoids writing unchanged properties to the database, but it achieves that by querying the database for the current values, which is trading one inefficiency for another. At this point, you might be wondering what happened to the Product object that was used to populate the HTML form fields and why can't it be used for change detection?

CHOOSING AN UPDATE STRATEGY

If your data model is relatively simple and your entity objects have few properties, then you should use the simplest update strategy and write the objects that you receive to the database, as shown in Listing 12-13, even if that means that values are written when they are not changed. This is an inefficient approach, but the inefficiencies will be small.

For more complex data models, the decision will depend on the relative costs of database server capacity and network traffic. If your major expense is network traffic, then you should perform an additional database read operation, as shown in Listing 12-14. This will increase the demand on the database but will reduce the amount of data sent over the network to and from the browser. If your major expense is provisioning the database server, then you should include the original data values in the HTML form, as shown in Listing 12-17. This approach avoids a database operation but does so by doubling up the data values included in the form and can require the features described in Chapter 21 to detect when the baseline data has been changed by another user.

Each HTTP request received by the application is processed by a new instance of the Home controller, and each controller object gets a new repository object and a new database context object. When the HTTP request has been handled, the controller, repository, and database objects are discarded, along with any Product objects that have been retrieved from the database. This means that each request must retrieve the data it requires from the database, even when an earlier request from the same client used performed the same queries.

However, the third strategy for performing updates is to take advantage of that original read operation by including the data it obtained in the response sent to the client and using it to avoiding updating unchanged values.

First, edit the Editor.cshtml file to add the hidden input elements shown in Listing 12-16.

Listing 12-16. Adding Elements in the Editor.cshtml File in the Views/Shared Folder

```
@model DataApp.Models.Product
@{
    ViewData["Title"] = ViewBag.CreateMode ? "Create" : "Edit";
    Layout = "_Layout";
}

<form asp-action="@(ViewBag.CreateMode ? "Create" : "Edit")" method="post">
    <input name="original.Id" value="@Model?.Id" type="hidden" />
    <input name="original.Name" value="@Model?.Name" type="hidden" />
    <input name="original.Category" value="@Model?.Category" type="hidden" />
    <input name="original.Price" value="@Model?.Price" type="hidden" />
    <div class="form-group">
        <label asp-for="Name"></label>
        <input asp-for="Name" class="form-control" />
    </div>
    <div class="form-group">
        <label asp-for="Category"></label>
        <input asp-for="Category" class="form-control" />
    </div>
```

```
    <div class="form-group">
        <label asp-for="Price"></label>
        <input asp-for="Price" class="form-control" />
    </div>
    <div class="text-center">
        <button class="btn btn-primary" type="submit">Save</button>
        <a asp-action="Index" class="btn btn-secondary">Cancel</a>
    </div>
</form>
```

The name attributes for these elements are prefixed with original followed by a period, which tells the MVC model binder that these elements should be used as properties for an action method parameter whose name is original. These elements will provide the original data values when the browser sends the POST request.

To receive the original data, edit the Home controller and add a parameter to the Edit method, as shown in Listing 12-17. The name of the parameter is original, which corresponds to the input elements in Listing 12-16, and the MVC model binder will create a Product object using the values from those input elements, providing the application with easy access to the original values.

Listing 12-17. Binding the Original Values in the HomeController.cs File in the Controllers Folder

```
using Microsoft.AspNetCore.Mvc;
using DataApp.Models;
using System.Linq;

namespace DataApp.Controllers {
    public class HomeController : Controller {
        private IDataRepository repository;

        public HomeController(IDataRepository repo) {
            repository = repo;
        }

        public IActionResult Index(string category = null, decimal? price = null) {
            var products = repository.GetFilteredProducts(category, price);
            ViewBag.category = category;
            ViewBag.price = price;
            return View(products);
        }

        public IActionResult Create() {
            ViewBag.CreateMode = true;
            return View("Editor", new Product());
        }

        [HttpPost]
        public IActionResult Create(Product product) {
            repository.CreateProduct(product);
            return RedirectToAction(nameof(Index));
        }
```

```
    public IActionResult Edit(long id) {
        ViewBag.CreateMode = false;
        return View("Editor", repository.GetProduct(id));
    }

    [HttpPost]
    public IActionResult Edit(Product product, Product original) {
        repository.UpdateProduct(product, original);
        return RedirectToAction(nameof(Index));
    }

    [HttpPost]
    public IActionResult Delete(long id) {
        repository.DeleteProduct(id);
        return RedirectToAction(nameof(Index));
    }
  }
}
```

The MVC model binder will create two Product objects, one of which contains the values from the input elements that may have been edited by the user and one of which contains the original values. The modified Edit method passes both objects to the repository, which must be updated to receive them. Change the UpdateProduct method defined by the IDataRepository interface, as shown in Listing 12-18.

Listing 12-18. Updating the Method in the IDataRepository.cs File in the Models Folder

```
using System.Collections.Generic;
using System.Linq;

namespace DataApp.Models {

    public interface IDataRepository {

        Product GetProduct(long id);

        IEnumerable<Product> GetAllProducts();

        IEnumerable<Product> GetFilteredProducts(string category = null,
            decimal? price = null);

        void CreateProduct(Product newProduct);

        void UpdateProduct(Product changedProduct, Product originalProduct = null);

        void DeleteProduct(long id);
    }
}
```

To follow the changes through, edit the EFDataRepository implementation class to add the optional parameter to the UpdateProduct method and to use it to detect changes, as shown in Listing 12-19.

Listing 12-19. Tracking Changes in the EFDataRepository.cs File in the Models Folder

```
...
public void UpdateProduct(Product changedProduct, Product originalProduct = null) {
    if (originalProduct == null) {
        originalProduct = context.Products.Find(changedProduct.Id);
    } else {
        context.Products.Attach(originalProduct);
    }
    originalProduct.Name = changedProduct.Name;
    originalProduct.Category = changedProduct.Category;
    originalProduct.Price = changedProduct.Price;
    context.SaveChanges();
}
...
```

If the UpdateProduct receives an originalProduct parameter, it is placed under the management of Entity Framework Core using the DbSet<T>.Attach method, which sets up the Entity Framework Core change tracking process and sets the associated EntityEntry.State property to Unmodified.

The property values from the other Product object are copied to the tracked object, and the change detection process will ensure that only changed values will be stored in the database.

Restart the application, click the Edit button for the Stadium product again, and change the Name field from Stadium (Small) to Stadium (Regular). When you click the Save button, the logging messages will show a SQL statement that only updates the property that has changed, like this:

```
...
UPDATE [Products] SET [Name] = @p0
WHERE [Id] = @p1;
...
```

No additional query is required to work out what has changed since the baseline data has been included in the HTTP POST request.

■ **Tip**   See Chapter 21 for details of how to detect when the baseline data has been changed since it was read from the database.

Deleting Data

The final data operation to implement is deletion, which is a relatively simple process when compared with updates. To add support for deleting rows from the database, edit the DeleteProduct method in the repository class to add the code shown in Listing 12-20.

Listing 12-20. Deleting Data in the EFDataRepository.cs File in the Models Folder

```
...
public void DeleteProduct(long id) {
    Product p = context.Products.Find(id);
    context.Products.Remove(p);
    context.SaveChanges();
}
...
```

The DbSet class defines a Remove method that accepts an entity object. When the SaveChanges method is called, Entity Framework Core will ask the database to remove the row from the database table. You can see how the Remove method results in a SQL command by examining the output from the application, which will contain an entry like this:

```
...
DELETE FROM [Products]
    WHERE [Id] = @p0;
...
```

The problem with the code in Listing 12-20 is that it uses the Find method to query the database to get the Product that should be deleted. This works, but it results in a database operation that can be avoided by creating a Product object directly, as shown in Listing 12-21.

■ **Tip** The DbSet<T> property also defines a RemoveRange method that can be used to delete multiple objects in a single method call, as demonstrated in Chapter 16.

Listing 12-21. Deleting Data in the EFDataRepository.cs File in the Models Folder

```
...
public void DeleteProduct(long id) {
    context.Products.Remove(new Product { Id = id });
    context.SaveChanges();
}
...
```

Only the key is used to identify the row in the database that will be deleted, so the delete operation can be performed by creating a new Product object with just an Id value and passing it to the Remove method. To see the effect, restart the application, navigate to http://localhost:5000, and click a Delete button to remove a product from the database, as shown in Figure 12-6. The result is the same but without the need to read data before deleting it.

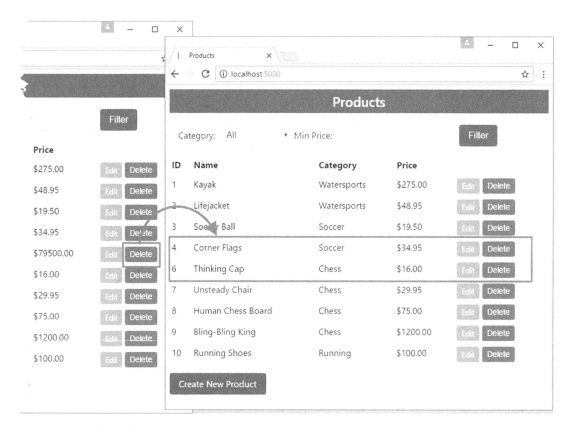

Figure 12-6. Deleting data

Summary

In this chapter, I explained how to perform basic data operations using Entity Framework Core. For the most part, these operations are easy to perform and fit well into the MVC model, although some thought must be given to the queries that are required to perform each task, which is a recurring theme when using Entity Framework Core. In the next chapter, I describe the Entity Framework Core migrations feature, which is used to prepare databases for storing application data.

CHAPTER 13

Understanding Migrations

In this chapter, I describe the migrations feature, which is how Entity Framework Core ensures the database reflects the data model in the application, even as that model changes. This is known as *code first*, meaning that you start with the data model classes you require and use migrations to create and manage the database. (This is as opposed to *database first*, where you work with an existing database, which I describe in Chapters 17 and 18.)

In this chapter, I explain how to create and apply migrations, how to assess the impact of migrations, and how to manage migrations using command-line tools and an API. Table 13-1 puts migrations in context.

Table 13-1. *Putting Migrations in Context*

Question	Answer
What are they?	Migrations are groups of commands that prepare databases for use with Entity Framework Core applications. They are used to create the database and then keep it synchronized with changes in the data model.
Why are they useful?	Migrations automate the process of creating and maintaining databases for storing application data. Without migrations, you would have to create the database using SQL commands and manually configure Entity Framework Core to use it.
How are they used?	Migrations are created and applied using the dotnet ef command-line tools.
Are there any pitfalls or limitations?	The error messages that Entity Framework Core produces when working with migrations are not always clear. The most common problem is creating migrations but not applying them to the database.
Are there any alternatives?	You create the database first and then create the data model classes for use with Entity Framework Core. See Chapter 17 for examples.

Caution Many of the commands described in this chapter change the structure of the database and can result in data loss. Do not use these commands on production databases until you are sure that you understand their effects and only after you have taken backups of critical data.

Table 13-2 summarizes the chapter.

Table 13-2. *Chapter Summary*

Problem	Solution	Listing
Create a new migration	Use the `dotnet ef migration add` command	12
See the changes that a migration contains	Use the `dotnet ef migrations script` command	3, 10, 13
Apply a migration to the database	Use the `dotnet ef database update` command	4-9, 15-17
List the migrations in a project	Use the `dotnet ef migrations list` command	14
Remove a migration	Use the `dotnet ef migrations remove` command	18-20
Reset the database	Use the `dotnet ef database update 0` command or the `dotnet ef database drop` command	21, 22
Manage migrations for multiple databases	Create a separate context class and specify its name when using the `dotnet ef` command	23-28, 30, 31
See the database contexts in a project	Use the `dotnet ef dbcontext list` command	29
Managing migrations programmatically	Use the Entity Framework Core migrations API	32-35
Seed the database programmatically	Use the migrations API to ensure that there are no pending updates before using the context class to add data to the database	36-39

Preparing for This Chapter

This chapter uses the `DataApp` project created in Chapter 11 and modified in Chapter 12. To prepare for this chapter, open a command prompt or PowerShell window in the `DataApp` project folder and run the command shown in Listing 13-1.

 Tip   If you don't want to follow the process of building the example project, you can download all of the required files from this book's source code repository, `https://github.com/apress/pro-ef-core-2-for-asp.net-core-mvc`.

Listing 13-1. Resetting the Database

```
dotnet ef database drop --force
```

This command removes the database, which will help ensure that you get the right expected results from the examples in this chapter. Next, start the application by running the command shown in Listing 13-2.

Listing 13-2. Starting the Example Application

```
dotnet run
```

The application will start, but when you use a browser to request the URL http://localhost:5000, you will see an error. The stack trace is long, and the error will be repeated several times, but here is the important part of the message:

```
...
SqlException: Cannot open database "DataAppDb" requested by the login.
...
```

Understanding Migrations

The reason that the error was reported in the previous section was because the database hasn't been prepared for the application. The connection string in the appsettings.json file specifies a database called DataAppDb, like this:

```
...
"DefaultConnection": "Server=(localdb)\\MSSQLLocalDB;Database=DataAppDb;
    MultipleActiveResultSets=true"
...
```

SQL Server doesn't know anything about the DataAppDb database at the moment, so when the application tried to read the data from it, an error occurred. Databases are prepared using Entity Framework Core *migrations*. A migration is a C# class that contains instructions for creating a database schema. When a migration is applied, the database, tables, and columns required to store entity data are created.

Working with the Initial Migration

There is already a migration in the example application, which was created in Chapter 11 and which was used by the application in earlier chapters. Open the DataApp/Migrations folder, and you will see three files. (One of these files is nested in the Solution Explorer and isn't visible until its parent item is expanded.) All three files are described in Table 13-3.

Table 13-3. *The Migration Files in the Example Project*

Name	Description
<timestamp>_Initial.cs	This is part of the Initial class, which applies the first migration to the database. It contains instructions for creating the database schema.
<timestamp>_Initial.Designer.cs	This is part of the Initial class, which applies the first migration to the database. It contains instructions creating for model objects.
EFDatabaseContextModelSnapshot.cs	This class contains a description of the entity classes used in the migration and is used to detect changes for creating further migrations.

The first two files are partial classes, which means that the code they contain is combined to form a single C# class. The name of these files starts with a timestamp that indicates when they were created and is followed the name of the migration they contain. The names in this case include _Initial because the migration was created in Chapter 11 using this command (you don't need to run this command again):

```
dotnet ef migrations add Initial
```

The convention for working with migrations is to use the name Initial for the first migration that is created in a project. Open the <timestamp>_Initial.cs file, and you will see the most important part of the migration, as follows:

```
using Microsoft.EntityFrameworkCore.Metadata;
using Microsoft.EntityFrameworkCore.Migrations;
using System;
using System.Collections.Generic;

namespace DataApp.Migrations {
    public partial class Initial : Migration {

        protected override void Up(MigrationBuilder migrationBuilder) {

            migrationBuilder.CreateTable(
                name: "Products",
                columns: table => new {
                    Id = table.Column<long>(nullable: false)
                        .Annotation("SqlServer:ValueGenerationStrategy",
                            SqlServerValueGenerationStrategy.IdentityColumn),
                    Category = table.Column<string>(nullable: true),
                    Name = table.Column<string>(nullable: true),
                    Price = table.Column<decimal>(nullable: false)
                },
                constraints: table => {
                    table.PrimaryKey("PK_Products", x => x.Id);
                });
        }

        protected override void Down(MigrationBuilder migrationBuilder) {
            migrationBuilder.DropTable(
                name: "Products");
        }
    }
}
```

■ **Note**   The exact code may change, especially if you are using a later version of Entity Framework Core or the database provider for SQL Server. But the purpose and general nature of the code will be close enough to understand what the migration does.

This part of the Initial class contains the methods that will be called to update the database. Each migration contains two methods, Up and Down, which are described in Table 13-4.

Table 13-4. The Migration Methods

Name	Description
Up()	This method contains statements that upgrade the database to store entity data.
Down()	This method contains statements that downgrade the database to its original state.

A migration can be used to upgrade or downgrade the database, a process that will make more sense shortly. For a newly created database, the upgrade process will create the table and columns needed to store the data, while the downgrade process will return the database to its original state. Both of these processes are described in the sections that follow.

UNDERSTANDING THE OTHER EF COMMANDS

Working with Entity Framework Core means using the command line to create and apply migrations. All of the commands that I use in this book start with dotnet ef, like this command from Chapter 11:

```
dotnet ef migration add Initial
```

This command creates a new migration. It is applied to the database using a similar command, shown later in the chapter in Listing 13-4:

```
dotnet ef database update
```

If you have used earlier versions of Entity Framework, you may be familiar with a different set of commands, such as Add-Migration and Update-Database. These were the original commands used to manage migrations and databases, but they are only supported by Visual Studio and work reliably only when used in the Package Manager Console, which is a PowerShell window with some additional features.

This style of command is still supported, but I have not used them in this book. These commands only work in a specific Visual Studio window, and they cause endless problems.

Understanding the Migration Upgrade

The Up method is responsible for upgrading the database. When dealing with the migration that is applied to a newly created database, Entity Framework Core creates a table for each DbSet<T> property in the context class. There is only one DbSet property in the context at the moment, called Products, and it has resulted in this statement in the migration:

```
...
migrationBuilder.CreateTable(
    name: "Products",
...
```

The parameter for the Up method is an instance of the `MigrationBuilder` class, which provides methods that are used to specify the changes that will be applied to the database. These methods are translated into database-specific commands by the database provider, which is how the C# statements in the migration are translated into SQL statements that SQL Server can execute.

The `MigrationBuilder.CreateTable` method creates a new database table. By default, Entity Framework Core uses the name of the `DbSet<T>` property as the name for the database table, which is why the `name` argument to the `CreateTable` is set to `Products` for the migration in the example application.

The other arguments to the `CreateTable` method configure the table. The `columns` argument is used to define a column for each of the properties defined by the entity class that the table will be used to store. The type of the `Products` property defined by the context class is `DbSet<Product>`, so Entity Framework Core adds columns to the table for each property that the `Product` class defines.

```
...
migrationBuilder.CreateTable(
    name: "Products",
    columns: table => new {
        Id = table.Column<long>(nullable: false)
            .Annotation("SqlServer:ValueGenerationStrategy",
                SqlServerValueGenerationStrategy.IdentityColumn),
        Category = table.Column<string>(nullable: true),
        Name = table.Column<string>(nullable: true),
        Price = table.Column<decimal>(nullable: false)
    },
...
```

Columns are defined for the Id, Name, Category, and Price properties. The Id property is configured so that the database will generate values when new rows are added to the table. Each column is configured with the .NET type for the corresponding Product property.

To finish the definition of the table, a constraint is added that nominates the Id column as the primary key.

```
...
migrationBuilder.CreateTable(
    name: "Products",
    columns: table => new {
        Id = table.Column<long>(nullable: false)
            .Annotation("SqlServer:ValueGenerationStrategy",
                SqlServerValueGenerationStrategy.IdentityColumn),
        Category = table.Column<string>(nullable: true),
        Name = table.Column<string>(nullable: true),
        Price = table.Column<decimal>(nullable: false)
    },
    constraints: table => {
        table.PrimaryKey("PK_Products", x => x.Id);
    });
}
...
```

Putting these pieces together, the Up method creates a new table called Products, with Id, Name, Category, and Price columns, configured so that the Id column is the primary key and values for the Id column will be generated by the database when new rows are created.

Understanding the Migration Downgrade

The Down method is used to return the database to its previous state, undoing the effect of the Up method. When dealing with a migration that will be applied to an empty database, the downgrade just has to remove the table that has been created to store entity data.

```
...
migrationBuilder.DropTable(name: "Products");
...
```

The MigrationBuilder.DropTable command removes a table from the database. In this case, the Products table will be removed, which returns the database to its original state.

Examining the Migration SQL

To see how the commands in the Initial migration class are translated into SQL statements, use a command prompt to run the command shown in Listing 13-3 in the DataApp folder.

Listing 13-3. Examining a Migration

```
dotnet ef migrations script
```

All of the Entity Framework Core command-line tools are invoked with dotnet ef, which targets the EF Core tools added to the project in Chapter 11. The migrations argument selects the tools that perform operations on migrations, and the script argument displays the SQL commands that the migration will execute in the database. For the Initial migration in the example project, the following SQL script will be generated:

```
...
IF OBJECT_ID(N'__EFMigrationsHistory') IS NULL
BEGIN
    CREATE TABLE [__EFMigrationsHistory] (
        [MigrationId] nvarchar(150) NOT NULL,
        [ProductVersion] nvarchar(32) NOT NULL,
        CONSTRAINT [PK___EFMigrationsHistory] PRIMARY KEY ([MigrationId])
    );
END;

GO

CREATE TABLE [Products] (
    [Id] bigint NOT NULL IDENTITY,
    [Category] nvarchar(max) NULL,
    [Name] nvarchar(max) NULL,
    [Price] decimal(18, 2) NOT NULL,
    CONSTRAINT [PK_Products] PRIMARY KEY ([Id])
);

GO
```

```
INSERT INTO [__EFMigrationsHistory] ([MigrationId], [ProductVersion])
VALUES (N'20180124114307_Initial', N'2.0.1-rtm-125');

GO
...
```

These statements create two tables. One table, called Products, corresponds to the instructions contained in the migration that were described in the previous section. The other table is called __EFMigrationsHistory, and it is used to keep track of which migrations have been applied to the database, the importance of which will become clear when you create additional migrations later in the chapter.

Applying the Migration

A migration doesn't take effect until it is applied to the database. Run the command shown in Listing 13-4 in the DataApp folder to apply the migration to the database.

Listing 13-4. Applying a Migration

```
dotnet ef database update
```

The dotnet ef command targets the Entity Framework Core tools; the database argument specifies that you want to perform an operation on the database, and the update argument tells Entity Framework Core to update the database by applying all of the migrations in the project (although there is only one migration at the moment). The project will be compiled, and the code in the Up method of the Initial class will be executed to generate the SQL commands that create and configure the Products table.

■ **Tip**   When you apply a migration with the dotnet ef database update command, the database that is specified in the connection string will be created if it doesn't already exist. This is how the DataAppDb database that the application is configured to use comes into being, even though the name of the database isn't part of the migration of the SQL script it produces.

Checking the Migration

Select Tools ➤ SQL Server ➤ New Query and enter **(localdb)\MSSQLLocalDB** in the Server Name field. Ensure that Windows Authentication is selected for the Authentication field and click the Database Name menu to select DataAppDb from the drop-down list, which will display a complete list of the databases that have been created using LocalDB. Once you have connected to the database, enter the SQL shown in Listing 13-5 into the editor window.

Listing 13-5. Inspecting the Products Table

```
USE DataAppDb

SELECT column_name, data_type FROM INFORMATION_SCHEMA.COLUMNS
WHERE TABLE_NAME = 'Products'

GO
```

Select Execute from the Visual Studio SQL menu to send the query to the database server. The result contains the name and type of each column in the Products table, showing the effect of the migration, as shown in Table 13-5, and showing how a row in the Products table contains columns for all of the data values needed to represent a Product object.

Table 13-5. *The Structure of the Products Table*

column_name	data_type
Id	bigint
Category	nvarchar
Name	nvarchar
Price	decimal

Seeding the Database and Running the Application

Now that the database schema has been created, Entity Framework Core will be able to read and store Product objects on behalf of the example application.

To provide the application with some data to work with, enter the SQL shown in Listing 13-6 into the SQL query window (or open a new one).

Listing 13-6. Seeding the Database

```
USE DataAppDb

INSERT INTO Products (Name, Category, Price)
VALUES
    ('Kayak', 'Watersports', 275),
    ('Lifejacket', 'Watersports', 48.95),
    ('Soccer Ball', 'Soccer', 19.50),
    ('Corner Flags', 'Soccer', 34.95),
    ('Stadium', 'Soccer', 79500),
    ('Thinking Cap', 'Chess', 16),
    ('Unsteady Chair', 'Chess', 29.95),
    ('Human Chess Board', 'Chess', 75),
    ('Bling-Bling King', 'Chess', 1200)
```

Select SQL ➤ Execute to seed the database and receive the following response that reports how many rows were changed by the command:

```
(9 row(s) affected)
```

Manually seeding databases is a slightly awkward process, but I show you how to handle this using C# code later in the chapter. Run the command shown in Listing 13-7 in the DataApp folder to start the example application.

Listing 13-7. Starting the Example Application

```
dotnet run
```

Open a new browser window and request the URL http://localhost:5000. You will see the data table, as shown in Figure 13-1. Stop the application with Ctrl+C once you have confirmed that the database is working and has been populated with the seed data.

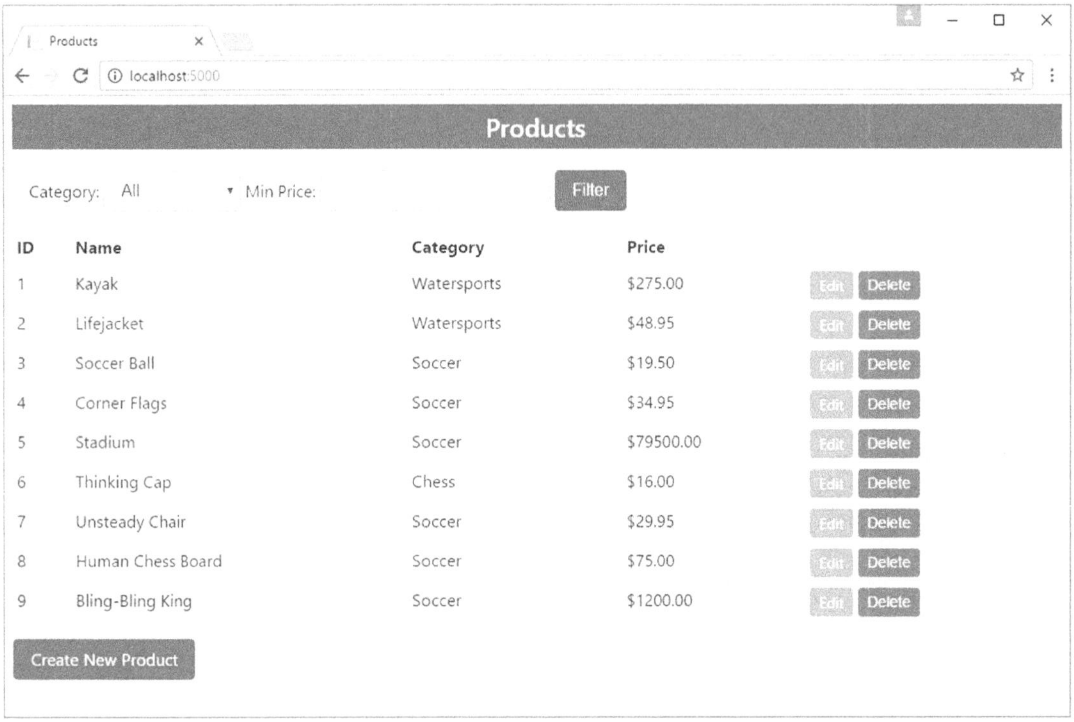

Figure 13-1. *Running the example application*

Before moving on, it is worth reflecting on the effect of the database migration. This section started without a database and no way to store Product objects. The migration, which was created in Chapter 11, is a set of C# files that contain instructions for upgrading or downgrading the database. When the migration was applied, the DataAppDb database was created, and the C# upgrade statements were translated into a SQL commands that were executed to create and configure the Products table, with columns for each of the properties defined by the Product class. Each row in the Products table represents a Product object, starting with the seed data created in Listing 13-6.

It is also worth reflecting on how much of the process was entirely automatic. Entity Framework Core discovered the database context class, identified the classes that need to be stored in the database, and worked out how to represent instances of those classes as relational data. Entity Framework Core can require some direction for more complex examples, as you will see in later chapters, but you can get a long way just by defining C# classes and letting Entity Framework Core figure out the details for you.

Creating Additional Migrations

The convenience of migrations becomes apparent when the data model in the MVC application changes. To see how Entity Framework Core handles changes to the data model, edit the Product class to add the enumeration and property shown in Listing 13-8.

Listing 13-8. Adding a Property in the Product.cs File in the Models Folder

```
namespace DataApp.Models {

    public enum Colors {
        Red, Green, Blue
    }

    public class Product {

        public long Id { get; set; }
        public string Name { get; set; }
        public string Category { get; set; }
        public decimal Price { get; set; }
        public Colors Color { get; set; }
    }
}
```

The Color property uses the Colors enum. Adding a property means that Product objects can no longer be stored in the database since there is no means of storing Color values.

Bringing the database into sync with the revised data model means creating and applying a new migration. To create the migration, run the command shown in Listing 13-9 in the DataApp folder.

Listing 13-9. Creating a New Database Migration

```
dotnet ef migrations add AddColorProperty
```

The dotnet ef migrations add command creates a new migration, which in this case is called AddColorProperty. You can use any name you like for migrations, and common naming strategies include describing the data model change that the migration reflects or using incremental version numbers.

When you run the command in Listing 13-9, new files are added to the Migrations folder. Open the <timestamp>_AddColorProperty.cs file to see the changes that migration will apply to the database, which are as follows:

```
using Microsoft.EntityFrameworkCore.Migrations;
using System;
using System.Collections.Generic;

namespace DataApp.Migrations {
    public partial class AddColorProperty : Migration {

        protected override void Up(MigrationBuilder migrationBuilder) {
            migrationBuilder.AddColumn<int>(
                name: "Color",
                table: "Products",
                nullable: false,
                defaultValue: 0);
        }
```

```
    protected override void Down(MigrationBuilder migrationBuilder) {
        migrationBuilder.DropColumn(
            name: "Color",
            table: "Products");
    }
  }
}
```

The Up method will update the schema to reflect the change in the data model, which in this case means adding a column called Color to the Products table. The Down method returns the database to its previous state by dropping the Color column.

Run the command in Listing 13-10 in the DataApp folder to see the SQL statements that the new migration will produce.

Listing 13-10. Inspecting the Migration SQL Statements

```
dotnet ef migrations script Initial AddColorProperty
```

Specifying the names of migrations when using the dotnet ef migrations script command will show the statements required to update the database from the first migration to the second and will produce the following result:

```
...
ALTER TABLE [Products] ADD [Color] int NOT NULL DEFAULT 0;

GO

INSERT INTO [__EFMigrationsHistory] ([MigrationId], [ProductVersion])
VALUES (N'<timestamp>_AddColorProperty', N'2.0.1-rtm-125');

GO
...
```

These statements add a Color property to the Products table and update the __EFMigrationsHistory table to reflect the application of the migration to the database.

Adding Another Property to the Data Model

I am going to create a third migration to show how changes to the database can be managed. Add the property shown in Listing 13-11 to the Product class.

Listing 13-11. Adding an Additional Property in the Product.cs File in the Models Folder

```
namespace DataApp.Models {

    public enum Colors {
        Red, Green, Blue
    }

    public class Product {
```

```
        public long Id { get; set; }
        public string Name { get; set; }
        public string Category { get; set; }
        public decimal Price { get; set; }
        public Colors Color { get; set; }
        public bool InStock { get; set; }
    }
}
```

The new addition is a bool property called InStock. To create a migration to add support for storing this property in the database, run the command shown in Listing 13-12 in the DataApp folder.

Listing 13-12. Creating a New Migration

```
dotnet ef migrations add AddInStockProperty
```

A new set of migration class files will be added to the Migrations folder of the project. Run the command shown in Listing 13-13 in the DataApp folder to see the SQL statements that will modify the Products table.

Listing 13-13. Displaying the SQL Statements for a Migration

```
dotnet ef migrations script AddColorProperty AddInStockProperty
```

This command will produce the following result:

```
...
ALTER TABLE [Products] ADD [InStock] bit NOT NULL DEFAULT 0;

GO

INSERT INTO [__EFMigrationsHistory] ([MigrationId], [ProductVersion])
VALUES (N'<timestamp>_AddInStockProperty', N'2.0.1-rtm-125');

GO
...
```

You can see how each change to the Product class produces a migration that will bring the data model and the database back in sync. When a migration is created, Entity Framework Core works out what changes have to be applied to the database automatically so that the migration only makes the modifications necessary to represent instances of the modified classes.

Managing Migrations

Creating a migration is only part of the process: a migration must also be applied to the database to ensure that the application data can be stored. The most common way to manage migrations is to use the dotnet ef command-line tools, which I describe in the sections that follow. Migrations can also be managed using an API provided by Entity Framework Core, which I describe in the "Managing Migrations Programmatically" section of this chapter.

Listing Migrations

You can see the list of migrations that have been created for the example project by running the command shown in Listing 13-14 in the DataApp folder.

Listing 13-14. Listing the Available Migrations

```
dotnet ef migrations list
```

This command lists all of the migrations that have been created for a project. There are three migrations in the DataApp project, which produces the following output (although you will see timestamps in the file names):

```
...
<timestamp>_Initial
<timestamp>_AddColorProperty
<timestamp>_AddInStockProperty
...
```

This is a list of the migrations that are defined in the project, which may not have been applied to the database yet. The migrations are listed in order, which means that you can easily tell that the AddColorProperty migration builds on the changes that are contained in the Initial migration and that the AddInStockProperty migration builds on AddColorProperty.

Applying All Migrations

The most common task is to apply all of the migrations that are defined in the project to bring the database up-to-date in a single step. To apply all of the migrations in the DataApp project, run the command shown in Listing 13-15 from the DataApp folder.

Listing 13-15. Applying All Migrations

```
dotnet ef database update
```

Entity Framework Core will use the __EFMigrationsHistory table to work out which migrations have already been applied and will bring the database up-to-date.

Select Tools ➤ SQL Server ➤ New Query, connect to the database, and enter the SQL shown in Listing 13-16.

Listing 13-16. Inspecting the Products Table

```
USE DataAppDb

SELECT column_name, data_type FROM INFORMATION_SCHEMA.COLUMNS
WHERE TABLE_NAME = 'Products'

GO
```

Select Execute from the Visual Studio SQL menu to send the query to the database server, which will provide a summary of the table structure, as shown in Table 13-6. The summary includes columns that correspond to the new properties added to the Product class in Listing 13-8 and Listing 13-11.

Table 13-6. *The Structure of the Products Table*

column_name	data_type
Id	bigint
Category	nvarchar
Name	nvarchar
Price	decimal
Color	int
InStock	bit

Updating to a Specific Migration

You can update the database to a specific migration, which can be useful when you need to roll back a set of changes or don't want to apply all of the migrations in a project in one go. Run the command in Listing 13-17 in the DataApp folder to migrate the database to the AddColorProperty migration.

Listing 13-17. Updating the Database to a Specific Migration

```
dotnet ef database update AddColorProperty
```

When the name of a migration is used with the dotnet ef database update command, Entity Framework Core examines the database to see which migrations have been applied and starts working toward the target migration, calling the Up or Down method to perform upgrades or downgrades as required to get to the target state.

In the case of the command in Listing 13-17, to update to the AddColorProperty migration, Entity Framework Core has to perform a downgrade from the AddInStockProperty migration, which has the effect of dropping the InStock column from the Products table. You can see the change to the table structure if you execute the SQL query in Listing 13-16 again, which will show the table structure in Table 13-7.

Table 13-7. *The Structure of the Products Table*

column_name	data_type
Id	bigint
Category	nvarchar
Name	nvarchar
Price	decimal
Color	int

Removing a Migration

Migrations are sometimes created by mistake or outlive their usefulness. Run the command shown in Listing 13-18 in the DataApp folder to remove the most recent migration added to the project.

Listing 13-18. Removing the Most Recent Migration

```
dotnet ef migrations remove
```

The command in Listing 13-18 removes the AddInStockProperty migration, which can be seen in the output that is produced.

```
...
Removing migration '<timestamp>_AddInStockProperty'.
Reverting model snapshot.
...
```

The message about reverting the model snapshot relates to the EFDatabaseContextModelSnapshot.cs file in the Migrations folder, which is used to compare the entity classes in the project with the most recent migrations. When you remove a migration, the snapshot used for comparisons is updated to reflect the change. This is especially useful if you are removing a migration because, for example, you misspelled the name, because it means that the next migration you create will reflect any changes in the model classes since the most recent remaining migration in the project.

⬚ **Tip**   You can remove only the most recent migration, which means you have to run the command in Listing 13-18 several times if you need to remove multiple migrations.

You will see a warning when the migration you are about to remove has already been applied to the database. This is important because you run the risk of putting the database into a state from which it cannot be upgraded because the schema doesn't match the state that the remaining migrations expect to find. To see the warning, run the command in Listing 13-19 in the DataApp folder.

Listing 13-19. Removing an Applied Migration

```
dotnet ef migrations remove
```

This command tells Entity Framework Core to remove the AddColorProperty migration, which has been applied to the database. You will see the following warning, and the migration will not be removed:

```
...
The migration '<timestamp>_AddColorProperty' has already been applied to the database.
Revert it and try again. If the migration has been applied to other databases, consider
reverting its changes using a new migration.
...
```

You can use the dotnet ef database update command to remove the migration from the database or use the --force argument, as shown in Listing 13-20, to tell Entity Framework Core to proceed anyway and remove the migration from the project. Run this command in the DataApp folder to force the removal of the migration, even though it has been applied to the database.

Listing 13-20. Forcing the Removal of an Applied Migration

```
dotnet ef migrations remove --force
```

When you force the removal of the migration, Entity Framework Core doesn't check the state of the database before removing the migration from the project. This is confirmed in the output from the command, shown here:

```
...
Removing migration '<timestamp>_AddColorProperty' without checking the database. If this
migration has been applied to the database, you will need to manually reverse the changes
it made.
Removing migration '<timestamp>_AddColorProperty'.
Reverting model snapshot.
...
```

Resetting the Database

There will be times when you want to undo all of the migrations that have been applied to the database and start over. This can be because you want to test that the migrations produce the expected schema or because you have forced the removal of a migration that had been applied to the database and the schema and the project are out of sync.

Run the command shown in Listing 13-21 in the DataApp folder to run the commands in the Down methods of all of the migrations in the project.

Listing 13-21. Downgrading all Migrations

```
dotnet ef database update 0
```

Using 0 as the argument to the dotnet ef database update command removes all of the migrations that have been applied to the database. This isn't quite the same as returning to the original starting point because the DataAppDb database and the __EFMigrationsHistory table still exist (although the table is empty since no migrations are applied). Run the command shown in Listing 13-22 to return to a completely clean state.

Listing 13-22. Dropping the Database

```
dotnet ef database drop --force
```

This command drops the DataAppDb database completely, including the __EFMigrationsHistory table. The --force argument can be omitted if you want to be prompted before dropping the database.

Working with Multiple Databases

All the examples so far in this chapter have assumed that the project relies on only one database. When the dotnet ef migrations and dotnet ef database commands are used, they inspect the project to find the context class, connect to the database using the associated connection string, and do their work.

When a project relies on multiple databases, which might be because there is one database for product data and another for user data, then the context class that the migration operation affects must be specified as part of the command line. The sections that follow add a second database to the example project and demonstrate how its migrations are created and applied.

DECIDING WHEN TO CREATE A DIFFERENT DATABASE

A database can contain multiple tables, each of which is able to store a different type of data object. For many projects, this means that all of the data that an application requires can be stored in a single database and accessed through a single context class.

The most common reason for using multiple databases is when a project relies on a third-party package that uses Entity Framework Core, such as ASP.NET Core Identity, which is used to manage user accounts, authentication, and authorization. The application's custom data (the equivalent of the product data in the example application) is stored in one database, and the identity data is stored in another. You may also need multiple databases if your project has to work with data from a legacy application or if different types of data have different performance or security requirements.

Extending the Data Model

The starting point for adding a second database to the example application is to create a new entity class, a new repository, and its implementation class. Begin by adding a file called Customer.cs to the Models folder and adding the code shown in Listing 13-23.

Listing 13-23. The Contents of the Customer.cs File in the Models Folder

```
namespace DataApp.Models {

    public class Customer {

        public long Id { get; set; }
        public string Name { get; set; }
        public string City { get; set; }
        public string Country { get; set; }
    }
}
```

The Customer class defines an Id property that will be used as the unique key, values for which will be generated by the database. The Name, String, and Country properties are conventional string values.

To create a context class for working with Customer objects, add a class file called EFCustomerContext.cs to the Models folder and add the code shown in Listing 13-24.

Listing 13-24. The Contents of the EFCustomerContext.cs File in the Models Folder

```
using Microsoft.EntityFrameworkCore;
using Microsoft.EntityFrameworkCore.Design;
using Microsoft.Extensions.DependencyInjection;

namespace DataApp.Models {
    public class EFCustomerContext : DbContext {

        public EFCustomerContext(DbContextOptions<EFCustomerContext> opts)
            : base(opts) { }
```

```
        public DbSet<Customer> Customers { get; set; }
    }
}
```

The EFCustomerContext class follows the standard pattern for a context, defining a constructor that receives a configuration object and a property that returns a DbSet<T> with a type parameter that indicates the type of objects that the context manages.

To create a repository for Customer objects, add a class file called CustomerRepository.cs to the Models folder and add the code shown in Listing 13-25. This file contains both the interface and the implementation class for simplicity.

Listing 13-25. The Contents of the CustomerRepository.cs File in the Models Folder

```
using System.Collections.Generic;

namespace DataApp.Models {

    public interface ICustomerRepository {

        IEnumerable<Customer> GetAllCustomers();

    }

    public class EFCustomerRepository : ICustomerRepository {
        private EFCustomerContext context;

        public EFCustomerRepository(EFCustomerContext ctx) {
            context = ctx;
        }

        public IEnumerable<Customer> GetAllCustomers() {
            return context.Customers;
        }
    }
}
```

The repository provides a GetAllCustomers method that returns all the Customer objects in the database. I have omitted the other standard data operations, as described in Chapter 12, to keep the example as simple as possible.

Configuring the Application

A connection string is required so that the database provider can reach the database server, authenticate itself, and use the new database. Edit the appsettings.json file and add the connection string shown in Listing 13-26.

Listing 13-26. Defining the Connection String in the appsettings.json File in the DataApp Folder

```
{
  "ConnectionStrings": {
    "DefaultConnection": "Server=(localdb)\\MSSQLLocalDB;Database=DataAppDb;MultipleActive
    ResultSets=true",
    "CustomerConnection": "Server=(localdb)\\MSSQLLocalDB;Database=CustomerDb;MultipleActive
    ResultSets=true"
  },
  "Logging": {
    "LogLevel": {
      "Default": "None",
      "Microsoft.EntityFrameworkCore": "Information"
    }
  }
}
```

The new connection string, called `CustomerConnection`, specifies a database called `CustomerDb` on the same LocalDB database server used for `Product` objects.

■ **Tip** The databases for the example application are both managed by the same database server, which is SQL Server accessed through the LocalDB feature. This isn't a requirement, and you can use separate database servers in an application and even mix and match database servers from different suppliers such that an application can use both SQL Server and MySQL databases, for example.

The next step is to configure Entity Framework Core to use the new database and configure the ASP.NET Core dependency injection feature to handle dependencies on the customer repository interface. Edit the ConfigureServices method in the Startup class to add the statements shown in Listing 13-27.

Listing 13-27. Configuring the Application in the Startup.cs File in the DataApp Folder

```
using System;
using System.Collections.Generic;
using System.Linq;
using System.Threading.Tasks;
using Microsoft.AspNetCore.Builder;
using Microsoft.AspNetCore.Hosting;
using Microsoft.AspNetCore.Http;
using Microsoft.Extensions.DependencyInjection;
using DataApp.Models;
using Microsoft.EntityFrameworkCore;
using Microsoft.Extensions.Configuration;

namespace DataApp {
    public class Startup {

        public Startup(IConfiguration config) => Configuration = config;

        public IConfiguration Configuration { get; }
```

```
        public void ConfigureServices(IServiceCollection services) {
            services.AddMvc();
            string conString = Configuration["ConnectionStrings:DefaultConnection"];
            services.AddDbContext<EFDatabaseContext>(options =>
                options.UseSqlServer(conString));

            string customerConString =
                Configuration["ConnectionStrings:CustomerConnection"];
            services.AddDbContext<EFCustomerContext>(options =>
                options.UseSqlServer(customerConString));

            services.AddTransient<IDataRepository, EFDataRepository>();
            services.AddTransient<ICustomerRepository, EFCustomerRepository>();
        }

        public void Configure(IApplicationBuilder app, IHostingEnvironment env) {
            app.UseDeveloperExceptionPage();
            app.UseStatusCodePages();
            app.UseStaticFiles();
            app.UseMvcWithDefaultRoute();
        }
    }
}
```

Creating and Applying Migrations

Now that there are two context classes in the application, the commands used earlier in the chapter won't work. To see the problem, run the command shown in Listing 13-28 in the DataApp folder.

Listing 13-28. Creating a Migration

```
dotnet ef migrations add Customers_Initial
```

This command displays the following error message:

```
...
More than one DbContext was found. Specify which one to use. Use the '-Context' parameter
for PowerShell commands and the '--context' parameter for dotnet commands.
...
```

When Entity Framework Core inspects the project, it finds two classes that are derived from DbContext, and it doesn't know which one the migration command should be applied to.

You don't have to search the project to find out which context classes have been discovered. Instead, run the command shown in Listing 13-29 in the DataApp folder, and Entity Framework Core will display a list of the context classes it finds.

Listing 13-29. Listing the Context Classes

```
dotnet ef dbcontext list
```

This command displays a list of the context classes that are in the project, as follows:

```
...
DataApp.Models.EFCustomerContext
DataApp.Models.EFDatabaseContext
...
```

The name of the class, with or without its namespace, can be used with the --context argument to select a context to operate on. Run the commands shown in Listing 13-30 in the DataApp folder to create the initial migration for the Customer class and to reflect the uncaptured changes in the Product class that were created when migrations were deleted earlier in the chapter, this time specifying the context that it applies to.

Listing 13-30. Specifying a Context When Creating a Migration

```
dotnet ef migrations add Initial --context EFCustomerContext
dotnet ef migrations add Current --context EFDatabaseContext
```

The same technique is required to apply migrations to the database. Run the commands shown in Listing 13-31 in the DataApp folder to apply the migrations for both databases.

Listing 13-31. Applying Migrations to the Databases

```
dotnet ef database update --context EFDatabaseContext
dotnet ef database update --context EFCustomerContext
```

Managing Migrations Programmatically

For most projects, the best way to manage migrations is to use the dotnet ef migrations and dotnet ef database command-line tools. But Entity Framework Core also provides an API for managing migrations programmatically, which can be useful when it isn't possible to use the command line. The migrations API can be used to create a migrations management tool that can be used to decide which migrations are applied to a database. In this section, I demonstrate how to create a migrations manager and demonstrate how the migrations API works.

■ **Caution**   Do not use ASP.NET Core Identity to manage access to the migrations management tool. Identity relies on Entity Framework Core for data storage, which means that you can easily apply a migration that prevents you from authenticating yourself and so prevents you from using the management tool. I generally install the migration management tool on its own, alongside the database server, to keep it separate from the public-facing MVC applications.

Creating the Migration Manager Class

The starting point for creating the migrations manager is to define a helper that will take care of dealing with the Entity Framework Core API in a way that is easy to consume from an MVC controller. Create a class file called MigrationsManager.cs in the Models folder and add the code shown in Listing 13-32.

Listing 13-32. The Contents of the MigrationsManager.cs File in the Models Folder

```
using System;
using System.Collections.Generic;
using System.Linq;
using Microsoft.Extensions.DependencyInjection;
using Microsoft.EntityFrameworkCore;
using Microsoft.EntityFrameworkCore.Migrations;
using Microsoft.EntityFrameworkCore.Infrastructure;

namespace DataApp.Models {

    public class MigrationsManager {
        private IEnumerable<Type> ContextTypes;
        private IServiceProvider provider;
        public IEnumerable<string> ContextNames;

        public MigrationsManager(IServiceProvider prov) {
            provider = prov;

            ContextTypes = provider.GetServices<DbContextOptions>()
                .Select(o => o.ContextType);
            ContextNames = ContextTypes.Select(t => t.FullName);
            ContextName = ContextNames.First();
        }

        public string ContextName { get; set; }

        public IEnumerable<string> AppliedMigrations
            => Context.Database.GetAppliedMigrations();

        public IEnumerable<string> PendingMigrations
            => Context.Database.GetPendingMigrations();

        public IEnumerable<string> AllMigrations
            => Context.Database.GetMigrations();

        public void Migrate(string contextName, string target = null) {
            Context.GetService<IMigrator>().Migrate(target);
        }

        public DbContext Context =>
            provider.GetRequiredService(Type.GetType(ContextName)) as DbContext;
    }
}
```

This class has three roles. The first is to get the types and names of the database context classes in the application. The manager class gets all of the DbContextOptions services that have been registered as services using the ASP.NET Core dependency injection feature and then, using these services, gets the associated context class by reading the ContextType property of each DbContextOptions object, like this:

```
...
ContextTypes = provider.GetServices<DbContextOptions>().Select(o => o.ContextType);
...
```

This is a somewhat awkward technique, but it is the same one used by Entity Framework Core to discover context classes.

The second role of the manager class is to take a string containing the type name of a context class and to obtain an instance of that class using the ASP.NET Core dependency injection feature, like this:

```
...
public DbContext Context =>
    provider.GetRequiredService(Type.GetType(ContextName)) as DbContext;
...
```

This is the bridge to the MVC part of the application, which will receive the name of the context that a migration should be applied to as a string in an HTML form and use it to set the value of the ContextName property, which is used to identify the context that the user wants to work with.

The third and final role is to perform migration objects on database contexts. The Microsoft.EntityFrameworkCore namespace includes extension methods that operate on migrations through the DatabaseFacade objects returned by the DbContext.Database property, as described in Table 13-8.

Table 13-8. *The DatabaseFacade Extension Methods for Migrations*

Name	Description
GetMigrations()	This method returns a sequence of string values, each of which is the name of a migration.
GetAppliedMigrations()	This method returns a sequence of string values, each of which is the name of a migration that has been applied to the database.
GetPendingMigrations()	This method returns a sequence of string values, each of which is the name of a migration that has not yet been applied to the database.
Migrate()	This method applies all pending migrations to the database.

The Migrate method doesn't allow a specific migration to be specified. Providing this functionality means using the IMigrator service, which is defined in the Microsoft.EntityFrameworkCore.Migrations namespace and which defines a Migrate method that does allow a migration to be specified, which is how I implemented the MigrationsManager class's Migrate method, as follows:

```
...
Context.GetService<IMigrator>().Migrate(target);
...
```

Using the methods described in Table 13-8 and the IMigrator service, the manager class is able to provide information about the migration status of each database context class and apply and remove individual migrations.

Creating the Migrations Controller and View

The next step is to create a controller and view that will provide access to the functionality offered by the MigrationsManager class. Add a class file called MigrationsController.cs to the Controllers folder and add the code shown in Listing 13-33.

Listing 13-33. The Contents of the MigrationsController.cs File in the Controllers Folder

```
using DataApp.Models;
using Microsoft.AspNetCore.Mvc;
using System.Linq;

namespace DataApp.Controllers {

    public class MigrationsController : Controller {
        private MigrationsManager manager;

        public MigrationsController(MigrationsManager mgr) {
            manager = mgr;
        }

        public IActionResult Index(string context) {
            ViewBag.Context = manager.ContextName = context
                ?? manager.ContextNames.First();
            return View(manager);
        }

        [HttpPost]
        public IActionResult Migrate(string context, string migration) {
            manager.ContextName = context;
            manager.Migrate(context, migration);
            return RedirectToAction(nameof(Index), new { context = context });
        }
    }
}
```

The Index action method is used to display details of the context classes and migrations in the project. The POST-only Migrate method is used to apply migrations to the database. To provide the controller with its view, create the Views/Migrations folder and add to it a Razor file called Index.cshtml with the markup shown in Listing 13-34.

Listing 13-34. The Contents of the Index.cshtml File in the Views/Migrations Folder

```
@using DataApp.Models
@model MigrationsManager
@{
    ViewData["Title"] = "Migrations";
    Layout = "_Layout";
}
```

```html
<div class="m-1 p-2">
    <form asp-action="Index" method="get" class="form-inline">
        <label class="m-1">Database Context:</label>
        <select name="context" class="form-control">
            @foreach (var name in Model.ContextNames) {
                <option selected="@(name == ViewBag.Context)">@name</option>
            }
        </select>
        <button class="btn btn-primary m-1">Select</button>
    </form>
</div>

<table class="table table-sm table-striped m-2">
    <thead>
        <tr><th>Migration Name</th><th>Status</th></tr>
    </thead>
    <tbody>
        @foreach (string m in Model.AllMigrations) {
            <tr>
                <td>@m</td>
                <td>
                    @(Model.AppliedMigrations.Contains(m)
                    ? "Applied" : "Pending")
                </td>
            </tr>
        }
    </tbody>
</table>

<div class="m-1 p-2">
    <form asp-action="Migrate" method="post" class="form-inline">
        <input type="hidden" name="context" value="@ViewBag.Context" />
        <label class="m-1">Migration:</label>
        <select name="migration" class="form-control">
            <option selected value="@Model.AllMigrations.Last()">All</option>
            @foreach (var m in Model.AllMigrations.Reverse()) {
                <option>@m</option>
            }
            <option value="0">None</option>
        </select>
        <button class="btn btn-primary m-1">Migrate</button>
    </form>
</div>
```

The view contains a form that is used to select the context class that is managed, a table that lists the migrations and their status, and a second form that is used to apply migrations.

Configuring the Application

The MigrationsManager class must be registered with the ASP.NET Core dependency injection system so that new instances can be created with the IServiceProvider object that is used to get context objects. Edit the ConfigureServices method of the Startup class to add the statement shown in Listing 13-35.

Listing 13-35. Registering the Helper Class in the Startup.cs File in the DataApp Folder

```
...
public void ConfigureServices(IServiceCollection services) {
    services.AddMvc();
    string conString = Configuration["ConnectionStrings:DefaultConnection"];
    services.AddDbContext<EFDatabaseContext>(options =>
        options.UseSqlServer(conString));

    string customerConString =
        Configuration["ConnectionStrings:CustomerConnection"];
    services.AddDbContext<EFCustomerContext>(options =>
        options.UseSqlServer(customerConString));

    services.AddTransient<IDataRepository, EFDataRepository>();
    services.AddTransient<ICustomerRepository, EFCustomerRepository>();
    services.AddTransient<MigrationsManager>();
}
...
```

The MigrationsManager class is registered using the AddTransient method, which means that every dependency on the class will be resolved with a new object.

Running the Migrations Manager

Restart the application using the dotnet run command and navigate to the URL http://localhost:5000/migrations. You can switch between context classes by picking an item using the select element at the top of the window and clicking the Select button. To upgrade or downgrade a database, select the migration you want and click the Migrate button, as shown in Figure 13-2. Examine the output from the application, and you will see the SQL statements that are sent to the database server to move between migrations.

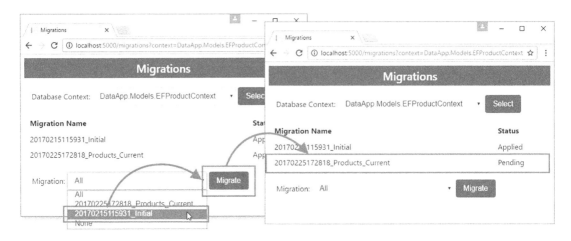

Figure 13-2. *Managing migrations programmatically*

Seeding Databases Programmatically

Many databases require some seed data so that the application has some baseline data to work with. This is often the case with product databases, where there is an initial set of products on sale to customers, as well as security databases, where there is at least one account in the database so that administrators can log in and perform initial configuration tasks.

So far in this part of the book, the databases have been seeded using raw SQL sent directly to the database server. This is an error-prone way of adding data to the database and doesn't use Entity Framework Core.

Entity Framework Core doesn't include any built-in support specifically for dealing with seed data, although it is in the published road map at the time of writing. Until there is a dedicated seeding feature, there are two techniques that you can use for seeding, which are described in the sections that follow. As I explain, each approach has benefits and drawbacks, but the overall effect is to populate the database so that you don't have to use raw SQL.

Both approaches rely on creating objects and storing them in the database using Entity Framework Core. To avoid repeating code for each approach, I created a class file called SeedData.cs in the Models folder and added the code shown in Listing 13-36.

⬛ **Caution**   The code in Listing 13-36 contains a method that removes the data from the database. This is useful when experimenting with Entity Framework Core because you can easily reset the database and try a different seeding technique. For real projects, caution is required to avoid deleting real production data, and you may want to mitigate the risk by not implementing the equivalent of the ClearData method in your own projects.

Listing 13-36. The Contents of the SeedData.cs File in the Models Folder

```
using Microsoft.EntityFrameworkCore;
using System.Linq;

namespace DataApp.Models {

    public static class SeedData {

        public static void Seed(DbContext context) {
            if (context.Database.GetPendingMigrations().Count() == 0) {
                if (context is EFDatabaseContext prodCtx
                        && prodCtx.Products.Count() == 0) {
                    prodCtx.Products.AddRange(Products);
                } else if (context is EFCustomerContext custCtx
                        && custCtx.Customers.Count() == 0) {
                    custCtx.Customers.AddRange(Customers);
                }
                context.SaveChanges();
            }
        }

        public static void ClearData(DbContext context) {
            if (context is EFDatabaseContext prodCtx
                    && prodCtx.Products.Count() > 0) {
                prodCtx.Products.RemoveRange(prodCtx.Products);
            } else if (context is EFCustomerContext custCtx
                    && custCtx.Customers.Count() > 0) {
                custCtx.Customers.RemoveRange(custCtx.Customers);
            }
            context.SaveChanges();
        }

        private static Product[] Products = {
            new Product { Name = "Kayak", Category = "Watersports",
                Price = 275, Color = Colors.Green, InStock = true },
            new Product { Name = "Lifejacket", Category = "Watersports",
                Price = 48.95m, Color = Colors.Red, InStock = true },
            new Product { Name = "Soccer Ball", Category = "Soccer",
                Price = 19.50m, Color = Colors.Blue, InStock = true },
            new Product { Name = "Corner Flags", Category = "Soccer",
                Price = 34.95m, Color = Colors.Green, InStock = true },
            new Product { Name = "Stadium", Category = "Soccer",
                Price = 79500, Color = Colors.Red, InStock = true },
            new Product { Name = "Thinking Cap", Category = "Chess",
                Price = 16, Color = Colors.Blue, InStock = true },
            new Product { Name = "Unsteady Chair", Category = "Chess",
                Price = 29.95m, Color = Colors.Green, InStock = true },
            new Product { Name = "Human Chess Board", Category = "Chess",
                Price = 75, Color = Colors.Red, InStock = true },
            new Product { Name = "Bling-Bling King", Category = "Chess",
                Price = 1200, Color = Colors.Blue, InStock = true }};
```

```
        private static Customer[] Customers = {
            new Customer { Name = "Alice Smith",
                City = "New York", Country = "USA" },
            new Customer { Name = "Bob Jones",
                City = "Paris", Country = "France" },
            new Customer { Name = "Charlie Davies",
                City = "London", Country = "UK" }};
    }
}
```

The SeedData class defines static properties that define the `Product` and `Customer` objects used for seeding and defines methods that use the static properties to populate and clear the database. Each method receives a database context object, identifies the type of the context, and then adds or removes the data.

The Seed method, which is responsible for adding seed data to a database, starts by checking that there are no pending migrations, like this:

```
...
if (context.Database.GetPendingMigrations().Count() == 0) {
...
```

Programmatically seeding a database can be tricky because the objects used to populate the database must match the structure of the database table that Entity Framework Core will use to store them. If there is a mismatch, then Entity Framework Core won't be able to store the data, and the seeding will fail. Checking that there are no pending migrations before trying to store the seed data helps reduce the risk of a mismatch, but you must still take care to ensure that all changes to the data model classes have been captured in a migration before trying to seed the database.

Creating a Seeding Tool

The first approach is to create a tool for seeding the database, similar to the one I created earlier in the chapter for managing migrations. In fact, to avoid duplicating code, I am going to extend the migrations tool so that it can seed the database as well.

This is the best approach for seeding databases in production systems. The drawback is that seeding requires a developer or administrator to explicitly perform an action to add the seed data to the database, which can be frustrating during development (for which the technique described in the "Seeding During Startup" section is more suitable).

The first step is to add new action methods to the `Migrations` controller that can be used to seed and clear the databases, as shown in Listing 13-37.

Listing 13-37. Adding Actions in the MigrationsController.cs File in the Controllers Folder

```
using DataApp.Models;
using Microsoft.AspNetCore.Mvc;
using System.Linq;

namespace DataApp.Controllers {

    public class MigrationsController : Controller {
        private MigrationsManager manager;
```

```
    public MigrationsController(MigrationsManager mgr) {
        manager = mgr;
    }

    public IActionResult Index(string context) {
        ViewBag.Context = manager.ContextName = context
            ?? manager.ContextNames.First();
        return View(manager);
    }

    [HttpPost]
    public IActionResult Migrate(string context, string migration) {
        manager.ContextName = context;
        manager.Migrate(context, migration);
        return RedirectToAction(nameof(Index), new { context = context });
    }

    [HttpPost]
    public IActionResult Seed(string context) {
        manager.ContextName = context;
        SeedData.Seed(manager.Context);
        return RedirectToAction(nameof(Index), new { context = context });
    }

    [HttpPost]
    public IActionResult Clear(string context) {
        manager.ContextName = context;
        SeedData.ClearData(manager.Context);
        return RedirectToAction(nameof(Index), new { context = context });
    }
    }
}
```

The new action methods, called Seed and Clear, can be targeted only using a POST request. Each method receives the name of the database context class as its argument, which is used with the MigrationsManager class created in Listing 13-32 to get hold of a context object that can be passed to one of the methods defined by the SeedData class.

With the action methods in place, I can create buttons that will seed and clear the database, as shown in Listing 13-38.

Listing 13-38. Adding Buttons in the Index.chstml File in the Views/Migrations Folder

```
@using DataApp.Models
@model MigrationsManager
@{
    ViewData["Title"] = "Migrations";
    Layout = "_Layout";
}
```

```
<!-- ...elements omitted for brevity... -->

<div class="m-1 p-2">
    <form method="post">
        <input type="hidden" name="context" value="@ViewBag.Context" />
        <button class="btn btn-primary" asp-action="Seed">Seed Database</button>
        <button class="btn btn-danger" asp-action="Clear">Clear Database</button>
    </form>
</div>
```

The new elements define a form, with the actions specified by each button element through the asp-action tag helper attribute. To see the result, start the application using dotnet run, navigate to http://localhost:5000/migrations, and click either the Seed or Clear button, which are shown in Figure 13-3.

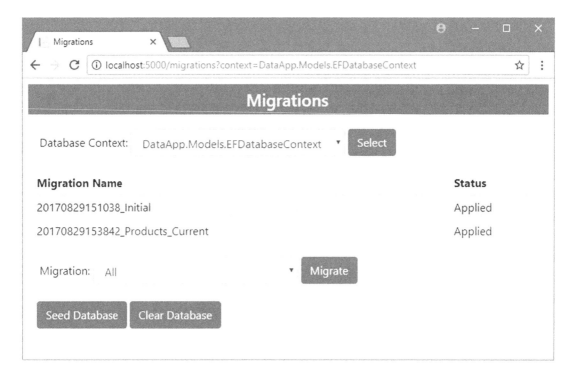

Figure 13-3. *Adding seeding support to the migrations tool*

Seeding During Startup

The other way to seed a database is to do so automatically during application startup. This is something that should be done only during development, especially if there are going to be multiple instances of the application running in production; otherwise, more than one instance of the application can try to seed the database simultaneously, causing problems and preventing a clean startup.

The advantage of this approach is that it is automatic. If the database has no pending migrations and is empty, then the database will be seeded. The database can be seeded as part of the application startup by adding the statements shown in Listing 13-39 to the Startup class.

Listing 13-39. Seeding the Database in the Startup.cs File in the DataApp Folder

```
using System;
using System.Collections.Generic;
using System.Linq;
using System.Threading.Tasks;
using Microsoft.AspNetCore.Builder;
using Microsoft.AspNetCore.Hosting;
using Microsoft.AspNetCore.Http;
using Microsoft.Extensions.DependencyInjection;
using DataApp.Models;
using Microsoft.EntityFrameworkCore;
using Microsoft.Extensions.Configuration;

namespace DataApp {
    public class Startup {

        public Startup(IConfiguration config) => Configuration = config;

        public IConfiguration Configuration { get; }

        public void ConfigureServices(IServiceCollection services) {
            services.AddMvc();
            string conString = Configuration["ConnectionStrings:DefaultConnection"];
            services.AddDbContext<EFDatabaseContext>(options =>
                options.UseSqlServer(conString));

            string customerConString =
                Configuration["ConnectionStrings:CustomerConnection"];
            services.AddDbContext<EFCustomerContext>(options =>
                options.UseSqlServer(customerConString));

            services.AddTransient<IDataRepository, EFDataRepository>();
            services.AddTransient<ICustomerRepository, EFCustomerRepository>();
            services.AddTransient<MigrationsManager>();
        }

        public void Configure(IApplicationBuilder app, IHostingEnvironment env,
                EFDatabaseContext prodCtx, EFCustomerContext custCtx) {
            app.UseDeveloperExceptionPage();
            app.UseStatusCodePages();
            app.UseStaticFiles();
            app.UseMvcWithDefaultRoute();

            if (env.IsDevelopment()) {
                SeedData.Seed(prodCtx);
                SeedData.Seed(custCtx);
            }
        }
    }
}
```

Declaring parameters on the Configure method allows me to receive context objects for the databases, which can then be passed to the SeedData.Seed method. To prevent seeding the databases automatically in production, I check the environment to make sure that the application is running in development. The result is that the database is seeded automatically when the application starts, which you can see by clearing the database using the tool created in the previous section and then restarting the application.

AVOIDING PROBLEMS WITH THE COMMAND LINE TOOLS

With Entity Framework Core 2, Microsoft changed the way that database contexts are discovered, which means that the code added in Listing 13-39 will be executed even when the command-line tools are used to manage migrations or apply them to a database. This means that it is possible to get into a situation where the seeding code is trying to populate a database with data that it is unable to store or that doesn't exist. If this happens, you will see an exception when you run the dotnet ef command. To work around this issue, comment out the calls to the SeedData.Seed method that were added in Listing 13-39 until you have finished working with the migrations, at which point you can safely uncomment them again.

Summary

In this chapter, I explained how migrations are used to keep the database schema consistent with the application and to prepare databases so they can store the application's data. I demonstrated the process for creating new migrations, showed you how to upgrade and downgrade the database, and explained how to apply and manage migrations using the Entity Framework Core API. I finished the chapter by showing you how to seed the database for production and development environments. In the next chapter, I explain how to create relationships between objects and represent them in the database.

CHAPTER 14

Creating Data Relationships

The foundation of Entity Framework Core is the way that it represents instances of .NET classes as rows in a relational database table. When you create relationships between classes, Entity Framework Core responds by creating corresponding relationships in the database. For the most part, the process of creating data relationships is intuitive and natural, although there are many options and some advanced features present pitfalls for the unwary.

In this chapter, I demonstrate how to create relationships between classes in the data model, show you how Entity Framework Core responds to these changes, and explain how you can use relationships in an ASP.NET Core MVC application. Table 14-1 puts this chapter in context.

Table 14-1. *Putting Data Relationships in Context*

Question	Answer
What are they?	Relationships allow the database to store associations between objects in the database.
Why are they useful?	Relationships allow you to more naturally model data using .NET objects and then store them and their associations to other objects.
How are they used?	Relationships are created by adding properties to data model classes and then using a migration to update the database. When storing data, Entity Framework Core will try to store related data automatically, although that doesn't always work as you might expect.
Are there any pitfalls or limitations?	Relationships are complicated because the way that databases manage data associations doesn't always reflect the natural behavior of .NET objects. Some effort can be required to get the behavior you require.
Are there any alternatives?	You don't have to use relationships at all and can just store individual objects if you prefer, although that will limit you to applications with simple data models.

© Adam Freeman 2018
A. Freeman, *Pro Entity Framework Core 2 for ASP.NET Core MVC*,
https://doi.org/10.1007/978-1-4842-3435-8_14

Table 14-2 summarizes the chapter.

Table 14-2. *Chapter Summary*

Problem	Solution	Listing
Create a relationship	Add a navigation property and create and apply a migration	1–4, 10
Include related data in a query	Use the Include and ThenInclude methods	5–9, 22–29
Store or update related data	Use the methods provided by the context class	12–15
Delete related data	Use the method provided by the context class	16
Create a required relationship	Add a foreign key property with a non-nullable type	17–21

Preparing for This Chapter

This chapter uses the DataApp project created in Chapter 11 and modified in the chapters since. To prepare for this chapter, open a command prompt in the DataApp folder and run the command shown in Listing 14-1.

Tip   If you don't want to follow the process of building the example project, you can download all of the required files from this book's source code repository, `https://github.com/apress/pro-ef-core-2-for-asp.net-core-mvc`.

Listing 14-1. Resetting the Database

```
dotnet ef database drop --force --context EFDatabaseContext
```

This command removes the database used to store Product objects, which will help ensure that you get the right expected results from the examples in this chapter. The application won't have a database or data to work with until later in the chapter, after I have demonstrated the process for creating a data relationship.

Creating a Relationship

The best way to understand data relationships is to create one. To get started, I am going to add a new entity class to the application to represent a supplier for a product. Add a class file called Supplier.cs in the Models folder and add the code shown in Listing 14-2.

Listing 14-2. The Contents of the Supplier.cs File in the Models Folder

```
namespace DataApp.Models {

    public class Supplier {
        public long Id { get; set; }
        public string Name { get; set; }
        public string City { get; set; }
        public string State { get; set; }
    }
}
```

The new class defines an Id property that will be used to store primary key values in the database and defines Name, City, and State properties that provide a basic description of a supplier. There is nothing special about this class at the moment, and it follows the same pattern used in earlier examples.

Adding a Navigation Property

To create a data relationship, add the property shown in Listing 14-3 to the Product class, which will allow each Product object to be associated with a Supplier object.

Listing 14-3. Adding a Property in the Product.cs File in the Models Folder

```
namespace DataApp.Models {

    public enum Colors {
        Red, Green, Blue
    }

    public class Product {

        public long Id { get; set; }
        public string Name { get; set; }
        public string Category { get; set; }
        public decimal Price { get; set; }
        public Colors Color { get; set; }
        public bool InStock { get; set; }

        public Supplier Supplier { get; set; }
    }
}
```

The new property, called Supplier, creates a relationship so that each Product object can be associated with one Supplier object. This is known as a *navigation property* because it allows navigation from one object to another. In this case, if you start with a Product object, you can use the navigation property to access the related Supplier object.

NAMING NAVIGATION PROPERTIES

In Listing 14-3, I used the name Supplier for the navigation property that creates the relationship with a Supplier object. You don't have to use the name of the related class for a navigation property, although it is commonly convenient to do so, as it was in this case. You can use any legal name for a C# property, and there is an example later in the chapter where I name a property Location to create a relationship with an instance of a class called ContactLocation.

To understand how Entity Framework Core deals with relationships, it helps to think about the effect the Supplier property has on the .NET objects in the application without worrying about the database. The changes to the data model mean that each Product object can be related to a Supplier object, as illustrated in Figure 14-1.

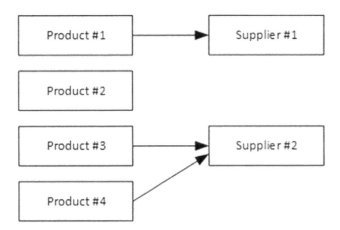

Figure 14-1. *Creating a relationship between data model classes*

A Product object's Supplier property can be null, which means that a Product object does not have to be related to a Supplier. And a Product object's Supplier property doesn't have to be unique, which means multiple Product objects can be related to the same Supplier.

Creating the Migration

To see how Entity Framework Core handles the addition of the navigation property, run the command shown in Listing 14-4 in the DataApp project folder to create a migration.

Listing 14-4. Creating a Migration

```
dotnet ef migrations add Add_Supplier --context EFDatabaseContext
```

Entity Framework Core will create a migration called Add_Supplier, and if you examine the Up methods in the <timestamp>_Add_Supplier.cs file in the Migrations folder, you will be able to see how Entity Framework Core will update the database. The Up method contains four statements that will update the database. The first statement adds a new column to the existing table in the database.

```
...
migrationBuilder.AddColumn<long>(name: "SupplierId", table: "Products",
    nullable: true);
...
```

This is the column that Entity Framework Core will use to keep track of which Supplier object is associated with a Product object. The arguments to the AddColumn method will create a column called SupplierId on the existing Products table. The nullable argument is set to true, which means that null values are allowed in the new column so that a Product object that isn't related to a Supplier can still be stored in the database.

The second statement in the migration's Up method creates a new table that will be used to store Supplier objects.

```
...
migrationBuilder.CreateTable(
    name: "Supplier",
    columns: table => new {
        Id = table.Column<long>(nullable: false)
            .Annotation("SqlServer:ValueGenerationStrategy",
                SqlServerValueGenerationStrategy.IdentityColumn),
        City = table.Column<string>(nullable: true),
        Name = table.Column<string>(nullable: true),
        State = table.Column<string>(nullable: true)
    },
    constraints: table => {
        table.PrimaryKey("PK_Supplier", x => x.Id);
    });
...
```

The arguments to the CreateTable method will create a table called Supplier that has Id, Name, City, and State columns that correspond to the properties defined by the Supplier class. The Id column is configured as the primary key, and the database server will be responsible for generating values for this column when new rows are added to the table.

■ **Tip**   Notice that the name of the table is Supplier, while the name of the existing table is Products. The convention Entity Framework Core follows is to use the name of the DbSet<T> property when it creates a table for an entity class that is accessible through a context class and to use the name of the navigation property for an entity class that can be accessed only through a relationship.

The next statement creates an index, which is used to speed up database queries:

```
...
migrationBuilder.CreateIndex(name: "IX_Products_SupplierId",
    table: "Products", column: "SupplierId");
...
```

The index isn't directly related to representing the relationship between Product and Supplier objects, and I will skip over it for the purposes of this chapter. The final statement in the Up method is responsible for creating the link between the rows in the Products and Supplier tables:

```
...
migrationBuilder.AddForeignKey(
    name: "FK_Products_Supplier_SupplierId", table: "Products",
    column: "SupplierId", principalTable: "Supplier",
    principalColumn: "Id", onDelete: ReferentialAction.Restrict);
...
```

The `AddForeignKey` method is used to configure the `SupplierId` column added to the `Products` table to create a foreign key relationship with the `Id` column on the new `Supplier` table. This helps protect the integrity of the database by ensuring that a row in the `Product` table can only have a value for the `SupplierId` column that corresponds to a valid row in the `Supplier` table (or have a value of `null`, indicating that there is no relationship to a `Supplier`).

The combined effect of the statements in the migration's Up method is to update the database to reflect the changes in the data model, as illustrated in Figure 14-2.

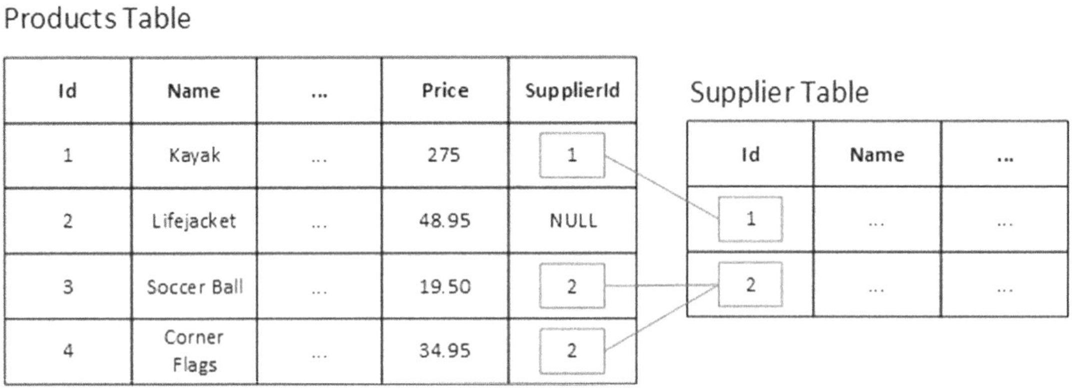

Products Table

Id	Name	...	Price	SupplierId
1	Kayak	...	275	1
2	Lifejacket	...	48.95	NULL
3	Soccer Ball	...	19.50	2
4	Corner Flags	...	34.95	2

Supplier Table

Id	Name	...
1	...	...
2	...	...

Figure 14-2. *The effect of a data relationship on the database*

The `Supplier` table allows Entity Framework Core to store `Supplier` objects, and the `SupplierId` column added to the `Products` table will be used to keep track of the relationships between `Product` and `Supplier` objects.

Querying and Displaying the Related Data

I explain how to perform the complete set of data operations on related data in this chapter, but I am going to start with the most basic task, which is to display the related data values to the user. By default, Entity Framework Core doesn't follow navigation properties to load related data. This is to prevent queries from returning data that isn't required. To load the `Supplier` data related to a `Product` object, add the statement shown in Listing 14-5 to the repository implementation class.

Listing 14-5. Querying Related Data in the EFDataRepository.cs File in the Models Folder

```
using System;
using System.Collections.Generic;
using System.Linq;
using Newtonsoft.Json;
using Microsoft.EntityFrameworkCore.ChangeTracking;
using Microsoft.EntityFrameworkCore;

namespace DataApp.Models {

    public class EFDataRepository : IDataRepository {
        private EFDatabaseContext context;
```

```
public EFDataRepository(EFDatabaseContext ctx) {
    context = ctx;
}

public Product GetProduct(long id) {
    return context.Products.Include(p => p.Supplier).First(p => p.Id == id);
}

public IEnumerable<Product> GetAllProducts() {
    Console.WriteLine("GetAllProducts");
    return context.Products.Include(p => p.Supplier);
}

public IEnumerable<Product> GetFilteredProducts(string category = null,
        decimal? price = null, bool includeRelated = true) {

    IQueryable<Product> data = context.Products;
    if (category != null) {
        data = data.Where(p => p.Category == category);
    }
    if (price != null) {
        data = data.Where(p => p.Price >= price);
    }
    if (includeRelated) {
        data = data.Include(p => p.Supplier);
    }
    return data;
}

public void CreateProduct(Product newProduct) {
    newProduct.Id = 0;
    context.Products.Add(newProduct);
    context.SaveChanges();
    Console.WriteLine($"New Key: {newProduct.Id}");
}

public void UpdateProduct(Product changedProduct,
        Product originalProduct = null) {
    if (originalProduct == null) {
        originalProduct = context.Products.Find(changedProduct.Id);
    } else {
        context.Products.Attach(originalProduct);
    }
    originalProduct.Name = changedProduct.Name;
    originalProduct.Category = changedProduct.Category;
    originalProduct.Price = changedProduct.Price;
    context.SaveChanges();
}
```

```
        public void DeleteProduct(long id) {
            Product p = context.Products.Find(id);
            context.Products.Remove(p);
            context.SaveChanges();
        }
    }
}
```

The Include extension method is defined in the `Microsoft.EntityFrameworkCore` namespace and is called on objects that implement the `IQueryable<T>` interface to include related data. The argument to the Include method is an expression that selects the navigation property that Entity Framework Core should follow to get the related data. In the listing, I select the `Supplier` object. The Include method can be incorporated into queries like other LINQ methods, like this:

```
...
return context.Products.Include(p => p.Supplier);
...
```

Not all LINQ extension methods can be used on the object returned by the Include method, so you may have to rework some queries when using related data. The `Find` method, which I used in earlier examples to locate a specific `Product` in the database, cannot be used with Include, so I replaced it with the `First` method, which works in a similar way, like this:

```
...
return context.Products.Include(p => p.Supplier).First(p => p.Id == id);
...
```

You can decide whether to include related data in a query at runtime. In Listing 14-5, I changed the `GetFilteredProducts` method so the Include method is called when the value of the `includeRelated` parameter is `true` but not otherwise, like this:

```
...
if (includeRelated) {
    data = data.Include(p => p.Supplier);
}
...
```

To work the support for selectively including related data through to the rest of the application, change the signature of the `IDataRepository` interface, as shown in Listing 14-6.

FUTURE SUPPORT FOR LAZY LOADING

Earlier versions of Entity Framework supported a feature called *lazy loading*, which Microsoft has announced will be included in a future release of Entity Framework Core. In lazy loading, related data is loaded from the database automatically when a navigation property is read. For the example application, this would mean that reading the value of the `Supplier` property on a `Product` object will automatically trigger a SQL query for the data required to create a `Supplier` object.

Lazy loading sounds like a good idea and is often enabled as a convenience feature, allowing the MVC part of the application to be written without having to create Entity Framework Core queries that include or exclude different sets of related data for different actions. Everything just works like magic, and Entity Framework Core makes sure that the data that the MVC part of the application needs is available. But behind the scenes, extra SQL queries are generated when the navigation properties are read, increasing the load on the database server and increasing the time taken to process HTTP requests.

My advice is to avoid lazy loading. Instead, define repository methods or properties that return data in all of the combinations that the MVC part of the application requires, with or without related data. Put another way, avoid any feature that generates database queries automatically.

Listing 14-6. Adding a Parameter in the IDataRepository.cs File in the Models Folder

```
using System.Collections.Generic;
using System.Linq;

namespace DataApp.Models {

    public interface IDataRepository {

        Product GetProduct(long id);

        IEnumerable<Product> GetAllProducts();

        IEnumerable<Product> GetFilteredProducts(string category = null,
            decimal? price = null, bool includeRelated = true);

        void CreateProduct(Product newProduct);

        void UpdateProduct(Product changedProduct,
            Product originalProduct = null);

        void DeleteProduct(long id);
    }
}
```

Next, add a parameter to the action method so that the controller can get a value for whether to include related data from the HTTP request through the MVC model binding process, as shown in Listing 14-7.

Listing 14-7. Adding an Action Parameter in the HomeController.cs File in the Controllers Folder

```
using Microsoft.AspNetCore.Mvc;
using DataApp.Models;
using System.Linq;

namespace DataApp.Controllers {
    public class HomeController : Controller {
        private IDataRepository repository;

        public HomeController(IDataRepository repo) {
            repository = repo;
        }
```

```
    public IActionResult Index(string category = null,
            decimal? price = null, bool includeRelated = true) {
        var products = repository
            .GetFilteredProducts(category, price, includeRelated);
        ViewBag.category = category;
        ViewBag.price = price;
        ViewBag.includeRelated = includeRelated;
        return View(products);
    }

    // ...other actions omitted for brevity...
    }
}
```

One drawback of the way that Entity Framework Core handles related data is that there is no good way of working out whether the value for a navigation property is null. This is either because there is no related data for a specific object or because related data was not selected using the Include method. To work around this, I have used a ViewBag property so that the view will know whether related data has been requested.

Updating the View to Display Related Data

Now that all of the code changes are in place, I can display the related data using Razor. The model data will include Supplier objects when they have been requested, and there is a ViewBag property that can be used to configure a form element, as shown in Listing 14-8.

Listing 14-8. Displaying Related Data in the Index.cshtml File in the Views/Home Folder

```
@model IEnumerable<DataApp.Models.Product>
@{
    ViewData["Title"] = "Products";
    Layout = "_Layout";
}

<div class="m-1 p-2">
    <form asp-action="Index" method="get" class="form-inline">
        <label class="m-1">Category:</label>
        <select name="category" class="form-control">
            <option value="">All</option>
            <option selected="@(ViewBag.category == "Watersports")">
                Watersports
            </option>
            <option selected="@(ViewBag.category == "Soccer")">Soccer</option>
            <option selected="@(ViewBag.category == "Chess")">Chess</option>
        </select>
        <label class="m-1">Min Price:</label>
        <input class="form-control" name="price" value="@ViewBag.price" />
        <div class="form-check m-1">
            <label class="form-check-label">
                <input class="form-check-input" type="checkbox"
                        name="includeRelated" value="true"
```

```
                        checked="@(ViewBag.includeRelated == true)"/>
                    Related Data
                </label>
                <input type="hidden" name="includeRelated" value="false" />
            </div>
            <button class="btn btn-primary m-1">Filter</button>
        </form>
    </div>
<table class="table table-sm table-striped">
    <thead>
        <tr>
            <th>ID</th><th>Name</th><th>Category</th><th>Price</th>
            @if (ViewBag.includeRelated) {
                <th>Supplier</th>
            }
        </tr>
    </thead>
    <tbody>
        @foreach (var p in Model) {
            <tr>
                <td>@p.Id</td><td>@p.Name</td>
                <td>@p.Category</td><td>$@p.Price.ToString("F2")</td>
                @if (ViewBag.includeRelated) {
                    <td>@p.Supplier?.Name</td>
                }
                <td>
                    <form asp-action="Delete" method="post">
                        <a asp-action="Edit" class="btn btn-sm btn-warning"
                           asp-route-id="@p.Id">
                            Edit
                        </a>
                        <input type="hidden" name="id" value="@p.Id" />
                        <button type="submit" class="btn btn-danger btn-sm">
                            Delete
                        </button>
                    </form>
                </td>
            </tr>
        }
    </tbody>
</table>
<a asp-action="Create" class="btn btn-primary">Create New Product</a>
```

I have added a checkbox that will control whether related data is included in the request. When the user has selected related data, the `ViewBag.includeRelated` property will be `true`, and the view uses this value to display an additional column in the table. The value of the column is obtained by reading the `Name` property of the `Supplier` object related to the `Product` object that is being displayed, like this:

```
...
<td>@p.Supplier?.Name</td>
...
```

The Razor view has no knowledge of the source of the Supplier objects because Entity Framework Core populates navigation properties with regular .NET objects.

Preparing the Database

I will demonstrate how to perform the complete set of data operations on related data, but it helps to have some initial data to demonstrate how queries with the Include method work. To add Supplier objects to the database, make the changes shown in Listing 14-9 to the seed data class.

Listing 14-9. Seeding the Database with Suppliers in the SeedData.cs File in the Models Folder

```
...
private static Product[] Products {
    get {
        Product[] products = new Product[] {
            new Product { Name = "Kayak", Category = "Watersports",
                Price = 275, Color = Colors.Green, InStock = true },
            new Product { Name = "Lifejacket", Category = "Watersports",
                Price = 48.95m, Color = Colors.Red, InStock = true },
            new Product { Name = "Soccer Ball", Category = "Soccer",
                Price = 19.50m, Color = Colors.Blue, InStock = true },
            new Product { Name = "Corner Flags", Category = "Soccer",
                Price = 34.95m, Color = Colors.Green, InStock = true },
            new Product { Name = "Stadium", Category = "Soccer",
                Price = 79500, Color = Colors.Red, InStock = true },
            new Product { Name = "Thinking Cap", Category = "Chess",
                Price = 16, Color = Colors.Blue, InStock = true },
            new Product { Name = "Unsteady Chair", Category = "Chess",
                Price = 29.95m, Color = Colors.Green, InStock = true },
            new Product { Name = "Human Chess Board", Category = "Chess",
                Price = 75, Color = Colors.Red, InStock = true },
            new Product { Name = "Bling-Bling King", Category = "Chess",
                Price = 1200, Color = Colors.Blue, InStock = true }};

        Supplier s1 = new Supplier { Name = "Surf Dudes",
            City = "San Jose", State = "CA" };
        Supplier s2 = new Supplier { Name = "Chess Kings",
            City = "Seattle", State = "WA" };

        products.First().Supplier = s1;
        foreach (Product p in  products.Where(p => p.Category == "Chess")) {
            p.Supplier = s2;
        }
        return products;
    }
}
...
```

I have replaced the static array of Product objects in the SeedData class with a property whose getter creates two Supplier objects and associates them with Product objects. The Surf Dudes supplier is associated with the first Product object, Kayak, while the Chess Kings supplier is associated with all the Product objects in the Chess category.

Next, prepare the database for the application by applying the migrations, including the new one that defines the Supplier relationship. To apply the migrations, run the command shown in Listing 14-10 in the DataApp project folder.

Listing 14-10. Preparing the Database

```
dotnet ef database update --context EFDatabaseContext
```

To start the application, open a command prompt, navigate to the DataApp folder, and start the application by running the command shown in Listing 14-11.

Listing 14-11. Starting the Example Application

```
dotnet run
```

The application will seed the database with Product and Supplier objects, which may take a moment to complete. Once the application has started, open a browser window and navigate to http://localhost:5000. You will see the new column in the table that contains the names of the suppliers for those Product objects that are related to a Supplier object, as shown in Figure 14-3. Notice that not all Product objects are related to a Supplier and, of those that are, more than one has a relationship with the same Supplier.

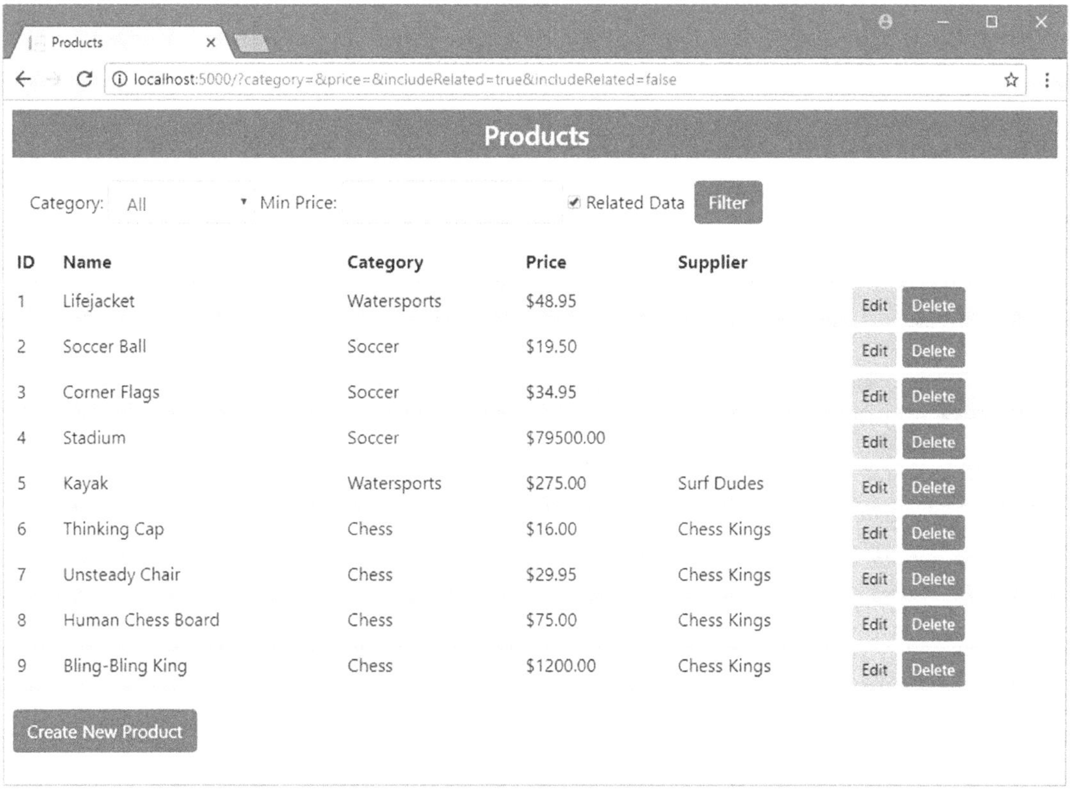

Figure 14-3. *Running the example application*

If you examine the console output from the application, you will see the query that Entity Framework Core uses to get the related data.

```
...
SELECT [p].[Id], [p].[Category], [p].[Color], [p].[InStock], [p].[Name],
       [p].[Price], [p].[SupplierId], [p.Supplier].[Id], [p.Supplier].[City],
       [p.Supplier].[Name], [p.Supplier].[State]
FROM [Products] AS [p]
LEFT JOIN [Supplier] AS [p.Supplier] ON [p].[SupplierId] = [p.Supplier].[Id]
...
```

The query uses the relationship between the Products and Supplier tables to perform a join so that all of the data that is required can be obtained in a single query. If you uncheck the Related Data option and click the Filter button, the query to the database won't request Supplier data, and the Supplier column won't be shown in the table displayed by the browser.

Creating and Updating Related Data

The process for creating or updating related data is performed through the navigation properties and done using standard .NET objects.

For the example application—in common with most real projects—there are three different scenarios in which a Supplier object is stored in the database or an existing Supplier object is updated.

- New Product and Supplier objects are created at the same time.

- A new Supplier object is created and associated with an existing Product object.

- An existing Supplier object is modified after it has been associated with a Product object.

To prepare for these operations, I added a view called Supplier.cshtml to the Views/Shared folder with the content shown in Listing 14-12.

Listing 14-12. The Contents of the Supplier.cshtml File in the Views/Shared Folder

```
@model DataApp.Models.Product

<input type="hidden" asp-for="Supplier.Id" />
<div class="form-group">
    <label asp-for="Supplier.Name"></label>
    <input asp-for="Supplier.Name" class="form-control" />
</div>
<div class="form-group">
    <label asp-for="Supplier.City"></label>
    <input asp-for="Supplier.City" class="form-control" />
</div>
<div class="form-group">
    <label asp-for="Supplier.State"></label>
    <input asp-for="Supplier.State" class="form-control" />
</div>
```

The model for this view is a `Product` object. This may seem odd in a view that will be used to work with `Supplier` data, but following the MVC conventions and using the `asp-for` tag helper sets up the HTML elements so that the MVC model binding process will create a `Supplier` object using the values from the `input` elements and assign it to the `Supplier` property of the `Product` object it creates.

Edit the `Editor.cshtml` view in the `Views/Home` folder, as shown in Listing 14-13, to incorporate the view from Listing 14-12 and add some structure to the view content.

Listing 14-13. Using a Partial View in the Editor.cshtml File in the Views/Home Folder

```
@model DataApp.Models.Product
@{
    ViewData["Title"] = ViewBag.CreateMode ? "Create" : "Edit";
    Layout = "_Layout";
}

<form asp-action="@(ViewBag.CreateMode ? "Create" : "Edit")" method="post">
    <input name="original.Id" value="@Model?.Id" type="hidden" />
    <input name="original.Name" value="@Model?.Name" type="hidden" />
    <input name="original.Category" value="@Model?.Category" type="hidden" />
    <input name="original.Price" value="@Model?.Price" type="hidden" />
    <div class="row m-1">
        <div class="col-6">
            <h5 class="bg-info text-center p-2 text-white">Product</h5>
            <div class="form-group">
                <label asp-for="Name"></label>
                <input asp-for="Name" class="form-control" />
            </div>
            <div class="form-group">
                <label asp-for="Category"></label>
                <input asp-for="Category" class="form-control" />
            </div>
            <div class="form-group">
                <label asp-for="Price"></label>
                <input asp-for="Price" class="form-control" />
            </div>
        </div>
        <div class="col-6">
            <h5 class="bg-info text-center p-2 text-white">Supplier</h5>
            @Html.Partial("Supplier", Model)
        </div>
    </div>
    <div class="text-center">
        <button class="btn btn-primary" type="submit">Save</button>
        <a asp-action="Index" class="btn btn-secondary">Cancel</a>
    </div>
</form>
```

The Bootstrap styles applied to the `div` elements in Listing 14-13 create a simple grid so that the form elements are displayed in two columns, one for the fields defined by the `Product` class and one for the `Supplier` class. You will see the layout that has been created in the next section.

Creating a New Supplier When Creating a New Product

The first scenario is the simplest: new `Product` and `Supplier` objects are added to the database at the same time. This requires no further changes to the application because the existing code that creates new `Product` object will automatically deal with `Supplier` objects.

Start the application, using a browser to navigate to `http://localhost:5000`, and click the Create New Product button.

Fill out both columns in the form, as shown in Figure 14-4, and click the Save button. If you want to re-create the `Product` and `Supplier` shown in the figure, then use the values shown in Table 14-3.

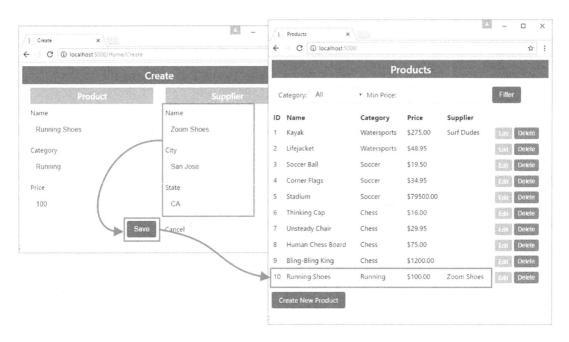

Figure 14-4. *Creating a supplier along with a new product*

Table 14-3. *The Product and Supplier Details Used in the Figure*

Field	Value
Product Name	Running Shoes
Category	Running
Price	100
Supplier Name	Zoom Shoes
City	San Jose
State	CA

When you clicked the Save button, the browser sent an HTTP POST request to the server that contained values from the input elements defined in Listing 14-12. These input elements were rendered by Razor so they would be recognized as properties for a Supplier object by the MVC model binder. For example, here is how the element for the City property was rendered:

```
...
<input class="form-control" type="text"
    id="Supplier_City" name="Supplier.City" value="">
...
```

The model binder uses the values in the HTML form to create a Product object and a Supplier object, which is assigned to the Product object's Supplier navigation property. The Product object is used as an argument to the Home controller's Create method, which passes it on to the repository's CreateProduct method. The repository's CreateProduct method adds the Product object to the collection managed by the context object and calls the SaveChanges method. Entity Framework Core inspects the Product object and sees that is Id value is zero, which indicates that it is a new object to be stored in the database. Entity Framework Core also follows the Product.Supplier navigation property to inspect the Supplier object and see that it too has an Id value of zero and is a new object to be stored in the database. These objects are stored as new rows in the Products and Supplier tables, and the value of the SupplierId column on the Products row is set to the value of the Id column on the Supplier row to record the relationship between the objects.

If you examine the logging messages produced by the application, you will see the two sets of SQL statements that stored the data. The first pair of statements creates the row in the Supplier table, which stores the Supplier object and gets the primary key value that the database server assigned.

```
...
INSERT INTO [Supplier] ([City], [Name], [State])
VALUES (@p0, @p1, @p2);

SELECT [Id]
FROM [Supplier]
WHERE @@ROWCOUNT = 1 AND [Id] = scope_identity();
...
```

The second pair of statement creates the row in the Products table and gets the primary key that the database server assigned.

```
...
INSERT INTO [Products] ([Category], [Color], [InStock],
    [Name], [Price], [SupplierId])
VALUES (@p3, @p4, @p5, @p6, @p7, @p8);

SELECT [Id]
FROM [Products]
WHERE @@ROWCOUNT = 1 AND [Id] = scope_identity();
...
```

The result is that Entity Framework Core seamlessly works with the objects that were created by the MVC model binder and stores two new rows in the database to represent the new objects and the relationship between them, as illustrated in Figure 14-5.

Products Table

Id	Name	...	Price	SupplierId
1	Kayak	...	275	1
2	Lifejacket	...	48.95	NULL
3	Soccer Ball	...	19.50	2
4	Corner Flags	...	34.95	2
4	Running Shoes	...	100	3

Supplier Table

Id	Name	...
1	...	...
2	...	...
3	Zoom Shoes	...

Figure 14-5. *Creating new Product and Supplier objects*

Updating a Supplier when Updating a Product

A change is required to the context class to create or update a Supplier object when the Product object it is related to has previously been stored in the database. This is because of the technique I used earlier to take advantage of the change detection features that Entity Framework Core provides to reduce the number of database queries that are performed and that must be extended to include the Supplier data. To include the Supplier data in the HTML form sent to the client, add the elements shown in Listing 14-14 to the Supplier.cshtml view.

Listing 14-14. Adding Existing Values in the Supplier.cshtml File in the Views/Shared Folder

```
@model DataApp.Models.Product

<input name="original.Supplier.Id" value="@Model.Supplier?.Id" type="hidden" />
<input name="original.Supplier.Name" value="@Model.Supplier?.Name" type="hidden" />
<input name="original.Supplier.City" value="@Model.Supplier?.City" type="hidden" />
<input name="original.Supplier.State" value="@Model.Supplier?.State" type="hidden" />

<input type="hidden" asp-for="Supplier.Id" />
<div class="form-group">
    <label asp-for="Supplier.Name"></label>
    <input asp-for="Supplier.Name" class="form-control" />
</div>
<div class="form-group">
    <label asp-for="Supplier.City"></label>
    <input asp-for="Supplier.City" class="form-control" />
</div>
<div class="form-group">
    <label asp-for="Supplier.State"></label>
    <input asp-for="Supplier.State" class="form-control" />
</div>
```

These hidden `input` elements are the counterparts to the ones in the `Editor.cshtml` view. To ensure that changes made by the user are written to the database, edit the `UpdateProduct` method of the `EFDataRepository` class to add the statement shown in Listing 14-15.

Listing 14-15. Including Supplier Data in the EFDataRepository.cs File in the Models Folder

```
...
public void UpdateProduct(Product changedProduct, Product originalProduct = null) {
    if (originalProduct == null) {
        originalProduct = context.Products.Find(changedProduct.Id);
    } else {
        context.Products.Attach(originalProduct);
    }
    originalProduct.Name = changedProduct.Name;
    originalProduct.Category = changedProduct.Category;
    originalProduct.Price = changedProduct.Price;
    originalProduct.Supplier.Name = changedProduct.Supplier.Name;
    originalProduct.Supplier.City = changedProduct.Supplier.City;
    originalProduct.Supplier.State = changedProduct.Supplier.State;
    context.SaveChanges();
}
...
```

These statements copy the `Name`, `City`, and `State` values to the object that is being tracked by Entity Framework Core to ensure that changed values will be stored in the database. Notice that I have not copied the `Supplier.Id` property; this value is managed by Entity Framework Core or the database server and is best left alone when performing an update.

To test the changes, restart the application, navigate to `http://localhost:5000`, and click the Edit button for the Thinking Cap product. To see the effect of updating both related objects, make the changes shown in Table 14-4.

Table 14-4. *The Values for Editing the of the Thinking Cap Product and Supplier*

Field	Value
Product Name	Thinking Cap (Medium)
Supplier Name	The Pawn Brokers
City	Chicago
State	IL

Click the Save button, and the browser will send the modified data to the application. The `Product` and `Supplier` objects will be created from the request data by the model builder, and Entity Framework Core will save the changes to the database. Since the `Supplier` object is related to all of the `Product` objects in the `Chess` category, the change will be reflected in several rows in the table, as shown in Figure 14-6.

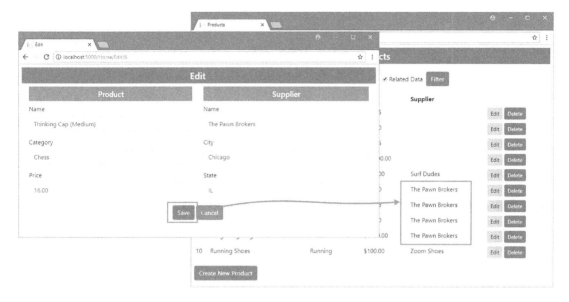

Figure 14-6. *Updating a Product and Supplier*

Deleting Related Data

By default, Entity Framework Core won't follow a navigation property to remove related data from the database. This means that deleting a `Product` object doesn't remove the `Supplier` object it is related to.

This is because the `Supplier` object may be related to other `Product` objects and removing it from the database would make the database inconsistent, which the database server works hard to avoid. There are features that make it easier to perform delete operations, which I describe in later chapters, but for the moment, I am going to demonstrate just the default configuration and explain the pitfall it presents.

To see how the delete operation is handled, start the application, navigate to `http://localhost:5000`, and click the Delete button for Unsteady Chair product, which is related to the The Pawn Brokers product. The operation removes the product but leaves the `Supplier` object, which is still related to the other products in the `Chess` category, as shown in Figure 14-7.

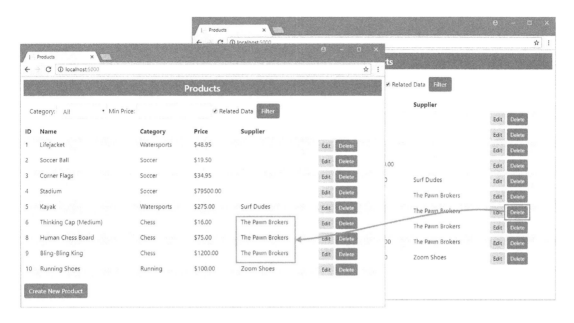

Figure 14-7. *Deleting an object that has related data*

You can tell Entity Framework Core to delete related data, although the database server will cause an exception if doing so would make the database inconsistent. To see how this works, make the changes shown in Listing 14-16 to the DeleteProduct method in the EFDataRepository class.

Listing 14-16. Deleting Related Data in the EFDataRepository.cs File in the Models Folder

```
...
public void DeleteProduct(long id) {
    Product p = this.GetProduct(id);
    context.Products.Remove(p);
    if (p.Supplier != null) {
        context.Remove<Supplier>(p.Supplier);
    }
    context.SaveChanges();
}
...
```

The statements in Listing 14-16 call the GetProduct method, which retrieves a Product and its related Supplier from the database. The Product object is deleted through the Remove method provided by the context object's DbSet<Product> property. There is no direct access to the Supplier data, but the context object's Remove<T> method can be used to remove any object from the database, like this:

```
...
context.Remove<Supplier>(p.Supplier);
...
```

To test this code, restart the application, navigate to `http://localhost:5000`, and click the Delete button for the Running Shoes product, as shown in Figure 14-8. This is the only `Product` object that is related to the Zoom Shoes `Supplier` object, which means that deleting these objects doesn't create any inconsistencies and both are removed.

Figure 14-8. *Deleting related data*

To see how the database server prevents an inconsistency, click the Delete button for the Human Chess Board product. Since the related `Supplier` for this `Product` is also related to other `Product` objects, deleting it would leave rows in the `Products` table with values in their `SupplierId` columns that refer to a nonexistent row in the `Supplier` table. The exception in Figure 14-9 shows how the database server won't perform an operation that would cause this problem.

Figure 14-9. *A delete operation that would cause database inconsistencies*

320

As things stand, the delete operation is not especially helpful, but I will return to this topic later in the chapter and explain how using different a type of relationship can make delete operations more useful and predictable.

Creating a Required Relationship

The Product and Supplier classes have an optional relationship, reflecting the fact that a Product doesn't *have* to be related to a Supplier. This is the default type of relationship and mirrors the way that objects work in the MVC part of the application, where a property that refers to another object may be null.

Some relationships need to be more formal, where it is important that an object of one type always be related to an object of some other type. In these situations, you can create a *required relationship*, which reconfigures the database to enforce the relationship on behalf of the application.

Creating a required relationship means telling Entity Framework Core how it should create the foreign key column that tracks the relationship in the database. Here are the statements from the migration that create the relationship between the Products and Supplier tables:

```
...
migrationBuilder.AddColumn<long>(name: "SupplierId",
    table: "Products", nullable: true);
...
migrationBuilder.AddForeignKey(name: "FK_Products_Supplier_SupplierId",
    table: "Products", column: "SupplierId", principalTable: "Supplier",
    principalColumn: "Id", onDelete: ReferentialAction.Restrict);
...
```

Entity Framework Core hasn't been provided with any information about the foreign key relationship and has used some sensible defaults, including allowing null values in the column that tracks relationships and creating a foreign key relationship with a name that combines the names of the tables and columns involved.

Creating a Foreign Key Property

Overriding the defaults is done by creating a property that provides Entity Framework Core with details about how the foreign key should be created. This is a *foreign key property*, and it is defined in the same class that contains the navigation property. In Listing 14-17, I have defined a foreign key property in the Product class that configures the relationship to Supplier objects.

Listing 14-17. Adding a Foreign Key Property in the Product.cs File in the Models Folder

```
namespace DataApp.Models {

    public enum Colors {
        Red, Green, Blue
    }

    public class Product {

        public long Id { get; set; }
        public string Name { get; set; }
        public string Category { get; set; }
```

```
        public decimal Price { get; set; }
        public Colors Color { get; set; }
        public bool InStock { get; set; }

        public long SupplierId { get; set; }
        public Supplier Supplier { get; set; }
    }
}
```

The name of the property tells Entity Framework Core which navigation property it relates to by combining the navigation property name or the related class name with the name of the primary key. For the Product class, both of these conventions lead to a property called SupplierId, which Entity Framework Core will detect as the foreign key property for the Supplier navigation property. (In Chapter 18, I show you how to override the convention for property names.)

The type of the foreign key property tells Entity Framework Core whether the relationship is optional or required. The relationship will be optional if the foreign key property type can be set to null (such as when the type long? is used) and required if null values are not possible (such as when the type long is used). In Listing 14-17, I used long as the property type; this tells Entity Framework Core to create a required relationship since long values cannot be set to null.

Run the command shown in Listing 14-18 in the DataApp project folder to create a migration that will modify the database to apply the attribute.

Listing 14-18. Creating a Migration

```
dotnet ef migrations add Required --context EFDatabaseContext
```

If you examine the statements in the Up method of the <timestamp>_Required.cs file in the Migrations folder, you will see how the change will be applied to the database, as follows:

```
...
protected override void Up(MigrationBuilder migrationBuilder) {
    migrationBuilder.DropForeignKey(name: "FK_Products_Supplier_SupplierId",
        table: "Products");

    migrationBuilder.AlterColumn<long>(name: "SupplierId", table: "Products",
        nullable: false, oldClrType: typeof(long), oldNullable: true);

    migrationBuilder.AddForeignKey(name: "FK_Products_Supplier_SupplierId",
        table: "Products", column: "SupplierId", principalTable: "Supplier",
        principalColumn: "Id", onDelete: ReferentialAction.Cascade);
}
...
```

The migration will re-create the foreign key relationship between the Products and Supplier tables to reflect the new property on the Product class. The most important statement is the one that alters the SupplierId column, and its nullable argument is the one that is used to prevent null values.

```
...
migrationBuilder.AlterColumn<long>(name: "SupplierId", table: "Products",
    nullable: false, oldClrType: typeof(long), oldNullable: true);
...
```

The altered column is no longer allowed to store `null` values, and the foreign key requires that values correspond to a row in the `Supplier` table, which is how required relationships are managed.

Dropping the Database and Preparing the Seed Data

You will get an error if you try to apply the migration to the database because there are rows in the `Products` table that contain NULL values and are no longer allowed.

In a real project, you should prepare the database for the migration by removing the data that does not meet the new requirements. For the example application, I am going to remove the database entirely, update the seed data, and then re-create it to ensure that all of the data is valid. First, run the command shown in Listing 14-19 in the `DataApp` project folder to drop the database.

Listing 14-19. Dropping the Database

```
dotnet ef database drop --force --context EFDatabaseContext
```

Next, update the getter for the `Products` property defined by the `SeedData` class so that all the `Product` objects that are stored are related to a `Supplier` object, as shown in Listing 14-20.

Listing 14-20. Ensuring Data Relationships in the SeedData.cs File in the Models Folder

```
...
private static Product[] Products {
    get {
        Product[] products = new Product[] {
            new Product { Name = "Kayak", Category = "Watersports",
                Price = 275, Color = Colors.Green, InStock = true },
            new Product { Name = "Lifejacket", Category = "Watersports",
                Price = 48.95m, Color = Colors.Red, InStock = true },
            new Product { Name = "Soccer Ball", Category = "Soccer",
                Price = 19.50m, Color = Colors.Blue, InStock = true },
            new Product { Name = "Corner Flags", Category = "Soccer",
                Price = 34.95m, Color = Colors.Green, InStock = true },
            new Product { Name = "Stadium", Category = "Soccer",
                Price = 79500, Color = Colors.Red, InStock = true },
            new Product { Name = "Thinking Cap", Category = "Chess",
                Price = 16, Color = Colors.Blue, InStock = true },
            new Product { Name = "Unsteady Chair", Category = "Chess",
                Price = 29.95m, Color = Colors.Green, InStock = true },
            new Product { Name = "Human Chess Board", Category = "Chess",
                Price = 75, Color = Colors.Red, InStock = true },
            new Product { Name = "Bling-Bling King", Category = "Chess",
                Price = 1200, Color = Colors.Blue, InStock = true }};

        Supplier acme = new Supplier { Name = "Acme Co",
            City = "New York", State = "NY" };
        Supplier s1 = new Supplier { Name = "Surf Dudes",
            City = "San Jose", State = "CA" };
        Supplier s2 = new Supplier { Name = "Chess Kings",
            City = "Seattle", State = "WA" };
```

```
        foreach (Product p in products) {
            if (p == products[0]) {
                p.Supplier = s1;
            } else if (p.Category == "Chess") {
                p.Supplier = s2;
            } else {
                p.Supplier = acme;
            }
        }
        return products;
    }
}
...
```

The changes to the seed data keep the relationships that I set up previously and use the Acme Co supplier for all other products.

Updating and Seeding the Database

Run the command shown in Listing 14-21 in the DataApp project folder to prepare the database, including the required relationship between Product and Supplier objects.

Listing 14-21. Updating the Database to Include the Changed Relationship

```
dotnet ef database update --context EFDatabaseContext
```

Once Entity Framework Core has applied the migrations, start the application using dotnet run and use a browser to request the http://localhost:5000 URL. During application startup, the database will be seeded with data that meets the constraints applied to the database so that all Product objects are related to a Supplier, as shown in Figure 14-10.

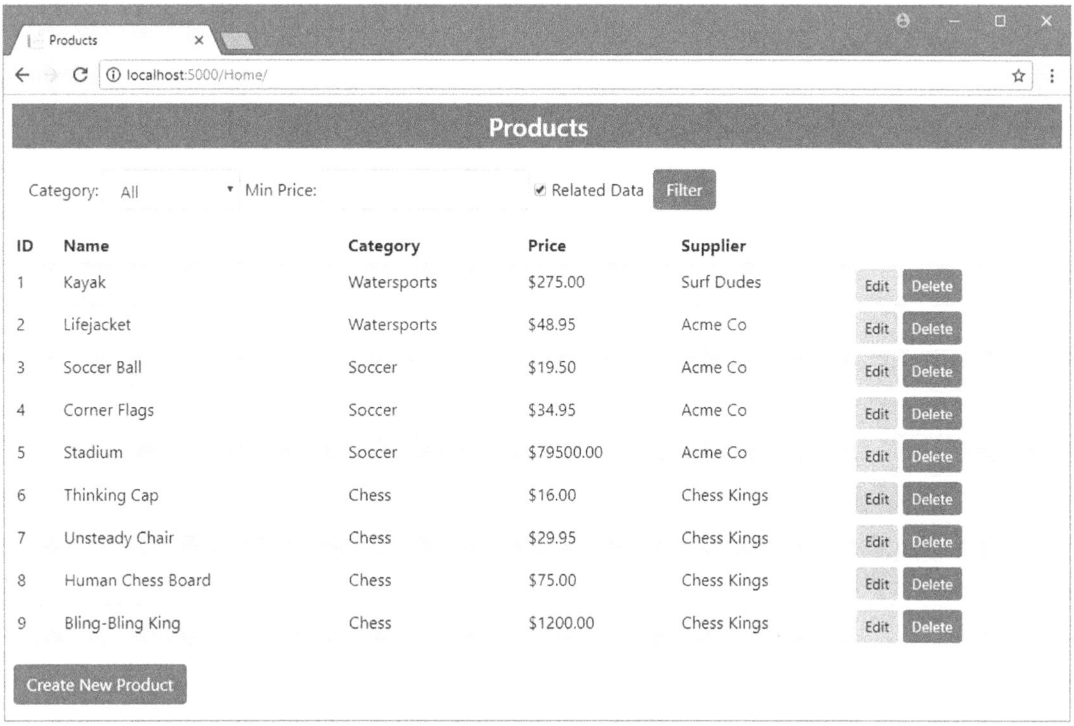

Figure 14-10. *Creating a relationship*

Understanding the Required Relationship Delete Operation

The foreign key property resulted in two important changes in the migration created in Listing 14-21. The first was to prevent null values from being stored in the SupplierId column, which changed the relationship from optional to required. The second change makes a surprising difference to the way the database works and causes a lot of confusion.

When the navigation property was added to the Product class in Listing 14-3 before the foreign key property was defined, the migration that was created configured the foreign key relationship like this:

```
...
migrationBuilder.AddForeignKey(
    name: "FK_Products_Supplier_SupplierId", table: "Products",
    column: "SupplierId", principalTable: "Supplier",
    principalColumn: "Id", onDelete: ReferentialAction.Restrict);
...
```

The onDelete argument tells the database what to do when the row that the Product depends on in the Supplier table is deleted, using values from the ReferentialAction enum. The Restrict value is used for optional relationships and configures the database so that a Supplier cannot be deleted while there are rows in the Products table that depend on it. This is the reason that there was an error when deleting a Supplier earlier in the chapter.

325

When you create a required relationship, the foreign key is reconfigured with a different
ReferentialAction value, like this:

```
...
migrationBuilder.AddForeignKey(
    name: "FK_Products_Supplier_SupplierId", table: "Products",
    column: "SupplierId", principalTable: "Supplier",
    principalColumn: "Id", onDelete: ReferentialAction.Cascade);
...
```

When the Cascade value is used, deleting a Supplier causes a *cascade delete*, which means that any
other Product objects that depend on that Supplier are also deleted. To see the effect of the cascade, start
the application with dotnet run, navigate to http://localhost:5000, and click the Delete button for the
Unsteady Chair product. Not only will this Product be deleted, but so will all of the others that are related to
the Chess Kings supplier, as shown in Figure 14-11.

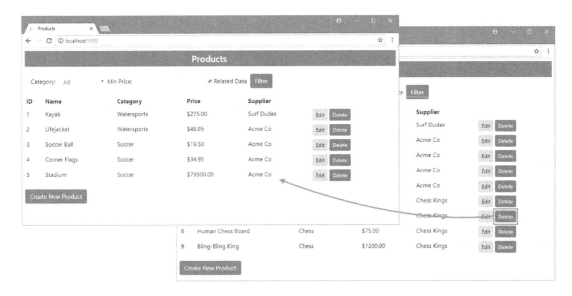

Figure 14-11. *The effect of a cascade delete*

It is important to understand that it is the act of deleting the Supplier object that triggers the cascade
delete. You can remove a Product object from the database, and the Supplier will be unaffected. When you
remove a Supplier, the cascade delete is responsible for removing the rows from the Products database that
have a foreign key relationship with the row from the Supplier table that is being deleted.

Bear in mind that it is the database server and not Entity Framework Core that performs the cascade
delete. The configuration of the database that was applied by the migration tells the database server what to
do when a row is deleted. I explain how to take control of this behavior directly in Chapter 22.

Querying for Multiple Relationships

Most applications contain more than one data relationship. The process for creating, updating, and deleting more complex related data is the same, but a different technique is required to tell Entity Framework Core to follow all of the navigation properties to ensure that you get the data you require.

To demonstrate how this works, I added a class file called ContactLocation.cs to the Models folder and added the code shown in Listing 14-22.

Listing 14-22. The Contents of the ContactLocation.cs File in the Models Folder

```
namespace DataApp.Models {

    public class ContactLocation {
        public long Id { get; set; }
        public string LocationName { get; set; }
        public string Address { get; set; }
    }
}
```

Next, I created a class file called ContactDetails.cs in the Models folder and added the code shown in Listing 14-23.

Listing 14-23. The Contents of the ContactDetails.cs File in the Models Folder

```
namespace DataApp.Models {

    public class ContactDetails {
        public long Id { get; set; }
        public string Name { get; set; }
        public string Phone { get; set; }
        public ContactLocation Location { get; set; }
    }
}
```

The ContactDetails class defines a navigation property called Location that creates a relationship with a ContactLocation object. To complete the additions, I added a navigation property to the Supplier class, as shown in Listing 14-24.

Listing 14-24. Adding a Navigation Property in the Supplier.cs File in the Models Folder

```
namespace DataApp.Models {

    public class Supplier {
        public long Id { get; set; }
        public string Name { get; set; }
        public string City { get; set; }
        public string State { get; set; }

        public ContactDetails Contact { get; set; }
    }
}
```

The Contact property creates a relationship with the ContactDetails class. The overall result is a chain of relationships between classes, as illustrated in Figure 14-12.

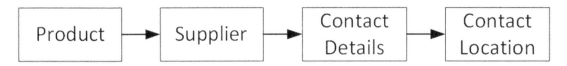

Figure 14-12. *Creating a chain of navigation properties*

Updating and Seeding the Database

To create a migration that will allow the database to store instances of the new classes, run the command shown in Listing 14-25 in the DataApp project folder.

Tip   If you get out of sequence with the command in this chapter and start to see Invalid Column Name exceptions, then comment out the statements in the Startup class that seed the database and run the commands in Listing 14-26 and then Listing 14-25. Once the database is updated, uncomment the statements in the Startup class and start the application.

Listing 14-25. Creating a Migration

```
dotnet ef migrations add AdditionalTypes --context EFDatabaseContext
```

If you examine the C# statements in the <timestamp>_AdditionalTypes.cs file that has been created in the Migrations folder, you will see that Entity Framework Core has followed the conventions explained earlier in the chapter to create tables that will store ContentDetails and ContactLocation objects.

To drop and re-create the database so that it can be reseeded, run the commands in Listing 14-26 in the DataApp project folder.

Listing 14-26. Re-creating the Database

```
dotnet ef database drop --force --context EFDatabaseContext
dotnet ef database update --context EFDatabaseContext
```

To ensure that there is some data to query when the database is seeded, add the statements shown in Listing 14-27 to the getter of the Products property in the SeedData class.

Listing 14-27. Expanding the Seed Data in the SeedData.cs File in the Models Folder

```
...
private static Product[] Products {
    get {
        Product[] products = new Product[] {
            new Product { Name = "Kayak", Category = "Watersports",
                Price = 275, Color = Colors.Green, InStock = true },
            new Product { Name = "Lifejacket", Category = "Watersports",
                Price = 48.95m, Color = Colors.Red, InStock = true },
```

```
        new Product { Name = "Soccer Ball", Category = "Soccer",
            Price = 19.50m, Color = Colors.Blue, InStock = true },
        new Product { Name = "Corner Flags", Category = "Soccer",
            Price = 34.95m, Color = Colors.Green, InStock = true },
        new Product { Name = "Stadium", Category = "Soccer",
            Price = 79500, Color = Colors.Red, InStock = true },
        new Product { Name = "Thinking Cap", Category = "Chess",
            Price = 16, Color = Colors.Blue, InStock = true },
        new Product { Name = "Unsteady Chair", Category = "Chess",
            Price = 29.95m, Color = Colors.Green, InStock = true },
        new Product { Name = "Human Chess Board", Category = "Chess",
            Price = 75, Color = Colors.Red, InStock = true },
        new Product { Name = "Bling-Bling King", Category = "Chess",
            Price = 1200, Color = Colors.Blue, InStock = true }};

    ContactLocation hq = new ContactLocation {
        LocationName = "Corporate HQ", Address = "200 Acme Way"
    };
    ContactDetails bob = new ContactDetails {
        Name = "Bob Smith", Phone = "555-107-1234", Location = hq
    };

    Supplier acme = new Supplier { Name = "Acme Co",
        City = "New York", State = "NY", Contact = bob };
    Supplier s1 = new Supplier { Name = "Surf Dudes",
        City = "San Jose", State = "CA" };
    Supplier s2 = new Supplier { Name = "Chess Kings",
        City = "Seattle", State = "WA" };

    foreach (Product p in products) {
        if (p == products[0]) {
            p.Supplier = s1;
        } else if (p.Category == "Chess") {
            p.Supplier = s2;
        } else {
            p.Supplier = acme;
        }
    }
    return products;
    }
}
...
```

The changes create a new contact for Bob Smith at headquarters and assign him as the contact for the Acme Co supplier.

Querying the Chain of Navigation Properties

The ThenInclude method is used to extend the scope of a query to follow navigation properties defined by the types selected using the Include method. Listing 14-28 uses the ThenInclude method to tell Entity Framework Core to follow the navigation properties defined by the Supplier and ContactDetails classes so that all of the relationships illustrated by Figure 14-12 are included in the query.

Listing 14-28. Following Navigation Properties in the EFDatabaseRepository.cs File in the Models Folder

```
...
public Product GetProduct(long id) {
    return context.Products.Include(p => p.Supplier)
        .ThenInclude(s => s.Contact).ThenInclude(c => c.Location)
        .First(p => p.Id == id);
}
...
```

The argument to the ThenInclude method is a lambda function that operates on the type selected by the previous call to the Include or ThenInclude method and selects the navigation property that you want to follow. By combining the Include and ThenInclude methods, you can navigate around a complex model to incorporate all of the data you require in a query.

To display the additional related data, add the elements shown in Listing 14-29 to the Supplier.cshtml view.

Listing 14-29. Displaying Related Data in the Supplier.cshtml File in the Views/Shared Folder

```
@model DataApp.Models.Product

<input name="original.Supplier.Id" value="@Model.Supplier?.Id" type="hidden" />
<input name="original.Supplier.Name" value="@Model.Supplier?.Name" type="hidden" />
<input name="original.Supplier.City" value="@Model.Supplier?.City" type="hidden" />
<input name="original.Supplier.State" value="@Model.Supplier?.State" type="hidden" />

<input type="hidden" asp-for="Supplier.Id" />
<div class="form-group">
    <label asp-for="Supplier.Name"></label>
    <input asp-for="Supplier.Name" class="form-control" />
</div>
<div class="form-group">
    <label asp-for="Supplier.City"></label>
    <input asp-for="Supplier.City" class="form-control" />
</div>
<div class="form-group">
    <label asp-for="Supplier.State"></label>
    <input asp-for="Supplier.State" class="form-control" />
</div>
@if (Model.Supplier?.Contact != null) {
    <div class="form-group">
        <label asp-for="Supplier.Contact.Name"></label>
        <input asp-for="Supplier.Contact.Name" class="form-control" readonly />
    </div>
    <div class="form-group">
        <label asp-for="Supplier.Contact.Phone"></label>
        <input asp-for="Supplier.Contact.Phone" class="form-control" readonly />
    </div>
    <div class="form-group">
        <label asp-for="Supplier.Contact.Location.LocationName"></label>
        <input asp-for="Supplier.Contact.Location.LocationName"
                class="form-control" readonly />
    </div>
}
```

The additions are read-only elements that display values from the extended related data. To test the query, use `dotnet run` to start the application, navigate to `http://localhost:5000`, and click the Edit button for one of the products whose supplier is Acme Co. You will see the contact details, as shown in Figure 14-13.

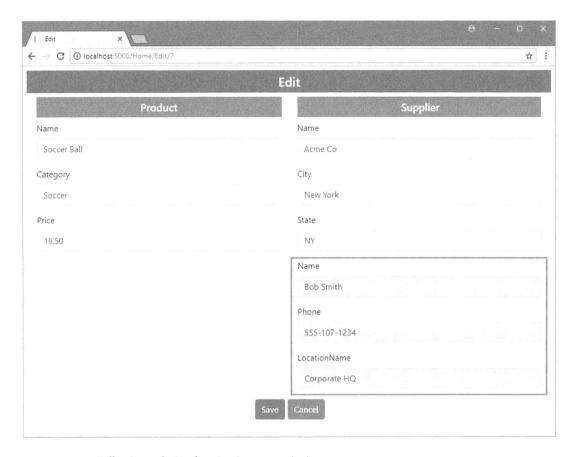

Figure 14-13. *Following a chain of navigation properties in a query*

Summary

In this chapter, I explained how navigation properties are used to create relationships between data and how these are reflected in the database and consumed by Entity Framework Core. In the next chapter, I show you how to use different relationship features.

░░ ░░ ░░

CHAPTER 15

Working with Relationships Part 1

In this chapter, I show you how to access related data directly and, once you have done this, how you can complete a relationship so that navigation can be performed in both directions between the objects in the relationship. This chapter focuses on one-to-many relationships, which are the easiest to create but which require care when performing queries or updating the database. In Chapter 16, I describe other types of data relationships that Entity Framework Core supports. Table 15-1 summarizes the chapter.

Table 15-1. *Chapter Summary*

Problem	Solution	Listing
Access related data directly rather than through a navigation property	Add a DbSet<T> property to the context class and then create and apply a migration	1–7
Access related data by type	Use the DbContext.Set<T>() method	8–12
Navigate a relationship in both directions	Complete the relationship with a navigation property	13–15, 20–33
Force execution of a query	Use explicit loading	16
Compose data relationships across multiple queries	Rely on the fixing up feature	17–19

Preparing for This Chapter

This chapter uses the DataApp project created in Chapter 11 and modified in the chapters since. To prepare for this chapter, open a command prompt in the DataApp folder and run the commands shown in Listing 15-1.

> ░ **Tip**   If you don't want to follow the process of building the example project, you can download all of the required files from this book's source code repository, https://github.com/apress/pro-ef-core-2-for-asp.net-core-mvc.

Listing 15-1. Resetting the Database

```
dotnet ef database drop --force --context EFDatabaseContext
dotnet ef database update --context EFDatabaseContext
```

These commands remove and re-create the database used to store Product objects, which will help ensure that you get the expected results from the examples in this chapter. Start the application using dotnet run and use a browser to navigate to http://localhost:5000. The application will seed the database as it starts, and you will see the list of products shown in Figure 15-1.

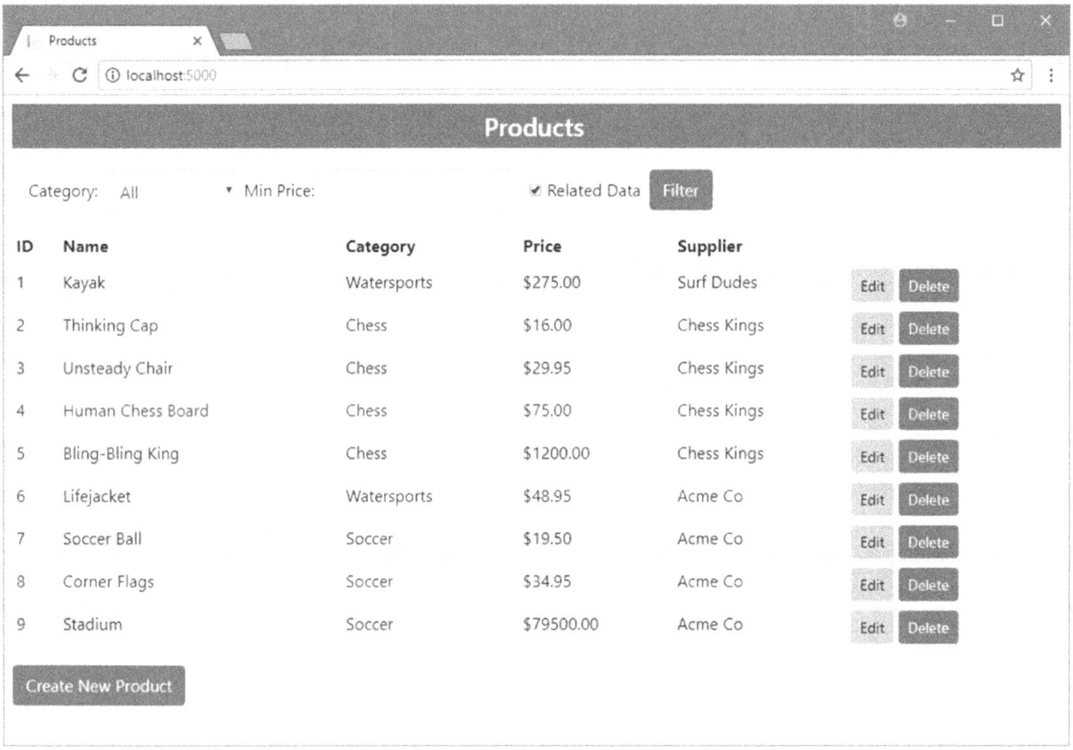

Figure 15-1. *Running the example application*

Directly Accessing Related Data

In most applications, at least some of the related data has its own lifecycle and workflows that users need to perform. In the DataApp application, for example, you can easily imagine that an administrator might need to make a change to reflect an address change. This is difficult because I can only access the data in the database by starting with a Product object and following its navigation properties. If I want to update a ContactLocation object, for example, I have to start by searching for a Product that is related to the Supplier I want to modify, query for that Product, and then follow the navigation properties to get the Supplier and ContactDetails objects. Only then will I be able to access the ContactLocation object that I want to modify.

To avoid this kind of issue, you can access related data directly. In the sections that follow, I show you two different approaches to accessing related data and explain when each should be used.

Promoting Related Data

For data that plays an important role in the application, such that it has its own management tools and lifecycle, the best approach is to promote the data so it can be accessed through a DbSet<T> property defined by the context class.

This is the most disruptive approach because it requires a new migration to be created and applied, but it puts the related data on a first-class footing in the application and follows the conventions that many developers are accustomed to.

To promote the Supplier data so that it can be accessed directly, I added a property to the EFDatabaseContext class, as shown in Listing 15-2.

Listing 15-2. Promoting Related Data in the EFDatabaseContext.cs File in the Models Folder

```
using Microsoft.EntityFrameworkCore;

namespace DataApp.Models {
    public class EFDatabaseContext : DbContext {

        public EFDatabaseContext(DbContextOptions<EFDatabaseContext> opts)
            : base(opts) { }

        public DbSet<Product> Products { get; set; }
        public DbSet<Supplier> Suppliers { get; set; }
    }
}
```

The new property returns a DbSet<Supplier> object that can be used to query and operate on the Supplier objects in the database. A new migration is required when you define DbSet<T> properties, so run the commands shown in Listing 15-3 in the DataApp project folder to create and apply a migration.

Listing 15-3. Creating and Applying a Migration

```
dotnet ef migrations add PromoteSuppliers --context EFDatabaseContext
dotnet ef database update --context EFDatabaseContext
```

If you examine the Up method of the <timestamp>_PromoteSuppliers.cs file that has been created in the Migrations folder, you will see that promoting the Supplier data has led to the database table that contains the related data being renamed, like this:

```
...
migrationBuilder.RenameTable(name: "Supplier", newName: "Suppliers");
...
```

The name change is caused by the switch from one Entity Framework Core convention to another. In Listing 15-3, I have followed the convention of using the plural form of the class name for the property—Suppliers, in this case—which Entity Framework Core will use as the name of the table used to store the Supplier objects in the database. However, there is already a Supplier table in the database, which was created using the convention of using the name of the navigation property defined in Chapter 14. The convention for the DbSet<T> property takes precedence and has led to the table that contains Supplier objects being renamed.

Consuming the Promoted Data

Once you have promoted the data, you can access it using the techniques described in earlier chapters. To provide a repository for Supplier objects, I added a class file called SupplierRepository.cs to the Models folder and defined the interface and class shown in Listing 15-4.

Listing 15-4. The Contents of the SupplierRepository.cs File in the Models Folder

```
using System.Collections.Generic;

namespace DataApp.Models {

    public interface ISupplierRepository {

        Supplier Get(long id);
        IEnumerable<Supplier> GetAll();
        void Create(Supplier newDataObject);
        void Update(Supplier changedDataObject);
        void Delete(long id);
    }

    public class SupplierRepository : ISupplierRepository {
        private EFDatabaseContext context;

        public SupplierRepository(EFDatabaseContext ctx) => context = ctx;

        public Supplier Get(long id) {
            return context.Suppliers.Find(id);
        }

        public IEnumerable<Supplier> GetAll() {
            return context.Suppliers;
        }

        public void Create(Supplier newDataObject) {
            context.Add(newDataObject);
            context.SaveChanges();
        }

        public void Update(Supplier changedDataObject) {
            context.Update(changedDataObject);
            context.SaveChanges();
        }

        public void Delete(long id) {
            context.Remove(Get(id));
            context.SaveChanges();
        }
    }
}
```

I have used simple operations in this repository, avoiding the more complex optimizations described in Chapter 12. In Listing 15-5, I have registered the repository in the Startup class so that it can be consumed as a service in the rest of the application.

Listing 15-5. Registering the Promoted Repository in the Startup.cs File in the DataApp Folder

```
...
public void ConfigureServices(IServiceCollection services) {
    services.AddMvc();
    string conString = Configuration["ConnectionStrings:DefaultConnection"];
    services.AddDbContext<EFDatabaseContext>(options =>
        options.UseSqlServer(conString));

    string customerConString =
        Configuration["ConnectionStrings:CustomerConnection"];
    services.AddDbContext<EFCustomerContext>(options =>
        options.UseSqlServer(customerConString));

    services.AddTransient<IDataRepository, EFDataRepository>();
    services.AddTransient<ICustomerRepository, EFCustomerRepository>();
    services.AddTransient<MigrationsManager>();
    services.AddTransient<ISupplierRepository, SupplierRepository>();
}
...
```

To provide a controller for the Supplier data, I added a class called RelatedDataController.cs to the Controllers folder and defined the class shown in Listing 15-6.

Listing 15-6. The Contents of the RelatedDataController.cs File in the Controllers Folder

```
using DataApp.Models;
using Microsoft.AspNetCore.Mvc;

namespace DataApp.Controllers {

    public class RelatedDataController : Controller {
        private ISupplierRepository supplierRepo;

        public RelatedDataController(ISupplierRepository repo)
            => supplierRepo = repo;

        public IActionResult Index() => View(supplierRepo.GetAll());
    }
}
```

The controller defines a single action method that queries the repository for all the Supplier objects in the database and passes them to the default view. For the view, I created the Views/RelatedData folder and added to it a view called Index.cshtml with the content shown in Listing 15-7.

Listing 15-7. The Contents of the Index.cshtml File in the Views/RelatedData Folder

```
@model IEnumerable<DataApp.Models.Supplier>

@{
    ViewData["Title"] = "Suppliers";
    Layout = "_Layout";
}

<table class="table table-striped table-sm">
    <tr><th>ID</th><th>Name</th><th>City</th><th>State</th></tr>
    @foreach (var s in Model.OrderBy(s => s.Id)) {
        <tr>
            <td>@s.Id</td>
            <td>@s.Name</td>
            <td>@s.City</td>
            <td>@s.State</td>
        </tr>
    }
</table>
```

To see the effect of promoting the Supplier data, start the application and navigate to http://localhost:5000/relateddata to see the result shown in Figure 15-2.

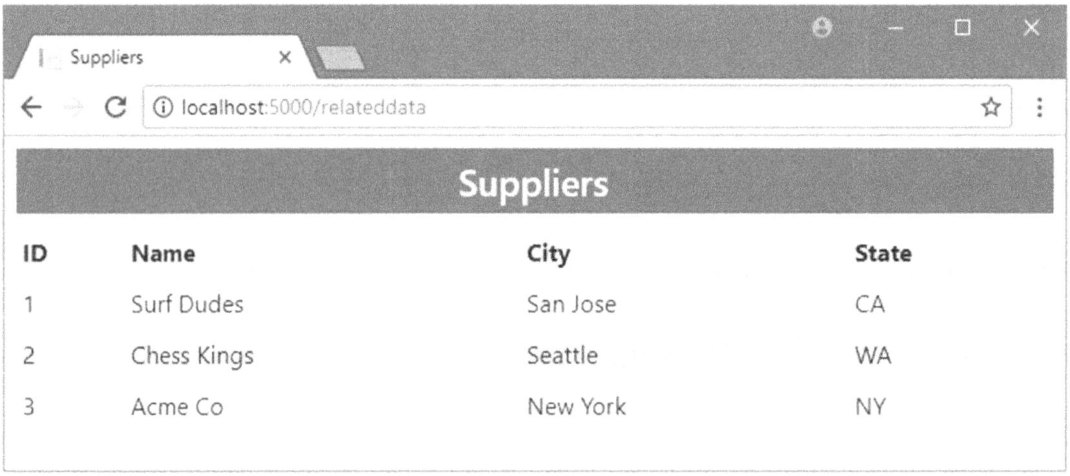

Figure 15-2. *Promoting related data*

Accessing Related Data Using a Type Parameter

The alternative to promoting data is to use a set of methods that are provided by the database context class and that allow the data type to be specified as a type parameter. This is a useful feature for dealing with data for which you require occasional or limited access for specific operations and for which promotion to a DbSet<T> property is not warranted. Table 15-2 describes the DbContext methods that accept a type parameter and can be used to access data without needing to promote it.

Table 15-2. *The DbContext Methods with Type Parameters*

Name	Description
Set<T>()	This method returns a DbSet<T> object that can be used to query the database.
Find<T>(key)	This method queries the database for the object of type T that has the specified key.
Add<T>(newObject)	This method adds a new object of type T to the database.
Update<T>(changedObject)	This method updates an object of type T.
Remove<T>(dataObject)	This method removes an object of type T from the database.

One advantage of these methods is that they can be used to create a generic repository that can be used to provide access to a specific type when it is configured as a service in the Startup class. I added a class file called GenericRepository.cs to the Models folder and defined the interface and class shown in Listing 15-8.

Listing 15-8. The Contents of the GenericRepository.cs File in the Models Folder

```
using System.Collections.Generic;

namespace DataApp.Models {

    public interface IGenericRepository<T> where T : class {

        T Get(long id);

        IEnumerable<T> GetAll();

        void Create(T newDataObject);

        void Update(T changedDataObject);

        void Delete(long id);
    }

    public class GenericRepository<T> : IGenericRepository<T> where T : class {
        protected EFDatabaseContext context;

        public GenericRepository(EFDatabaseContext ctx) => context = ctx;

        public virtual T Get(long id) {
            return context.Set<T>().Find(id);
        }

        public virtual IEnumerable<T> GetAll() {
            return context.Set<T>();
        }
```

```
        public virtual void Create(T newDataObject) {
            context.Add<T>(newDataObject);
            context.SaveChanges();
        }

        public virtual void Delete(long id) {
            context.Remove<T>(Get(id));
            context.SaveChanges();
        }

        public virtual void Update(T changedDataObject) {
            context.Update<T>(changedDataObject);
            context.SaveChanges();
        }
    }
}
```

The IGenericRepository<T> interface defines the operations that a repository must provide to work with the type T. The where clause restricts the type parameter to classes, which is a constraint imposed by Entity Framework Core. The GenericRepository<T> class implements the interface using the same basic techniques I used for the Supplier class but performed using the methods described in Table 15-2.

Tip   The methods in Listing 15-8 are marked as virtual so that I can create more specialized implementations of the repository class without having to make wide-ranging changes to the application.

The specific types that the interface and implementation class will be used for are configured when the dependency injection service is created in the Startup class. In Listing 15-9, I have defined services for the ContactDetails and ContactLocation classes.

Listing 15-9. Creating Services in the Startup Class in the DataApp Folder

```
...
public void ConfigureServices(IServiceCollection services) {
    services.AddMvc();
    string conString = Configuration["ConnectionStrings:DefaultConnection"];
    services.AddDbContext<EFDatabaseContext>(options =>
        options.UseSqlServer(conString));

    string customerConString =
        Configuration["ConnectionStrings:CustomerConnection"];
    services.AddDbContext<EFCustomerContext>(options =>
        options.UseSqlServer(customerConString));

    services.AddTransient<IDataRepository, EFDataRepository>();
    services.AddTransient<ICustomerRepository, EFCustomerRepository>();
    services.AddTransient<MigrationsManager>();
    services.AddTransient<ISupplierRepository, SupplierRepository>();
```

```
    services.AddTransient<IGenericRepository<ContactDetails>,
        GenericRepository<ContactDetails>>();
    services.AddTransient<IGenericRepository<ContactLocation>,
        GenericRepository<ContactLocation>>();
}
...
```

To display the data obtained through the generic context methods, I added action methods to the RelatedData controller, as shown in Listing 15-10. These methods query for all of the available objects of each type, although all of the standard data operations can be used.

Listing 15-10. Querying for Data in the RelatedDataController.cs File in the Controllers Folder

```
using DataApp.Models;
using Microsoft.AspNetCore.Mvc;

namespace DataApp.Controllers {

    public class RelatedDataController : Controller {
        private ISupplierRepository supplierRepo;
        private IGenericRepository<ContactDetails> detailsRepo;
        private IGenericRepository<ContactLocation> locsRepo;

        public RelatedDataController(ISupplierRepository sRepo,
                IGenericRepository<ContactDetails> dRepo,
                IGenericRepository<ContactLocation> lRepo) {
            supplierRepo = sRepo;
            detailsRepo = dRepo;
            locsRepo = lRepo;
        }

        public IActionResult Index() => View(supplierRepo.GetAll());

        public IActionResult Contacts() => View(detailsRepo.GetAll());
        public IActionResult Locations() => View(locsRepo.GetAll());
    }
}
```

■ **Caution**   You may be tempted to build on the idea of accessing data classes using type parameters and set up a generic handler and controller in the ASP.NET Core pipeline that doesn't require action methods and views for each class. This may seem like a good idea, but it should be avoided because it provides access to all of the data in the database, which is rarely a good idea. Use type parameters behind the scenes to keep the application simple but explicitly grant access to classes on an individual basis.

The generic repositories are received through the constructor in the normal way and used by the Contacts and Locations action methods, both of which use the default view. To display the ContactDetails objects, I created a file called Contacts.cshtml in the Views/RelatedData folder, with the content shown in Listing 15-11.

Listing 15-11. The Contents of the Contacts.cshtml File in the Views/RelatedData Folder

```
@model IEnumerable<DataApp.Models.ContactDetails>
@{
    ViewData["Title"] = "ContactDetails";
    Layout = "_Layout";
}
<table class="table table-striped table-sm">
    <tr><th>ID</th><th>Name</th><th>Phone</th></tr>
    @foreach (var s in Model) {
        <tr><td>@s.Id</td><td>@s.Name</td><td>@s.Phone</td></tr>
    }
</table>
```

The view displays the ContactDetails properties in a table. To provide a corresponding view for the ContactLocation objects, I added a file called Locations.cshtml to the Views/RelatedData folder with the content shown in Listing 15-12.

Listing 15-12. The Contents of the Locations.cshtml File in the Views/RelatedData Folder

```
@model IEnumerable<DataApp.Models.ContactLocation>
@{
    ViewData["Title"] = "ContactLocations";
    Layout = "_Layout";
}
<table class="table table-striped table-sm">
    <tr><th>ID</th><th>Name</th></tr>
    @foreach (var s in Model) {
        <tr><td>@s.Id</td><td>@s.LocationName</td></tr>
    }
</table>
```

To access the related data through the generic repositories, restart the application and navigate to the http://localhost:5000/relateddata/contacts and http://localhost:5000/relateddata/locations URLs, which target the action methods defined in Listing 15-10 and produce the results shown in Figure 15-3.

Figure 15-3. *Accessing related data via a generic repository*

Completing a Data Relationship

Promoting the related data has made it easier to access, but working with it can be improved further. At the moment, the relationships between classes flow in only one direction. I can start with a Product object, for example, and follow a navigation property to get the related Supplier data, but I can't start with a Supplier and navigate in the opposite direction. To address this shortfall, Entity Framework Core allows me to define properties that allow navigation in the other direction, which is known as *completing the relationship*.

There is a range of different types of relationship that you can create between classes, but when you first define a navigation property, Entity Framework Core assumes that you want to create a one-to-many relationship and that the navigation property has been added to the class at the "many" end of the relationship. This is what happened when I added a navigation property to the Product class in Chapter 14: Entity Framework Core created a one-to-many relationship that allowed each Supplier object to be related to many Product objects and configured the database accordingly.

■ **Tip** I describe how to create other types of relationships in Chapter 16.

Completing a one-to-many relationship is easy and requires a navigation property to be added to the class at the "one" end of the relationship. This is known as the *inverse* property, and to complete the relationship between the Product and Supplier class, I added the inverse navigation property shown in Listing 15-13 to the Supplier class.

Listing 15-13. Completing a Relationship in the Supplier.cs File in the Models Folder

```
using System.Collections.Generic;

namespace DataApp.Models {

    public class Supplier {
        public long Id { get; set; }
        public string Name { get; set; }
        public string City { get; set; }
        public string State { get; set; }

        public ContactDetails Contact { get; set; }
        public IEnumerable<Product> Products { get; set; }
    }
}
```

The navigation property returns an enumeration of the other class in the relationship, which is Product in this case. This reflects the fact that each Supplier object can be related to many Product objects, and using IEnumerable<Product> allows Entity Framework Core to provide the complete set of related data.

■ **Note** You don't have to create a new migration when you complete a one-to-many relationship. A new migration is required for other types of relationships, as demonstrated in Chapter 16.

Querying Related Data in a One-to-Many Relationship

Once you have completed the relationship, you can start with an object of either type in the relationship and navigate in both directions. In the case of the example application, this means that I can start with a Supplier object and follow the Products property to navigate to the set of related Product objects, just as long as the related data has been included in the request. Including related data in a completed one-to-many relationship can be performed in a number of different ways, as I explain in the sections that follow.

Querying for All Related Data

If you want the complete set of related data, then you can use the Include or ThenInclude method to extend the query by selecting the navigation property. In Listing 15-14, I have used the Include method to follow the Supplier.Products method defined in Listing 15-13 and query for all of the Product objects that are related to each Supplier.

Listing 15-14. Querying for All Data in the SupplierRepository.cs File in the Models Folder

```
using System.Collections.Generic;
using Microsoft.EntityFrameworkCore;
using System.Linq;

namespace DataApp.Models {

    public interface ISupplierRepository {

        Supplier Get(long id);
        IEnumerable<Supplier> GetAll();
        void Create(Supplier newDataObject);
        void Update(Supplier changedDataObject);
        void Delete(long id);
    }

    public class SupplierRepository : ISupplierRepository {
        private EFDatabaseContext context;

        public SupplierRepository(EFDatabaseContext ctx) => context = ctx;

        public Supplier Get(long id) {
            return context.Suppliers.Find(id);
        }

        public IEnumerable<Supplier> GetAll() {
            return context.Suppliers.Include(s => s.Products);
        }

        public void Create(Supplier newDataObject) {
            context.Add(newDataObject);
            context.SaveChanges();
        }
```

```
    public void Update(Supplier changedDataObject) {
        context.Update(changedDataObject);
        context.SaveChanges();
    }

    public void Delete(long id) {
        context.Remove(Get(id));
        context.SaveChanges();
    }
  }
}
```

The changes in the repository tell Entity Framework Core to query for all the Product objects associated with a Supplier object. Additional changes are required to display the related data to the user and to start building out the set of data operations. To display the Product objects related to a Supplier, I added the content shown in Listing 15-15 to the Index.cshtml file in the Views/RelatedData folder.

Listing 15-15. Displaying Related Data in the Index.cshtml File in the Views/RelatedData Folder

```
@model IEnumerable<DataApp.Models.Supplier>

@{
    ViewData["Title"] = "Suppliers";
    Layout = "_Layout";
}

<table class="table table-striped table-sm">
    <tr><th>ID</th><th>Name</th><th>City</th><th>State</th></tr>
    @foreach (var s in Model.OrderBy(s => s.Id)) {
        <tr>
            <td>@s.Id</td>
            <td>@s.Name</td>
            <td>@s.City</td>
            <td>@s.State</td>
        </tr>
        @if (s.Products != null) {
            @foreach (var p in s.Products) {
                <tr class="table-dark">
                    <td></td>
                    <td>@p.Name</td>
                    <td>@p.Category</td>
                    <td>@p.Price</td>
                </tr>
            }
        }
    }
</table>
```

The changes to the view display a summary of each Product object after the Supplier object it is related to. To see the effect, start the application and navigate to http://localhost:5000/relateddata. The Product objects are shown in dark colored rows, as illustrated by Figure 15-4.

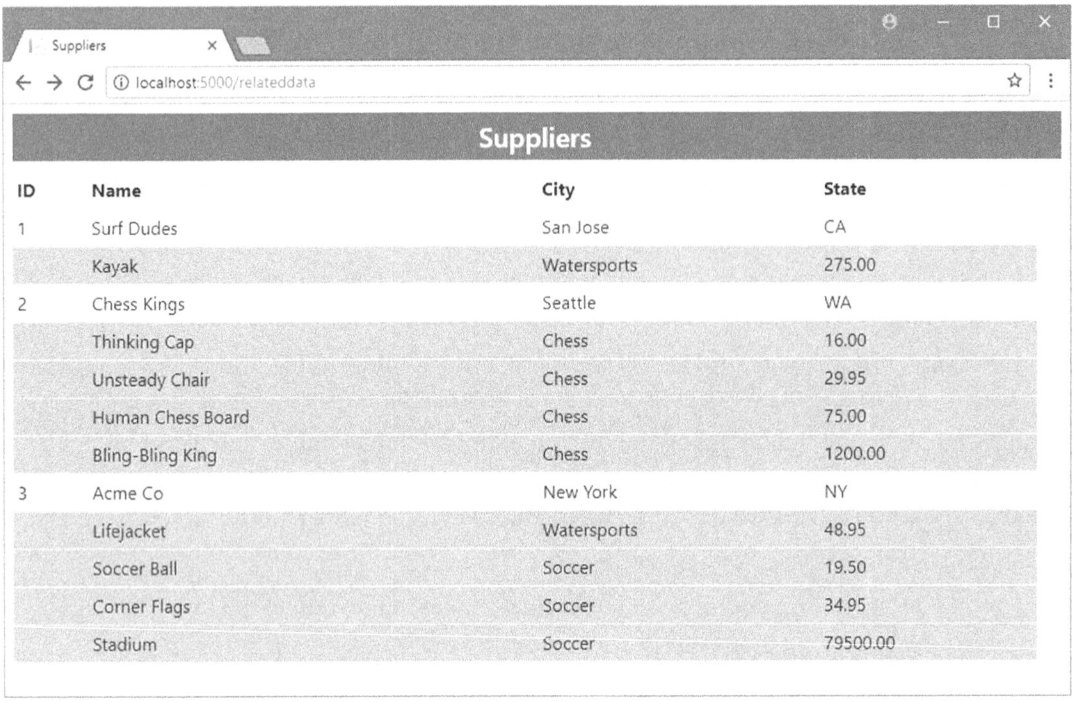

ID	Name	City	State
1	Surf Dudes	San Jose	CA
	Kayak	Watersports	275.00
2	Chess Kings	Seattle	WA
	Thinking Cap	Chess	16.00
	Unsteady Chair	Chess	29.95
	Human Chess Board	Chess	75.00
	Bling-Bling King	Chess	1200.00
3	Acme Co	New York	NY
	Lifejacket	Watersports	48.95
	Soccer Ball	Soccer	19.50
	Corner Flags	Soccer	34.95
	Stadium	Soccer	79500.00

Figure 15-4. *Querying for all related data in a one-to-many relationship*

When considering the different ways that related data in a one-to-many relationship can be obtained, it is helpful to examine the query that was used to get the data from the database. If you examine the logging output produced by the application, you will see that using the `Supplier` data is requested first, like this:

```
...
SELECT [s].[Id], [s].[City], [s].[ContactId], [s].[Name], [s].[State]
FROM [Suppliers] AS [s]
ORDER BY [s].[Id]
...
```

To get the related data, a second query is sent, which obtains the related `Product` data, like this:

```
...
SELECT [s.Products].[Id], [s.Products].[Category], [s.Products].[Color],
    [s.Products].[InStock], [s.Products].[Name], [s.Products].[Price],
    [s.Products].[SupplierId]
FROM [Products] AS [s.Products]
INNER JOIN (
    SELECT [s0].[Id]
    FROM [Suppliers] AS [s0]
) AS [t] ON [s.Products].[SupplierId] = [t].[Id]
ORDER BY [t].[Id]
...
```

Querying Using Explicit Loading

Using the Include method to follow a one-to-many navigation property doesn't provide any way to filter the related data, which means that it is all retrieved from the database. If you want to be more selective, then Entity Framework Core provides two ways to filter the data that is queried. The first of these techniques is called *explicit loading*, which I have used to replace the Include method in Listing 15-16.

Listing 15-16. Using Explicit Loading in the SupplierRepository.cs File in the Models Folder

```
...
public IEnumerable<Supplier> GetAll() {
    IEnumerable<Supplier> data = context.Suppliers.ToArray();
    foreach (Supplier s in data) {
        context.Entry(s).Collection(e => e.Products)
            .Query()
            .Where(p => p.Price > 50)
            .Load();
    }
    return data;
}
...
```

Explicit loading relies on the DbContext.Entry method, which I used in Chapter 12 to access change tracking data. Calling the Entry method defined by the context object returns an EntityEntry object that provides two methods for accessing related data, as described in Table 15-3.

Table 15-3. The EntityEntry Methods for Related Data

Name	Description
Reference(name)	This method is used for navigation properties that target a single object, specified either as a string or using a lambda expression to select a property.
Collection(name)	This method is used for navigation properties that target a collection, specified either as a string or using a lambda expression to select a property.

Once you have used the Reference or Collection method to select the navigation property, the Query method is used to get an IQueryable object that can be used with LINQ to filter the data that will be loaded. In Listing 15-16, the Where method is used to filter the related data based on price, telling Entity Framework Core to query only for those related Product objects whose Price value exceeds 50.

The Load method is used to force execution of the query. This isn't usually required because the query will be executed automatically when the IQueryable<T> is enumerated by the Razor view or by a LINQ method. In this case, however, the Load method is required because the IQueryable<T> objects returned by the Query method are never enumerated. Without the Load method, the related data queries would not be executed, and only the Supplier objects would be passed to the Razor view. (The Load method has the same effect as ToArray or ToList but doesn't create and return a collection of objects.)

> **Note**   Notice that I have used the `ToArray` method in Listing 15-6 before enumerating the `Supplier` objects in a `foreach` loop. The `ToArray` method forces execution of the query that obtains the `Supplier` data, avoiding the situation where one query is performed when the `IQueryable<Supplier>` is enumerated by the `foreach` loop in the repository method and a duplicate query is triggered by the `foreach` loop in the Razor view.

To see the effect of using explicit loading, restart the application and navigate to `http://localhost:5000/relateddata`. The `Product` data that is displayed contains only the filtered objects, as shown in Figure 15-5.

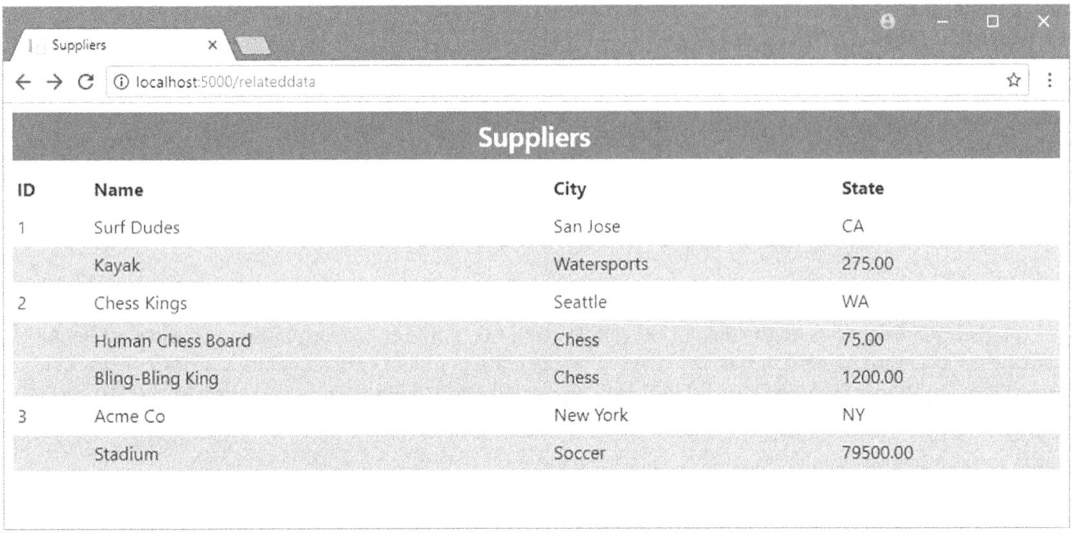

ID	Name	City	State
1	Surf Dudes	San Jose	CA
	Kayak	Watersports	275.00
2	Chess Kings	Seattle	WA
	Human Chess Board	Chess	75.00
	Bling-Bling King	Chess	1200.00
3	Acme Co	New York	NY
	Stadium	Soccer	79500.00

Figure 15-5. *Using explicit loading to filter data*

The drawback of using explicit loading is that it generates many queries for the database. If you examine the logging messages created by the application, you will see that the first query is for the `Supplier` data, as shown here:

```
...
SELECT [s].[Id], [s].[City], [s].[ContactId], [s].[Name], [s].[State]
FROM [Suppliers] AS [s]
...
```

As each `Supplier` object is processed by the `foreach` method and the related data is explicitly loaded, another query is sent to the database, like this one:

```
...
SELECT [e].[Id], [e].[Category], [e].[Color], [e].[InStock], [e].[Name],
    [e].[Price], [e].[SupplierId]
FROM [Products] AS [e]
WHERE ([e].[SupplierId] = @__get_Item_0) AND ([e].[Price] > 50.0)
...
```

There are three `Supplier` objects stored in the database, which means that four requests in total are needed to get the data for this example. The number of queries can add up for large numbers of objects, which means that the explicit loading technique is most effective when there are a small number of objects for which related data is required. If you are working with larger numbers of objects, then the technique in the next section may be more suitable.

Querying Using the Fixing Up Feature

Entity Framework Core supports a feature called *fixing up*, where the data retrieved by a database context object is cached and used to populate the navigation properties of objects that are created for subsequent queries. This is a feature that, used carefully, can allow complex queries to be created that obtain related data more efficiently than explicit loading or following a navigation property using the `Include` method. In Listing 15-17, I have relied on the fixing up feature to obtain the `Supplier` objects and the related `Product` objects whose `Price` value exceeds 50.

Listing 15-17. Relying on Fixing Up in the SupplierRepository.cs File in the Models Folder

```
...
public IEnumerable<Supplier> GetAll() {
    context.Products.Where(p => p.Supplier != null && p.Price > 50).Load();
    return context.Suppliers;
}
...
```

There are two queries required for this example. The first uses the context object's `Products` property to retrieve all of the `Product` objects that are related to a `Supplier` and whose `Price` property is greater than 50. The sole purpose of this query is to populate the Entity Framework Core cache with data objects, so I have used the `Load` method to force evaluation of the query.

The second query uses the context object's `Suppliers` property to retrieve the `Supplier` objects. This query will be executed when the sequence of objects is enumerated in the Razor view, so the `Load` method isn't required. When the second query is executed, Entity Framework Core will automatically examine the data cached from the first request and use that data to populate the `Supplier.Products` navigation properties with the appropriate `Product` objects. The result is the same outcome as when I used explicit loading, as shown in Figure 15-6.

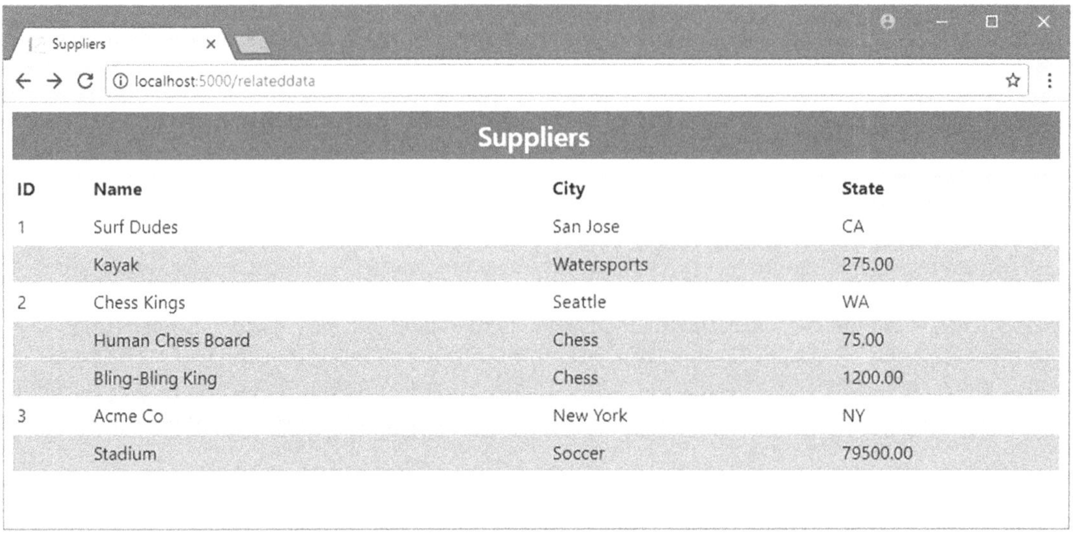

Figure 15-6. Using fixing up to filter data

Caution Using the fixing up feature can require some trial and error and requires careful attention to the queries that are sent to the database. It is possible to get all of the data you require with fewer queries than the explicit loading technique, but it is surprisingly easy to miss the mark and either query for too much or too little data or to generate more requests than you intended.

If you look at the logging messages generated by the application, you will see the queries that were sent to the database. The first query retrieves the Product objects that met the criteria specified by the Where method.

```
...
SELECT [p].[Id], [p].[Category], [p].[Color], [p].[InStock], [p].[Name],
    [p].[Price], [p].[SupplierId]
FROM [Products] AS [p]
WHERE [p].[SupplierId] IS NOT NULL AND ([p].[Price] > 50.0)
...
```

The second query retrieves all of the available Supplier data.

```
...
SELECT [s].[Id], [s].[City], [s].[ContactId], [s].[Name], [s].[State]
FROM [Suppliers] AS [s]
...
```

The fixing up process uses the data from the first query to populate the navigation properties of the objects created from the second query. This process is entirely automatic and will be performed whenever the same database context object is used to make multiple queries (which is one of the reasons why you should be careful about the lifecycle of repository objects configured in the Startup class, so that you don't get fixed-up data when you are not expecting it).

Understanding the Fixing Up Pitfall

The fixing up feature means Entity Framework Core will populate navigation properties with objects that it has previously created. When used carefully, the fixing up process is a powerful tool for selecting just the data that is required without endlessly querying the database. But the fixing up process cannot be disabled and presents a pitfall for the unwary if you follow navigation properties without considering the queries that have been made.

To demonstrate the problem, I created a view called `SupplierRelated.cshtml` in the `Views/Home` folder and added the content shown in Listing 15-18 to present a `Supplier` and its list of `Product` objects to the user.

Listing 15-18. The Contents of the SupplierRelated.cshtml File in the Views/Home Folder

```
@model DataApp.Models.Supplier

@if (Model?.Products == null) {
    <tr><td colspan="6" class="text-center table-dark">No Related Data</td></tr>
} else {
    @foreach (Product p in Model?.Products) {
        <tr class="table-dark">
            <td colspan="3"></td>
            <td>@p.Name</td>
            <td>@p.Category</td>
            <td>@p.Price</td>
        </tr>
    }
}
```

This view receives a `Supplier` as its model and follows the `Products` navigation property to create a simple table of related `Products`. To use this view, I made the change shown in Listing 15-19 to the `Index.cshtml` view in the `Views/Home` folder.

Listing 15-19. Displaying Related Data in the Index.chstml File in the Views/Home Folder

```
...
<tbody>
    @foreach (var p in Model) {
        <tr>
            <td>@p.Id</td><td>@p.Name</td><td>@p.Category</td>
            <td>$@p.Price.ToString("F2")</td>
            @if (ViewBag.includeRelated) {
                <td>@p.Supplier?.Name</td>
            }
            <td>
                <form asp-action="Delete" method="post">
                    <a asp-action="Edit" class="btn btn-sm btn-warning"
                        asp-route-id="@p.Id">
                        Edit
                    </a>
```

```
            <input type="hidden" name="id" value="@p.Id" />
            <button type="submit" class="btn btn-danger btn-sm">
                Delete
            </button>
        </form>
    </td>
</tr>
<tr>
    <td colspan="6">@Html.Partial("SupplierRelated", p.Supplier)</td>
</tr>
}
</tbody>
...
```

To see the problem, restart the application and navigate to http://localhost:5000. The fixing up process is applied to populate navigation properties as Entity Framework Core processes the response from the database server, which means that the data is inconsistent, as shown in Figure 15-7.

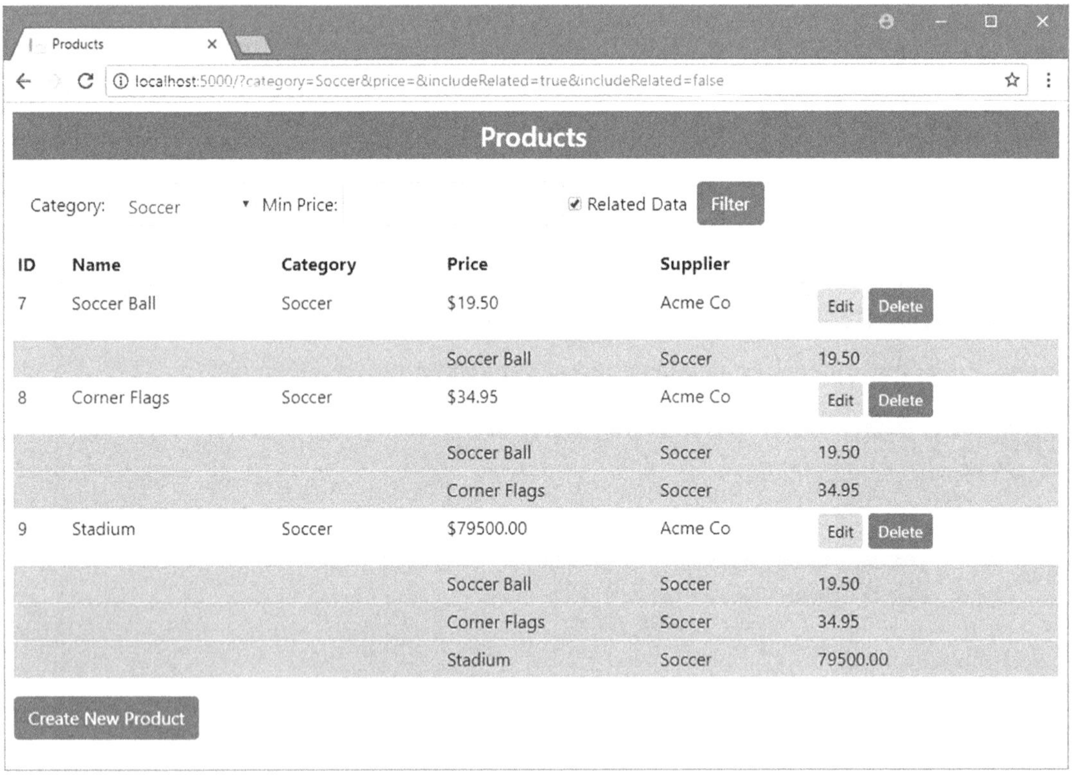

Figure 15-7. *Navigating to data beyond the scope of the query*

The figure shows the Products in the Soccer category, and you can see that the related data is different for each item. This happens because I have followed navigation properties beyond the related data specified in the query, starting with a Product object, moving on to the related Supplier, and then coming back again to the related Products. Entity Framework Core uses fixed-up data to populate the Supplier.Products property but only has the Product objects that have been created so far to work with, which increases with each Product object that is processed and produces the inconsistent results shown in the figure. To avoid this type of problem, do not navigate using properties that you have not selected using the Include or ThenInclude method or fixed up using a previous query.

Working with Related Data in a One-to-Many Relationship

One of the most important characteristics of completed relationships is that operations can be performed using the navigation properties at both ends of the relationship. In the sections that follow, I show you to use the navigation properties in the one-to-many relationship between the Supplier and Product classes to perform different operations.

To prepare for this section, I changed the query used for Supplier objects in the SupplierRepository class so that all of the related Product objects are included, as shown in Listing 15-20.

Listing 15-20. Changing the Queries in the SupplierRepository.cs File in the Models Folder

```
...
public IEnumerable<Supplier> GetAll() {
    return context.Suppliers.Include(p => p.Products);
}
...
```

To separate this example from the others in this chapter, I added a class file called SuppliersController.cs in the Controllers folder and defined the controller shown in Listing 15-21.

Listing 15-21. The Contents of the SuppliersController.cs File in the Controllers Folder

```
using DataApp.Models;
using Microsoft.AspNetCore.Mvc;

namespace DataApp.Controllers {

    public class SuppliersController : Controller {
        private ISupplierRepository supplierRepository;

        public SuppliersController(ISupplierRepository supplierRepo) {
            supplierRepository = supplierRepo;
        }

        public IActionResult Index() {
            return View(supplierRepository.GetAll());
        }
    }
}
```

The controller defines a single action method that passes all of the Supplier objects to the default view. To display the Supplier objects and their related Product objects, I created the Views/Suppliers folder and added to it a file called Index.cshtml with the content shown in Listing 15-22.

Listing 15-22. The Contents of the Index.cshtml File in the Views/Suppliers Folder

```
@model IEnumerable<DataApp.Models.Supplier>

@{
    ViewData["Title"] = "Suppliers";
    Layout = "_Layout";
}

@foreach (Supplier s in Model) {
    <h4 class="bg-info text-center text-white p-1">@s.Name</h4>
    <div class="container-fluid">
        @if (s.Products == null || s.Products.Count() == 0) {
            <div class="p-1 text-center">No Products</div>
        } else {
            @foreach (Product p in s.Products) {
                <div class="row p-1">
                    <div class="col">@p.Name</div>
                    <div class="col">@p.Category</div>
                    <div class="col">@p.Price</div>
                </div>
            }
        }
    </div>
}
```

To see the content generated by the view, restart the application and navigate to http://localhost:5000/suppliers. The name of each Supplier is displayed, along with details of the related Product objects, as shown in Figure 15-8.

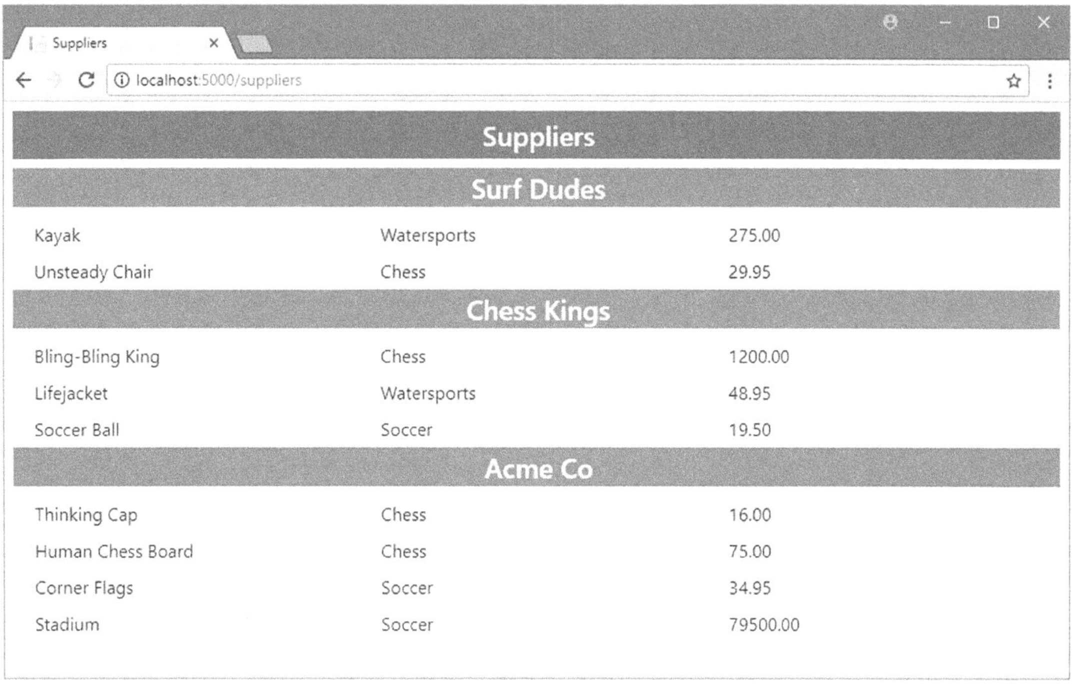

Figure 15-8. *Displaying Supplier and Product objects*

Updating Related Objects

Earlier in this chapter, I showed you how to edit the values of Product objects that were retrieved from the database directly using the DbSet<Product> property defined by the database context class. This is the simplest and most direct way to perform updates, but you can also make changes by starting with a Supplier object and accessing the Product objects you want to modify through a navigation property. To show how to perform edits via a navigation property, I started by creating a view called Editor.cshtml in the Views/Suppliers folder and adding the content shown in Listing 15-23.

Listing 15-23. The Contents of the Editor.cshtml File in the Views/Suppliers Folder

```
@model Supplier
@{
    int counter = 0;
}

<form asp-action="Update" method="post">
    <input type="hidden" asp-for="Id" />
    <input type="hidden" asp-for="Name" />
    <input type="hidden" asp-for="City" />
    <input type="hidden" asp-for="State" />

    @foreach (Product p in Model.Products) {
        <div class="row">
            <input type="hidden" name="Products[@counter].Id" value="@p.Id" />
```

```
            <div class="col">
                <input name="Products[@counter].Name" value="@p.Name"
                    class="form-control"/>
            </div>
            <div class="col">
                <input name="Products[@counter].Category" value="@p.Category"
                    class="form-control" />
            </div>
            <div class="col">
                <input name="Products[@counter].Price" value="@p.Price"
                    class="form-control"/>
            </div>
            @{ counter++; }
        </div>
    }
    <div class="row">
        <div class="col text-center m-1">
            <button class="btn btn-sm btn-danger" type="submit">Save</button>
            <a class="btn btn-sm btn-secondary" asp-action="Index">Cancel</a>
        </div>
    </div>
</form>
```

This view will be used to allow the user to edit the property values for all the Product objects related to a Supplier. The slightly awkward structure relies on incrementing an int called counter, which is used to create HTML elements that will be correctly parsed as an array of Product objects by the MVC model binder. The property values are presented in a grid of input elements and will be submitted to an action called Update when the user clicks the Save button.

To incorporate the Editor view into the application, I added the elements shown in Listing 15-24 to the Index.cshtml view in the Views/Suppliers folder.

Listing 15-24. Incorporating the Editor in the Index.cshtml File in the Views/Suppliers Folder

```
@model IEnumerable<DataApp.Models.Supplier>

@{
    ViewData["Title"] = "Suppliers";
    Layout = "_Layout";
}

@foreach (Supplier s in Model) {
    <h4 class="bg-info text-center text-white p-1">
        @s.Name
        <a asp-action="Edit" asp-route-id="@s.Id"
                class="btn btn-sm btn-warning">
            Edit
        </a>
    </h4>
    <div class="container-fluid">
        @if (s.Products == null || s.Products.Count() == 0) {
            <div class="p-1 text-center">No Products</div>
```

```
        } else if (ViewBag.SupplierEditId == s.Id) {
            @Html.Partial("Editor", s);
        } else {
            @foreach (Product p in s.Products) {
                <div class="row p-1">
                    <div class="col">@p.Name</div>
                    <div class="col">@p.Category</div>
                    <div class="col">@p.Price</div>
                </div>
            }
        }
    }
    </div>
}
```

The first addition adds an Edit button alongside the name of each Supplier, which targets the Edit action and includes the Id of the Supplier object. This will start the editing process by setting a SupplierEditId property in the ViewBag, which is used by the second addition in Listing 15-24 to display the Editor view.

To provide the support required by the views, I added the action methods shown in Listing 15-25 to the Suppliers controller.

Listing 15-25. Adding Actions in the SuppliersController.cs File in the Controllers Folder

```
using DataApp.Models;
using Microsoft.AspNetCore.Mvc;

namespace DataApp.Controllers {

    public class SuppliersController : Controller {
        private ISupplierRepository supplierRepository;

        public SuppliersController(ISupplierRepository supplierRepo) {
            supplierRepository = supplierRepo;
        }

        public IActionResult Index() {
            ViewBag.SupplierEditId = TempData["SupplierEditId"];
            return View(supplierRepository.GetAll());
        }

        public IActionResult Edit(long id) {
            TempData["SupplierEditId"] = id;
            return RedirectToAction(nameof(Index));
        }

        [HttpPost]
        public IActionResult Update(Supplier supplier) {
            supplierRepository.Update(supplier);
            return RedirectToAction(nameof(Index));
        }
    }
}
```

To see how the editing process works, restart the application, navigate to http://localhost:5000/ suppliers, and click the Edit button for Chess Kings. Use the input elements to make changes and click the Save button to update the database, as shown in Figure 15-9.

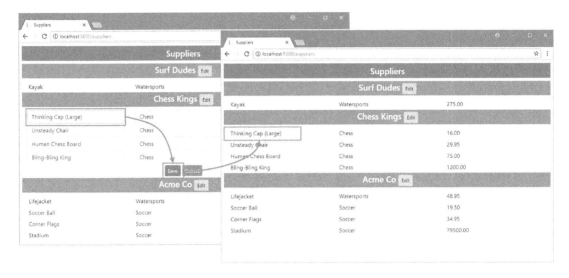

Figure 15-9. *Editing property values via a navigation property*

When you click the Save button, the browser sends an HTTP request that contains the values required by the MVC model binder to create a Supplier object and a collection of Product objects. The MVC binder automatically assigns the Product collection to the Supplier.Products property, which is then used to update the database. Entity Framework Core can't perform change tracking on these objects (because they were created by the MVC model binder), so the Supplier object must include values for all of its properties, which you can see I included in the Editor view.

Note   Bear in mind that completing a relationship doesn't prevent you from operating on objects directly. For example, completing the Product/Supplier relationship doesn't mean that I can only update Product objects through the Supplier.Products navigation property; I can still query directly for Product objects and update them individually. Completing a relationship opens up new ways of working and allows you to choose the one that is most convenient for your project.

Creating New Related Objects

The technique that I described in the previous section can be easily adapted to create new related objects. When Entity Framework Core processes the collection of Product objects that have been created by the MVC model binder, any Product object whose Id property value is zero will be added to the database as a new object. This is a convenient way of creating new objects that will automatically be associated with a Supplier. This is a useful way to create new objects without breaking the required relationship constraint between Product and Supplier objects.

To add support for creating new `Product` object, I added a view called `Create.cshtml` in the Views/Suppliers folder and added the content shown in Listing 15-26.

Listing 15-26. The Contents of the Create.cshtml File in the Views/Suppliers Folder

```
@model Supplier
@{
    int counter = 0;
}

<form asp-action="Update" method="post">
    <input type="hidden" asp-for="Id" />
    <input type="hidden" asp-for="Name" />
    <input type="hidden" asp-for="City" />
    <input type="hidden" asp-for="State" />

    @foreach (Product p in Model.Products) {
        <input type="hidden" name="Products[@counter].Id" value="@p.Id" />
        <input type="hidden" name="Products[@counter].Name" value="@p.Name" />
        <input type="hidden" name="Products[@counter].Category"
            value="@p.Category" />
        <input type="hidden" name="Products[@counter].Price" value="@p.Price" />
        counter++;
    }
    <div class="row">
        <div class="col">
            <input name="Products[@counter].Name" value="" class="form-control" />
        </div>
        <div class="col">
            <input name="Products[@counter].Category" class="form-control" />
        </div>
        <div class="col">
            <input name="Products[@counter].Price" class="form-control" />
        </div>
    </div>
    <div class="row">
        <div class="col text-center m-1">
            <button class="btn btn-sm btn-danger" type="submit">Save</button>
            <a class="btn btn-sm btn-secondary" asp-action="Index">Cancel</a>
        </div>
    </div>
</form>
```

When updating data through a navigation property, you must take care to include all of the existing objects in the HTML form. When Entity Framework Core receives the collection of `Product` objects, for example, it assumes that it has received the complete set and will try to break relationships with any `Product` object that is not in the collection. As a consequence, you must include form data values for all of the existing data as well as creating elements so that the user can enter new ones, which is what I have done in Listing 15-26.

To integrate the new view into the application, I added the elements shown in Listing 15-27 to the `Index.cshtml` view in the Views/Suppliers folder.

Listing 15-27. Using a Partial View in the Index.cshtml File in the Views/Suppliers Folder

```
@model IEnumerable<DataApp.Models.Supplier>

@{
    ViewData["Title"] = "Suppliers";
    Layout = "_Layout";
}

@foreach (Supplier s in Model) {
    <h4 class="bg-info text-center text-white p-1">
        @s.Name
        <a asp-action="Edit" asp-route-id="@s.Id"
            class="btn btn-sm btn-warning">Edit</a>
        <a asp-action="Create" asp-route-id="@s.Id"
            class="btn btn-sm btn-danger">Add</a>
    </h4>
    <div class="container-fluid">
        @if (s.Products == null || s.Products.Count() == 0) {
            <div class="p-1 text-center">No Products</div>
        } else if (ViewBag.SupplierEditId == s.Id) {
            @Html.Partial("Editor", s);
        } else {
            @foreach (Product p in s.Products) {
                <div class="row p-1">
                    <div class="col">@p.Name</div>
                    <div class="col">@p.Category</div>
                    <div class="col">@p.Price</div>
                </div>
            }
            if (ViewBag.SupplierCreateId == s.Id) {
                @Html.Partial("Create", s);
            }
        }
    </div>
}
```

The Add button sends a request to an action called `Create`, and the content in the `Create.cshtml` view
will be shown when the ViewBag contains a `SupplierCreateId` property whose value corresponds to the
Id property of the Supplier being processed. To support the new view features, I added the action method
shown in Listing 15-28 to the Suppliers controller.

Listing 15-28. Adding an Action in the SuppliersController.cshtml File in the Controllers Folder

```
using DataApp.Models;
using Microsoft.AspNetCore.Mvc;

namespace DataApp.Controllers {

    public class SuppliersController : Controller {
        private ISupplierRepository supplierRepository;
```

```
public SuppliersController(ISupplierRepository supplierRepo) {
    supplierRepository = supplierRepo;
}

public IActionResult Index() {
    ViewBag.SupplierEditId = TempData["SupplierEditId"];
    ViewBag.SupplierCreateId = TempData["SupplierCreateId"];
    return View(supplierRepository.GetAll());
}

public IActionResult Edit(long id) {
    TempData["SupplierEditId"] = id;
    return RedirectToAction(nameof(Index));
}

[HttpPost]
public IActionResult Update(Supplier supplier) {
    supplierRepository.Update(supplier);
    return RedirectToAction(nameof(Index));
}

public IActionResult Create(long id) {
    TempData["SupplierCreateId"] = id;
    return RedirectToAction(nameof(Index));
}
}
}
```

The Create method sets the ViewBag property that is used to display the Create.cshtml view and then redirects the browser. Notice that I don't have to add an action method to handle the create operation. As far as Entity Framework Core is concerned, this operation is an update on an existing Supplier object, which is performed through the Update method.

To see the effect, restart the application, navigate to http://localhost:5000/suppliers, and click the Add button for one of the suppliers. Fill out the form and click Save, and you will see that a new Product object has been created, as illustrated in Figure 15-10.

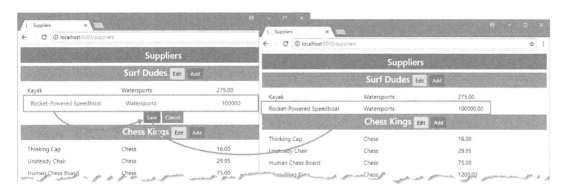

Figure 15-10. *Creating new related data*

Changing Relationships

The create and update operations are made simple by the fact that the Product objects are associated with a Supplier. A little more work is required when it comes to changing the Supplier that a Product object is related to, especially for a required relationship because the database server will not perform updates that affect the integrity of the database.

To add support for changing a relationship, I added a view called RelationshipEditor.cshtml to the Views/Suppliers folder and added the content shown in Listing 15-29.

Listing 15-29. The Contents of the RelationshipEditor.cshtml File in the Views/Suppliers Folder

```
@model ValueTuple<Supplier, IEnumerable<Supplier>>
@{
    int counter = 0;
}

<form asp-action="Change" method="post">
    <input type="hidden" name="Id" value="@Model.Item1.Id" />
    <input type="hidden" name="Name" value="@Model.Item1.Name" />
    <input type="hidden" name="City" value="@Model.Item1.City" />
    <input type="hidden" name="State" value="@Model.Item1.State" />

    @foreach (Product p in Model.Item1.Products) {
        <input type="hidden" name="Products[@counter].Id" value="@p.Id" />
        <input type="hidden" name="Products[@counter].Name" value="@p.Name" />
        <input type="hidden" name="Products[@counter].Category"
            value="@p.Category" />
        <input type="hidden" name="Products[@counter].Price" value="@p.Price" />

        <div class="row">
            <div class="col">@p.Name</div>
            <div class="col">@p.Category</div>
            <div class="col">
                <select name="Products[@counter].SupplierId">
                    @foreach (Supplier s in Model.Item2) {
                        if (p.Supplier == s) {
                            <option selected value="@s.Id">@s.Name</option>
                        } else {
                            <option value="@s.Id">@s.Name</option>
                        }
                    }
                </select>
            </div>
        </div>

        counter++;
    }
```

```
    <div class="row">
        <div class="col text-center m-1">
            <button class="btn btn-sm btn-danger" type="submit">Save</button>
            <a class="btn btn-sm btn-secondary" asp-action="Index">Cancel</a>
        </div>
    </div>
</form>
```

The model for this view is a tuple that contains a Supplier object and an enumeration of Suppliers. This is an ungainly approach, but, as you will see, this entire process can be awkward, and receiving two data objects as the view model makes it easier to generate the HTML elements that allow the user to make changes. The view generates a form with hidden elements that contain the Supplier and Product values that are not to be changed, along with a select element that allows a different Supplier to be selected for each Product. The form targets an action method called Change, which I will define shortly.

To incorporate the new partial view into the application, I added the elements shown in Listing 15-30 to the Index.cshtml view in the Views/Suppliers folder.

Listing 15-30. Incorporating a Partial View in the Index.cshtml File in the Views/Suppliers Folder

```
@model IEnumerable<DataApp.Models.Supplier>

@{
    ViewData["Title"] = "Suppliers";
    Layout = "_Layout";
}

@foreach (Supplier s in Model) {
    <h4 class="bg-info text-center text-white p-1">
        @s.Name
        <a asp-action="Edit" asp-route-id="@s.Id"
            class="btn btn-sm btn-warning">Edit</a>
        <a asp-action="Create" asp-route-id="@s.Id"
            class="btn btn-sm btn-danger">Add</a>
        <a asp-action="Change" asp-route-id="@s.Id"
            class="btn btn-sm btn-primary">Change</a>
    </h4>
    <div class="container-fluid">
        @if (s.Products == null || s.Products.Count() == 0) {
            <div class="p-1 text-center">No Products</div>
        } else if (ViewBag.SupplierEditId == s.Id) {
            @Html.Partial("Editor", s);
        } else if (ViewBag.SupplierRelationshipId == s.Id) {
            @Html.Partial("RelationshipEditor", (s, Model));
        } else {
            @foreach (Product p in s.Products) {
                <div class="row p-1">
                    <div class="col">@p.Name</div>
                    <div class="col">@p.Category</div>
                    <div class="col">@p.Price</div>
                </div>
            }
```

```
                if (ViewBag.SupplierCreateId == s.Id) {
                    @Html.Partial("Create", s);
                }
            }
        }
    </div>
}
```

The new elements add a Change button that targets the Change action on the controller, which will set a ViewBag property called SupplierRelationshipId, which is used to decide when to show the partial view created in Listing 15-29. To add the actions that the views rely on, I added the methods shown in Listing 15-31 to the SuppliersController class.

Listing 15-31. Adding Actions in the SuppliersController.cs File in the Controllers Folder

```
using DataApp.Models;
using Microsoft.AspNetCore.Mvc;
using System.Collections.Generic;
using System.Linq;

namespace DataApp.Controllers {

    public class SuppliersController : Controller {
        private ISupplierRepository supplierRepository;

        public SuppliersController(ISupplierRepository supplierRepo) {
            supplierRepository = supplierRepo;
        }

        public IActionResult Index() {
            ViewBag.SupplierEditId = TempData["SupplierEditId"];
            ViewBag.SupplierCreateId = TempData["SupplierCreateId"];
            ViewBag.SupplierRelationshipId = TempData["SupplierRelationshipId"];
            return View(supplierRepository.GetAll());
        }

        public IActionResult Edit(long id) {
            TempData["SupplierEditId"] = id;
            return RedirectToAction(nameof(Index));
        }

        [HttpPost]
        public IActionResult Update(Supplier supplier) {
            supplierRepository.Update(supplier);
            return RedirectToAction(nameof(Index));
        }

        public IActionResult Create(long id) {
            TempData["SupplierCreateId"] = id;
            return RedirectToAction(nameof(Index));
        }
```

```
    public IActionResult Change(long id) {
        TempData["SupplierRelationshipId"] = id;
        return RedirectToAction(nameof(Index));
    }

    [HttpPost]
    public IActionResult Change(Supplier supplier) {
        IEnumerable<Product> changed = supplier.Products
            .Where(p => p.SupplierId != supplier.Id);
        if (changed.Count() > 0) {
            IEnumerable<Supplier> allSuppliers
                = supplierRepository.GetAll().ToArray();
            Supplier currentSupplier
                = allSuppliers.First(s => s.Id == supplier.Id);
            foreach(Product p in changed) {
                Supplier newSupplier
                    = allSuppliers.First(s => s.Id == p.SupplierId);
                newSupplier.Products = newSupplier.Products
                    .Append(currentSupplier.Products
                        .First(op => op.Id == p.Id)).ToArray();
                supplierRepository.Update(newSupplier);
            }
        }
        return RedirectToAction(nameof(Index));
    }
}
}
```

The code in the Change method that accepts POST requests is convoluted because there is some conflict between features. I have queried the database to get the complete set of Supplier objects and their related Product objects so that I can update the relationships that the user has changed. Entity Framework Core tracks the objects that it has created, which means that I can't perform database updates using the objects that are created by the MVC model binder without generating an exception. This means I have to process the objects created by the MVC model binder to figure out what has to change and then translate those changes into the objects that Entity Framework Core has created, which can be used to update the database. (Don't spend too much time following the code in Listing 15-31 because I show simpler approaches in the sections that follow.)

To see how relationships can be changed, restart the application, navigate to http://localhost:5000/suppliers, and click one of the Change buttons. Use the drop-down lists to change relationships and click the Save button to update the database. The Product objects whose relationships you edited will be shown alongside their new Supplier, as illustrated in Figure 15-11.

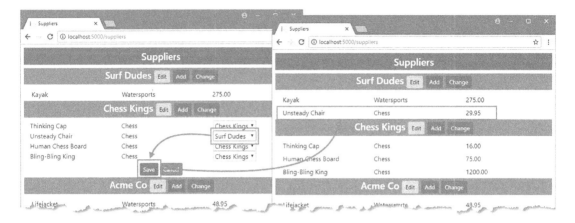

Figure 15-11. *Changing relationships between objects*

Simplifying the Relationship Change Code

The code required to handle the updates in Listing 15-31 relies on a series of LINQ queries to get the data from the database and merge the changes from the objects created from the HTTP request. This approach works around the Entity Framework Core object tracking system, which underpins features such as change tracking and fixing up. These are useful features, but the tracking system gets in the way for other operations.

I can simplify the code required to handle the changes by disabling the object tracking feature, as shown in Listing 15-32, which means I can use the objects created by the MVC model binder to update the database.

Listing 15-32. Disabling Change Tracking in the SuppliersController.cs File in the Models Folder

```
using DataApp.Models;
using Microsoft.AspNetCore.Mvc;
using System.Collections.Generic;
using System.Linq;
using Microsoft.EntityFrameworkCore;

namespace DataApp.Controllers {

    public class SuppliersController : Controller {
        private ISupplierRepository supplierRepository;
        private EFDatabaseContext dbContext;

        public SuppliersController(ISupplierRepository supplierRepo,
                EFDatabaseContext context) {
            supplierRepository = supplierRepo;
            dbContext = context;
        }

        public IActionResult Index() {
            ViewBag.SupplierEditId = TempData["SupplierEditId"];
            ViewBag.SupplierCreateId = TempData["SupplierCreateId"];
```

```
        ViewBag.SupplierRelationshipId = TempData["SupplierRelationshipId"];
        return View(supplierRepository.GetAll());
    }

    public IActionResult Edit(long id) {
        TempData["SupplierEditId"] = id;
        return RedirectToAction(nameof(Index));
    }

    [HttpPost]
    public IActionResult Update(Supplier supplier) {
        supplierRepository.Update(supplier);
        return RedirectToAction(nameof(Index));
    }

    public IActionResult Create(long id) {
        TempData["SupplierCreateId"] = id;
        return RedirectToAction(nameof(Index));
    }

    public IActionResult Change(long id) {
        TempData["SupplierRelationshipId"] = id;
        return RedirectToAction(nameof(Index));
    }

    [HttpPost]
    public IActionResult Change(Supplier supplier) {
        IEnumerable<Product> changed
            = supplier.Products.Where(p => p.SupplierId != supplier.Id);
        IEnumerable<long> targetSupplierIds
            = changed.Select(p => p.SupplierId).Distinct();
        if (changed.Count() > 0) {
            IEnumerable<Supplier> targetSuppliers = dbContext.Suppliers
                .Where(s =>  targetSupplierIds.Contains(s.Id))
                .AsNoTracking().ToArray();
            foreach(Product p in changed) {
                Supplier newSupplier
                    = targetSuppliers.First(s => s.Id == p.SupplierId);
                newSupplier.Products = newSupplier.Products == null
                    ? new Product[] { p }
                        : newSupplier.Products.Append(p).ToArray();
            }
            dbContext.Suppliers.UpdateRange(targetSuppliers);
            dbContext.SaveChanges();
        }
        return RedirectToAction(nameof(Index));
    }
}
}
```

For the sake of simplicity, I have used the data context class directly, rather than work the changes through the repository interface and implementation class. The code in Listing 15-33 is simpler (although it may not look like it) because the tracking feature has been disabled by using the AsNoTracking extension method in the query that retrieves the Supplier and related Product objects from the database.

```
...
IEnumerable<Supplier> targetSuppliers = dbContext.Suppliers
    .Where(s =>  targetSupplierIds.Contains(s.Id))
    .AsNoTracking().ToArray();
...
```

When the AsNoTracking method is used, Entity Framework Core doesn't keep track of the objects that it has created, and this allows me to use the Product objects created by the MVC model binder to update the database.

One reason that the code in Listing 15-32 is simpler than Listing 15-31 is that I don't have to retrieve the Product objects related to each Supplier in order to perform the updates. Entity Framework Core doesn't update data that has not been queried from the database, so excluding Product objects from the query means that the existing relationships are not affected by the changes specified by the user.

■ **Caution**   The AsNoTracking method should be used with caution because it prevents other useful features, such as change detection and fixing up, from working.

Further Simplifying the Relationship Change Code

The previous two listings have demonstrated that it is possible to change relationships from the "one" end of a one-to-many relationship but that doing so is awkward. There is a much simpler way of solving this problem, which can be understood by thinking about how the relationship is represented in the database.

In the case of the example application, the Product class has a SupplierId property that is used to store the value of the Id property for the Supplier it is related to. The Products property defined by the Supplier class is for convenient navigation only, and when the relationship for a Product is changed, Entity Framework Core only has to update the row in the Products table to reflect the change, even when you perform those changes via the IEnumerable<Product> navigation property.

Once you realize how the update is performed, you can dramatically simplify the code required to perform updates by operating on the Product objects directly, as shown in Listing 15-33.

Listing 15-33. Performing Direct Updates in the SuppliersController.cs File in the Controllers Folder

```
...
[HttpPost]
public IActionResult Change(long Id, Product[] products) {
    dbContext.Products.UpdateRange(products.Where(p => p.SupplierId != Id));
    dbContext.SaveChanges();
    return RedirectToAction(nameof(Index));
}
...
```

Changing the parameters for the action method tells the MVC model binder that I require the Id value for the Supplier whose relationships the user is changing and the set of Products related to that Supplier.

I use LINQ to filter out those Product objects that have not changed and pass those that have to the DbSet<T>.UpdateRange method provided by the database context class, which allows me to update several objects at once. I call the SaveChanges method to send the changes to the database and then redirect the browser to the Index action.

The result is the same as the code in Listing 15-31 and Listing 15-32 but simpler and easier to understand. As this example demonstrates, while it is possible to perform updates using either navigation property in a one-to-many relationship, giving thought to how the updates will be reflected into the database can give insight into whether a simpler result can be obtained by giving preference to one property over another.

Summary

In this chapter, I demonstrated how to access related data directly, either by promoting the data with a context property or by using the context methods that accept a type parameter. Once you have promoted data, you will often want to navigate from it to other parts of the data model, and I showed you how to complete a relationship by adding a navigation property to define a one-to-many relationship, which is the most common in ASP.NET Core MVC and Entity Framework Core development. I explained the different ways to query related data in a one-to-many relationship and how to create and update related data through the one-to-many navigation property. I finished this chapter by showing that it is possible to edit relationships through the navigation property but that simpler results can be obtained by considering how relationships are represented in the database. In the next chapter, I continue demonstrating the Entity Framework Core features for using relationships.

CHAPTER 16

Working with Relationship Part 2

The one-to-many relationships that I described in Chapter 15 are not the only types of relationship that Entity Framework Core supports. In this chapter, I show you how to define *one-to-one* and *many-to-many* relationships, demonstrate how to query for related data when using these relationships, and explain how to manage these relationships in the database. Table 16-1 summarizes the chapter.

Table 16-1. *Chapter Summary*

Problem	Solution	Listing
Define a completed one-to-one relationship	Add reciprocal navigation properties and add a foreign key property to the dependent entity class	1–7
Update related objects	Deal with the related objects separately to ensure that you add and update data correctly	8–16
Define a many-to-many relationship	Create a junction class that has one-to-many relationships on the two related data types	17–28

Preparing for This Chapter

This chapter uses the DataApp project created in Chapter 11 and modified in the subsequent chapters. To prepare for this chapter, open a command prompt in the DataApp folder and run the commands shown in Listing 16-1.

Tip If you don't want to follow the process of building the example project, you can download all of the required files from this book's source code repository, https://github.com/apress/pro-ef-core-2-for-asp.net-core-mvc.

Listing 16-1. Resetting the Database

```
dotnet ef database drop --force --context EFDatabaseContext
dotnet ef database update --context EFDatabaseContext
```

These commands remove and re-create the database used to store Product objects and their related Supplier, ContactDetails, and ContactLocation objects, which will help ensure that you get the right expected results from the examples in this chapter.

© Adam Freeman 2018
A. Freeman, *Pro Entity Framework Core 2 for ASP.NET Core MVC*,
https://doi.org/10.1007/978-1-4842-3435-8_16

Start the application using `dotnet run` and use a browser to navigate to `http://localhost:5000`. The application will seed the database as it starts, and you will see the list of products shown in Figure 16-1.

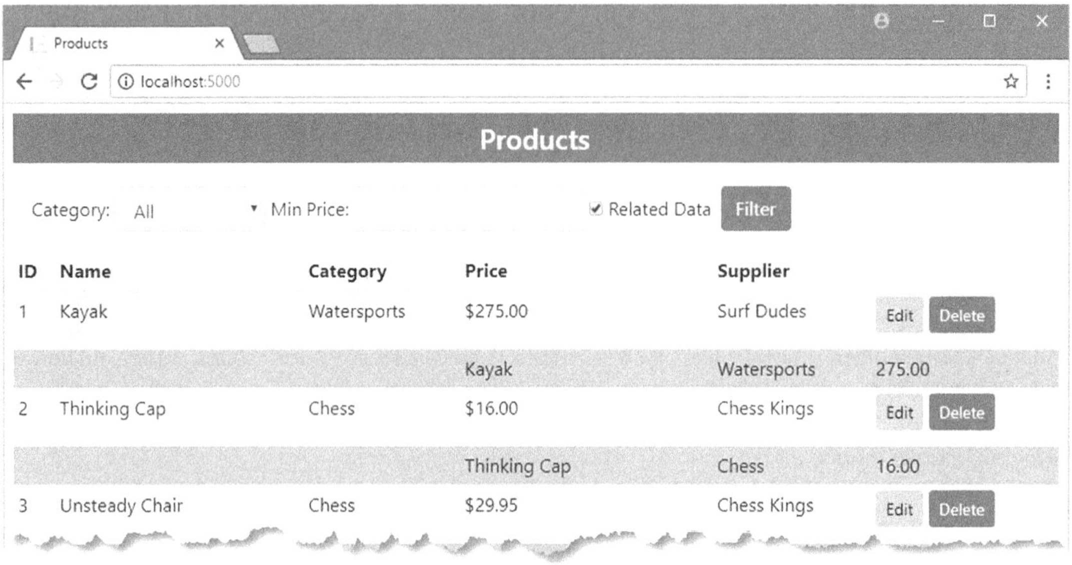

Figure 16-1. *Running the example application*

Completing a One-to-One Relationship

In a one-to-one relationship, an object of one type is related to a single object of another type. Two steps are required to complete a one-to-one relationship, and in the sections that follow, I explain both steps as I complete a relationship between the `Supplier` and `ContactDetails` classes so that each `Supplier` object will be related to one `ContactDetails` object.

Defining the Navigation Property

The first step is to define the navigation property. This is the inverse of the property that I defined in Chapter 14 that created the relationship between the `Supplier` and `ContactDetails` classes. When only one navigation property is defined, Entity Framework Core assumes that a one-to-many relationship is required, and it is only when both navigation properties are defined that a one-to-one relationship can be created. In Listing 16-2, I have added the navigation property to the `ContactDetails` class that completes the relationship.

Listing 16-2. Adding a Property in the ContactDetails.cs File in the Models Folder

```
namespace DataApp.Models {

    public class ContactDetails {
        public long Id { get; set; }
        public string Name { get; set; }
        public string Phone { get; set; }
        public ContactLocation Location { get; set; }
```

372

```
        public Supplier Supplier { get; set; }
    }
}
```

The Supplier property returns a single Supplier object, rather than the IEnumerable<T> returned by a navigation property for a one-to-many relationship. The single object result of the navigation property tells Entity Framework Core that this is a one-to-one relationship. The name of the navigation property is not taken into account when determining the relationship type.

Selecting the Dependent Entity Class

The second step is to decide which class in the relationship is the *dependent entity* and define the foreign key property on it. Entity Framework Core stores objects as rows in database tables. When you create a relationship between classes, Entity Framework Core adds a column to one of the tables and uses it to record the primary key value of the related object. The foreign key column and class whose table contains the foreign key column is called the *dependent entity*, while the other class (whose table doesn't contain the foreign key column) is called the *principal entity*.

In a one-to-many relationship, the "many" class is always the dependent entity, and Entity Framework Core always knows where the foreign key column should be defined. But either class can be the dependent entity in a one-to-one relationship, and only the foreign key property gives Entity Framework Core the information it needs to put the foreign key column in the right place in the database.

For this example, I am going to make the ContactDetails class the dependent entity, so I defined the foreign key property shown in Listing 16-3, following the conventions described in Chapter 14.

HOW TO SELECT THE DEPENDENT ENTITY CLASS

When you create a relationship between classes, it can be hard to know where the foreign key property should go. The question to ask yourself is "Should an object of X type be able to exist without a related object of Y type?" If the answer is yes, then X is your principal entity, and the foreign key property should be defined in class Y, which is the dependent entity. If the answer is no, then Y is the principal, and the property should be added to class X, which is dependent. In the case of the DataApp application, for example, the question is "Should a Supplier be able to exist without a related ContactDetails object?"

Sometimes the answer to this question is obvious, which makes it easy to work out where to put the foreign key property. For the example application, it makes sense for a product suppler to be able to exist without a contact, but it makes no sense for the reverse to be true. That is why I made the ContactDetails class the dependent entity.

Often, however, it isn't clear-cut, especially when dealing with abstract concepts that lack real-world counterparts. For these relationships, the best you can do is make an informed guess and see how the application takes shape. This isn't ideal, but working with data isn't always easy, and you can always correct a mistake by moving the foreign key property and then creating and applying a new migration.

Listing 16-3. Defining a Foreign Key Property in the ContactDetails.cs File in the Models Folder

```
namespace DataApp.Models {

    public class ContactDetails {
        public long Id { get; set; }
        public string Name { get; set; }
        public string Phone { get; set; }
        public ContactLocation Location { get; set; }

        public long SupplierId { get; set; }
        public Supplier Supplier { get; set; }
    }
}
```

The type of the foreign key property determines whether the one-to-one relationship is required or optional. I specified long as the type for the property in Listing 16-3, which will create a required relationship, meaning that a ContactDetails object cannot be stored in the database unless it is related to a Supplier object. If I had used a type that can be set to null, such as long?, then an optional relationship would have been created.

■ **Caution**   Always complete a relationship with a foreign key property. If you don't specify a foreign key property in a one-to-one relationship, then Entity Framework Core may try to guess which class is the dependent entity, which can lead to unexpected results.

Creating and Applying the Migration

You can create a migration once you have defined the navigation and foreign key properties. Run the command shown in Listing 16-4 to create a new migration that will change the relationship between ContactDetails and Supplier objects.

Listing 16-4. Creating a Migration for a One-to-One Relationship

```
dotnet ef migrations add CompleteOneToOne --context EFDatabaseContext
```

To understand how completing the relationship will change the database, open the <timestamp>_ CompleteOneToOne.cs file that has been created in the Migrations folder and examine the Up method.

When there was only a navigation property, Entity Framework Core created a one-to-many relationship in which the Supplier class was the dependent entity. To reflect the new relationship, the migration removes the existing foreign key column and creates a new one on the ContactDetails table, which makes the ContactDetails class the dependent entity. To reflect the fact that the relationship is one-to-one, the migration includes this statement:

```
...
migrationBuilder.CreateIndex(
    name: "IX_ContactDetails_SupplierId", table: "ContactDetails",
    column: "SupplierId", unique: true);
...
```

The one-to-one relationship is represented by creating an index that requires unique values in the foreign key column. This ensures that a ContactDetails object can be related to a single Supplier object only.

░ **Tip**   The migration cannot be applied to the database because the existing data conflicts with the new constraints imposed by the migration. I will drop and re-create the database so that it will be reseeded when the application is started.

Working with One-to-One Relationships

Once you have completed the relationship, performing operations on related data through a one-to-one relationship is straightforward, as described in the sections that follow.

Querying Related Data in a One-to-One Relationship

Querying data in a one-to-one relationship is a simple task because you know that you have only one related object to deal with. The Include method is used to tell Entity Framework Core to follow a navigation property and query for the related object in a one-to-one relationship. You can start the query with the objects at either end of the relationship, and for this chapter I am going to query for ContactDetails objects and navigate to the related Supplier objects.

To demonstrate working with one-to-one relationships, I added a class file called One2OneController.cs in the Controllers folder and used it to define the controller shown in Listing 16-5.

░ **Note**   As explained in Chapter 11, I recommend using a repository in real projects, but I am working directly with the database context class in this controller to avoid having to make three changes (controller, repository interface, and implementation class) each time I demonstrate a different feature or operation.

Listing 16-5. The Contents of the One2OneController.cs File in the Controllers Folder

```
using DataApp.Models;
using Microsoft.AspNetCore.Mvc;
using Microsoft.EntityFrameworkCore;

namespace DataApp.Controllers {

    public class One2OneController : Controller {
        private EFDatabaseContext context;

        public One2OneController(EFDatabaseContext ctx) => context = ctx;

        public IActionResult Index () {
            return View(context.Set<ContactDetails>().Include(cd => cd.Supplier));
        }
    }
}
```

The controller defines an action method called Index that queries the database for all of the ContactDetails objects and related Supplier objects and uses them as the view model for the default view.

To display the data to the user, I created the Views/One2One folder and added to it a new view file called Index.cshtml with the content shown in Listing 16-6.

Listing 16-6. The Contents of the Index.cshtml File in the Views/One2One Folder

```
@model IEnumerable<DataApp.Models.ContactDetails>
@{
    ViewData["Title"] = "ContactDetails";
    Layout = "_Layout";
}
<table class="table table-striped table-sm">
    <tr>
        <th>ID</th>
        <th>Name</th>
        <th>Phone</th>
        <th></th>
        <th class="table-dark text-center" colspan="4">Supplier</th>
    </tr>
    @foreach (var s in Model) {
        <tr>
            <td>@s.Id</td>
            <td>@s.Name</td>
            <td>@s.Phone</td>
            <td>
                <form>
                    <button class="btn btn-sm btn-warning"
                            asp-action="Edit" asp-route-id="@s.Id">
                        Edit
                    </button>
                </form>
            </td>
            @if (s.Supplier != null) {
                <td class="table-dark">@s.Supplier.Id</td>
                <td class="table-dark">@s.Supplier.Name</td>
                <td class="table-dark">@s.Supplier.City</td>
                <td class="table-dark">@s.Supplier.State</td>
            } else {
                <td colspan="4" class="table-dark text-center">
                    No Related Supplier
                </td>
            }
        </tr>
    }
</table>
<a class="btn btn-primary" asp-action="Create">Create</a>
```

The view creates a table with each row displaying a ContactDetails object and its related Supplier. There are also button and anchor elements that target action methods that do not yet exist on the controller but that I will used to demonstrate different features in later sections.

Updating the Database and Running the Application

You will get an error if you try to apply the migration created in the database because the data that it already contains conflicts with the changes that the migration contains. For a production database, you would take the time to migrate the data, but for a development project, the database can be dropped and re-created. Run the commands shown in Listing 16-7 in the DataApp project folder to drop the database and apply the migration for the one-to-one relationship.

Listing 16-7. Dropping and Re-creating the Database

```
dotnet ef database drop --force --context EFDatabaseContext
dotnet ef database update --context EFDatabaseContext
```

Start the application using dotnet run and navigate to http://localhost:5000/one2one. The database will be seeded when the application starts, and the requested URL will target the Index action method defined in the controller in Listing 16-5, which selects the view created in Listing 16-6 and display the results shown in Figure 16-2.

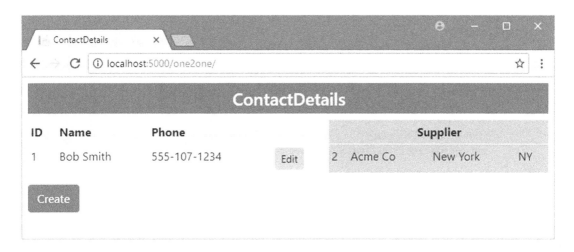

Figure 16-2. *Displaying related data in a one-to-one relationship*

Creating and Updating Related Objects

You can create and update related objects through either navigation property in a one-to-one relationship. This means, for example, that you can operate on a Supplier object through a ContactDetails object's Supplier property or, equally, operate on a ContactDetails object through a Supplier object's Contact property. I am focusing on the ContactDetails data in this section, so I added the action methods shown in Listing 16-8 to the One2One controller to handle the editing and creation processes.

Listing 16-8. Adding Action Methods in the One2OneController.cs File in the Controllers Folder

```
using DataApp.Models;
using Microsoft.AspNetCore.Mvc;
using Microsoft.EntityFrameworkCore;
using System.Linq;
```

```
namespace DataApp.Controllers {

    public class One2OneController : Controller {
        private EFDatabaseContext context;

        public One2OneController(EFDatabaseContext ctx) => context = ctx;

        public IActionResult Index () {
            return View(context.Set<ContactDetails>().Include(cd => cd.Supplier));
        }

        public IActionResult Create() => View("ContactEditor");

        public IActionResult Edit(long id) {
            return View("ContactEditor",
                context.Set<ContactDetails>()
                    .Include(cd => cd.Supplier).First(cd => cd.Id == id));
        }

        [HttpPost]
        public IActionResult Update(ContactDetails details) {
            if (details.Id == 0) {
                context.Add<ContactDetails>(details);
            } else {
                context.Update<ContactDetails>(details);
            }
            context.SaveChanges();
            return RedirectToAction(nameof(Index));
        }
    }
}
```

These actions follow the same pattern used in earlier chapters. The Create and Edit methods are used to select a view called ContactEditor that will allow the user to create or modify an object, with the EditContact method using the repository to query for the object that the user has selected. The Update method is used to receive POST requests containing the data entered by the user and calls the context object's Add or Update method to update the database.

To provide the view that will allow the user to create or edit an object, I created a view called ContactEditor.cshtml in the Views/One2One folder and added the elements shown in Listing 16-9.

Listing 16-9. The Contents of the ContactEditor.cshtml File in the Views/One2One Folder

```
@model DataApp.Models.ContactDetails
@{
    ViewData["Title"] = Model == null ? "Create" : "Edit";
    Layout = "_Layout";
}
```

```
<form asp-action="Update" method="post">
    <input type="hidden" asp-for="Id" />
    <input type="hidden" asp-for="Supplier.Id" />
    <h4>Contact Details</h4>
    <div class="p-1 m-1">
        <div class="form-row">
            <div class="form-group col">
                <label asp-for="Name" class="form-control-label"></label>
                <input asp-for="Name" class="form-control" />
            </div>
            <div class="form-group col">
                <label asp-for="Phone" class="form-control-label"></label>
                <input asp-for="Phone" class="form-control" />
            </div>
        </div>
    </div>
    <h4>Supplier</h4>
    <div class="p-1 m-1">
        <div class="form-row">
            <div class="form-group col">
                <label asp-for="Supplier.Name" class="form-control-label"></label>
                <input asp-for="Supplier.Name" class="form-control" />
            </div>
            <div class="form-group col">
                <label asp-for="Supplier.City" class="form-control-label"></label>
                <input asp-for="Supplier.City" class="form-control" />
            </div>
            <div class="form-group col">
                <label asp-for="Supplier.State" class="form-control-label"></label>
                <input asp-for="Supplier.State" class="form-control" />
            </div>
        </div>
        @if (ViewBag.Suppliers != null) {
            @Html.Partial("RelationshipEditor", Model.SupplierId)
        }
    </div>
    <div class="text-center m-1">
        <button type="submit" class="btn btn-primary">Save</button>
        <a asp-action="Index" class="btn btn-secondary">Cancel</a>
    </div>
</form>
```

The most important elements in this view are the ones that the user won't see: the `hidden` elements that will include the Id property values of the `ContactDetails` and `Supplier` objects. If the value of these properties is zero, then new object will be created; for any other value an existing object will be updated. (This view also refers to a partial view that I will create in the next section.)

Start the application using `dotnet run`, navigate to `http://localhost:5000/one2one`, and click the Create button. Fill out the input elements and click the Save button to create new `ContactDetails` and `Supplier` objects, which will then be displayed, as shown in Figure 16-3.

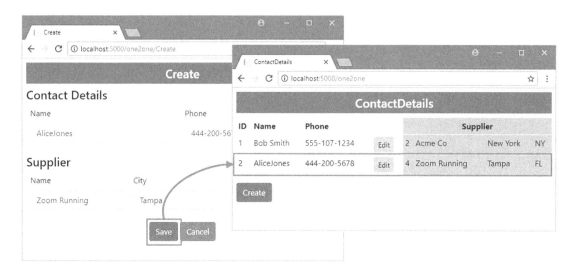

Figure 16-3. *Creating new objects via a navigation property*

Click the Edit button for the newly created object and change the value of the Name field for the Supplier object. When you click the Save button, Entity Framework Core will follow the navigation property of the ContactDetails object that is created by the MVC model binder and use it to update the database, as shown in Figure 16-4.

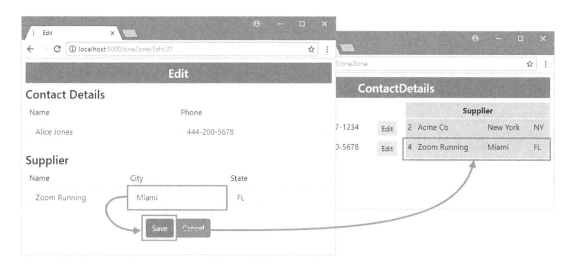

Figure 16-4. *Updating existing objects via a navigation property*

Changing One-to-One Relationships

Care must be taken when changing the relationships between objects, especially with required relationships. Entity Framework Core doesn't enforce the restrictions on relationships before sending updates to the database, and it is easy to perform an update that violates the referential integrity of the database, producing an error. In the sections that follow, I show you how to update both required and optional relationships, starting with the existing required relationship that is already configured in the database for the example application.

Changing a Required One-to-One Relationship

The challenge with a required relationship is that you must avoid storing any dependent entity that is not related to a principal entity. For the example application, that means that every ContactDetails object must be associated with a Supplier object. Attempting to store or update a ContactDetails object that isn't related to a Supplier will cause an error.

A required relationship is applied in only one direction; the dependent entity must be related to a principal entity but a principal does not have to be related to a dependent. For the example application, this means that Supplier objects can exist without being related to a ContactDetails object. This corresponds to how relationships are represented in the database, where the foreign key column is defined on the table used to store dependent entities but the table for the principal entity contains no information about the relationship at all.

This presents two different scenarios for changing an object's relationship. The first is when you want to change a relationship so that a dependent entity will be related to a principal entity that is not currently in a relationship. For the example application, this means that there are unattached (or "spare") Supplier objects available, and one of these becomes related to a ContactDetails object, replacing the existing Supplier. At the end of this operation, the Supplier that the ContactDetails object was originally related to becomes one of the spares.

The second scenario is when you want to create a relationship to a Supplier that is already related to another object. You can't leave the existing ContactDetails object unattached without violating the database constraints, so you must create a relationship with another Supplier, typically by performing a swap.

To add support for changing an existing relationship, I made the changes shown in Listing 16-10 to the One2One controller.

Listing 16-10. Changing Relationships in the One2OneController.cs File in the Controllers Folder

```
using DataApp.Models;
using Microsoft.AspNetCore.Mvc;
using Microsoft.EntityFrameworkCore;
using System.Linq;

namespace DataApp.Controllers {

    public class One2OneController : Controller {
        private EFDatabaseContext context;

        public One2OneController(EFDatabaseContext ctx) => context = ctx;

        public IActionResult Index () {
            return View(context.Set<ContactDetails>().Include(cd => cd.Supplier));
        }

        public IActionResult Create() => View("ContactEditor");

        public IActionResult Edit(long id) {
            ViewBag.Suppliers = context.Suppliers.Include(s => s.Contact);
            return View("ContactEditor",
                context.Set<ContactDetails>()
                    .Include(cd => cd.Supplier).First(cd => cd.Id == id));
        }
```

```
    [HttpPost]
    public IActionResult Update(ContactDetails details) {
        if (details.Id == 0) {
            context.Add<ContactDetails>(details);
        } else {
            context.Update<ContactDetails>(details);
        }
        context.SaveChanges();
        return RedirectToAction(nameof(Index));
    }
  }
}
```

I am going to build up this feature step-by-step because it can be confusing. The only change I have made at the moment is to create a ViewBag property that will provide the view with the Supplier data. This will ensure that a partial view called RelationshipEditor.cshtml is included in the output when the user edits an object, which provides me with the opportunity to present a list of existing Supplier objects with which a relationship can be established. I created a view file with the name RelationshipEditor.cshtml in the Views/One2One folder and added the content shown in Listing 16-11.

Listing 16-11. The Contents of the RelationshipEditor.cshtml File in the Views/One2One Folder

```
@model long

<div class="p-1 m-1">
    @foreach (Supplier s in ViewBag.Suppliers) {
        @if (s.Id != Model) {
            <div class="form-row">
                <div class="form-group col">
                    <input type="radio" name="targetSupplierId" value="@s.Id" />
                    @if (s.Contact == null) {
                        <input type="hidden" name="spares" value="@s.Id" />
                    }
                </div>
                <div class="form-group col-1">
                    <label class="form-control-label">@s.Id</label>
                </div>
                <div class="form-group col">
                    <label class="form-control-label">@s.Name</label>
                </div>
                <div class="form-group col">
                    <label class="form-control-label">@s.City</label>
                </div>
                <div class="form-group col">
                    <label class="form-control-label">@s.State</label>
                </div>
                <div class="form-group col">
                    <label class="form-control-label">
                        @(s.Contact == null ? "(None)" : s.Contact.Name)
                    </label>
```

```
            </div>
        </div>
    }
  }
</div>
```

This partial view enumerates a sequence of `Supplier` objects to present a list to the user, allowing a `Supplier` to be chosen using a radio button that includes a form data value called `targetSupplierId` in the HTTP POST request that will be sent to the application. There is also a collection of values called `spares` that contain the primary key values of the `Supplier` objects that are free, which I will use to work out whether there is an existing relationship to change.

Use `dotnet run` to start the application, navigate to `http://localhost:5000/one2one`, and click the Edit button for one of the `ContactDetails` objects that is shown. In addition to the `input` elements from the previous examples, you will see a list of the `Supplier` objects, excluding the one that the current object is related to, as shown in Figure 16-5.

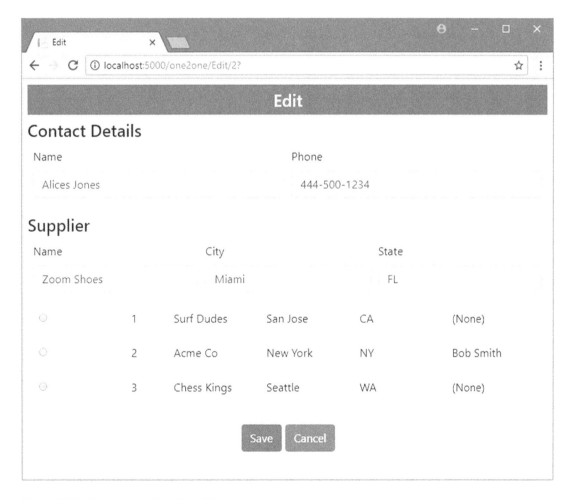

Figure 16-5. *Displaying a list of suppliers*

Now that all of the preparation is complete, I can add the code that will change the relationship. The first scenario is when the user selects a Supplier object that is not currently related to a ContactDetails object. This is an easy change to make because all I have to do is change the value of the SupplierId property of the ContactDetails object to the primary key of the "spare" Supplier. This change will break the relationship with the current Supplier and create a relationship with the new Supplier. Listing 16-12 shows the changes that are required to the controller to handle this type of change.

Listing 16-12. Changing Relationships in the One2OneController.cs File in the Controllers Folder

```
...
[HttpPost]
public IActionResult Update(ContactDetails details,
        long? targetSupplierId, long[] spares) {
    if (details.Id == 0) {
        context.Add<ContactDetails>(details);
    } else {
        context.Update<ContactDetails>(details);
        if (targetSupplierId.HasValue) {
            if (spares.Contains(targetSupplierId.Value)) {
                details.SupplierId = targetSupplierId.Value;
            }
        }
    }
    context.SaveChanges();
    return RedirectToAction(nameof(Index));
}
...
```

The new targetSupplierId parameter will have a value when the user selects one of the existing Supplier objects, while the spares parameter will contain the primary key values of the Supplier objects that are not in a relationship. The new statements in the action method use the parameters to see whether the user has selected an existing spare Supplier and, if so, sets the SupplierId property to create a relationship.

To see the effect of this code, restart the application, and navigate to http://localhost:5000/one2one. Click one of the Edit buttons and select the radio button for one of the Supplier objects that is shown with (None) in the final column, indicating that it is spare. Click the Save button, and you will see that the ContactDetails object is now related to the Supplier you selected, as illustrated by Figure 16-6.

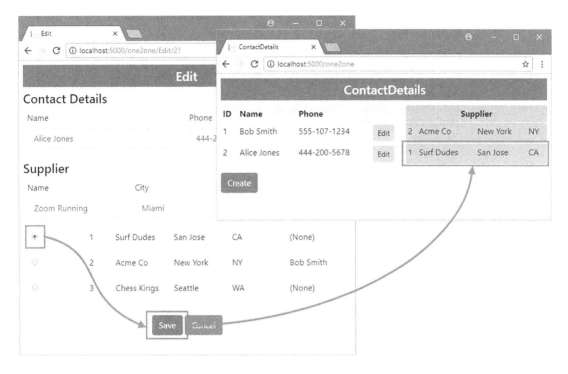

Figure 16-6. *Selecting a free supplier*

The second scenario is the one that causes confusion. When you want to create a relationship with a Supplier that is not spare, additional steps are required to update the database while preserving its referential integrity. In Listing 16-13, I have added the statements to the Update action method that will handle this process.

Listing 16-13. Changing Existing Relationships in the One2OneController.cs File in the Controllers Folder

```
...
[HttpPost]
public IActionResult Update(ContactDetails details,
        long? targetSupplierId, long[] spares) {
    if (details.Id == 0) {
        context.Add<ContactDetails>(details);
    } else {
        context.Update<ContactDetails>(details);
        if (targetSupplierId.HasValue) {
            if (spares.Contains(targetSupplierId.Value)) {
                details.SupplierId = targetSupplierId.Value;
            } else {
                ContactDetails targetDetails = context.Set<ContactDetails>()
                    .FirstOrDefault(cd => cd.SupplierId == targetSupplierId);
```

385

```
                    targetDetails.SupplierId = details.Supplier.Id;
                    Supplier temp = new Supplier { Name = "temp" };
                    details.Supplier = temp;
                    context.SaveChanges();

                    temp.Contact = null;
                    details.SupplierId = targetSupplierId.Value;
                    context.Suppliers.Remove(temp);
                }
            }
        }
        context.SaveChanges();
        return RedirectToAction(nameof(Index));
}
...
```

If the Supplier that the user has selected is already related to a ContactDetails object, then some shuffling has to be done. First, I query the database for the ContactDetails object that is related to the Supplier that the user wants and change its SupplierId property so that it is related to the object that the user is editing. (I walk through a specific example at the end of this section, which will help you make sense of what is happening in this sequence of updates.)

I can't update the database at this point because two ContactDetails objects are related to the same Supplier, which isn't allowed in the database. And, since this is a required one-to-one relationship, I can't store either ContactDetails object unless it is related to a Supplier.

So, the next step is to create a *new* Supplier object, which I assign to a variable called temp, and use it to create a relationship with the ContactDetail object that is being edited. At this point, I call the SaveChanges method to store the changes, and a new row will be created in the Suppliers table for the temp object.

As a result of the update, the Supplier object that the user has selected is a spare and is available for use. I assign its primary key value to the SupplierId property of the ContactDetails object that is being edited, tell Entity Framework Core to delete the temporary Supplier object, and then call the SaveChanges method again. The second update removes the row from the temp object and creates the ContactDetails/Supplier relationship that the user requested.

Tip This kind of multistage operation is usually performed inside a transaction so that the changes applied by the first update can be automatically undone if the second update in the operation fails for some reason. See Chapter 24 for details of how transactions work and how they are supported by Entity Framework Core.

To see how this works, restart the application using dotnet run, navigate to http://localhost:5000/one2one, and click one of the Edit buttons. Select the radio button for a Supplier that is already related to a ContactDetails object and click the Save button. The new code added to the action method in Listing 16-13 will update the database so that the relationships between the ContactDetails and Supplier objects are swapped over, as shown in Figure 16-7.

Figure 16-7. *Selecting a supplier that is already related to a contact details object*

I selected the Alice Jones ContactDetails object, which is related to the Surf Dudes Supplier and told the application that I want it to be related to the Acme Co Supplier instead. The Acme Co Supplier is related to the Bob Smith ContactDetails object. Here are the actions I perform to achieve the update required by the user:

1. Change the Bob Smith object's SupplierId property to the Id value of the Surf Dudes object.

2. Create a temporary Supplier object and assign it to the Alice Jones Supplier property.

3. Update the database so that the Acme Co object is not in a relationship with a ContactDetails object and is "spare."

4. Change the Alice Jones SupplierId property to the Id value of the Acme Co object.

5. Delete the temporary Supplier object.

6. Update the database again, which stores the relationship between the Alice Jones and Acme Co objects and removes the temporary Supplier.

This is an undeniably awkward process—and one that causes a lot of confusion—but it ensures that the constraints in the database are honored and avoids any errors from the database server.

Changing an Optional One-to-One Relationship

The process is simpler when you are working with an optional one-to-one relationship because you don't have to worry about ensuring that every ContactDetails object is related to a Supplier object, only that you avoid duplicate foreign key values. Changing the type of the foreign key property to one that can be set to null will change the required relationship to an optional one. In Listing 16-14, I have changed the type of the foreign ley property defined by the ContactDetails navigation property.

Listing 16-14. Changing a Property Type in the ContactDetails.cs File in the Models Folder

```
namespace DataApp.Models {

    public class ContactDetails {
        public long Id { get; set; }
        public string Name { get; set; }
        public string Phone { get; set; }
        public ContactLocation Location { get; set; }

        public long? SupplierId { get; set; }
        public Supplier Supplier { get; set; }
    }
}
```

Run the commands shown in Listing 16-15 in the DataApp project folder to update the database to reflect the relationship change. (The database doesn't have to be dropped and re-created because the change loosens the restrictions in the database.)

Listing 16-15. Creating and Applying a Migration

```
dotnet ef migrations add OptionalOneToOne --context EFDatabaseContext
dotnet ef database update --context EFDatabaseContext
```

Now that the relationship is optional, I can simplify the code in the controller's Update method, as shown in Listing 16-16.

Listing 16-16. Simplifying the Update Method in the One2OneController.cs File in the Controllers Folder

```
...
[HttpPost]
public IActionResult Update(ContactDetails details,
        long? targetSupplierId, long[] spares) {
    if (details.Id == 0) {
        context.Add<ContactDetails>(details);
    } else {
        context.Update<ContactDetails>(details);
        if (targetSupplierId.HasValue) {
            if (spares.Contains(targetSupplierId.Value)) {
                details.SupplierId = targetSupplierId.Value;
            } else {
                ContactDetails targetDetails = context.Set<ContactDetails>()
                    .FirstOrDefault(cd => cd.SupplierId == targetSupplierId);
                targetDetails.SupplierId = null;
```

```
            details.SupplierId = targetSupplierId.Value;
            context.SaveChanges();
        }
      }
    }
    context.SaveChanges();
    return RedirectToAction(nameof(Index));
}
...
```

Swapping the related objects is no longer required because ContactDetails can now be stored in the database without a relationship to a Supplier object. When the user selects a Supplier, I query the database to find the ContactDetails object to which it is related and set its SupplierId property to null. This is an important step because the SupplierId values must still be unique and two ContactDetails objects cannot be related to the same Supplier.

To see the effect, restart the application, repeat the editing process, and select a Supplier that is already related to a ContactDetails object. When you click the Save button, you will see that the old relationship has been broken and that the ContactDetails object is shown as unrelated, as illustrated in Figure 16-8.

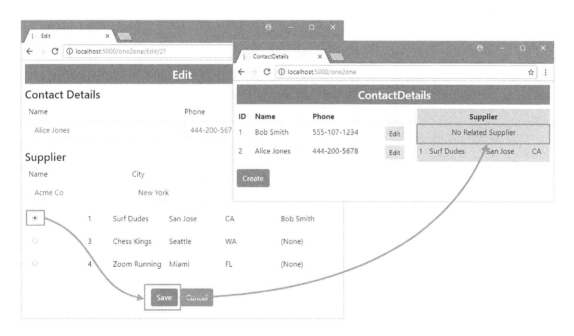

Figure 16-8. *Selecting a related Supplier when using an optional relationship*

Defining Many-to-Many Relationships

Entity Framework Core can be used to create and manage many-to-many relationships, where each object of one type can have nonexclusive relationships with multiple objects of another type. Some applications can't get by with only one-to-one and one-to-many relationships, so the sections that follow demonstrate how to define and use a many-to-many relationship, even though the Entity Framework Core support for doing so is awkward.

389

To prepare for this example, I added a class file called Shipment.cs to the Models folder and used it to define the class shown in Listing 16-17. This class will be one of the participants in the many-to-many relationship.

Listing 16-17. The Contents of the Shipment.cs File in the Models Folder

```
namespace DataApp.Models {

    public class Shipment {
        public long Id { get; set; }
        public string ShipperName {get; set;}
        public string StartCity { get; set; }
        public string EndCity { get; set; }
    }
}
```

The Shipment class will represent a shipment of products. To keep track of which products have been shipped, I am going to create a many-to-many relationship with the Product class. This means that a Product object can be related to many Shipment objects (indicating that products are delivered in multiple shipments), and a Shipment object can be related to multiple Product objects (indicating that a shipment can contain multiple products).

Creating the Junction Class

Entity Framework Core can represent a many-to-many relationship only by combining two one-to-many relationships and using a *junction class* to join them together. Don't worry if this doesn't make immediate sense because it will start to become clearer as you see how the different pieces fit together.

To create the junction class, I added a class file called ProductShipmentJunction.cs to the Models folder and used it to define the class shown in Listing 16-18.

Listing 16-18. The Contents of the ProductShipmentJunction.cs File in the Models Folder

```
namespace DataApp.Models {

    public class ProductShipmentJunction {

        public long Id { get; set; }

        public long ProductId { get; set; }
        public Product Product { get; set; }

        public long ShipmentId { get; set; }
        public Shipment Shipment { get; set; }
    }
}
```

The sole purpose of the junction class is to act as a container for two one-to-many relationships. The ProductShipmentJunction class defines two sets of navigation and foreign key properties that create relationships with the Product and Shipment classes and is the dependent entity in both relationships.

Completing the Many-to-Many Relationship

Completing the relationship means adding navigation properties to both the Product and Supplier classes to complete the individual one-to-many relationships and to allow navigation from one class to the other, via the junction class. In Listing 16-19, I have added the navigation property to the Product class.

Listing 16-19. Adding a Navigation Property in the Product.cs File in the Models Folder

```
using System.Collections.Generic;

namespace DataApp.Models {

    public enum Colors {
        Red, Green, Blue
    }

    public class Product {

        public long Id { get; set; }
        public string Name { get; set; }
        public string Category { get; set; }
        public decimal Price { get; set; }
        public Colors Color { get; set; }
        public bool InStock { get; set; }

        public long SupplierId { get; set; }
        public Supplier Supplier { get; set; }

        public IEnumerable<ProductShipmentJunction>
            ProductShipments { get; set; }
    }
}
```

The new navigation property completes the relationship with the junction class and not the Shipment class. In Listing 16-20, I have added the corresponding property to the Shipment class, completing its relationship with the junction class.

Listing 16-20. Adding a Navigation Property in the Shipment.cs File in the Models Folder

```
using System.Collections.Generic;

namespace DataApp.Models {

    public class Shipment {
        public long Id { get; set; }
        public string ShipperName {get; set;}
        public string StartCity { get; set; }
        public string EndCity { get; set; }

        public IEnumerable<ProductShipmentJunction>
            ProductShipments { get; set; }
    }
}
```

Both of the entity classes define navigation properties that return IEnumerable<ProductShipmentJunction> and have no direct relationship with one another. This makes navigation and data operations more complicated but does build on a familiar foundation to provide the many-to-many feature, as you will see in the sections that follow.

Run the commands shown in Listing 16-21 in the DataApp project folder to create a migration that will update the database so that it can store the Shipment object and represent the many-to-many relationship.

Listing 16-21. Creating a Migration

```
dotnet ef migrations add ManyToMany --context EFDatabaseContext
```

If you examine the Up method in the <timestamp>_ManyToMany.cs file that has been created in the Migrations folder, you will see that two new tables have been added. Entity Framework Core has detected the new navigation property on the Product class and determined that it needs to store the ProductShipmentJunction and Shipment objects. The ProductShipmentJunction class is the dependent entity in both of its relationships, and this is the table to which Entity Framework Core adds the foreign key columns that will be used to represent relationships with the Product and Supplier classes. The result is a one-to-many relationship between the ProductShipmentJunction class and the Product class and a one-to-many relationship between the ProductShipmentJunction class and the Shipment class, as shown in Figure 16-9.

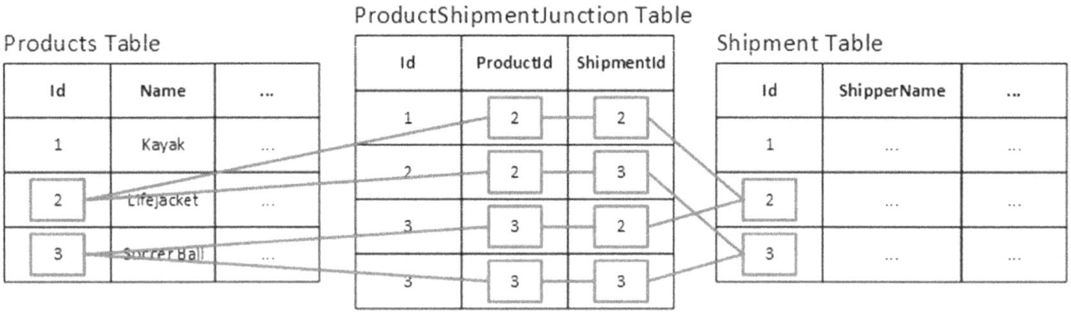

Figure 16-9. *Understanding how many-to-many relationships will be represented in the database*

Each ProductShipmentJunction object acts as a junction between a Product and Shipment object, and the collection of ProductShipmentJunction objects returned by the navigation properties will provide access to the complete set of related objects, albeit indirectly, as you will see in the sections that follow.

Preparing the Application

To have some data to work with, I have added some Shipment objects to the seed data class, as shown in Listing 16-22. There are no relationships created by the new objects, and they will exist in isolation when they are stored in the database. I'll show you how to create and manage the relationships shortly.

Listing 16-22. Adding Data in the SeedData.cs File in the Models Folder

```
using Microsoft.EntityFrameworkCore;
using System.Linq;

namespace DataApp.Models {

    public static class SeedData {
```

```
public static void Seed(DbContext context) {
    if (context.Database.GetPendingMigrations().Count() == 0) {
        if (context is EFDatabaseContext prodCtx
                && prodCtx.Products.Count() == 0) {
            prodCtx.Products.AddRange(Products);
            prodCtx.Set<Shipment>().AddRange(Shipments);
        } else if (context is EFCustomerContext custCtx
                && custCtx.Customers.Count() == 0) {
            custCtx.Customers.AddRange(Customers);
        }
        context.SaveChanges();
    }
}

public static void ClearData(DbContext context) {
    if (context is EFDatabaseContext prodCtx
            && prodCtx.Products.Count() > 0) {
        prodCtx.Products.RemoveRange(prodCtx.Products);
        prodCtx.Set<Shipment>()
            .RemoveRange(prodCtx.Set<Shipment>());
    } else if (context is EFCustomerContext custCtx
            && custCtx.Customers.Count() > 0) {
        custCtx.Customers.RemoveRange(custCtx.Customers);
    }
    context.SaveChanges();
}

public static Shipment[] Shipments {
    get {
        return new Shipment[] {
            new Shipment { ShipperName = "Express Co",
                StartCity = "New York", EndCity = "San Jose"},
            new Shipment { ShipperName = "Tortoise Shipping",
                StartCity = "Boston", EndCity = "Chicago"},
            new Shipment { ShipperName = "Air Express",
                StartCity = "Miami", EndCity = "Seattle"}
        };
    }
}

private static Product[] Products {
    get {
        // ...statements omitted for brevity...
    }
}

private static Customer[] Customers = {
    new Customer { Name = "Alice Smith",
        City = "New York", Country = "USA" },
    new Customer { Name = "Bob Jones",
        City = "Paris", Country = "France" },
```

```
            new Customer { Name = "Charlie Davies",
                City = "London", Country = "UK" }};
    }
}
```

The new `Shipments` property returns an array of `Shipment` objects, which are added to the database using the `Set<T>.AddRange` method in the `Seed` method. The `ClearData` method has also been updated to remove `Shipment` objects from the database, also using the `Set<T>` feature.

The seed data will be applied only to an empty database, so run the commands shown in Listing 16-23 in the `DataApp` folder to drop and re-create the database with all of the migrations, including the one created in Listing 16-22 that adds support for the many-to-many relationship.

Listing 16-23. Dropping and Re-creating the Database

```
dotnet ef database drop --force --context EFDatabaseContext
dotnet ef database update --context EFDatabaseContext
```

Querying for Many-to-Many Data

The approach required for many-to-many relationships has an effect on the way that queries are performed. Be careful when writing the code that queries a one-to-one database because it is easy to focus just on the classes that are important to the application and forget about the role of the junction class.

To create a basic query, I added a class file called `Many2ManyController.cs` in the `Controllers` folder and used it to define the controller shown in Listing 16-24.

Listing 16-24. The Contents of the Many2ManyController.cs File in the Controllers Folder

```
using DataApp.Models;
using Microsoft.AspNetCore.Mvc;
using Microsoft.EntityFrameworkCore;
using System.Collections.Generic;
using System.Linq;

namespace DataApp.Controllers {

    public class Many2ManyController : Controller {
        private EFDatabaseContext context;

        public Many2ManyController(EFDatabaseContext ctx) => context = ctx;

        public IActionResult Index() {
            return View(new ProductShipmentViewModel {
                Products = context.Products.Include(p => p.ProductShipments)
                    .ThenInclude(ps => ps.Shipment).ToArray(),
                Shipments = context.Set<Shipment>().Include(s => s.ProductShipments)
                    .ThenInclude(ps => ps.Product).ToArray()
            });
        }
    }
```

```
        public class ProductShipmentViewModel {
            public IEnumerable<Product> Products { get; set; }
            public IEnumerable<Shipment> Shipments { get; set; }
        }
    }
```

The Many2Many controller defines an Index action method that passes a ProductShipmentViewModel object to the default view. The ProductShipmentViewModel class allows me to pass both the Product and Shipment data to the view in a consistent way.

The query statements in the Index action populate the properties of the view model objects with data, using the custom context property for Product objects and the Set<T> method to query the Shipment data. In both cases, the Include method is used to follow the navigation property to the junction class, and the ThenInclude method is used to include the other type in the relationship.

You must take the junction class into account when you want to display the related data in this kind of relationship. To provide the Index action defined in Listing 16-24 with a view, I created the Views/Many2Many folder and added to it a Razor file called Index.cshtml with the content shown in Listing 16-25.

Listing 16-25. The Contents of the Index.cshtml File in the Views/Many2Many Folder

```
@model DataApp.Controllers.ProductShipmentViewModel
@{
    ViewData["Title"] = "Many To Many";
    Layout = "_Layout";
}

<h4>Shipments</h4>
<table class="table table-sm table-striped">
    <tr><th>ID</th><th>Name</th><th>Product Names</th><th></th></tr>
    @if (Model.Shipments?.Count() > 0) {
        @foreach (Shipment s in Model.Shipments) {
            <tr>
                <td>@s.Id</td><td>@s.ShipperName</td>
                <td>
                    @(string.Join(", ", s.ProductShipments
                        .Select(ps => ps.Product.Name)))
                </td>
                <td>
                    <a asp-action="EditShipment" asp-route-id="@s.Id"
                        class="btn btn-sm btn-primary">Edit</a>
                </td>
        </tr>
        }
    } else {
        <tr><td colspan="3" class="text-center">No Data</td></tr>
    }
</table>
```

```
<h4>Products</h4>
<table class="table table-sm table-striped">
    <tr><th>ID</th><th>Name</th><th>Shipment Names</th></tr>
    @if (Model.Products?.Count() > 0) {
        @foreach (Product p in Model.Products) {
            <tr>
                <td>@p.Id</td><td>@p.Name</td>
                <td colspan="2">
                    @(string.Join(", ", p.ProductShipments
                        .Select(ps => ps.Shipment.ShipperName)))
                </td>
            </tr>
            }
        } else {
            <tr><td colspan="3" class="text-center">No Data</td></tr>
        }
</table>
```

The view displays tables that contain details of the Product and Shipment objects, with links that target actions I'll add later in this chapter to demonstrate how relationships are changed. Each table row uses navigation properties to reach through the junction class to get the collection of related objects, which are then processed using LINQ and the string.Join method to create an array of names.

■ **Tip**   The view evaluates the sequences of data objects more than once, which is why I used the ToArray method in the queries in Listing 16-25, as described in Chapter 15, to prevent duplicate queries from being sent to the database.

Start the application using dotnet run and navigate to http://localhost:5000/many2many. The database will have been seeded with the data in Listing 16-25 during startup, but there are no many-to-many relationships currently, which produces the result shown in Figure 16-10.

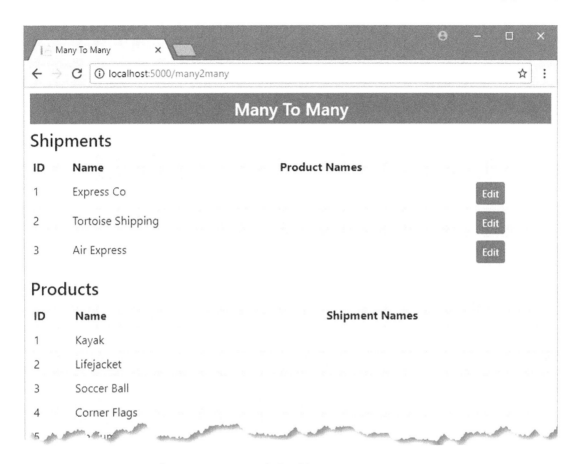

Figure 16-10. *Querying with a many-to-many relationship*

Managing Many-to-Many Relationships

To begin adding support for managing relationships, I added the action method shown in Listing 16-26 to the Many2Many controller. The action method queries the database for the object that the user has selected and passes it to a view called ShipmentEditor.

Listing 16-26. Adding an Action in the Many2ManyController.cs File in the Controllers Folder

```
using DataApp.Models;
using Microsoft.AspNetCore.Mvc;
using Microsoft.EntityFrameworkCore;
using System.Collections.Generic;
using System.Linq;

namespace DataApp.Controllers {

    public class Many2ManyController : Controller {
        private EFDatabaseContext context;

        public Many2ManyController(EFDatabaseContext ctx) => context = ctx;
```

```
    public IActionResult Index() {
        return View(new ProductShipmentViewModel {
            Products = context.Products.Include(p => p.ProductShipments)
                .ThenInclude(ps => ps.Shipment).ToArray(),
            Shipments = context.Set<Shipment>().Include(s => s.ProductShipments)
                .ThenInclude(ps => ps.Product).ToArray()
        });
    }

    public IActionResult EditShipment (long id) {
        ViewBag.Products = context.Products.Include(p => p.ProductShipments);
        return View("ShipmentEditor", context.Set<Shipment>().Find(id));
    }
}

public class ProductShipmentViewModel {
    public IEnumerable<Product> Products { get; set; }
    public IEnumerable<Shipment> Shipments { get; set; }
}
}
```

To allow the user to edit the relationships for a Shipment object, I need the object itself and the complete collection of Product objects so that I can show which ones are currently related and which are not, which means that I also need to get the ProductShipmentJunction objects. I get the Product and ProductShipmentJunction objects in a single query, using the Include method, and assign the results to the ViewBag.Products property, which provides access to the Products and the means to work out whether they are related to the Shipment that the user has selected. For the Shipment object itself, I use the database context object's Set<T> method to query the database with the Find method and pass the Shipment object as the model to the View method.

To provide the action method with its view, I added a view file called ShipmentEditor.cshtml to the Views/Many2Many folder and added the content shown in Listing 16-27.

Listing 16-27. The Contents of the ShipmentEditor.cshtml in the Views/Many2Many Folder

```
@model DataApp.Models.Shipment
@{
    ViewData["Title"] = "Many To Many";
    Layout = "_Layout";
}

<div class="m-1 p-1">
    <div class="row">
        <div class="col"><strong>Name</strong></div>
        <div class="col"><strong>Start</strong></div>
        <div class="col"><strong>End</strong></div>
    </div>
    <div class="row">
        <div class="col">@Model.ShipperName</div>
        <div class="col">@Model.StartCity</div>
        <div class="col">@Model.EndCity</div>
    </div>
</div>
```

```
<form asp-action="UpdateShipment" method="post" class="p-2">
    <input type="hidden" name="id" value="@Model.Id" />
    <h4>Products</h4>
    @foreach (Product p in ViewBag.Products) {
        <div class="form-row">
            <div class="form-group col-1">
                @if (p.ProductShipments.Any(ps => ps.ShipmentId == Model.Id)) {
                    <input type="checkbox" name="pids" value="@p.Id" checked />
                } else {
                    <input type="checkbox" name="pids" value="@p.Id" />
                }
            </div>
            <div class="form-group col">
                <label class="form-control-label">@p.Name</label>
            </div>
            <div class="form-group col">
                <label class="form-control-label">@p.Category</label>
            </div>
            <div class="form-group col">
                <label class="form-control-label">@p.Price.ToString("C2")</label>
            </div>
        </div>
    }
    <div class="text-center">
        <button class="btn btn-primary" type="submit">Save</button>
        <a asp-action="Index" class="btn btn-secondary">Cancel</a>
    </div>
</form>
```

The Shipment object is used to display property values to the user and to provide the value for the hidden input element in the form. The collection of Product objects is used to display a grid of details, with the ProductShipmentJunction objects being used to determine whether the Product is related to the Shipment model object.

When the user clicks the Save button presented by the view, the HTML form is sent to an action called UpdateShipment. In Listing 16-28, I have added the action method to the Many2Many controller along with the code required to update the database to reflect the relationships that the user has selected.

⁓ **Note** The code in Listing 16-28 updates only the many-to-many relationship and does not update any other aspect of the Shipment object. See Chapter18 for a demonstration of updating an object and its many-to-many relationships in a single action method.

Listing 16-28. Updating Relationships in the Many2ManyController.cs File in the Controllers Folder

```
using DataApp.Models;
using Microsoft.AspNetCore.Mvc;
using Microsoft.EntityFrameworkCore;
using System.Collections.Generic;
using System.Linq;
```

```
namespace DataApp.Controllers {

    public class Many2ManyController : Controller {
        private EFDatabaseContext context;

        public Many2ManyController(EFDatabaseContext ctx) => context = ctx;

        public IActionResult Index() {
            return View(new ProductShipmentViewModel {
                Products = context.Products.Include(p => p.ProductShipments)
                    .ThenInclude(ps => ps.Shipment).ToArray(),
                Shipments = context.Set<Shipment>().Include(s => s.ProductShipments)
                    .ThenInclude(ps => ps.Product).ToArray()
            });
        }

        public IActionResult EditShipment (long id) {
            ViewBag.Products = context.Products.Include(p => p.ProductShipments);
            return View("ShipmentEditor", context.Set<Shipment>().Find(id));
        }

        public IActionResult UpdateShipment(long id, long[] pids) {
            Shipment shipment = context.Set<Shipment>()
                .Include(s => s.ProductShipments).First(s => s.Id == id);
            shipment.ProductShipments = pids.Select(pid
                => new ProductShipmentJunction {
                        ShipmentId = id, ProductId = pid
                    }).ToList();
            context.SaveChanges();
            return RedirectToAction(nameof(Index));
        }
    }

    public class ProductShipmentViewModel {
        public IEnumerable<Product> Products { get; set; }
        public IEnumerable<Shipment> Shipments { get; set; }
    }
}
```

The new action method receives the Id value of the Shipment object that the user has edited and an array of the Id values for the Product objects for which relationships are required.

The first step in updating the relationships is to query the database to get the Shipment object and its related junction objects. This is an important step because if you do not retrieve the junction object from the database, Entity Framework Core won't delete any existing relationships that are no longer required.

⚠ Caution   If you do not query for the existing relationships, then you will find that new relationships are added to the database but that ones that the user deselects are left unchanged.

The next step is to replace the collection of junction objects with ones that contain just the relationships that the user has chosen, like this:

```
...
shipment.ProductShipments = pids.Select(pid =>
    new ProductShipmentJunction { ShipmentId = id, ProductId = pid }).ToList();
...
```

The LINQ Select method is used to project a sequence of ProductShipmentJunction objects whose foreign key properties are set to represent one of the relationships that the user has chosen. (The ToList method is required to create a variable-length collection, which is what Entity Framework Core expects to work with.)

No explicit action is required to delete the existing relationships that are no longer required. When the SaveChanges method is called, Entity Framework Core will use the collection of junction objects created by the action method to update the database, creating and deleting data as required.

To see the result, restart the application, navigate to http://localhost:5000/many2many, and click the Edit button for one of the shipments. Check the Product objects for which a relationship is required and click the Save button. You will see that the relationships are reflected in both the Shipments and Products sections of the list and that each object can be related to multiple other objects, as shown in Figure 16-11.

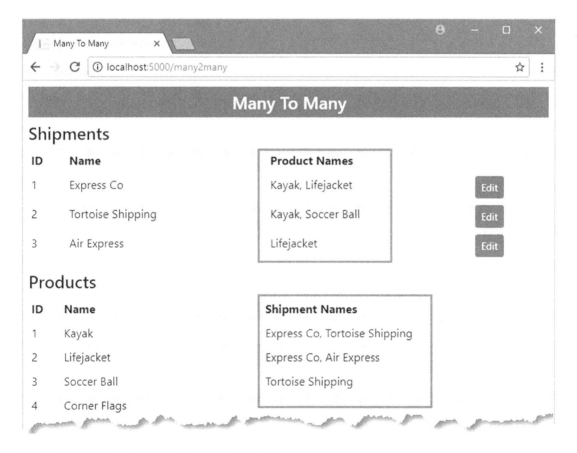

Figure 16-11. Managing many-to-many relationships

Summary

In this chapter, I explained how Entity Framework Core supports one-to-one and many-to-many relationships. I showed you how to define these relationships, how to perform queries on related data, and how to update these relationships on behalf of the user. In the next chapter, I show you how to use Entity Framework Core with an existing database.

CHAPTER 17

Scaffolding an Existing Database

The examples in earlier chapters start with the C# classes that define the model and use them to create a database, which is known as *code-first* development. A different approach is required for projects that need to use an existing database, known as *database-first* development, and in this chapter, I show you how to use the Entity Framework Core *scaffolding* feature, which inspects a database and automatically generates a data model. This feature is best suited to simple databases, while more complex projects are better served by manual data modeling, which I describe in Chapter 18. Table 17-1 puts this chapter in context.

Table 17-1. *Putting Database Scaffolding in Context*

Question	Answer
What is it?	Scaffolding is the process of building a data model so that Entity Framework Core can use an existing database.
Why is it useful?	Not all projects are able to create a new database. Scaffolding inspects an existing database and creates a data model automatically.
How is it used?	Scaffolding is performed using a command-line tool.
Are there any pitfalls or limitations?	The scaffolding process can't deal with all database features and can get bogged down with large and complex databases.
Are there any alternatives?	You can model the database manually, as described in Chapter 18.

© Adam Freeman 2018
A. Freeman, *Pro Entity Framework Core 2 for ASP.NET Core MVC*,
https://doi.org/10.1007/978-1-4842-3435-8_17

Table 17-2 summarizes the chapter.

Table 17-2. *Chapter Summary*

Problem	Solution	Listing
Scaffold an existing database	Run the command line tool and then adjust the context class for use with Entity Framework Core	1–23
Reflect database changes in the application	Rescaffold the database	24–30

Preparing for This Chapter

This chapter depends on a database that is created without using Entity Framework Core in order to simulate a database that already exists. To do this, I am going to use the Visual Studio features for executing SQL queries to create and populate a database, as described in the sections that follow.

■ **Note**   I build up the database step-by-step in the listings that follow to make the process easier to follow. However, typing complex SQL statements is an error-prone process, and the best way to create the database is to download the SQL file that I included in the project for this chapter, which can be downloaded from the GitHub repository for this book (`https://github.com/apress/pro-ef-core-2-for-asp.net-core-mvc`).

Understanding the Example Existing Database

To help put the SQL that appears in this part of the chapter in context, I will describe the database that I am going create. The database will be called ZoomShoesDb, and it will represent the product database for the fictional Zoom running shoe company. Table 17-3 lists the table that I will add to the database and the relationships between them. Real databases are much more complex than the example, but it contains all of the characteristics that I need to demonstrate the Entity Framework Core features for working with an existing database.

Table 17-3. *The Tables in the Example Database*

Name	Description
Shoes	This table will be the centerpiece of the database and will contain details of the products produced by the company. This table has relationships with all of the other tables.
Categories	This table contains the set of categories used to describe the company's running shoes. It has a many-to-many relationship with the Shoes table through the ShoeCategoryJunction table.
ShoeCategory Junction	This is the junction table for the many-to-many relationship between the Shoes and Categories tables.
Colors	This table contains the set of color combinations in which shoes are available and has a one-to-many relationship with the Shoes table.
SalesCampaigns	This table contains details of the sales campaign for each shoe and has a one-to-one relationship with the Shoes table.

Connecting to the Database Server

Start Visual Studio without opening or creating a new project. Select Tools ➤ SQL Server ➤ New Query and enter **(localdb)\MSSQLLocalDB** in the Server Name field. (Note that there is only one backslash—the \ character—in the database name, rather than the two that are required when defining a connection string in the appsettings.json file.)

Ensure that Windows Authentication is selected for the Authentication field and ensure that <default> is selected for the Database Name field, as shown in Figure 17-1, and click the Connect button. Visual Studio will open a new query window into which SQL statements can be entered and executed.

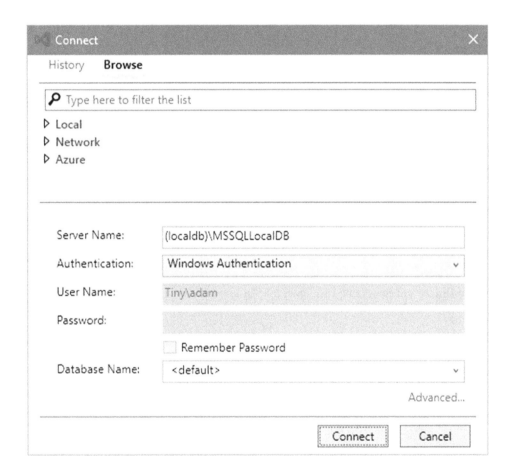

Figure 17-1. *Connecting to the database server*

Creating the Database

The first step is to create the database. Enter the statements shown in Listing 17-1 into the editor window, right-click, and select Execute from the pop-up menu.

■ **Note**   If you are using Visual Studio Code, click Execute Query from the menu when you right-click the editor pane.

Listing 17-1. Creating the Database

```
USE master

DROP DATABASE IF EXISTS ZoomShoesDb
GO

CREATE DATABASE ZoomShoesDb
GO

USE ZoomShoesDb
GO
```

The DROP DATABASE command deletes the ZoomShoesDb database if it already exists, which means that you can return to the listing and start over if you make a mistake while preparing the database for this chapter. The CREATE DATABASE command creates the database, and the USE command tells the database server that the commands that follow are to be applied to the ZoomShoesDb database.

Creating the Colors Table

The order in which tables are created is important because the database server won't allow foreign key relationships to be defined on tables that don't exist. The Colors table has to be created before the Shoes table, for example, so that the Shoes table can be defined with a foreign key column that will be used for the one-to-many relationship described in Table 17-3. Enter the SQL shown in Listing 17-2 in the SQL editor window, right-click, and select Execute from the pop-up menu to create and populate the Colors table.

Listing 17-2. Creating and Populating the Colors Table

```
CREATE TABLE Colors (
        Id bigint IDENTITY(1,1) NOT NULL,
        Name nvarchar(max) NOT NULL,
        MainColor nvarchar(max) NOT NULL,
        HighlightColor nvarchar(max) NOT NULL,
CONSTRAINT PK_Colors PRIMARY KEY (Id));

SET IDENTITY_INSERT dbo.Colors ON
INSERT dbo.Colors (Id, Name, MainColor, HighlightColor)
        VALUES (1, N'Red Flash', N'Red', N'Yellow'),
                        (2, N'Cool Blue', N'Dark Blue', N'Light Blue'),
                        (3, N'Midnight', N'Black', N'Black'),
                        (4, N'Beacon', N'Yellow', N'Green')
SET IDENTITY_INSERT dbo.Colors OFF
GO
```

The CREATE TABLE command creates the Colors table, which has Id, Name, MainColor, and HighlightColor columns, with the Id column used as the primary key column. The INSERT command populates the table, with the SET IDENTITY command used to temporarily allow data to be added with values for the Id column. The Colors table is configured so that the database server is responsible for generating values for the Id column, but I need to specify the values when populating the database so that I can set up the relationships between tables correctly.

To test that you have created the table correctly, replace the text in the editor window with the SQL query shown in Listing 17-3.

Listing 17-3. Querying the Colors Table

```
SELECT * FROM Colors
```

Right-click in the editor window and select Execute from the pop-up menu; you should see the output in Table 17-4, reflecting the structure and contents of the Colors table.

■ **Caution** If you don't get the expected results, then return to Listing 17-1 and start over. You may be tempted to carry on regardless, but you will not get the expected results later in the chapter.

Table 17-4. The Structure and Data of the Colors Table

Id	Name	MainColor	HighlightColor
1	Red Flash	Red	Yellow
2	Cool Blue	Dark Blue	Light Blue
3	Midnight	Black	Black

Creating the Shoes Table

The Shoes table contains details of the products that are produced by the shoe company. To create the table, replace the text in the editor window with the SQL shown in Listing 17-4 and then right-click and select Execute from the pop-up menu.

Listing 17-4. Creating and Populating the Shoes Table

```
CREATE TABLE Shoes (
        Id bigint IDENTITY(1,1) NOT NULL,
        Name nvarchar(max) NOT NULL,
        ColorId bigint NOT NULL,
        Price decimal(18, 2) NOT NULL,
 CONSTRAINT PK_Shoes PRIMARY KEY (Id ),
 CONSTRAINT FK_Shoes_Colors FOREIGN KEY(ColorId) REFERENCES dbo.Colors (Id))

SET IDENTITY_INSERT dbo.Shoes ON
INSERT dbo.Shoes (Id, Name, ColorId, Price)
        VALUES (1, N'Road Rocket', 2, 145.0000),
                (2, N'Trail Blazer', 4, 150.0000),
                (3, N'All Terrain Monster', 3, 250.0000),
                (4, N'Track Star', 1, 120.0000)
SET IDENTITY_INSERT dbo.Shoes OFF
GO
```

The CREATE TABLE command creates a table with Id, Name, ColorId, and Price columns. The Id column holds the primary keys, and there is a foreign key relationship between the ColorId column and the Id column of the Colors table.

To ensure that the Shoes table has been created and populated correctly, replace the contents of the editor window with the query shown in Listing 17-5.

Listing 17-5. Querying the Shoes Table

```
SELECT * FROM Shoes
```

Right-click in the editor window and select Execute from the pop-up menu, and you should see the output in Table 17-5, reflecting the structure and contents of the Shoes table.

Table 17-5. The Structure and Data of the Shoes Table

Id	Name	ColorId	Price
1	Road Rocket	2	145.00
2	Trail Blazer	4	150.00
3	All Terrain Monster	3	250.00
4	Track Star	1	120.00

Creating the SalesCampaigns Table

The SalesCampaigns table has a one-to-one relationship with the Shoes table and contains details of the sales campaign associated with each shoe product, where the Shoes table is the principal entity in the relationship. To create and populate the table, replace the contents of the editor with the SQL shown in Listing 17-6. Right-click in the editor window and select Execute from the pop-up menu to create and populate the table.

Listing 17-6. Creating and Populating the SalesCampaigns Table

```
CREATE TABLE SalesCampaigns(
        Id bigint IDENTITY(1,1) NOT NULL,
        Slogan nvarchar(max) NULL,
        MaxDiscount int NULL,
        LaunchDate date NULL,
        ShoeId bigint NOT NULL,
 CONSTRAINT PK_SalesCampaigns PRIMARY KEY (Id),
 CONSTRAINT FK_SalesCampaigns_Shoes FOREIGN KEY(ShoeId)
        REFERENCES dbo.Shoes (Id),
 INDEX IX_SalesCampaigns_ShoeId UNIQUE (ShoeId))

SET IDENTITY_INSERT dbo.SalesCampaigns ON
INSERT dbo.SalesCampaigns (Id, Slogan, MaxDiscount,
        LaunchDate, ShoeId) VALUES
        (1, N'Jet-Powered Shoes for the Win!', 20, CAST(N'2019-01-01' AS Date), 1),
        (2, N'"Blaze" a Trail with Side-Mounted Flame Throwers ',
                15, CAST(N'2019-05-03' AS Date), 2),
        (3, N'All Surfaces. All Weathers. Victory Guaranteed.',
```

```
              5, CAST(N'2020-01-01' AS Date), 3),
        (4, N'Contains an Actual Star to Dazzle Competitors',
              25, CAST(N'2020-01-01' AS Date), 4)
SET IDENTITY_INSERT dbo.SalesCampaigns OFF
GO
```

The SalesCampaigns table has Id, Slogan, MaxDiscount, LauchDate, and ShoeId columns. The Id column is used to store primary keys, and the ShoeId column is a foreign key column that stores values from the Id column of the Shoes table. There is also an index that requires unique values on the ShoeId column and enforces the one-to-one relationship with the Shoes table.

To ensure that the table has been created and populated correctly, replace the contents of the editor window with the query shown in Listing 17-7.

Listing 17-7. Querying the SalesCampaigns Table

```
select * from SalesCampaigns
```

Right-click in the editor window and select Execute from the pop-up menu, and you should see the output in Table 17-6, reflecting the structure and contents of the table.

Table 17-6. The Structure and Data of the SalesCampaigns Table

Id	Slogan	MaxDiscount	LaunchDate	ShoeId
1	Jet-Powered Shoes for the Win!	20	2019-01-01	1
2	"Blaze" a Trail with Side-Mounted Flame Throwers	15	2019-05-03	2
3	All Surfaces. All Weathers. Victory Guaranteed.	5	2020-01-01	3
4	Contains an Actual Star to Dazzle Competitors	25	2020-01-01	4

Creating the Categories and ShoeCategoryJunction Tables

To complete the database, I am going to create the Categories table and the ShoeCategoryJunction table that will allow a many-to-many relationship with the Shoes table. To create and populate these tables, replace the contents of the editor window with the SQL that is shown in Listing 17-8. Right-click in the editor window and select Execute to perform the actions specified by the SQL commands.

Listing 17-8. Creating the Categories and ShoeCategoryJunction Tables

```
CREATE TABLE Categories(
        Id bigint IDENTITY(1,1) NOT NULL,
        Name nvarchar(max) NOT NULL,
 CONSTRAINT PK_Categories PRIMARY KEY (id));

SET IDENTITY_INSERT dbo.Categories ON
INSERT dbo.Categories (Id, Name) VALUES
        (1, N'Road/Tarmac'), (2, N'Track'), (3, N'Trail'), (4, N'Road to Trail')
SET IDENTITY_INSERT dbo.Categories OFF
GO
```

409

```
CREATE TABLE ShoeCategoryJunction(
        Id bigint IDENTITY(1,1) NOT NULL,
        ShoeId bigint NOT NULL,
        CategoryId bigint NOT NULL,
 CONSTRAINT PK_ShoeCategoryJunction PRIMARY KEY (Id),
 CONSTRAINT FK_ShoeCategoryJunction_Categories FOREIGN KEY(CategoryId)
        REFERENCES dbo.Categories (Id),
CONSTRAINT FK_ShoeCategoryJunction_Shoes FOREIGN KEY(ShoeId)
        REFERENCES dbo.Shoes (Id))

SET IDENTITY_INSERT dbo.ShoeCategoryJunction ON
INSERT dbo.ShoeCategoryJunction (Id, ShoeId, CategoryId)
        VALUES (1, 1, 1), (2, 2, 3), (3, 2, 4), (4, 3, 1),
            (5, 3, 2), (6, 3, 3), (7, 3, 4), (8, 4, 2)
SET IDENTITY_INSERT dbo.ShoeCategoryJunction OFF
GO
```

The Categories table has Id and Name columns, with the Id column used for primary keys. The ShoeCategoryJunction has Id, ShoeId, and CategoryId columns, with the Id column used for primary keys and the other columns used for foreign key relationships with the Shoes and Categories tables. This is the same approach to handling many-to-many relationships that I described in Chapter 16.

To ensure that the table has been created and populated correctly, replace the contents of the editor window with the query shown in Listing 17-9.

Listing 17-9. Querying the Categories and ShoeCategoryJunction Tables

```
SELECT * FROM Categories
INNER JOIN ShoeCategoryJunction
ON Categories.Id = ShoeCategoryJunction.ShoeId
```

Right-click in the editor window and select Execute from the pop-up menu, and you should see the output in Table 17-7, which combines the structure and content of the two tables.

Table 17-7. *The Structure and Data for the Categories and ShoeCategoryJunction Tables*

Id	Name	Id	ShoeId	CategoryId
1	Road/Tarmac	1	1	1
2	Track	2	2	3
2	Track	3	2	4
3	Trail	4	3	1
3	Trail	5	3	2
3	Trail	6	3	3
3	Trail	7	3	4
4	Road to Trail	8	4	2

Creating the ASP.NET Core MVC Project

In addition to the database, I need an ASP.NET Core MVC project so that I can demonstrate how Entity Framework Core can be used with an existing database. To create the project, select New ➤ Project from the Visual Studio File menu, select the ASP.NET Core Web Application template, and set the name of the project to be ExistingDb, as shown in Figure 17-2. (You will be prompted to save the contents of the SQL editor window. As long as you received the expected results for each query, you won't need the SQL statements again.) Click the OK button to proceed with the project creation process.

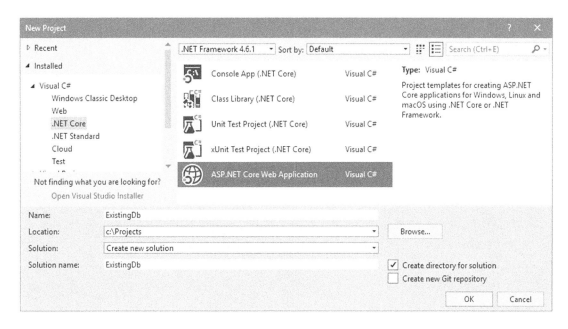

Figure 17-2. *Creating the new ASP.NET Core MVC project*

Ensure that .NET Core and ASP.NET Core 2.0 are selected in the menu at the top of the window and select the Empty project template, as shown in Figure 17-3. Click the OK button to complete the configuration process and create the new project.

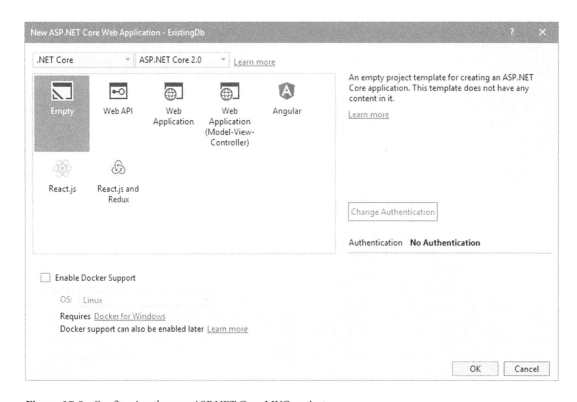

Figure 17-3. *Configuring the new ASP.NET Core MVC project*

Adding the Tools NuGet Package

The metapackage that Visual Studio adds to new projects contains the ASP.NET Core MVC and Entity Framework Core functionality, but a manual addition is required to set up the Entity Framework Core command-line tools. Right-click the ExistingDb project item in the Solution Explorer, select Edit ExistingDb. csproj from the pop-up menu, and add the configuration element shown in Listing 17-10.

Listing 17-10. Adding the Tools Package in the ExistingDb.csproj File in the ExistingDb Folder

```
<Project Sdk="Microsoft.NET.Sdk.Web">

  <PropertyGroup>
    <TargetFramework>netcoreapp2.0</TargetFramework>
  </PropertyGroup>

  <ItemGroup>
    <Folder Include="wwwroot\" />
  </ItemGroup>
```

```
  <ItemGroup>
    <PackageReference Include="Microsoft.AspNetCore.All" Version="2.0.5" />
    <DotNetCliToolReference Include="Microsoft.EntityFrameworkCore.Tools.DotNet"
        Version="2.0.0"    />
  </ItemGroup>

</Project>
```

Save the file, and the package will be downloaded and installed, providing the project with the command-line tools that are required for the examples in this chapter.

Configuring ASP.NET Core Middleware and Services

The Empty project template requires configuration to set up the middleware and services in the `Startup` class required for an MVC application, as shown in Listing 17-11.

Listing 17-11. Configuring Middleware and Services in the Startup.cs File in the ExistingDb Folder

```
using System;
using System.Collections.Generic;
using System.Linq;
using System.Threading.Tasks;
using Microsoft.AspNetCore.Builder;
using Microsoft.AspNetCore.Hosting;
using Microsoft.AspNetCore.Http;
using Microsoft.Extensions.DependencyInjection;

namespace ExistingDb {
    public class Startup {

        public void ConfigureServices(IServiceCollection services) {
            services.AddMvc();
        }

        public void Configure(IApplicationBuilder app, IHostingEnvironment env) {
            app.UseDeveloperExceptionPage();
            app.UseStatusCodePages();
            app.UseStaticFiles();
            app.UseMvcWithDefaultRoute();
        }
    }
}
```

I have not added any configuration statements for Entity Framework Core. I'll set up the services required to work with the database later in the chapter.

Adding a Controller and View and Installing Bootstrap

The final preparation for this chapter is to create a simple controller and view so that the application can be tested and to install the Bootstrap CSS package so that I can easily style the HTML content displayed to the user. For the controller, I created the Controllers folder and added to it a class file called HomeController. cs, with the content shown in Listing 17-12.

Listing 17-12. The Contents of the HomeController.cs File in the Controllers Folder

```
using Microsoft.AspNetCore.Mvc;

namespace ExistingDb.Controllers {

    public class HomeController : Controller {

        public IActionResult Index() {
            return View();
        }
    }
}
```

I will build on this controller later in the chapter, but at the moment there is one action method that selects the default view. To create the view, I created the Views/Home folder and added to it a file called Index.cshtml, to which I added the content shown in Listing 17-13.

Listing 17-13. The Contents of the Index.cshtml File in the Views/Home Folder

```
@{
    ViewData["Title"] = "Existing Database";
    Layout = "_Layout";
}

<h2 class="bg-info p-1 m-1 text-white">Placeholder for Data</h2>
```

To provide a shared layout for the views in the example application, I created the Views/Shared folder and added to it a file called _Layout.cshtml with the content shown in Listing 17-14.

Listing 17-14. The Contents of the _Layout.cshtml File in the Views/Shared Folder

```
<!DOCTYPE html>
<html>
<head>
    <meta name="viewport" content="width=device-width" />
    <title>@ViewData["Title"]</title>
    <link rel="stylesheet" href="~/lib/bootstrap/dist/css/bootstrap.min.css" />
</head>
<body>
    <div class="p-2">
        @RenderBody()
    </div>
</body>
</html>
```

To install the Bootstrap CSS package, I used the the JSON File template (found in the ASP.NET Core ➤ Web ➤ General category) to create a file called .bowerrc with the content shown in Listing 17-15. (It is important to pay attention to this file name: it starts with a period, contains the letter r twice and has no file extension).

Listing 17-15. The Contents of the .bowerrc File in the ExistingDb Folder

```
{
  "directory": "wwwroot/lib"
}
```

I used the JSON File template again to create a file called bower.json, with the content shown in Listing 4-9.

Listing 17-16. The Contents of the bower.json File in the ExistingDb Folder

```
{
  "name": "asp.net",
  "private": true,
  "dependencies": {
    "bootstrap": "4.0.0"
  }
}
```

When you save the changes to the file, the Bootstrap package will be downloaded and installed in the wwwroot/lib folder.

Testing the Example Application

To simplify the process of working with the application, edit the Properties/launchSettings.json file and change the two URLs that it contains so they both specify port 5000, as shown in Listing 17-17. This is the port that I will use in the URLs to demonstrate different features of the example application.

Listing 17-17. Changing Ports in the launchSettings.json File in the Properties Folder

```
{
  "iisSettings": {
    "windowsAuthentication": false,
    "anonymousAuthentication": true,
    "iisExpress": {
      "applicationUrl": "http://localhost:5000/",
      "sslPort": 0
    }
  },
  "profiles": {
    "IIS Express": {
      "commandName": "IISExpress",
      "launchBrowser": true,
      "environmentVariables": {
        "ASPNETCORE_ENVIRONMENT": "Development"
      }
    },
    "ExistingDb": {
```

```
      "commandName": "Project",
      "launchBrowser": true,
      "environmentVariables": {
        "ASPNETCORE_ENVIRONMENT": "Development"
      },
      "applicationUrl": "http://localhost:5000/"
    }
  }
}
```

Start the application using `dotnet run` in the `ExistingDb` project folder and use a browser to navigate to `http://localhost:5000` to see the placeholder content, as shown in Figure 17-4.

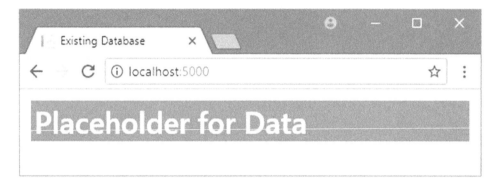

Figure 17-4. *Running the example application*

Scaffolding an Existing Database

The easiest way to work with an existing database is to use the Entity Framework Core scaffolding feature, which inspects a database and creates the context and model classes required to perform queries and other data operations.

Even if you create a data model for an existing database manually, as I describe in Chapter 18, it can still be worth using the scaffolding feature to make sure that the description of the database that you have been provided is correct. In the sections that follow, I show you how to use the scaffolding feature and explain how to use the data model it creates in an ASP.NET Core MVC application.

Performing the Scaffold Process

The scaffolding process is performed using a command-line tool contained in the package added to the example project in Listing 17-10. Run the command shown in Listing 17-18 in the `ExistingDb` project folder to inspect the example database and generate a data model.

■ **Tip** The layout of the page makes it difficult to show complex commands, but you must take care to enter all parts of Listing 17-18 into a single line in the command prompt.

Listing 17-18. Scaffolding an Existing Database

```
dotnet ef dbcontext scaffold "Server=(localdb)\MSSQLLocalDB;Database=ZoomShoesDb"
"Microsoft.EntityFrameworkCore.SqlServer" --output-dir "Models/Scaffold" --context
ScaffoldContext
```

The basic command is `dotnet ef dbcontext scaffold`, which runs the scaffolding process. The first two arguments are required and provide the connection string for the database that is to be modeled and the name of the database provider. There are two optional arguments in Listing 17-18: the `--output-dir` argument specifies the directory (and namespace) for the C# classes generated by the scaffolding process, and the `--context` argument specifies the name of the context class used to access the database.

DEALING WITH PROBLEM DATABASES

The scaffolding process that results from the command in Listing 17-18 is seamless because the example database is simple and created specifically for this chapter. When you scaffold a real database, it is important to keep a close eye on the output from the `dotnet ef` command because this is where any problem will be reported.

Some issues will just be warnings, where some aspect of the database cannot be mapped cleanly into Entity Framework Core, resulting in a compromise in the data model that is created. But there can also be showstoppers where Entity Framework Core doesn't know how to proceed. For these situations, you can either model the database manually, as described in Chapter 18, or restrict the scope of the scaffolding process by using the `--table` argument to select the tables that you want to work with and exclude those that cause problems.

In Listing 17-18, I provided the connection string for the example database created at the start of the chapter and selected the SQL Server provider. The optional arguments specify that the data model classes should be placed in the `Models/Scaffold` folder and that the context class should be called `ScaffoldContext`.

The command will take a moment to run. When it is complete, you will see that a `Models/Scaffold` folder is shown in the Solution Explorer, containing a class that represents each table in the database, along with a context class called `ScaffoldContext`.

Each class that has been generated by the scaffolding process follows roughly the same style that I described in earlier chapters. For example, here are the contents of the `Shoes.cs` file, which will be used to represent rows of data from the Shoes table in the database:

```
using System;
using System.Collections.Generic;

namespace ExistingDb.Models.Scaffold {

    public partial class Shoes {

        public Shoes() {
            ShoeCategoryJunction = new HashSet<ShoeCategoryJunction>();
        }
```

```
        public long Id { get; set; }
        public string Name { get; set; }
        public long ColorId { get; set; }
        public decimal Price { get; set; }

        public Colors Color { get; set; }
        public SalesCampaigns SalesCampaigns { get; set; }
        public ICollection<ShoeCategoryJunction> ShoeCategoryJunction { get; set; }
    }
}
```

You can see how this class matches up with the ones created in earlier chapters. The Id, Name, ColorId, and Price properties correspond to the columns added to the Shoes table. The Color, SalesCampaigns, and ShoeCategoryJunction properties allow navigation to related data, corresponding to the relationships between the tables in the database.

There are some small differences. The class name, for example, is Shoes because the scaffolding process uses the names of the database table. And the constructor initializes the collection for the ShoeCategoryJunction property, which is something that I omitted in earlier chapters, preferring to deal with null values when there is no data available, rather than an empty collection.

The scaffolding process also creates a context class, which has DbSet<T> properties for each of the tables in the database. The context also overrides the OnConfiguring and OnModelCreating methods, which were not required in earlier chapters. Here are the contents of the ScaffoldContext.cs file, with some of the statements from the OnModelCreating method removed for brevity:

```
using System;
using Microsoft.EntityFrameworkCore;
using Microsoft.EntityFrameworkCore.Metadata;

namespace ExistingDb.Models.Scaffold {

    public partial class ScaffoldContext : DbContext {

        public virtual DbSet<Categories> Categories { get; set; }
        public virtual DbSet<Colors> Colors { get; set; }
        public virtual DbSet<SalesCampaigns> SalesCampaigns { get; set; }
        public virtual DbSet<ShoeCategoryJunction> ShoeCategoryJunction { get; set; }
        public virtual DbSet<Shoes> Shoes { get; set; }

        protected override void OnConfiguring(DbContextOptionsBuilder
                optionsBuilder) {
            if (!optionsBuilder.IsConfigured) {
                optionsBuilder.UseSqlServer(
                    @"Server=(localdb)\MSSQLLocalDB;Database=ZoomShoesDb");
            }
        }

        protected override void OnModelCreating(ModelBuilder modelBuilder) {
```

```
        // ...statements omitted for brevity...

        modelBuilder.Entity<Shoes>(entity => {
            entity.Property(e => e.Name).IsRequired();

            entity.HasOne(d => d.Color)
                .WithMany(p => p.Shoes)
                .HasForeignKey(d => d.ColorId)
                .OnDelete(DeleteBehavior.ClientSetNull)
                .HasConstraintName("FK_Shoes_Colors");
        });
    }
  }
}
```

The functionality provided by the code in these methods was elsewhere in earlier chapters. The OnConfiguring method contains the connection string for the database, which is defined in a settings file in ASP.NET Core MVC projects. The OnModelCreating method contains the statements that create the mapping between the database and the data model classes, and these statements were part of the snapshot class created by migrations. I'll move the connection string to its normal location shortly, and I explain the purpose of the statements in the OnModelCreating method in Chapter 18.

Using a Scaffolded Data Model in the ASP.NET Core MVC

Once you have created the data model, it can be used in an ASP.NET Core MVC with just a few changes, as I describe in the sections that follow.

Creating the Configuration File

The first step is to create a configuration file to contain the connection string that the scaffolding process put into the context class (and which won't work for ASP.NET Core MVC applications). I used the ASP.NET Configuration File item template to add a file called appsettings.json to the project and make the changes shown in Listing 17-19.

Listing 17-19. The Contents of the appsettings.json File in the ExistingDb Folder

```
{
  "ConnectionStrings": {
    "DefaultConnection": "Server=(localdb)\\MSSQLLocalDB;Database=ZoomShoesDb;MultipleActiv
eResultSets=true"
  },
  "Logging": {
    "LogLevel": {
      "Default": "None",
      "Microsoft.EntityFrameworkCore": "Information"
    }
  }
}
```

In addition to changing the connection string, I have added the Logging configuration section so that Entity Framework Core will display details of the queries it sends to the database server. The logging changes are not required to get the data model working but are useful so that you can see how Entity Framework Core works with the database.

Updating the Context Class

The context class created by the scaffolding process must be modified before it can be used with the rest of the ASP.NET Core MVC application. Remove or comment out the OnConfiguring method and replace it with a constructor that accepts its configuration options through dependency injection, as shown in Listing 17-20.

Listing 17-20. Updating the Context in the ScaffoldContext.cs File in the Models/Scaffold Folder

```
using System;
using Microsoft.EntityFrameworkCore;
using Microsoft.EntityFrameworkCore.Metadata;

namespace ExistingDb.Models.Scaffold {

    public partial class ScaffoldContext : DbContext {

        public virtual DbSet<Categories> Categories { get; set; }
        public virtual DbSet<Colors> Colors { get; set; }
        public virtual DbSet<SalesCampaigns> SalesCampaigns { get; set; }
        public virtual DbSet<ShoeCategoryJunction> ShoeCategoryJunction { get; set; }
        public virtual DbSet<Shoes> Shoes { get; set; }

        public ScaffoldContext(DbContextOptions<ScaffoldContext> options)
            : base(options) { }

        //protected override void OnConfiguring(DbContextOptionsBuilder
        //        optionsBuilder) {
        //    if (!optionsBuilder.IsConfigured) {
        //        optionsBuilder.UseSqlServer
        //            (@"Server=(localdb)\MSSQLLocalDB;Database=ZoomShoesDb");
        //    }
        //}

        protected override void OnModelCreating(ModelBuilder modelBuilder) {

            // ...statements omitted for brevity...

        }
    }
}
```

Registering Middleware and Services

The scaffolding process doesn't configure Entity Framework Core for use with ASP.NET Core MVC or register the context class as a service for dependency injection. To get the different parts of the application working together, I add the statements shown in Listing 17-21 to the Startup class.

Listing 17-21. Configuring the Application in the Startup.cs File in the ExistingDb Folder

```
using System;
using System.Collections.Generic;
using System.Linq;
using System.Threading.Tasks;
using Microsoft.AspNetCore.Builder;
using Microsoft.AspNetCore.Hosting;
using Microsoft.AspNetCore.Http;
using Microsoft.Extensions.DependencyInjection;
using Microsoft.Extensions.Configuration;
using ExistingDb.Models.Scaffold;
using Microsoft.EntityFrameworkCore;

namespace ExistingDb {
    public class Startup {

        public Startup(IConfiguration config) => Configuration = config;

        public IConfiguration Configuration { get; }

        public void ConfigureServices(IServiceCollection services) {
            services.AddMvc();
            string conString = Configuration["ConnectionStrings:DefaultConnection"];
            services.AddDbContext<ScaffoldContext>(options =>
                options.UseSqlServer(conString));
        }

        public void Configure(IApplicationBuilder app, IHostingEnvironment env) {
            app.UseDeveloperExceptionPage();
            app.UseStatusCodePages();
            app.UseStaticFiles();
            app.UseMvcWithDefaultRoute();
        }
    }
}
```

Updating the Controller and View

The rest of the application is ready, and all that remains is to update the controller so that it gets the data from the database and displays it to the user. In Listing 17-22, I have added statements to the Home controller that query the database for data. I am only going to add some basic features because I am going make changes to the data model and I don't want to have to work every change through multiple action methods and views.

Listing 17-22. Querying for Data in the HomeController.cs File in the Controllers Folder

```
using Microsoft.AspNetCore.Mvc;
using ExistingDb.Models.Scaffold;
using Microsoft.EntityFrameworkCore;

namespace ExistingDb.Controllers {

    public class HomeController : Controller {
        private ScaffoldContext context;

        public HomeController(ScaffoldContext ctx) => context = ctx;

        public IActionResult Index() {
            return View(context.Shoes
                .Include(s => s.Color)
                .Include(s => s.SalesCampaigns)
                .Include(s => s.ShoeCategoryJunction)
                    .ThenInclude(junct => junct.Category));
        }
    }
}
```

Working with a scaffolding data model is just the same as using one that has been created with a migration. In Listing 17-22, I have queried the database using the Shoes property defined by the context class and followed the navigation properties to the related data with the Include and ThenInclude methods.

To enable the ASP.NET Core MVC tag helpers and provide easy access to the model classes in views, I added a file called _ViewImports.cshtml in the Views folder with the content shown in Listing 17-23.

Listing 17-23. The Contents of the _ViewImports.cshtml File in the Views Folder

```
@using ExistingDb.Models.Scaffold
@addTagHelper *, Microsoft.AspNetCore.Mvc.TagHelpers
```

To display the data to the user, I replace the contents of the Index.cshtml file in the Views/Home folder with the elements shown in Listing 17-24.

Listing 17-24. Displaying Data in the Index.cshtml File in the Views/Home Folder

```
@model IEnumerable<Shoes>
@{
    ViewData["Title"] = "Existing Database";
    Layout = "_Layout";
}

<div class="container-fluid">
    <h4 class="bg-primary p-3 text-white">Zoom Shoes</h4>
    <table class="table table-striped">
        <thead>
            <tr>
                <th>Name</th><th>Price</th><th>Color</th>
                <th>Slogan</th><th>Categories</th>
```

```
            </tr>
        </thead>
        <tbody>
            @foreach (Shoes s in Model) {
                <tr>
                    <td>@s.Name</td>
                    <td>$@s.Price.ToString("F2")</td>
                    <td>@s.Color.Name</td>
                    <td>@s.SalesCampaigns?.Slogan</td>
                    <td>
                        @String.Join(", ", s.ShoeCategoryJunction
                    .Select(j => j.Category.Name))
                    </td>
                </tr>
            }
        </tbody>
    </table>
</div>
```

Start the application using `dotnet run` and navigate to `http://localhost:5000`; you will see a table containing details of the data in the database, accessed through the data model created using the scaffolding process, as shown in Figure 17-5.

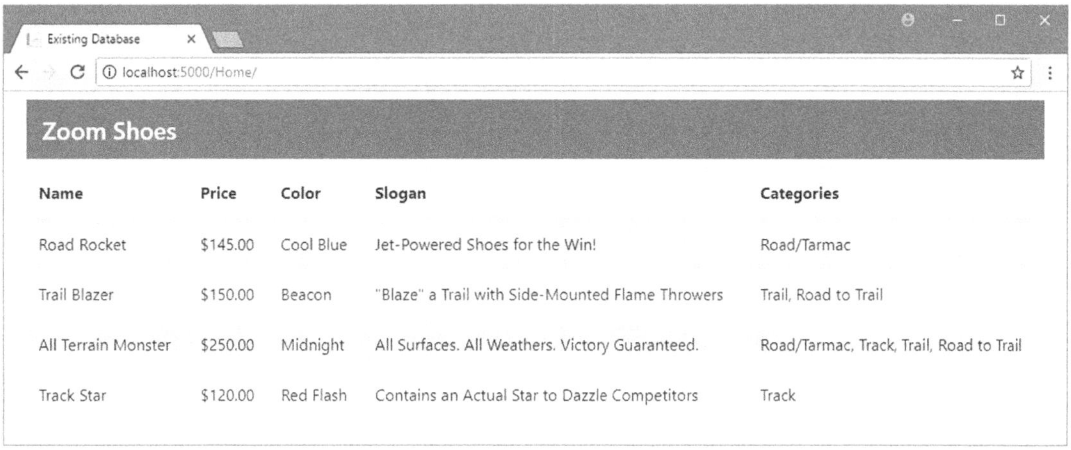

Figure 17-5. *Using a scaffolded data model*

Responding to Database Changes

If you don't have sole use of an existing database, you may have to respond to changes that are made for the benefit of other applications. In the sections that follow, I simulate a change to the database and demonstrate how to update the scaffolded data model to accommodate the change in the application.

Modifying the Database

To simulate a change to the database, select Tools ➤ SQL Server ➤ New Query and connect to the database using the steps described at the start of this chapter. Paste the SQL shown in Listing 17-25 into the editor, right-click, and select Execute from the pop-up menu.

■ **Tip** If you want to reset the database, then you can execute the SQL statements in Listings 17-1 to 17-6. (This process is easier if you download the project for this chapter from the GitHub repository, which contains SQL files that contain all of the require statements.)

Listing 17-25. Changing the Database

```
USE ZoomShoesDb

CREATE TABLE Fittings (
        Id bigint IDENTITY(1,1) NOT NULL,
        Name nvarchar(max) NOT NULL,
CONSTRAINT PK_Fittings PRIMARY KEY (Id));
GO

SET IDENTITY_INSERT Fittings ON
INSERT Fittings (Id, Name)
        VALUES (1, N'Narrow'),
                        (2, N'Standard'),
                        (3, N'Wide'),
                        (4, N'Big Foot')
SET IDENTITY_INSERT Fittings OFF
GO

ALTER TABLE Shoes
    ADD FittingId bigint
ALTER TABLE Shoes
    ADD CONSTRAINT FK_Shoes_Fittings FOREIGN KEY(FittingId) REFERENCES Fittings (Id)
GO

UPDATE Shoes SET FittingId = 2
GO

SELECT * from Shoes
```

These statements add a `Fittings` table and add a foreign key property on the `Shoes` table that references the primary key column of the new table. The final statement queries the table to show the effect of the change and will produce the data shown in Table 17-8.

Table 17-8. *The Effect of Adding a Column to the Shoes Table*

Id	Name	ColorId	Price	FittingId
1	Road Rocket	2	145.00	2
2	Trail Blazer	4	150.00	2
3	All Terrain Monster	3	250.00	2
4	Track Star	1	120.00	2

This type of change causes problems for the ASP.NET Core MVC application because the data model doesn't have any representation of the `OutOfStock` column. Queries of the `Shoes` database won't contain all of the data in the table, and the application won't be able to store new objects in the `Shoes` table because the required value for the `OutOfStock` column will be missing.

Updating the Data Model

Updating the data model to reflect the change in the database means repeating the scaffolding process. Run the command shown in Listing 17-26 in the `ExistingDb` project folder, ensuring that you include the two additional arguments shown in bold.

Listing 17-26. Updating the Data Model

```
dotnet ef dbcontext scaffold "Server=(localdb)\MSSQLLocalDB;Database=ZoomShoesDb"
"Microsoft.EntityFrameworkCore.SqlServer" --output-dir "Models/Scaffold" --context
ScaffoldContext --force --no-build
```

The `--force` argument tells Entity Framework Core to replace the existing data model classes with new ones. The `--no-build` argument prevents the project from being built before the scaffolding process is performed. It is easy to get into a situation where the scaffolding process generates a data model that is out of sync with the rest of the application, such as controllers and views. Entity Framework Core tries to build the project by default before scaffolding a database, and a failed build—commonly because a property or data model class has been removed—will prevent the scaffolding process from being performed. Using the `--no-build` argument avoids this problem and lets you update the rest of the application once the database has been scaffolded.

Updating the Context Class

The scaffolding process will replace the context class, overwriting the changes required to support an ASP. NET Core MVC application. When the scaffolding process is complete, repeat the process of commenting out the OnConfiguring method and adding a constructor that receives a configuration options argument, as shown in Listing 17-27.

Listing 17-27. Updating the Context in the ScaffoldContext.cs File in the Models/Scaffold Folder

```
using System;
using Microsoft.EntityFrameworkCore;
using Microsoft.EntityFrameworkCore.Metadata;

namespace ExistingDb.Models.Scaffold {
    public partial class ScaffoldContext : DbContext {
        public virtual DbSet<Categories> Categories { get; set; }
        public virtual DbSet<Colors> Colors { get; set; }
        public virtual DbSet<Fittings> Fittings { get; set; }
        public virtual DbSet<SalesCampaigns> SalesCampaigns { get; set; }
        public virtual DbSet<ShoeCategoryJunction> ShoeCategoryJunction { get; set; }
        public virtual DbSet<Shoes> Shoes { get; set; }

        public ScaffoldContext(DbContextOptions<ScaffoldContext> options)
            : base(options) { }

        //protected override void OnConfiguring(DbContextOptionsBuilder
        //      optionsBuilder) {
        //    if (!optionsBuilder.IsConfigured) {
        //        optionsBuilder.UseSqlServer
        //            (@"Server=(localdb)\MSSQLLocalDB;Database=ZoomShoesDb");
        //    }
        //}

        protected override void OnModelCreating(ModelBuilder modelBuilder) {

            // ...statements omitted for brevity...
        }
    }
}
```

Updating the Controllers and Views

Depending on the changes to the database, you will also have to update the rest of the project to ensure that the application works correctly. For the example application, that means updating the Home controller to follow the new navigation property added to the Shoes class to include the related data in its queries and updating the view to display that data. Listing 17-28 shows the change to the controller.

Listing 17-28. Following a New Navigation Property in the HomeController.cs File in the Controllers Folder

```
using Microsoft.AspNetCore.Mvc;
using ExistingDb.Models.Scaffold;
using Microsoft.EntityFrameworkCore;

namespace ExistingDb.Controllers {

    public class HomeController : Controller {
        private ScaffoldContext context;

        public HomeController(ScaffoldContext ctx) => context = ctx;

        public IActionResult Index() {
            return View(context.Shoes
                .Include(s => s.Color)
                .Include(s => s.SalesCampaigns)
                .Include(s => s.ShoeCategoryJunction)
                    .ThenInclude(junct => junct.Category)
                .Include(s => s.Fitting));
        }
    }
}
```

To display the additional data to the user, Listing 17-29 adds a column to the table in the Index.cshtml view.

Listing 17-29. Displaying Additional Data in the Index.cshtml File in the Views/Home Folder

```
@model IEnumerable<Shoes>
@{
    ViewData["Title"] = "Existing Database";
    Layout = "_Layout";
}

<div class="container-fluid">
    <h4 class="bg-primary p-3 text-white">Zoom Shoes</h4>
    <table class="table table-striped">
        <thead>
            <tr>
                <th>Name</th>
                <th>Price</th>
                <th>Color</th>
                <th>Slogan</th>
                <th>Categories</th>
                <th>Fitting</th>
            </tr>
        </thead>
        <tbody>
            @foreach (Shoes s in Model) {
                <tr>
                    <td>@s.Name</td>
```

```
            <td>$@s.Price.ToString("F2")</td>
            <td>@s.Color.Name</td>
            <td>@s.SalesCampaigns?.Slogan</td>
            <td>
                @String.Join(", ", s.ShoeCategoryJunction
            .Select(j => j.Category.Name))
            </td>
            <td>@s.Fitting.Name</td>
        </tr>
    }
    </tbody>
</table>
</div>
```

To see the effect of the database change, start the application using `dotnet run` and navigate to `http://localhost:5000`, which will produce the result shown in Figure 17-6.

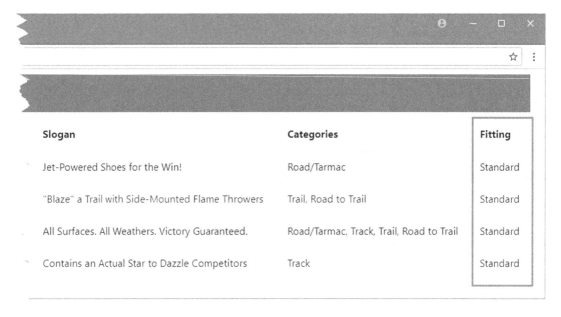

Figure 17-6. *Displaying data from the updated database*

Adding Persistent Data Model Features

Many data models are simply classes that act as collections of data and navigation properties to represent the data in the database. But some applications require additional code in the data model classes to perform tasks such as validation or to synthesize data that isn't available in the database. Re-creating the data model each time the database changes can present a problem because the model classes are overwritten, meaning that any additional logic will be lost.

To address this, Entity Framework Core creates partial classes when it creates the data model during the scaffolding process. As an example, here is the definition of the Shoes class that Entity Framework Core created:

```
...
public partial class Shoes {
...
```

Partial classes can be defined in multiple files, which allows any additional logic required by the application to be defined separately from the file created by the scaffolding process and ensures that it will survive changes in the database. To demonstrate how this works, I created the Models/Logic folder and added to it a class file called Shoes.cs with the code shown in Listing 17-30.

Listing 17-30. The Contents of the Shoes.cs File in the Models/Logic Folder

```
namespace ExistingDb.Models.Scaffold {

    public partial class Shoes {

        public decimal PriceIncTax => this.Price * 1.2m;
    }
}
```

The different parts of a partial class must be defined in the same namespace, which is why this class is in the ExistingDb.Models.Scaffold namespace, even though the class file is in the Logic folder. One part of a partial class can access the members of the other parts, which means that the PriceIncTax property is able to read the value of the Price property.

■ **Caution**   Defining additional logic for model classes in a partial class means that the code will not be affected when the data model is re-created, but you must still ensure the code remains useful and accurate following a database change.

In Listing 17-31, I have updated the view that displays the data to use the property defined in Listing 17-30.

Listing 17-31. Using a Partial Class Property in the Index.cshtml File in the Views/Home Folder

```
...
<tbody>
    @foreach (Shoes s in Model) {
        <tr>
            <td>@s.Name</td>
            <td>$@s.PriceIncTax.ToString("F2")</td>
            <td>@s.Color.Name</td>
            <td>@s.SalesCampaigns?.Slogan</td>
            <td>
```

```
            @String.Join(", ", s.ShoeCategoryJunction
        .Select(j => j.Category.Name))
        </td>
        <td>@s.Fitting.Name</td>
    </tr>
}
</tbody>
...
```

To see the effect of the additional logic, start the application with `dotnet run` and navigate to `http://localhost:5000`, which will show the prices with a 20 percent increase for tax, as illustrated by Figure 17-7.

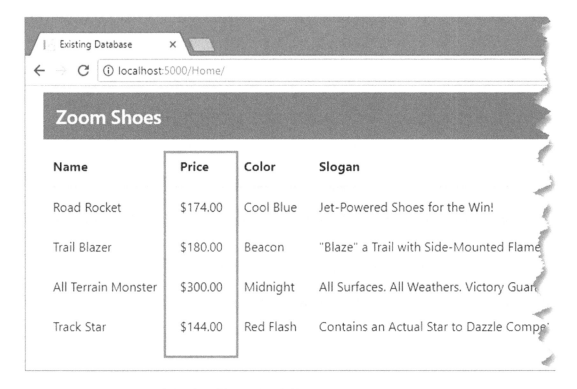

Figure 17-7. *Using a partial class for additional model logic*

Summary

In this chapter, I showed you how to use an existing database by using the Entity Framework Core scaffolding feature, which inspects the database and creates the context and entity classes required to use it. This is a useful feature for simple databases, but it can be more difficult to use in more complex projects. In the next chapter, I show you to create the data model manually, rather than relying on the scaffolding process.

CHAPTER 18

Manually Modeling a Database

In Chapter 17, I used the scaffolding process to automatically create a data model for an existing database. The scaffolding process is convenient, but it doesn't provide much in the way of fine-grained control, and the result can be awkward to use. In this chapter, I show you how to manually model a database. This process requires more work but produces a data model that is more natural to work with and easier to manage when the database changes. Table 18-1 puts this chapter in context.

Table 18-1. *Putting Manual Database Modeling in Context*

Question	Answer
What is it?	Manual modeling creates a data model for a database without using scaffolding.
Why is it useful?	The scaffolding feature can't always cope with large and complex databases.
How is it used?	The Fluent API is used to configure the data model in the context class.
Are there any pitfalls or limitations?	If you are modeling only part of the database, you must ensure that there are no dependencies on the parts you exclude.
Are there any alternatives?	The only alternative is to use the scaffolding views.

Table 18-2 summarizes the chapter.

Table 18-2. *Chapter Summary*

Problem	Solution	Listing
Manually model a database	Create a context class and use the Fluent API to configure the data model	1–11, 19–32
Manually model a relationship	Define navigation properties and configure the relationships using attributes or Fluent API statements	12–18

A. Freeman, *Pro Entity Framework Core 2 for ASP.NET Core MVC*,
https://doi.org/10.1007/978-1-4842-3435-8_18

Preparing for This Chapter

This chapter uses the ExistingDb project created in Chapter 17 and relies on the database that was created in that chapter. If you have jumped directly to this chapter, you will need to follow the steps outlined at the start of Chapter 17 to create the database that the examples in this chapter rely on.

Tip You can download the project, which contains files with the SQL statements required to create the database, as part of the free source code download for this book, available at `https://github.com/apress/pro-ef-core-2-for-asp.net-core-mvc`.

To ensure that the database has been created and contains the expected data, start the application using `dotnet run` and navigate to `http://localhost:5000`, which will produce the result shown in Figure 18-1.

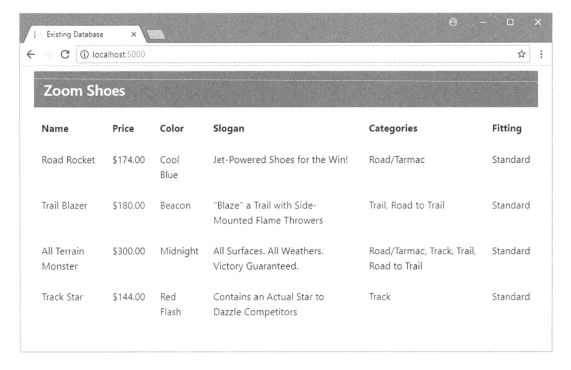

Figure 18-1. *Running the example application*

Creating a Manual Data Model

Before starting to model an existing database, you must understand its schema and know which parts of the database you need for the ASP.NET Core MVC application. Running the scaffolding process described in Chapter 18 can be a useful starting point if you have not been provided with a detailed description of the database and its design, even if you use the scaffolded data model only for reference as you build a model manually.

Creating the Context and Entity Classes

The starting point for a manually created data model is to create a context class. I created a Models/Manual folder and added to it a class file called ManualContext.cs, which I used to define the class shown in Listing 18-1.

Listing 18-1. The Contents of the ManualContext.cs File in the Models/Manual Folder

```
using Microsoft.EntityFrameworkCore;

namespace ExistingDb.Models.Manual {

    public class ManualContext : DbContext {

        public ManualContext(DbContextOptions<ManualContext> options)
            : base(options) { }

        public DbSet<Shoe> Shoes { get; set; }
    }
}
```

The ManualContext class is derived from DbContext, has a constructor that receives a configuration object that is passed on to the superclass constructor, and defines a DbSet<T> property called Shoes that provides access to a collection of Shoe objects. If this seems familiar, it is because you can get a long way toward modeling a database just by following the conventions that have been used in earlier chapters. To define the Shoe class used by the context, I added a class file called Shoe.cs in the Models/Manual folder and added the code shown in Listing 18-2.

Listing 18-2. The Contents of the Shoe.cs File in the Models/Manual Folder

```
namespace ExistingDb.Models.Manual {

    public class Shoe {
        public long Id { get; set; }
        public string Name { get; set; }
        public decimal Price { get; set; }
    }
}
```

The Shoe class contains properties for some of the columns in the Shoes table, although I have not yet created the navigation properties. To make the new context available for use by the rest of the application, I created the service shown in Listing 18-3.

Listing 18-3. Creating a Service in the Startup.cs File in the ExistingDb Folder

```
using System;
using System.Collections.Generic;
using System.Linq;
using System.Threading.Tasks;
using Microsoft.AspNetCore.Builder;
using Microsoft.AspNetCore.Hosting;
using Microsoft.AspNetCore.Http;
using Microsoft.Extensions.DependencyInjection;
```

```
using Microsoft.Extensions.Configuration;
using ExistingDb.Models.Scaffold;
using Microsoft.EntityFrameworkCore;
using ExistingDb.Models.Manual;

namespace ExistingDb {
    public class Startup {

        public Startup(IConfiguration config) => Configuration = config;

        public IConfiguration Configuration { get; }

        public void ConfigureServices(IServiceCollection services) {
            services.AddMvc();
            string conString = Configuration["ConnectionStrings:DefaultConnection"];

            services.AddDbContext<ScaffoldContext>(options =>
                options.UseSqlServer(conString));

            services.AddDbContext<ManualContext>(options =>
                options.UseSqlServer(conString));
        }

        public void Configure(IApplicationBuilder app, IHostingEnvironment env) {
            app.UseDeveloperExceptionPage();
            app.UseStatusCodePages();
            app.UseStaticFiles();
            app.UseMvcWithDefaultRoute();
        }
    }
}
```

The new context uses the same connection string as the context created by the scaffolding process, since both are connecting to the same database.

Creating the Controller and View

To test the initial data model, I created a class file called `ManualController.cs` in the `Controllers` folder and added the code shown in Listing 18-4.

Listing 18-4. The Contents of the ManualController.cs File in the Controllers Folder

```
using ExistingDb.Models.Manual;
using Microsoft.AspNetCore.Mvc;

namespace ExistingDb.Controllers {

    public class ManualController : Controller {
        private ManualContext context;
```

```
        public ManualController(ManualContext ctx) => context = ctx;

        public IActionResult Index() => View(context.Shoes);
    }
}
```

The Index action passes the DbSet<Shoe> object returned by the context's Shoes property to the default view. To provide the action with its view, I created the Views/Manual folder and added to it a view called Index.cshtml with the content shown in Listing 18-5.

Listing 18-5. The Contents of the Index.cshtml File in the Views/Manual Folder

```
@using ExistingDb.Models.Manual
@model IEnumerable<Shoe>
@{
    ViewData["Title"] = "Manual Data Model";
    Layout = "_Layout";
}

<div class="container-fluid">
    <h4 class="bg-primary p-3 text-white">Zoom Shoes</h4>
    <table class="table table-striped table-sm">
        <tr><th>Id</th><th>Name</th><th>Price</th></tr>
        @foreach (Shoe s in Model) {
            <tr>
                <td>@s.Id</td>
                <td>@s.Name</td>
                <td>$@s.Price.ToString("F2")</td>
            </tr>
        }
    </table>
</div>
```

The view displays a table containing the Id, Name, and Price values for each Shoe object in the sequence received from the action method. To test the manual data model, start the application using dotnet run and navigate to http://localhost:5000/manual, which will produce the result shown in Figure 18-2.

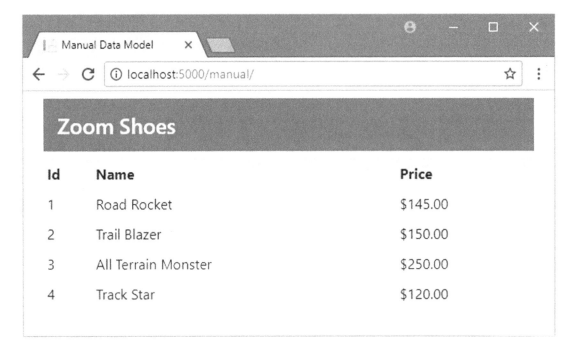

Figure 18-2. *Testing the manual data model*

Understanding the Basic Data Model Conventions

As the previous section showed, it is easy to create a data model manually if you are able to follow the conventions that Entity Framework Core expects. Even in a simple data model like the one I created in the previous section, I relied on several conventions to get the data from the database. I'll explain each of them in due course, but I am going to focus on these most basic conventions:

- The name of the property in the context class corresponds to the name of the database table so that the Shoes property in the context class corresponds to the Shoes table in the database. (If there is no context class property and data is accessed through the Set<T> method, then the name of the entity class is used as the table name.)

- The names of the properties in the entity class correspond to the names of the columns in the database table so that the Id, Name, and Price properties will be used to represent the values in the Id, Name, and Price columns in the Shoes table.

- The primary key will be represented by a property called Id or <Type>Id so that the primary key for the Shoe class will be a property called Id or ShoeId.

These are the conventions that you have already become accustomed to from earlier chapters when migrations were used to create a database from context and entity classes. Entity Framework Core uses the same conventions when working with an existing database, which means that the mapping between objects and the database can be set up without needing any explicit configuration.

Overriding the Data Model Conventions

Entity Framework Core conventions are convenient when the design of the database aligns with what you need in the application. But this rarely happens, especially if you are trying to integrate an existing database into a project. Entity Framework Core provides two different ways in which you can override the conventions so that you can create a data model that suits the ASP.NET Core MVC part of the project while still providing access to the data in the database: attributes and the Fluent API. Attributes are easy to use but don't provide access to the full range of Entity Framework Core features. The Fluent API is more complex but provides greater control over how the data model is mapped to the database. I introduce both approaches in the sections that follow and demonstrate how they can be used to override the three basic conventions described previously.

Using Attributes to Override Data Model Conventions

The basic data model conventions can be overridden using the attributes described in Table 18-3, which are applied to the entity model class.

Table 18-3. *The Attributes for Overriding the Basic Data Model Conventions*

Name	Description
Table	This attribute specifies the database table and overrides the name of the property in the context class.
Column	This attribute specifies the column that provides values for the property it is applied to.
Key	This attribute is used to identify the property that will be assigned the primary key value.

I added a file called Style.cs to the Models/Manual folder and used it to define the class shown in Listing 18-6 to demonstrate how these attributes work.

Listing 18-6. The Contents of the Style.cs File in the Models/Manual Folder

```
using System.ComponentModel.DataAnnotations;
using System.ComponentModel.DataAnnotations.Schema;

namespace ExistingDb.Models.Manual {

    [Table("Colors")]
    public class Style {

        [Key]
        [Column("Id")]
        public long UniqueIdent  { get; set; }

        [Column("Name")]
        public string StyleName { get; set; }

        public string MainColor { get; set; }
        public string HighlightColor { get; set; }
    }
}
```

The Table attribute tells Entity Framework Core that the source of data for this class is the Colors table. I used the Key attribute to specify that the UniqueIdent property should be used for primary key values, along with the Column attribute to ensure that the Id column will be used as the source for those values. I used the Column attribute to tell Entity Framework Core that values for the StyleName property should be assigned values from the Name column.

You only have to apply attributes for the changes you require, which allows me to rely on the conventions for the MainColor and HighlightColor properties, which will be assigned values from the columns of the same name. To complete this example, I added a property to the context class to make accessing the data more convenient, as shown in Listing 18-7.

Listing 18-7. Adding a Convenience Property in the ManualContext.cs File in the Models/Manual Folder

```
using Microsoft.EntityFrameworkCore;

namespace ExistingDb.Models.Manual {

    public class ManualContext : DbContext {

        public ManualContext(DbContextOptions<ManualContext> options)
            : base(options) { }

        public DbSet<Shoe> Shoes { get; set; }

        public DbSet<Style> ShoeStyles { get; set; }
    }
}
```

I'll use this property to access the data in the next section, after I have introduced the Fluent API.

CHOOSING BETWEEN ATTRIBUTES AND THE FLUENT API

The basic data model conventions can be overridden using either attributes or the Fluent API, so you can choose whichever approach feels most natural. Some developers prefer annotating classes with attributes because it is more consistent with how ASP.NET Core MVC features such as validation and authorization work. Other developers prefer to describe the data model in the context class so that all of changes from the regular conventions can be seen and understood in a single place.

There are some advanced features that can be used only through the Fluent API. If you need to use these features to model a database, then you have no choice but to do so using the Fluent API, even if you prefer working with attributes. That said, as this chapter has demonstrated, you can mix and match attributes and the Fluent API to create a data model, which means that you can use attributes for the features they support if that is your preference. If so, bear in mind that Fluent API statements take precedence over attributes and that the attributes will be quietly ignored if you override the same convention using the Fluent API.

Using the Fluent API to Override Model Conventions

The Fluent API is used to override the data model conventions by describing parts of the data model programmatically. Attributes are suitable for making simple changes, but eventually you will have to deal with a situation for which there is no suitable attribute, and that requires an advanced feature that only the Fluent API supports.

■ **Note** In this chapter, I am using the Fluent API to model an existing database, but it can also be used to fine-tune the migrations in a code-first application, as demonstrated in Part 3.

To show an equivalent example to the use of attributes in the previous section, I added a file called ShoeWidth.cs to the Models/Manual folder and used it to define the class shown in Listing 18-8.

Listing 18-8. The Contents of the ShoeWidth.cs File in the Models/Manual Folder

```
namespace ExistingDb.Models.Manual {

    public class ShoeWidth {

        public long UniqueIdent { get; set; }

        public string WidthName { get; set; }
    }
}
```

I am going to use the ShoeWidth class to represent the data in the Fittings table. The class does not follow the Entity Framework Core conventions: the class name does not match the database table name, and I want to use the UniqueIdent and WidthName properties for the Id and Name columns.

Rather than modify the entity class, the Fluent API is applied in the context class by overriding the OnModelCreating method, as shown in Listing 18-9.

Listing 18-9. Using the Fluent API in the ManualContext.cs File in the Models/Manual Folder

```
using Microsoft.EntityFrameworkCore;

namespace ExistingDb.Models.Manual {

    public class ManualContext : DbContext {

        public ManualContext(DbContextOptions<ManualContext> options)
            : base(options) { }

        public DbSet<Shoe> Shoes { get; set; }

        public DbSet<Style> ShoeStyles { get; set; }

        public DbSet<ShoeWidth> ShoeWidths { get; set; }

        protected override void OnModelCreating(ModelBuilder modelBuilder) {
```

```
        modelBuilder.Entity<ShoeWidth>().ToTable("Fittings");
        modelBuilder.Entity<ShoeWidth>().HasKey( t => t.UniqueIdent);
        modelBuilder.Entity<ShoeWidth>()
            .Property(t => t.UniqueIdent)
            .HasColumnName("Id");

        modelBuilder.Entity<ShoeWidth>()
            .Property(t => t.WidthName)
            .HasColumnName("Name");
    }
  }
}
```

The OnModelCreating method receives a ModelBuilder object, on which the Fluent API is used. The most important method defined by the ModelBuilder class is Entity<T>, which allows an entity class to be described to Entity Framework Core and overrides the conventions that would otherwise be used.

The Entity<T> method returns an EntityTypeBuilder<T> object, which defines a series of methods that are used to describe the data model to Entity Framework Core. Table 18-4 describes the EntityTypeBuilder<T> methods used in Listing 18-9.

■ **Tip**   The Fluent API methods that select an entity class property, such as the HasKey and Property methods described in Table 18-4, are overloaded so that properties can be specified as strings or using a lambda expression. Lambda expressions avoid typos that cause errors only when the application is running, so these are the methods that I use in this book.

Table 18-4.   *The EntityTypeBuilder<T> Methods Used in Listing 18-9*

Name	Description
ToTable(table)	This method is used to specify the table for the entity class, equivalent to the Table attribute.
HasKey(selector)	This method is used to specify the key property for an entity class, equivalent to the Key attribute. The argument is a lambda expression that selects the key property.
Property(selector)	This method is used to select a property so that it can be described in more detail, as described in the following text.

The ToTable and HasKey methods are used on their own to specify the database table and the primary key property for the ShoeWidth class. The Property method is used to select a property for further configuration and returns a PropertyBuilder<T> object where T is the type returned by the selected property. The PropertyBuilder<T> class defines a number of methods that are used to provide fine-grained control over a property and that I will describe throughout this chapter and the chapters that follow. The PropertyBuilder<T> method that I used in Listing 18-9 is the HasColumnName method, which is used to select the database table column that will provide values for the selected property and which is described in Table 18-5 for quick reference.

Table 18-5. *The PropertyBuilder<T> Method Used in Listing 18-9*

Name	Description
HasColumnName(name)	This method is used to select the column that will provide values for the selected property, equivalent to using the Column attribute.

Using the Customized Data Model

Regardless of whether you use the attributes or the Fluent API, once you have overridden the conventions to create the data model that your application requires, you can use the context class and the entity classes as you would normally. To complete this section, I added statements to the Index action of the Manual controller that pass the ShoeStyle and ShoeWidth objects to the default view using the ViewBag, as shown in Listing 18-10.

Listing 18-10. Using the Customized Model in the ManualController.cs File in the Controllers Folder

```
using ExistingDb.Models.Manual;
using Microsoft.AspNetCore.Mvc;

namespace ExistingDb.Controllers {

    public class ManualController : Controller {
        private ManualContext context;

        public ManualController(ManualContext ctx) => context = ctx;

        public IActionResult Index() {
            ViewBag.Styles = context.ShoeStyles;
            ViewBag.Widths = context.ShoeWidths;
            return View(context.Shoes);
        }
    }
}
```

To display the data to the user, I added the content shown in Listing 18-11 to the Index.cshtml view in the Views/Manual folder.

Listing 18-11. Displaying Additional Data in the Index.cshtml File in the Views/Manual Folder

```
@using ExistingDb.Models.Manual
@model IEnumerable<Shoe>
@{
    ViewData["Title"] = "Manual Data Model";
    Layout = "_Layout";
}

<div class="container-fluid">
    <h4 class="bg-primary p-3 text-white">Zoom Shoes</h4>
    <table class="table table-striped table-sm">
        <tr><th>Id</th><th>Name</th><th>Price</th></tr>
        @foreach (Shoe s in Model) {
```

```
            <tr>
                <td>@s.Id</td>
                <td>@s.Name</td>
                <td>$@s.Price.ToString("F2")</td>
            </tr>
        }
    </table>
    <div class="row">
        <div class="col">
            <h5 class="bg-primary p-2 text-white">Styles</h5>
            <table class="table table-striped table-sm">
                <tr>
                    <th>UniqueIdent</th><th>Style Name</th>
                    <th>Main Color</th><th>Highlight Color</th>
                </tr>
                @foreach (Style s in ViewBag.Styles) {
                    <tr>
                        <td>@s.UniqueIdent</td>
                        <td>@s.StyleName</td>
                        <td>@s.MainColor</td>
                        <td>@s.HighlightColor</td>
                    </tr>
                }
            </table>
        </div>
        <div class="col">
            <h5 class="bg-primary p-2 text-white">Widths</h5>
            <table class="table table-striped table-sm">
                <tr><th>UniqueIdent</th><th>Name</th></tr>
                @foreach (ShoeWidth s in ViewBag.Widths) {
                    <tr><td>@s.UniqueIdent</td><td>@s.WidthName</td></tr>
                }
            </table>
        </div>
    </div>
</div>
```

To test both techniques for overriding the data model conventions, start the application using dotnet run and navigate to http://localhost:5000/manual. During startup, Entity Framework Core will use the attributes and the Fluent API statements as it builds the data model so that the queries made by the action method are seamlessly mapped into the database, producing the result shown in Figure 18-3.

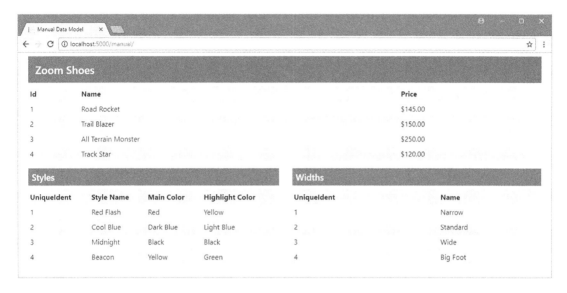

Figure 18-3. *Overriding the data model*

RESPONDING TO DATABASE CHANGES

You must ensure that you update your data model when changes are made to the database. There is no automatic update process, such as when using the scaffolding feature described in Chapter 17.

If you don't update the data model correctly, you will create a mismatch between Entity Framework Core and the database. This kind of problem won't become apparent until runtime and can cause subtle issues that manifest only for specific operations or with certain data values.

Ensure that you understand the impact that database changes will have on the application and adhere to a testing regime that minimizes the chances of errors making their way to production systems.

Modeling Relationships

Although I have set up three classes to represent the data in the database, each exists in isolation and must be queried individually. Defining the relationships between the classes means adding navigation and foreign key properties, following the same conventions used for code-first development. Listing 18-12 shows the changes to the Shoes class to add the navigation and foreign key property that models one side of the one-to-many relationship between the Shoes and Colors tables in the database.

Listing 18-12. Adding Properties in the Shoes.cs File in the Models/Manual Folder

```
namespace ExistingDb.Models.Manual {

    public class Shoe {
        public long Id { get; set; }
        public string Name { get; set; }
        public decimal Price { get; set; }

        public long ColorId { get; set; }
        public Style Color { get; set; }
    }
}
```

When modeling an existing database, the most important property is the one that maps to the foreign key column in the database table used to store the dependent entity, which is the Shoe class in this example. The convention for the name of the navigation property is to drop the column name from the foreign key property so that the navigation property for the relationship stored in the ColorId property will be Color. Notice that the type returned by the Color property is Style; Entity Framework Core applies the changes applied to the data model consistently, which means that the attributes used to specify the Style class as the representation of the data in the Colors table continues even when defining relationships.

To complete the relationship, I added the inverse navigation property to the Style class, as shown in Listing 18-13.

Listing 18-13. Completing the Relationship in the Style.cs File in the Models/Manual Folder

```
using System.ComponentModel.DataAnnotations;
using System.ComponentModel.DataAnnotations.Schema;
using System.Collections.Generic;

namespace ExistingDb.Models.Manual {

    [Table("Colors")]
    public class Style {

        [Key]
        [Column("Id")]
        public long UniqueIdent  { get; set; }

        [Column("Name")]
        public string StyleName { get; set; }

        public string MainColor { get; set; }
        public string HighlightColor { get; set; }

        public IEnumerable<Shoe> Shoes { get; set; }
    }
}
```

Overriding the Relationship Conventions Using Attributes

The relationship defined in Listing 18-12 reveals the underlying structure of the database through the changes that have been applied to the model, with the result that you follow a property called Color to get a Style object.

One drawback with overriding the data model conventions is that, once you start, you need to keep going and work the changes all the way through, including ensuring that the name of navigation and foreign key properties is consistent with the other changes that you have made. In Listing 18-14, I have used attributes to override the default relationship conventions for the foreign key and navigation properties in the Shoe class.

Listing 18-14. Overriding Conventions in the Shoe.cs File in the Models/Manual Folder

```
using System.ComponentModel.DataAnnotations.Schema;

namespace ExistingDb.Models.Manual {

    public class Shoe {
        public long Id { get; set; }
        public string Name { get; set; }
        public decimal Price { get; set; }

        [Column("ColorId")]
        public long StyleId { get; set; }

        [ForeignKey("StyleId")]
        public Style Style { get; set; }
    }
}
```

Two attributes are required to create a relationship with properties that are consistent with the rest of the data model. The Column attribute tells Entity Framework Core that the StyleId property should be mapped to the ColorId column, while the ForeignKey attribute is used to specify that the StyleId property is the foreign key property for the Style navigation property. Together, these attributes allow properties whose names are consistent with the rest of the data model to express the relationship, without needing to expose details of the underlying database structure.

The property that I added to the Styles class in Listing 18-14 doesn't require an attribute because it follows the regular relationship contentions and Entity Framework Core will recognize it as an inverse navigation property to the Shoe class. However, if you can't use the conventional name for this type of property, then you can use the InverseProperty attribute to tell Entity Framework Core which class the property relates to, as shown in Listing 18-15.

Listing 18-15. Identifying an Inverse Navigation Property in the Styles.cs File in the Models/Manual Folder

```
using System.ComponentModel.DataAnnotations;
using System.ComponentModel.DataAnnotations.Schema;
using System.Collections.Generic;

namespace ExistingDb.Models.Manual {

    [Table("Colors")]
    public class Style {
```

```
    [Key]
    [Column("Id")]
    public long UniqueIdent  { get; set; }

    [Column("Name")]
    public string StyleName { get; set; }

    public string MainColor { get; set; }
    public string HighlightColor { get; set; }

    [InverseProperty(nameof(Shoe.Style))]
    public IEnumerable<Shoe> Products { get; set; }
    }
}
```

The argument for the InverseProperty attribute is the name of the other property in the relationship, which can be specified as a string or using the nameof function to avoid typos. In the listing, the InverseProperty attribute has allowed me to change the name of the inverse property to Products.

For future quick reference, Table 18-6 describes the attributes used to override the relationship conventions in this section. (The Column attribute is described in Table 18-3.)

Table 18-6. *The Attributes Used to Override Relationship Conventions*

Name	Description
ForeignKey(property)	This attribute is used to identify the foreign key property for a navigation property.
InverseProperty(name)	This attribute is used to specify the name of the property at the other end of the relationship.

Overriding the Relationship Conventions Using the Fluent API

If you prefer using the Fluent API, then you can use the Entity<T> method to select an entity class, followed by the Property method, which allows you to select and configure individual properties. To show how the Fluent API can be used to describe relationships, in Listing 18-16 I added a foreign key and navigation property to the Shoe class to create a relationship with the ShoeWidth class, which represents data from the Fittings database table.

Listing 18-16. Defining Properties in the Shoe.cs File in the Models/Manual Folder

```
using System.ComponentModel.DataAnnotations.Schema;

namespace ExistingDb.Models.Manual {

    public class Shoe {
        public long Id { get; set; }
        public string Name { get; set; }
        public decimal Price { get; set; }
```

```
        [Column("ColorId")]
        public long StyleId { get; set; }

        [ForeignKey("StyleId")]
        public Style Style { get; set; }

        public long WidthId { get; set; }
        public ShoeWidth Width { get; set;  }
    }
}
```

To complete the relationship, I added the inverse navigation property shown in Listing 18-17 to the ShoeWidth class.

Listing 18-17. Adding a Navigation Property in the ShoeWidth.cs File in the Models/Manual Folder

```
using System.Collections.Generic;

namespace ExistingDb.Models.Manual {

    public class ShoeWidth {

        public long UniqueIdent { get; set; }

        public string WidthName { get; set; }

        public IEnumerable<Shoe> Products { get; set; }
    }
}
```

These properties do not follow the relationship conventions and have not been decorated with attributes, which means that Entity Framework Core won't be able to determine their purpose. To describe the role of these properties in the data model, I added the statements shown in Listing 18-18 to the OnModelCreating method of the ManualContext class.

Listing 18-18. Overriding Conventions in the ManualContext.cs File in the Models/Manual Folder

```
using Microsoft.EntityFrameworkCore;

namespace ExistingDb.Models.Manual {

    public class ManualContext : DbContext {

        public ManualContext(DbContextOptions<ManualContext> options)
            : base(options) { }

        public DbSet<Shoe> Shoes { get; set; }

        public DbSet<Style> ShoeStyles { get; set; }

        public DbSet<ShoeWidth> ShoeWidths { get; set; }

        protected override void OnModelCreating(ModelBuilder modelBuilder) {
```

```
modelBuilder.Entity<ShoeWidth>().ToTable("Fittings");
modelBuilder.Entity<ShoeWidth>().HasKey( t => t.UniqueIdent);
modelBuilder.Entity<ShoeWidth>()
    .Property(t => t.UniqueIdent)
    .HasColumnName("Id");

modelBuilder.Entity<ShoeWidth>()
    .Property(t => t.WidthName)
    .HasColumnName("Name");

modelBuilder.Entity<Shoe>()
    .Property(s => s.WidthId).HasColumnName("FittingId");

modelBuilder.Entity<Shoe>()
    .HasOne(s => s.Width).WithMany(w => w.Products)
    .HasForeignKey(s => s.WidthId).IsRequired(true);
        }
    }
}
```

Two configuration statements are required to configure the properties defined in Listing 18-17 and Listing 18-18 to represent the relationship between the Shoes and Fittings tables. The first statement uses the same methods shown in the previous section, which tell Entity Framework Core that the values for the Shoe.WidthId property should be read from the FittingId column. The second statement uses the methods that the Fluent API provides specifically for describing relationships, as described in Table 18-7.

***Table 18-7.** The EntityBuilder<T> Methods for Describing Relationships*

Name	Description
HasOne(property)	This method is used to start describing a relationship where the selected entity class has a relationship with a single object of another type. The argument selects the navigation property, either by name or by using a lambda expression.
HasMany(property)	This method is used to start describing a relationship where the selected entity class has a relationship with many objects of another type. The argument selects the navigation property, either by name or by using a lambda expression.

You start with one of the methods shown the table and describe the other end of the relationship using one of the methods described in Table 18-8, which tells Entity Framework Core whether this is a one-to-one or one-to-many relationship.

***Table 18-8.** The Fluent API Methods for Completing the Description of a Relationship*

Name	Description
WithMany(property)	This method is used to select the inverse navigation property in a one-to-many relationship.
WithOne(property)	This method is used to select the inverse navigation property in a one-to-one relationship.

Once you have selected the navigation properties for both ends of the relationship, you can configure the relationship by chaining calls to the methods described in Table 18-9.

Table 18-9. *The Fluent API Relationship Configuration Methods*

Name	Description
HasForeignKey(property)	This method is used to select the foreign key property for the relationship.
IsRequired(required)	This method is used to specify whether the relationship is required or optional.

The combination of methods I used in Listing 18-18 tells Entity Framework Core that the Shoe class is the dependent entity in a required one-to-many relationship with the ShoeWidth class and that the WidthId property is the foreign key property. Combined with the statement that maps the WidthId property to the foreign key column in the database, Entity Framework Core has all of the information it needs to understand the relationship and how the entity classes are mapped to the database tables.

Completing the Data Model

To complete the data model, I need to define classes to represent the SalesCampaigns and Categories tables and describe the relationships between them. I added a file called SalesCampaign.cs to the Models/Manual folder and used it to define the class shown in Listing 18-19.

Listing 18-19. The Contents of the SalesCampaign.cs File in the Models/Manual Folder

```
using System;
using System.ComponentModel.DataAnnotations.Schema;

namespace ExistingDb.Models.Manual {

    [Table("SalesCampaigns")]
    public class SalesCampaign {

        public long Id { get; set; }
        public string Slogan { get; set; }
        public int? MaxDiscount { get; set; }
        public DateTime? LaunchDate { get; set; }

        public long ShoeId { get; set; }
        public Shoe Shoe { get; set; }
    }
}
```

I used the Table attribute to specify the table that will be used to create SalesCampaign objects, allowing me to keep the names of the classes consistent in the data model. The properties defined by the SalesCampaign class directly map to the columns in the database table, with the exception of the Shoe property, which is a navigation property for the one-to-one relationship with the Shoe class.

The Categories table has a many-to-many relationship, which means that I need to define the entity and junction classes. For the entity, I created a file called Category.cs in the Models/Manual folder and used it to define the class shown in Listing 18-20.

Listing 18-20. The Contents of the Category.cs File in the Models/Manual Folder

```
using System.Collections.Generic;

namespace ExistingDb.Models.Manual {

    public class Category {
        public long Id { get; set; }
        public string Name { get; set; }

        public IEnumerable<ShoeCategoryJunction> Shoes { get; set; }
    }
}
```

To represent the junction required by this relationship, I created a class file called ShoeCategoryJunction.cs in the Models/Manual folder and defined the class shown in Listing 18-21.

Listing 18-21. The Contents of the ShoeCategoryJunction.cs File in the Models/Manual Folder

```
namespace ExistingDb.Models.Manual {

    public class ShoeCategoryJunction {

        public long Id { get; set; }
        public long ShoeId { get; set; }
        public long CategoryId { get; set; }

        public Category Category { get; set; }
        public Shoe Shoe { get; set; }
    }
}
```

This class defines properties that correspond to the columns in the junction table in the database, along with navigation properties that use the class names in the data model, which are used instead of the conventional names. The name of the class is the same as the name of the junction table in the database. Since the junction class conforms to all of the conventions, no attributes or Fluent API statements are required to configure the class or its relationships.

In Listing 18-22, I have added the navigation properties required for both the SalesCampaign class and the junction class for the relationship with the Category class from Listing 18-21.

Listing 18-22. Adding Navigation Properties to the Shoe.cs File in the Models/Manual Folder

```
using System.ComponentModel.DataAnnotations.Schema;
using System.Collections.Generic;

namespace ExistingDb.Models.Manual {

    public class Shoe {
        public long Id { get; set; }
        public string Name { get; set; }
        public decimal Price { get; set; }
```

```
        [Column("ColorId")]
        public long StyleId { get; set; }

        [ForeignKey("StyleId")]
        public Style Style { get; set; }

        public long WidthId { get; set; }
        public ShoeWidth Width { get; set; }

        public SalesCampaign Campaign { get; set; }
        public IEnumerable<ShoeCategoryJunction> Categories { get; set; }
    }
}
```

To provide convenient access to the Category objects, I added a DbSet<T> property to the context class, as shown in Listing 18-23.

Listing 18-23. Configuring a Relationship in the ManualContext.cs File in the Models/Manual Folder

```
using Microsoft.EntityFrameworkCore;

namespace ExistingDb.Models.Manual {

    public class ManualContext : DbContext {

        public ManualContext(DbContextOptions<ManualContext> options)
            : base(options) { }

        public DbSet<Shoe> Shoes { get; set; }

        public DbSet<Style> ShoeStyles { get; set; }

        public DbSet<ShoeWidth> ShoeWidths { get; set; }

        public DbSet<Category> Categories { get; set; }

        protected override void OnModelCreating(ModelBuilder modelBuilder) {

            // ...statements omitted for brevity...
        }
    }
}
```

Using the Manually Created Data Model

Now that the data model is complete, I can use the data in the ASP.NET Core MVC part of the application and let Entity Framework Core handle mapping it to the database where the conventions have not been followed. In the sections that follow, I demonstrate the process for querying and updating data.

Querying Data in a Manually Created Data Model

I expanded the query in the Index action of the Manual controller to include all of the available data and added ViewBag properties for each data type, as shown in Listing 18-24, to demonstrate querying for all the relationships in the model.

Listing 18-24. Querying for Additional Data in the ManualController.cs File in the Models/Manual Folder

```
using ExistingDb.Models.Manual;
using Microsoft.AspNetCore.Mvc;
using Microsoft.EntityFrameworkCore;

namespace ExistingDb.Controllers {

    public class ManualController : Controller {
        private ManualContext context;

        public ManualController(ManualContext ctx) => context = ctx;

        public IActionResult Index() {
            ViewBag.Styles = context.ShoeStyles.Include(s => s.Products);
            ViewBag.Widths = context.ShoeWidths.Include(s => s.Products);
            ViewBag.Categories = context.Categories
                .Include(c => c.Shoes).ThenInclude(j => j.Shoe);
            return View(context.Shoes.Include(s => s.Style)
                .Include(s => s.Width).Include(s => s.Categories)
                    .ThenInclude(j => j.Category));
        }
    }
}
```

To display the data to the user, I added the elements shown in Listing 18-25 to the Index view used by the action method.

Listing 18-25. Displaying Data in the Index.cshtml File in the Views/Manual Folder

```
@using ExistingDb.Models.Manual
@model IEnumerable<Shoe>
@{
    ViewData["Title"] = "Manual Data Model";
    Layout = "_Layout";
}

<div class="container-fluid">
    <h4 class="bg-primary p-3 text-white">Zoom Shoes</h4>
    <table class="table table-striped table-sm">
        <tr>
            <th>Id</th><th>Name</th><th>Price</th><th>Styles</th>
            <th>Widths</th><th>Categories</th><th></th>
        </tr>
        @foreach (Shoe s in Model) {
            <tr>
```

```
            <td>@s.Id</td>
            <td>@s.Name</td>
            <td>$@s.Price.ToString("F2")</td>
            <td class="table-primary">@s.Width?.WidthName</td>
            <td class="table-secondary">@s.Style?.StyleName</td>
            <td class="table-success">
                @string.Join(", ", s.Categories.Select(c => c.Category.Name))
            </td>
            <td class="text-center">
                <a asp-action="Edit" asp-route-id="@s.Id"
                        class="btn btn-sm btn-primary">Edit</a>
            </td>
        </tr>
    }
</table>
<div class="row">
    <div class="col">
        <h5 class="bg-primary p-2 text-white">Styles</h5>
        <table class="table table-striped table-sm">
            <tr><th>UniqueIdent</th><th>Name</th><th>Products</th></tr>
            @foreach (Style s in ViewBag.Styles) {
                <tr>
                    <td>@s.UniqueIdent</td>
                    <td>@s.StyleName</td>
                    <td class="table-secondary">
                        @String.Join(", ", s.Products.Select(p => p.Name))
                    </td>
                </tr>
            }
        </table>
    </div>
    <div class="col">
        <h5 class="bg-primary p-2 text-white">Widths</h5>
        <table class="table table-striped table-sm">
            <tr><th>UniqueIdent</th><th>Name</th><td>Products</td></tr>
            @foreach (ShoeWidth s in ViewBag.Widths) {
                <tr>
                    <td>@s.UniqueIdent</td>
                    <td>@s.WidthName</td>
                    <td class="table-primary">
                        @String.Join(", ", s.Products.Select(p => p.Name))
                    </td>
                </tr>
            }
        </table>
    </div>
    <div class="col">
        <h5 class="bg-primary p-2 text-white">Categories</h5>
        <table class="table table-striped table-sm">
            <tr><th>Id</th><th>Name</th><th>Products</th></tr>
            @foreach (Category c in ViewBag.Categories) {
```

```
            <tr>
                <td>@c.Id</td>
                <td>@c.Name</td>
                <td class="table-success">
                    @String.Join(", ", c.Shoes.Select(j => j.Shoe.Name))
                </td>
            </tr>
        }
        </table>
    </div>
    </div>
</div>
```

Start the application and navigate to http://localhost:5000/manual to see the new content, which is shown in Figure 18-4.

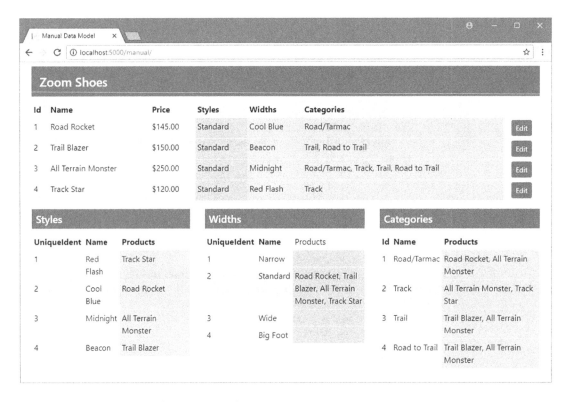

Figure 18-4. Using a manually created database

The additions in Listing 18-25 result in a series of tables that display the data in the database, demonstrating that working with a manually created data model works in just the same way as one that has been scaffolded or used as the basis for a migration. Entity Framework Core automatically takes care of dealing with any deviation from the conventions, which you can see by examining the output from the application. Here is one of the queries used to get the data displayed in the figure; you can see how the names of classes and properties that have differed from the convention are translated into the tables and columns in the database:

```
...
SELECT [c.Shoes].[Id], [c.Shoes].[CategoryId], [c.Shoes].[ShoeId], [s.Shoe].[Id],
    [s.Shoe].[Name], [s.Shoe].[Price], [s.Shoe].[ColorId], [s.Shoe].[FittingId]
FROM [ShoeCategoryJunction] AS [c.Shoes]
INNER JOIN [Shoes] AS [s.Shoe] ON [c.Shoes].[ShoeId] = [s.Shoe].[Id]
INNER JOIN (
    SELECT [c0].[Id]
    FROM [Categories] AS [c0]
) AS [t] ON [c.Shoes].[CategoryId] = [t].[Id]
ORDER BY [t].[Id]
...
```

■ **Caution**   Creating a manual data model results in a more natural development experience in the ASP.NET Core MVC part of the application, but it works only when you accurately model the database. Entity Framework Core doesn't validate that the model you create accurately describes the database, and any problems will only become apparent when the application tries to query or update the database.

Updating Data in a Manually Created Data Model

I added an anchor element to the view in Listing 18-25 that targets an action called Edit. In this section, I am going to implement the action method to emphasize that working with a manually created database is just the same as one that has been scaffolded or used to create a migration. In Listing 18-26, I added methods to the controller that will allow the user to start the editing process and update an existing Shoe object.

Listing 18-26. Adding Actions in the ManualController.cs File in the Controllers Folder

```
using ExistingDb.Models.Manual;
using Microsoft.AspNetCore.Mvc;
using Microsoft.EntityFrameworkCore;
using System.Linq;
using System.Collections.Generic;

namespace ExistingDb.Controllers {

    public class ManualController : Controller {
        private ManualContext context;

        public ManualController(ManualContext ctx) => context = ctx;
```

```
    public IActionResult Index() {
        ViewBag.Styles = context.ShoeStyles.Include(s => s.Products);
        ViewBag.Widths = context.ShoeWidths.Include(s => s.Products);
        ViewBag.Categories = context.Categories
            .Include(c => c.Shoes).ThenInclude(j => j.Shoe);
        return View(context.Shoes.Include(s => s.Style)
            .Include(s => s.Width).Include(s => s.Categories)
                .ThenInclude(j => j.Category));
    }

    public IActionResult Edit(long id) {
        ViewBag.Styles = context.ShoeStyles;
        ViewBag.Widths = context.ShoeWidths;
        ViewBag.Categories = context.Categories;
        return View(context.Shoes.Include(s => s.Style)
            .Include(s => s.Campaign)
            .Include(s => s.Width).Include(s => s.Categories)
            .ThenInclude(j => j.Category).First(s => s.Id == id));
    }

    [HttpPost]
    public IActionResult Update(Shoe shoe, long[] newCategoryIds,
            ShoeCategoryJunction[] oldJunctions) {

        IEnumerable<ShoeCategoryJunction> unchangedJunctions
            = oldJunctions.Where(j => newCategoryIds.Contains(j.CategoryId));

        context.Set<ShoeCategoryJunction>()
            .RemoveRange(oldJunctions.Except(unchangedJunctions));

        shoe.Categories = newCategoryIds.Except(unchangedJunctions
            .Select(j => j.CategoryId))
            .Select(id => new ShoeCategoryJunction {
                ShoeId = shoe.Id, CategoryId = id
            }).ToList();

        context.Shoes.Update(shoe);
        context.SaveChanges();
        return RedirectToAction(nameof(Index));
    }
  }
}
```

The Edit action queries the database for a single object and all of its related data so that the current details can be displayed for editing. The ViewBag is used to pass additional data to the view so that the user can be presented with the range of options available for changing the related data.

The Update method receives a Shoe object, which will be created by the ASP.NET Core MVC model binder from HTTP form data and used to update the database. The Update method also receives an array containing the primary key values of the Category objects that the user wants the Shoe to be related to and an array of junction objects, which I will ensure is included in the HTTP request data so that I don't have to query the database just to figure out which junction objects have to be deleted.

In Chapter 16, I showed you how to update a many-to-many relationship separately from the objects in that relationship, which I did by querying the database for the object at one end of the relationships and its related data, which provided Entity Framework Core with enough information to update the junction table.

That technique won't work for this chapter because I want to update the Shoe object and the many-to-many relationship at the same time, and if I query the database for the Shoe, then the Entity Framework Core change tracking feature will throw an exception when I use the Update method with the Shoe created by the MVC model binder.

To perform the update, I remove any outdated relationships by comparing the selected categories with those that were originally related and removing those that are not required by passing the objects to the RemoveRange method, like this:

```
...
IEnumerable<ShoeCategoryJunction> unchangedJunctions
    = oldJunctions.Where(j => newCategoryIds.Contains(j.CategoryId));

context.Set<ShoeCategoryJunction>()
    .RemoveRange(oldJunctions.Except(unchangedJunctions));
...
```

I did not define a context property for the junction data, so I perform the delete operation by getting a DbSet<T> object using the Set<T> method. To avoid creating duplicate relationships, I compare the original set of junction objects with the categories that the user has chosen, ensuring that I only create new objects to fill in the gaps, like this:

```
...
shoe.Categories = newCategoryIds.Except(unchangedJunctions.Select(j => j.CategoryId))
    .Select(id => new ShoeCategoryJunction {
        ShoeId = shoe.Id, CategoryId = id
    }).ToList();
...
```

I remove unwanted relationships and create new ones, while carefully leaving those that are unchanged untouched in the database. In this way, I am able to perform the update using the objects created by the ASP.NET Core MVC model binder.

Creating the Partial Views

To complete the example, I need to create a partial view for each of the objects that will allow the user to perform an edit. I started by adding a file called EditShoe.cshtml in the Views/Manual folder and then added the content shown in Listing 18-27.

Listing 18-27. The Contents of the EditShoe.cshtml File in the Views/Manual Folder

```
@using ExistingDb.Models.Manual
@model Shoe

<input type="hidden" asp-for="Id" />
<h4>Product Details</h4>
<div class="p-1 m-1">
```

```
    <div class="form-row">
        <div class="form-group col">
            <label asp-for="Name" class="form-control-label"></label>
            <input asp-for="Name" class="form-control" />
        </div>
        <div class="form-group col">
            <label asp-for="Price" class="form-control-label"></label>
            <input asp-for="Price" class="form-control" />
        </div>
    </div>
</div>
```

Each partial view will contain just the elements required to perform editing of one aspect of the data presented to the user, and, in this case, there are two input elements that allow the Name and Price properties of a Shoe object to be edited. Next, I added a file called EditStyle.cshtml in the Views/Manual folder and added the content shown in Listing 18-28.

Listing 18-28. The Contents of the EditStyle.cshtml File in the Views/Manual Folder

```
@using ExistingDb.Models.Manual
@model Shoe

<label><strong>Style:</strong></label>
<select asp-for="StyleId" class="form-control">
    @foreach (Style s in ViewBag.Styles) {
        if (s.UniqueIdent == Model.StyleId) {
            <option value="@s.UniqueIdent" selected>@s.StyleName</option>
        } else {
            <option value="@s.UniqueIdent">@s.StyleName</option>
        }
    }
</select>
```

This partial view displays a select element that is used to choose the Style object to which the Shoe being edited is related. I have taken a similar approach with the ShoeWidth object, creating a file called EditWidth.cshtml in the Views/Manual folder with the content shown in Listing 18-29.

Listing 18-29. The Contents of the EditWidth.cshtml File in the Views/Manual Folder

```
@using ExistingDb.Models.Manual
@model Shoe

<label>Width:</label>
<select asp-for="WidthId" class="form-control">
    @foreach (ShoeWidth w in ViewBag.Widths) {
        if (w.UniqueIdent == Model.WidthId) {
            <option value="@w.UniqueIdent" selected>@w.WidthName</option>
        } else {
            <option value="@w.UniqueIdent">@w.WidthName</option>
        }
    }
</select>
```

There is a one-to-one relationship with the SalesCampaign class, so I have chosen to present the user with input elements to change the property values by creating a file called EditCampaign.cshtml in the Views/Manual folder and adding the content shown in Listing 18-30.

Listing 18-30. The Contents of the EditCampaign.cshtml File in the Views/Manual Folder

```
@using ExistingDb.Models.Manual
@model Shoe

<div class="form-row">
    <input type="hidden" asp-for="Campaign.Id" />
    <label><strong>Sales Campaign:</strong></label>
</div>
<div class="form-row">
    <div class="form-group col">
        <label asp-for="Campaign.Slogan" class="form-control-label"></label>
        <input asp-for="Campaign.Slogan" class="form-control" />
    </div>
</div>
<div class="form-row">
    <div class="form-group col">
        <label class="form-control-label">Max Discount:</label>
        <input asp-for="Campaign.MaxDiscount" class="form-control" />
    </div>
    <div class="form-group col">
        <label class="form-control-label">Launch Date:</label>
        <input type="date" asp-for="Campaign.LaunchDate" class="form-control" />
    </div>
</div>
```

The final partial view will allow the user to select which Category objects the Shoe object being edited is related to. This is a more complex view because I have included hidden elements that the ASP.NET Core MVC model binder will use to create the junction objects I use to avoid having to query the database to determine the current set of relationships in the Update action method. I added a view file called EditCategory.cshtml in the Views/Manual folder and added the content shown in Listing 18-31.

Listing 18-31. The Contents of the EditCategory.cshtml File in the Views/Manual Folder

```
@using ExistingDb.Models.Manual
@model Shoe

@{ int index = 0; }

@foreach (var junc in Model.Categories) {
    <input type="hidden" name="oldJunctions[@index].Id" value="@junc.Id" />
            <input type="hidden" name="oldJunctions[@index].CategoryId"
                    value="@junc.CategoryId" />
    index++;
}
```

```
@foreach (Category c in ViewBag.Categories) {
    <div class="form-group col">
        <label class="form-check-label">
            @if (c.Shoes?.Any(s => s.ShoeId == Model.Id) == true) {
                <input type="checkbox" name="newCategoryIds" value="@c.Id"
                        checked class="form-check-input" />
            } else {
                <input type="checkbox" name="newCategoryIds" value="@c.Id"
                        class="form-check-input" />
            }
            @c.Name
        </label>
    </div>
}
```

The awkward foreach loop with the index counter is used to generate data that will be correctly processed by the ASP.NET Core MVC model binder. The other elements generate a series of labels and checkboxes that are used to select the categories for a shoe.

Creating the Editor View

All that remains is to create a view that will incorporate the partial views to present the user with a single editor. I added a file called Edit.cshtml to the Views/Manual folder with the content shown in Listing 18-32.

Listing 18-32. The Contents of the Edit.cshtml File in the Views/Manual Folder

```
@using ExistingDb.Models.Manual
@model Shoe
@{
    ViewData["Title"] = "Manual Data Model";
    Layout = "_Layout";
}

<form asp-action="Update" method="post">
    @Html.Partial("EditShoe", Model)
    <div class="p-1 m-1">
        <div class="form-row">
            <div class="form-group col">@Html.Partial("EditStyle", Model)</div>
            <div class="form-group col">@Html.Partial("EditWidth", Model)</div>
        </div>
        @Html.Partial("EditCampaign", Model)
        <div class="form-row">
            <label><strong>Categories:</strong></label>
        </div>
        <div class="form-row">@Html.Partial("EditCategory", Model)</div>
    </div>
    <div class="text-center m-1">
        <button type="submit" class="btn btn-primary">Save</button>
        <a asp-action="Index" class="btn btn-secondary">Cancel</a>
    </div>
</form>
```

To check that the code and views for updating data in a manually created data model works, start the application, navigate to `http://localhost:5000/manual`, and click the Edit button for the All Terrain Monster product. Change the Width option to Big Foot and uncheck the Trail category. Click the Save button, and you will see the changes you made reflected in the overview, as shown in Figure 18-5.

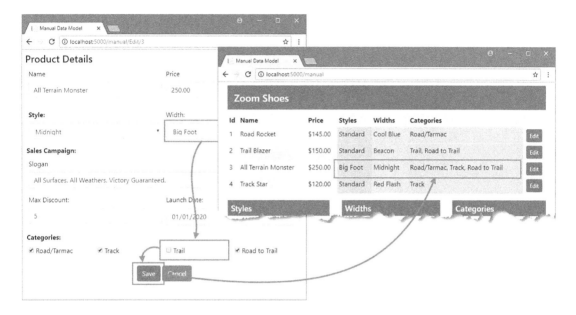

Figure 18-5. *Editing data in a manually created data mode*

Summary

In this chapter, I demonstrated the process for manually modeling a database. This is a process that requires care and attention but can produce a data model that is easier to use in the ASP.NET Core MVC part of the application when compared with the scaffolding process described in Chapter 17. In Part 3, I describe the advanced Entity Framework Core features.

PART III

Advanced Entity Framework Core 2

In Part 3 of this book, I describe the advanced features that Entity Framework Core provides. These are not features that will be needed in every project but they can be invaluable when you need to go beyond the standard features described in Part 2.

CHAPTER 19

Working with Keys

Selecting the most suitable keys for your data sets the foundation for the rest of the data model. In earlier chapters, you have seen the role that keys play in uniquely identifying objects, the conventions that Entity Framework Core uses to select properties to use as keys, and how these conventions are overridden. In this chapter, I describe the advanced key features that Entity Framework Core provides. Like many of the features described in this part of the book, you are unlikely to need the advanced key features in every project that uses Entity Framework Core, but the ability to take control of how keys are used can be important for those unusual occasions when the standard features can't deliver the functionality your application required.

Entity Framework Core isn't able to generate migrations that make substantial changes to keys, which means that most of the examples in this chapter require the database to be reset or for earlier migrations to be removed. This emphasizes the importance of choosing your key strategy as early as possible so as to avoid having to make complex changes to databases that can result in data loss. Table 19-1 puts this chapter in context.

Table 19-1. *Putting Advanced Key Features in Context*

Question	Answer
What are they?	These features allow you to change the way that keys are created and used.
Why are they useful?	Not all applications can work with the default primary key features, especially when working with an existing database.
How are they used?	These features are applied using Fluent API statements in the database context class.
Are there any pitfalls or limitations?	These features require careful thought because it is easy to select properties whose values do not uniquely identify an object.
Are there any alternatives?	These features are optional, and you can use the basic features described in Part 2.

> **Note** Many of the advanced features can be applied only using the Fluent API and have no corresponding attributes. I have added notes when there are attributes available, but the focus of this chapter—and the other chapters in this part of the book—is firmly on the use of the Fluent API.

© Adam Freeman 2018
A. Freeman, *Pro Entity Framework Core 2 for ASP.NET Core MVC*,
https://doi.org/10.1007/978-1-4842-3435-8_19

Table 19-2 summarizes the chapter.

Table 19-2. *Chapter Summary*

Problem	Solution	Listing
Change how primary key values are generated	Use the Fluent API key generation methods	14–16
Use natural keys	Use the IsUnique method to ensure that values area not duplicated in the database	17, 18, 25–27
Use additional properties to identify objects	Create an alternate key	19–24
Use multiple properties to identify objects	Create a composite key	28–32

Preparing for This Chapter

For this chapter, I create a new project so that I can demonstrate the more advanced features that Entity Framework Core supports. To create the project, select New ➤ Project from the Visual Studio File menu and use the ASP.NET Core Web Application template to create a new project called AdvancedApp, as shown in Figure 19-1.

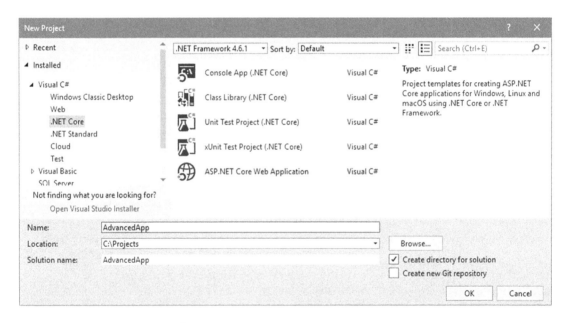

Figure 19-1. *Creating a new application*

■ **Tip** If you don't want to follow the process of building the example project, you can download all of the required files from this book's source code repository, available at `https://github.com/apress/pro-ef-core-2-for-asp.net-core-mvc`.

Click the OK button to move to the next dialog. Ensure that ASP.NET Core 2.0 is selected from the list and click the Empty template, as shown in Figure 19-2. Click OK to close the dialog window and create the project.

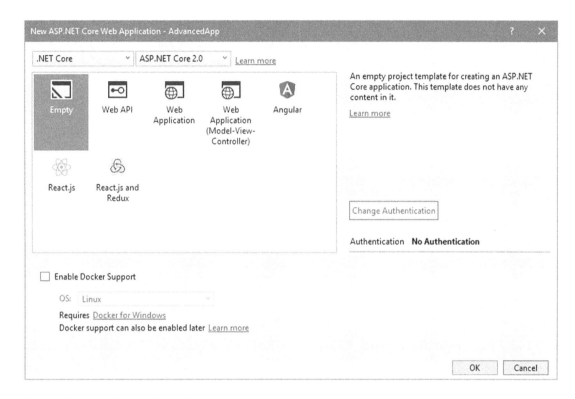

Figure 19-2. *Configuring the project*

Creating the Data Model

The data model for this chapter will represent employees in a simplified HR database, just to provide some variety from the product-based examples I used in earlier chapters. I created a folder called Models and added to it a class file called Employee.cs, which I used to define the class shown in Listing 19-1.

Listing 19-1. The Contents of the Employee.cs File in the Models Folder

```
namespace AdvancedApp.Models {

    public class Employee {

        public long Id { get; set; }
        public string SSN { get; set; }
        public string FirstName { get; set; }
        public string FamilyName { get; set; }
        public decimal Salary { get; set; }
    }
}
```

467

The Employee class has properties for a person's Social Security number, name, and salary. A real HR database would require additional details, but this is enough to get started.

To create the database context class, I added a class file called AdvancedContext.cs to the Models folder and defined the class shown in Listing 19-2.

Listing 19-2. The Contents of the AdvancedContext.cs File in the Models Folder

```
using Microsoft.EntityFrameworkCore;

namespace AdvancedApp.Models {

    public class AdvancedContext : DbContext {

        public AdvancedContext(DbContextOptions<AdvancedContext> options)
            : base(options) { }

        public DbSet<Employee> Employees { get; set; }

        protected override void OnModelCreating(ModelBuilder modelBuilder) {

        }
    }
}
```

The context class defines a DbSet property to provide convenient access to the Employee objects in the database and override the OnModelCreating method so that the Fluent API can be used to configure the database. No configuration statements are required at the moment because I am happy using the default conventions for the Employee class.

Creating the Controller and Views

For the ASP.NET Core MVC part of the application, I started by creating the Controllers folder and adding to it a class file called HomeController.cs, which I used to define the controller shown in Listing 19-3. The controller defines an Index action that will display data to the user and defines an Update action that will create and update objects. I introduce the ability to soft-delete objects (meaning they are hidden from the user but still in the database) in Chapter 20 and to really delete objects in Chapter 22.

Listing 19-3. The Contents of the HomeController.cs File in the Controllers Folder

```
using AdvancedApp.Models;
using Microsoft.AspNetCore.Mvc;

namespace AdvancedApp.Controllers {

    public class HomeController : Controller {
        private AdvancedContext context;

        public HomeController(AdvancedContext ctx) => context = ctx;

        public IActionResult Index() {
            return View(context.Employees);
        }
```

```
    public IActionResult Edit(long id) {
        return View(id == default(long)
            ? new Employee() : context.Employees.Find(id));
    }

    [HttpPost]
    public IActionResult Update(Employee employee) {

        if (employee.Id == default(long)) {
            context.Add(employee);
        } else {
            context.Update(employee);
        }
        context.SaveChanges();
        return RedirectToAction(nameof(Index));
    }
  }
}
```

To provide the controller with its views, I created a Views/Home folder and added to it a file called Index. cshtml with the content shown in Listing 19-4. This view displays a table showing the details of the Employee objects read from the database, along with buttons that will allow objects to be created and modified.

Listing 19-4. The Contents of the Index.cshtml File in the Views/Home Folder

```
@model IEnumerable<Employee>
@{
    ViewData["Title"] = "Advanced Features";
    Layout = "_Layout";
}
<h3 class="bg-info p-2 text-center text-white">Employees</h3>
<table class="table table-sm table-striped">
    <thead>
        <tr>
            <th>Key</th>
            <th>SSN</th>
            <th>First Name</th>
            <th>Family Name</th>
            <th>Salary</th>
            <th></th>
        </tr>
    </thead>
    <tbody>
        <tr class="placeholder"><td colspan="7" class="text-center">No Data</td></tr>
        @foreach (Employee e in Model) {
            <tr>
                <td>@e.Id</td>
                <td>@e.SSN</td>
                <td>@e.FirstName</td>
                <td>@e.FamilyName</td>
                <td>@e.Salary</td>
                <td class="text-right">
```

```
                <a asp-action="Edit" asp-route-id="@e.Id"
                    class="btn btn-sm btn-primary">Edit</a>
            </td>
        </tr>
    }
    </tbody>
</table>
<div class="text-center">
    <a asp-action="Edit" class="btn btn-primary">Create</a>
</div>
```

To allow the user to create or edit an Employee object, I added a file called Edit.cshtml to the Views/Home folder, with the content shown in Listing 19-5.

Listing 19-5. The Contents of the Edit.cshtml File in the Views/Home Folder

```
@model Employee
@{
    ViewData["Title"] = "Advanced Features";
    Layout = "_Layout";
}

<h4 class="bg-info p-2 text-center text-white">
    Create/Edit
</h4>
<form asp-action="Update" method="post">
    <input type="hidden" asp-for="Id" />
    <div class="form-group">
        <label class="form-control-label" asp-for="SSN"></label>
        <input class="form-control" asp-for="SSN" />
    </div>
    <div class="form-group">
        <label class="form-control-label" asp-for="FirstName"></label>
        <input class="form-control" asp-for="FirstName" />
    </div>
    <div class="form-group">
        <label class="form-control-label" asp-for="FamilyName"></label>
        <input class="form-control" asp-for="FamilyName" />
    </div>
    <div class="form-group">
        <label class="form-control-label" asp-for="Salary"></label>
        <input class="form-control" asp-for="Salary" />
    </div>
    <div class="text-center">
        <button type="submit" class="btn btn-primary">Save</button>
        <a class="btn btn-secondary" asp-action="Index">Cancel</a>
    </div>
</form>
```

To provide a common layout for the view, I created the Views/Shared folder and added to it a file called _Layout.cshtml with the content shown in Listing 19-6.

Listing 19-6. The Contents of the _Layout.cshtml File in the Views/Shared Folder

```
<!DOCTYPE html>
<html>
<head>
    <meta name="viewport" content="width=device-width" />
    <title>@ViewData["Title"]</title>
    <link rel="stylesheet" href="~/lib/bootstrap/dist/css/bootstrap.min.css" />
    <style>
        .placeholder { visibility: collapse }
        .placeholder:only-child { visibility: visible }
    </style>
</head>
<body>
    <div class="p-2">
        @RenderBody()
    </div>
</body>
</html>
```

The layout includes a link for the file that contains the Bootstrap CSS styles and some custom CSS that will display the element added to the placeholder class in the Index.cshtml view when there is no data to display.

To enable tag helpers and import the package that contains the model classes for use in the views, I added a file called _ViewImports.cshtml in the Views folder and added the content shown in Listing 19-7.

Listing 19-7. The Contents of the _ViewImports.cshtml File in the Views Folder

```
@using AdvancedApp.Models
@addTagHelper *, Microsoft.AspNetCore.Mvc.TagHelpers
```

Configuring the Application

To install the NuGet package that provides the Entity Framework Core command-line tools, I right-clicked the AdvancedApp project item in the Solution Explorer, selected Edit AdvancedApp.csproj from the pop-up menu, and added the element shown in Listing 19-8.

Listing 19-8. Adding a NuGet Package in the AdvancedApp.csproj File in the AdvancedApp Folder

```
<Project Sdk="Microsoft.NET.Sdk.Web">

  <PropertyGroup>
    <TargetFramework>netcoreapp2.0</TargetFramework>
  </PropertyGroup>

  <ItemGroup>
    <Folder Include="wwwroot\" />
  </ItemGroup>
```

```
  <ItemGroup>
    <PackageReference Include="Microsoft.AspNetCore.All" Version="2.0.5" />
    <DotNetCliToolReference Include="Microsoft.EntityFrameworkCore.Tools.DotNet"
        Version="2.0.0" />
  </ItemGroup>

</Project>
```

To configure the details of the database for the example application, I used the ASP.NET Configuration File item template to add a file called appsettings.json to the AdvancedApp project folder and added the configuration settings shown in Listing 19-9. In addition to the connection string, I configured the logging system so that Entity Framework Core will display details of the SQL queries and commands that it sends to the database server.

Listing 19-9. The Contents of the appsettings.json File in the AdvancedApp Folder

```
{
  "ConnectionStrings": {
    "DefaultConnection": "Server=(localdb)\\MSSQLLocalDB;Database=AdvancedDb;MultipleActive
ResultSets=true"
  },
  "Logging": {
    "LogLevel": {
      "Default": "None",
      "Microsoft.EntityFrameworkCore": "Information"
    }
  }
}
```

To enable the ASP.NET Core MVC and Entity Framework Core middleware, I added the configuration statements shown in Listing 19-10 to the Startup class.

Listing 19-10. Configuring Middleware in the Startup.cs File in the AdvancedApp Folder

```
using System;
using System.Collections.Generic;
using System.Linq;
using System.Threading.Tasks;
using Microsoft.AspNetCore.Builder;
using Microsoft.AspNetCore.Hosting;
using Microsoft.AspNetCore.Http;
using Microsoft.Extensions.DependencyInjection;
using Microsoft.Extensions.Configuration;
using Microsoft.EntityFrameworkCore;
using AdvancedApp.Models;

namespace AdvancedApp {
    public class Startup {

        public Startup(IConfiguration config) => Configuration = config;

        public IConfiguration Configuration { get; }
```

```
public void ConfigureServices(IServiceCollection services) {
    services.AddMvc();
    string conString = Configuration["ConnectionStrings:DefaultConnection"];
    services.AddDbContext<AdvancedContext>(options =>
        options.UseSqlServer(conString));
}

public void Configure(IApplicationBuilder app, IHostingEnvironment env) {
    app.UseDeveloperExceptionPage();
    app.UseStatusCodePages();
    app.UseStaticFiles();
    app.UseMvcWithDefaultRoute();
}
}
}
```

I used the the JSON File template (found in the ASP.NET Core ➤ Web ➤ General category) to create a file called .bowerrc with the content shown in Listing 19-11. (It is important to pay attention to this file name: it starts with a period, contains the letter r twice and has no file extension).

Listing 19-11. The Contents of the .bowerrc File in the AdvancedApp Folder

```
{
  "directory": "wwwroot/lib"
}
```

I used the JSON File template again to create a file called bower.json, with the content shown in Listing 19-12.

Listing 19-12. The Contents of the bower.json File in the AdvancedApp Folder

```
{
  "name": "asp.net",
  "private": true,
  "dependencies": {
    "bootstrap": "4.0.0"
  }
}
```

When you save the file, Visual Studio will download the Bootstrap package and install it into the wwwroot/lib folder.

To simplify the process of working with the application, edit the Properties/launchSettings.json file and change the two URLs that it contains so they both specify port 5000, as shown in Listing 19-13. This is the port that I will use in the URLs to demonstrate different features of the example application.

Listing 19-13. Changing Ports in the launchSettings.json File in the Properties Folder

```json
{
  "iisSettings": {
    "windowsAuthentication": false,
    "anonymousAuthentication": true,
    "iisExpress": {
      "applicationUrl": "http://localhost:5000/",
      "sslPort": 0
    }
  },
  "profiles": {
    "IIS Express": {
      "commandName": "IISExpress",
      "launchBrowser": true,
      "environmentVariables": {
        "ASPNETCORE_ENVIRONMENT": "Development"
      }
    },
    "AdvancedApp": {
      "commandName": "Project",
      "launchBrowser": true,
      "environmentVariables": {
        "ASPNETCORE_ENVIRONMENT": "Development"
      },
      "applicationUrl": "http://localhost:5000/"
    }
  }
}
```

Creating the Database and Testing the Application

Run the commands shown in Listing 19-14 in the AdvancedApp project folder to create and apply the migration that will set up the database to store Employee objects.

Listing 19-14. Creating and Applying a Database Migration

```
dotnet ef migrations add Initial
dotnet ef database update
```

I will drop and re-create the database in the next section, but it is important to make sure that the example application is working before proceeding. Start the application using dotnet run and navigate to http://localhost:5000. There is no data in the database currently, and you will see the placeholder content. Click the Create button, fill out the form fields, and click the Save button to store a new Employee object in the database, producing a result similar to the one shown in Figure 19-3.

Figure 19-3. *Running the example application*

Managing Key Generation

When working with SQL Server, there are two strategies that can be used to produce the values used for primary keys, which are configured using the methods described in Table 19-3.

Table 19-3. *The Key Generation Methods*

Name	Description
ForSqlServerUseIdentityColumns()	This method selects the Identity strategy for key generation.
ForSqlServerUseSequenceHiLo()	This method specifies the Hi-Lo strategy for key generation.

■ **Note** Not all database servers support these key strategies. See the documentation for your database provider package to see what strategies are available.

Understanding the Identity Strategy

The Identity strategy is used by default. When Entity Framework Core stores a new object, it relies on the database server to create a unique primary key value. This means that storing an object requires two operations, which you can see if you click the Create button, fill out the form, click the Save button, and examine the logging messages generated by the application. The first operation inserts the new data into the database, like this:

```
...
INSERT INTO [Employees] ([FamilyName], [FirstName], [SSN], [Salary])
VALUES (@p0, @p1, @p2, @p3);
...
```

475

Entity Framework Core has not included a value for the Id property because it knows that the value will be assigned by the database server (and, in fact, providing a value for an UPDATE results in an error). The second operation queries the database to get the primary key that the database generated when it inserted the new data into the table, like this:

```
...
SELECT [Id]
FROM [Employees]
WHERE @@ROWCOUNT = 1 AND [Id] = scope_identity();
...
```

The advantage of this approach is simplicity. The applications using the database don't have to coordinate with one another to avoid duplicate keys or have any knowledge of how keys are generated. The disadvantage is that an additional query is required to obtain the key value.

Tip　If you are not sure what key strategy to follow, then use the Identity strategy because it is the easiest to work with and least likely to cause you any problems.

Understanding the Hi-Lo Key Strategy

The Hi-Lo strategy is an optimization that allows Entity Framework Core to create primary key values, instead of the database server, while still ensuring those values are unique. A little work is required to see how this strategy works because Entity Framework Core migrations are unable to change the strategy of a primary key that has been created in an earlier migration. The first step is to apply the Fluent API method from Table 19-3 in the context class to select the Hi-Lo strategy, as shown in Listing 19-15.

Listing 19-15.　Selecting a Key Strategy in the AdvancedContext.cs File in the Models Folder

```
using Microsoft.EntityFrameworkCore;

namespace AdvancedApp.Models {

    public class AdvancedContext : DbContext {

        public AdvancedContext(DbContextOptions<AdvancedContext> options)
            : base(options) { }

        public DbSet<Employee> Employees { get; set; }

        protected override void OnModelCreating(ModelBuilder modelBuilder) {

            modelBuilder.Entity<Employee>()
                .Property(e => e.Id).ForSqlServerUseSequenceHiLo();
        }
    }
}
```

The strategy is applied by selecting a property and calling the ForSqlServerUseSequenceHiLo methods described in Table 19-3. To apply the change to the key generation strategy, I need to remove the existing migration and create a new one so that the data model is created in a single migration and no change in Identity strategy is required. Run the commands shown in Listing 19-16 in the AdvancedApp project folder to remove the existing migration and create a replacement.

Listing 19-16. Resetting Migrations

```
dotnet ef migrations remove --force
dotnet ef migrations add HiLoStrategy
```

If you examine the Up method in the `<timestamp>_ HiLoStrategy.cs` file in the Migrations folder, you will see that a new sequence called EntityFrameworkHiLoSequence has been set up, like this:

```
...
protected override void Up(MigrationBuilder migrationBuilder) {
    migrationBuilder.CreateSequence(
        name: "EntityFrameworkHiLoSequence",
        incrementBy: 10);

    migrationBuilder.CreateTable(
        name: "Employees",
        columns: table => new {
            Id = table.Column<long>(nullable: false),
            FamilyName = table.Column<string>(nullable: true),
            FirstName = table.Column<string>(nullable: true),
            SSN = table.Column<string>(nullable: true),
            Salary = table.Column<decimal>(nullable: false)
        },
        constraints: table => {
            table.PrimaryKey("PK_Employees", x => x.Id);
        });
}
...
```

The new sequence will be used to create primary key values, as I explain shortly. Run the commands shown in Listing 19-17 in the AdvancedApp project folder to drop and re-create the database using the new migration.

Listing 19-17. Recreating the Database

```
dotnet ef database drop --force
dotnet ef database update
```

Using the Hi-Lo Strategy

In the Hi-Lo strategy, Entity Framework Core takes responsibility for generating primary keys based on an initial seed value obtained from the database server. When an application needs to store an object, Entity Framework Core gets the next value from the EntityFrameworkHiLoSequence sequence and treats this as the first number in a block of ten primary key values that it can create without needing to refer to the database server or coordinate with other applications. For example, if the next sequence value is 100, then Entity Framework Core knows that it can create objects using the primary keys 100, 101, 102, and so on, through to 109. Once the block of primary keys has been used up, the next value from the sequence is read. Each application (or instance of the same application) follows the same process to get its own block of keys, ensuring that no key values are duplicated. The database server ensures that each request for a sequence value gets a different result, ensuring that there are no duplicate blocks of keys assigned.

To see how this strategy works, start the application, navigate to `http://localhost:5000`, and go through the process of creating and storing a new `Employee` object. There won't be any obvious difference in the way that the ASP.NET Core MVC part of the application behaves, and the changes are visible only if you examine the Entity Framework Core logging messages.

When you store a new object, Entity Framework Core gets the next value from the sequence, like this:

```
...
SELECT NEXT VALUE FOR [EntityFrameworkHiLoSequence]
...
```

The sequence value is the start of the block of ten primary keys that Entity Framework Core can use without needing any further checks. This is known as the "high" part of the key, which gives the Hi-Lo strategy part of its name. The "low" part comes from incrementing the sequence value to generate the block of keys, which are included in the `INSERT` operation, like this:

```
...
INSERT INTO [Employees] ([Id], [FamilyName], [FirstName], [SSN], [Salary])
VALUES (@p0, @p1, @p2, @p3, @p4);
...
```

Unlike the Identity strategy, Entity Framework Core doesn't have to query the database to determine the primary key value. Each block of keys is shared between the context objects created by an application, so Entity Framework Core only has to query for the next value in the sequence after it has stored ten new objects.

■ **Caution**   Do not rely on Entity Framework Core using a specific sequence of keys. The implementation of the Hi-Lo strategy may change or may be implemented differently if you switch to a different database provider.

The advantage of this strategy is that it doesn't require a query after each insert operation to discover the primary key. The disadvantage is that all of the applications using the database must understand and follow the Hi-Lo strategy for it to work.

Understanding Hi-Lo Key Exhaustion

This strategy can exhaust the possible range of keys because the unused keys in a block will be "lost" when an application is restarted, so you must select a data type for the primary keys that provides adequate capacity. To see how ranges of keys are left unused, stop and restart the application, navigate to `http://localhost:5000`, click the Create button, and store another `Employee` object in the database. A new sequence value will be read from the database and used as the "high" component of the key, producing the results shown in Figure 19-4. The keys in the range 2 to 10 that were in the block received by the previous instance of the application will not be used.

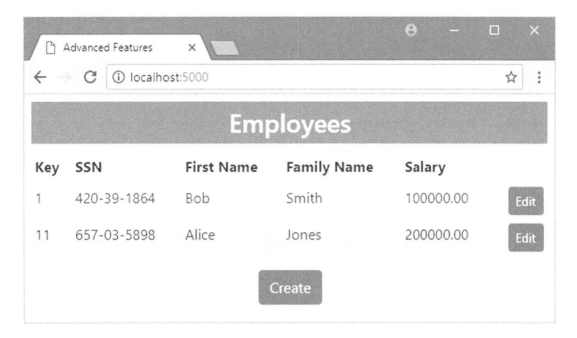

Figure 19-4. *Skipping key ranges with the Hi-Lo strategy*

Working with Natural Keys

Some data types have their own *natural keys*, which means that there is some aspect of the data that can uniquely identify an object. In the case of the Employee class, the SSN property might be a natural key in countries where Social Security numbers can be relied on to be unique.

UNDERSTANDING SURROGATE KEYS

Even though the Employee data has a natural key, I still added a dedicated primary key property to the Employee class, which I used to demonstrate the key generation strategies in the previous section. This is known as a *surrogate key*, and its purpose is solely to identify an object; it has no relationship to the rest of the values that make up an object. It can be difficult to make data model changes that affect the primary key, as you will see in the examples in this chapter, and using a surrogate key helps minimize the impact of future changes to the data model. The data in the example application might happily use Social Security numbers if it needed to support only one country, but a change to support other countries might require the SSN property to be removed or modified. This is much harder to do when a surrogate key has not been used.

Ensuring Unique Values for Natural Keys

Even though I am not using the natural key to uniquely identify Employee objects, it is still important to ensure that there are no duplicate values for the SSN property stored in the database. This will help prevent mistyped entries from being entered by users and help minimize problems if I need to change the data model later. The simplest way to prevent duplicates is to create an index for a property, as shown in Listing 19-18.

Listing 19-18. Creating an Index in the AdvancedContext.cs File in the Models Folder

```
using Microsoft.EntityFrameworkCore;

namespace AdvancedApp.Models {

    public class AdvancedContext : DbContext {

        public AdvancedContext(DbContextOptions<AdvancedContext> options)
            : base(options) { }

        public DbSet<Employee> Employees { get; set; }

        protected override void OnModelCreating(ModelBuilder modelBuilder) {

            modelBuilder.Entity<Employee>()
                .Property(e => e.Id).ForSqlServerUseSequenceHiLo();

            modelBuilder.Entity<Employee>()
                .HasIndex(e => e.SSN).HasName("SSNIndex").IsUnique();
        }
    }
}
```

Indexes are created by selecting the class using the Entity method and calling the HasIndex method to choose the property for which the index will be created. The HasName method is used to specify a name for the index, and when working with natural keys, you must also call the IsUnique method to add a constraint to the database to prevent duplicate values.

⬛ **Note**   Indexes can be created only using the Fluent API. There is no attribute support for this feature.

The listing sets up a unique index for the SSN property, which can be added to the database by creating and applying a migration using the commands shown in Listing 19-19, which must be run in the AdvancedApp project folder.

Listing 19-19. Creating and Applying a Migration

```
dotnet ef migrations add UniqueIndex
dotnet ef database update
```

If you examine the Up method of the `<timestamp>_UniqueIndex.cs` file that has been added to the Migrations folder, you will see how the Fluent API statement in Listing 19-18 has altered the database to enforce uniqueness for the natural key.

```
...
protected override void Up(MigrationBuilder migrationBuilder) {

    migrationBuilder.AlterColumn<string>(name: "SSN",
        table: "Employees", type: "nvarchar(450)", nullable: true,
        oldClrType: typeof(string), oldNullable: true);

    migrationBuilder.CreateIndex(name: "SSNIndex",
        table: "Employees", column: "SSN", unique: true,
        filter: "[SSN] IS NOT NULL");
}
...
```

The first statement in the Up method changes the data type of the SSN column so that it has a fixed size. The second statement creates the index, setting the unique argument to true, so that duplicate entries are prohibited. Start the application, navigate to `http://localhost:5000`, and try to store a new Employee object whose SSN value is the same as the existing entry; you will see the error message shown in Figure 19-5.

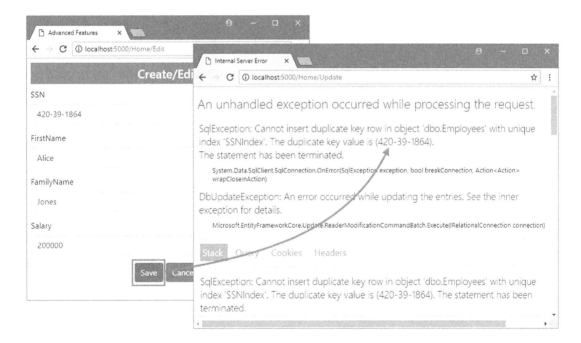

Figure 19-5. *Enforcing unique values for a natural key*

Creating an Alternate Key

A different approach is required if you need to create relationships using natural key values. In these situations, an *alternate key* is required, which ensures unique values and also configures the database so that an object can be uniquely identified by an additional key, as well as with the primary key.

UNDERSTANDING WHEN ALTERNATE KEYS ARE USEFUL

In most applications, you can safely create relationships using the primary key, which is what Entity Framework Core will do by default. If you only need to avoid duplicate values, then create a unique index instead of creating an alternate key, as described in the previous section. Being able to create a relationship on an alternate key is important only if you expect the alternate key value to be moved to another object in the future and you want to seamlessly transfer existing relationships, which is something that most applications don't have to worry about.

To demonstrate the use of an alternate key, I added a file called `SecondaryIdentity.cs` to the `Models` folder and used it to define the class shown in Listing 19-20.

Listing 19-20. The Contents of the SecondaryIdentity.cs in the Models Folder

```
namespace AdvancedApp.Models {

    public class SecondaryIdentity {
        public long Id { get; set; }
        public string Name { get; set; }
        public bool InActiveUse { get; set; }

        public string PrimarySSN { get; set; }
        public Employee PrimaryIdentity { get; set; }
    }
}
```

This class will represent another name by which an employee is known. The `SecondaryIdentity` class defines an `PrimaryIdentity` property that forms part of the relationship with the `Employee` class, and the `PrimarySSN` property will be used as the foreign key property. To complete the relationship, I added the inverse navigation property to the `Employee` class shown in Listing 19-21.

Listing 19-21. Completing the Relationship in the Employee.cs File in the Models Folder

```
namespace AdvancedApp.Models {

    public class Employee {

        public long Id { get; set; }
        public string SSN { get; set; }
        public string FirstName { get; set; }
        public string FamilyName { get; set; }
        public decimal Salary { get; set; }
```

```
        public SecondaryIdentity OtherIdentity { get; set; }
    }
}
```

The `OtherIdentity` property returns a `SecondaryIdentity` object, which tells Entity Framework Core that this is a one-to-one relationship.

By default, Entity Framework Core will use the primary key of the `Employee` class for the foreign key column in the relationship between the `SecondaryIdentity` and `Employee` classes. I added the Fluent API statements shown in Listing 19-22 to the context class to override this convention and use the alternate key instead.

⬛ **Note**   Alternate keys can be created only using the Fluent API. There is no attribute support for this feature.

Listing 19-22. Using an Alternate Key in the AdvancedContext.cs File in the Models Folder

```
using Microsoft.EntityFrameworkCore;

namespace AdvancedApp.Models {

    public class AdvancedContext : DbContext {

        public AdvancedContext(DbContextOptions<AdvancedContext> options)
            : base(options) { }

        public DbSet<Employee> Employees { get; set; }

        protected override void OnModelCreating(ModelBuilder modelBuilder) {

            modelBuilder.Entity<Employee>()
                .Property(e => e.Id).ForSqlServerUseSequenceHiLo();

            //modelBuilder.Entity<Employee>()
            //    .HasIndex(e => e.SSN).HasName("SSNIndex").IsUnique();

            modelBuilder.Entity<Employee>().HasAlternateKey(e => e.SSN);

            modelBuilder.Entity<SecondaryIdentity>()
                .HasOne(s => s.PrimaryIdentity)
                .WithOne(e => e.OtherIdentity)
                .HasPrincipalKey<Employee>(e => e.SSN)
                .HasForeignKey<SecondaryIdentity>(s => s.PrimarySSN);
        }
    }
}
```

The first new statement in Listing 19-22 creates the alternate key using the `HasAlternateKey` method, which has the same effect as creating a unique index, except that Entity Framework Core will allow relationships to be created using the selected property. This method is required to prepare a property as an alternate key only if you are not going to set up the relationship immediately, but I tend to include it anyway, just to make my intentions obvious.

The second new statement in Listing 19-22 sets up the relationship between the two classes. The HasOne and WithOne methods are used to select the navigation properties, and the HasPrincipalKey<T> and HasForeignKey<T> methods are used to select the alternate key and foreign key properties.

The result is that the SSN property will be configured as an alternate key, which is used as the foreign key in the relationship with the SecondaryIdentity class. Run the commands shown in Listing 19-23 in the AdvancedApp project folder to create and apply the change to the database.

Listing 19-23. Creating and Applying a Database Migration

```
dotnet ef migrations add AlternateKey
dotnet ef database update
```

If you examine the Up method in the <timestamp>_AlternateKey.cs file that has been added to the Migrations folder, you will see the foreign key constraint that has been applied to the PrimarySSN column in the table that has been created to store SecondaryIdentity objects.

```
...
constraints: table => {
    table.PrimaryKey("PK_SecondaryIdentity", x => x.Id);
    table.ForeignKey(
        name: "FK_SecondaryIdentity_Employees_PrimarySSN",
        column: x => x.PrimarySSN,
        principalTable: "Employees",
        principalColumn: "SSN",
        onDelete: ReferentialAction.Restrict);
});
...
```

Once you have defined the alternate key, you can use it to create relationships just as you would with a primary key. To work through the changes into the ASP.NET Core MVC part of the application, I added the elements shown in Listing 19-24 to the Edit.cshtml view so that the user can create or edit a SecondaryIdentity object along with the Employee object it is related to.

Listing 19-24. Adding Elements in the Edit.cshtml File in the Views/Home Folder

```
@model Employee
@{
    ViewData["Title"] = "Advanced Features";
    Layout = "_Layout";
}

<h4 class="bg-info p-2 text-center text-white">
    Create/Edit
</h4>
<form asp-action="Update" method="post">
    <input type="hidden" asp-for="Id" />
    <div class="form-group">
        <label class="form-control-label" asp-for="SSN"></label>
        <input class="form-control" asp-for="SSN" />
    </div>
```

```
    <div class="form-group">
        <label class="form-control-label" asp-for="FirstName"></label>
        <input class="form-control" asp-for="FirstName" />
    </div>
    <div class="form-group">
        <label class="form-control-label" asp-for="FamilyName"></label>
        <input class="form-control" asp-for="FamilyName" />
    </div>
    <div class="form-group">
        <label class="form-control-label" asp-for="Salary"></label>
        <input class="form-control" asp-for="Salary" />
    </div>

    <input type="hidden" asp-for="OtherIdentity.Id" />
    <div class="form-group">
        <label class="form-control-label">Other Identity Name:</label>
        <input class="form-control" asp-for="OtherIdentity.Name" />
    </div>

    <div class="form-check">
        <label class="form-check-label">
            <input class="form-check-input" type="checkbox"
                    asp-for="OtherIdentity.InActiveUse" />
            In Active Use
        </label>
    </div>

    <div class="text-center">
        <button type="submit" class="btn btn-primary">Save</button>
        <a class="btn btn-secondary" asp-action="Index">Cancel</a>
    </div>
</form>
```

I also modified the Edit method in the Home controller so that the query for an Employee object follows the navigation property to include the related data and pass it to the view, as shown in Listing 19-25.

Listing 19-25. Including Related Data in the HomeController.cs File in the Controllers Folder

```
using AdvancedApp.Models;
using Microsoft.AspNetCore.Mvc;
using Microsoft.EntityFrameworkCore;
using System.Linq;

namespace AdvancedApp.Controllers {

    public class HomeController : Controller {
        private AdvancedContext context;

        public HomeController(AdvancedContext ctx) => context = ctx;
```

```
    public IActionResult Index() {
        return View(context.Employees);
    }

    public IActionResult Edit(long id) {
        return View(id == default(long)
            ? new Employee() : context.Employees.Include(e => e.OtherIdentity)
                .First(e => e.Id == id));
    }

    [HttpPost]
    public IActionResult Update(Employee employee) {
        if (employee.Id == default(long)) {
            context.Add(employee);
        } else {
            context.Update(employee);
        }
        context.SaveChanges();
        return RedirectToAction(nameof(Index));
    }
  }
}
```

The query in the Edit method uses the Include method to follow the navigation property and the First method to find the object with the Id value specified by the user. To check that the alternate key is working, start the application using dotnet run, navigate to http://localhost:5000, and create or edit an Employee object. With the addition of the new relationship (and the alternate key it uses), you can provide details of a second identity, as shown in Figure 19-6.

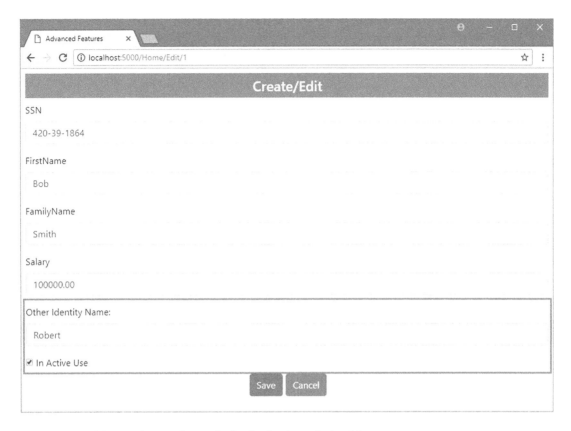

Figure 19-6. *Using an alternate key as the foreign key in a relationship*

■ **Tip** Don't make any change to the SSN, FirstName, or FamilyName properties of objects that have been stored in the database. The properties that form the key cannot be changed unless the database is specifically configured to allow it.

Using Natural Keys as Primary Keys

If you don't want to use a surrogate key—typically because you have confidence that there will be no data model changes—you can select a property to use as the primary key and take responsibility for generating unique values, although this is not a decision to be taken lightly because you are responsible for ensuring that each value is unique. Natural keys can be messy and cannot always be relied on to be as unique as might have been assumed during the project design phase. To demonstrate the use of a natural key as the primary key, I reconfigured the data model using Fluent API statements, telling Entity Framework Core to ignore the existing primary key property and use the SSN property instead, as shown in Listing 19-26.

░ **Note**   You can select any property as the primary key by using the Key attribute. The rest of this example is the same, including the changes required to deal with keys that the user/application is responsible for generating.

Listing 19-26. Using a Natural Key in the AdvancedContext.cs File in the Models Folder

```
using Microsoft.EntityFrameworkCore;

namespace AdvancedApp.Models {

    public class AdvancedContext : DbContext {

        public AdvancedContext(DbContextOptions<AdvancedContext> options)
            : base(options) { }

        public DbSet<Employee> Employees { get; set; }

        protected override void OnModelCreating(ModelBuilder modelBuilder) {

            modelBuilder.Entity<Employee>().Ignore(e => e.Id);
            modelBuilder.Entity<Employee>().HasKey(e => e.SSN);

            modelBuilder.Entity<SecondaryIdentity>()
                .HasOne(s => s.PrimaryIdentity)
                .WithOne(e => e.OtherIdentity)
                .HasPrincipalKey<Employee>(e => e.SSN)
                .HasForeignKey<SecondaryIdentity>(s => s.PrimarySSN);
        }
    }
}
```

I have used the Ignore method to exclude the Id property from the data model and the HasKey method to select the SSN property as the primary key. No change is required to the statement that configures the relationship between the Employee and SecondaryIdentity classes, although the call to the HasPrincipalKey method could be removed since Entity Framework Core will use the SSN property in this relationship by default now that it is the primary key.

Run the commands shown in Listing 19-27 in the AdvancedApp project folder to create and apply a migration that will change the primary key.

Listing 19-27. Resetting and Updating the Database

```
dotnet ef migrations remove --force
dotnet ef migrations add NaturalPrimaryKey
dotnet ef database drop --force
dotnet ef database update
```

Entity Framework Core struggles to make changes that involve keys, and trying to add a migration changes the primary key won't work because the migration will try to remove a constraint set up for the alternate key that is used by the relationship created on it. To work around this problem, I removed the migration that set up the alternate key, created a migration that selects the SSN property as the primary key, and then re-created the database.

To work the changes through into the ASP.NET Core MVC part of the application, I updated the controller so that it uses the SSN property as the primary key, as shown in Listing 19-28.

Listing 19-28. Using the New Primary Key in the HomeController.cs File in the Controllers Folder

```
using AdvancedApp.Models;
using Microsoft.AspNetCore.Mvc;
using Microsoft.EntityFrameworkCore;
using System.Linq;

namespace AdvancedApp.Controllers {

    public class HomeController : Controller {
        private AdvancedContext context;

        public HomeController(AdvancedContext ctx) => context = ctx;

        public IActionResult Index() {
            return View(context.Employees);
        }

        public IActionResult Edit(string SSN) {
            return View(string.IsNullOrWhiteSpace(SSN)
                ? new Employee() : context.Employees.Include(e => e.OtherIdentity)
                    .First(e => e.SSN == SSN));
        }

        [HttpPost]
        public IActionResult Update(Employee employee) {
            if (context.Employees.Count(e => e.SSN == employee.SSN) == 0) {
                context.Add(employee);
            } else {
                context.Update(employee);
            }
            context.SaveChanges();
            return RedirectToAction(nameof(Index));
        }
    }
}
```

The most important change is to the Update method. When I was relying on the database server to generate key values, I could determine whether a request was an update or create operation by checking for the default value of the key type. I can't do that now that the user is responsible for providing a value key value, so I have queried the database to check to see whether there is an existing object with the key value included in the request, which I perform using the LINQ Count method.

Start the application using `dotnet run`, navigate to `http://localhost:5000`, click the Create button, and store a new `Employee` object in the database. If you examine the log messages generated by the application, you will see that the query in the `Update` method results in this operation:

```
...
SELECT COUNT(*)
FROM [Employees] AS [e]
WHERE [e].[SSN] = @__employee_SSN_0
...
```

This check allows me to determine whether the key specified by the user is already in the database without loading the data and tripping over the Entity Framework Core data cache when I perform an update using an object created by the MVC model binder.

Creating Composite Keys

A *composite key* uniquely identifies an object by combining values from two or more columns in the database table or properties from the entity class. You won't need to create composite keys when using the identity or Hi-Lo strategies to generate key values because they will always be unique, but a composite key can be useful when using a natural key that is unique only when combined with another value. Social Security numbers are often treated as unique in the United States, but some studies have estimated that there are 40 million numbers that are used by more than one person, through a combination of confusion, errors, and fraud. At the moment, the example application will generate an exception if an attempt is made to create an `Employee` object that uses an SSN value already stored in the database, but in this section, I am going to relax the rules about SSN uniqueness by identifying objects through a combination of properties, as shown in Listing 19-29.

Note   Composite keys can be created only by using the Fluent API. There is no attribute support for this feature.

Listing 19-29. Creating a Composite Key in the AdvancedContext.cs File in the Models Folder

```
using Microsoft.EntityFrameworkCore;

namespace AdvancedApp.Models {

    public class AdvancedContext : DbContext {

        public AdvancedContext(DbContextOptions<AdvancedContext> options)
            : base(options) { }

        public DbSet<Employee> Employees { get; set; }

        protected override void OnModelCreating(ModelBuilder modelBuilder) {

            modelBuilder.Entity<Employee>().Ignore(e => e.Id);
            modelBuilder.Entity<Employee>()
                .HasKey(e => new { e.SSN, e.FirstName, e.FamilyName });
```

```
        modelBuilder.Entity<SecondaryIdentity>()
            .HasOne(s => s.PrimaryIdentity)
            .WithOne(e => e.OtherIdentity)
            .HasPrincipalKey<Employee>(e => new { e.SSN,
                e.FirstName, e.FamilyName })
            .HasForeignKey<SecondaryIdentity>(s => new { s.PrimarySSN,
                s.PrimaryFirstName, s.PrimaryFamilyName });
        }
    }
}
```

Composite keys are created by creating an object that selects the properties that should be used in the key, which are the SSN, FirstName, and FamilyName properties in this example. There can be duplicate values for each of these properties in the database, just as long as each object has a unique combination of values. The properties that make up the key have to be used to create relationships too, which you can see reflected in the lambda expressions used in the HasPrincipalKey method, which configures the one side of the relationship with the SecondaryIdentity class.

```
...
.HasPrincipalKey<Employee>(e => new { e.SSN, e.FirstName, e.FamilyName })
...
```

For the HasForeignKey method, I have specified some additional foreign key properties for keeping track of the related Employee object using the composite key, and I have defined those properties on the SecondaryIdentity class in Listing 19-30.

Listing 19-30. Adding Foreign Key Properties in the SecondaryIdentity.cs File in the Models Folder

```
namespace AdvancedApp.Models {

    public class SecondaryIdentity {
        public long Id { get; set; }
        public string Name { get; set; }
        public bool InActiveUse { get; set; }

        public string PrimarySSN { get; set; }
        public string PrimaryFamilyName { get; set; }
        public string PrimaryFirstName { get; set; }
        public Employee PrimaryIdentity { get; set; }
    }
}
```

Run the commands shown in Listing 19-31 in the AdvancedApp project folder to create a new migration and apply it to the database. Entity Framework Core struggles to make the changes required to the primary key, so these commands remove the migration from the previous section, add a new migration, and then re-create the database.

Listing 19-31. Creating and Applying a Database Migration

```
dotnet ef migrations remove --force
dotnet ef migrations add CompositeKey
dotnet ef database drop --force
dotnet ef database update
```

If you examine the Up method in the `<timestamp>_CompositeKey.cs` file in the `Migrations` folder, you will find a statement that will configure the primary key for the `Employees` table using a combination of the properties selected in Listing 19-29.

```
...
migrationBuilder.AddPrimaryKey(
    name: "PK_Employees",
    table: "Employees",
    columns: new[] { "SSN", "FirstName", "FamilyName" });
...
```

When you create a composite key, the change has to be worked through the rest of the application. In Listing 19-32, I have updated the controller so that it will use all of the key properties when querying the database.

Listing 19-32. Using the Composite Key in the HomeController.cs File in the Controllers Folder

```
using AdvancedApp.Models;
using Microsoft.AspNetCore.Mvc;
using Microsoft.EntityFrameworkCore;
using System.Linq;

namespace AdvancedApp.Controllers {

    public class HomeController : Controller {
        private AdvancedContext context;

        public HomeController(AdvancedContext ctx) => context = ctx;

        public IActionResult Index() {
            return View(context.Employees);
        }

        public IActionResult Edit(string SSN, string firstName, string familyName) {
            return View(string.IsNullOrWhiteSpace(SSN)
                ? new Employee() : context.Employees.Include(e => e.OtherIdentity)
                    .First(e => e.SSN == SSN
                        && e.FirstName == firstName
                        && e.FamilyName == familyName));
        }
    }
```

```
    [HttpPost]
    public IActionResult Update(Employee employee) {
        if (context.Employees.Count(e => e.SSN == employee.SSN
                && e.FirstName == employee.FirstName
                && e.FamilyName == employee.FamilyName) == 0) {
            context.Add(employee);
        } else {
            context.Update(employee);
        }
        context.SaveChanges();
        return RedirectToAction(nameof(Index));
    }
  }
}
```

Without these changes, the controller won't query the database using the full primary key, which will lead to some odd results, either selecting the wrong object for editing or failing to insert a new object if it has an SSN value that is already in the database.

⬛ **Tip** Some methods, such as Find, accept a series of key values that are used to query the database. When you use these methods, you must provide values in the same order that you used to define the composite key in the context class. For the example application, this means querying using the values of the SSN, FirstName, and FamilyName properties in this order because that's how I defined the composite key.

The final change is to add some additional attributes that select an object for editing in the Index.cshtml file, as shown in Listing 19-33, so that the Edit method defined by the controller receives all of the primary key values.

Listing 19-33. Using the Composite Key in the Index.cshtml File in the Views/Home Folder

```
@model IEnumerable<Employee>
@{
    ViewData["Title"] = "Advanced Features";
    Layout = "_Layout";
}
<h3 class="bg-info p-2 text-center text-white">Employees</h3>
<table class="table table-sm table-striped">
    <thead>
        <tr>
            <th>Key</th>
            <th>SSN</th>
            <th>First Name</th>
            <th>Family Name</th>
            <th>Salary</th>
            <th></th>
        </tr>
    </thead>
```

```
<tbody>
    <tr class="placeholder"><td colspan="7" class="text-center">No Data</td></tr>
    @foreach (Employee e in Model) {
        <tr>
            <td>@e.Id</td>
            <td>@e.SSN</td>
            <td>@e.FirstName</td>
            <td>@e.FamilyName</td>
            <td>@e.Salary</td>
            <td class="text-right">
                <a asp-action="Edit" asp-route-ssn="@e.SSN"
                    asp-route-firstname="@e.FirstName"
                    asp-route-familyname="@e.FamilyName"
                    class="btn btn-sm btn-primary">Edit</a>
            </td>
        </tr>
    }
</tbody>
</table>
<div class="text-center">
    <a asp-action="Edit" class="btn btn-primary">Create</a>
</div>
```

The `asp-route-` attributes provide the composite key values required to identify an object when the user edits an `Employee`. To ensure that the composite key is working, start the application, navigate to `http://localhost:5000`, and create new `Employee` objects using the data values shown in Table 19-4.

Table 19-4. *The Data for Checking the Composite Key*

SSN	FirstName	FamilyName	Salary	Other Name	In Active Use
420-39-1864	Bob	Smith	100000	Robert	Checked
420-39-1864	Alice	Jones	200000	Allie	Checked
420-39-1864	Bob	Smith	150000	Bobby	Unchecked

All three rows in the table contain the same value for the SSN property, but you will see an exception only when trying to create the third object, which has the same combination of values for the three properties used in the primary key. This is noted in the exception message displayed by the application, shown in Figure 19-7.

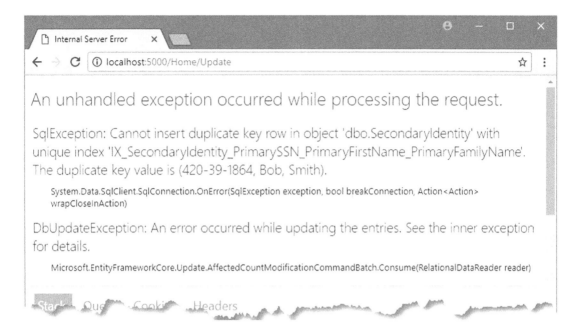

Figure 19-7. *Trying to create a duplicate composite key*

The error message includes details of the duplicate key, which demonstrates that it is the combination of primary key properties that are being used to identify objects, like this:

```
...
The duplicate key value is (420-39-1864, Bob, Smith).
...
```

When the combination of values forms the key, then individual properties can be duplicated, as this example demonstrates.

Summary

In this chapter, I demonstrated the advanced Entity Framework Core features for working with keys. I explained the Identity and Hi-Lo key generation strategies and how to work with natural keys in different ways: ensuring unique values, using them to create relationships, and as primary keys. In the next chapter, I describe the advanced features for queries.

CHAPTER 20

Queries

The Entity Framework Core support for querying with LINQ makes working with data a natural process for .NET developers. In the sections that follow, I describe the advanced features that Entity Framework Core provides for controlling queries, which can be useful if you can't get the behavior you require using the techniques described in earlier chapters. Table 20-1 puts this chapter in context.

Table 20-1. *Putting Advanced Query Features in Context*

Question	Answer
What are they?	The advanced query features allow you to override the default Entity Framework Core behavior.
Why are they useful?	These features can be useful when working with existing databases or when you have specific performance requirements.
How are they used?	These features are applied as part of LINQ queries.
Are there any pitfalls or limitations?	These features can unexpectedly change the behavior of applications or alter query results and should be used with caution.
Are there any alternatives?	These are specialized features that most projects will not require.

Table 20-2 summarizes the chapter.

Table 20-2. *Chapter Summary*

Problem	Solution	Listing
Query for read-only data	Disable the change tracking feature	1–7
Filter the data produced by all queries	Apply a query filter	8–12
Override a query filter	Use the IgnoreQueryFilters method	13, 14
Query for data using a search expression	Use the Like function	15
Perform concurrent queries	Use the asynchronous query methods	16, 17
Speed up query reuse	Explicitly compile the query	18
Detect client evaluation of queries	Enable exception reporting when queries include client evaluation	19, 21

© Adam Freeman 2018
A. Freeman, *Pro Entity Framework Core 2 for ASP.NET Core MVC*,
https://doi.org/10.1007/978-1-4842-3435-8_20

Preparing for This Chapter

In this chapter, I continue to use the AdvancedApp project that I created in Chapter 19. To prepare for this chapter, I have modified the view used to create and edit Employee objects so the values of the composite primary key cannot be changed, as shown in Listing 20-1.

■ **Tip** If you don't want to follow the process of building the example project, you can download all of the required files from this book's source code repository, available at https://github.com/apress/pro-ef-core-2-for-asp.net-core-mvc.

Listing 20-1. Disabling Key Changes in the Edit.cshtml File in the Views/Home Folder

```
@model Employee
@{
    ViewData["Title"] = "Advanced Features";
    Layout = "_Layout";
}

<h4 class="bg-info p-2 text-center text-white">
    Create/Edit
</h4>
<form asp-action="Update" method="post">
    <input type="hidden" asp-for="Id" />
    <div class="form-group">
        <label class="form-control-label" asp-for="SSN"></label>
        <input class="form-control" asp-for="SSN" readonly="@Model.SSN" />
    </div>
    <div class="form-group">
        <label class="form-control-label" asp-for="FirstName"></label>
        <input class="form-control" asp-for="FirstName"
            readonly="@Model.FirstName" />
    </div>
    <div class="form-group">
        <label class="form-control-label" asp-for="FamilyName"></label>
        <input class="form-control" asp-for="FamilyName"
            readonly="@Model.FamilyName"/>
    </div>
    <div class="form-group">
        <label class="form-control-label" asp-for="Salary"></label>
        <input class="form-control" asp-for="Salary" />
    </div>
    <input type="hidden" asp-for="OtherIdentity.Id" />
    <div class="form-group">
        <label class="form-control-label">Other Identity Name:</label>
        <input class="form-control" asp-for="OtherIdentity.Name" />
    </div>
```

```
    <div class="form-check">
        <label class="form-check-label">
            <input class="form-check-input" type="checkbox"
                    asp-for="OtherIdentity.InActiveUse" />
            In Active Use
        </label>
    </div>
    <div class="text-center">
        <button type="submit" class="btn btn-primary">Save</button>
        <a class="btn btn-secondary" asp-action="Index">Cancel</a>
    </div>
</form>
```

Next, run the commands shown in Listing 20-2 in the AdvancedApp project folder to drop and re-create the database.

Listing 20-2. Dropping and Re-creating the Database

```
dotnet ef database drop --force
dotnet ef database update
```

Start the application using dotnet run, navigate to http://localhost:5000, click the Create button, and use the values shown in Table 20-3 to store three Employee objects.

Table 20-3. *The Data Values for Creating Example Objects*

SSN	FirstName	FamilyName	Salary	Other Name	In Active Use
420-39-1864	Bob	Smith	100000	Robert	Checked
657-03-5898	Alice	Jones	200000	Allie	Checked
300-30-0522	Peter	Davies	180000	Pete	Checked

When you have created all three objects, you should see the layout illustrated in Figure 20-1.

499

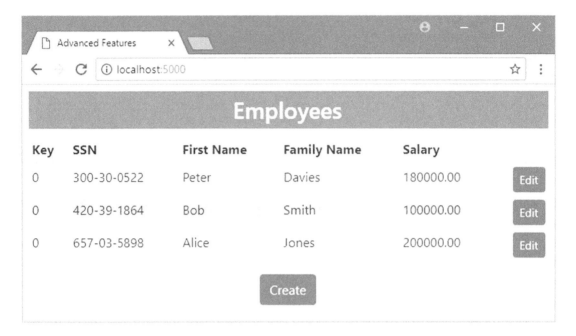

Figure 20-1. *Running the example application*

Managing Change Tracking for Query Results

The change tracking feature is one of the features that makes Entity Framework Core convenient to use. When you query the database, Entity Framework Core starts tracking the objects that it creates to represent the data. When you call the SaveChanges method, Entity Framework Core identifies the properties whose values have changed and updates the database accordingly.

As useful as this feature can be, it isn't always needed for every query made in ASP.NET Core MVC applications. Many HTTP requests that are received by an MVC application target action methods that only read data from the database and make no changes. If you are reading data, then there is no benefit gained from the work that Entity Framework Core has to do to set up change tracking for the objects it creates because there will never be any changes to detect.

You can control whether change tracking is performed for a query using the methods shown in Table 20-4, which are called on IQueryable<T> objects.

Table 20-4. *The Methods Used to Configure Change Tracking*

Name	Description
AsNoTracking()	This method disables change tracking for the results of the query to which it is applied.
AsTracking()	This method enables change tracking for the results of the query to which it is applied.

The methods described in Table 20-4 are applied to control change tracking for individual queries. By default, change tracking is enabled, so in Listing 20-3 I have disabled tracking for the read-only queries made by the Home controller.

Listing 20-3. Disabling Change Tracking in the HomeController.cs File in the Controllers Folder

```
using AdvancedApp.Models;
using Microsoft.AspNetCore.Mvc;
using Microsoft.EntityFrameworkCore;
using System.Linq;

namespace AdvancedApp.Controllers {

    public class HomeController : Controller {
        private AdvancedContext context;

        public HomeController(AdvancedContext ctx) => context = ctx;

        public IActionResult Index() {
            return View(context.Employees.AsNoTracking());
        }

        public IActionResult Edit(string SSN, string firstName, string familyName) {
            return View(string.IsNullOrWhiteSpace(SSN)
                ? new Employee() : context.Employees.Include(e => e.OtherIdentity)
                    .AsNoTracking()
                    .First(e => e.SSN == SSN
                        && e.FirstName == firstName
                        && e.FamilyName == familyName));
        }

        [HttpPost]
        public IActionResult Update(Employee employee) {
            if (context.Employees.Count(e => e.SSN == employee.SSN
                    && e.FirstName == employee.FirstName
                    && e.FamilyName == employee.FamilyName) == 0) {
                context.Add(employee);
            } else {
                context.Update(employee);
            }
            context.SaveChanges();
            return RedirectToAction(nameof(Index));
        }
    }
}
```

I have added the AsNotTracking method to the queries in the Index and Edit action methods. The AsTracking and AsNotTracking methods are applied to IQueryable<T> objects, which means they have to be included in the chain of methods that create a query before methods such as First that narrow a result to a single object.

There is no discernable effect of disabling change tracking, but Entity Framework Core is no longer setting up tracking for objects that are used for read-only actions.

Removing Individual Objects from Change Tracking

A common problem with change tracking in ASP.NET Core MVC applications arises when you try to perform an update using an object created by the MVC model binder that has the same primary key as an object that has been loaded by an Entity Framework Core query that is using change tracking. To demonstrate this problem, I have modified the Update method in the Home controller, as shown in Listing 20-4.

Listing 20-4. Mixed Objects in the HomeController.cs File in the Controllers Folder

```
...
[HttpPost]
public IActionResult Update(Employee employee) {
    if (context.Employees.Find(employee.SSN, employee.FirstName,
            employee.FamilyName) == null) {
        context.Add(employee);
    } else {
        context.Update(employee);
    }
    context.SaveChanges();
    return RedirectToAction(nameof(Index));
}
...
```

I have changed the query in the listing so that it uses the Find method to determine whether a key has already been used. This is an artificial problem because the original code showed that passing a lambda expression to the LINQ Count method worked without causing any problems, but this is such a common issue that it is worth demonstrating the issue even if you have already seen one technique that avoids it.

Start the application using dotnet run and navigate to http://localhost:5000. Click the Edit button for an Employee and then click the Save button; you will see the error illustrated by Figure 20-2.

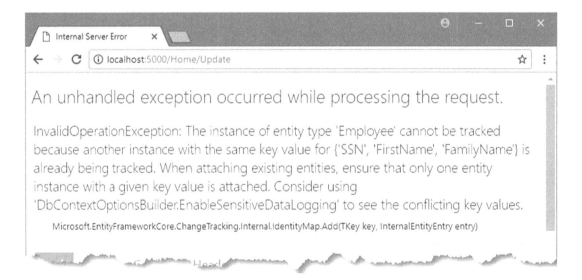

Figure 20-2. *An exception caused by the change tracking feature*

The error message reports that only one object with a specific key can be tracked. This problem has arisen because Entity Framework Core has placed the Employee object created as the result of the Find method into change tracking, and this object has the same primary key as the Employee object that the MVC model binder created and that has been passed to the Update method. Entity Framework Core can't perform change tracking on two objects with the same key because it won't be able to reconcile any conflicting changes that are made to them, so the exception is thrown.

The simplest way of avoiding this problem is to use queries that produce simple results that are not subject to change tracking, such as the original code for this listing that relied on the LINQ Count method. Entity Framework Core only performs change tracking on entity objects, so any query that produces a nonentity result, such as an int value, isn't subject to change tracking. You can also use the AsNoTracking method, described in the previous section, which will exclude all the objects created by a query from change tracking.

If neither of these approaches is suitable, you can explicitly remove an object from change tracking. This doesn't avoid the work that Entity Framework Core performs to track the object, but it does prevent Entity Framework Core from throwing an exception.

In Listing 20-5, I have modified the Update method so that the Employee object created by Entity Framework Core is removed from change tracking so that it won't conflict with the Employee object created by the MVC model binder.

Listing 20-5. Removing an Object from Tracking in the HomeController.cs File in the Controllers Folder

```
...
[HttpPost]
public IActionResult Update(Employee employee) {
    Employee existing = context.Employees.Find(employee.SSN,
        employee.FirstName, employee.FamilyName);
    if (existing  == null) {
        context.Add(employee);
    } else {
        context.Entry(existing).State = EntityState.Detached;
        context.Update(employee);
    }
    context.SaveChanges();
    return RedirectToAction(nameof(Index));
}
...
```

The object being tracked is passed to the context object's Entry method, and the State property is assigned the EntityState.Detached value. The result is that Entity Framework Core removes the object from change tracking, which means that it no longer conflicts with the object with the same primary key that is created from the HTTP request by the MVC model binder.

Changing the Default Change Tracking Behavior

If the majority of your queries do not modify objects, then it can be simpler to disable tracking for all of the queries made by a context object and use the AsTracking method to enable it for just those queries that need it.

In Listing 20-6, I have disabled tracking for all queries in the AdvancedContext class. There is only one context in the example application, but the change in the listing would not affect other contexts, each of which must be configured in the same way.

Listing 20-6. Disabling Change Tracking in the AdvancedContext.cs File in the Models Folder

```
using Microsoft.EntityFrameworkCore;

namespace AdvancedApp.Models {

    public class AdvancedContext : DbContext {

        public AdvancedContext(DbContextOptions<AdvancedContext> options)
                : base(options) {
            ChangeTracker.QueryTrackingBehavior = QueryTrackingBehavior.NoTracking;
        }

        public DbSet<Employee> Employees { get; set; }

        protected override void OnModelCreating(ModelBuilder modelBuilder) {

            modelBuilder.Entity<Employee>().Ignore(e => e.Id);
            modelBuilder.Entity<Employee>()
                .HasKey(e => new { e.SSN, e.FirstName, e.FamilyName });

            modelBuilder.Entity<SecondaryIdentity>()
                .HasOne(s => s.PrimaryIdentity)
                .WithOne(e => e.OtherIdentity)
                .HasPrincipalKey<Employee>(e => new { e.SSN,
                    e.FirstName, e.FamilyName })
                .HasForeignKey<SecondaryIdentity>(s => new { s.PrimarySSN,
                    s.PrimaryFirstName, s.PrimaryFamilyName });
        }
    }
}
```

The ChangeTracker property defined by the DbContext class returns a ChangeTracker object whose QueryTrackingBehavior property is configured using the enumeration of the same name. Table 20-5 shows the values for the QueryTrackingBehavior enumeration.

Table 20-5. *The QueryTrackingBehavior Values*

Name	Description
NoTracking	This value disables change tracking for the queries made by the context object.
TrackAll	This value enables change tracking for the queries made by the context object.

If you disable change tracking by default, then you must use the AsTracking method in any query where you rely on tracking to detect changes. In Listing 20-7, I have modified the query in the Update method of the Home controller so that the value for the Salary property is applied to an Employee object read from the database, which will work only if Entity Framework Core is allowed to use change tracking to detect the modified value.

Listing 20-7. Enabling Tracking on a Query in the HomeController.cs File in the Controllers Folder

```
...
[HttpPost]
public IActionResult Update(Employee employee) {
    Employee existing = context.Employees
        .AsTracking()
        .First(e => e.SSN == employee.SSN && e.FirstName == employee.FirstName
            && e.FamilyName == employee.FamilyName);
    if (existing  == null) {
        context.Add(employee);
    } else {
        existing.Salary = employee.Salary;
    }
    context.SaveChanges();
    return RedirectToAction(nameof(Index));
}
...
```

Without the `AsTracking` method, Entity Framework Core won't be able to detect the change and will not update the database.

Using a Query Filter

A query filter is applied to all of the queries made in the application for a specific entity class. One useful application of the query filter is to implement a "soft delete" feature that marks objects that are deleted without removing them from the database, allowing data to be restored if it has been deleted by mistake.

Note I describe the advanced features for really deleting data in Chapter 22.

To prepare, I added a property to the `Employee` class that will indicate when an object stored in the database has been soft-deleted by the user, as shown in Listing 20-8.

Listing 20-8. Adding a Property in the Employee.cs File in the Models Folder

```
namespace AdvancedApp.Models {

    public class Employee {

        public long Id { get; set; }
        public string SSN { get; set; }
        public string FirstName { get; set; }
        public string FamilyName { get; set; }
        public decimal Salary { get; set; }

        public SecondaryIdentity OtherIdentity { get; set; }

        public bool SoftDeleted { get; set; } = false;
    }
}
```

The next step is to add a query filter that excludes soft-deleted Employee objects from query results, as shown in Listing 20-9. I have also commented out the line that disables change tracking to keep the example as simple as possible.

Listing 20-9. Defining a Query Filter in the AdvancedContext.cs File in the Models Folder

```
using Microsoft.EntityFrameworkCore;

namespace AdvancedApp.Models {

    public class AdvancedContext : DbContext {

        public AdvancedContext(DbContextOptions<AdvancedContext> options)
                : base(options) {
            //ChangeTracker.QueryTrackingBehavior = QueryTrackingBehavior.NoTracking;
        }

        public DbSet<Employee> Employees { get; set; }

        protected override void OnModelCreating(ModelBuilder modelBuilder) {

            modelBuilder.Entity<Employee>()
                .HasQueryFilter(e => !e.SoftDeleted);

            modelBuilder.Entity<Employee>().Ignore(e => e.Id);
            modelBuilder.Entity<Employee>()
                .HasKey(e => new { e.SSN, e.FirstName, e.FamilyName });

            modelBuilder.Entity<SecondaryIdentity>()
                .HasOne(s => s.PrimaryIdentity)
                .WithOne(e => e.OtherIdentity)
                .HasPrincipalKey<Employee>(e => new { e.SSN,
                    e.FirstName, e.FamilyName })
                .HasForeignKey<SecondaryIdentity>(s => new { s.PrimarySSN,
                    s.PrimaryFirstName, s.PrimaryFamilyName });
        }
    }
}
```

Query filters are created by selecting a class with the Entity method and then calling the HasQueryFilter method. The filter is applied to all queries for the selected class, and only those objects for which the lambda expression returns true will be included in the query results. In the listing, I have defined a query filter that selects Employee objects whose SoftDeleted value is false.

To implement the soft-delete feature, I have updated the Home controller, as shown in Listing 20-10. I have added a Delete action that sets an Employee object's SoftDeleted property to true, which will ensure that objects that are soft-deleted won't be excluded by the query filter.

Listing 20-10. Supporting Soft Delete in the HomeController.cs File in the Controllers Folder

```
using AdvancedApp.Models;
using Microsoft.AspNetCore.Mvc;
using Microsoft.EntityFrameworkCore;
using System.Linq;

namespace AdvancedApp.Controllers {

    public class HomeController : Controller {
        private AdvancedContext context;

        public HomeController(AdvancedContext ctx) => context = ctx;

        public IActionResult Index() {
            return View(context.Employees.AsNoTracking());
        }

        public IActionResult Edit(string SSN, string firstName, string familyName) {
            return View(string.IsNullOrWhiteSpace(SSN)
                ? new Employee() : context.Employees.Include(e => e.OtherIdentity)
                    .AsNoTracking()
                    .First(e => e.SSN == SSN
                        && e.FirstName == firstName
                        && e.FamilyName == familyName));
        }

        [HttpPost]
        public IActionResult Update(Employee employee) {
            Employee existing = context.Employees
                .AsTracking()
                .First(e => e.SSN == employee.SSN
                    && e.FirstName == employee.FirstName
                    && e.FamilyName == employee.FamilyName);
            if (existing  == null) {
                context.Add(employee);
            } else {
                existing.Salary = employee.Salary;
            }
            context.SaveChanges();
            return RedirectToAction(nameof(Index));
        }

        [HttpPost]
        public IActionResult Delete(Employee employee) {
            context.Attach(employee);
            employee.SoftDeleted = true;
            context.SaveChanges();
            return RedirectToAction(nameof(Index));
        }
    }
}
```

To allow the user to use the soft-delete feature, I added elements to the Index.cshtml view, as shown in Listing 20-11, that will send an HTTP POST request containing the Employee primary key values to the Delete action method.

Listing 20-11. Adding Elements to the Index.cshtml File in the Views/Home Folder

```
@model IEnumerable<Employee>
@{
    ViewData["Title"] = "Advanced Features";
    Layout = "_Layout";
}
<h3 class="bg-info p-2 text-center text-white">Employees</h3>
<table class="table table-sm table-striped">
    <thead>
        <tr>
            <th>Key</th>
            <th>SSN</th>
            <th>First Name</th>
            <th>Family Name</th>
            <th>Salary</th>
            <th></th>
        </tr>
    </thead>
    <tbody>
        <tr class="placeholder"><td colspan="7" class="text-center">No Data</td></tr>
        @foreach (Employee e in Model) {
            <tr>
                <td>@e.Id</td>
                <td>@e.SSN</td>
                <td>@e.FirstName</td>
                <td>@e.FamilyName</td>
                <td>@e.Salary</td>
                <td class="text-right">
                    <form>
                        <input type="hidden" name="SSN" value="@e.SSN" />
                        <input type="hidden" name="Firstname" value="@e.FirstName" />
                        <input type="hidden" name="FamilyName"
                            value="@e.FamilyName" />
                        <button type="submit" asp-action="Delete" formmethod="post"
                                class="btn btn-sm btn-danger">Delete</button>
                        <button type="submit" asp-action="Edit" formmethod="get"
                                class="btn btn-sm btn-primary">
                            Edit
                        </button>
                    </form>
                </td>
            </tr>
        }
    </tbody>
</table>
<div class="text-center">
    <a asp-action="Edit" class="btn btn-primary">Create</a>
</div>
```

The form element and its contents are used for the delete and editing features. Each button element is configured with the action and HTTP method that should be used when the user clicks it, replacing the anchor element I used previously.

Run the commands shown in Listing 20-12 in the AdvancedApp project folder to create a new migration and apply it to the database.

Listing 20-12. Creating and Applying a Database Migration

```
dotnet ef migrations add SoftDelete
dotnet ef database update
```

To see the effect of the soft-delete, start the application using dotnet run, navigate to http://localhost:5000, and delete an Employee object. When you delete the object, it will disappear from the table of Employee objects, as shown in Figure 20-3.

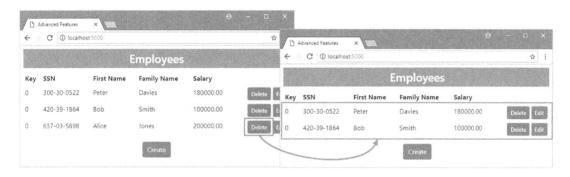

Figure 20-3. *Soft-deleting data*

Overriding a Query Filter

Being able to soft-delete an object is useful only if there are also facilities for undeleting objects. This means I need to override the filter so that I can query the database for the soft-deleted objects and present them to the user. I added a class file called DeleteController.cs to the Controllers folder and used it to define the controller shown in Listing 20-13.

Listing 20-13. The Contents of the DeleteController.cs File in the Controllers Folder

```
using AdvancedApp.Models;
using Microsoft.AspNetCore.Mvc;
using Microsoft.EntityFrameworkCore;
using System.Linq;

namespace AdvancedApp.Controllers {

    public class DeleteController : Controller {
        private AdvancedContext context;

        public DeleteController(AdvancedContext ctx) => context = ctx;
```

```
    public IActionResult Index() {
        return View(context.Employees.Where(e => e.SoftDeleted)
            .Include(e => e.OtherIdentity).IgnoreQueryFilters());
    }

    [HttpPost]
    public IActionResult Restore(Employee employee) {
        context.Employees.IgnoreQueryFilters()
            .First(e => e.SSN == employee.SSN
                && e.FirstName == employee.FirstName
                && e.FamilyName == employee.FamilyName).SoftDeleted = false;
        context.SaveChanges();
        return RedirectToAction(nameof(Index));
    }
  }
}
```

The Index and Restore action methods both need to query for soft-deleted objects, which the query filter excludes. To ensure these queries have access to the data they require, I called the IgnoreQueryFilters method, like this:

```
...
return View(context.Employees.Where(e => e.SoftDeleted)
    .Include(e => e.OtherIdentity).IgnoreQueryFilters());
...
```

This method makes the query without applying the query filter. To provide the controller with a view, I created the Views/Delete folder and added to it a file called Index.cshtml with the content shown in Listing 20-14.

Listing 20-14. The Contents of the Index.cshtml File in the Views/Delete Folder

```
@model IEnumerable<Employee>
@{
    ViewData["Title"] = "Advanced Features";
    Layout = "_Layout";
}
<h3 class="bg-info p-2 text-center text-white">Deleted Employees</h3>
<table class="table table-sm table-striped">
    <thead>
        <tr>
            <th>SSN</th>
            <th>First Name</th>
            <th>Family Name</th>
            <th></th>
        </tr>
    </thead>
    <tbody>
        <tr class="placeholder"><td colspan="4" class="text-center">No Data</td></tr>
        @foreach (Employee e in Model) {
            <tr>
```

```
        <td>@e.SSN</td>
        <td>@e.FirstName</td>
        <td>@e.FamilyName</td>
        <td class="text-right">
            <form method="post">
                <input type="hidden" name="SSN" value="@e.SSN" />
                <input type="hidden" name="FirstName" value="@e.FirstName" />
                <input type="hidden" name="FamilyName"
                        value="@e.FamilyName" />
                <button asp-action="Restore"
                    class="btn btn-sm btn-success">Restore</button>
            </form>
        </td>
    </tr>
}
    </tbody>
</table>
```

Start the application using `dotnet run` and navigate to `http://localhost:5000/delete`; you will see a list of the soft-deleted objects. Click the Restore button to set an object's `SoftDeleted` property to `false`, which will restore it to the main data table presented by the `Home` controller, as shown in Figure 20-4.

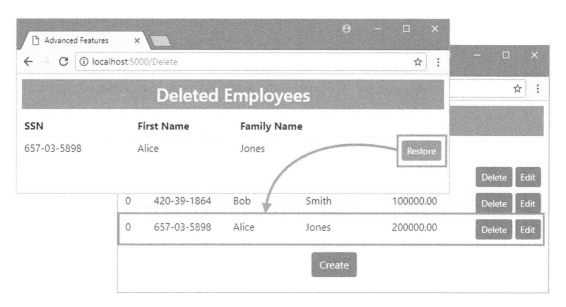

Figure 20-4. *Restoring a soft-deleted object*

Querying Using Search Patterns

Entity Framework Core supports the SQL LIKE expression, which means that queries can be performed using search patterns. In Listing 20-15, I have modified the Index action of the Home controller so that it receives a search term parameter that is used to create a LIKE query.

Listing 20-15. Using a Search Pattern in the HomeController.cs File in the Controllers Folder

```
using AdvancedApp.Models;
using Microsoft.AspNetCore.Mvc;
using Microsoft.EntityFrameworkCore;
using System.Linq;

namespace AdvancedApp.Controllers {

    public class HomeController : Controller {
        private AdvancedContext context;

        public HomeController(AdvancedContext ctx) => context = ctx;

        public IActionResult Index(string searchTerm) {
            IQueryable<Employee> data = context.Employees;
            if (!string.IsNullOrEmpty(searchTerm)) {
                data = data.Where(e => EF.Functions.Like(e.FirstName, searchTerm));
            }
            return View(data);
        }

        public IActionResult Edit(string SSN, string firstName, string familyName) {
            return View(string.IsNullOrWhiteSpace(SSN)
                ? new Employee() : context.Employees.Include(e => e.OtherIdentity)
                    .AsNoTracking()
                    .First(e => e.SSN == SSN
                        && e.FirstName == firstName
                        && e.FamilyName == familyName));
        }

        [HttpPost]
        public IActionResult Update(Employee employee) {
            Employee existing = context.Employees
                .AsTracking()
                .First(e => e.SSN == employee.SSN
                    && e.FirstName == employee.FirstName
                    && e.FamilyName == employee.FamilyName);
            if (existing  == null) {
                context.Add(employee);
            } else {
                existing.Salary = employee.Salary;
            }
            context.SaveChanges();
            return RedirectToAction(nameof(Index));
        }
    }
```

```
        [HttpPost]
        public IActionResult Delete(Employee employee) {
            context.Attach(employee);
            employee.SoftDeleted = true;
            context.SaveChanges();
            return RedirectToAction(nameof(Index));
        }
    }
}
```

There is no direct support for LIKE in LINQ, which results in an awkward syntax. The EF.Functions. Like method is used to access the LIKE functionality within a Where clause and receives the property that will be matched and the search term as parameters. In the listing, I have used the Like method to search for Employee objects whose FirstName value matches the search term parameter received by the action method. Search terms can be expressed using four wildcards, which are described in Table 20-6.

Table 20-6. *The SQL LIKE Wildcards*

Wildcard	Description
%	This wildcard matches any string of zero or more characters.
_	This wildcard matches any single character.
[chars]	This wildcard matches any single character within a set.
[^chars]	This wildcard matches any single character not within a set.

To see how the search works, start the application using dotnet run, ensure that all of the sample Employee objects have been restored from soft-deletion, and then navigate to the following URL:

http://localhost:5000?searchTerm=%[ae]%

This search term specified in the URL query string will match any first name that contains the letter A or E. If you examine the logging messages generated by the application, you will see the query that Entity Framework Core has sent to the database server.

```
...
SELECT [e].[SSN], [e].[FirstName], [e].[FamilyName], [e].[Salary], [e].[SoftDeleted]
FROM [Employees] AS [e]
WHERE ([e].[SoftDeleted] = 0) AND [e].[FirstName] LIKE @__searchTerm_1
...
```

The important part of the query is the LIKE keyword, which I have highlighted. This ensures that only objects that match the search term will be read from the database.

Of the three objects created using the data in Table 20-3, only Alice and Peter will be matched by the search term, producing the results shown in Figure 20-5.

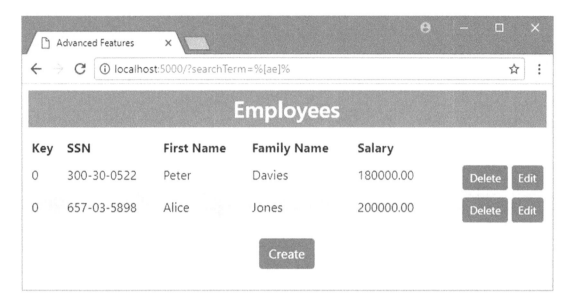

Figure 20-5. *Using a search term in a query*

AVOIDING THE LIKE EVALUATION PITFALL

Care must be taken to apply the EF.Functions.Like method only to IQueryable<T> objects. You must avoid calling the Like method on an IEnumerable<T> object like this:

```
...
public IActionResult Index(string searchTerm) {
    IEnumerable<Employee> data = context.Employees;
    if (!string.IsNullOrEmpty(searchTerm)) {
        data = data.Where(e => EF.Functions.Like(e.FirstName, searchTerm));
    }
    return View(data);
}
...
```

The results will look the same, but if you examine the query sent to the database server, you will see that the LIKE keyword is not included in the query.

```
...
SELECT [e].[SSN], [e].[FirstName], [e].[FamilyName], [e].[Salary], [e].[SoftDeleted]
FROM [Employees] AS [e]
WHERE [e].[SoftDeleted] = 0
...
```

Entity Framework Core will retrieve all the objects that could be matched by the search term, process them in the application, and discard the ones that are not required. For the example application, that means the query will load one extra object, but in a real project the amount of data that is loaded and then discarded can be significant.

Making Asynchronous Queries

Most queries made using Entity Framework Core are synchronous. In most applications, synchronous queries are perfectly acceptable because the query is the only activity performed by an ASP.NET Core MVC action method, which is also synchronous.

Entity Framework Core can also perform queries asynchronously, which can be useful if you are using an asynchronous action method *and* that action method needs to perform multiple activities concurrently *and* only one of those activities is a database query. The set of circumstances in which asynchronous queries are useful is so specific, in fact, that most ASP.NET Core MVC projects don't need to use them.

In Listing 20-16, I have rewritten the Index action so that it is asynchronous and takes advantage of the Entity Framework Core support for asynchronous queries.

Listing 20-16. Making an Asynchronous Query in the HomeController.cs File in the Controllers Folder

```
using AdvancedApp.Models;
using Microsoft.AspNetCore.Mvc;
using Microsoft.EntityFrameworkCore;
using System.Linq;
using System.Threading.Tasks;
using System.Net.Http;

namespace AdvancedApp.Controllers {

    public class HomeController : Controller {
        private AdvancedContext context;

        public HomeController(AdvancedContext ctx) => context = ctx;

        public async Task<IActionResult> Index(string searchTerm) {
            IQueryable<Employee> employees = context.Employees;
            if (!string.IsNullOrEmpty(searchTerm)) {
                employees = employees.Where(e =>
                    EF.Functions.Like(e.FirstName, searchTerm));
            }
            HttpClient client = new HttpClient();
            ViewBag.PageSize = (await client.GetAsync("http://apress.com"))
                .Content.Headers.ContentLength;
            return View(await employees.ToListAsync());
        }

        // ...other action methods omitted for brevity...
    }
}
```

The limitations of asynchronous queries make it difficult to create a useful example. In the listing, I used the HttpClient class to send an asynchronous HTTP GET request to apress.com while also querying the database.

AVOIDING THE CONCURRENT QUERY PITFALL

Microsoft specifically warns against using a context object to perform multiple asynchronous requests because the DbContext class has not been written to accommodate them. This leads some enterprising developers to use dependency injection to receive two context objects, each of which is used to perform a concurrent asynchronous request.

```
...
public HomeController(AdvancedContext ctx, AdvancedContext ctx2) {
...
```

The problem with this approach is that the ASP.NET Core MVC dependency injection feature will create just one context object and use it to resolve both dependencies, which means that there is one context object after all. My advice is to accept the limitations of asynchronous query support.

Entity Framework Core provides a series of methods that force asynchronous evaluation of a query. The most commonly used asynchronous methods are described in Table 20-7, but there are asynchronous equivalents for all of the methods that force query evaluation, such that the LastAsync method is the asynchronous counterpart to the Last method. No asynchronous versions of the methods used to create the query, such as Where, are required because they build up the query without executing it.

Table 20-7. *The Commonly Used Methods That Perform an Asynchronous Query*

Name	Description
LoadAsync()	This method forces asynchronous execution of a query but does nothing with the results. This is the counterpart to the Load method and is most often used with the fixing up process.
ToListAsync()	This method queries the database and returns the resulting objects in a list.
ToArrayAsync()	This method queries the database and returns the resulting objects in an array.
ToDictionaryAsync(key)	This method queries the database and returns the resulting objects in a dictionary, using the specified property as the source of key values.
CountAsync()	This method returns the number of objects stored in the database that match the specified predicate. If no predicate is specified, the number of stored objects matching the query is returned.
FirstAsync(predicate)	This method returns the first object that matches the specified predicate.
ForEachAsync(function)	This method invokes the specified function for each of the objects matched by the query.

> **Note** The ForEachAsync method doesn't have a synchronous counterpart but can be used to invoke a function for each object that is created from the results of a query.

In the listing, I used the ToListAsync method to query the database asynchronously and pass the List<Employee> that is produced to the View method. The List<T> class implements the IEnumerable<T> interface, which means that the existing view can enumerate the objects without any changes. To display the number of bytes read from apress.com by the asynchronous HTTP request in Listing 20-16, I added the element shown in Listing 20-17 to the Index view.

Listing 20-17. Adding an Element in the Index.cshtml File in the Views/Home Folder

```
@model IEnumerable<Employee>
@{
    ViewData["Title"] = "Advanced Features";
    Layout = "_Layout";
}
<h3 class="bg-info p-2 text-center text-white">Employees</h3>
<table class="table table-sm table-striped">

    <!-- ...table contents omitted for brevity... -->

</table>
@if (ViewBag.PageSize != null) {
    <h4 class="bg-info p-2 text-center text-white">
        Page Size: @ViewBag.PageSize bytes
    </h4>
}
<div class="text-center">
    <a asp-action="Edit" class="btn btn-primary">Create</a>
</div>
```

To test the asynchronous query, start the application using dotnet run and navigate to http://localhost:5000. You will see the page size element shown in Figure 20-6, along with the Employee data that was retrieved from the database at the same time. (You may see a different number of bytes displayed, since apress.com is often updated.)

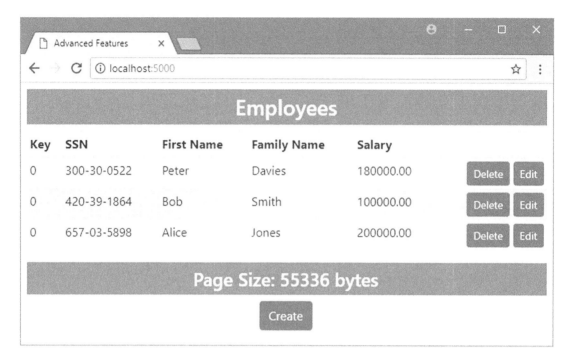

Figure 20-6. *Making concurrent queries*

Explicitly Compiling Queries

One of the most compelling Entity Framework Core features is the way that LINQ queries are translated into SQL. The translation process can be complex, and to improve performance, Entity Framework Core automatically keeps a cache of the queries it has processed and creates a hashed representation of every query that it processes to determine whether there is a cached translation available. If there is, then the cached translation is used; if not, then a new translation is created and put into the cache for future use.

You can improve the performance of this process by explicitly translating a query so that Entity Framework Core doesn't have to create the hash code and check the cache. This is known as *explicitly compiling* a query. In Listing 20-18, I have updated the Home controller so that the query performed by the Index action is explicitly compiled.

Listing 20-18. Compiling a Query in the HomeController.cs File in the Controllers Folder

```
using AdvancedApp.Models;
using Microsoft.AspNetCore.Mvc;
using Microsoft.EntityFrameworkCore;
using System.Linq;
using System.Threading.Tasks;
using System.Net.Http;
using System;
using System.Collections.Generic;

namespace AdvancedApp.Controllers {
```

```
public class HomeController : Controller {
    private AdvancedContext context;

    private static Func<AdvancedContext, string, IEnumerable<Employee>> query
        = EF.CompileQuery((AdvancedContext context, string searchTerm)
            => context.Employees
                    .Where(e => EF.Functions.Like(e.FirstName, searchTerm)));

    public HomeController(AdvancedContext ctx) => context = ctx;

    public IActionResult Index(string searchTerm) {
        return View(string.IsNullOrEmpty(searchTerm )
            ? context.Employees : query(context, searchTerm));
    }

    // ...other action methods omitted for brevity...
}
```

The statements that produce a compiled query can be difficult to read. The compilation is performed using the EF.CompileQuery method, like this:

```
...
EF.CompileQuery((AdvancedContext context, string searchTerm)
    => context.Employees.Where(e => EF.Functions.Like(e.FirstName, searchTerm)));
...
```

The argument to the CompileQuery method is a lambda expression that receives a context object and parameters that are used in the query and returns an IQueryable<T> as its result. In the listing, the lambda expression receives an AdvancedContext object and a string, and it uses them to create an IQueryable<Employee> that will query the database using the LIKE feature.

The result from the EF.CompileQuery method is a Func<AdvancedContext, string, IEnumerable<Employee>> object, which represents a function that accepts the context and string and produces a sequence of Employee objects.

```
...
private static Func<AdvancedContext, string, IEnumerable<Employee>> query
    = EF.CompileQuery((AdvancedContext context, string searchTerm)
        => context.Employees.Where(e => EF.Functions.Like(e.FirstName, searchTerm)));
...
```

Notice that the compiled function returns an IEnumerable<T> object, which means that any further operations that you perform on the result will be executed in memory rather than building on the request that is sent to the database. This makes sense since the purpose of this process is to create an immutable query, and it means you must ensure that every aspect of the query you require is included in the expression passed to the CompileQuery method.

Executing the query is done by invoking the function that is returned by the CompiledQuery method, like this:

```
...
return View(string.IsNullOrEmpty(searchTerm )
    ? context.Employees : query(context, searchTerm));
...
```

There is no visible difference in the way that a compiled query is executed, but behind the scenes, Entity Framework Core is able to skip the process of creating a hashed representation of the query and checking to see whether it has been translated previously.

AVOIDING THE EXCESSIVE QUERYING PITFALL

Notice that I check to see whether the `searchTerm` parameter for the `Index` action method is `null` outside of the explicitly compiled query. A common mistake when defining the query expression is including checks that are intended to be performed in the application, like this:

```
...
EF.CompileQuery((AdvancedContext context, string searchTerm)
    => context.Employees.Where(e => string.IsNullOrEmpty(searchTerm)
            || EF.Functions.Like(e.FirstName, searchTerm)));
...
```

The problem is that Entity Framework Core will incorporate the check for null values into the SQL query, like this, which may not be what you intended:

```
...
SELECT [e].[SSN], [e].[FirstName], [e].[FamilyName], [e].[Salary],
    [e].[SoftDeleted]
FROM [Employees] AS [e]
WHERE ([e].[SoftDeleted] = 0) AND ((@__searchTerm IS NULL
    OR (@__searchTerm = N'')) OR [e].[FirstName] LIKE @__searchTerm)
...
```

This is the opposite problem to the client evaluation pitfall that I describe in the next section, but both problems emphasize the importance of examining the SQL queries that Entity Framework produces to make sure they target exactly the data you intended.

Avoiding the Client Evaluation Pitfall

When you start working with Entity Framework Core, it can take a while before you have confidence that your LINQ queries will be translated into the SQL you require. As this book shows, there are lots of potential pitfalls that can result in too much data or too little data being retrieved from the database. There is one potential error that is so common that Entity Framework Core will warn you when it translates a query into SQL.

The problem occurs when Entity Framework Core is unable to see all of the details of a LINQ query and cannot translate it completely into SQL. This often occurs when a query is refactored so that the code that selects a set of data objects can be used more consistently throughout an application. Entity Framework Core splits up the query so that part of it is executed by the database server and part is executed by the client application. Not only does this increase the amount of processing that the application has to do, but it can dramatically increase the amount of data that a query retrieves from the database.

To demonstrate, I added a class file called `QueryController.cs` to the `Controllers` folder and used it to define the controller shown in Listing 20-19.

Listing 20-19. The Contents of the QueryController.cs File in the Controllers Folder

```
using AdvancedApp.Models;
using Microsoft.AspNetCore.Mvc;
using System.Linq;

namespace AdvancedApp.Controllers {

    public class QueryController : Controller {
        private AdvancedContext context;

        public QueryController(AdvancedContext ctx) => context = ctx;

        public IActionResult ServerEval() {
            return View("Query", context.Employees.Where(e => e.Salary > 150_000));
        }

        public IActionResult ClientEval() {
            return View("Query", context.Employees.Where(e => IsHighEarner(e)));
        }

        private bool IsHighEarner(Employee e) {
            return e.Salary > 150_000;
        }
    }
}
```

The controller defines two actions that query for Employee objects whose Salary value is greater than 150,000. The ServerEval method puts the filter expression directly in the Where clause of the LINQ expression, whereas the ClientEval method uses a separate method, which represents a typical refactoring process that allows the criteria for selecting high earners into a separate method.

To provide both actions with a view, I created the Views/Query folder and added to it a file called Query.cshtml with the content shown in Listing 20-20.

Listing 20-20. The Contents of the Query.cshtml File in the Views/Query Folder

```
@model IEnumerable<Employee>
@{
    ViewData["Title"] = "Advanced Features";
    Layout = "_Layout";
}
<h3 class="bg-info p-2 text-center text-white">Employees</h3>
<table class="table table-sm table-striped">
    <thead>
        <tr>
            <th>SSN</th>
            <th>First Name</th>
            <th>Family Name</th>
            <th>Salary</th>
        </tr>
    </thead>
```

```
    <tbody>
        <tr class="placeholder"><td colspan="4" class="text-center">No Data</td></tr>
        @foreach (Employee e in Model) {
            <tr>
                <td>@e.SSN</td>
                <td>@e.FirstName</td>
                <td>@e.FamilyName</td>
                <td>@e.Salary</td>
            </tr>
        }
    </tbody>
</table>
```

To see the difference in the way that queries are performed, start the application using dotnet run and navigate to http://localhost:5000/query/servereval and http://localhost:5000/query/clienteval, both of which will produce the results shown in Figure 20-7.

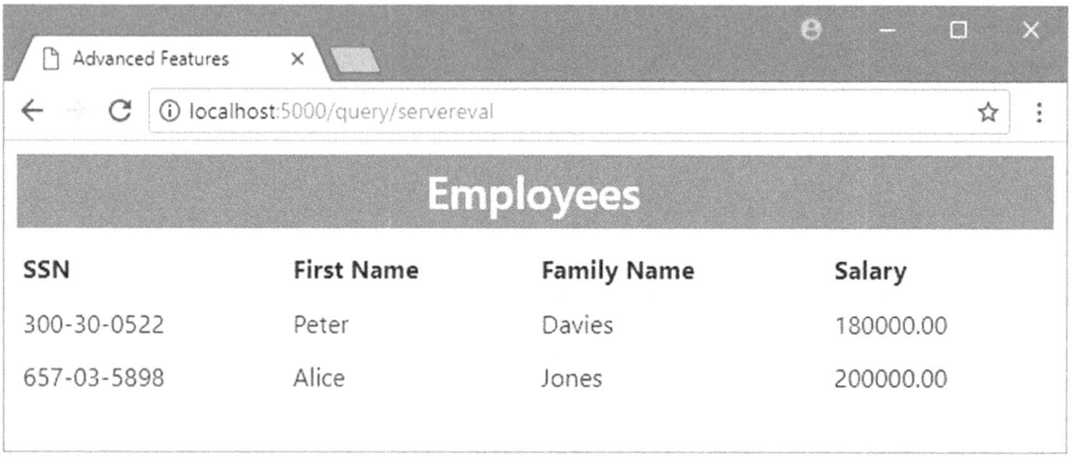

Figure 20-7. *Query results*

To understand the difference between the two action methods, you must examine the queries sent to the database server. The ServerEval action results in this query:

```
...
SELECT [e].[SSN], [e].[FirstName], [e].[FamilyName], [e].[Salary], [e].[SoftDeleted]
FROM [Employees] AS [e]
WHERE ([e].[SoftDeleted] = 0) AND ([e].[Salary] > 150000.0)
...
```

The WHERE clause in this query will retrieve only those Employee objects whose Salary value exceeds 150,000. This means that only the objects that will be subsequently displayed to the user are retrieved from the database.

By contrast, here is the query that is produced by the `ClientEval` action:

```
...
SELECT [e].[SSN], [e].[FirstName], [e].[FamilyName], [e].[Salary], [e].[SoftDeleted]
FROM [Employees] AS [e]
WHERE [e].[SoftDeleted] = 0
...
```

Entity Framework Core isn't able to see into the controller's `IsHighEarner` method and incorporate the logic it contains into the SQL query. Instead, Entity Framework Core translates the part of the query that it can see into SQL and then passes the objects it receives through the `IsHighEarner` method to produce the query result. The objects that are not selected by the `IsHighEarner` method are discarded, with the effect that more data is read from the database and more work is required by the application to produce the required results. In the example application, that means one additional object is read and created, but in a real application, the difference can be significant.

Throwing a Client Evaluation Exception

When part of a query has to be evaluated in the client, Entity Framework Core will display a warning message in the logging output, as follows:

```
The LINQ expression 'where value(AdvancedApp.Controllers.QueryController)
.IsHighEarner([e])' could not be translated and will be evaluated locally
```

This can be easy to miss in the flow of logging messages, and you may find that client evaluation of a query passes unnoticed until there are performance issues in a production application. During development, it can be useful to receive an exception when part of a query will be evaluated in the client, which will make the problem more noticeable. In Listing 20-21, I have changed the Entity Framework Core configuration so that an exception will be thrown.

Listing 20-21. Configuring Exceptions in the Startup.cs File in the AdvancedApp Folder

```csharp
using System;
using System.Collections.Generic;
using System.Linq;
using System.Threading.Tasks;
using Microsoft.AspNetCore.Builder;
using Microsoft.AspNetCore.Hosting;
using Microsoft.AspNetCore.Http;
using Microsoft.Extensions.DependencyInjection;
using Microsoft.Extensions.Configuration;
using Microsoft.EntityFrameworkCore;
using AdvancedApp.Models;
using Microsoft.EntityFrameworkCore.Diagnostics;

namespace AdvancedApp {
    public class Startup {

        public Startup(IConfiguration config) => Configuration = config;

        public IConfiguration Configuration { get; }
```

```
    public void ConfigureServices(IServiceCollection services) {
        services.AddMvc();
        string conString = Configuration["ConnectionStrings:DefaultConnection"];
        services.AddDbContext<AdvancedContext>(options =>
            options.UseSqlServer(conString).ConfigureWarnings(warning =>
                warning.Throw(RelationalEventId.QueryClientEvaluationWarning)));
    }

    public void Configure(IApplicationBuilder app, IHostingEnvironment env) {
        app.UseDeveloperExceptionPage();
        app.UseStatusCodePages();
        app.UseStaticFiles();
        app.UseMvcWithDefaultRoute();
    }
  }
}
```

The ConfigureWarnings method is used to configure the warnings produced by Entity Framework Core using a lambda expression that receives a WarningsConfigurationsBuilder object that defines the methods shown in Table 20-8.

Table 20-8. *The WarningsConfigurationBuilder Methods*

Name	Description
Ignore(event)	This method tells Entity Framework Core to ignore the specified event.
Log(event)	This method tells Entity Framework Core to log the specified event.
Throw(event)	This method tells Entity Framework Core to throw an exception for the specified event.

The methods in Table 20-8 are used with the RelationalEventId enumeration, which defines values that represent the diagnostic events likely to be encountered in an Entity Framework Core application. There are values for almost 30 different events, although most of them are related to the lifecycles of database connections and transactions and the creation and application of migrations. You can see a complete list of events at https://docs.microsoft.com/en-us/ef/core/api/microsoft. entityframeworkcore.infrastructure.relationaleventid. The value that I used in Listing 20-20 is QueryClientEvaluationWarning, which represents the event triggered by Entity Framework Core when part of a request will be evaluated by the client. To see the effect of the change, start the application using dotnet run and navigate to http://localhost:5000/query/clienteval. Rather than the easily missed warning, you will see the exception in Figure 20-8.

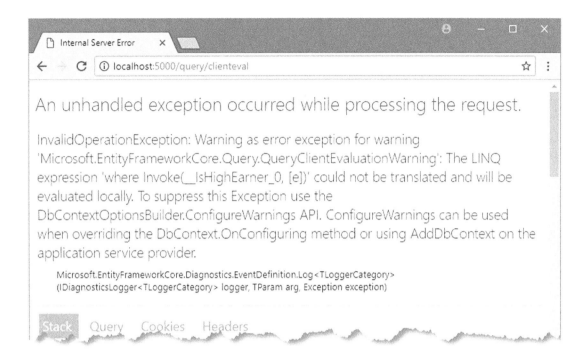

Figure 20-8. *The client query evaluation exception*

Summary

In this chapter, I described the advanced features that Entity Framework Core provides for querying data. I explained how to control the change tracking feature, how to use a query filter, how to perform queries using the SQL LIKE feature, and how to explicitly compile queries. I finished the chapter by demonstrating a common problem caused by refactoring queries and how to configure the application so that you will know when you encounter this problem in your own projects. In the next chapter, I describe the advanced features for storing data.

CHAPTER 21

Storing Data

In this chapter, I continue to describe the advanced features that Entity Framework Core provides, focusing on those that relate to adding or updating data. I show you how to select the data types used to store values, how to format or validate values, how to hide data values from the rest of the application, and how to detect concurrent updates by multiple clients. Table 21-1 puts this chapter in context.

Table 21-1. *Putting Advanced Storage Features in Context*

Question	Answer
What are they?	These features allow you to change the way that data is stored in the database, overriding the conventional behaviors. This can range from selecting specific SQL types to detecting when two users update the same data.
Why are they useful?	These features can be useful when you are modeling an existing database or when your application has specific needs that can't easily be met using the standard features.
How are they used?	These features are applied through a combination of model class members and Fluent API statements.
Are there any pitfalls or limitations?	Some of these features change the way that data is mapped onto data model objects, which can lead to odd results if it is not done carefully.
Are there any alternatives?	Most projects can use the standard Entity Framework Core features for storing data.

Table 21-2 summarizes the chapter.

© Adam Freeman 2018

A. Freeman, *Pro Entity Framework Core 2 for ASP.NET Core MVC*,
https://doi.org/10.1007/978-1-4842-3435-8_21

Table 21-2. *Chapter Summary*

Problem	Solution	Listing
Change the SQL data type used to represent a value	Use the HasColumnType or HasMaxLength method.	1–6
Process values before they are made available to the rest of the application or stored in the database	Use a backing field	7–11
Hide data values from the MVC part of the application	Use a shadow property	12–15
Set a default value	Use the HasDefaultValue method	16–20
Detect concurrent updates	Use a concurrency token or enable row versioning	21–30

Preparing for This Chapter

For this chapter, I am going to continue using the AdvancedApp project that I created in Chapter 19 and modified in Chapter 20. To prepare for this chapter, I have changed the code in the Home controller, as shown in Listing 21-1, to include related data in the query performed by the Index action and to tidy up the Update method so that all properties are updated.

■ **Tip** If you don't want to follow the process of building the example project, you can download all of the required files from this book's source code repository, available at https://github.com/apress/pro-ef-core-2-for-asp.net-core-mvc.

Listing 21-1. Simplifying Code in the HomeController.cs File in the Controllers Folder

```
using AdvancedApp.Models;
using Microsoft.AspNetCore.Mvc;
using Microsoft.EntityFrameworkCore;
using System.Linq;

namespace AdvancedApp.Controllers {

    public class HomeController : Controller {
        private AdvancedContext context;

        public HomeController(AdvancedContext ctx) => context = ctx;

        public IActionResult Index() {
            return View(context.Employees.Include(e => e.OtherIdentity));
        }

        public IActionResult Edit(string SSN, string firstName, string familyName) {
            return View(string.IsNullOrWhiteSpace(SSN)
```

```
                ? new Employee() : context.Employees.Include(e => e.OtherIdentity)
                    .First(e => e.SSN == SSN
                        && e.FirstName == firstName
                        && e.FamilyName == familyName));
        }


        [HttpPost]
        public IActionResult Update(Employee employee) {
            if (context.Employees.Count(e => e.SSN == employee.SSN
                    && e.FirstName == employee.FirstName
                    && e.FamilyName == employee.FamilyName) == 0) {
                context.Add(employee);
            } else {
                context.Update(employee);
            }
            context.SaveChanges();
            return RedirectToAction(nameof(Index));
        }


        [HttpPost]
        public IActionResult Delete(Employee employee) {
            context.Attach(employee);
            employee.SoftDeleted = true;
            context.SaveChanges();
            return RedirectToAction(nameof(Index));
        }
    }
}
```

To display details of the SecondaryIdentity objects to the user, I made the changes shown in Listing 21-2 to the Index.cshtml view in the Views/Home folder. I have also taken the opportunity to remove some of the content added in the previous chapter, which is no longer required.

Listing 21-2. Adding Content in the Index.cshtml File in the Views/Home Folder

```
@model IEnumerable<Employee>
@{
    ViewData["Title"] = "Advanced Features";
    Layout = "_Layout";
}
<h3 class="bg-info p-2 text-center text-white">Employees</h3>
<table class="table table-sm table-striped">
    <thead>
        <tr>
            <th>SSN</th>
            <th>First Name</th>
            <th>Family Name</th>
            <th>Salary</th>
            <th>Other Name</th>
            <th>In Use</th>
            <th></th>
        </tr>
    </thead>
```

```
        </thead>
        <tbody>
            <tr class="placeholder"><td colspan="7" class="text-center">No Data</td></tr>
            @foreach (Employee e in Model) {
                <tr>
                    <td>@e.SSN</td>
                    <td>@e.FirstName</td>
                    <td>@e.FamilyName</td>
                    <td>@e.Salary</td>
                    <td>@(e.OtherIdentity?.Name ?? "(None)")</td>
                    <td>@(e.OtherIdentity?.InActiveUse.ToString() ?? "(N/A)")</td>
                    <td class="text-right">
                        <form>
                            <input type="hidden" name="SSN" value="@e.SSN" />
                            <input type="hidden" name="Firstname" value="@e.FirstName" />
                            <input type="hidden" name="FamilyName"
                                value="@e.FamilyName" />
                            <button type="submit" asp-action="Delete" formmethod="post"
                                    class="btn btn-sm btn-danger">Delete</button>
                            <button type="submit" asp-action="Edit" formmethod="get"
                                    class="btn btn-sm btn-primary">
                                Edit
                            </button>
                        </form>
                    </td>
                </tr>
            }
        </tbody>
    </table>
    <div class="text-center">
        <a asp-action="Edit" class="btn btn-primary">Create</a>
    </div>
```

Next, run the commands shown in Listing 21-3 in the AdvancedApp project folder to drop and re-create the database.

Listing 21-3. Dropping and Re-creating the Database

```
dotnet ef database drop --force
dotnet ef database update
```

Start the application using dotnet run, navigate to http://localhost:5000, click the Create button, and use the values shown in Table 21-3 to store three Employee objects.

Table 21-3. *The Data Values for Creating Example Objects*

SSN	FirstName	FamilyName	Salary	Other Name	In Active Use
420-39-1864	Bob	Smith	100000	Robert	Checked
657-03-5898	Alice	Jones	200000	Allie	Checked
300-30-0522	Peter	Davies	180000	Pete	Checked

When you have created all three objects, you should see the layout illustrated in Figure 21-1.

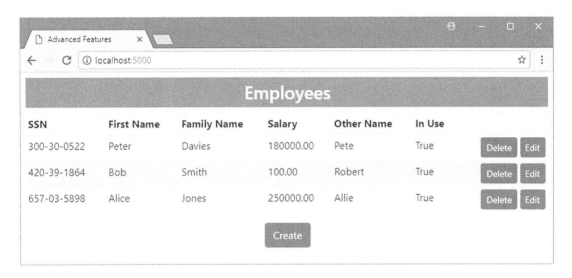

Figure 21-1. *Running the example application*

Specifying SQL Data Types

Entity Framework Core automatically takes care of mapping between .NET and SQL data types, both in a migration for a code-first project and during the scaffolding phase of a database-first project. Database servers don't always support the same data types—or implement them in the same way—and it is the responsibility of the database provider to make suitable type choices. This means migrations for the same data model that target two different database servers may use different SQL types, for example.

Most providers use similar types, but there are some variations. Table 21-4 shows the mappings that are used for the .NET Core primitive types for the official SQL Server database provider and one of the most popular MySQL providers.

■ **Caution**   These mappings may change for future releases of the database providers. Create a migration to definitively determine which data type a provider uses.

Table 21-4. *The Database Provider Mappings for .NET Core Primitive Types*

.NET Core Type	SQL Server Type	MySQL Type
int	int	int
long	bigint	bigint
bool	bit	bit
byte	tinyint	tinyint
double	float	double
char	int	tinyint
short	smallint	smallint
float	real	float
decimal	decimal(18,2)	decimal(65,30)
string	nvarchar(max)	longtext
TimeSpan	time	time(6)
DateTime	datetime2	datetime(6)
DateTimeOffset	datetimeoffset	datetime(6)
Guid	uniqueidentifier	char(36)

You can change the SQL data type used to store a value if the type selected by Entity Framework Core doesn't suit you. This feature is most frequently used to adjust the type to ensure sufficient precision for the values generated by an application or to select a smaller data type to restrict the values that can be stored.

The Salary property of the Employee class is expressed as a .NET decimal, which the SQL Server provider maps to the decimal(18,2) SQL type (meaning a number with 18 digits to the left of the decimal point and 2 to the right). This is more precision than I need to express an individual's income, and in Listing 21-4 I have told Entity Framework Core to use a less precise type, overriding the default type what was selected when the first migration was created in Chapter 19.

■ **Caution**   Entity Framework Core doesn't validate the types or maximum lengths that you specify, which means you must be sure that the types and sizes you select are suitable for your needs.

Listing 21-4. Changing a Data Type in the AdvancedContext.cs File in the Models Folder

```
using Microsoft.EntityFrameworkCore;

namespace AdvancedApp.Models {

    public class AdvancedContext : DbContext {

        public AdvancedContext(DbContextOptions<AdvancedContext> options)
            : base(options) {}

        public DbSet<Employee> Employees { get; set; }
```

```
        protected override void OnModelCreating(ModelBuilder modelBuilder) {

            modelBuilder.Entity<Employee>()
                .HasQueryFilter(e => !e.SoftDeleted);

            modelBuilder.Entity<Employee>().Ignore(e => e.Id);
            modelBuilder.Entity<Employee>()
                .HasKey(e => new { e.SSN, e.FirstName, e.FamilyName });

            modelBuilder.Entity<Employee>()
                .Property(e => e.Salary).HasColumnType("decimal(8,2)");

            modelBuilder.Entity<SecondaryIdentity>()
                .HasOne(s => s.PrimaryIdentity)
                .WithOne(e => e.OtherIdentity)
                .HasPrincipalKey<Employee>(e => new { e.SSN,
                    e.FirstName, e.FamilyName })
                .HasForeignKey<SecondaryIdentity>(s => new { s.PrimarySSN,
                    s.PrimaryFirstName, s.PrimaryFamilyName });
        }
    }
}
```

The HasColumnType method is used to specify a SQL type for a property that has been selected using the Property method. In the listing, I specified the type decimal(8,2), which reduces the number of digits to the left of the decimal point to eight.

■ **Note**　If you don't like using the Fluent API, you can specify the SQL type for a property by using the Column attribute and providing a TypeName argument: [Column(TypeName = "decimal(8, 2)")].

Specifying a Maximum Length

If you are working with a value that will be stored in the database using an array data type, such as string or int[], then you can provide guidance to Entity Framework Core about the amount of data that you need to store without having to explicitly select a SQL data type, which means that you can influence the data type selection without needing to make decisions that are specific to a single database provider or server. In Listing 21-5, I have used the Fluent API to set a maximum length for the Name property defined by the SecondaryIdentity class.

■ **Note**　If you prefer not to use the Fluent API, you can specify a maximum length by decorating a property with the MaxLength attribute.

Listing 21-5. Setting a Maximum Length in the AdvancedContext.cs File in the Models Folder

```
using Microsoft.EntityFrameworkCore;

namespace AdvancedApp.Models {

    public class AdvancedContext : DbContext {

        public AdvancedContext(DbContextOptions<AdvancedContext> options)
            : base(options) {}

        public DbSet<Employee> Employees { get; set; }

        protected override void OnModelCreating(ModelBuilder modelBuilder) {

            modelBuilder.Entity<Employee>()
                .HasQueryFilter(e => !e.SoftDeleted);

            modelBuilder.Entity<Employee>().Ignore(e => e.Id);
            modelBuilder.Entity<Employee>()
                .HasKey(e => new { e.SSN, e.FirstName, e.FamilyName });

            modelBuilder.Entity<Employee>()
                .Property(e => e.Salary).HasColumnType("decimal(8,2)");

            modelBuilder.Entity<SecondaryIdentity>()
                .HasOne(s => s.PrimaryIdentity)
                .WithOne(e => e.OtherIdentity)
                .HasPrincipalKey<Employee>(e => new { e.SSN,
                    e.FirstName, e.FamilyName })
                .HasForeignKey<SecondaryIdentity>(s => new { s.PrimarySSN,
                    s.PrimaryFirstName, s.PrimaryFamilyName });

            modelBuilder.Entity<SecondaryIdentity>()
                .Property(e => e.Name).HasMaxLength(100);
        }
    }
}
```

The HasMaxLength method is used to specify a maximum length, and I have used it to specify a maximum of 100 characters for the Name property.

Updating the Database

Changing a data type or specifying a maximum length requires a migration to update the database. Run the commands shown in Listing 21-6 in the AdvancedApp project folder to create and apply a new migration.

Listing 21-6. Creating and Applying a Database Migration

```
dotnet ef migrations add ChangeType
dotnet ef database update
```

If you examine the Up method in the <timestamp>_ChangeType.cs file in the Migrations folder, you will see the effect of the HasColumnType and HasMaxLength methods.

```
...
protected override void Up(MigrationBuilder migrationBuilder) {
    migrationBuilder.AlterColumn<string>(name: "Name", table: "SecondaryIdentity",
        maxLength: 100, nullable: true, oldClrType: typeof(string),
        oldNullable: true);

    migrationBuilder.AlterColumn<decimal>(name: "Salary",table: "Employees",
        type: "decimal(8,2)",nullable: false, oldClrType: typeof(decimal));
}
...
```

The data type that I specified in Listing 21-4 will accommodate numbers that have eight digits before the decimal place. To see what happens when a number exceeds the available storage, start the application using dotnet run, navigate to http://localhost:5000, and click the Edit button for one of the items shown. Change the value of the Salary field to 100000000 (one, followed by eight zeros) and click the Save button. Entity Framework Core will attempt to update the database, but because the Salary value has more digits than can be stored using the type specified, an error is reported, as shown in Figure 21-2. The specific error that you encounter will depend on the nature of the mismatch, but the point is that you must take care to ensure that the application will not try—or allow the user to try—to store values that cannot be represented by the database.

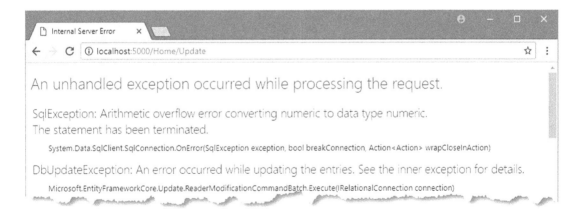

Figure 21-2. *Exceeding the available storage for a data value*

535

Validating or Formatting Data Values

In many applications, entity classes are just collections of properties that provide convenient access to the data in the database. In some situations, however, providing direct access to the data values can present a problem because some form of processing or validation is required.

Entity Framework Core supports *backing fields*, which store the value in the database but are not available to the rest of the application, which instead has access to the data mediated by a property. This is easier to understand with a demonstration, and in Listing 21-7 I have changed the Salary property in the Employee class so that it no longer provides direct access to the value in the database and uses a backing field instead.

Listing 21-7. Defining a Backing Field in the Employee.cs File in the Models Folder

```
using System;

namespace AdvancedApp.Models {

    public class Employee {
        private decimal databaseSalary;

        public long Id { get; set; }
        public string SSN { get; set; }
        public string FirstName { get; set; }
        public string FamilyName { get; set; }

        public decimal Salary {
            get => databaseSalary * 2;
            set => databaseSalary = Math.Max(0, value);
        }

        public SecondaryIdentity OtherIdentity { get; set; }

        public bool SoftDeleted { get; set; } = false;
    }
}
```

The backing field is called databaseSalary. The backing field must have a compatible type with the property you want to work with, and, in this case, the backing field and the Salary property both use the decimal type. By using a backing field, I can repurpose the Salary property to validate or transform the value that is stored in the database. In the listing, the Salary property's getter returns twice the value of the backing field, and the setter ensures that the minimum value that can be assigned to the backing field is zero, preventing negative values.

Adding a backing field to the entity class isn't enough because Entity Framework Core will just assume that it should continue using the Salary property. In Listing 21-8, I have used the Fluent API to tell Entity Framework Core about the backing field and how it should be used.

■ **Note** Backing fields can be configured only using the Fluent API. There is no attribute that supports this feature.

Listing 21-8. Setting Up a Backing Field in the AdvancedContext.cs File in the Models Folder

```
using Microsoft.EntityFrameworkCore;

namespace AdvancedApp.Models {

    public class AdvancedContext : DbContext {

        public AdvancedContext(DbContextOptions<AdvancedContext> options)
            : base(options) {}

        public DbSet<Employee> Employees { get; set; }

        protected override void OnModelCreating(ModelBuilder modelBuilder) {

            modelBuilder.Entity<Employee>()
                .HasQueryFilter(e => !e.SoftDeleted);

            modelBuilder.Entity<Employee>().Ignore(e => e.Id);
            modelBuilder.Entity<Employee>()
                .HasKey(e => new { e.SSN, e.FirstName, e.FamilyName });

            modelBuilder.Entity<Employee>()
                .Property(e => e.Salary).HasColumnType("decimal(8,2)")
                .HasField("databaseSalary")
                .UsePropertyAccessMode(PropertyAccessMode.Field);

            modelBuilder.Entity<SecondaryIdentity>()
                .HasOne(s => s.PrimaryIdentity)
                .WithOne(e => e.OtherIdentity)
                .HasPrincipalKey<Employee>(e => new { e.SSN,
                    e.FirstName, e.FamilyName })
                .HasForeignKey<SecondaryIdentity>(s => new { s.PrimarySSN,
                    s.PrimaryFirstName, s.PrimaryFamilyName });

            modelBuilder.Entity<SecondaryIdentity>()
                .Property(e => e.Name).HasMaxLength(100);
        }
    }
}
```

I am able to further configure the property by chaining calls to the existing Fluent API statement that selects the Salary property, which I used in the previous section to change the data type. I configure the backing field using the HasField method, specifying the name of the field as the argument. The way that the backing field is used is configured by calling the UsePropertyAccessMode method, specifying a value from the PropertyAccessMode enumeration, as described in Table 21-5.

■ **Tip**   You don't have to use UsePropertyAccessMode to configure a backing field, but doing so ensures that Entity Framework Core uses the field in the way that you expect and makes the purpose of the backing field obvious to other developers who are reading your Fluent API statements.

Table 21-5. *The PropertyAccessMode Values*

Name	Description
FieldDuringConstruction	This is the default behavior and tells Entity Framework Core to use the backing field when first creating the object and then to use the property for all other operations, including change detection.
Field	This value tells Entity Framework Core to ignore the property and always use the backing field.
Property	This value tells Entity Framework Core to always use the property and ignore the backing field.

Choosing the right PropertyAccessMode value is important because this value causes Entity Framework Core to behave in substantially different ways. In Listing 21-8, the backing field is always the "true" value, so I have used the Field value, which ensures that Entity Framework Core directly assigns the value in the database to the backing field when creating the object using query data and uses the backing field value when writing updates to the database.

No change to the database is required when you add a backing field because this feature only affects how the data values are mapped to the entity class. To see the effect of changes in this section, start the application using dotnet run and navigate to http://localhost:5000. When Entity Framework Core queries the data for Employee objects, it assigns the value from the Salary column to the backing field. When the Razor view enumerates the Employee objects, it reads the value of the Salary property, whose getter returns double the value stored in the database, producing the result shown in Figure 21-3.

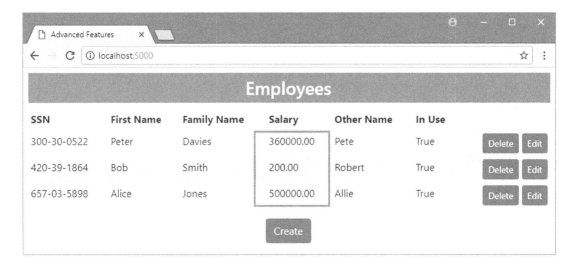

Figure 21-3. *Using a backing field to mediate access to values*

To see how changing the property value affects the backing field, click the Edit button for one of the Employee objects and enter **120000** (one hundred and twenty thousand without commas) into the Salary field.

I configured the backing field with the PropertyAccessMode.Field value, which means that the value of the backing field, rather than the property, is used to update the database. When Entity Framework Core performs change detection, it is the backing field value—and not the Salary property's getter—that is used to update the database. To confirm this is the case, select SQL Server ➤ New Query from the Visual Studio Tools menu, connect to the database, and execute the query shown in Listing 21-9.

Listing 21-9. Querying the Database

```
USE AdvancedDb
SELECT * FROM Employees
```

The results from the query show that the backing field was used when Entity Framework Core updated the Salary column in the Employees table, which will appear as shown in Table 21-6.

Table 21-6. *The Database Results*

FamilyName	FirstName	SSN	Salary
Davies	Peter	300-30-0522	180000
Jones	Alice	657-03-5898	200000
Smith	Bob	420-39-1864	120000

If I had used the FieldDuringConstruction value, then Entity Framework Core would have used the Salary property getter to obtain a value when updating the database.

The updated value is still read through the Salary property getter by the rest of the application, which remains unaware of the backing field. This is reflected in the view displayed by the ASP.NET Core MVC part of the application, as shown in Figure 21-4, which shows double the value stored in the database.

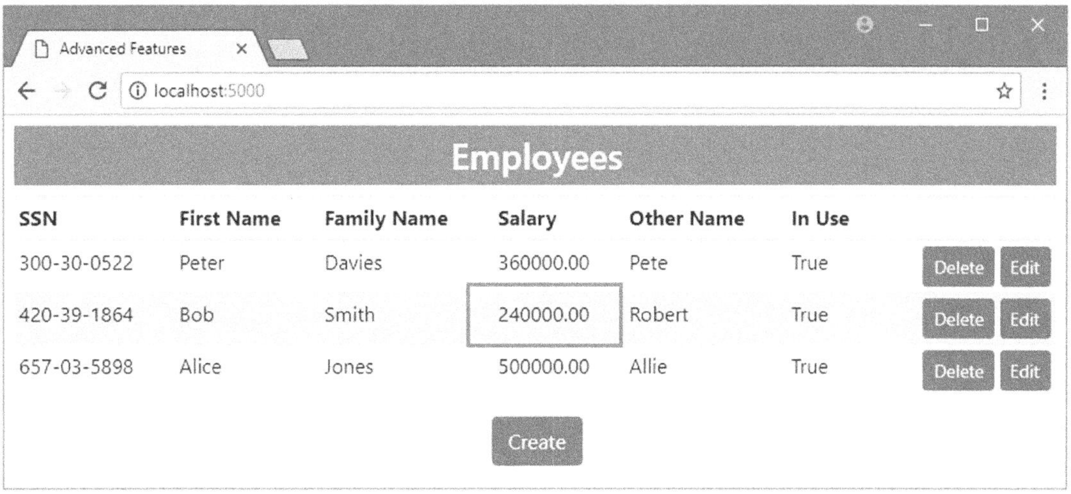

Figure 21-4. *Updating a value with a backing field*

Avoiding the Backing Field Selective Update Pitfall

Care must be taken when implementing setters that don't always update the backing field with which they are associated. To demonstrate the problem, I changed the setter for the Salary property so that it only updates the backing field for even values, as shown in Listing 21-10. I have also changed the getter for the Salary property so that it returns the unmodified value of the backing field, which will make the problem easier to understand.

539

Listing 21-10. Selectively Updating the Field in the Employee.cs File in the Models Folder

```
using System;

namespace AdvancedApp.Models {

    public class Employee {
        private decimal databaseSalary;

        public long Id { get; set; }
        public string SSN { get; set; }
        public string FirstName { get; set; }
        public string FamilyName { get; set; }

        public decimal Salary {
            get => databaseSalary;
            set {
                if (value % 2 == 0) {
                    databaseSalary = value;
                }
            }
        }

        public SecondaryIdentity OtherIdentity { get; set; }

        public bool SoftDeleted { get; set; } = false;
    }
}
```

Start the application using `dotnet run`, navigate to `http://localhost:5000`, and click one of the Edit buttons. Enter an odd number, such as **101**, in the Salary field and click the Save button. Instead of the value that you entered, Entity Framework Core will update the database with zero, as shown in Figure 21-5.

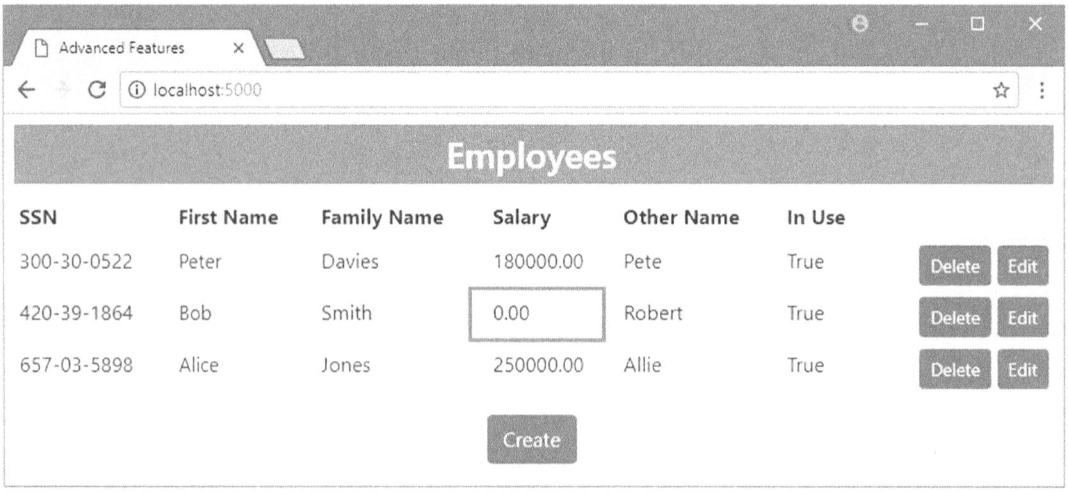

Figure 21-5. The effect of a selective backing field update

Only Entity Framework Core understands backing fields and how to use them. In an ASP.NET Core MVC application, the MVC model binder is also responsible for creating objects. When the browser sends an HTTP POST request to the controller, the model binder creates a new Employee object and sets the properties using the values sent by the user. Unlike when Entity Framework Core creates an Employee, the model binder ignores the backing field and uses the Salary property's setter to assign the value from the HTTP request. But the setter ignores the value assigned by the MVC model binder because it isn't an even number. This means the backing field has its default value (which is zero for decimal values) when the Employee object is handed over to the context object so that Entity Framework Core can perform an update.

The best way to avoid this problem is to write setters that always update their backing field. If this is not possible, then you can query the database so that Entity Framework Core creates an object with the existing values and apply the values from the HTTP request directly to it, as shown in Listing 21-11.

Listing 21-11. Setting Values Directly in the HomeController.cs File in the Controllers Folder

```
using AdvancedApp.Models;
using Microsoft.AspNetCore.Mvc;
using Microsoft.EntityFrameworkCore;
using System.Linq;

namespace AdvancedApp.Controllers {

    public class HomeController : Controller {
        private AdvancedContext context;

        public HomeController(AdvancedContext ctx) => context = ctx;

        public IActionResult Index() {
            return View(context.Employees.Include(e => e.OtherIdentity));
        }

        public IActionResult Edit(string SSN, string firstName, string familyName) {
            return View(string.IsNullOrWhiteSpace(SSN)
                ? new Employee() : context.Employees.Include(e => e.OtherIdentity)
                    .First(e => e.SSN == SSN
                        && e.FirstName == firstName
                        && e.FamilyName == familyName));
        }

        [HttpPost]
        public IActionResult Update(Employee employee, decimal salary) {
            Employee existing = context.Employees.Find(employee.SSN,
                employee.FirstName, employee.FamilyName);
            if (existing == null) {
                context.Add(employee);
            } else {
                existing.Salary = salary;
            }
            context.SaveChanges();
            return RedirectToAction(nameof(Index));
        }
    }
```

```
        [HttpPost]
        public IActionResult Delete(Employee employee) {
            context.Attach(employee);
            employee.SoftDeleted = true;
            context.SaveChanges();
            return RedirectToAction(nameof(Index));
        }
    }
}
```

I have changed the Update method so that it queries the database for the existing Employee object, which gives me an object created by Entity Framework Core and whose backing field is correctly initialized. I then assign the value specified by the user in the Salary field, which I receive by adding a salary parameter to the action method, like this:

```
...
public IActionResult Update(Employee employee, decimal salary) {
...
```

This provides me with the value that the user entered into the HTML form so that I can assign it to the Salary property.

```
...
existing.Salary = salary;
...
```

If the setter updates the backing field, then Entity Framework Core will detect the changed value and update the database. If the setter discards the new value (because it is odd numbered in this case), then Entity Framework Core will detect no change, and the original value stored in the database will be preserved.

Start the application, navigate to http://localhost:5000, and repeat the process of entering an even number, such as **100**, and then an odd number, such as **101**, into the Salary field. This time, when you save the changes, the odd number will be discarded, but the even number will still be stored in the database, as shown in Figure 21-6.

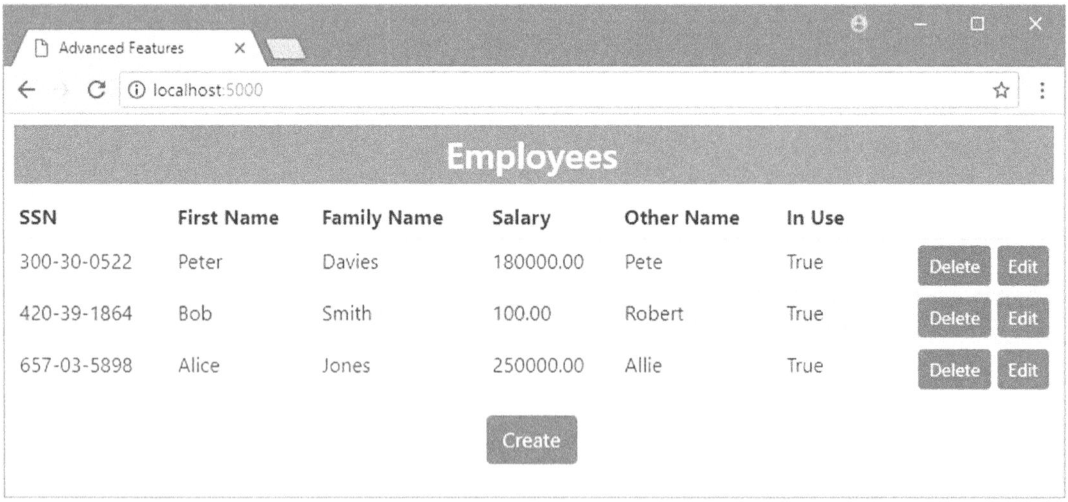

Figure 21-6. *Avoiding setting a backing field to the default value for its type*

Hiding Data Values from the MVC Application

Some types of data are needed to perform database operations but should not be accessible to the MVC part of the application, either because the data is sensitive or because you want to keep the focus of the application on the data that the user sees directly. In these situations, you can use *shadow properties*, which are properties that are defined in the data model but not in the entity class that represents that data.

Keeping track of the time that objects were stored in the database is the most common use for shadow properties, providing information that may be useful in diagnosing problems but which is not of interest to the user and should not be exposed through the ASP.NET Core MVC part of the application.

The Fluent API is used to create shadow properties. In Listing 21-12, I have added a shadow property called LastUpdated to the Employee class.

■ **Note** Shadow properties can be configured only using the Fluent API. There is no attribute that supports this feature.

Listing 21-12. Defining a Shadow Property in the AdvancedContext.cs File in the Models Folder

```
using Microsoft.EntityFrameworkCore;
using System;

namespace AdvancedApp.Models {

    public class AdvancedContext : DbContext {

        public AdvancedContext(DbContextOptions<AdvancedContext> options)
            : base(options) {}

        public DbSet<Employee> Employees { get; set; }

        protected override void OnModelCreating(ModelBuilder modelBuilder) {

            modelBuilder.Entity<Employee>()
                .HasQueryFilter(e => !e.SoftDeleted);

            modelBuilder.Entity<Employee>().Ignore(e => e.Id);
            modelBuilder.Entity<Employee>()
                .HasKey(e => new { e.SSN, e.FirstName, e.FamilyName });

            modelBuilder.Entity<Employee>()
                .Property(e => e.Salary).HasColumnType("decimal(8,2)")
                .HasField("databaseSalary")
                .UsePropertyAccessMode(PropertyAccessMode.Field);

            modelBuilder.Entity<Employee>().Property<DateTime>("LastUpdated");

            modelBuilder.Entity<SecondaryIdentity>()
                .HasOne(s => s.PrimaryIdentity)
                .WithOne(e => e.OtherIdentity)
                .HasPrincipalKey<Employee>(e => new { e.SSN,
```

543

```
                    e.FirstName, e.FamilyName })
            .HasForeignKey<SecondaryIdentity>(s => new { s.PrimarySSN,
                s.PrimaryFirstName, s.PrimaryFamilyName });

        modelBuilder.Entity<SecondaryIdentity>()
            .Property(e => e.Name).HasMaxLength(100);
        }
    }
}
```

The shadow property is defined by using the Entity method to select the class and then calling the Property method. This is a different version of the Property method from the one used in earlier examples. The argument specifies the name of the shadow property, and the type parameter is used to specify its data type; the Fluent API in the statement in Listing 21-12 tells Entity Framework Core that there is a DateTime property called LastUpdated.

░ **Tip**   You can chain additional calls to methods like IsRequired to configure shadow properties just like any other property.

Adding a shadow property to an existing database requires a migration. Run the commands shown in Listing 21-13 in the AdvancedDb project folder to create a migration called ShadowProperty and apply it to the database.

Listing 21-13. Creating and Applying a Migration

```
dotnet ef migrations add ShadowProperty
dotnet ef database update
```

If you examine the Up method of the <timestamp>_ShadowProperty.cs file that has been created in the Migrations folder, you can see how Entity Framework Core has set up a column for the shadow property, even though there is no corresponding property in the Employee class.

```
...
protected override void Up(MigrationBuilder migrationBuilder) {
    migrationBuilder.AddColumn<DateTime>(
        name: "LastUpdated",
        table: "Employees",
        nullable: false,
        defaultValue: new DateTime(1, 1, 1, 0, 0, 0, 0, DateTimeKind.Unspecified));
}
...
```

Accessing Shadow Property Values

Shadow properties can be accessed through the context class. In Listing 21-14, I have modified the Update action in the Advanced controller so that a value is assigned to the LastUpdated shadow property when a change is made to the database.

Listing 21-14. Updating a Shadow Property in the HomeController.cs File in the Controllers Folder

```
...
[HttpPost]
public IActionResult Update(Employee employee, decimal salary) {
    Employee existing = context.Employees.Find(employee.SSN,
        employee.FirstName, employee.FamilyName);
    if (existing == null) {
        context.Entry(employee)
            .Property("LastUpdated").CurrentValue = System.DateTime.Now;
        context.Add(employee);
    } else {
        existing.Salary = salary;
        context.Entry(existing)
            .Property("LastUpdated").CurrentValue = System.DateTime.Now;
    }
    context.SaveChanges();
    return RedirectToAction(nameof(Index));
}
...
```

I used the Entry method in Chapter 12 to access the Entity Framework Core changes detection feature, but the object that is returned is also used to access shadow properties through its Property method. The value of the shadow property can be read or set using the CurrentValue property, and in the listing I assign the current time to the shadow property.

■ **Note** Shadow properties can be accessed only through the context object, which means that even if you use the context directly in the controller, as I have done in this example, the MVC model binder will not be able to set a value for any shadow properties, even if the HTTP request contains one.

Including Shadow Properties in Queries

The static EF.Property method is used to include shadow properties in LINQ queries, which means that you can incorporate shadow properties into queries. In Listing 21-15, I have used the EF.Property method to order the objects in the database using the shadow property value.

Listing 21-15. Querying with a Shadow Property in the HomeController.cs File in the Controllers Folder

```
using AdvancedApp.Models;
using Microsoft.AspNetCore.Mvc;
using Microsoft.EntityFrameworkCore;
using System.Linq;
using System;

namespace AdvancedApp.Controllers {

    public class HomeController : Controller {
        private AdvancedContext context;
```

```
    public HomeController(AdvancedContext ctx) => context = ctx;

    public IActionResult Index() {
        return View(context.Employees.Include(e => e.OtherIdentity)
            .OrderByDescending(e => EF.Property<DateTime>(e, "LastUpdated")));
    }

    // ...other actions omitted for brevity...
  }
}
```

The EF.Property method accepts the object being queried and the name of the shadow property. There is a type parameter that must be set to the type used to define the property in the Fluent API statement. To see the use of the shadow property, start the application using dotnet run and navigate to http://localhost:5000.

Edit one of the Employee objects, and when you click the Save button, you will see that it appears in the first row in the table, as shown in Figure 21-7.

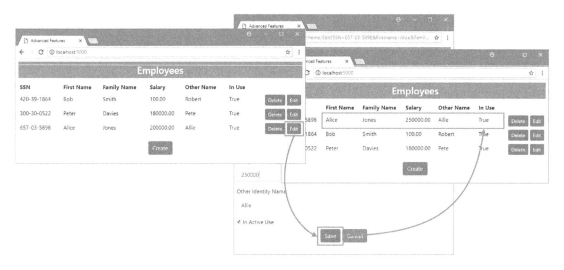

Figure 21-7. *Using a shadow property to order objects in a LINQ query*

Setting Default Values

When I set up the LastUpdated property in the previous section, I took responsibility for setting the value in two places: once when an object was stored in the database for the first time and again when an existing object was modified.

I can remove one of those statements by asking Entity Framework Core to set a default value for the LastUpdated property when a new object is stored. To set the default value for the LastUpdated property, I used the HasDefaultValue method in a Fluent API statement, as shown in Listing 21-16.

Note   Default values can be specified only using the Fluent API. There is no attribute that supports this feature.

Listing 21-16. Configuring a Default Value in the AdvancedContext.cs File in the Models Folder

```
using Microsoft.EntityFrameworkCore;
using System;

namespace AdvancedApp.Models {

    public class AdvancedContext : DbContext {

        public AdvancedContext(DbContextOptions<AdvancedContext> options)
            : base(options) {}

        public DbSet<Employee> Employees { get; set; }

        protected override void OnModelCreating(ModelBuilder modelBuilder) {

            modelBuilder.Entity<Employee>()
                .HasQueryFilter(e => !e.SoftDeleted);

            modelBuilder.Entity<Employee>().Ignore(e => e.Id);
            modelBuilder.Entity<Employee>()
                .HasKey(e => new { e.SSN, e.FirstName, e.FamilyName });

            modelBuilder.Entity<Employee>()
                .Property(e => e.Salary).HasColumnType("decimal(8,2)")
                .HasField("databaseSalary")
                .UsePropertyAccessMode(PropertyAccessMode.Field);

            modelBuilder.Entity<Employee>().Property<DateTime>("LastUpdated")
                .HasDefaultValue(new DateTime(2000, 1, 1));

            modelBuilder.Entity<SecondaryIdentity>()
                .HasOne(s => s.PrimaryIdentity)
                .WithOne(e => e.OtherIdentity)
                .HasPrincipalKey<Employee>(e => new { e.SSN,
                    e.FirstName, e.FamilyName })
                .HasForeignKey<SecondaryIdentity>(s => new { s.PrimarySSN,
                    s.PrimaryFirstName, s.PrimaryFamilyName });

            modelBuilder.Entity<SecondaryIdentity>()
                .Property(e => e.Name).HasMaxLength(100);
        }
    }
}
```

The HasDefaultValue method is used to specify a default value, which will be used when a new row is created in the database. You can override the default value by supplying a value for the property when storing an object, but if you do not, then the default value passed to the HasDefaultValue method will be used.

Setting a default value requires a new migration. Run the commands shown in Listing 21-17 in the AdvancedApp project folder to create a migration called DefaultValue and apply it to the database.

Listing 21-17. Creating and Applying a Database Migration

```
dotnet ef migrations add DefaultValue
dotnet ef database update
```

If you examine the Up method in the `<timestamp>_DefaultValue.cs` file that has been created in the Migrations folder, you will see that the default value associated with the LastUpdated column has been changed to January 1, 2000, reflecting the date specified in Listing 21-16.

```
...
protected override void Up(MigrationBuilder migrationBuilder) {
    migrationBuilder.AlterColumn<DateTime>(
        name: "LastUpdated",
        table: "Employees",
        nullable: false,
        defaultValue: new DateTime(2000, 1, 1, 0, 0, 0, 0, DateTimeKind.Unspecified),
        oldClrType: typeof(DateTime));
}
...
```

Displaying the Default Value

To work this example through the rest of the application, I am going to display the value of the LastUpdate property to the user. In Listing 21-18, I have promoted the LastUpdated property from a shadow property to one that can be accessed by the rest of the application by modifying the Employee class. This doesn't change the behavior of the property and just means that the property value doesn't have to be accessed via a context object.

Listing 21-18. Adding a Property in the Employee.cs File in the Models Folder

```
using System;

namespace AdvancedApp.Models {

    public class Employee {
        private decimal databaseSalary;

        public long Id { get; set; }
        public string SSN { get; set; }
        public string FirstName { get; set; }
        public string FamilyName { get; set; }

        public decimal Salary {
            get => databaseSalary;
            set {
                if (value % 2 == 0) {
                    databaseSalary = value;
                }
            }
        }
```

```
        public SecondaryIdentity OtherIdentity { get; set; }

        public bool SoftDeleted { get; set; } = false;

        public DateTime LastUpdated { get; set; }
    }
}
```

In Listing 21-19, I have modified the Update method in the Home controller to remove the statement that sets the LastUpdated property when new objects are stored, instead relying on the default value.

Listing 21-19. Disabling a Statement in the HomeController.cs File in the Controllers Folder

```
...
[HttpPost]
public IActionResult Update(Employee employee, decimal salary) {
    Employee existing = context.Employees.Find(employee.SSN,
        employee.FirstName, employee.FamilyName);
    if (existing == null) {
        //context.Entry(employee)
        //    .Property("LastUpdated").CurrentValue = System.DateTime.Now;
        context.Add(employee);
    } else {
        existing.Salary = salary;
        context.Entry(existing)
            .Property("LastUpdated").CurrentValue = System.DateTime.Now;
    }
    context.SaveChanges();
    return RedirectToAction(nameof(Index));
}
...
```

The final step is to add a column to the Index view used by the Home controller to display the value of the LastUpdated property, as shown in Listing 21-20.

Listing 21-20. Adding a Column in the Index.cshtml File in the Views/Home Folder

```
@model IEnumerable<Employee>
@{
    ViewData["Title"] = "Advanced Features";
    Layout = "_Layout";
}
<h3 class="bg-info p-2 text-center text-white">Employees</h3>
<table class="table table-sm table-striped">
    <thead>
        <tr>
            <th>SSN</th>
            <th>First Name</th>
            <th>Family Name</th>
            <th>Salary</th>
            <th>Other Name</th>
            <th>In Use</th>
```

```
                <th>Last Updated</th>
                <th></th>
            </tr>
        </thead>
        <tbody>
            <tr class="placeholder"><td colspan="8" class="text-center">No Data</td></tr>
            @foreach (Employee e in Model) {
                <tr>
                    <td>@e.SSN</td>
                    <td>@e.FirstName</td>
                    <td>@e.FamilyName</td>
                    <td>@e.Salary</td>
                    <td>@(e.OtherIdentity?.Name ?? "(None)")</td>
                    <td>@(e.OtherIdentity?.InActiveUse.ToString() ?? "(N/A)")</td>
                    <td>@e.LastUpdated.ToLocalTime()</td>
                    <td class="text-right">
                        <form>
                            <input type="hidden" name="SSN" value="@e.SSN" />
                            <input type="hidden" name="Firstname" value="@e.FirstName" />
                            <input type="hidden" name="FamilyName"
                                value="@e.FamilyName" />
                            <button type="submit" asp-action="Delete" formmethod="post"
                                    class="btn btn-sm btn-danger">Delete</button>
                            <button type="submit" asp-action="Edit" formmethod="get"
                                    class="btn btn-sm btn-primary">
                                Edit
                            </button>
                        </form>
                    </td>
                </tr>
            }
        </tbody>
    </table>
    <div class="text-center">
        <a asp-action="Edit" class="btn btn-primary">Create</a>
    </div>
```

To see a default value, start the application using dotnet run, navigate to http://localhost:5000, and click the Create button. Fill out the form fields and click the Save button; you will see that the new object is assigned a LastUpdated value of January 1, 2000, which is the default value I used in Listing 21-16, as shown in Figure 21-8. The dates displayed will be in the default locale for your system; the dates shown in the figure are in the format used in the United Kingdom.

■ **Tip**   If your database contained Employee objects before the LastUpdated column was added to the Employee table in the database and you have not edited those objects, you will see a LastUpdated value of Jan 01 0001, as shown in the figure. This is because the default value is applied only when creating a new object. The existing data in the database was assigned a value of all zeros when the LastUpdated column was created, and this is what is displayed.

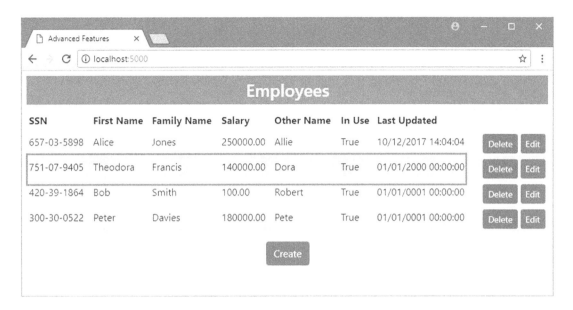

Figure 21-8. Assigning a default value

Detecting Concurrent Updates

Most ASP.NET Core MVC applications follow a query-and-update cycle when the user edits data. Existing data values are retrieved from the database in a query to provide the user with an initial state, and then an update is made with any changes. This can be a problem when there are several users performing this cycle concurrently, as illustrated in Figure 21-9.

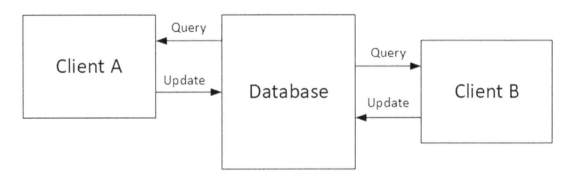

Figure 21-9. Concurrent updates

Client A and Client B query the same data and get the same values. Client A performs an update and, shortly after, so does Client B.

This can cause a range of problems, including updates that are silently overwritten and exceptions for seemingly valid updates. Some problems can take a while to manifest, as clients continue working with inconsistent or incomplete data.

Using Concurrency Tokens

Entity Framework Core can be configured to check a value associated with an object to make sure it hasn't changed since the data was read. The property that is selected for this check is known as a *concurrency token,* and this technique is useful when you don't want to—or unable to—make changes to the database to prevent concurrent updates. In Listing 21-21, I have configured the data model to make the Salary property a concurrency token for updates to Employee objects.

≋ **Caution**   As you will learn, the concurrency token feature has some serious limitations. There is a better alternative available if you are able to modify the database, as described in the next section.

Listing 21-21. Creating a Token in the AdvancedContext.cs File in the Models Folder

```
using Microsoft.EntityFrameworkCore;
using System;

namespace AdvancedApp.Models {

    public class AdvancedContext : DbContext {

        public AdvancedContext(DbContextOptions<AdvancedContext> options)
            : base(options) {}

        public DbSet<Employee> Employees { get; set; }

        protected override void OnModelCreating(ModelBuilder modelBuilder) {

            modelBuilder.Entity<Employee>()
                .HasQueryFilter(e => !e.SoftDeleted);

            modelBuilder.Entity<Employee>().Ignore(e => e.Id);
            modelBuilder.Entity<Employee>()
                .HasKey(e => new { e.SSN, e.FirstName, e.FamilyName });

            modelBuilder.Entity<Employee>()
                .Property(e => e.Salary).HasColumnType("decimal(8,2)")
                .HasField("databaseSalary")
                .UsePropertyAccessMode(PropertyAccessMode.Field)
                .IsConcurrencyToken();

            modelBuilder.Entity<Employee>().Property<DateTime>("LastUpdated")
                .HasDefaultValue(new DateTime(2000, 1, 1));

            modelBuilder.Entity<SecondaryIdentity>()
                .HasOne(s => s.PrimaryIdentity)
                .WithOne(e => e.OtherIdentity)
                .HasPrincipalKey<Employee>(e => new { e.SSN,
                    e.FirstName, e.FamilyName })
                .HasForeignKey<SecondaryIdentity>(s => new { s.PrimarySSN,
```

```
                        s.PrimaryFirstName, s.PrimaryFamilyName });

            modelBuilder.Entity<SecondaryIdentity>()
                .Property(e => e.Name).HasMaxLength(100);
        }
    }
}
```

The IsConcurrencyToken method is used to tell Entity Framework Core that it should include the existing value of the property in the query when it performs an update to make sure it hasn't changed. Using a concurrency token works only if Entity Framework Core knows the old value before it performs an update, which requires a little work in ASP.NET Core MVC applications to deal with objects created by the MVC model binder.

■ **Tip**   The ConcurrencyCheck attribute can be applied to tell Entity Framework Core to use a property as a concurrency token.

I don't want to unduly complete this example by having to deal with the effect of a setter that doesn't always update the backing field with which it is associated. In Listing 21-22, I have simplified the setter for the Salary property so that it simply updates the databaseSalary field.

Listing 21-22. Simplifying a Property Setter in the Employee.cs File in the Models Folder

```
using System;

namespace AdvancedApp.Models {

    public class Employee {
        private decimal databaseSalary;

        public long Id { get; set; }
        public string SSN { get; set; }
        public string FirstName { get; set; }
        public string FamilyName { get; set; }

        public decimal Salary {
            get => databaseSalary;
            set => databaseSalary = value;
        }

        public SecondaryIdentity OtherIdentity { get; set; }

        public bool SoftDeleted { get; set; } = false;

        public DateTime LastUpdated { get; set; }
    }
}
```

To provide Entity Framework Core with the old Salary value to check, I added a hidden input element to the Edit.cshtml view used by the Home controller, as shown in Listing 21-23. This will ensure that the Update action method receives the value of the Salary property that was read from the database.

Listing 21-23. Adding an Element in the Edit.cshtml File in the Views/Home Folder

```
@model Employee
@{
    ViewData["Title"] = "Advanced Features";
    Layout = "_Layout";
}

<h4 class="bg-info p-2 text-center text-white">
    Create/Edit
</h4>
<form asp-action="Update" method="post">
    <input type="hidden" asp-for="Id" />
    <input type="hidden" name="originalSalary" value="@Model.Salary" />
    <div class="form-group">
        <label class="form-control-label" asp-for="SSN"></label>
        <input class="form-control" asp-for="SSN" readonly="@Model.SSN"/>
    </div>
    <div class="form-group">
        <label class="form-control-label" asp-for="FirstName"></label>
        <input class="form-control" asp-for="FirstName"
                readonly="@Model.FirstName" />
    </div>
    <div class="form-group">
        <label class="form-control-label" asp-for="FamilyName"></label>
        <input class="form-control" asp-for="FamilyName"
                readonly="@Model.FamilyName" />
    </div>
    <div class="form-group">
        <label class="form-control-label" asp-for="Salary"></label>
        <input class="form-control" asp-for="Salary"/>
    </div>
    <input type="hidden" asp-for="OtherIdentity.Id"/>
    <div class="form-group">
        <label class="form-control-label">Other Identity Name:</label>
        <input class="form-control" asp-for="OtherIdentity.Name"/>
    </div>
    <div class="form-check">
        <label class="form-check-label">
            <input class="form-check-input" type="checkbox"
                    asp-for="OtherIdentity.InActiveUse"/>
            In Active Use
        </label>
    </div>
    <div class="text-center">
        <button type="submit" class="btn btn-primary">Save</button>
        <a class="btn btn-secondary" asp-action="Index">Cancel</a>
    </div>
</form>
```

To ensure that Entity Framework Core is able to use the original Salary value to perform the concurrency check, I added a parameter to the Update action on the Home controller to receive the value from the input element and apply it to the Employee object that is used to perform the update, as shown in Listing 21-24.

Listing 21-24. Updating the Action Method in the HomeController.cs File in the Controllers Folder

```
...
[HttpPost]
public IActionResult Update(Employee employee, decimal originalSalary) {
    if (context.Employees.Count(e => e.SSN == employee.SSN
            && e.FirstName == employee.FirstName
            && e.FamilyName == employee.FamilyName) == 0) {
        context.Add(employee);
    } else {
        Employee e = new Employee {
            SSN = employee.SSN, FirstName = employee.FirstName,
            FamilyName = employee.FamilyName, Salary = originalSalary
        };
        context.Employees.Attach(e);
        e.Salary = employee.Salary;
        e.LastUpdated = DateTime.Now;
    }
    context.SaveChanges();
    return RedirectToAction(nameof(Index));
}
...
```

The most important thing to remember is that querying the database in the Update method would undermine the purpose of the concurrency token because the query will return the value that is currently in the database and not the value that was stored at the time that the client requested the data that the user has been editing.

In the Update method, I create a new Employee object and set its Salary property using the value from the hidden input element. This sets the baseline for the Entity Framework Core change detection process using the data values that were current when the user started the edit operation. I put the Employee object under change management using the Attach method and change the Salary property using the value received in the HTTP POST request.

This sequence of steps is awkward, but it allows the concurrency token to be used in an ASP.NET Core MVC application, and it will make more sense when you see how this feature works.

A database migration isn't required when using a concurrency token because it affects only the queries sent by Entity Framework Core, not the database itself. Start the application using dotnet run, navigate to http://localhost:5000, click the Edit button for one of the objects shown in the table, change the Salary value, and click the Save button.

If you inspect the logging messages that are generated by the application, you will see the SQL command that Entity Framework Core sent to the database to perform the update.

```
...
UPDATE [Employees] SET [LastUpdated] = @p0, [Salary] = @p1
WHERE [SSN] = @p2 AND [FirstName] = @p3 AND [FamilyName] = @p4 AND [Salary] = @p5;
...
```

The WHERE clause, which I have highlighted, restricts the update so that it will only apply to a row in the Employees table that has a specific composite primary key and a specific Salary value. This prevents the update from being applied if another client has modified the concurrency token because no rows will match the WHERE clause of the UPDATE statement. Entity Framework Core checks to see how many rows have been changed by the UPDATE statement. If one row is updated, then it assumes that there have been no concurrent updates. If no rows are updated, then Entity Framework Core assumes that the concurrency token has been changed by another client and reports an error.

To see the error, open a second browser window and perform an interleaved update: click the Edit button for the same Employee in both browser windows, change the Salary value in both windows, and click the Save button in both windows. The second update will fail, and you will see the error message shown in Figure 21-10.

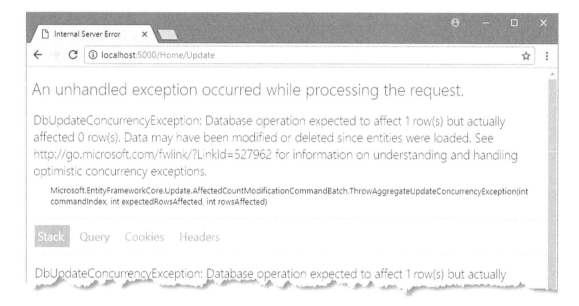

Figure 21-10. *A concurrency check failure*

The limitation of the concurrency check feature is that every update must modify the same column to indicate a change, and every update must know what a change to that column indicates. In the case of the example application, this means updates must modify the Salary property to signal to other clients that there has been a change; updates that affect only other properties won't prevent concurrent updates. Despite these problems, using a concurrency token can be useful if you can't modify the database and you are able to ensure that clients will update a specific property every time.

```
┌─────────────────────────────────────────────────────────────────────────────┐
│                        AVOIDING THE DATE PITFALL                              │
└─────────────────────────────────────────────────────────────────────────────┘
```

You might assume the limitations of the concurrency token can be avoided by using the `LastUpdated` property, which is updated each time an `Employee` object is updated and doesn't rely on the user to make a specific change. Unfortunately, you must ensure that Entity Framework Core will query for exactly the value stored in the database, and dates are subject to variations in precision and formatting. The `LastUpdated` values are stored in the database like this:

```
2017-11-10 09:11:42.3366667
```

But when Entity Framework Core reads these values and parses them into a `DateTime` object, the precision is lost, and the format is changed based on the locale configuration. At best, you will get a value like this:

```
10/11/2017 09:11:42
```

When Entity Framework Core performs an `UPDATE`, the date value specified in the `WHERE` clause won't match the value in the database, and no records will be matched. Entity Framework Core will think that the concurrency check has failed, and you will see the exception shown in Figure 21-10.

Using a Row Version to Detect Concurrent Updates

If your project allows you to make changes to the database, a more reliable alternative is a *row version*, which is a timestamp that is automatically updated when there is an update but is stored in a way that doesn't lead to formatting differences. In Listing 21-25, I have added a property to the `Employee` class that will be used for row versioning.

Listing 21-25. Adding a Property in the Employee.cs File in the Models Folder

```
using System;

namespace AdvancedApp.Models {

    public class Employee {
        private decimal databaseSalary;

        public long Id { get; set; }
        public string SSN { get; set; }
        public string FirstName { get; set; }
        public string FamilyName { get; set; }

        public decimal Salary {
            get => databaseSalary;
            set => databaseSalary = value;
        }
```

```
        public SecondaryIdentity OtherIdentity { get; set; }

        public bool SoftDeleted { get; set; } = false;

        public DateTime LastUpdated { get; set; }
        public byte[] RowVersion { get; set; }
    }
}
```

Row versioning is done using a byte array property, which avoids problems with data precision and formatting. In Listing 21-26, I have added a Fluent API statement that configures the new property so that it will be used by the row version feature. I have also commented out the method call that configures the Salary property as a concurrency token.

■ **Note**   You can tell Entity Framework Core about a row version property by applying the TimeStamp attribute to it, which is equivalent to using the Fluent API IsRowVersion method.

Listing 21-26. Adding a Row Version in the AdvancedContext.cs File in the Models Folder

```
using Microsoft.EntityFrameworkCore;
using System;

namespace AdvancedApp.Models {

    public class AdvancedContext : DbContext {

        public AdvancedContext(DbContextOptions<AdvancedContext> options)
            : base(options) {}

        public DbSet<Employee> Employees { get; set; }

        protected override void OnModelCreating(ModelBuilder modelBuilder) {

            modelBuilder.Entity<Employee>()
                .HasQueryFilter(e => !e.SoftDeleted);

            modelBuilder.Entity<Employee>().Ignore(e => e.Id);
            modelBuilder.Entity<Employee>()
                .HasKey(e => new { e.SSN, e.FirstName, e.FamilyName });

            modelBuilder.Entity<Employee>()
                .Property(e => e.Salary).HasColumnType("decimal(8,2)")
                .HasField("databaseSalary")
                .UsePropertyAccessMode(PropertyAccessMode.Field);
                //.IsConcurrencyToken();

            modelBuilder.Entity<Employee>().Property<DateTime>("LastUpdated")
                .HasDefaultValue(new DateTime(2000, 1, 1));
```

```
    modelBuilder.Entity<Employee>()
        .Property(e => e.RowVersion).IsRowVersion();

    modelBuilder.Entity<SecondaryIdentity>()
        .HasOne(s => s.PrimaryIdentity)
        .WithOne(e => e.OtherIdentity)
        .HasPrincipalKey<Employee>(e => new { e.SSN,
            e.FirstName, e.FamilyName })
        .HasForeignKey<SecondaryIdentity>(s => new { s.PrimarySSN,
            s.PrimaryFirstName, s.PrimaryFamilyName });

    modelBuilder.Entity<SecondaryIdentity>()
        .Property(e => e.Name).HasMaxLength(100);
    }
  }
}
```

The row version feature is configured by selecting a property and calling the IsRowVersion method. To prevent concurrent updates, the value for the RowVersion property that was stored in the database at the start of the edit operation must be included in the HTML sent to the client so that it can be received by the Update method when the user submits a change, just like the example in the previous section. In Listing 21-27, I have added a hidden input element to the Edit.cshtml view that contains the value of the RowVersion property.

Listing 21-27. Adding an Element in the Edit.cshtml File in the Views/Home Folder

```
@model Employee
@{
    ViewData["Title"] = "Advanced Features";
    Layout = "_Layout";
}

<h4 class="bg-info p-2 text-center text-white">
    Create/Edit
</h4>
<form asp-action="Update" method="post">
    <input type="hidden" asp-for="Id" />
    <input type="hidden" asp-for="RowVersion" />
    @*<input type="hidden" name="originalSalary" value="@Model.Salary" />*@
    <div class="form-group">
        <label class="form-control-label" asp-for="SSN"></label>
        <input class="form-control" asp-for="SSN" readonly="@Model.SSN" />
    </div>
    <div class="form-group">
        <label class="form-control-label" asp-for="FirstName"></label>
        <input class="form-control" asp-for="FirstName"
            readonly="@Model.FirstName" />
    </div>
    <div class="form-group">
        <label class="form-control-label" asp-for="FamilyName"></label>
        <input class="form-control" asp-for="FamilyName"
            readonly="@Model.FamilyName" />
    </div>
```

```
<div class="form-group">
    <label class="form-control-label" asp-for="Salary"></label>
    <input class="form-control" asp-for="Salary" />
</div>
<input type="hidden" asp-for="OtherIdentity.Id" />
<div class="form-group">
    <label class="form-control-label">Other Identity Name:</label>
    <input class="form-control" asp-for="OtherIdentity.Name" />
</div>
<div class="form-check">
    <label class="form-check-label">
        <input class="form-check-input" type="checkbox"
                asp-for="OtherIdentity.InActiveUse" />
        In Active Use
    </label>
</div>
<div class="text-center">
    <button type="submit" class="btn btn-primary">Save</button>
    <a class="btn btn-secondary" asp-action="Index">Cancel</a>
</div>
</form>
```

To use the value received included in the POST request, I updated the Update method of the Home controller, as shown in Listing 21-28.

The technique for performing the update is essentially the same as for the previous example, and it is important not to query the database for the current RowVersion value, which would undermine the purpose of the concurrency check.

Listing 21-28. Using a Row Version in the HomeController.cs File in the Controllers Folder

```
...
[HttpPost]
public IActionResult Update(Employee employee) {
    if (context.Employees.Count(e => e.SSN == employee.SSN
            && e.FirstName == employee.FirstName
            && e.FamilyName == employee.FamilyName) == 0) {
        context.Add(employee);
    } else {
        Employee e = new Employee {
            SSN = employee.SSN, FirstName = employee.FirstName,
            FamilyName = employee.FamilyName, RowVersion = employee.RowVersion
        };
        context.Employees.Attach(e);
        e.Salary = employee.Salary;
        e.LastUpdated = DateTime.Now;
    }
    context.SaveChanges();
    return RedirectToAction(nameof(Index));
}
...
```

Notice that I don't have to change the RowVersion property when I perform the update. The database server will generate a new RowVersion value for each update, which Entity Framework Core uses in its WHERE clause for the UPDATE statement.

Finally, I need to a hidden element to the Index view used by the Home controller so that the soft-delete feature works correctly, as shown in Listing 21-29.

▪ **Tip**   Notice that I used the asp-for tag helper to set the value of the input element. The RowVersion property type is a byte array, and the tag helper concatenates the array elements to form a string that the MVC model binder can parse in the subsequent HTTP POST request.

Listing 21-29. Adding an Element to the Index.cshtml File in the Views/Home Folder

```
@model IEnumerable<Employee>
@{
    ViewData["Title"] = "Advanced Features";
    Layout = "_Layout";
}
<h3 class="bg-info p-2 text-center text-white">Employees</h3>
<table class="table table-sm table-striped">
    <thead>
        <tr>
            <th>SSN</th>
            <th>First Name</th>
            <th>Family Name</th>
            <th>Salary</th>
            <th>Other Name</th>
            <th>In Use</th>
            <th>Last Updated</th>
            <th></th>
        </tr>
    </thead>
    <tbody>
        <tr class="placeholder"><td colspan="8" class="text-center">No Data</td></tr>
        @foreach (Employee e in Model) {
            <tr>
                <td>@e.SSN</td>
                <td>@e.FirstName</td>
                <td>@e.FamilyName</td>
                <td>@e.Salary</td>
                <td>@(e.OtherIdentity?.Name ?? "(None)")</td>
                <td>@(e.OtherIdentity?.InActiveUse.ToString() ?? "(N/A)")</td>
                <td>@e.LastUpdated.ToLocalTime()</td>
                <td class="text-right">
                    <form>
                        <input type="hidden" name="SSN" value="@e.SSN" />
                        <input type="hidden" name="Firstname" value="@e.FirstName" />
                        <input type="hidden" name="FamilyName"
                               value="@e.FamilyName" />
```

```
                    <input type="hidden" name="RowVersion"
                            asp-for="@e.RowVersion" />
                    <button type="submit" asp-action="Delete" formmethod="post"
                            class="btn btn-sm btn-danger">
                        Delete
                    </button>
                    <button type="submit" asp-action="Edit" formmethod="get"
                            class="btn btn-sm btn-primary">
                        Edit
                    </button>
                </form>
            </td>
        </tr>
    }
    </tbody>
</table>
<div class="text-center">
    <a asp-action="Edit" class="btn btn-primary">Create</a>
</div>
```

The drawback of the row version approach is that it requires changes to the database. Run the commands shown in Listing 21-30 in the AdvancedApp project folder to create and apply a migration called RowVersion.

Listing 21-30. Creating and Applying a Database Migration

```
dotnet ef migrations add RowVersion
dotnet ef database update
```

If you use two browser windows to perform interleaved updates, you will see the same error message that is shown in Figure 21-10. The difference is that all updates will trigger a change in the RowVersion value. This means all updates—regardless of the properties they modify—will cause a change that can be used to detect concurrent updates.

Summary

In this chapter, I described the features that Entity Framework Core provides for taking control of the way that data is created or stored in the database. I explained how to change the SQL type used to store a property in the database, how to validate or format data using a backing field, how to use shadow properties for data that you don't want the rest of the application to access, and how to set default values when objects are stored in the database. I finished the chapter by showing you how to detect concurrent updates using the concurrency token and row version features. In the next chapter, I describe the advanced features available for deleting data.

CHAPTER 22

Deleting Data

Deleting data can be a surprisingly complex task, especially when it comes to dealing with related data or modeling an existing database. In this chapter, I describe the Entity Framework Core features for dealing with deleting data, demonstrate how each of them works, and explain when they are useful. Table 22-1 puts this chapter into context.

Table 22-1. *Putting Advanced Delete Features in Context*

Question	Answer
What are they?	These features allow you to specify how the database server responds to requests to delete data.
Why are they useful?	There are several different ways that related data can be handled when an object is deleted, and selecting the right one will ensure your application has access to the data it needs.
How are they used?	These features are applied through a combination of Fluent API statements and changes to the repository classes in the project.
Are there any pitfalls or limitations?	Care must be taken not to cause an unexpected cascade delete in the database and remove more data than was intended. Equally, you can create orphaned data by not removing enough data.
Are there any alternatives?	You can rely on the default behaviors that Entity Framework Core applies to the database.

Table 22-2 summarizes the chapter.

Table 22-2. *Chapter Summary*

Problem	Solution	Listing
Change the delete behavior	Use the OnDelete method	1–19

Preparing for This Chapter

I continue using the AdvancedApp project, but some changes are required to prepare for this chapter. To display details of SecondaryIdentity objects, I created a file called SecondaryIdentities.cshtml in the Views/Home folder and added the content shown in Listing 22-1 to create a partial view.

■ **Tip** If you don't want to follow the process of building the example project, you can download all of the required files from this book's source code repository, available at https://github.com/apress/pro-ef-core-2-for-asp.net-core-mvc.

Listing 22-1. The Contents of the SecondaryIdentities.cshtml File in the Views/Home Folder

```
<h3 class="bg-info p-2 text-center text-white">Secondary Identities</h3>
<table class="table table-sm table-striped">
    <thead>
        <tr>
            <th>Key</th>
            <th>Name</th>
            <th>Active Use</th>
            <th>Foreign SSN</th>
            <th>Foreign FamilyName</th>
            <th>Foreign FirstName</th>
        </tr>
    </thead>
    <tbody>
        <tr class="placeholder"><td colspan="6" class="text-center">No Data</td></tr>
        @foreach (SecondaryIdentity ident in ViewBag.Secondaries) {
            <tr>
                <td>@ident.Id</td>
                <td>@ident.Name</td>
                <td>@ident.InActiveUse</td>
                <td>@(ident.PrimarySSN ?? "(null)")</td>
                <td>@(ident.PrimaryFirstName ?? "(null)")</td>
                <td>@(ident.PrimaryFamilyName ?? "(null)")</td>
            </tr>
        }
    </tbody>
</table>
```

To incorporate the partial view into the display shown to the user, I added the element shown in Listing 22-2 to the Index view used by the Home controller. I also removed the In Use and Last Updated columns from the table that displays the Employees objects.

Listing 22-2. Adding a Partial View in the Index.cshtml File in the Views/Home Folder

```
@model IEnumerable<Employee>
@{
    ViewData["Title"] = "Advanced Features";
    Layout = "_Layout";
}
<h3 class="bg-info p-2 text-center text-white">Employees</h3>
<table class="table table-sm table-striped">
    <thead>
        <tr>
            <th>SSN</th>
```

```
                <th>First Name</th>
                <th>Family Name</th>
                <th>Salary</th>
                <th>Other Name</th>
                @*<th>In Use</th>*@
                @*<th>Last Updated</th>*@
                <th></th>
            </tr>
        </thead>
        <tbody>
            <tr class="placeholder"><td colspan="8" class="text-center">No Data</td></tr>
            @foreach (Employee e in Model) {
                <tr>
                    <td>@e.SSN</td>
                    <td>@e.FirstName</td>
                    <td>@e.FamilyName</td>
                    <td>@e.Salary</td>
                    <td>@(e.OtherIdentity?.Name ?? "(None)")</td>
                    @*<td>@(e.OtherIdentity?.InActiveUse.ToString() ?? "(N/A)")</td>*@
                    @*<td>@e.LastUpdated.ToLocalTime()</td>*@
                    <td class="text-right">
                        <form>
                            <input type="hidden" name="SSN" value="@e.SSN" />
                            <input type="hidden" name="Firstname" value="@e.FirstName" />
                            <input type="hidden" name="FamilyName"
                                    value="@e.FamilyName" />
                            <input type="hidden" name="RowVersion"
                                    asp-for="@e.RowVersion" />
                            <button type="submit" asp-action="Delete" formmethod="post"
                                     class="btn btn-sm btn-danger">
                                Delete
                            </button>
                            <button type="submit" asp-action="Edit" formmethod="get"
                                     class="btn btn-sm btn-primary">
                                Edit
                            </button>
                        </form>
                    </td>
                </tr>
            }
        </tbody>
    </table>
    @Html.Partial("SecondaryIdentities")
    <div class="text-center">
        <a asp-action="Edit" class="btn btn-primary">Create</a>
    </div>
```

For the Home controller, I changed the Index action to provide access to the SecondaryIdentity objects through the ViewBag, as shown in Listing 22-3. I also changed the Delete method to remove the soft-delete feature and performed a conventional delete, similar to those used in earlier chapters. (I restore the soft-delete feature at the end of the chapter.)

Listing 22-3. Making Changes in the HomeController.cs File in the Controllers Folder

```csharp
using AdvancedApp.Models;
using Microsoft.AspNetCore.Mvc;
using Microsoft.EntityFrameworkCore;
using System.Linq;
using System;

namespace AdvancedApp.Controllers {

    public class HomeController : Controller {
        private AdvancedContext context;

        public HomeController(AdvancedContext ctx) => context = ctx;

        public IActionResult Index() {
            ViewBag.Secondaries = context.Set<SecondaryIdentity>();
            return View(context.Employees.Include(e => e.OtherIdentity)
                .OrderByDescending(e => EF.Property<DateTime>(e, "LastUpdated")));
        }

        public IActionResult Edit(string SSN, string firstName, string familyName) {
            return View(string.IsNullOrWhiteSpace(SSN)
                ? new Employee() : context.Employees.Include(e => e.OtherIdentity)
                    .First(e => e.SSN == SSN
                        && e.FirstName == firstName
                        && e.FamilyName == familyName));
        }

        [HttpPost]
        public IActionResult Update(Employee employee) {
            if (context.Employees.Count(e => e.SSN == employee.SSN
                    && e.FirstName == employee.FirstName
                    && e.FamilyName == employee.FamilyName) == 0) {
                context.Add(employee);
            } else {
                Employee e = new Employee {
                    SSN = employee.SSN, FirstName = employee.FirstName,
                    FamilyName = employee.FamilyName,
                    RowVersion = employee.RowVersion
                };
                context.Employees.Attach(e);
                e.Salary = employee.Salary;
                e.LastUpdated = DateTime.Now;
            }
            context.SaveChanges();
            return RedirectToAction(nameof(Index));
        }
}
```

```
        [HttpPost]
        public IActionResult Delete(Employee employee) {
            context.Remove(employee);
            context.SaveChanges();
            return RedirectToAction(nameof(Index));
        }
    }
}
```

Next, run the commands shown in Listing 22-4 in the AdvancedApp project folder to drop and re-create the database.

Listing 22-4. Dropping and Re-creating the Database

```
dotnet ef database drop --force
dotnet ef database update
```

Start the application using dotnet run, navigate to http://localhost:5000, click the Create button, and use the values shown in Table 22-3 to store three Employee objects.

Table 22-3. *The Data Values for Creating Example Objects*

SSN	FirstName	FamilyName	Salary	Other Name	In Active Use
420-39-1864	Bob	Smith	100000	Robert	Checked
657-03-5898	Alice	Jones	200000	Allie	Checked
300-30-0522	Peter	Davies	180000	Pete	Checked
751-07-9405	Theodora	Francis	140000	Dora	Checked

When you have created all four objects, you should see the layout illustrated in Figure 22-1.

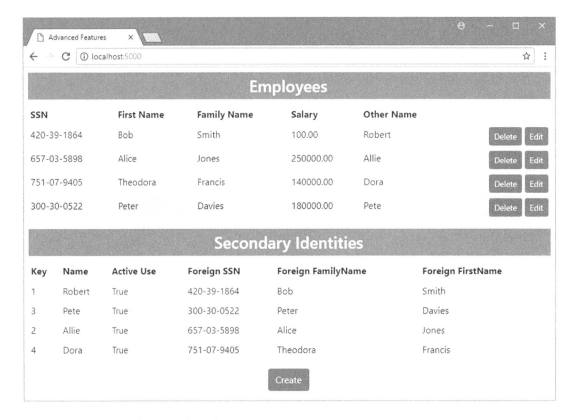

Figure 22-1. *Running the example application*

Understanding Delete Constraints

The context's Remove method is used to delete data from the database. Passing an object to this method tells Entity Framework Core that the corresponding data in the database is no longer required and a DELETE command should be sent to the database server when the SaveChanges method is called.

A common problem arises in ASP.NET Core MVC applications when the object that is to be deleted has a relationship to other data stored in the database. You can see an example by clicking the Delete button for one of the Employee objects displayed by the application. The database server won't allow the data to be deleted, and you will see the exception in Figure 22-2.

Figure 22-2. *Attempting to delete data*

When you delete the principal entity in a relationship, one of three things will happen to the dependent entity, based on the data model configuration.

- The dependent entity will be deleted. This means that deleting an Employee object would also delete its related SecondaryIdentity.

- The dependent entity's foreign key properties are set to null. This would mean that deleting an Employee would cause the related SecondaryIdentity object's SSN, PrimaryFirstName, and PrimaryFamily name properties to be set to null.

- No change is made to the dependent entity.

The third option really means you have to manage related data in the application, taking responsibility to ensure that you don't attempt any operation that would delete data on which a relationship depends. Database servers work hard to ensure the integrity of the databases they manage and will report errors rather than allow a reference problem to be created.

When a relationship is defined, Entity Framework Core follows a set of conventions to select the delete behavior, using one of the values defined by the DeleteBehavior enumeration, as described in Table 22-4.

Table 22-4. *The DeleteBehavior Values*

Name	Description
Cascade	The dependent entity is deleted automatically along with the principal entity.
SetNull	The primary key of the dependent entity is set to null by the database server.
ClientSetNull	The primary key of the dependent entity is set to null by Entity Framework Core.
Restrict	No change is made to the dependent entity.

The relationship between the Employee and SecondaryIdentity classes is configured in the CompositeKey migration. If you examine the Up method in the <timestamp>_CompositeKey.cs file in the Migrations folder, you will find the statement that sets the delete behavior.

```
...
migrationBuilder.CreateTable(name: "SecondaryIdentity",
    columns: table => new {
        Id = table.Column<long>(type: "bigint", nullable: false)
            .Annotation("SqlServer:ValueGenerationStrategy",
                SqlServerValueGenerationStrategy.IdentityColumn),

        ...column definitions omitted for brevity...

    },
    constraints: table => {
        table.PrimaryKey("PK_SecondaryIdentity", x => x.Id);
        table.ForeignKey(name: "FK_SecondaryIdentity_Employees_
            PrimarySSN_PrimaryFirstName_PrimaryFamilyName",
                columns: x => new { x.PrimarySSN, x.PrimaryFirstName,
                    x.PrimaryFamilyName },
                principalTable: "Employees",
                principalColumns: new[] { "SSN", "FirstName", "FamilyName" },
                onDelete: ReferentialAction.Restrict);
    });
...
```

This relationship has been configured with the Restrict behavior. No change was made to the SecondaryIdentity object when its related Employee was deleted, causing the exception shown in Figure 22-2.

Configuring the Delete Behavior

The most reliable way to get the behavior you require is to select the desired delete behavior using the Fluent API, explicitly configuring the data model with a DeleteBehavior value. The descriptions in the table may seem simple enough, but there are some complications. These behaviors can be different for required and optional relationships. In addition, just to make things more difficult, Entity Framework Core will only perform some operations on related data that has been loaded from the database, which can be confusing in an ASP.NET Core MVC application, where objects are often created by the MVC model binder and will require special handling. In the sections that follow, I explain how each of the delete behaviors works.

DECIDING WHICH DELETE BEHAVIOR TO USE

The choice of delete behavior can be confusing, and it can be difficult to figure out which one you need, even after you have seen the demonstrations of each behavior in the sections that follow. Here is my advice if you find yourself uncertain where to begin.

If you are working with a required relationship, then you should start with the Cascade behavior, but do some testing to make sure that a single delete operation doesn't propagate through the database and remove more data than you expected.

If you are working with an optional relationship, then you should start with the SetNull behavior if your database server supports it and the ClientSetNull behavior otherwise. But if you have no plan to deal with orphaned data, then use the Cascade behavior instead.

Avoid the Restrict behavior unless you are modeling a database that has specific demands that cannot be dealt with using the other behaviors. The Restrict behavior lets you take complete control of the delete process, but that can be harder to implement than you might expect, and it is easy to make mistakes.

Using the Cascade Delete Behavior

The DeleteBehavior.Cascade value configures the database so that dependent entities are removed from the database when the principal entity they are related to is deleted. The cascade behavior is the easiest to work with, but caution is required because you can easily delete more data than you expected since the database server will continue to follow relationships and delete data to ensure the integrity of the database. If you apply the cascade behavior too freely, you can find that a delete operation can get out of control and have far-reaching consequences.

In Listing 22-5, I have added a Fluent API statement to the context class to select the cascade behavior for the Employee/SecondaryIdentity relationship.

Note   The delete behavior for a relationship can be specified only using the Fluent API. There is no attribute support for this feature.

Listing 22-5. Configuring the Delete Behavior in the AdvancedContext.cs File in the Models Folder

```
using Microsoft.EntityFrameworkCore;
using System;

namespace AdvancedApp.Models {

    public class AdvancedContext : DbContext {

        public AdvancedContext(DbContextOptions<AdvancedContext> options)
            : base(options) {}

        public DbSet<Employee> Employees { get; set; }

        protected override void OnModelCreating(ModelBuilder modelBuilder) {

            modelBuilder.Entity<Employee>()
                .HasQueryFilter(e => !e.SoftDeleted);

            modelBuilder.Entity<Employee>().Ignore(e => e.Id);
            modelBuilder.Entity<Employee>()
                .HasKey(e => new { e.SSN, e.FirstName, e.FamilyName });
```

```
            modelBuilder.Entity<Employee>()
                .Property(e => e.Salary).HasColumnType("decimal(8,2)")
                .HasField("databaseSalary")
                .UsePropertyAccessMode(PropertyAccessMode.Field);
                //.IsConcurrencyToken();

            modelBuilder.Entity<Employee>().Property<DateTime>("LastUpdated")
                .HasDefaultValue(new DateTime(2000, 1, 1));

            modelBuilder.Entity<Employee>()
                .Property(e => e.RowVersion).IsRowVersion();

            modelBuilder.Entity<SecondaryIdentity>()
                .HasOne(s => s.PrimaryIdentity)
                .WithOne(e => e.OtherIdentity)
                .HasPrincipalKey<Employee>(e => new { e.SSN,
                    e.FirstName, e.FamilyName })
                .HasForeignKey<SecondaryIdentity>(s => new { s.PrimarySSN,
                    s.PrimaryFirstName, s.PrimaryFamilyName })
                .OnDelete(DeleteBehavior.Cascade);

            modelBuilder.Entity<SecondaryIdentity>()
                .Property(e => e.Name).HasMaxLength(100);
        }
    }
}
```

The OnDelete method is used to configure a relationship's delete behavior and accepts a DeleteBehavior value as its argument. This method is used as part of the chain of method calls that define the relationship between two classes.

Run the commands shown in Listing 22-6 in the AdvancedApp project folder to create and apply a migration to the database that will change the delete behavior.

Listing 22-6. Creating and Applying a Migration

```
dotnet ef migrations add CascadeDelete
dotnet ef database update
```

To see the effect of the change, start the application using dotnet run, navigate to http://localhost:5000, and click the Delete button for one of the Employee objects. The Employee and its related SecondaryIdentity object will be removed from the database, as shown in Figure 22-3.

■ **Tip**   If you run out of objects to delete, then click the Create button, fill out the fields, and click Save to store new data in the database. The values you choose are not important because all of the examples in this chapter are focused just on deleting data.

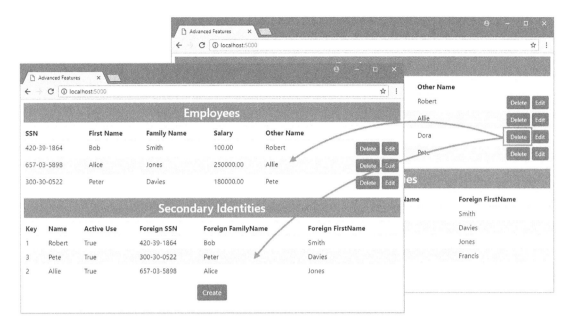

Figure 22-3. *Using the cascade delete behavior*

The cascade behavior is implemented by the database server, which automatically removes the related data from the database. You can see this by examining the logging messages generated by the application. When you clicked the Delete button, Entity Framework Core sent the following SQL to the database:

```
...
DELETE FROM [Employees]
WHERE [SSN] = @p0 AND [FirstName] = @p1 AND [FamilyName] = @p2
    AND [RowVersion] = @p3;
...
```

Entity Framework Core only has to delete the principal entity and can rely on the database server to deal with removing the related data to preserve the integrity of the database.

Setting Foreign Keys to Null

Two of the DeleteBehavior values, SetNull and ClientSetNull, respond to deleting the principal entity by leaving the dependent entity in the database but setting the foreign key to null. This has the effect of breaking the relationship between the two objects so that the principal can be deleted without violating the referential integrity of the database.

■ **Caution** This behavior can be used only for optional relationships. Using this behavior on a required relationship will produce an exception.

573

The difference between the SetNull and ClientSetNull behaviors is who takes responsibility for modifying the dependent entity. With the SetNull behavior, the database server will set the foreign key property of the dependent entity to null. With the ClientSetNull behavior, Entity Framework Core takes responsibility for updating the dependent entity.

Not all databases support the SetNull behavior—although SQL Server does—but SetNull has the advantage of consistency because the ClientSetNull behavior will work only if Entity Framework Core is made aware of the related data, either because it has been loaded as part of a query or because the MVC model binder creates an object that contains its primary key. I demonstrate the different ways these behaviors are used in the sections that follow.

Relying on the Database Server to Change Foreign Keys

If your database server supports it, then the SetNull behavior can be used to update dependent entities even if they have not been loaded by Entity Framework Core. Of the two delete behaviors that set foreign keys to null, this is the one that is easiest to work with because you don't have to make sure that Entity Framework Core is tracking the objects that have to be modified. In Listing 22-7, I have selected the SetNull behavior for the Employee/SecondaryIdentity relationship by changing the argument to the OnDelete method.

Listing 22-7. Changing the Delete Behavior in the AdvancedContext.cs File in the Models Folder

```
...
modelBuilder.Entity<SecondaryIdentity>()
    .HasOne(s => s.PrimaryIdentity)
    .WithOne(e => e.OtherIdentity)
    .HasPrincipalKey<Employee>(e => new { e.SSN,
            e.FirstName, e.FamilyName })
    .HasForeignKey<SecondaryIdentity>(s => new { s.PrimarySSN,
            s.PrimaryFirstName, s.PrimaryFamilyName })
    .OnDelete(DeleteBehavior.SetNull);
...
```

Run the commands shown in Listing 22-8 in the AdvancedApp project folder to create a new migration and apply it to the database.

Listing 22-8. Creating and Applying a Database Migration

```
dotnet ef migrations add SetNullDelete
dotnet ef database update
```

To see how the delete behavior works, start the application using dotnet run, navigate to http://localhost:5000, and click one of the Delete buttons. You will see that the Employee object is removed from the database and the foreign key properties of the related SecondaryIdentity object are set to null, as shown in Figure 22-4.

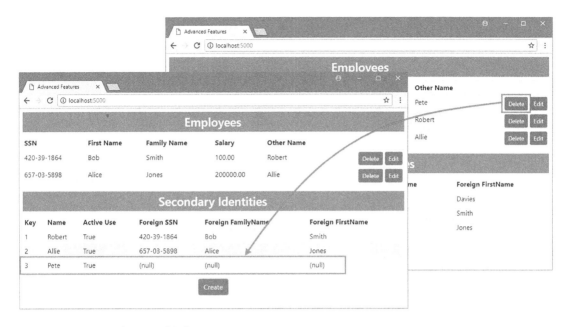

Figure 22-4. *Using the SetNull behavior*

If you examine the logging messages produced by the application, you can see the DELETE command that Entity Framework Core used to remove the Employee object.

```
...
DELETE FROM [Employees]
WHERE [SSN] = @p0 AND [FirstName] = @p1 AND [FamilyName] = @p2
    AND [RowVersion] = @p3;
...
```

No command is sent to update the related SecondaryIdentity object, and it is the database server that updates the foreign key properties of any dependent entities to null.

■ **Caution**   Since the SetNull behavior doesn't delete dependent entities from the database, you can end up with "orphaned" data. You should use this behavior only if the application is likely to reuse the dependent entities left in the database. For the example application, there is now a SecondaryIdentity object in the database that is not associated with an Employee, and the application provides no means to use the existing object when creating a new Employee, effectively orphaning the data. Orphaned data can cause unexpected problems, especially if there are uniqueness constraints applied to natural keys, which will stop new objects from being created with the same key values as used by orphans.

Relying on Entity Framework Core to Update Foreign Keys

With the `ClientSetNull` behavior, Entity Framework Core will update the foreign key properties of dependent entities when the principal entity is deleted. This is useful if your database server doesn't support the `SetNull` behavior, although it requires some additional work in ASP.NET Core MVC applications because Entity Framework Core will update only those objects that have been loaded from the database or manually added to change tracking. This means that either using an additional query to load related data from the database or including additional information in the HTTP request that the user sends to initiate the delete operation.

To configure the `ClientSetNull` behavior, I changed the value passed to the `OnDelete` method in the context class, as shown in Listing 22-9.

Listing 22-9. Changing the Delete Behavior in the AdvancedContext.cs File in the Models Folder

```
...
modelBuilder.Entity<SecondaryIdentity>()
    .HasOne(s => s.PrimaryIdentity)
    .WithOne(e => e.OtherIdentity)
    .HasPrincipalKey<Employee>(e => new { e.SSN,
            e.FirstName, e.FamilyName })
    .HasForeignKey<SecondaryIdentity>(s => new { s.PrimarySSN,
            s.PrimaryFirstName, s.PrimaryFamilyName })
    .OnDelete(DeleteBehavior.ClientSetNull);
...
```

A new migration is required to configure the database. Run the commands shown in Listing 22-10 in the AdvancedApp folder to create the migration and apply it to the database.

Listing 22-10. Creating and Applying a Database Migration

```
dotnet ef migrations add ClientSetNullDelete
dotnet ef database update
```

If you examine the `Up` method in the `<timestamp>_ClientSetNullDelete.cs` file that has been added to the `Migrations` folder, you will see that the delete behavior has been changed, as follows:

```
...
protected override void Up(MigrationBuilder migrationBuilder) {
    migrationBuilder.DropForeignKey(
        name: "FK_SecondaryIdentity_Employees
            _PrimarySSN_PrimaryFirstName_PrimaryFamilyName",
        table: "SecondaryIdentity");

    migrationBuilder.AddForeignKey(
        name: "FK_SecondaryIdentity_Employees
            _PrimarySSN_PrimaryFirstName_PrimaryFamilyName",
        table: "SecondaryIdentity",
        columns: new[] { "PrimarySSN", "PrimaryFirstName", "PrimaryFamilyName" },
        principalTable: "Employees",
        principalColumns: new[] { "SSN", "FirstName", "FamilyName" },
        onDelete: ReferentialAction.Restrict);
}
...
```

The migration changes the behavior back to `Restrict` so that the database server takes no action when an `Employee` object is deleted. That makes sense because the `ClientSetNull` behavior relies on Entity Framework Core to update the foreign key values, rather than the database server.

If you start the application using `dotnet run`, navigate to `http://localhost:5000`, and click a Delete button, you will see the error message shown in Figure 22-5.

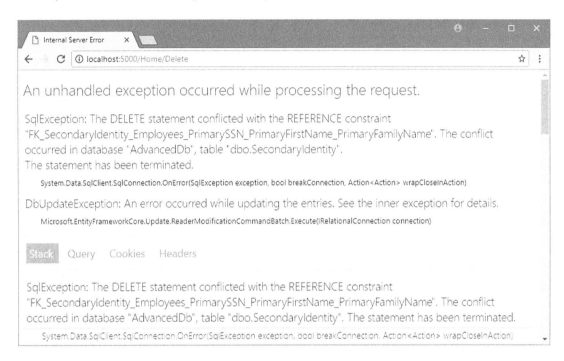

Figure 22-5. *Deleting a principal entity*

This is what happens if you select the `ClientSetNull` behavior but don't provide Entity Framework Core with access to the dependent entities that are related to the object being deleted. The effect is equivalent to specifying the `Restrict` behavior because the database server won't make any changes to the dependent entities and Entity Framework Core doesn't know about them.

Using a Query to Load Related Data

One way to make sure that Entity Framework Core knows that there are related objects to delete is to perform a database query to load the data, as shown in Listing 22-11.

Listing 22-11. Querying for Related Data in the HomeController.cs File in the Controllers Folder

```
...
[HttpPost]
public IActionResult Delete(Employee employee) {

    context.Set<SecondaryIdentity>().FirstOrDefault(id =>
        id.PrimarySSN == employee.SSN
        && id.PrimaryFirstName == employee.FirstName
        && id.PrimaryFamilyName == employee.FamilyName);
```

```
    context.Employees.Remove(employee);
    context.SaveChanges();
    return RedirectToAction(nameof(Index));
}
...
```

It is enough to load the data that will be deleted, and I don't have to do anything with the object that Entity Framework Core creates other than ensure that it is being tracked.

■ **Tip** I have used the Find method, which executes a query immediately. If your related data can be accessed only through a LINQ query that creates an IQueryable<T>, then you should call the Load method to force evaluation of the query. Otherwise, Entity Framework Core won't execute the query, the data won't be loaded, and the foreign key properties won't be set to null.

Start the application using dotnet run, navigate to http://localhost:5000, and click a Delete button. As with the SetNull behavior, the Employee object will be removed from the database, and the foreign key properties of the related SecondaryIdentity object will be set to null, as shown in Figure 22-6.

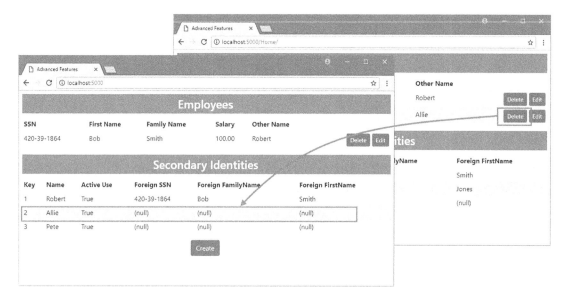

Figure 22-6. Using the ClientSetNull behavior

If you examine the logging messages generated by the application, you will see that Entity Framework Core has taken responsibility for dealing with both objects. First you will see this command, which sets the foreign key values of the SecondaryIdentity object to null:

```
...
UPDATE [SecondaryIdentity] SET [PrimaryFamilyName] = @p0, [PrimaryFirstName] = @p1,
    [PrimarySSN] = @p2
WHERE [Id] = @p3;
...
```

This ensures that the Employee object can be deleted without causing referential integrity problems. The delete operation is performed with this command:

```
...
DELETE FROM [Employees]
WHERE [SSN] = @p4 AND [FirstName] = @p5 AND [FamilyName] = @p6
    AND [RowVersion] = @p7;
...
```

Avoiding Related Data Query

Entity Framework Core only needs the primary key of the dependent entity to perform an update. You can avoid the additional query in Listing 22-11 by including an additional value in the HTTP POST request that targets the Delete operation and use it to give Entity Framework Core the information it requires. In Listing 22-12, I have added an element to the Index view for the primary key of the related SecondaryIdentity object.

Listing 22-12. Adding an Element in the Index.cshtml File in the Views/Home Folder

```
@model IEnumerable<Employee>
@{
    ViewData["Title"] = "Advanced Features";
    Layout = "_Layout";
}
<h3 class="bg-info p-2 text-center text-white">Employees</h3>
<table class="table table-sm table-striped">
    <thead>
        <tr>
            <th>SSN</th>
            <th>First Name</th>
            <th>Family Name</th>
            <th>Salary</th>
            <th>Other Name</th>
            <th></th>
        </tr>
    </thead>
    <tbody>
        <tr class="placeholder"><td colspan="8" class="text-center">No Data</td></tr>
        @foreach (Employee e in Model) {
            <tr>
                <td>@e.SSN</td>
                <td>@e.FirstName</td>
```

```
            <td>@e.FamilyName</td>
            <td>@e.Salary</td>
            <td>@(e.OtherIdentity?.Name ?? "(None)")</td>
            <td class="text-right">
                <form>
                    <input type="hidden" name="SSN" value="@e.SSN" />
                    <input type="hidden" name="Firstname" value="@e.FirstName" />
                    <input type="hidden" name="FamilyName"
                            value="@e.FamilyName" />
                    <input type="hidden" name="RowVersion"
                            asp-for="@e.RowVersion" />
                    <input type="hidden" name="OtherIdentity.Id"
                            value="@e.OtherIdentity.Id" />
                    <button type="submit" asp-action="Delete" formmethod="post"
                            class="btn btn-sm btn-danger">
                        Delete
                    </button>
                    <button type="submit" asp-action="Edit" formmethod="get"
                            class="btn btn-sm btn-primary">
                        Edit
                    </button>
                </form>
            </td>
        </tr>
    }
    </tbody>
</table>
@Html.Partial("SecondaryIdentities")
<div class="text-center">
    <a asp-action="Edit" class="btn btn-primary">Create</a>
</div>
```

In Listing 22-13, I have commented out the query in the Delete action method. The new value included in the HTTP POST request allows the MVC model binder to create a SecondaryIdentity object, which Entity Framework Core will use to update the database before performing the deleting operation.

Listing 22-13. Disabling a Query in the HomeController.cs File in the Controllers Folder

```
...
[HttpPost]
public IActionResult Delete(Employee employee) {

    //context.Set<SecondaryIdentity>().FirstOrDefault(id =>
    //     id.PrimarySSN == employee.SSN
    //     && id.PrimaryFirstName == employee.FirstName
    //     && id.PrimaryFamilyName == employee.FamilyName);

    context.Employees.Remove(employee);
    context.SaveChanges();
    return RedirectToAction(nameof(Index));
}
...
```

Start the application using `dotnet run`, navigate to `http://localhost:5000`, and click a Delete button. The foreign key properties of the related `SecondaryIdentity` object will be set to `null`, just as with the previous example, but without the need to perform an additional query in the `Delete` action method.

Taking Control of the Delete Operation

The `Restrict` behavior tells Entity Framework Core and the database server to make no changes to dependent entities. If you select this behavior, then you are responsible for ensuring that your delete operation can be performed without causing an error. In Listing 22-14, I have selected the delete behavior in the context class.

Listing 22-14. Selecting the Restrict Behavior in the AdvancedContext.cs File in the Models Folder

```
...
modelBuilder.Entity<SecondaryIdentity>()
    .HasOne(s => s.PrimaryIdentity)
    .WithOne(e => e.OtherIdentity)
    .HasPrincipalKey<Employee>(e => new { e.SSN,
            e.FirstName, e.FamilyName })
    .HasForeignKey<SecondaryIdentity>(s => new { s.PrimarySSN,
            s.PrimaryFirstName, s.PrimaryFamilyName })
    .OnDelete(DeleteBehavior.Restrict);
...
```

Run the commands shown in Listing 22-15 in the `AdvancedApp` project folder to create a new migration and apply it to the database.

Listing 22-15. Creating and Applying a Database Migration

```
dotnet ef migrations add RestrictDelete
dotnet ef database update
```

Re-creating the Cascade Behavior

If you want to delete related data, then you must either query the database for the objects you want to remove or ensure there is enough data in the HTTP POST request to create an object that will let Entity Framework Core perform a delete operation.

In Listing 22-12 I added a hidden `input` element to the `Index.cshtml` view that includes the primary key value of the `SecondaryIdentity` object in the request to delete an `Employee`. In Listing 22-16, I take use this value to tell Entity Framework Core to include the related object in the delete operation.

Listing 22-16. Deleting Related Data in the HomeController.cs File in the Controllers Folder

```
...
[HttpPost]
public IActionResult Delete(Employee employee) {
    if (employee.OtherIdentity != null) {
        context.Set<SecondaryIdentity>().Remove(employee.OtherIdentity);
    }
```

```
    context.Employees.Remove(employee);
    context.SaveChanges();
    return RedirectToAction(nameof(Index));
}
...
```

Start the application using dotnet run, navigate to http://localhost:5000, and click a Delete button (you may need to create new objects so you have something to delete). Examine the logging messages generated by the application, and you will see two operations that remove data from the database. The first removes the SecondaryIdentity object.

```
...
DELETE FROM [SecondaryIdentity]
WHERE [Id] = @p0;
...
```

Removing the dependent entity clears the way for the second operation, which removes the principal entity.

```
...
DELETE FROM [Employees]
WHERE [SSN] = @p1 AND [FirstName] = @p2 AND [FamilyName] = @p3
    AND [RowVersion] = @p4;
...
```

Re-creating the Set Null Behavior

If you want to take responsibility for setting foreign key properties to null, then you can use the Attach method to put an object created by the MVC model binder under Entity Framework Core change tracking and then set the values of the foreign key properties, as shown in Listing 22-17.

Note   This will work only for optional relationships. You will receive an error if you try to set the foreign key property to null in a required relationship.

Listing 22-17. Setting Foreign Key Properties in the HomeController.cs File in the Controllers Folder

```
...
[HttpPost]
public IActionResult Delete(Employee employee) {
    if (employee.OtherIdentity != null) {
        SecondaryIdentity identity =
            context.Set<SecondaryIdentity>().Find(employee.OtherIdentity.Id);
        identity.PrimarySSN = null;
        identity.PrimaryFirstName = null;
        identity.PrimaryFamilyName = null;
    }
    employee.OtherIdentity = null;
    context.Employees.Remove(employee);
    context.SaveChanges();
```

```
        return RedirectToAction(nameof(Index));
}
...
```

I query the database to get the current foreign key values, set the properties to null, and set the OtherIdentity navigation property to null on the Employee object. When Entity Framework Core updates the database, it sends UPDATE and DELETE commands just like the ones used by the ClientSetNull behavior.

Reinstating the Soft-Delete Feature

I am going to finish this chapter by reinstating the soft-delete feature and move the permanent delete feature into the separate Delete controller.

In Listing 22-18, I modified the Home controller so that the Delete action performs the soft delete. I also changed the query for related data in the Index action so that the SecondaryIdentity objects are accessed through the Employee navigation properties. This will ensure that the query is subject to the query filter so that SecondaryIdentity objects whose foreign key properties are null will not be displayed.

Listing 22-18. Updating Actions in the HomeController.cs File in the Controllers Folder

```
using AdvancedApp.Models;
using Microsoft.AspNetCore.Mvc;
using Microsoft.EntityFrameworkCore;
using System.Linq;
using System;
using System.Collections.Generic;

namespace AdvancedApp.Controllers {

    public class HomeController : Controller {
        private AdvancedContext context;

        public HomeController(AdvancedContext ctx) => context = ctx;

        public IActionResult Index() {
            IEnumerable<Employee> data = context.Employees
                .Include(e => e.OtherIdentity)
                .OrderByDescending(e => e.LastUpdated)
                .ToArray();
            ViewBag.Secondaries = data.Select(e => e.OtherIdentity);
            return View(data);
        }

        public IActionResult Edit(string SSN, string firstName, string familyName) {
            return View(string.IsNullOrWhiteSpace(SSN)
                ? new Employee() : context.Employees.Include(e => e.OtherIdentity)
                    .First(e => e.SSN == SSN
                        && e.FirstName == firstName
                        && e.FamilyName == familyName));
        }
```

```
    [HttpPost]
    public IActionResult Update(Employee employee) {
        if (context.Employees.Count(e => e.SSN == employee.SSN
                && e.FirstName == employee.FirstName
                && e.FamilyName == employee.FamilyName) == 0) {
            context.Add(employee);
        } else {
            Employee e = new Employee {
                SSN = employee.SSN, FirstName = employee.FirstName,
                FamilyName = employee.FamilyName,
                RowVersion = employee.RowVersion
            };
            context.Employees.Attach(e);
            e.Salary = employee.Salary;
            e.LastUpdated = DateTime.Now;
        }
        context.SaveChanges();
        return RedirectToAction(nameof(Index));
    }

    [HttpPost]
    public IActionResult Delete(Employee employee) {
        context.Employees.Attach(employee);
        employee.SoftDeleted = true;
        context.SaveChanges();
        return RedirectToAction(nameof(Index));
    }
  }
}
```

Query filters only apply to queries for the class they are applied to, which means you may get inconsistent results if you use queries that start at different ends of a relationship. In the Index action, I changed the query for SecondaryIdentity objects so that it selects a subset of the results from a query for Employee objects. This ensures that only SecondaryIdentity objects that are related to Employee objects that have not been soft-deleted will be displayed to the user.

░ **Tip**   To ensure that only one query is performed, I used the ToArray method to force execution of the query. Without this method, there would be duplicate queries when the Employee and SecondaryIdentity objects are enumerated by the view.

Next, I added buttons to the Index view used by the Delete controller so that soft-deleted objects can be removed from the database, either individually or in bulk, as shown in Listing 22-19.

Listing 22-19. Adding Elements in the Index.cshtml File in the Views/Delete Folder

```
@model IEnumerable<Employee>
@{
    ViewData["Title"] = "Advanced Features";
    Layout = "_Layout";
}
```

```
<h3 class="bg-info p-2 text-center text-white">Deleted Employees</h3>
<table class="table table-sm table-striped">
    <thead>
        <tr>
            <th>SSN</th>
            <th>First Name</th>
            <th>Family Name</th>
            <th></th>
        </tr>
    </thead>
    <tbody>
        <tr class="placeholder"><td colspan="4" class="text-center">No Data</td></tr>
        @foreach (Employee e in Model) {
            <tr>
                <td>@e.SSN</td>
                <td>@e.FirstName</td>
                <td>@e.FamilyName</td>
                <td class="text-right">
                    <form method="post">
                        <input type="hidden" name="SSN" value="@e.SSN" />
                        <input type="hidden" name="FirstName" value="@e.FirstName" />
                        <input type="hidden" name="FamilyName"
                                value="@e.FamilyName" />
                        <input type="hidden" name="RowVersion"
                                asp-for="@e.RowVersion" />
                        <input type="hidden" name="OtherIdentity.Id"
                                value="@e.OtherIdentity.Id" />
                        <button asp-action="Restore" class="btn btn-sm btn-success">
                            Restore
                        </button>
                        <button asp-action="Delete" class="btn btn-sm btn-danger">
                            Delete
                        </button>
                    </form>
                </td>
            </tr>
        }
    </tbody>
</table>
<div class="text-center">
    <form method="post" asp-action="DeleteAll">
        <button type="submit" class="btn btn-danger">Delete All</button>
    </form>
</div>
```

To complete the feature, I added the actions shown in Listing 22-20 to the Delete controller, corresponding to the elements added in Listing 22-19.

Listing 22-20. Adding Actions in the DeleteController.cs File in the Controllers Folder

```
using AdvancedApp.Models;
using Microsoft.AspNetCore.Mvc;
using Microsoft.EntityFrameworkCore;
using System.Linq;
using System.Collections.Generic;

namespace AdvancedApp.Controllers {

    public class DeleteController : Controller {
        private AdvancedContext context;

        public DeleteController(AdvancedContext ctx) => context = ctx;

        public IActionResult Index() {
            return View(context.Employees.Where(e => e.SoftDeleted)
                .Include(e => e.OtherIdentity).IgnoreQueryFilters());
        }

        [HttpPost]
        public IActionResult Restore(Employee employee) {
            context.Employees.IgnoreQueryFilters()
                .First(e => e.SSN == employee.SSN
                    && e.FirstName == employee.FirstName
                    && e.FamilyName == employee.FamilyName).SoftDeleted = false;
            context.SaveChanges();
            return RedirectToAction(nameof(Index));
        }

        [HttpPost]
        public IActionResult Delete(Employee e) {
            if (e.OtherIdentity != null) {
                context.Remove(e.OtherIdentity);
            }
            context.Employees.Remove(e);
            context.SaveChanges();
            return RedirectToAction(nameof(Index));
        }

        [HttpPost]
        public IActionResult DeleteAll() {
            IEnumerable<Employee> data = context.Employees
                .IgnoreQueryFilters()
                .Include(e => e.OtherIdentity)
                .Where(e => e.SoftDeleted).ToArray();
            context.RemoveRange(data.Select(e => e.OtherIdentity));
            context.RemoveRange(data);
            context.SaveChanges();
            return RedirectToAction(nameof(Index));
        }
    }
}
```

The action methods must ensure that the SecondaryIdentity objects related to the Employee objects are also removed from the database because the data model is configured with the Restrict delete behavior. To test the soft-delete/hard-delete feature, start the application using dotnet run, navigate to http://localhost:5000, and click the Delete button for one or more Employee objects. Navigate to http://localhost:5000/delete, and you can use the buttons shown in Figure 22-7 to restore the objects, permanently delete a single soft-deleted object, or delete all of the soft-deleted objects.

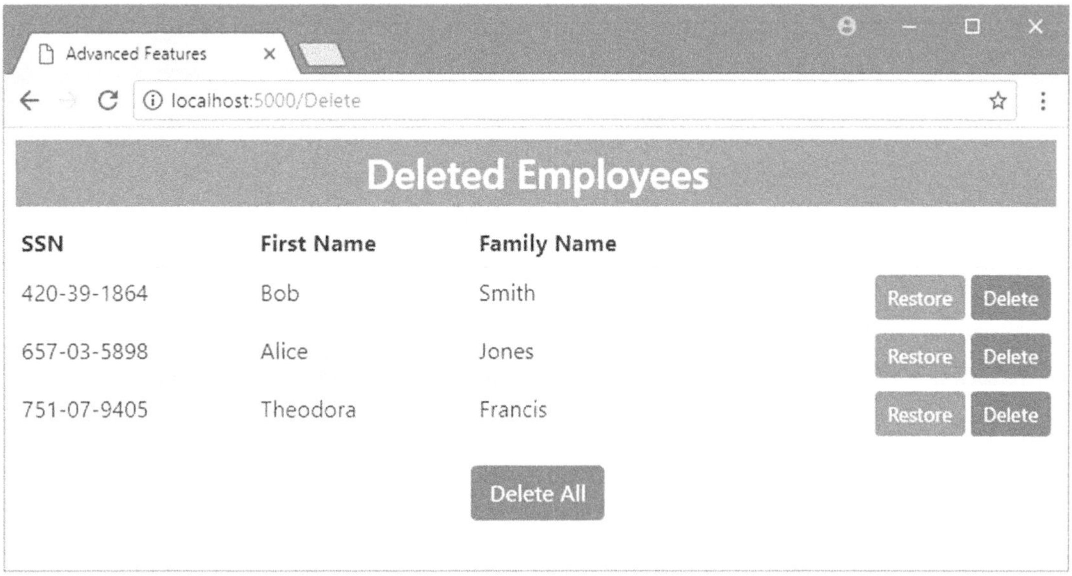

Figure 22-7. *Restoring and completing the soft-delete feature*

Summary

In this chapter, I described the different behaviors that Entity Framework Core supports for deleting data. I showed the differences between the Cascade and SetNull/ClientSetNull behaviors and how to take control of the delete process using the Restrict behavior. I completed this chapter by restoring the soft-delete feature and adding support for permanently deleting an object from its soft-deleted state. In the next chapter, I describe the features that Entity Framework Core provides for using advanced features provided by database servers.

CHAPTER 23

Using Database Server Features

Even with its advanced features, Entity Framework Core aims to cover the most commonly needed features provided by database servers. But, knowing that this won't be enough for some projects, Microsoft has also included support for working directly with the database server, which can be invaluable if your project has specialized requirements or if you are modeling a complex database.

In this chapter, I demonstrate how to use SQL directly to access features that Entity Framework Core doesn't support directly, including views, stored procedures, and table-valued functions. I also demonstrate the range of features that Entity Framework Core provides for working with data values that are generated by the database server. Table 23-1 puts this chapter in context.

Caution   All Entity Framework Core features are subject to variation between database servers and provider packages, but this is especially the case for the examples in this chapter. These examples have been tested using SQL Server and the default Microsoft database provider. You may have to make changes to the examples if you are using a different database server or provider package.

Table 23-1. *Putting Database Features in Context*

Question	Answer
What are they?	Database servers provide advanced features that cannot be accessed using the normal Entity Framework Core techniques. Entity Framework Core include a set of tools for working with these features so that you can go beyond the basic set of features common to all database servers.
Why are they useful?	These features are useful for increasing the amount of work undertaken by the database server on behalf of the application or when you need a particular feature that cannot be accessed otherwise. If you are working with an existing database, you may have to use these features to get and store data.
How are they used?	These features are accessed through a combination of methods that are included in LINQ queries and Fluent API statements that configure the data model.
Are there any pitfalls or limitations?	Working directly with database features makes it harder to test your application code and requires a good understanding of advanced database server features and the SQL required to use them.
Are there any alternatives?	No. The techniques described in this chapter are the only way to access the database server features.

© Adam Freeman 2018
A. Freeman, *Pro Entity Framework Core 2 for ASP.NET Core MVC*,
https://doi.org/10.1007/978-1-4842-3435-8_23

Table 23-2 summarizes the chapter.

Table 23-2. *Chapter Summary*

Problem	Solution	Listing
Execute SQL commands	Use the `FromSql` or `ExecuteSqlCommand` methods	1–18
Update data model objects to reflect server-generated values	Use the `HasDefaultValueSql` or `HasSequence` method or the `ValueGeneratedOnXXX` methods	19–25, 30–33
Ensure that values are unique	Use the `HasIndex` method	26–29

Preparing for This Chapter

In this chapter, I continue to work with the AdvancedApp project that I have been using since Chapter 19. Some of the queries in this chapter do not include related data, so I changed the Index view used by the Home controller as shown in Listing 23-1.

■ **Tip**   If you don't want to follow the process of building the example project, you can download all of the required files from this book's source code repository, available at `https://github.com/apress/pro-ef-core-2-for-asp.net-core-mvc`.

Listing 23-1. Dealing with Missing Related Data in the Index.cshtml File in the Views/Home Folder

```
@model IEnumerable<Employee>
@{
    ViewData["Title"] = "Advanced Features";
    Layout = "_Layout";
}
<h3 class="bg-info p-2 text-center text-white">Employees</h3>
<table class="table table-sm table-striped">
    <thead>
        <tr>
            <th>SSN</th>
            <th>First Name</th>
            <th>Family Name</th>
            <th>Salary</th>
            <th>Other Name</th>
            <th></th>
        </tr>
    </thead>
    <tbody>
        <tr class="placeholder"><td colspan="8" class="text-center">No Data</td></tr>
        @foreach (Employee e in Model) {
            <tr>
                <td>@e.SSN</td>
                <td>@e.FirstName</td>
                <td>@e.FamilyName</td>
```

```html
                    <td>@e.Salary</td>
                    <td>@(e.OtherIdentity?.Name ?? "(None)")</td>
                    <td class="text-right">
                        <form>
                            <input type="hidden" name="SSN" value="@e.SSN" />
                            <input type="hidden" name="Firstname" value="@e.FirstName" />
                            <input type="hidden" name="FamilyName"
                                    value="@e.FamilyName" />
                            <input type="hidden" name="RowVersion"
                                    asp-for="@e.RowVersion" />
                            <input type="hidden" name="OtherIdentity.Id"
                                    value="@e.OtherIdentity?.Id" />
                            <button type="submit" asp-action="Delete" formmethod="post"
                                    class="btn btn-sm btn-danger">
                                Delete
                            </button>
                            <button type="submit" asp-action="Edit" formmethod="get"
                                    class="btn btn-sm btn-primary">
                                Edit
                            </button>
                        </form>
                    </td>
                </tr>
            }
        </tbody>
</table>
@if (ViewBag.Secondaries != null) {
    @Html.Partial("SecondaryIdentities")
}
<div class="text-center">
    <a asp-action="Edit" class="btn btn-primary">Create</a>
</div>
```

I also need to start this chapter without a query filter, so I commented out the Fluent API statement in the context class that filters out soft-deleted objects, as shown in Listing 23-2.

Listing 23-2. Disabling the Query Filter in the AdvancedContext.cs File in the Models Folder

```csharp
using Microsoft.EntityFrameworkCore;
using System;

namespace AdvancedApp.Models {

    public class AdvancedContext : DbContext {

        public AdvancedContext(DbContextOptions<AdvancedContext> options)
            : base(options) {}

        public DbSet<Employee> Employees { get; set; }

        protected override void OnModelCreating(ModelBuilder modelBuilder) {
```

```
//modelBuilder.Entity<Employee>()
//      .HasQueryFilter(e => !e.SoftDeleted);

modelBuilder.Entity<Employee>().Ignore(e => e.Id);
modelBuilder.Entity<Employee>()
    .HasKey(e => new { e.SSN, e.FirstName, e.FamilyName });

modelBuilder.Entity<Employee>()
    .Property(e => e.Salary).HasColumnType("decimal(8,2)")
    .HasField("databaseSalary")
    .UsePropertyAccessMode(PropertyAccessMode.Field);

modelBuilder.Entity<Employee>().Property<DateTime>("LastUpdated")
    .HasDefaultValue(new DateTime(2000, 1, 1));

modelBuilder.Entity<Employee>()
    .Property(e => e.RowVersion).IsRowVersion();

modelBuilder.Entity<SecondaryIdentity>()
    .HasOne(s => s.PrimaryIdentity)
    .WithOne(e => e.OtherIdentity)
    .HasPrincipalKey<Employee>(e => new { e.SSN,
        e.FirstName, e.FamilyName })
    .HasForeignKey<SecondaryIdentity>(s => new { s.PrimarySSN,
        s.PrimaryFirstName, s.PrimaryFamilyName })
    .OnDelete(DeleteBehavior.Restrict);

modelBuilder.Entity<SecondaryIdentity>()
    .Property(e => e.Name).HasMaxLength(100);
        }
    }
}
```

Some of the examples in this chapter require client-side evaluation of queries, so I have commented out the statement in the Startup class that tells Entity Framework Core to throw an exception when part of a query will be evaluated in the application, as shown in Listing 23-3.

Listing 23-3. Disabling the Client-Side Exception in the Startup.cs File in the AdvancedApp Folder

```
using System;
using System.Collections.Generic;
using System.Linq;
using System.Threading.Tasks;
using Microsoft.AspNetCore.Builder;
using Microsoft.AspNetCore.Hosting;
using Microsoft.AspNetCore.Http;
using Microsoft.Extensions.DependencyInjection;
using Microsoft.Extensions.Configuration;
using Microsoft.EntityFrameworkCore;
using AdvancedApp.Models;
using Microsoft.EntityFrameworkCore.Diagnostics;
```

```
namespace AdvancedApp {
    public class Startup {

        public Startup(IConfiguration config) => Configuration = config;

        public IConfiguration Configuration { get; }

        public void ConfigureServices(IServiceCollection services) {
            services.AddMvc();
            string conString = Configuration["ConnectionStrings:DefaultConnection"];
            services.AddDbContext<AdvancedContext>(options =>
                options.UseSqlServer(conString));
                    //.ConfigureWarnings(warning => warning.Throw(
                    // RelationalEventId.QueryClientEvaluationWarning)));
        }

        public void Configure(IApplicationBuilder app, IHostingEnvironment env) {
            app.UseDeveloperExceptionPage();
            app.UseStatusCodePages();
            app.UseStaticFiles();
            app.UseMvcWithDefaultRoute();
        }
    }
}
```

Next, run the commands shown in Listing 23-4 in the AdvancedApp project folder to drop and re-create the database.

Listing 23-4. Dropping and Re-creating the Database

```
dotnet ef database drop --force
dotnet ef database update
```

Start the application using dotnet run, navigate to http://localhost:5000, click the Create button, and use the values shown in Table 23-3 to store three Employee objects.

Table 23-3. *The Data Values for Creating Example Objects*

SSN	FirstName	FamilyName	Salary	Other Name	In Active Use
420-39-1864	Bob	Smith	100000	Robert	Checked
657-03-5898	Alice	Jones	200000	Allie	Checked
300-30-0522	Peter	Davies	180000	Pete	Checked

When you have created all three objects, you should see the layout illustrated in Figure 23-1.

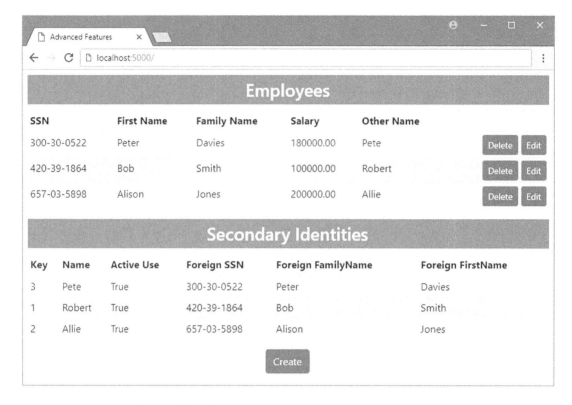

Figure 23-1. *Running the example application*

Using SQL Directly

Entity Framework Core does a good job of providing access to the database server features that most projects need, but every database server has unique features, and using them means working directly with SQL. In the sections that follow, I explain the different ways that Entity Framework Core supports working with SQL and demonstrate how each of them works.

Caution   These features should be used only if you can't get the results you require using the standard Entity Framework Core features. Using SQL directly makes your application harder to test and maintain and can restrict your application so that it will work with only one database server. If you are not using SQL Server, you may not get the expected results from the examples in this chapter.

Querying Using SQL

Entity Framework Core supports the FromSql method for querying a database using SQL directly. To demonstrate, I have changed the Index action of the Home controller so that it queries the database using SQL, as shown in Listing 23-5.

Listing 23-5. Querying Using SQL in the HomeController.cs File in the Controllers Folder

```csharp
using AdvancedApp.Models;
using Microsoft.AspNetCore.Mvc;
using Microsoft.EntityFrameworkCore;
using System.Linq;
using System;
using System.Collections.Generic;

namespace AdvancedApp.Controllers {

    public class HomeController : Controller {
        private AdvancedContext context;

        public HomeController(AdvancedContext ctx) => context = ctx;

        public IActionResult Index() {
            IEnumerable<Employee> data = context.Employees
                .FromSql(@"SELECT * FROM Employees
                            WHERE SoftDeleted = 0
                            ORDER BY Salary DESC");
            //ViewBag.Secondaries = data.Select(e => e.OtherIdentity);
            return View(data);
        }

        public IActionResult Edit(string SSN, string firstName, string familyName) {
            return View(string.IsNullOrWhiteSpace(SSN)
                ? new Employee() : context.Employees.Include(e => e.OtherIdentity)
                    .First(e => e.SSN == SSN
                        && e.FirstName == firstName
                        && e.FamilyName == familyName));
        }


        [HttpPost]
        public IActionResult Update(Employee employee) {
            if (context.Employees.Count(e => e.SSN == employee.SSN
                    && e.FirstName == employee.FirstName
                    && e.FamilyName == employee.FamilyName) == 0) {
                context.Add(employee);
            } else {
                Employee e = new Employee {
                    SSN = employee.SSN, FirstName = employee.FirstName,
                    FamilyName = employee.FamilyName,
                    RowVersion = employee.RowVersion
                };
                context.Employees.Attach(e);
                e.Salary = employee.Salary;
                e.LastUpdated = DateTime.Now;
            }
            context.SaveChanges();
            return RedirectToAction(nameof(Index));
        }
```

```
        [HttpPost]
        public IActionResult Delete(Employee employee) {
            context.Employees.Attach(employee);
            employee.SoftDeleted = true;
            context.SaveChanges();
            return RedirectToAction(nameof(Index));
        }
    }
}
```

The FromSql method is used to create a query that includes raw SQL, and in the example, I selected data from the Employees table that hasn't been soft-deleted and ordered the results by Salary value.

There are restrictions in the SQL you can use with the FromSql method. First, and most important, you must ensure that your results include columns for every property of the entity class that Entity Framework Core will create, and those columns must have the same names as those properties. You can only query for a specific entity class through its DbSet<T>, and related data cannot be included, which means you can't query for classes unless they are part of the data model. Finally, Entity Framework Core will not create related objects, even if you include a JOIN in the raw SQL query. (See the "Composing Complex Queries" section for details of a different technique for getting related data.)

To see the SQL as it is sent to the database server, start the application using dotnet run and navigate to http://localhost:5000. Examine the log messages produced by the application, and you will see the query that corresponds to the raw SQL from Listing 23-5.

```
...
SELECT * FROM Employees
WHERE SoftDeleted = 0
ORDER BY Salary DESC
...
```

Since there is no related data retrieved from the database, only details of the Employee objects will be displayed to the user, as shown in Figure 23-2.

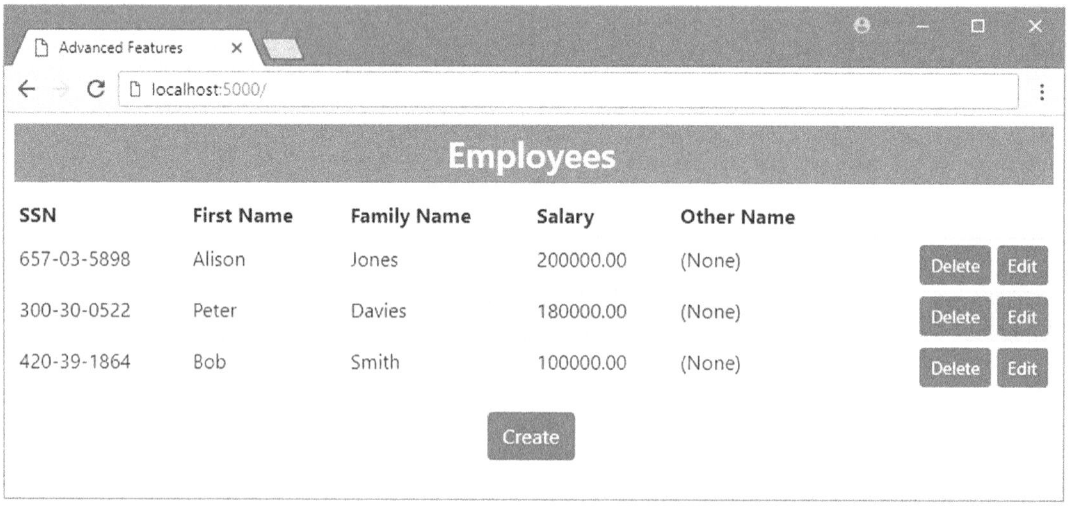

Figure 23-2. *Querying the database using raw SQL*

Querying Using Parameters

To prevent SQL injection attacks, you must parametrize any user input that is included in a SQL query. The simplest way to do this is to rely on the string interpolation feature that includes values by name in a SQL string and automatically ensures they are handled safely. In Listing 23-6, I have changed the query made by the Index action so that it accepts a parameter whose value is taken from the HTTP request and used to select data.

Listing 23-6. Using a Query Parameter in the HomeController.cs File in the Controllers Folder

```
...
public IActionResult Index(decimal salary = 0) {
    IEnumerable<Employee> data = context.Employees
        .FromSql($@"SELECT * FROM Employees
                    WHERE SoftDeleted = 0
                        AND Salary > {salary}
                    ORDER BY Salary DESC");
    //ViewBag.Secondaries = data.Select(e => e.OtherIdentity);
    return View(data);
}
...
```

Prefixing the string with a dollar sign allows me to include values by name so that `{salary}` safely incorporates the value into the query. To see the SQL that is generated, start the application using `dotnet run` and navigate to `http://localhost:5000`. In the logging messages generated by the application, you will see this query:

```
...
SELECT * FROM Employees
WHERE SoftDeleted = 0 AND Salary > @p0
ORDER BY Salary DESC
...
```

Entity Framework Core has sent a query that uses a safe parameter rather than incorporating the value directly into the SQL string. If you navigate to `http://localhost:5000?salary=100000`, you will see that the data is filtered so that only `Employee` objects whose `Salary` value exceeds 100,000 are displayed, as shown in Figure 23-3.

Figure 23-3. *Querying with user input*

OTHER WAYS OF PASSING PARAMETERS IN QUERIES

If you don't want to use string interpolation, you can pass parameters safely as arguments to the `FromSql` method, like this:

```
...
context.Employees.FromSql(@"SELECT * FROM Employees
                    WHERE SoftDeleted = 0 AND Salary > {0}
                    ORDER BY Salary DESC", salary);
...
```

The arguments are consumed in the order they are specified and referred to in the SQL string using a zero-based index. If you are working with a string that contains the name of the parameters that the query requires, then you can use the `SqlParameter` class to provide the values to the query.

```
...
SqlParameter min = new SqlParameter("minSalary", salary);

IEnumerable<Employee> data = context.Employees
    .FromSql(@"SELECT * FROM Employees
    WHERE SoftDeleted = 0 AND Salary > @minSalary
    ORDER BY Salary DESC", min);
...
```

Both of these techniques produce queries that match the string interpolation technique shown in Listing 23-6.

Composing Complex Queries

If your database server and provider package support it, Entity Framework Core is able to use raw SQL as the foundation for a more complex query, which is composed using standard LINQ methods or other Entity Framework Core features. As an example, I have uncommented the Fluent API statement in the context class to enable the query filter that excludes soft-deleted objects, as shown in Listing 23-7.

Listing 23-7. Enabling the Query Filter in the AdvancedContext.cs File in the Models Folder

```
using Microsoft.EntityFrameworkCore;
using System;

namespace AdvancedApp.Models {

    public class AdvancedContext : DbContext {

        public AdvancedContext(DbContextOptions<AdvancedContext> options)
            : base(options) {}

        public DbSet<Employee> Employees { get; set; }

        protected override void OnModelCreating(ModelBuilder modelBuilder) {
```

```
        modelBuilder.Entity<Employee>()
            .HasQueryFilter(e => !e.SoftDeleted);

        modelBuilder.Entity<Employee>().Ignore(e => e.Id);
        modelBuilder.Entity<Employee>()
            .HasKey(e => new { e.SSN, e.FirstName, e.FamilyName });

        // ...other statements omitted for brevity...
    }
  }
}
```

In Listing 23-8, I have changed the query made in the Index action method so that related data is included and the results are ordered using the LastUpdated property.

Listing 23-8. Composing a Complex Query in the HomeController.cs File in the Controllers Folder

```
...
public IActionResult Index(decimal salary = 0) {
    IEnumerable<Employee> data = context.Employees
        .FromSql($@"SELECT * FROM Employees
                    WHERE SoftDeleted = 0
                        AND Salary > {salary}")
        .Include(e => e.OtherIdentity)
        .OrderByDescending(e => e.Salary)
        .OrderByDescending(e => e.LastUpdated).ToArray();
    ViewBag.Secondaries = data.Select(e => e.OtherIdentity);
    return View(data);
}
...
```

Entity Framework Core generates a query that combines the raw SQL passed to the FromSql method with an additional query that represents the LINQ methods. To see the composed query, start the application using dotnet run, navigate to http://localhost:5000?salary=100000, and examine the logging messages, which will contain this query:

```
...
SELECT [e].[SSN], [e].[FirstName], [e].[FamilyName], [e].[LastUpdated],
    [e].[RowVersion], [e].[Salary], [e].[SoftDeleted], [e.OtherIdentity].[Id],
    [e.OtherIdentity].[InActiveUse], [e.OtherIdentity].[Name],
    [e.OtherIdentity].[PrimaryFamilyName], [e.OtherIdentity].[PrimaryFirstName],
    [e.OtherIdentity].[PrimarySSN]
FROM (
    SELECT * FROM Employees
    WHERE SoftDeleted = 0 AND Salary > @p0
) AS [e]
LEFT JOIN [SecondaryIdentity] AS [e.OtherIdentity] ON
    ((([e].[SSN] = [e.OtherIdentity].[PrimarySSN])
    AND ([e].[FirstName] = [e.OtherIdentity].[PrimaryFirstName]))
    AND ([e].[FamilyName] = [e.OtherIdentity].[PrimaryFamilyName])
WHERE [e].[SoftDeleted] = 0
ORDER BY [e].[LastUpdated] DESC, [e].[Salary] DESC
...
```

The inner part of the query is the string that I passed to the FromSql method, which has been surrounded by an outer query that uses SELECT to get the column names that Entity Framework Core requires to create Employee and SecondaryIdentity objects, the JOIN to get the related data, the WHERE clause to exclude soft-deleted data, and the ORDER BY clause that will sort the data by LastUpdated value.

The mix of raw SQL and standard LINQ methods can make queries more manageable and testable than those created purely with raw SQL. That said, this technique does put limits on the raw SQL part of the query. For example, notice that I have moved the WHERE clause that selects data based on the Salary value into a LINQ OrderByDescending method in Listing 23-8. One of the restrictions placed on raw SQL in composed queries is that ORDER BY clauses cannot be used.

Using Raw SQL to Query Stored Procedures

Stored procedures are often encountered when working with a database that predates the ASP.NET Core MVC application or where there are specific performance or data management requirements. Entity Framework Core supports querying a stored procedure, although the database server or provider may place restrictions on the types of queries that can be made.

Listing 23-9 contains the SQL statements required to create a simple stored procedure that queries the database for Employee objects whose Salary value exceeds a specified amount. Select SQL Server ➤ New Query from the Visual Studio Tools menu, connect to the database, and execute the SQL to create the stored procedure.

■ **Tip**   You can download a file containing the SQL statements in Listing 23-9 as part of the free source code download that accompanies this book at https://github.com/apress/pro-ef-core-2-for-asp.net-core-mvc.

Listing 23-9.   A Simple Stored Procedure

```
USE AdvancedDb
GO

DROP PROCEDURE IF EXISTS GetBySalary;
GO

CREATE PROCEDURE GetBySalary
        @SalaryFilter decimal
AS
        SELECT * from Employees
        WHERE Salary > @SalaryFilter AND SoftDeleted = 0
        ORDER BY Salary DESC
GO
```

Entity Framework Core can't query the stored procedure using its standard features, which means that the FromSql method must be used. In Listing 23-10 I have changed the query in the Index action of the Home controller so that it queries the database using the stored procedure.

Listing 23-10. Querying Using a Stored Procedure in the HomeController.cs File in the Controllers Folder

```
...
public IActionResult Index(decimal salary = 0) {
    IEnumerable<Employee> data = context.Employees
        .FromSql($"Execute GetBySalary @SalaryFilter = {salary}")
        .IgnoreQueryFilters();
    //ViewBag.Secondaries = data.Select(e => e.OtherIdentity);
    return View(data);
}
...
```

The types of query that you can perform with a stored procedure are limited. Related data cannot be included, for example, which is why I removed the Include. I have removed the OrderByDescending methods and added the IgnoreQueryFilters methods to prevent client-side execution. Entity Framework Core cannot compose complex queries using stored procedures, so you must either ensure that the procedure does all of the filtering and processing that you require or accept that client-side evaluation may be required. To test the stored procedure query, start the application using dotnet run and navigate to http://localhost:5000?salary=150000. If you examine the logging messages generated by the application, you can see that the stored procedure was queried like this:

```
...
Execute GetHighEarners @SalaryFilter = @p0
...
```

Since there is no related data, the results will include only Employee data, as shown in Figure 23-4.

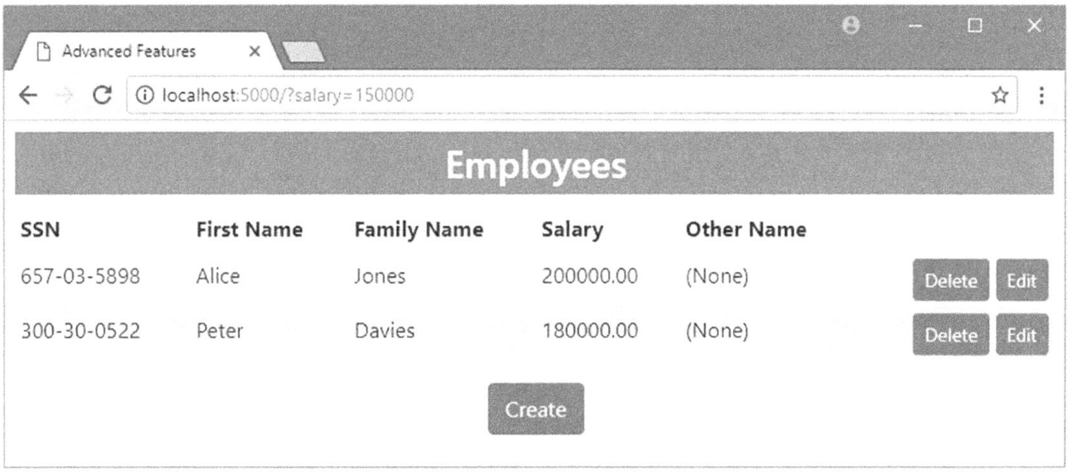

Figure 23-4. *Querying with a stored procedure*

Composing Complex Queries with Views

If you are able to influence or change the design of the database, then Entity Framework Core has more flexible support for views, which are virtual tables whose contents are generated by a query. Listing 23-11 contains the SQL statements required to create a simple view that contains all of the Employee data that has not been soft-deleted. Views are typically more complex or synthesize data by performing calculations, but this simple view is enough to demonstrate how they are used with Entity Framework Core. Select SQL Server ➤ New Query from the Visual Studio Tools menu, connect to the database, and execute the SQL to create the view.

Listing 23-11. A Simple View

```
USE AdvancedDb
GO

DROP VIEW IF EXISTS NotDeletedView
GO

CREATE VIEW NotDeletedView
AS
        SELECT * FROM Employees
        WHERE SoftDeleted = 0
GO
```

To query the view, I have updated the Index action on the Home controller, as shown in Listing 23-12. Since a view returns a table, Entity Framework Core is able to compose a query by mixing raw SQL and normal LINQ query methods.

Listing 23-12. Querying a View in the HomeController.cs File in the Controllers Folder

```
...
public IActionResult Index(decimal salary = 0) {
    IEnumerable<Employee> data = context.Employees
        .FromSql($@"SELECT * from NotDeletedView
                    WHERE Salary > {salary}")
        .Include(e => e.OtherIdentity)
        .OrderByDescending(e => e.Salary)
        .OrderByDescending(e => e.LastUpdated)
        .IgnoreQueryFilters()
        .ToArray();
    ViewBag.Secondaries = data.Select(e => e.OtherIdentity);
    return View(data);
}
...
```

The view is the source of the data in the query and is complemented by the Include and OrderByDescending methods. I added the IgnoreQueryFilters method because the view already excludes soft-deleted data, making the query filter redundant. Start the application, navigate to http://localhost:5000, and examine the logging messages to see the composed query that was sent to the database server.

```
...
SELECT [e].[SSN], [e].[FirstName], [e].[FamilyName], [e].[LastUpdated],
    [e].[RowVersion], [e].[Salary], [e].[SoftDeleted], [e.OtherIdentity].[Id],
```

```
    [e.OtherIdentity].[InActiveUse], [e.OtherIdentity].[Name],
    [e.OtherIdentity].[PrimaryFamilyName], [e.OtherIdentity].[PrimaryFirstName],
    [e.OtherIdentity].[PrimarySSN]
FROM (SELECT * from NotDeletedView WHERE Salary > @p0) AS [e]
LEFT JOIN [SecondaryIdentity] AS [e.OtherIdentity]
    ON (([e].[SSN] = [e.OtherIdentity].[PrimarySSN])
    AND ([e].[FirstName] = [e.OtherIdentity].[PrimaryFirstName]))
    AND ([e].[FamilyName] = [e.OtherIdentity].[PrimaryFamilyName])
ORDER BY [e].[LastUpdated] DESC, [e].[Salary] DESC
...
```

Since the composed query includes related data, the user is presented with both Employee and SecondaryIdentity objects, as shown in Figure 23-5.

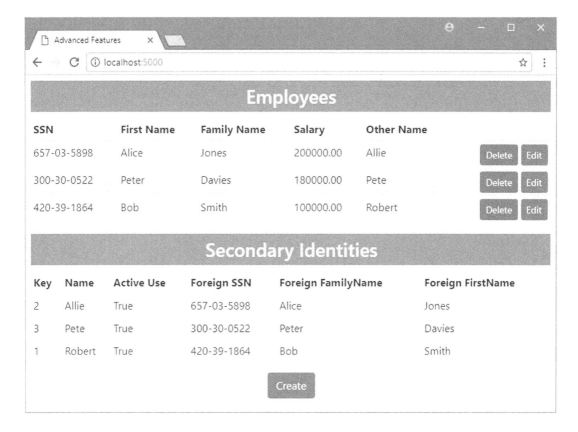

Figure 23-5. *Querying using a view*

Composing Complex Queries Using Table-Valued Functions

A table-valued function is like a cross between a view and a stored procedure. Like a stored procedure, a table-valued function can accept parameters, and it produces a table as its result, just like a view. When working with Entity Framework Core, table-valued functions can often replace stored procedures with the advantage of allowing complex queries to be composed.

603

Listing 23-13 contains the SQL statements required to create a table-valued function that performs the same query as the stored procedure created in Listing 23-9. Select SQL Server ➤ New Query from the Visual Studio Tools menu, connect to the database, and execute the SQL to create the function.

■ **Tip**   Entity Framework Core also supports scalar functions, which are functions that return a single value, rather than the table of results produced by a table-valued function. Rather than use SQL directly, you can create a method in the context class, and Entity Framework Core will know that a call to this method in a query should result in the function being executed. At the time of writing, this feature is limited and works for only a limited number of result types. Search online for the Fluent API `HasDbFunction` method for details.

Listing 23-13. A Table-Valued Function

```
USE AdvancedDb
GO

DROP FUNCTION IF EXISTS GetSalaryTable
GO

CREATE FUNCTION GetSalaryTable(@SalaryFilter decimal)
RETURNS @employeeInfo TABLE
(
    SSN nvarchar(450),
    FirstName nvarchar(450),
    FamilyName nvarchar(450),
    Salary decimal(8, 2),
    LastUpdated datetime2(7),
    SoftDeleted bit
) AS
    BEGIN
        INSERT INTO @employeeInfo
        SELECT SSN, FirstName, FamilyName, Salary, LastUpdated, SoftDeleted
        FROM Employees
        WHERE Salary > @SalaryFilter AND SoftDeleted = 0
            ORDER BY Salary DESC
        RETURN
    END
GO
```

This SQL creates a function called `GetSalaryTable` that returns a table of almost all of the columns that Entity Framework Core needs to create `Employee` objects. The exception is the `RowVersion` column because its SQL data type cannot be used in functions.

As noted earlier, raw SQL queries must produce values for all the properties that Entity Framework Core needs to create an object. To prevent an exception when Entity Framework Core processes the query results, I have configured the data model to ignore the `RowVersion` property in the `Employee` class, as shown in Listing 23-14.

■ **Caution**   Make sure you understand the impact of ignoring properties to get this kind of query to work. In this case, disabling the RowVersion property disables protection against concurrent updates when the user soft-deletes an object. Other operations are unaffected because the queries made by the other action methods in the Home controller do not use the table-valued function.

Listing 23-14. Ignoring a Property in the AdvancedContext.cs File in the Models Folder

```
using Microsoft.EntityFrameworkCore;
using System;

namespace AdvancedApp.Models {

    public class AdvancedContext : DbContext {

        public AdvancedContext(DbContextOptions<AdvancedContext> options)
            : base(options) {}

        public DbSet<Employee> Employees { get; set; }

        protected override void OnModelCreating(ModelBuilder modelBuilder) {

            modelBuilder.Entity<Employee>()
                .HasQueryFilter(e => !e.SoftDeleted);

            modelBuilder.Entity<Employee>().Ignore(e => e.Id);
            modelBuilder.Entity<Employee>()
                .HasKey(e => new { e.SSN, e.FirstName, e.FamilyName });

            modelBuilder.Entity<Employee>()
                .Property(e => e.Salary).HasColumnType("decimal(8,2)")
                .HasField("databaseSalary")
                .UsePropertyAccessMode(PropertyAccessMode.Field);

            modelBuilder.Entity<Employee>().Property<DateTime>("LastUpdated")
                .HasDefaultValue(new DateTime(2000, 1, 1));

            modelBuilder.Entity<Employee>()
                .Ignore(e => e.RowVersion);
            //  .Property(e => e.RowVersion).IsRowVersion();

            modelBuilder.Entity<SecondaryIdentity>()
                .HasOne(s => s.PrimaryIdentity)
                .WithOne(e => e.OtherIdentity)
                .HasPrincipalKey<Employee>(e => new { e.SSN,
                    e.FirstName, e.FamilyName })
                .HasForeignKey<SecondaryIdentity>(s => new { s.PrimarySSN,
                    s.PrimaryFirstName, s.PrimaryFamilyName })
                .OnDelete(DeleteBehavior.Restrict);
```

```
            modelBuilder.Entity<SecondaryIdentity>()
                .Property(e => e.Name).HasMaxLength(100);
        }
    }
}
```

To use the table-values function, I changed the query in the Index action of the Home controller, as shown in Listing 23-15.

Listing 23-15. Querying a Table-Valued Function in the HomeController.cs File in the Controllers Folder

```
...
public IActionResult Index(decimal salary = 0) {
    IEnumerable<Employee> data = context.Employees
        .FromSql($@"SELECT * from GetSalaryTable({salary})")
        .Include(e => e.OtherIdentity)
        //.OrderByDescending(e => e.Salary)
        .OrderByDescending(e => e.LastUpdated)
        .IgnoreQueryFilters()
        .ToArray();
    ViewBag.Secondaries = data.Select(e => e.OtherIdentity);
    return View(data);
}
...
```

The table-valued function is used as the target for the raw SQL query and receives a parameter that is used to filter by Salary value. Since Entity Framework Core is able to perform complex queries when table-valued functions are used, I am able to include related data and order the results. (I have commented out the OrderByDescending for the Salary property since the function already sorts the data using the Salary value.)

To see the effect, start the application using dotnet run and navigate to http://localhost:5000. In the logging messages generated by the application, you will see the query that Entity Framework Core has composed to target the table-valued function.

```
...
SELECT [e].[SSN], [e].[FirstName], [e].[FamilyName], [e].[LastUpdated], [e].[Salary],
    [e].[SoftDeleted], [e.OtherIdentity].[Id], [e.OtherIdentity].[InActiveUse],
    [e.OtherIdentity].[Name], [e.OtherIdentity].[PrimaryFamilyName],
    [e.OtherIdentity].[PrimaryFirstName], [e.OtherIdentity].[PrimarySSN]
FROM (SELECT * from GetSalaryTable(@p0)) AS [e]
LEFT JOIN [SecondaryIdentity] AS [e.OtherIdentity]
    ON (([e].[SSN] = [e.OtherIdentity].[PrimarySSN])
    AND ([e].[FirstName] = [e.OtherIdentity].[PrimaryFirstName]))
    AND ([e].[FamilyName] = [e.OtherIdentity].[PrimaryFamilyName])
ORDER BY [e].[LastUpdated] DESC
...
```

The composed query follows the same structure shown in earlier examples. As this is a composed query, related data is loaded and displayed to the user, as shown in Figure 23-6.

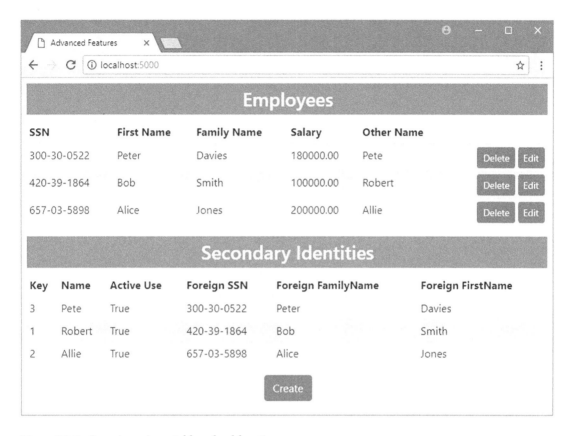

Figure 23-6. *Querying using a table-valued function*

Calling Stored Procedures or Other Operations

Not all stored procedures are used to query for data, which means that the FromSql method cannot always be used. Although Entity Framework Core doesn't automatically expose stored procedures through the context class, they can still be used. Listing 23-16 contains SQL statements that create two stored procedures that restore soft-deleted data or remove it permanently. Select SQL Server ➤ New Query from the Visual Studio Tools menu, connect to the database, and execute the SQL to create the function.

Listing 23-16. Two Stored Procedures

```
USE AdvancedDb
GO

DROP PROCEDURE IF EXISTS RestoreSoftDelete
DROP PROCEDURE IF EXISTS PurgeSoftDelete
GO

CREATE PROCEDURE RestoreSoftDelete
AS
    BEGIN
        UPDATE Employees
```

```
            SET SoftDeleted = 0 WHERE SoftDeleted = 1
    END
GO

CREATE PROCEDURE PurgeSoftDelete
AS
    BEGIN
        DELETE from SecondaryIdentity WHERE Id IN
            ( SELECT Id from Employees emp
            INNER JOIN SecondaryIdentity ident on ident.PrimarySSN = emp.SSN
            AND ident.PrimaryFirstName = emp.FirstName
            AND ident.PrimaryFamilyName = emp.FamilyName
            WHERE SoftDeleted = 1)
    END
    BEGIN
        DELETE FROM Employees
        WHERE SoftDeleted = 1
    END
```

Stored procedures that do not return data are called using the ExecuteSqlCommand, which I have used in Listing 23-17 to update the Delete controller.

Listing 23-17. Calling Stored Procedures in the DeleteController.cs File in the Controllers Folder

```
using AdvancedApp.Models;
using Microsoft.AspNetCore.Mvc;
using Microsoft.EntityFrameworkCore;
using System.Linq;
using System.Collections.Generic;

namespace AdvancedApp.Controllers {

    public class DeleteController : Controller {
        private AdvancedContext context;

        public DeleteController(AdvancedContext ctx) => context = ctx;

        public IActionResult Index() {
            return View(context.Employees.Where(e => e.SoftDeleted)
                .Include(e => e.OtherIdentity).IgnoreQueryFilters());
        }

        [HttpPost]
        public IActionResult Restore(Employee employee) {
            context.Employees.IgnoreQueryFilters()
                .First(e => e.SSN == employee.SSN
                    && e.FirstName == employee.FirstName
                    && e.FamilyName == employee.FamilyName).SoftDeleted = false;
            context.SaveChanges();
            return RedirectToAction(nameof(Index));
        }
```

```
        [HttpPost]
        public IActionResult Delete(Employee e) {
            if (e.OtherIdentity != null) {
                context.Remove(e.OtherIdentity);
            }
            context.Employees.Remove(e);
            context.SaveChanges();
            return RedirectToAction(nameof(Index));
        }

        [HttpPost]
        public IActionResult DeleteAll() {
            context.Database.ExecuteSqlCommand("EXECUTE PurgeSoftDelete");
            return RedirectToAction(nameof(Index));
        }

        [HttpPost]
        public IActionResult RestoreAll() {
            context.Database.ExecuteSqlCommand("EXECUTE RestoreSoftDelete");
            return RedirectToAction(nameof(Index));
        }

    }
}
```

SQL features that do not return data are accessed through the context class's Database.
ExecuteSqlCommand method, which accepts a SQL string (and optional parameters). In the listing, I have used the ExecuteSqlCommand method to call the stored procedures defined in Listing 23-16.

The DeleteAll action in Listing 23-17 can already be used by the user, and in Listing 23-18 I have added an HTML element to the Index view used by the Delete controller so that the RestoreAll method can be targeted.

Listing 23-18. Adding an Element in the Index.cshtml File in the Views/Delete Folder

```
@model IEnumerable<Employee>
@{
    ViewData["Title"] = "Advanced Features";
    Layout = "_Layout";
}
<h3 class="bg-info p-2 text-center text-white">Deleted Employees</h3>
<table class="table table-sm table-striped">
    <thead>
        <tr>
            <th>SSN</th>
            <th>First Name</th>
            <th>Family Name</th>
            <th></th>
        </tr>
    </thead>
    <tbody>
        <tr class="placeholder"><td colspan="4" class="text-center">No Data</td></tr>
        @foreach (Employee e in Model) {
            <tr>
```

609

```
            <td>@e.SSN</td>
            <td>@e.FirstName</td>
            <td>@e.FamilyName</td>
            <td class="text-right">
                <form method="post">
                    <input type="hidden" name="SSN" value="@e.SSN" />
                    <input type="hidden" name="FirstName" value="@e.FirstName" />
                    <input type="hidden" name="FamilyName"
                        value="@e.FamilyName" />
                    <input type="hidden" name="RowVersion"
                        asp-for="@e.RowVersion" />
                    <input type="hidden" name="OtherIdentity.Id"
                        value="@e.OtherIdentity.Id" />
                    <button asp-action="Restore" class="btn btn-sm btn-success">
                        Restore
                    </button>
                    <button asp-action="Delete" class="btn btn-sm btn-danger">
                        Delete
                    </button>
                </form>
            </td>
        </tr>
    }
    </tbody>
</table>
<div class="text-center">
    <form method="post" asp-action="DeleteAll">
        <button type="submit" class="btn btn-danger">Delete All</button>
        <button type="submit" class="btn btn-success" asp-action="RestoreAll">
            Restore All
        </button>
    </form>
</div>
```

To confirm that the stored procedures are being called, start the application using dotnet run, navigate to http://localhost:5000, and use the Delete buttons to soft-delete Employee objects. You can then navigate to http://localhost:5000/delete and use the Delete All or Restore All button to invoke the stored procedures, as shown in Figure 23-7.

Figure 23-7. *Calling a stored procedure*

Using Server-Generated Values

In Chapter 19, you saw how the database server can take responsibility for generating unique keys, but this isn't the only type of value that the database server can create. In the sections that follow, I explain the different Entity Framework Core features that support working with data values generated by the database server.

Using Database Server–Generated Default Values

For many properties, using the HasDefaultValue method with a fixed value, as shown in Chapter 21, can be useful because it allows you to define a convenient baseline for the objects that you store in the database.

In some projects, however, it can be useful to ask the database server to generate a default value each time a new object is stored, although the range of default values the database can generate is limited. As an example, I added a new property to the Employee class, as shown in Listing 23-19. Rather than add a new property for each different kind of server-generated value, I have added a property whose purpose is just to act as a placeholder so I can display values easily.

Listing 23-19. Adding a Property to the Employee.cs File in the Models Folder

```
using System;

namespace AdvancedApp.Models {

    public class Employee {
        private decimal databaseSalary;

        public long Id { get; set; }
        public string SSN { get; set; }
        public string FirstName { get; set; }
        public string FamilyName { get; set; }

        public decimal Salary {
            get => databaseSalary;
            set => databaseSalary = value;
        }
```

```
        public SecondaryIdentity OtherIdentity { get; set; }

        public bool SoftDeleted { get; set; } = false;

        public DateTime LastUpdated { get; set; }
        public byte[] RowVersion { get; set; }

        public string GeneratedValue { get; set; }
    }
}
```

Asking the database server to generate a default value for a property is done using the Fluent API HasDefaultValueSql method, which is similar to the HasDefaultValue method but tells the database server to execute a SQL expression to get the default value. In Listing 23-20, I have configured the new property using the HasDefaultValueSql method.

Listing 23-20. Configuring the Default Value in the AdvancedContext.cs File in the Models Folder

```
using Microsoft.EntityFrameworkCore;
using System;

namespace AdvancedApp.Models {

    public class AdvancedContext : DbContext {

        public AdvancedContext(DbContextOptions<AdvancedContext> options)
            : base(options) {}

        public DbSet<Employee> Employees { get; set; }

        protected override void OnModelCreating(ModelBuilder modelBuilder) {

            modelBuilder.Entity<Employee>()
                .HasQueryFilter(e => !e.SoftDeleted);

            modelBuilder.Entity<Employee>().Ignore(e => e.Id);
            modelBuilder.Entity<Employee>()
                .HasKey(e => new { e.SSN, e.FirstName, e.FamilyName });

            modelBuilder.Entity<Employee>()
                .Property(e => e.Salary).HasColumnType("decimal(8,2)")
                .HasField("databaseSalary")
                .UsePropertyAccessMode(PropertyAccessMode.Field);

            modelBuilder.Entity<Employee>().Property<DateTime>("LastUpdated")
                .HasDefaultValue(new DateTime(2000, 1, 1));

            modelBuilder.Entity<Employee>()
                .Ignore(e => e.RowVersion);
//      .Property(e => e.RowVersion).IsRowVersion();
```

```
modelBuilder.Entity<Employee>().Property(e => e.GeneratedValue)
    .HasDefaultValueSql("GETDATE()");

modelBuilder.Entity<SecondaryIdentity>()
    .HasOne(s => s.PrimaryIdentity)
    .WithOne(e => e.OtherIdentity)
    .HasPrincipalKey<Employee>(e => new { e.SSN,
        e.FirstName, e.FamilyName })
    .HasForeignKey<SecondaryIdentity>(s => new { s.PrimarySSN,
        s.PrimaryFirstName, s.PrimaryFamilyName })
    .OnDelete(DeleteBehavior.Restrict);

modelBuilder.Entity<SecondaryIdentity>()
    .Property(e => e.Name).HasMaxLength(100);
        }
    }
}
```

In the listing, I have used the SQL GETDATE function to get a timestamp. There are restrictions on the SQL expression that can be used to generate default values, which means that the range of values is limited. References to other columns in the same table are not allowed, for example, which makes sense because the default value is set when the data is stored. As a result, using SQL to specify default values generally involves invoking functions or using constants. It is for this reason that most demonstrations of default values rely on the SQL GETDATE function that I used in this example. There are more flexible options available, as I describe in the sections that follow.

To receive a value for the GeneratedValue property, I have changed the query in the Index action of the Home controller so that it no longer queries using the GetSalaryTable function, which returns a subset of the values that Entity Framework Core requires, as shown in Listing 23-21.

Listing 23-21. Revising the Query in the HomeController.cs File in the Controllers Folder

```
...
public IActionResult Index() {
    IEnumerable<Employee> data = context.Employees
        //.FromSql($@"SELECT * from GetSalaryTable({salary})")
        .Include(e => e.OtherIdentity)
        //.OrderByDescending(e => e.Salary)
        .OrderByDescending(e => e.LastUpdated)
        .IgnoreQueryFilters()
        .ToArray();
    ViewBag.Secondaries = data.Select(e => e.OtherIdentity);
    return View(data);
}
...
```

Configuring the database requires a new migration. Run the commands shown in Listing 23-22 in the AdvancedApp project folder to create a migration called GeneratedDefaultValue and apply it to the example database.

613

Listing 23-22. Creating and Applying a Database Migration

```
dotnet ef migrations add GeneratedDefaultValue
dotnet ef database update
```

To display the default value to the user, I added the elements shown in Listing 23-23 to the Index view used by the Home controller.

Listing 23-23. Adding Elements in the Index.cshtml File in the Views/Home Folder

```
@model IEnumerable<Employee>
@{
    ViewData["Title"] = "Advanced Features";
    Layout = "_Layout";
}
<h3 class="bg-info p-2 text-center text-white">Employees</h3>
<table class="table table-sm table-striped">
    <thead>
        <tr>
            <th>SSN</th>
            <th>First Name</th>
            <th>Family Name</th>
            <th>Salary</th>
            <th>Other Name</th>
            <th>Generated</th>
            <th></th>
        </tr>
    </thead>
    <tbody>
        <tr class="placeholder"><td colspan="8" class="text-center">No Data</td></tr>
        @foreach (Employee e in Model) {
            <tr>
                <td>@e.SSN</td>
                <td>@e.FirstName</td>
                <td>@e.FamilyName</td>
                <td>@e.Salary</td>
                <td>@(e.OtherIdentity?.Name ?? "(None)")</td>
                <td>@e.GeneratedValue</td>
                <td class="text-right">
                    <form>
                        <input type="hidden" name="SSN" value="@e.SSN" />
                        <input type="hidden" name="Firstname" value="@e.FirstName" />
                        <input type="hidden" name="FamilyName"
                                value="@e.FamilyName" />
                        <input type="hidden" name="RowVersion"
                                asp-for="@e.RowVersion" />
                        <input type="hidden" name="OtherIdentity.Id"
                                value="@e.OtherIdentity?.Id" />
                        <button type="submit" asp-action="Delete" formmethod="post"
                                class="btn btn-sm btn-danger">
                            Delete
                        </button>
```

```
                        <button type="submit" asp-action="Edit" formmethod="get"
                                class="btn btn-sm btn-primary">
                            Edit
                        </button>
                    </form>
                </td>
            </tr>
        }
    </tbody>
</table>
@if (ViewBag.Secondaries != null) {
    @Html.Partial("SecondaryIdentities")
}
<div class="text-center">
    <a asp-action="Edit" class="btn btn-primary">Create</a>
</div>
```

To see a default value generated by the database server, start the application using dotnet run, navigate to http://localhost:5000, click the Create button, and store a new object. When it stores the new data, the database server will evaluate the SQL expression I used in Listing 23-21 and produce a result similar to the one shown in Figure 23-8.

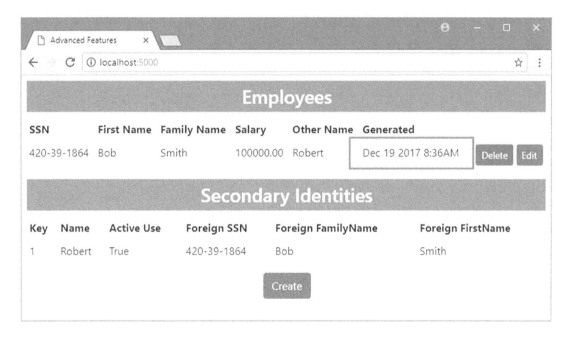

Figure 23-8. *Generating a default value*

One consequence of having the database server generate default values is that Entity Framework Core has to query the database to find out what value was assigned. If you examine the logging messages generated by the application, you will see an INSERT command was used to store the new object in the database, like this:

```
...
INSERT INTO [Employees] ([SSN], [FirstName], [FamilyName], [Salary], [SoftDeleted])
VALUES (@p0, @p1, @p2, @p3, @p4);
...
```

Immediately after the INSERT you will see a query where Entity Framework Core requests the GeneratedValue and LastUpdated values that were assigned by the database, like this:

```
...
SELECT [GeneratedValue], [LastUpdated]
FROM [Employees]
WHERE @@ROWCOUNT = 1 AND [SSN] = @p0 AND [FirstName] = @p1 AND [FamilyName] = @p2;
...
```

Entity Framework Core uses these values to update the properties of the object that has been stored, which ensures that any subsequent operations performed on that object have a complete set of values.

Incorporating Sequential Values

One way to increase the flexibility of a server-generated default value is to incorporate a sequence, where the database server will generate unique values on request. This is similar to the feature that generates key values that I described in Chapter 19, but it can be applied to any property and can be included in a generated value.

In Listing 23-24, I have added a sequence to the data model and used it as part of the SQL expression that produces a value for the GeneratedValue property.

Listing 23-24. Using a Sequence in the AdvancedContext.cs File in the Models Folder

```
using Microsoft.EntityFrameworkCore;
using System;

namespace AdvancedApp.Models {

    public class AdvancedContext : DbContext {

        public AdvancedContext(DbContextOptions<AdvancedContext> options)
            : base(options) {}

        public DbSet<Employee> Employees { get; set; }

        protected override void OnModelCreating(ModelBuilder modelBuilder) {

            modelBuilder.Entity<Employee>()
                .HasQueryFilter(e => !e.SoftDeleted);

            modelBuilder.Entity<Employee>().Ignore(e => e.Id);
```

```
        modelBuilder.Entity<Employee>()
            .HasKey(e => new { e.SSN, e.FirstName, e.FamilyName });

        modelBuilder.Entity<Employee>()
            .Property(e => e.Salary).HasColumnType("decimal(8,2)")
            .HasField("databaseSalary")
            .UsePropertyAccessMode(PropertyAccessMode.Field);

        modelBuilder.Entity<Employee>().Property<DateTime>("LastUpdated")
            .HasDefaultValue(new DateTime(2000, 1, 1));

        modelBuilder.Entity<Employee>()
            .Ignore(e => e.RowVersion);
//      .Property(e => e.RowVersion).IsRowVersion();

        modelBuilder.HasSequence<int>("ReferenceSequence")
            .StartsAt(100)
            .IncrementsBy(2);

        modelBuilder.Entity<Employee>().Property(e => e.GeneratedValue)
            .HasDefaultValueSql(@"'REFERENCE_'
                + CONVERT(varchar, NEXT VALUE FOR ReferenceSequence)");

        modelBuilder.Entity<SecondaryIdentity>()
            .HasOne(s => s.PrimaryIdentity)
            .WithOne(e => e.OtherIdentity)
            .HasPrincipalKey<Employee>(e => new { e.SSN,
                e.FirstName, e.FamilyName })
            .HasForeignKey<SecondaryIdentity>(s => new { s.PrimarySSN,
                s.PrimaryFirstName, s.PrimaryFamilyName })
            .OnDelete(DeleteBehavior.Restrict);

        modelBuilder.Entity<SecondaryIdentity>()
            .Property(e => e.Name).HasMaxLength(100);
    }
  }
}
```

Sequences are created using the HasSequence method, where the type parameter sets the data type for the sequential values and the method argument is the name assigned to the sequence. I used the name ReferenceSequence, but in a real project, you should make your sequence name as meaningful as you can because a single sequence can be used anywhere in the database.

The HasSequence method returns a SequenceBuilder object that can be used to configure the sequence using the methods described in Table 23-4.

Table 23-4. *The Sequence Configuration Methods*

Name	Description
StartsAt(value)	This method is used to specify the starting value for the sequence.
IncrementsBy(value)	This method is used to specify the amount by which the sequence is incremented after a value is generated.
IsCyclic(cycles)	This method is used to specify whether the sequence starts over when the maximum value is reached.
HasMax(value)	This method is used to specify a maximum value for the sequence.
HasMin(value)	This method is used to specify a minimum value for the sequence.

In the listing, I used the StartsAt method to specify 100 as the starting value and the IncrementsBy method to create a sequence that is incremented by two after each new value is generated. To use the sequence, I changed the expression passed to the HasDefaultValueSql method so that the next value of the sequence is converted to a string and prefixed with REFERENCE_.

Applying the sequence requires a new migration. Run the commands shown in Listing 23-25 in the AdvancedApp project folder to create a migration called Sequence and apply it to the database.

Listing 23-25. Creating and Applying a Database Migration

```
dotnet ef migrations add Sequence
dotnet ef database update
```

To see the effect, start the application using dotnet run, navigate to http://localhost:5000, click the Create button, and store a new object in the database. When the results are displayed, you will see that the sequence has been used to create the default value for the new object, as shown in Figure 23-9.

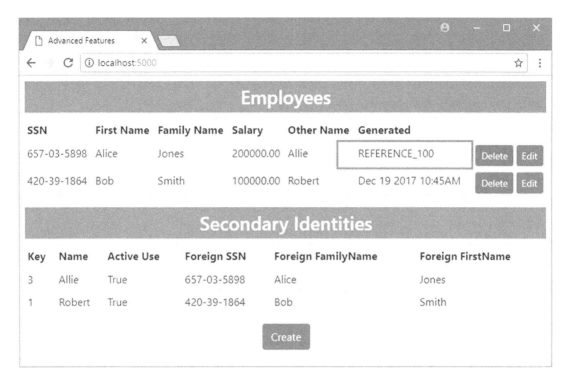

Figure 23-9. *Using a sequence to generate default values*

AVOIDING THE SEQUENCE PITFALLS

There are two common pitfalls that arise when using sequences. The first pitfall is to be too restrictive when using the methods described in Table 23-4, resulting in a pool of available values that is too small to meet the needs of the application. Sometime after development, all of the possible sequence values will be used up, and the database server will begin reporting errors.

The second pitfall is the most common attempt at correcting an exhausted sequence, which is to quickly apply the IsCyclic method so that the sequence will start over. Values in a cyclic sequence are not guaranteed to be unique, which means that the same value may be assigned several times and cause problems for applications that assume that sequence values are unique.

When creating a sequence, select a data type that provides a big enough range of values for your application. If you require unique values, then consider using an alternate key, as described in Chapter 19.

Computing Values in the Database

A computed column is one that the database server calculates using values already in the database. This can be a useful way of generating values that would otherwise have to be computed repeatedly each time a query is performed and that may otherwise require client-side query evaluation.

As an example, I changed the query in the Index action of the Home controller so that the user can apply a search term for the combined FirstName and FamilyName values, as shown in Listing 23-26.

Listing 23-26. Querying with a Search Term in the HomeController.cs File in the Controllers Folder

```
...
public IActionResult Index(string searchTerm) {
    IQueryable<Employee> query = context.Employees.Include(e => e.OtherIdentity);
    if (!string.IsNullOrEmpty(searchTerm)) {
        query = query.Where(e => EF.Functions
            .Like($"{e.FirstName[0]}{e.FamilyName}", searchTerm));
    }
    IEnumerable<Employee> data = query.ToArray();
    ViewBag.Secondaries = data.Select(e => e.OtherIdentity);
    return View(data);
}
...
```

The query takes the first character of the FirstName property, concatenates it with the value of the FamilyName property, and performs a search using the Like method. Start the application using dotnet run and navigate to http://localhost:5000?searchTerm=%ajon%. The search term is %ajon%, which will match an Employee such as Alice Jones, although you may need to change the search term to match the data you stored. You will see the following warning in the logging messages generated by the application:

```
...
The LINQ expression 'where __Functions_0.Like(Format("{0}{1}", [e].FamilyName, Convert([e].
FirstName.get_Chars(0), Object)), __searchTerm_1)' could not be translated and will be
evaluated locally.
...
```

As I explained in Chapter 20, the Like method will be evaluated in the client if the query cannot be translated into SQL, and that is what will happen for this example.

A computed column can help avoid client-side evaluation by generating values that can be queried in the database. In Listing 23-27, I changed the configuration of the GeneratedValue property so that it is a computed column that will contain the combined name values.

Listing 23-27. Defining a Computed Column in the AdvancedContext.cs File in the Models Folder

```
using Microsoft.EntityFrameworkCore;
using System;

namespace AdvancedApp.Models {

    public class AdvancedContext : DbContext {

        public AdvancedContext(DbContextOptions<AdvancedContext> options)
            : base(options) {}

        public DbSet<Employee> Employees { get; set; }

        protected override void OnModelCreating(ModelBuilder modelBuilder) {
```

```
        modelBuilder.Entity<Employee>()
            .HasQueryFilter(e => !e.SoftDeleted);

        modelBuilder.Entity<Employee>().Ignore(e => e.Id);
        modelBuilder.Entity<Employee>()
            .HasKey(e => new { e.SSN, e.FirstName, e.FamilyName });

        modelBuilder.Entity<Employee>()
            .Property(e => e.Salary).HasColumnType("decimal(8,2)")
            .HasField("databaseSalary")
            .UsePropertyAccessMode(PropertyAccessMode.Field);

        modelBuilder.Entity<Employee>().Property<DateTime>("LastUpdated")
            .HasDefaultValue(new DateTime(2000, 1, 1));

        modelBuilder.Entity<Employee>()
            .Ignore(e => e.RowVersion);
//       .Property(e => e.RowVersion).IsRowVersion();

        modelBuilder.HasSequence<int>("ReferenceSequence")
            .StartsAt(100)
            .IncrementsBy(2);

        modelBuilder.Entity<Employee>().Property(e => e.GeneratedValue)
            //.HasDefaultValueSql(@"'REFERENCE_'
            //    + CONVERT(varchar, NEXT VALUE FOR ReferenceSequence)");
            .HasComputedColumnSql(@"SUBSTRING(FirstName, 1, 1)
                                    + FamilyName PERSISTED");
        modelBuilder.Entity<Employee>().HasIndex(e => e.GeneratedValue);

        modelBuilder.Entity<SecondaryIdentity>()
            .HasOne(s => s.PrimaryIdentity)
            .WithOne(e => e.OtherIdentity)
            .HasPrincipalKey<Employee>(e => new { e.SSN,
                e.FirstName, e.FamilyName })
            .HasForeignKey<SecondaryIdentity>(s => new { s.PrimarySSN,
                s.PrimaryFirstName, s.PrimaryFamilyName })
            .OnDelete(DeleteBehavior.Restrict);

        modelBuilder.Entity<SecondaryIdentity>()
            .Property(e => e.Name).HasMaxLength(100);
        }
    }
}
```

Computed columns are configured using the HasComputedColumnSql method, which receives a SQL expression that will be used to generate the property values. In this case, the SQL expression creates the same concatenated name that I used earlier.

```
...
.HasComputedColumnSql(@"SUBSTRING(FirstName, 1, 1) + FamilyName PERSISTED");
...
```

The PERSISTED keyword tells the database server to permanently store the values in the database, rather than generate them for every query. I have also created an index for the GeneratedValue property using the Fluent API HasIndex method; this is not a requirement for computed columns, but it will improve search performance.

Adding a computed column requires an update to the database. Run the commands shown in Listing 23-28 in the AdvancedApp project folder to create a new migration and apply it to the database.

■ **Tip** The database server will automatically recalculate the computed column value when any of the values it depends on changes. In the case of the example, this means that the SearchName property will be recalculated if the FirstName or FamilyName value changes.

Listing 23-28. Creating and Applying a Database Migration

```
dotnet ef migrations add ComputedColumn
dotnet ef database update
```

Querying Using a Computed Column

Once a computed column has been defined, it can be used in a query just like any other column. In Listing 23-29, I have updated the query in the Index action of the Home controller so that the Like operation is performed on the property that corresponds to the computed column.

Listing 23-29. Using a Computed Column in the HomeController.cs File in the Controllers Folder

```
...
public IActionResult Index(string searchTerm) {
    IQueryable<Employee> query = context.Employees.Include(e => e.OtherIdentity);
    if (!string.IsNullOrEmpty(searchTerm)) {
        query = query.Where(e => EF.Functions.Like(e.GeneratedValue, searchTerm));
    }
    IEnumerable<Employee> data = query.ToArray();
    ViewBag.Secondaries = data.Select(e => e.OtherIdentity);
    return View(data);
}
...
```

Start the application using dotnet run and navigate to http://localhost:5000?searchTerm=%ajon%; you will see the results shown in Figure 23-10, although you may need to change the search term to match the data in your database. If you examine the logging messages generated by the application, you will see that the LIKE operation is performed as part of the SQL query.

```
...
SELECT [e].[SSN], [e].[FirstName], [e].[FamilyName], [e].[GeneratedValue],
    [e].[LastUpdated], [e].[Salary], [e].[SoftDeleted], [e.OtherIdentity].[Id],
    [e.OtherIdentity].[InActiveUse], [e.OtherIdentity].[Name],
    [e.OtherIdentity].[PrimaryFamilyName], [e.OtherIdentity].[PrimaryFirstName],
    [e.OtherIdentity].[PrimarySSN]
FROM [Employees] AS [e]
```

```
LEFT JOIN [SecondaryIdentity] AS [e.OtherIdentity]
    ON ((([e].[SSN] = e.OtherIdentity].[PrimarySSN])
        AND ([e].[FirstName] = [e.OtherIdentity].[PrimaryFirstName]))
        AND ([e].[FamilyName] = [e.OtherIdentity].[PrimaryFamilyName])
WHERE ([e].[SoftDeleted] = 0) AND [e].[GeneratedValue] LIKE @__searchTerm_1
...
```

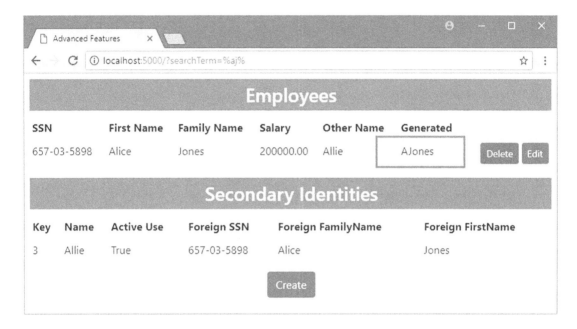

Figure 23-10. *Querying using a computed column*

Modeling Automatically Generated Values

In some projects, you may have to deal with values that are generated by the database server but that you have not configured in the database. This is most often because the database contains triggers, which generate values automatically when data is inserted or modified in the database.

To prepare for this example, run the commands shown in Listing 23-30 in the AdvancedApp project folder. These commands remove the most recent migration from the project and re-create the database, which avoids a problem where Entity Framework Core will try to remove a column while it is still being used by an index.

Listing 23-30. Removing a Migration and Dropping the Database

```
dotnet ef database drop --force
dotnet ef migrations remove --force
dotnet ef database update
```

Listing 23-31 contains the SQL statements required to create a simple trigger that updates the GeneratedValue property when an Employee object is stored or updated in the database. Select SQL Server ➤ New Query from the Visual Studio Tools menu, connect to the database, and execute the SQL to create the trigger.

Listing 23-31. Creating a Trigger in the Database

```
USE AdvancedDb
GO

DROP TRIGGER IF EXISTS GeneratedValueTrigger
GO

CREATE TRIGGER GeneratedValueTrigger ON Employees
        AFTER   INSERT, UPDATE
AS
BEGIN
        DECLARE @Salary decimal(8,0), @SSN nvarchar(450),
                @First nvarchar(450), @Family nvarchar(450)

        SELECT @Salary = INSERTED.Salary, @SSN = INSERTED.SSN,
                @First = INSERTED.FirstName, @Family = INSERTED.FamilyName
        FROM INSERTED

        UPDATE dbo.Employees SET GeneratedValue = FLOOR(@Salary /2)
        WHERE SSN = @SSN AND FirstName = @First AND FamilyName = @Family
END
```

This trigger is executed when a row in the Employee table is updated and sets the GeneratedValue property to half of the Salary value.

Entity Framework Core doesn't have support for setting up features like triggers in the database, but you can ensure that it checks to get the values that the database server produces so that subsequent operations performed using the same objects don't have incomplete or stale data.

There are four Fluent API methods that can be used to tell Entity Framework Core how values are generated for a property, as described in Table 23-5.

Table 23-5. *The Fluent API Methods for Generating Property Values*

Name	Description
ValueGeneratedNever()	This method tells Entity Framework Core that values will never be generated for this property, which is the default behavior.
ValueGeneratedOnAdd()	This method tells Entity Framework Core that values will be generated for this property when a new object is stored in the database.
ValueGeneratedOnUpdate()	This method tells Entity Framework Core that values will be generated for this property when an existing object is updated.
ValueGeneratedOnAddOrUpdate()	This method tells Entity Framework Core that values will be generated when a new object is stored in the database or when an existing object is updated.

I am going to add a trigger to the database that will generate a value for the GeneratedValue column when a row is inserted or updated in the SecondaryIdentity table. To configure the data model, I changed the configuration of the GenerateValue property to remove the computed column and tell Entity Framework Core to query for generated values when data is inserted or updated, as shown in Listing 23-32.

UNDERSTANDING THE LIMITATIONS OF THE GENERATED VALUE METHODS

The methods described in Table 23-5 do not configure the database to generated values; they only tell Entity Framework Core when it should query to get generated values that have already been configured. This means that these methods are useful for modeling existing databases but will not have an effect when used in a code-first project.

Even in a database-first project, these methods are useful only if you need to make a series of queries using the same database context object, such as with the fixing up feature. The additional queries that Entity Framework Core makes when the methods in Table 23-5 are used are not useful if you will discard the context—and its cached data—after the create or update operation is performed, which is the case in most ASP.NET Core MVC applications.

Listing 23-32. Configuring a Property in the AdvancedContext.cs File in the Models Folder

```
using Microsoft.EntityFrameworkCore;
using System;

namespace AdvancedApp.Models {

    public class AdvancedContext : DbContext {

        public AdvancedContext(DbContextOptions<AdvancedContext> options)
            : base(options) {}

        public DbSet<Employee> Employees { get; set; }

        protected override void OnModelCreating(ModelBuilder modelBuilder) {

            modelBuilder.Entity<Employee>()
                .HasQueryFilter(e => !e.SoftDeleted);

            modelBuilder.Entity<Employee>().Ignore(e => e.Id);
            modelBuilder.Entity<Employee>()
                .HasKey(e => new { e.SSN, e.FirstName, e.FamilyName });

            modelBuilder.Entity<Employee>()
                .Property(e => e.Salary).HasColumnType("decimal(8,2)")
                .HasField("databaseSalary")
                .UsePropertyAccessMode(PropertyAccessMode.Field);

            modelBuilder.Entity<Employee>().Property<DateTime>("LastUpdated")
                .HasDefaultValue(new DateTime(2000, 1, 1));
```

```
        modelBuilder.Entity<Employee>()
            .Ignore(e => e.RowVersion);
//          .Property(e => e.RowVersion).IsRowVersion();

        modelBuilder.HasSequence<int>("ReferenceSequence")
            .StartsAt(100)
            .IncrementsBy(2);

        modelBuilder.Entity<Employee>().Property(e => e.GeneratedValue)
            .ValueGeneratedOnAddOrUpdate();

        modelBuilder.Entity<SecondaryIdentity>()
            .HasOne(s => s.PrimaryIdentity)
            .WithOne(e => e.OtherIdentity)
            .HasPrincipalKey<Employee>(e => new { e.SSN,
                e.FirstName, e.FamilyName })
            .HasForeignKey<SecondaryIdentity>(s => new { s.PrimarySSN,
                s.PrimaryFirstName, s.PrimaryFamilyName })
            .OnDelete(DeleteBehavior.Restrict);

        modelBuilder.Entity<SecondaryIdentity>()
            .Property(e => e.Name).HasMaxLength(100);
    }
  }
}
```

Changing the configuration of the property requires an update to the database. Run the commands shown in Listing 23-33 in the AdvancedApp project folder to create a new migration and apply it to the database.

Listing 23-33. Creating and Applying a Migration

```
dotnet ef migrations add AutomaticallyGenerated
dotnet ef database update
```

Start the application using dotnet run, navigate http://localhost:5000, click the Create button, and store a new Employee object. When the data is stored, the trigger will set the GeneratedValue column for the new row in the database, producing the result shown in Figure 23-11.

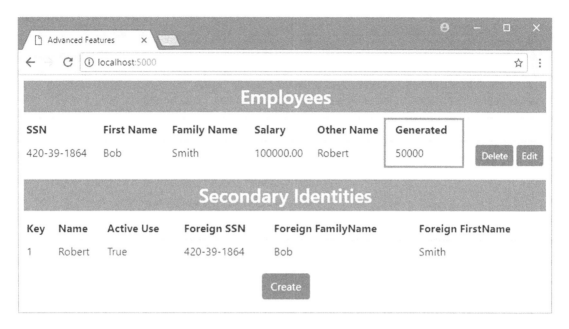

Figure 23-11. *Querying for an automatically generated value*

What's important for this example, however, is that Entity Framework Core will query for GeneratedValue after performing an INSERT or UPDATE command. In the logging messages that are produced by the application, you will see the INSERT statement used to store the object you created, like this:

```
...
INSERT INTO [Employees] ([SSN], [FirstName], [FamilyName], [Salary], [SoftDeleted])
VALUES (@p0, @p1, @p2, @p3, @p4);
...
```

Immediately after this command, you will see a query that gets the values of the properties that will be generated by the database server, as follows:

```
...
SELECT [GeneratedValue], [LastUpdated]
FROM [Employees]
WHERE @@ROWCOUNT = 1 AND [SSN] = @p0 AND [FirstName] = @p1 AND [FamilyName] = @p2;
...
```

MODELING GENERATED VALUES USING ATTRIBUTES

If you prefer not to use the Fluent API, then you can tell Entity Framework Core about properties for which the database server generates values using the DatabaseGenerated attribute, which accepts a value from the DatabaseGeneratedOption enumeration as its argument, like this:

```
...
[DatabaseGenerated(Computed)]
public string GeneratedValue { get; set; }
...
```

Three DatabaseGeneratedOption values are available. The None value indicates that the database will never generate a value, the Identity option indicates that the database will generate a value when a new object is stored, and the Computed value tells Entity Framework Core that the database will generate a value when a new object is stored or an existing object is updated.

Summary

In this chapter, I described the Entity Framework Core features for working directly with SQL. I showed you how to include SQL directly in your queries and how to create complex queries using different database server features, including views, stored procedures, and table-valued functions. I also explained the different ways that the database server can generate data values and how these can be incorporated in an application. In the next chapter, I explain how Entity Framework Core supports transactions.

CHAPTER 24

Using Transactions

In this chapter, I describe the way that Entity Framework Core supports transactions, which are used to ensure that multiple operations are performed as a single unit of work. If all of the operations can be performed without problems, then the changes are applied to the database, which is known as *committing* the transaction. If one or more operation will fail, then the database is not modified, and the changes are abandoned, which is known as *rolling back* the transaction. (I am simplifying a little here because transactions can be complicated, but this the essence of how transactions work.)

I start by describing the behavior that Entity Framework Core applies by default and then show you how take control of transactions directly, including how to disable them. Table 24-1 puts this chapter in context.

Note Not all database servers support transactions. The examples in this chapter are for SQL Server, and you may see different behavior if you use a different database server.

Table 24-1. *Putting Transactions in Context*

Question	Answer
What are they?	Transactions allow changes to be grouped together so that they are all applied if they all succeed and none are applied if any of them fails.
Why are they useful?	Transactions allow related operations to be grouped together to ensure consistency in the data used by the application, beyond the relational consistency enforced by the database server.
How are they used?	Transactions are enabled by default, but there is also an API for configuring how transactions are used.
Are there any pitfalls or limitations?	Transactions can impact performance, and it is possible to create deadlocks because updates must be queued when transactions are being processed.
Are there any alternatives?	Applications can make corrective updates to simulate the effect of rolling back a transaction, but this is hard to do correctly.

Table 24-2 summarizes the chapter.

© Adam Freeman 2018
A. Freeman, *Pro Entity Framework Core 2 for ASP.NET Core MVC*,
https://doi.org/10.1007/978-1-4842-3435-8_24

Table 24-2. *Chapter Summary*

Problem	Solution	Listing
Perform updates in isolation	Call SaveChanges after each update	5
Disable automatic transactions	Use the AutoTransactionsEnabled property	6, 7
Use transactions explicitly	Use the BeginTransaction, CommitTransaction, and RollbackTransaction methods	8, 9
Specify the transaction isolation level	Use the IsolationLevel enumeration	10

Preparing for This Chapter

In this chapter, I continue using the AdvancedApp project that I created in Chapter 19 and have been using in every chapter since. In Chapter 23, I used raw SQL to create features such as stored procedures and views, and these are no longer required. Run the commands shown in Listing 24-1 in the AdvancedApp folder to drop and re-create the database.

Listing 24-1. Resetting the Database

```
dotnet ef database drop --force
dotnet ef database update
```

To prepare for this chapter, I added a class file called MultiController.cs in the Controllers folder and used it to define the class shown in Listing 24-2.

Listing 24-2. The Contents of the MultiController.cs File in the Controllers Folder

```
using AdvancedApp.Models;
using Microsoft.AspNetCore.Mvc;
using Microsoft.Extensions.Logging;

namespace AdvancedApp.Controllers {

    public class MultiController : Controller {
        private AdvancedContext context;
        private ILogger<MultiController> logger;

        public MultiController(AdvancedContext ctx, ILogger<MultiController> log) {
            context = ctx;
            logger = log;
        }

        public IActionResult Index() {
            return View("EditAll", context.Employees);
        }

        [HttpPost]
        public IActionResult UpdateAll(Employee[] employees) {
            context.UpdateRange(employees);
```

```
            context.SaveChanges();
            return RedirectToAction(nameof(Index));
        }
    }
}
```

To provide the new controller with a view, I created the Views/Multi folder and added to it a file called EditAll.cshtml with the content shown in Listing 24-3.

■ **Tip**   If you don't want to follow the process of building the example project, you can download all of the required files from this book's source code repository, available at https://github.com/apress/pro-ef-core-2-for-asp.net-core-mvc.

Listing 24-3. The Contents of the EditAll.cshtml File in the Views/Multi Folder

```
@model IEnumerable<Employee>
@{
    ViewData["Title"] = "Advanced Features";
    Layout = "_Layout";
    int counter = 0;
}

<h4 class="bg-info p-2 text-center text-white">
    Edit All
</h4>
<form asp-action="UpdateAll" method="post">
    <div class="container">
        @foreach (Employee e in Model) {
            <div class="form-row">
                <div class="col">
                    <input class="form-control" name="Employees[@counter].SSN"
                        value="@e.SSN" readonly />
                </div>
                <div class="col">
                    <input class="form-control" name="Employees[@counter].FirstName"
                        value="@e.FirstName" readonly />
                </div>
                <div class="col">
                    <input class="form-control" name="Employees[@counter].FamilyName"
                        value="@e.FamilyName" readonly />
                </div>
                <div class="col">
                    <input class="form-control" name="Employees[@counter].Salary"
                        value="@e.Salary" />
                </div>
            </div>
             counter++;
        }
```

```
    </div>
    <div class="text-center m-2">
        <button type="submit" class="btn btn-primary">Save All</button>
        <a class="btn btn-secondary" asp-action="Index"
            asp-controller="Home">
                Cancel
        </a>
    </div>
</form>
```

Start the application using dotnet run, navigate to http://localhost:5000, click the Create button, and use the details in Table 24-3 to populate the database.

***Table 24-3.** The Data Values for the Example Applicaiton*

SSN	FirstName	FamilyName	Salary	Other Name	In Active Use
420-39-1864	Bob	Smith	100000	Robert	Checked
657-03-5898	Alice	Jones	200000	Allie	Checked
300-30-0522	Peter	Davies	180000	Pete	Checked

When you have finished adding data, you should see the results in Figure 24-1.

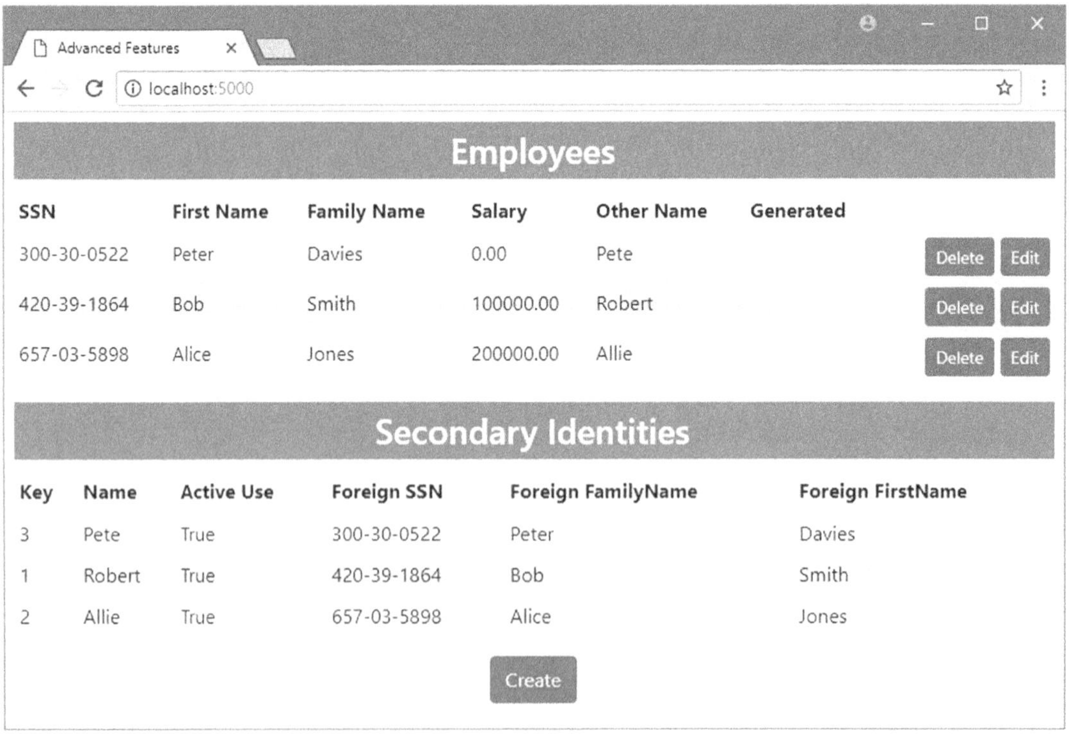

***Figure 24-1.** Running the example application*

Understanding the Default Behavior

Transactions are such a fundamental part of working with a database that Entity Framework Core uses them automatically. To reveal how transactions are used, I changed the configuration for the logging system so that Entity Framework Core will report more detailed messages, as shown in Listing 24-4.

Listing 24-4. Changing the Logging Level in the appsettings.json File in the AdvancedApp Folder

```
{
  "ConnectionStrings": {
    "DefaultConnection": "Server=(localdb)\\MSSQLLocalDB;Database=AdvancedDb;MultipleActive
    ResultSets=true"
  },
  "Logging": {
    "LogLevel": {
      "Default": "None",
      "Microsoft.EntityFrameworkCore": "Information",
      "Microsoft.EntityFrameworkCore.Database.Transaction":  "Debug"
    }
  }
}
```

The new entry requests Debug-level messages from the classes that handle Entity Framework Core transactions. To see how transactions are used by default, start the application using dotnet run, navigate to http://localhost:5000/multi, and change the Salary values as described in Table 24-4.

Table 24-4. *The Salary Values for a Successful Transaction*

Name	Salary Value
Bob Smith	150000
Alice Jones	250000

Click the Save All button, and Entity Framework Core will update the database. If you examine the logging messages from the database, you can see the sequence of events (although it can be hard to find individual messages in the stream of output that is generated by the Debug logging setting). First, Entity Framework Core creates a new transaction.

```
...
Beginning transaction with isolation level 'ReadCommitted'.
...
```

I explain what isolation levels are later, but what's important for this section is that a transaction has been started.

I haven't provided Entity Framework Core with a baseline for change detection, so every object is updated, resulting in three UPDATE statements, each of which is followed by a SELECT statement to determine the values generated by the database.

```
...
UPDATE [Employees] SET [LastUpdated] = @p0, [Salary] = @p1, [SoftDeleted] = @p2
WHERE [SSN] = @p3 AND [FirstName] = @p4 AND [FamilyName] = @p5;
SELECT [GeneratedValue]
```

633

```
FROM [Employees]
WHERE @@ROWCOUNT = 1 AND [SSN] = @p3 AND [FirstName] = @p4 AND [FamilyName] = @p5;

UPDATE [Employees] SET [LastUpdated] = @p6, [Salary] = @p7, [SoftDeleted] = @p8
WHERE [SSN] = @p9 AND [FirstName] = @p10 AND [FamilyName] = @p11;
SELECT [GeneratedValue]
FROM [Employees]
WHERE @@ROWCOUNT = 1 AND [SSN] = @p9 AND [FirstName] = @p10 AND [FamilyName] = @p11;

UPDATE [Employees] SET [LastUpdated] = @p12, [Salary] = @p13, [SoftDeleted] = @p14
WHERE [SSN] = @p15 AND [FirstName] = @p16 AND [FamilyName] = @p17;
SELECT [GeneratedValue]
FROM [Employees]
WHERE @@ROWCOUNT = 1 AND [SSN] = @p15 AND [FirstName] = @p16 AND [FamilyName] = @p17;
...
```

The database server hasn't reported any errors with these commands, and Entity Framework Core doesn't have any further work to perform; therefore, the transaction is committed, which applies the changes to the database and which is reported with this message:

```
...
Committing transaction.
...
```

Until the transaction is committed, the changes are not applied to the database and can be discarded if the transaction is rolled back. To see a rollback in action, navigate to http://localhost:5000/multi and change the Salary values as described in Table 24-5.

Table 24-5. *The Salary Values for a Failed Transaction*

Name	Salary Value
Bob Smith	900000000
Alice Jones	300000

The value for Bob Smith's Salary is too large to be represented using the data type configured in the data model, and you will see an exception when you click the Save All button. The exception interrupts the update, and the transaction is not committed. Since both the updates from Table 24-5 are performed within the same transaction, neither update is applied to the database.

Performing Independent Changes

One potential drawback of the default transaction behavior is that it prevents successful updates from being applied to the database if they are grouped with an update that fails. In the previous section, for example, you saw how the valid update for Alice Jones failed because it was grouped with the failed update for Bob Smith. If you want to isolate each update so that it isn't affected by other failures, then you can call the SaveChanges method for each update, as shown in Listing 24-5.

Listing 24-5. Performing Independent Changes in the MultiController.cs File in the Controllers Folder

```
using AdvancedApp.Models;
using Microsoft.AspNetCore.Mvc;
using Microsoft.Extensions.Logging;
using System;
using Microsoft.EntityFrameworkCore;

namespace AdvancedApp.Controllers {

    public class MultiController : Controller {
        private AdvancedContext context;
        private ILogger<MultiController> logger;

        public MultiController(AdvancedContext ctx, ILogger<MultiController> log) {
            context = ctx;
            logger = log;
        }

        public IActionResult Index() {
            return View("EditAll", context.Employees);
        }

        [HttpPost]
        public IActionResult UpdateAll(Employee[] employees) {
            foreach (Employee e in employees) {
                try {
                    context.Update(e);
                    context.SaveChanges();
                } catch (Exception) {
                    context.Entry(e).State = EntityState.Detached;
                }
            }
            return RedirectToAction(nameof(Index));
        }
    }
}
```

Each `Employee` object is passed to the context object's `Update` method individually, after which the `SaveChanges` method is called. I use a `try...catch` block to ensure that exceptions thrown by an update do no disrupt subsequent updates.

The effect is that a separate transaction will be used for each update, which you can see by starting the application using `dotnet run`, navigating to `http://localhost:5000/multi`, and applying the changes in Table 24-5. The update for Bob Smith will still fail, but this time the update for Alice Jones will be applied to the database, as shown in Figure 24-2.

■ **Tip**   Notice that I alter the change tracking status of `Employee` objects whose updates have failed to `Detached` in the `catch` clause of the `try...catch` block. Without this change, Entity Framework Core will include the failed update the next time that the `SaveChanges` method is called, causing another error and preventing the other update from being applied.

Figure 24-2. *Applying updates in their own transactions*

If you examine the logging messages generated by the application, you will see that a separate transaction is created and committed for each object. The exception thrown for the Bob Smith update prevents the transaction for that change from being committed but does not affect the other changes from being applied to the database.

Disabling Automatic Transactions

If you don't want Entity Framework Core to automatically use transactions, then you can disable this feature by changing the configuration of the context object. Context objects define a `Database` property that returns a `DatabaseFacade` object that provides access to the transaction features. This class defines the property described in Table 24-6 and which is used to control the automatic transaction feature.

Table 24-6. *The DatabaseFacade Property for Automatic Transactions*

Name	Description
`AutoTransactionsEnabled`	Setting this property to `false` will disable the automatic transactions feature.

In Listing 24-6, I have used the property described in Table 24-6 to disable the automatic transaction feature for the `AdvancedContext` class. This property must be set for each object that is created, which means that using the constructor ensures consistent results in a ASP.NET Core MVC application where dependency injection is used.

Listing 24-6. Disabling Automatic Transactions in the AdvancedContext.cs File in the Models Folder

```
using Microsoft.EntityFrameworkCore;
using System;

namespace AdvancedApp.Models {

    public class AdvancedContext : DbContext {

        public AdvancedContext(DbContextOptions<AdvancedContext> options)
                : base(options) {
```

```
        Database.AutoTransactionsEnabled = false;
    }

    public DbSet<Employee> Employees { get; set; }

    protected override void OnModelCreating(ModelBuilder modelBuilder) {
        // ...Fluent API statements omitted for brevity...
    }
}
}
```

In Listing 24-7, I have returned the UpdateAll method to its original implementation, such that all of the updates are performed with a single call to the SaveChanges method. This would have previously meat that all of the updates were performed in a single transaction.

Listing 24-7. Performing Updates in the MultiController.cs File in the Controllers Folder

```
using AdvancedApp.Models;
using Microsoft.AspNetCore.Mvc;
using Microsoft.Extensions.Logging;
using System;
using Microsoft.EntityFrameworkCore;

namespace AdvancedApp.Controllers {

    public class MultiController : Controller {
        private AdvancedContext context;
        private ILogger<MultiController> logger;

        public MultiController(AdvancedContext ctx, ILogger<MultiController> log) {
            context = ctx;
            logger = log;
        }

        public IActionResult Index() {
            return View("EditAll", context.Employees);
        }

        [HttpPost]
        public IActionResult UpdateAll(Employee[] employees) {
            context.UpdateRange(employees);
            context.SaveChanges();
            return RedirectToAction(nameof(Index));
        }
    }
}
```

To see how the configuration change alters the outcome, start the application using dotnet run and navigate to http://localhost:5000/multi. Make the changes shown in Table 24-7 and click the Save Changes button.

Table 24-7. *The Salary Changes to Test Disabling Automatic Transactions*

Name	Salary Value
Peter Davies	200000
Bob Smith	900000000
Alice Jones	200000

When you click the Save All button, you will see an exception because the value for Bob Smith is too large for the data type used to store Salary values in the database. But, since there is no transaction to be rolled back, the other changes are applied to the database, as shown in Figure 24-3.

░ **Tip** You may not always see the same outcome when working without transactions because the database server or provider package may respond in different ways. The important point to note is that you can't rely on all of the updates being rolled back if one of them fails.

Figure 24-3. *Working without automatic transactions*

Using Explicit Transactions

The default behavior is sufficient for most projects, but you can have Entity Framework Core use a transaction explicitly to group together separate operations. This can be useful if you need to change the way that transactions are configured or need to perform additional tasks before deciding whether to commit or roll back a set of updates.

In Listing 24-8, I have revised the UpdateAll method of the Multi controller so that it uses a transaction explicitly.

Listing 24-8. Using a Transaction in the MultiController.cs File in the Controllers Folder

```
using AdvancedApp.Models;
using Microsoft.AspNetCore.Mvc;
using Microsoft.Extensions.Logging;
```

```
using System;

namespace AdvancedApp.Controllers {

    public class MultiController : Controller {
        private AdvancedContext context;
        private ILogger<MultiController> logger;

        public MultiController(AdvancedContext ctx, ILogger<MultiController> log) {
            context = ctx;
            logger = log;
        }

        public IActionResult Index() {
            return View("EditAll", context.Employees);
        }

        [HttpPost]
        public IActionResult UpdateAll(Employee[] employees) {
            context.Database.BeginTransaction();
            try {
                context.UpdateRange(employees);
                context.SaveChanges();
                context.Database.CommitTransaction();
            } catch (Exception) {
                context.Database.RollbackTransaction();
            }
            return RedirectToAction(nameof(Index));
        }
    }
}
```

Direct access to transactions is through the context object's `Database` properties, which returns a `DatabaseFacade` object that defines the transaction-related members described in Table 24-8.

Table 24-8. *The DatabaseFacade Transaction Members*

Name	Description
BeginTransaction()	This method creates a new transaction. There is an asynchronous version of this method called BeginTransactionAsync.
CommitTransaction()	This method commits the current transaction.
RollbackTransaction()	This method rolls back the current transaction.
CurrentTransaction	This property returns the current transaction.

In the listing, I call `BeginTransaction` to start a new transaction and then perform the updates. When the SaveChanges method is called, Entity Framework Core sends the SQL commands to the database server to perform the updates but does not automatically commit the transaction, unlike when the automatic transaction feature is used. Instead, the changes are not applied to the database until the `CommitTransaction` method is called. I have used a try...catch block to deal with any errors reported by the database server by calling the `RollbackTransaction` method, which will abandon changes.

UNDERSTANDING TRANSACTION DISPOSAL

You will often see transactions created with a `using` clause that takes the result from the `BeginTransaction` method, like this:

```
...
using (var transaction = context.Database.BeginTransaction()) {
    // ...operations are performed...
    context.Database.CommitTransaction();
}
...
```

A transaction is automatically rolled back when it is disposed, and the idea of the `using` clause is to ensure that disposal happens as soon as the transaction is no longer required, preventing transactions from stacking up and waiting to be rolled back and have their objects destroyed.

You don't have to worry about disposing of transactions in an ASP.NET Core MVC application because objects are disposed when an action method completes. That means that a transaction will be rolled back after an action method is executed unless you explicitly call the `CommitTransaction` or `RollbackTransaction` method.

Including Other Operations in a Transaction

The previous example shows how you work directly with transactions but doesn't perform any tasks that wouldn't have worked identically using automatic transactions. One common reason for using transactions directly is to perform some additional work after the updates have been sent to the database before determining whether they should be committed or rolled back. As a demonstration, I have added a validation query to the UpdateAll method that queries the database to place a cap on the cumulative value of the Salary properties and rolls back the transaction if the total amount is too large, as shown in Listing 24-9.

Listing 24-9. Performing Additional Work in the MultiController.cs File in the Controllers Folder

```
using AdvancedApp.Models;
using Microsoft.AspNetCore.Mvc;
using Microsoft.Extensions.Logging;
using System;
using System.Linq;

namespace AdvancedApp.Controllers {

    public class MultiController : Controller {
        private AdvancedContext context;
        private ILogger<MultiController> logger;

        public MultiController(AdvancedContext ctx, ILogger<MultiController> log) {
            context = ctx;
            logger = log;
        }
```

```
    public IActionResult Index() {
        return View("EditAll", context.Employees);
    }

    [HttpPost]
    public IActionResult UpdateAll(Employee[] employees) {
        context.Database.BeginTransaction();
        context.UpdateRange(employees);
        context.SaveChanges();
        if (context.Employees.Sum(e => e.Salary) < 1_000_000) {
            context.Database.CommitTransaction();
        } else {
            context.Database.RollbackTransaction();
            throw new Exception("Salary total exceeds limit");
        }
        return RedirectToAction(nameof(Index));
    }
    }
}
```

After the SaveChanges method is called, I use the Sum method to get the total of the Salary values. I commit the transaction if the total is less than one million and roll it back and throw an exception otherwise. To see the effect, start the application, navigate to `http://localhost:5000/multi`, and change the Salary values. Click the Save All button, and either you will see how your changes are applied or an exception is shown and the changes are discarded, as shown in Figure 24-4.

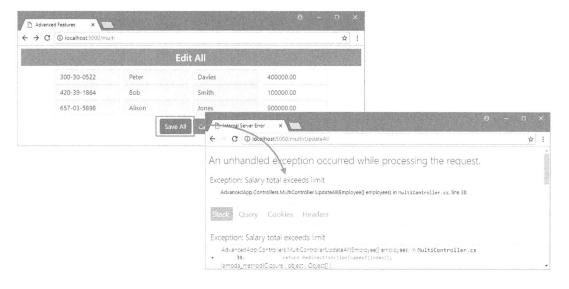

Figure 24-4. *Performing additional work in a transaction*

This sort of additional check isn't possible when using the automatic transaction feature because the transaction will be committed as soon as the SaveChanges method is called. By working directly with the transaction, I can perform additional tasks before deciding the outcome.

Changing the Transaction Isolation Level

The isolation level of a transaction specifies how the database server handles updates that have not yet been committed. In some applications, it can be important to isolate the changes made by one client from other clients until they are committed. In other applications, this kind of isolation is less important, and performance can be improved by reducing the extent to which clients are shielded from the uncommitted changes made by others. The isolation level for a transaction is specified by passing a value from the IsolationLevel enumeration, as described in Table 24-9.

Table 24-9. *The IsolationLevel Values*

Name	Description
Chaos	This value is poorly defined, but when it is supported, it typically behaves as though transactions are disabled. Changes made to the database are visible to other clients before they are committed, and there is often no rollback support. SQL Server does not support this isolation level.
ReadUncomitted	This value represents the lowest level of isolation that is commonly supported. Transactions using this isolation level can read changes made by other transactions that have not been committed.
ReadComitted	This value is the default level of isolation that is used if no value is specified. Other transactions can still insert or delete data between the updates made by the current transaction, which can result in inconsistent query results.
RepeatableRead	This value represents a higher level of isolation that prevents other transactions from modifying data that the current transaction has read, which ensures consistent query results.
Serializable	This value increases the RepeatableRead isolation level by preventing other transactions from adding data to regions of the database that have been read by the current transaction.
Snapshot	This value represents the highest level of isolation and ensures that transactions each work with their own data snapshot. This isolation level requires a change to the database that cannot be performed using Entity Framework Core. See here for details: https://docs.microsoft.com/en-us/dotnet/framework/data/adonet/sql/snapshot-isolation-in-sql-server.

The higher the isolation level, the less interaction there is between transactions, but the more locking that the database server has to use, which has a performance impact if there are multiple clients trying to modify the same data simultaneously. The trade-off when selecting an isolation level is between performance and inconsistent data. For many applications, especially in ASP.NET Core MVC projects, there is little need to change the isolation level because the default value will provide an acceptable trade-off. For some applications, however—especially those with particularly complex databases—the risk of interaction between transactions can be an issue.

AVOIDING THE HIGH ISOLATION LEVEL PITFALL

You might be tempted to select a high level of transactional isolation just to be on the safe side. This will certainly avoid the three problems described in this chapter but may also slow down your application. Database servers increase transactional isolation by locking access to parts of the database; the higher the level of transactional isolation, the more locking is required and the more likelihood there is that updates will start to be queued, making clients wait until earlier transactions have completed. The wrong choice of isolation level will offer no advantage to the application but can drag down performance.

Understanding Dirty Reads, Phantom Rows, and Nonrepeatable Reads

There are three potential problems that can occur when transactions interfere with one another. When you decide on an isolation level for your transaction, you are really telling the database which of these potential problems you are willing to accept and how much performance you are willing to sacrifice to avoid them. To demonstrate all three problems, I made some changes to the Multi controller, as shown in Listing 24-10.

Listing 24-10. Using Isolation Levels in the MultiController.cs File in the Controllers Folder

```
using AdvancedApp.Models;
using Microsoft.AspNetCore.Mvc;
using Microsoft.Extensions.Logging;
using System;
using System.Linq;
using System.Data;
using Microsoft.EntityFrameworkCore;

namespace AdvancedApp.Controllers {

    public class MultiController : Controller {
        private AdvancedContext context;
        private ILogger<MultiController> logger;
        private IsolationLevel level = IsolationLevel.ReadUncommitted;

        public MultiController(AdvancedContext ctx, ILogger<MultiController> log) {
            context = ctx;
            logger = log;
        }

        public IActionResult Index() {
            context.Database.BeginTransaction(level);
            return View("EditAll", context.Employees);
        }

        [HttpPost]
        public IActionResult UpdateAll(Employee[] employees) {
            context.Database.BeginTransaction(level);
            context.UpdateRange(employees);
```

```
            Employee temp = new Employee {
                SSN = "00-00-0000",
                FirstName = "Temporary",
                FamilyName = "Row",
                Salary = 0
            };
            context.Add(temp);
            context.SaveChanges();
            System.Threading.Thread.Sleep(5000);
            context.Remove(temp);
            context.SaveChanges();
            if (context.Employees.Sum(e => e.Salary) < 1_000_000) {
                context.Database.CommitTransaction();
            } else {
                context.Database.RollbackTransaction();
                logger.LogError("Salary total exceeds limit");
            }
            return RedirectToAction(nameof(Index));
        }

        public string ReadTest() {
            decimal firstSum = context.Employees.Sum(e => e.Salary);
            System.Threading.Thread.Sleep(5000);
            decimal secondSum = context.Employees.Sum(e => e.Salary);
            return $"Repeatable read results - first: {firstSum}, "
                + $"second: {secondSum}";
        }
    }
}
```

The isolation level is set as an argument to the BeginTransaction method, which is an extension method defined in the Microsoft.EntityFrameworkCore namespace. In the listing, I have selected the ReadUncommitted level, which I use in a transaction that queries the database in the Index action and updates the database in the UpdateAll action. In the UpdateAll method, I perform the updates received from the user, add a temporary Employee to the database, and then remove it again. The transaction is committed only if the sum of the Salary values is less than one million; otherwise, it is rolled back. To slow down the UpdateAll method and make it easier to see the effects of transactions interacting, I have added a call to the Thread.Sleep method that delays the transaction being committed or rolled back by five seconds.

To see two of the potential problems, start the application using dotnet run, open two browser windows, and navigate to http://localhost:5000/multi for both. Change the Salary value for Alice Jones to 900000 in the first browser window and click Save All. Reload the other browser before the five-second sleep period elapses, and you will see the results shown in Figure 24-5.

⬚ Caution You won't always be able to re-create these problems, especially in real projects where conditions are harder to control. You should select your isolation level based on the level of isolation you need in principle, even if you can't re-create a specific problem during testing.

Figure 24-5. Changes made by another transaction

Even though the changes are subsequently rolled back, there is a period when the ReadUncomitted isolation level has allowed the changes to be read in another transaction. The temporary row is an example of a phantom row, and the Salary value displayed for Alice is an example of a dirty read.

To see the third problem, navigate to http://localhost:5000/multi/readtest in one of the windows. This request targets the ReadTest action added in Listing 24-10, which performs the same query on the database before and after a five-second pause. This method returns a string so that I don't have to add a view to the project, and it will produce a result that shows the same value for both reads, like this:

```
Repeatable read results - first: 500000.00, second: 500000.00
```

Use the other browser window to navigate to http://localhost:5000/multi, change Alice's Salary to 90000, and click the Save All button. Before the five seconds elapses, reload the first browser window to repeat the two queries. This time, you will see that each query received a different result.

```
Repeatable read results - first: 1200000.00, second: 500000.00
```

This is the nonrepeatable read problem where two queries made by the same transaction return different results. If you change the isolation level used by the transaction in the controller, you will find these problems are not seen.

Summary

In this chapter, I described the way that Entity Framework Core supports transactions, starting with the automatic transaction feature and moving on to working with transactions directly. I explained how to disable transactions, how to perform additional work as part of a transaction, and how to tell Entity Framework Core when to commit or roll back changes to the database. I finished the chapter by explaining the different isolation levels that can be used with transactions and the trade-off that each represents in terms of performance.

That's all I have to tell you about Entity Framework Core for ASP.NET Core MVC development. I started by introducing the basics of working with database, described common problems you are likely to encounter, and described all of the key Entity Framework Core features. I hope that you have enjoyed reading this book as much as I enjoyed writing it, and I wish you every success in your ASP.NET Core MVC and Entity Framework Core projects.

Index

Get the eBook for only $5!

Why limit yourself?

With most of our titles available in both PDF and ePUB format, you can access your content wherever and however you wish—on your PC, phone, tablet, or reader.

Since you've purchased this print book, we are happy to offer you the eBook for just $5.

To learn more, go to http://www.apress.com/companion or contact support@apress.com.

Apress®

CPSIA information can be obtained
at www.ICGtesting.com
Printed in the USA
LVHW101104050219
606447LV00008B/149/P